S0-DNN-020

The Running and Maintenance of the Marine Diesel Engine

Other Books of Interest

By S. J. Christensen

LAMB'S QUESTIONS AND ANSWERS ON THE MARINE DIESEL ENGINE

By W. Ker Wilson

VIBRATION ENGINEERING

By D. Rutherford

TANKER CARGO HANDLING

By B. Baxter

NAVAL ARCITECTURE: EXAMPLES AND THEORY

By M. D. Jackson

WELDING: METHODS AND METALLURGY

By T. Walton and B. Baxter

KNOW YOUR OWN SHIP
(Construction, stability, loading, trim, tonnage and freeboard)

By J. Mackerle

AIR-COOLED AUTOMOTIVE ENGINES

Frontispiece

Opposed-piston turbocharged engine
(Doxford, type 76J9)

Cylinder bore 760 mm. Combined piston stroke 2,180 mm. Maximum power, trial rating: 23,000 h.p., at 121 r.p.m. Continuous duty power rating: 20,000 h.p., at 115 r.p.m. Length 59 ft 2 in. Height 33 ft 6 in. Weight 580 tons.

THE

RUNNING AND MAINTENANCE OF THE MARINE DIESEL ENGINE

JOHN LAMB, O.B.E.

M.I.Mech.E., M.I.Mar.E., F.Inst.P.

Denny Gold Medallist 1947 and 1953
Akroyd Stuart Prizeman 1949 and 1952

A reference book for the seagoing marine engineer, the engineer superintendent, and those qualifying for D.O.T. Certificates • Based on the experience acquired by the Author during 14 years at sea, 14 years as Superintendent Engineer, 10 years as Chief Marine Superintendent, and 10 years head of Marine Research with Shell Petroleum Limited.

SIXTH EDITION, REWRITTEN
With 274 illustrations

Fifth Impression

Charles Griffin and Company Ltd

London and High Wycombe

CHARLES GRIFFIN & COMPANY LIMITED
Registered Office: Charles Griffin House, Crendon Street,
High Wycombe, Bucks, HP13 6LE, England

First Edition – – – 1920
Second Edition, Revised – 1921
Third Edition, Revised – 1927
2nd Impression – 1928
Fourth Edition, Revised – 1930
2nd Impression – 1935
3rd Impression – 1936
4th Impression – 1937
5th Impression – 1938
Fifth Edition, Revised – 1939
2nd Impression – 1942
3rd Impression – 1943
4th Impression – 1945
5th Impression – 1946
6th Impression – 1948
7th Impression – 1949
Sixth Edition, Revised – 1958
2nd Impression – 1965
3rd Impression – 1973
4th Impression – 1976
5th Impression – 1982

ISBN 0 85264 105 2

Printed in Great Britain by
J. W. Arrowsmith Ltd., Bristol

Preface to the Sixth Edition

As with the five previous editions of this book, this new, rewritten edition retains its essentially practical character. The aim in writing has been to avoid including anything superfluous to the requirements of those whose duty it is to operate diesel engines – and it is, in fact, a "working tool" and practical guide, not a textbook. It does not give a detailed description of every make of engine as at present constructed, but rather provides the fundamental knowledge which will enable the engineer to understand the principles of operation of the different types and enable him to obtain the best results from all engines now in service.

To accomplish this, various parts mostly common to all makes of engines must, of course, be described and illustrated throughout the book, but the policy adopted in previous editions, of including the least possible amount of descriptive matter, has been continued. For the benefit of those preparing for examinations, however, an up-to-date general description of a few of the principal makes of engines will be found at the end of the book.

After serving for four years in steamships, I made my first contact with diesel engines in the year 1914 when appointed Second Engineer of a ship propelled by two-stroke engines. Although I have since been closely associated with other types of ships' propelling machinery, this contact has been maintained without interruption until the present time.

Most of the early motorships were propelled by twin screws, a feature appreciated by pioneer operating engineers, as it was generally, though not always, possible to keep one of those open-fronted, drip-lubricated, relatively high-speed engines working until the other had been fitted with a spare cylinder head, piston, crankshaft, crankpin, or crosshead bearing.

Difficulties were also experienced with the smaller parts, such as fuel-pump plungers seizing, exhaust and fuel valves burning, piston cooling gear failing, air-compressors catching fire, high-pressure fuel and compressed-air pipes corroding and bursting, fuel-valve nozzles and exhaust ports choking, cylinder-head valve springs breaking, and other troubles far too numerous to mention, or even remember!

Conditions at sea are now much less arduous, but some of the foregoing difficulties still occur. In days gone by, the endless work and worry was unavoidable owing to lack of knowledge, but when difficulties arise to-day the cause is often failure to take full advantage of the knowledge now readily available.

The reception given to my literary efforts during the past forty years has been most gratifying, and if the demand for this edition equals that for previous editions – a sure indication that the book is meeting a real need – I will feel well repaid for my labours.

I desire to thank many firms who have courteously lent blocks or permitted reproduction of illustrations from their lists, and my publishers, whose co-operation has proved of the greatest value to me.

JOHN LAMB

MONKSEATON,
NORTHUMBERLAND.
August, 1958

Publishers' Note to Fifth Impression

It is with pleasure that the steady continuing demand for this book calls for a further reprint. Although John Lamb died in 1958 his highly popular book lives on.

The ordered sequence of chapters fully describe the components of the marine diesel engine and ancillary equipment, and give a wealth of practical hints and information on handling and maintaining them. Augmenting this, details are given of many problems and solutions with which the author was involved with earlier designs – knowledge of which, beyond the academic, will stand the reader in good stead in analysing difficulties he may meet in the engine-room – however automated and developed this may become. It is not for nothing that a seagoing engineer once described it as "the book that bears the stamp of having been handed up from the engine-room".

During his working life, the author was concerned with a remarkably wide range of engine types, makes and powers: two- and four-stroke, single- and double-acting and opposed-piston, unsupercharged and supercharged, experimental, etc. – right up to the very largest engines producing high powers even when run on heavy residual oils – the very introduction of which fuels into worldwide diesel propulsion to-day was due to his initiative. In his position as Head of Marine Research of one of the largest tanker fleets in the world, many different technical advances in engines and in tankers were originated by him.

Oct. 1981 C. GRIFFIN & CO., LTD.

List of Contents

CHAPTER 1

Fundamentals of diesel engine operation

The diesel engine has now been with us long enough to ensure that all design difficulties have been overcome. Experience has, in fact, shown that it is, as regards reliability, second to none as a means of propelling ships in any part of the world, starting promptly and working regularly in climates ranging from the extremely hot to the extremely cold. The only exceptions are when designers in their eagerness to reduce the weight of an engine, or the space occupied for a given power developed, are carried beyond the point of discretion. Such indiscretions, however, are extremely rare ; and since much is to be desired in the directions mentioned if the low-speed diesel engine is to lead in the race for supremacy, improvements in design should be encouraged, provided deviations from current practice do not reduce the high standard of reliability expected of ships' machinery or make maintenance more difficult.

If a well-established make of engine gives trouble or is costly to keep in order, the cause in 99 cases in every 100 is improper handling. The odd instance may be due to shoddy work by shore labour during periodical refits, but this does not exonerate ships' engineer officers, as supervision at such times is as much their responsibility as is operating the engine at sea. Accidents can happen, of course, but apart from failure of materials because of latent defects, the author knows of only one that might be called unavoidable, and that is an explosion in the crankcase. Even this sort of accident can result only if some part in the crankcase is allowed to become really hot.

In nearly every case serious operating difficulties will be found to have small beginnings, and if by regular and frequent inspection minor faults are detected and remedied in time such difficulties will not occur. For instance, in the case of a four-year-old airless injection engine which came to the author's attention, exhaust valve lids and seats burnt and had to be frequently changed, while several pistons had cracked. In addition, an unbelievable amount of lubricating oil had to be injected into the cylinders in an endeavour to stop gas from blowing past the pistons—as though the fitting of the piston rings had been omitted at the last overhaul. The fuel valves of this engine were supplied from a common rail and operated by cams through a system of levers.

The trouble appeared to be due to the fuel being injected too late because the exhaust temperatures were much too high for the power developed, so the timing of the fuel valves was checked. The timing was found to be reasonably correct so no alterations were made on this occasion. This probable cause of the trouble having been ruled out for the time being, it was decided to start the engine and make more careful observations of the symptoms.

Unfortunately, indicator diagrams could not be obtained, because the indicator operating gear had been removed and could not be found, but it was evident that a power output corresponding to the exhaust temperature and fuel consumed was not being developed. Thoughts were again focussed on the timing of the fuel valves and a further check confirmed the readings previously obtained. Even so, it was decided to advance the beginning of the injection period from 3° to 6° before top dead centre of the crank. This had the effect of increasing slightly the engine revolutions, which indicated that the fault lay in the timing of injection.

The engine was stopped several times subsequently to advance the timing a few degrees. Each adjustment effected an increase in the engine revolutions, and finally it was observed that the exhaust gas temperature was lower by some 15°C. To obtain the last adjustment it was necessary to lift the camshaft and alter its position relative to the crankshaft, after which the fuel valves were found to be opening 20° before top dead centre when the engine was at rest and no pressure present in the fuel valves.

The explanation was that the particular amount of spring in the rather indirect fuel-valve operating gear, aggravated greatly by lost motion due to wear in the various connections, was such that when the engine was in motion and the fuel valves charged with fuel at the working pressure of 4,000 lb/sq.in., the fuel-injection period was delayed. This had the effect of creating abnormally high cylinder temperatures throughout the cycle, with the consequences described earlier.

On another occasion the author investigated the cause of excessive piston rod wear and leakage of gas past the piston rod packing of a double-acting engine. This particular packing consisted of a number of segmental cast-iron rings held against the rod by inward-springing steel rings. On the underside of the uppermost cast-iron rings slots were provided, the intention of the builders presumably being to prevent gas which might leak past the upper surface from accumulating and exerting a pressure behind the rings, and so cause them to bear unduly against the piston rod. Each segmental ring had a total end clearance of 1 mm, and the pressure exerted by the inward-springing steel ring was alone depended upon to keep the rings in contact with the piston rod.

This packing had given very good results, there being no leakage of gas, while the wear rate of the piston rods was negligible so long as the packing was kept properly adjusted and lubricated. Some time after new engineers were appointed to the ship the glands began to leak, and the packing was taken down for examination. The cause of the leakage was thought to be due to the top packing rings having been fitted upside down. Consequently, after the rings had been refitted, the surface containing the slots was uppermost, it being wrongly assumed that the object of the slots was to allow gas under pressure to reach the space behind the packing rings and assist the inward-springing steel rings in pressing them against the piston rods.

This certainly had the effect of stopping the leakage of gas at the glands for a time, but after a year, during which the end clearances of the packing rings had to be readjusted several times, it was found impossible to stop the leakage in the usual way. This was, of course, due to the piston rods having worn at the upper end to such an extent that the ship had to be taken out of service while the piston rods were machined to a uniform diameter, and new packing made and fitted in the proper manner.

There is no doubt that many of the troubles encountered, and much of the expense incurred, are due to running certain small but important parts, which may or may not be known to be out of order, too long. This may be due to the owners not appreciating the necessity for providing an adequate supply of small inexpensive spare parts in addition to the larger and more costly ones, or to the ship's staff not being aware of the serious effect that slight wear of such parts has upon the general operation of an engine.

For instance, if the small needle valve of an airless-injection engine fuel valve has measurable clearance in a sideways direction, the valve may not always reseat squarely. Such a fault, which cannot very well be corrected if new spare parts are not on board, is likely to cause carbonising of the spray nozzles, which will be followed by improper combustion and jamming of piston rings, as well as causing excessive wear of the cylinder liner. On the other hand, it may be that new spare parts are on board but that the engineers, who may not have been accustomed to working to such fine tolerances, do not appreciate that working fits without measurable clearance are not only possible but necessary. Scores of such instances could be quoted, but the foregoing may suffice to show that the ship's engineer officers cannot always be justly blamed for operating difficulties if owners persist in being penny wise and pound foolish.

There are many parts of a diesel engine which must periodically be taken out of service and which can be reconditioned on board and made fit for further service. Generally such parts will not be required for some time, but it occasionally happens that a part recently fitted is not satisfactory and a further change is necessary. It is good practice, therefore, to recondition the parts taken out of service at the very first opportunity so that they will be available if required. Often has a ship to be stopped at sea for periods longer than necessary because of neglect to take this simple precaution, and all too often the wisdom of keeping all small as well as large spare parts ready for immediate use is not fully appreciated. If the small parts must be kept in a corner of a dark store they should be periodically inspected, cleaned, and re-coated with some corrosion preventative.

The temperatures occurring in the cylinders of diesel engines, whence most troubles originate, are high compared with those prevailing in steam engines and turbines, but if they are not allowed to exceed the normal figure no trouble with the parts surrounding the combustion space will result, so long as they are properly cooled and the correct quantity of suitable oil is supplied to lubricate the piston rings.

Abnormally high cylinder temperatures result from unequal power distribution in a line of cylinders when an engine is working at the full rated power, and after-burning is due to bad combustion of fuel. If in consequence of either or both of these faults the normal temperature of the burning gases in the cylinder is exceeded, the very thin film of lubricating oil on the cylinder walls, so essential for the efficient lubrication of the piston rings, is destroyed and excessive wear of the cylinder liners and piston rings will take place. In most other machines excessive wear can be prevented by the expenditure of more lubricating oil, but such troubles are not so easily overcome in the case of diesel engine cylinders. A proportion of the oil in excess of the quantity required to form a film of the correct thickness on the cylinder walls will be carbonised and cause the piston rings to jam in their grooves and blow-past the pistons will occur. In addition to increasing the fuel consumption, per unit power developed, abnormally high cylinder temperatures may also lead to cracking of pistons and cylinder heads, and other equally serious troubles.

It will thus be seen that a great number of serious operating troubles are likely to result from allowing an engine to run unbalanced as regards power output from the individual cylinders, or the fuel to enter the cylinders in such a state that it will not burn completely in the allotted time. The power balance of a diesel engine cannot, unfortunately, be maintained as easily as that of a steam reciprocating engine, because of the greater pressures and temperatures and because the conditions prevailing in the cylinder are dependent upon the correct adjustment of very small parts. The power distribution of a diesel engine must, therefore, be frequently checked.

The temperature of the exhaust gases from individual cylinders is now widely used as a guide to the power developed, it being assumed that if the temperature of the exhaust gases from each cylinder is the same, the power output of the various cylinders will be the same also. This assumption holds good so long as the recording instrument is working properly, the condition of the various cylinder-head valves perfect, the compression pressure and timing of fuel-injection correct, and the devices for atomising the fuel are in good order. Unless every one of these conditions is fulfilled, however, the temperature of the exhaust gases is not a reliable guide to the power developed.

From this it will be appreciated that the temperature of the exhaust gases from the individual cylinders can be relied upon for the purpose of balancing the power output of a line of cylinders, and so ensuring the required power being developed under conditions which are least likely to bring about operating troubles and high maintenance costs, but only if certain parts of the engine are in good working order and properly adjusted. In other words, in order to ensure the successful operation of any well-designed and constructed diesel engine, not only must it be given proper attention whilst operating, but every part must be maintained in good order by regular and careful readjustment, otherwise the most careful and skilful attention possible whilst operating will not prevent involuntary stoppages at sea.

It is, therefore, essential for an operating engineer to know the exact conditions of the parts subjected to wear and tear, and the length of service which may be expected before a complete overhaul becomes necessary. This is possible only by systematic opening-up and close observation of various parts during the first year or so. The ability to make the necessary adjustments is not sufficient. The art of diagnosing the cause of excessive wear and other faults must be developed, and the knowledge necessary to suggest means that will reduce the wear rate or prevent a recurrence of faults must be acquired.

There are some things, however, for which the operating engineer cannot be held responsible. To compare test-bed results with those obtained in service is not quite fair. Engines on shop trials are not subjected to anything comparable to the severe strains resulting from sudden variation in load, as when a ship is in a heavy sea ; the fuel and lubricating oil systems are relatively clean and, besides consuming only fuel from which some of the impurities have had ample time to settle out, there is a much larger staff in attendance than is the case at sea.

After going through this book, most readers will agree that the useful life of most parts depends almost entirely upon the knowledge and skill of the operating engineer. With such qualities it is even in his power to obtain reasonably good results from the main parts of an engine built at a time when materials of construction were inferior and design not so far advanced as they are to-day. On the other hand, the modern engine, which if handled skilfully gives the desired good results, will, if placed in the charge of an incompetent engineer, give endless trouble and the cost of upkeep will be so great that the advantages of the diesel engine in the way of fuel economy and other directions will be lost.

All who are fully conversant with the progress made during recent years with ships' machinery will agree that the responsibilities of the operating engineer have increased very considerably. Not only are the Ministry of Transport examinations more exacting than they were before the advent of present-day machinery, but to operate a modern installation successfully requires executive ability, organising capabilities, and resourcefulness far in advance of previous requirements.

Many engineers serve their entire apprenticeship constructing diesel engines and never get the opportunity to acquire a practical knowledge of steam-driven machinery. Such a state of affairs is regrettable for several reasons, chief amongst which is that the majority of ships are neither wholly steam-driven nor wholly diesel-driven. For reasons not quite clear, some junior engineers who have served their apprenticeship in this way look upon boilers and any machinery driven by steam as inferior, and consider electrically driven machines not worth bothering about, even though they must realise that the safety and efficiency of most ships depend just as much upon the proper working of the steam and electrical auxiliary machinery as upon the main propelling engines. Many do, of course, make a thorough study of the steam-driven and other machinery when they go to sea and the opportunity denied them during their apprenticeship occurs, but the matter is of sufficient importance for the employers of engineering apprentices to offer facilities for progressive apprentices to acquire an all-round experience, even when it means an exchange of apprentices with a firm engaged upon a different class of machinery.

These remarks are prompted not only because of the vast difference occasionally observed in the condition of the different classes of machinery in a ship, but because it is unwise and unfair for a junior engineer without the necessary experience and knowledge to be placed in charge of steam-driven and electrical machinery, no matter how reliable such machinery may be.

Until something in the nature proposed is inaugurated, engineers whose experience has been confined to diesel engines should, in addition to making themselves more proficient in other respects, devote a reasonable amount of their time and energies to acquiring a knowledge of any machinery the practical experience of which has been denied them. By so doing, not only will they benefit themselves and their employers, but they will render valuable service to the nation, since the degree of efficiency attained by ships' operating engineers has a very far-reaching effect.

CHAPTER 2

Cycle of operations in diesel engine cylinders

The diesel engine can operate equally well on both the four-stroke (Otto) and two-stroke (Clerk) cycles of operations, both of which will now be described.

Four-stroke cycle

The diagrams in Fig. 1 illustrate the four piston strokes of the four-stroke cycle as applied to this type of diesel engine in its simplest form, i.e., an engine in which the suction created by the outward movement of the pistons draws the air for combustion into the cylinders.

(1) Beginning at the left-hand diagram, on the first down-stroke of the piston pure air at atmospheric pressure is drawn into the cylinder through the open air-inlet valve in the cylinder head. About the end of this stroke the cylinder is full of air and the air-inlet valve closes.

(2) The return stroke of the piston compresses the air in the cylinder to about 500 lb/sq.in., which raises it to a temperature in the neighbourhood of 1,200°F (650°C). All cylinder-head valves are closed during this stroke.

(3) The third stroke is the working stroke of the cycle. At the beginning of this stroke injection of fuel into the cylinder begins and the hot dense air therein causes the fuel to ignite and burn. Although at this stage the piston is moving out of the cylinder and increasing the volume of the space in which combustion is taking place, the burning fuel maintains the pressure acting on the piston. Injection of fuel ceases after about one-fifth of this stroke has been completed. Combustion having taken place, expansion of the gases proceeds and continues to drive the piston outward until near the end of the stroke, when the exhaust valve in the cylinder head opens. Some of the burnt gases then escape and the pressure in the cylinder is instantly reduced to the pressure in the exhaust pipe, i.e. near atmospheric.

(4) During the fourth stroke (second up-stroke) of the cycle the burnt gases remaining in the cylinder are expelled through the

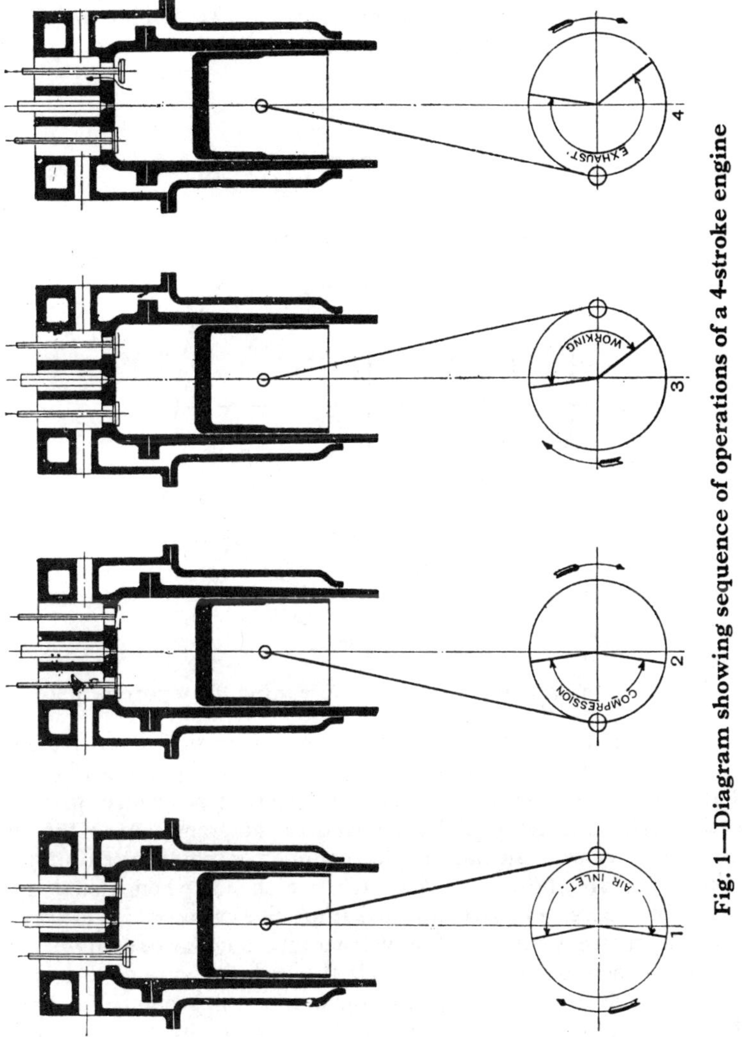

Fig. 1—Diagram showing sequence of operations of a 4-stroke engine

open exhaust valve by the inward-moving piston, after which the cycle of operations is repeated.

For reasons which will be given in a later chapter, the air-inlet and exhaust valves do not open and close exactly at the moment the motion of the piston is reversed, as will be observed from the diagram shown in Fig. 2, which represents the two revolutions of the crank, or the four strokes of the cycle.

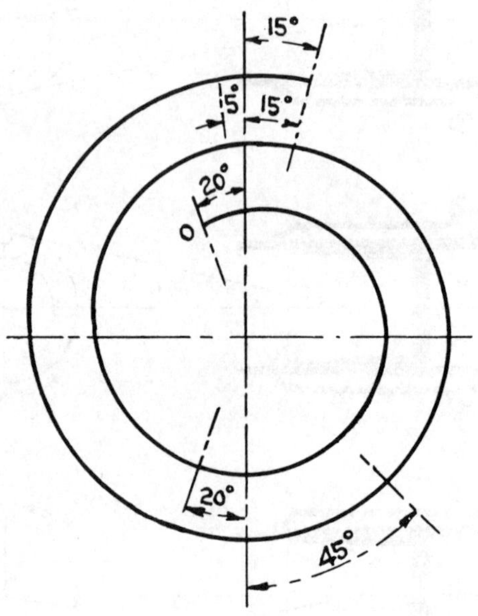

Fig. 2—Timing diagram of 4-stroke engine (unsupercharged)

Beginning at 0 and moving in a clockwise direction, it will be seen that the air-inlet valve begins to open 20° before the top dead centre of the crank and closes 20° after the bottom dead centre, giving a total angular opening of 220°, referred to the crank. After the air-inlet valve closes, the air in the cylinder is compressed until a point 5° before the top dead centre is reached, when injection of fuel commences, and is continued until the crank is 15° over the top dead centre, giving the fuel valve a total angular opening of 20°.

During the next stage of the cycle the high-pressure gases expand and continue to force the piston outward until a point 45° before the bottom centre is reached, when the exhaust valve opens and the products of combustion are released and then expelled by the next inward stroke of the piston, the exhaust valve closing 15° after the top centre.

In practice the opening and closing points of these valves vary according to the type of engine and speed of rotation, but the foregoing timings are a fair average for a simple unsupercharged four-stroke engine running at about 100 revolutions per minute. The valve timings for supercharged engines will be given later.

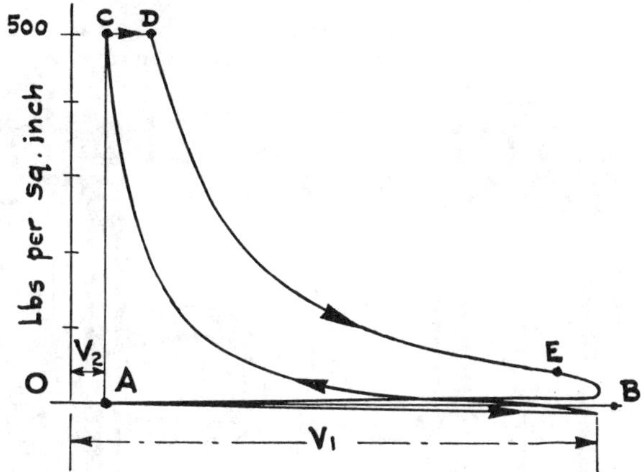

Fig. 3—Theoretical indicator diagram (4-stroke unsupercharged engine)

The four-stroke theoretical indicator diagram given in Fig. 3 shows how the power necessary to do external work is produced. The line *OB* represents the atmospheric pressure line, and the vertical line *AC* the maximum pressure of the cycle, so that the vertical distance above or below the atmospheric line to any point of the diagram represents the pressure in the cylinder at that point.

The distance V_1 represents the total volume of the cylinder, and V_2 the clearance volume, therefore the horizontal distance from the vertical line 0–500 to any point along the line V_1 represents the cylinder volume at that point. Consequently the length of the diagram *AB* represents the stroke of the piston, and the ratio of *AB* to *AO* (the volume swept by the piston to the clearance volume) expresses the compression ratio, which has a value of about 15 to 1.

It will be noted that the air-admission line starting from *A* falls slightly below the atmospheric line. This must be so because a slight vacuum in the cylinder during this stroke is necessary to induce the air to flow into it. The curve terminating at *C* is the compression stroke, from which will be seen how the pressure rises as the cylinder volume decreases. The horizontal line *CD* at the end of the compression curve represents the combustion period. During this short period the maximum pressure in the cylinder remains constant because the burning fuel imparts heat to the air. Injection of fuel begins at the end of the compression stroke and is continued at such a rate that the expansion of the air prevents the pressure in the

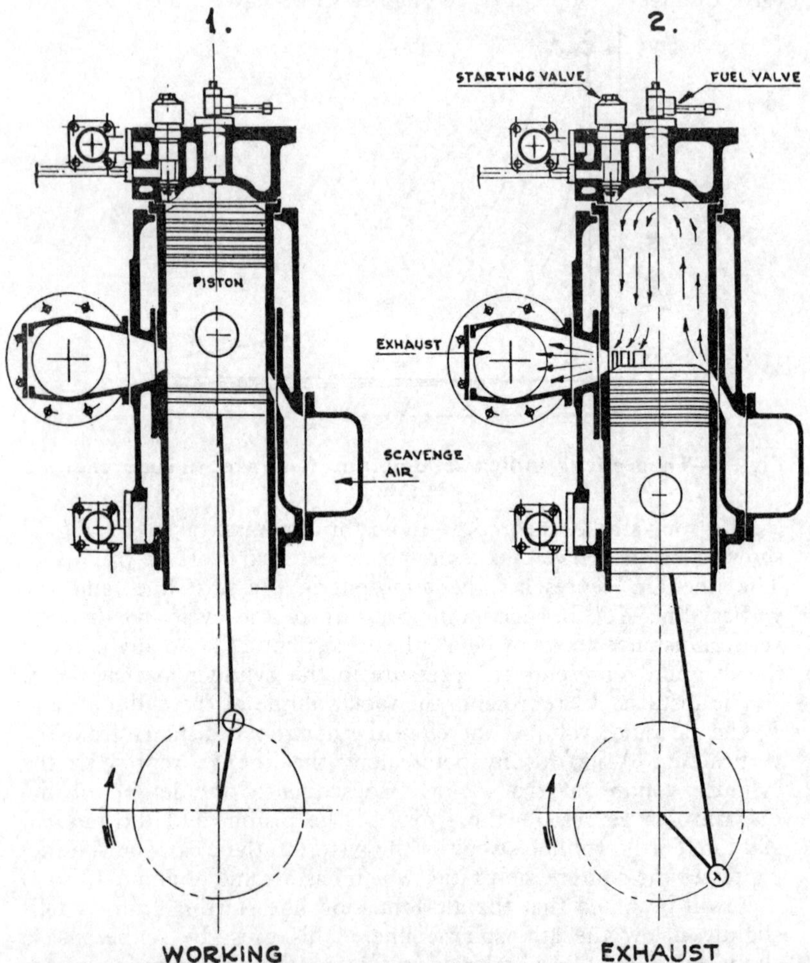

Fig. 4—Diagram showing sequence of

cylinder falling as the cylinder volume increases. This illustrates what is meant by the expression " combustion at constant pressure."

At *D* injection of fuel ceases, and the pressure in the cylinder therefore begins to fall as the cylinder volume increases and the gases expand. The gases continue to expand and the pressure in the cylinder to fall more slowly until the end of the expansion line

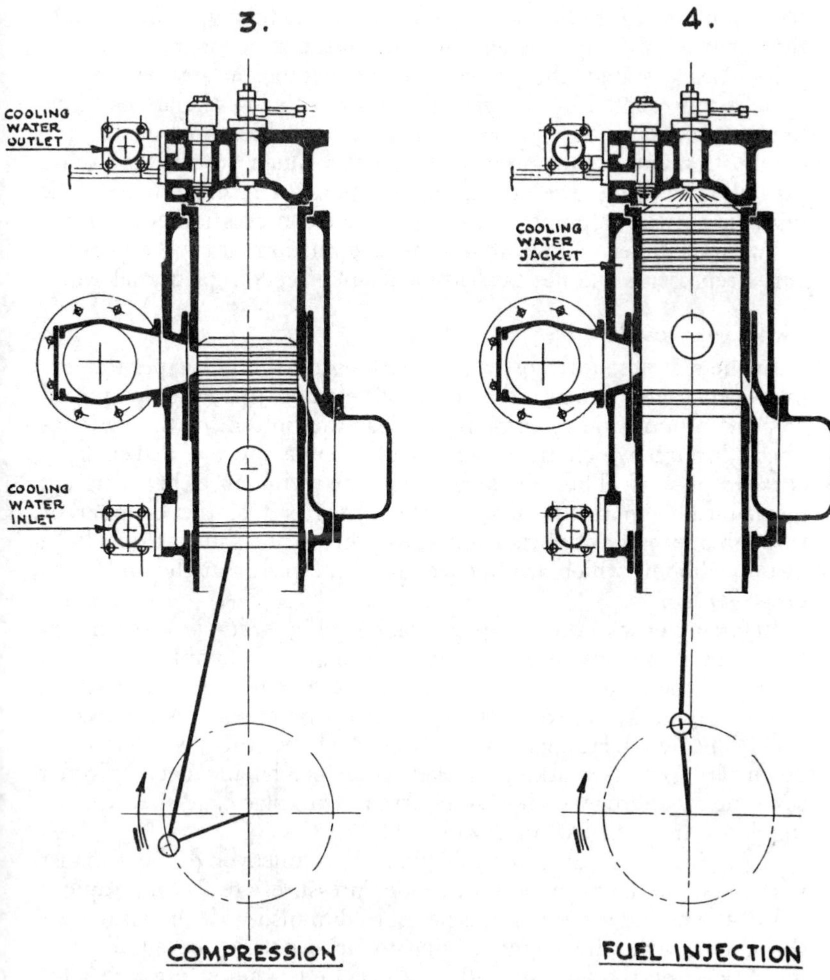

operations of a 2-stroke engine

DE is reached, when the exhaust valve opens and puts the cylinder into communication with the atmosphere. This rapid release accelerates the drop in pressure, as shown at the end of the line *DE*. At this point the cylinder volume remains more or less constant, since the motion of the piston is in process of being reversed.

The beginning of the exhaust line is, it will be noted, slightly above the atmospheric line owing to the mass of gas having to be set in motion and to the slight resistance to the flow of gases through the exhaust valve and passages leading to the atmosphere.

As already stated, the pressure in the cylinder at any part of the cycle is represented by the distance above or below the atmospheric line, consequently it will be evident that the pressures during the combustion and expansion periods are very much greater than those prevailing during the compression period : furthermore, the distance between a point on any part of the compression curve and a point immediately above it on the combustion line or expansion curve represents the net pressure available for doing external work.

Two-stroke cycle

In the simplest form of engine working on this principle the air-inlet stroke and exhaust stroke are eliminated by the employment of ports around the circumference near the bottom of the cylinder liner, through which the products of combustion are driven by a current of air. This air may enter the cylinder either through mechanically operated valves at the upper end of the cylinder or through a number of ports, similar to exhaust ports, near the bottom of the cylinder, which are uncovered by the piston at the end of its down-stroke.

Referring now to the two-page diagram, Fig. 4, it will be seen that the cycle of operations in this type of engine is completed in two strokes of the piston or one revolution of the crank. The four stages in the two strokes forming the cycle of operations are as follows:—

(1) The left-hand diagram of Fig. 4 shows the piston moving downwards on its working stroke ; the fuel having been injected as in the four-stroke engine, combustion takes place and the expanding gases drive the piston downwards.

(2) In the next diagram the piston has uncovered the exhaust ports, and the burnt gases, still under pressure, are flowing rapidly out of the cylinder. When the pressure diminishes to almost that of the atmosphere, the piston begins to uncover the scavenging (air inlet) ports on the opposite side of the cylinder, admitting air under slight pressure. This drives out the remainder of the burnt gases and leaves the cylinder full of air.

(3) In the next stage in the cycle of operations the piston has

moved upwards and closed the scavenging and exhaust ports. Compression of the air thus begins.

(4) At the end of the compression stroke the air in the cylinder is at the same pressure and temperature as with four-stroke engines, and fuel is injected and combustion takes place in exactly the same way.

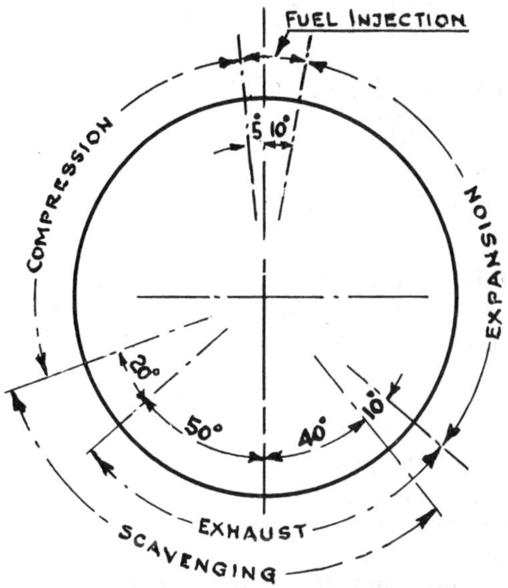

Fig. 5—Timing diagram of an unsupercharged 2-stroke engine

(Cut-off of scavenging air controlled)

Referring to the timing diagram shown in Fig. 5, it will be seen that the admission of fuel begins at 5° before the top dead centre and finishes at 10° after, making a total angular opening of 15°. The fuel injection period is slightly less than in four-stroke engines because release of the burnt gases must, owing to the use of ports, take place earlier.

Expansion of gases takes place until the crank reaches a point 50° from the bottom dead centre, when the piston uncovers the exhaust ports and the products of combustion are released. About 10° later the scavenging air is admitted and the remaining burnt gases are driven out of the cylinder. The air left in the cylinder is trapped and compressed, after which the cycle of operations is repeated.

A two-stroke theoretical indicator diagram is shown in Fig. 6. The compression curve is indicated by *BC*, while *CD* is the

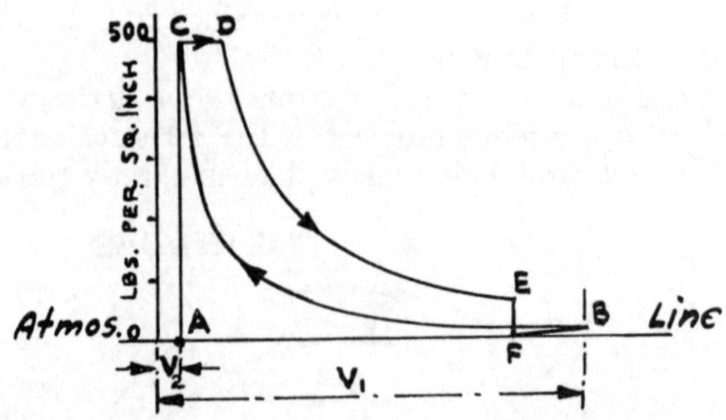

Fig. 6—Theoretical indicator diagram (2-stroke unsupercharged engine)

fuel-injection line and *DE* the expansion curve. At the end of the expansion curve the gaseous contents of the cylinder are at a pressure well above that prevailing in the exhaust passages, so that the cylinder pressure falls rapidly to the pressure of the atmosphere, indicated by *F*. At this point the scavenging ports open and the pressure rises to that of the scavenging air, which is the pressure in the cylinder when the piston begins its compression stroke at *B*.

In practice the burnt gases usually flow out of the cylinder through a row of ports around the circumference of the cylinder, the opening and closing of which is controlled by the piston, while the scavenging air enters through a similar row of ports and its flow is controlled by either the piston or valves. When the latter are used the timing of cut-off is shown in Fig. 5. Scavenging ports are always located in such a position that they are wholly uncovered when the piston is at the end of its out-stroke, but may be above, below or opposite the exhaust ports. The object in every case is to expel as much as possible of the burnt gases and re-charge the cylinder with air at scavenging pressure before compression begins.

The subject of scavenging will be dealt with more fully in a later chapter. This applies also to the fuel-injection process, which in modern engines is not strictly in accordance with the true diesel cycle of operations. Furthermore, all four-stroke and most two-stroke diesel engines are now supercharged and the points at which the exhausting and air-inlet processes begin and end are different from those given in this chapter. The timings of such engines will also be dealt with in a later chapter.

CHAPTER 3

Thermodynamics of the diesel heat cycle

Having now a knowledge of how the diesel engine works, we can pass on to a study of the behaviour of the gases in the cylinder during the various stages of the cycle of operations, but before doing so it would perhaps be as well to define some of the terms it will be necessary to use.

Temperature

This term merely denotes the " hotness " of a body. The fact that one body is hotter, or has a higher temperature, than another, does not mean that the hotter one necessarily contains more heat. Moreover, heat will always flow from a hot body to one at a lower temperature in contact with it, but this does not necessarily imply that the rise in temperature of the colder body will be equal to the fall in temperature of the hotter body, even though the mass in each case is equal and the transfer takes place without loss.

Absolute temperatures are those reckoned from an imaginary low temperature of such an order that if it were possible to reach such a temperature the volume of a gas would be zero. It is known that the volume of a gas decreases at a uniform rate for each degree drop in temperature over the range within which readings are obtainable, so that if this were to hold good for all temperatures, however low, the volume of the gas would be zero at a temperature of approximately −459°F (−273°C).

Unit of heat

This is generally termed the " British Thermal Unit " (B.T.U.) and is the quantity of heat required to raise the temperature of 1 lb of water 1°F, the temperature of the water being that of maximum density, namely, 39·2°F (4°C). The unit of heat employed on the Continent is the " Calorie," and is the quantity of heat required to raise the temperature of one kilogram of water from 4° to 5°C.

Specific heat

The quantity of heat required to raise the temperature of 1 lb of water 1°F is, as just mentioned, 1 heat unit or 1 B.T.U., but the heat required to raise the temperature of other substances a similar amount varies according to the nature of the substance. Therefore, the term " specific heat " denotes the number of heat units required to raise the temperature of unit weight of the substance in question through 1°F.

Water is taken as the standard substance because it has a greater capacity for heat than any other known liquid, as well as most solids. Gases have two different specific heats according to whether heat is applied at constant volume or constant pressure. The following table gives the specific heats of various materials :—

Water	1·000
Petroleum fuel	0·434
Lubricating oil	0·500
Mercury (liquid)	0·033
Air at constant pressure	0·238
,, ,, ,, volume	0·169
Steam at constant pressure	0·475
,, ,, ,, volume	0·370
Cast iron	0·130
Mild steel	0·116
Tin	0·056
Brass	0·094

Thus it will be seen that 0·434 heat units are required to raise the temperature of 1 lb of petroleum 1°F. Furthermore, that whilst it requires one heat unit to raise the temperature of 1 lb of water 1°F, the same quantity of heat will raise the temperature of 1 lb of petroleum $\frac{1}{0{\cdot}434} = 2{\cdot}3$°F (1·3°C), and mercury no less than $\frac{1}{0{\cdot}033} = 30$°F (16·6°C).

Mechanical equivalent of heat

When heat is transformed into work, or work into heat, the quantity of heat is equivalent to the amount of work done. Joule discovered that 778 foot-pounds of work were equivalent to one heat unit (B.T.U.). Therefore the quantity of heat required to change the temperature of 1 lb of water one degree F is capable of doing 778 ft lb of work.

Thermal efficiency

It is well known that the quantity of heat supplied in the fuel to any form of power producer, such as an internal combustion engine, is greater than that which comes away from it in the cooling water, exhaust gases, and by radiation, and that the missing part is the quantity of heat which has been converted into mechanical work. The thermal efficiency or heat efficiency of an engine, therefore, is a measure of the perfection with which the heat supplied is converted into mechanical work—the greater the proportion of heat converted into mechanical work the higher the thermal efficiency of the engine.

The thermal efficiency of a diesel engine is expressed in two ways, namely, "indicated thermal efficiency" and "brake thermal efficiency." The former represents the quantity of heat which is converted into work in the engine cylinders, and the latter the quantity available for doing external work. The quantity of heat supplied is found from the weight of fuel of known heat value consumed, the quantity converted into work in the engine cylinders from indicated diagrams, while the quantity available for doing useful or external work is found by means of a water brake or torsionmeter connected to the end of the crankshaft.

Mechanical efficiency

This term represents the ratio of the work done by an engine, or the work it is capable of doing, to the work done in the cylinders. The former is generally referred to as external work and the latter as internal work; the difference between work done internally and externally representing the work lost in overcoming frictional and other resistances in the engine itself, such as the power required to drive attached pumps, etc. The mechanical efficiency, therefore, of a reciprocating engine is obtained by dividing the brake h.p. by the indicated h.p. In an imaginary frictionless engine these two measures of power would be equal and the mechanical efficiency would be 100 per cent.

Heat transfer

The transfer of heat takes place either by what is termed conduction, convection, or radiation. Conduction is the gradual transfer of heat from one mass to another, whether liquid, solid, or gaseous. The rate at which the heat flows, usually measured in heat units per second per unit area, is directly proportional to the difference in temperature. The measure of conductivity is the quantity of heat in heat units that flows per second across a face one square foot in area, when the temperature drop is one degree per foot of distance the heat travels.

Convection is the transmission of heat through a substance by actual mixing of the particles as a result of circulation. Convection, therefore, is the principal means by which temperature is equalised in liquids and gases. It cannot occur in solids as the parts of such substances are fixed relatively one to another.

Radiation is the transfer of heat through space by wave motion. Heat radiation is in character precisely similar to light. Both travel at the same speed, the only difference between them being that light waves have a shorter wave-length than heat waves.

In the case of internal combustion engine cylinders, the heat in the burning and expanding gases is transferred to the comparatively cool walls mainly by radiation and convection. The heat when received by the cylinder walls passes through them by conduction and is carried away in the cooling water by convection.

Volumetric efficiency

This term refers to machines used to pump liquids or gases and is the ratio of the maximum theoretical capacity of the machine to the actual capacity. In the case of positive displacement pumps it is the volume of gas or liquid drawn into the cylinders of reciprocating machines or the casing of rotary machines, divided by the volume swept by the piston or rotors, respectively. In the case of internal combustion engines, it is the measure of the thoroughness with which the suction stroke of the cycle performs its function of recharging the cylinders with pure air for the next combustion process.

Isothermal compression and expansion

When a gas such as air is compressed or expanded so that its pressure is varied and, during the process, its temperature remains the same, it is said to have been compressed or expanded isothermally. To effect this, the heat generated when a gas is compressed has to be conducted away as fast as it is produced; and an equivalent quantity of the heat lost when a gas is expanded must be added to maintain the temperature.

Adiabatic compression and expansion

When a gas is compressed or expanded and its pressure varied without loss or gain of heat, to or from an external source, it is said to have been compressed or expanded adiabatically.

Boyle's Law

This law states that if the temperature of a gas be kept constant by the extraction or addition of heat when the gas is compressed or expanded, the volume of the gas will vary inversely as the pressure. In other words, the pressure of a mass of gas multiplied by its volume at any point of the compression or expansion process equals a constant if the temperature remains unaltered.

In symbols:

$$PV = \text{Constant.}$$

Charles's Law

This law states that if the pressure be kept constant, equal volumes of different gases increase equally if the temperature rise is the same; also, that if a mass of gas be heated under constant pressure, equal increments in its volume correspond very closely to equal increases in temperature. In other words, the volume of gas is proportional to its absolute temperature if the pressure is constant. It follows from this and Boyle's Law that the pressure of gas is proportional to its absolute temperature if the volume is constant.

Compression ratio

The compression ratio when applied to an internal combustion engine or gas-compressing machine is found by dividing the volume of the cylinder contents at the beginning of compression (not necessarily at the beginning of the compression stroke of the piston) by the volume at the end of the compression process.

To obtain a terminal compression temperature in the region of 1,200°F (650°C) atmospheric air must be compressed to about 500 lb/sq.in. The clearance volume necessary for this compression is, say, 8 to 6 per cent of the stroke (swept) volume.

Maximum efficiency

The conditions necessary to ensure the maximum efficiency of any internal combustion engine are:—(1) the largest possible cylinder volume with minimum surface, so that the least possible proportion of heat is lost by passing through the surrounding walls; (2) the highest possible speed of working, so that the least possible time is allowed for the transfer of heat from the hot gases to the comparatively cool cylinder walls; (3) the maximum ratio of expansion, so that the greatest possible proportion of heat in the gases will be converted into mechanical work; and (4) the highest possible compression ratio, because the efficiency of the engine increases with the compression ratio, as will be seen by inspection of the expression for the ideal efficiency of the diesel engine, namely,

$$\text{Efficiency} = 1 - \left(\frac{1}{r}\right)^{\gamma-1}, \text{ where } r \text{ is the ratio of compression.}$$

The greater r is, the smaller the value of the second term in the expression and, therefore, the greater the efficiency of the engine.

Proceeding now to a detailed examination of the changes in state of the gases which result in a diesel engine cylinder, the simplest form of atmospheric (unsupercharged) four-stroke engine will be taken first.

Air-inlet stroke

The air drawn from the atmosphere on this stroke has a temperature of, say, 60°F (15·6°C), and an absolute pressure of 14·7 lb/sq.in., but after it has entered the cylinder its temperature may be expected to have increased a certain amount owing to its making contact during its passage with the hot cylinder walls and to its mixing with hot burnt gases left in the cylinder compression space from the previous cycle. As we are dealing with slow-running engines the initial and final pressure will be practically the same, i.e. atmospheric, so that the only change in the state of the gas during this stroke is change of temperature.

Taking first the rise in temperature due to the air making contact with the hot cylinder walls, this factor can doubtless be neglected, since only a very small proportion of the air taken in must make contact, and because during the greater part of the stroke the air is slightly wire-drawn as it passes through the cylinder-head valve, which has the effect of reducing its temperature a few degrees. It is probable therefore that, were the whole of the burnt gases from the previous cycle expelled, the temperature of the air in the cylinder at the end of the air-inlet stroke would not be very different from the atmospheric temperature. The difference would be slightly greater, i.e. temperature higher, the lower the piston speed, because of the longer time allowed for the air to become heated.

The exact increase in temperature resulting from mixture with the burnt gases left in the cylinder depends mainly upon the actual weight of air drawn into the cylinder and the temperature of the burnt gases left in the cylinder, both rather uncertain values. These values can, however, be assumed and a fairly accurate measure of the increase in temperature obtained in the following manner.

We will assume that at the beginning of the air-inlet stroke the cylinder clearance space, which is, say $\frac{1}{15}$ the volume swept by the piston, is filled with burnt gases at a temperature of 1,000°F (538°C), or 1,459°F (811°C) Absolute, and that it has the same weight per unit volume and the same specific heat value as air. If, for the sake of simplifying explanation and calculation, we assume that the burnt gases and fresh air do not mix until the end of the stroke—actually, of course, they do mix, but the result is unaffected by such an assumption—the burnt gases and the air have the following values at the end of the stroke:—

	Burnt gases	Air
Pressure, lb/sq.in. Absolute . . .	14·7	14·7
Volume in units of clearance space . .	1	15
Temperature °F Absolute . . .	1,459	519
,, °C ,, . . .	811	288·6

We will now assume that the burnt gases and air mix together, the temperature of the former being reduced and the latter increased in the process. As the pressure remains constant during the process, the burnt gases will contract in volume and the air will expand, the amounts depending upon the respective changes in their absolute temperatures. As the combined volume and the pressure do not alter during the mixing, the mean temperature of the burnt gases and air, or in other words, the final temperature at the end of the air inlet stroke, is determined as follows, taking the volume and temperature values already given:

The burnt gases give up heat to the air, and if we neglect the heat given up by the cylinder walls, the heat lost by the burnt gases, which we will represent by H_1, is equal to the heat gained by the air, which will be represented by H_2. Therefore $H_1 = H_2$.

The burnt gases and air have practically the same weight for equal volumes, so that the respective weights can be taken as 1 and 15. Therefore, by substituting the given values in the general formula:

$$*H = p \times W(T_1 - T_2)$$

we get

$$H_1 = 0{\cdot}24 \times 1\,(1{,}459 - T) = H_2$$
$$= 0{\cdot}24 \times 15\,(T - 519)$$

* p represents the specific heat of air at constant pressure. Actually its value is 0·238. See page 18.

$$\text{Therefore} \quad 1{,}459 - T = 15 \times T - 15 \times 519$$
$$16T = 1{,}459 + 15 \times 519$$
$$\text{and} \quad T = \frac{9{,}244}{16} = 578°\text{F Absolute.}$$

The mean temperature of the cylinder contents at the end of the suction or air-inlet stroke is therefore 578 – 459 = 119°F (48·3°C) when the atmospheric temperature is 60°F (15·6°C).

Since the power any engine is capable of developing is directly proportional to the amount of air drawn into the cylinder on the air-inlet stroke, or, in other words, since the power output depends upon the volumetric efficiency, the pressure and temperature of the cylinder contents at the end of the stroke are of importance. The nearer the pressure and temperature are to those of the atmosphere, the greater will be the volumetric efficiency.

From this it will be clear that if the pressure and temperature of the air in the cylinder were equal to those of the atmosphere, the volumetric efficiency would be 100 per cent and, consequently, the lower the pressure and the higher the temperature, the lower will be the volumetric efficiency. In practice the volumetric efficiency can never be 100 per cent, not only because the air in the cylinder is slightly higher in temperature and slightly lower in pressure than that of the atmosphere, but also because the piston must have an end working clearance. Any air under pressure left in the working clearance will, of course, expand and reduce the amount of air taken in and, therefore, the volumetric efficiency. The volumetric efficiency of low-speed diesel engines varies from 90 to 95 per cent. Higher piston speeds and higher exhaust temperatures result in a lower volumetric efficiency, even in a properly designed and well operated engine.

Compression stroke

The compression of air in the cylinder of a diesel engine is not isothermal, because the temperature increases during the process; nor is it adiabatic, because some of the heat generated during the process passes through the surrounding walls into the cooling water. As, therefore, the temperature changes during the process and heat is lost also, the law which covers the actual conditions in the diesel engine lies between the isothermal and adiabatic laws, and is represented by the equation:

$$P_1 \times V_1^n = P_2 \times V_2^n = \text{Constant} \qquad (1)$$

the power index n having a value between unity, for the isothermal law, and 1·408, for the adiabatic law. The figure 1·408 is the ratio of the specific heat of air at constant pressure to that at constant volume. These values are given on page 18.

The more heat that is lost during the process the nearer will the compression approach the isothermal condition, and, consequently, the nearer will the power index n in the foregoing equation approach unity; while conversely, the less heat lost the more nearly is the compression adiabatic and the closer is the power index to 1·408. In practice the amount of heat lost is such that the power index n ranges between 1·32 and 1·37, so that the figure 1·35 may be taken to represent average conditions. The equation representing the changes in pressure and volume during compression in the diesel engine cylinder therefore becomes:

$$P_1 \times V_1^{1\cdot 35} = P_2 \times V_2^{1\cdot 35} \qquad (2)$$

As the weight of air in the cylinder during compression remains constant, the changes which occur are confined to temperature, pressure, and volume. The changes which occur are all in accordance with the general law expressed by the following equation, which embodies both Boyle's and Charles's laws given on page 21:

$$\frac{P_1 \times V_1}{T_1} = \frac{P_2 \times V_2}{T_2} = \text{Constant} \qquad (3)$$

where P_1 = absolute initial pressure
P_2 = absolute final pressure
V_1 = initial volume
V_2 = final volume
T_1 = absolute initial temperature
T_2 = absolute final temperature.

Combining the two equations just given, the following equation connecting pressures and volumes with the temperature results:—

From equation (2),
$$P_1 = P_2\left(\frac{V_2}{V_1}\right)^{1\cdot 35}$$

Substituting in equation (3),
$$\frac{P_2V_1\left(\frac{V_2}{V_1}\right)^{1\cdot 35}}{T_1} = \frac{P_2V_2}{T_2}$$

Therefore
$$T_2 = \frac{T_1V_2}{V_1\left(\frac{V_2}{V_1}\right)^{1\cdot 35}} = T_1 \times \frac{V_2}{V_1} \times \left(\frac{V_1}{V_2}\right)^{1\cdot 35}$$

$$= T_1 \times \left(\frac{V_1}{V_2}\right)^{0\cdot 35}$$

Also from equation (3), $$V_1 = \frac{P_2V_2T_1}{P_1T_2}$$

and substituting in equation (1),

$$P_1\left(\frac{P_2V_2T_1}{P_1T_2}\right)^n = P_2V_2^n$$

Therefore $$\frac{P_1P_2^nT_1^n}{P_1^nT_2^n} = P_2$$

$$\frac{P_2}{P_2^n} = \frac{T_1^n}{P_1^{n-1}\,T_2^n}$$

$$\frac{1}{P_2^{n-1}} = \frac{T_1^n}{P_1^{n-1}\,T_2^n}$$

$$\left(\frac{P_1}{P_2}\right)^{n-1} = \left(\frac{T_1}{T_2}\right)^n$$

$$\left(\frac{P_1}{P_2}\right)^{\frac{n-1}{n}} = \frac{T_1}{T_2}$$

Therefore $T_1 = T_2 \times \left(\dfrac{P_1}{P_2}\right)^{0\cdot259}$ or $T_2 = T_1 \times \left(\dfrac{P_2}{P_1}\right)^{0\cdot259}$

We are now in a position to calculate the pressure and temperature of the air in the cylinder of a diesel engine at the end of the compression stroke, and for purposes of illustration will assume that the air at the beginning of the compression stroke has the values already given; that is:

$$P_1 = 14{\cdot}7;\quad V_1 = 16;\quad T_1 = 578;\quad V_2 = 1$$

As has already been stated, the equation connecting pressures and volumes is:

$$P_1 \times V_1^{1\cdot35} = P_2 \times V_2^{1\cdot35}$$

so that $$P_2 = P_1 \times \left(\frac{V_1}{V_2}\right)^{1\cdot35}$$

Substituting the assumed values, we have:

$$P_2 = 14{\cdot}7 \times \left(\frac{16}{1}\right)^{1\cdot35}$$

$= 623$ lb/sq.in. Absolute

$= 608{\cdot}3$ lb/sq.in. by gauge.

The temperature of the air at the end of the compression stroke is given by the equation:

$$T_2 = T_1\left(\frac{V_1}{V_2}\right)^{0\cdot35}$$

Substituting known values, we have:

$$T_2 = 578 \times \left(\frac{16}{1}\right)^{0 \cdot 35}$$

$$= 1{,}525°\text{F Absolute} = 1{,}066°\text{F on thermometer scale.}$$

This proves that, in the general case given, a compression ratio of 16 gives a final pressure of 608·3 lb/sq.in. by gauge and that when air is compressed to this pressure under the conditions prevailing in the diesel engine a temperature of 1,066°F (575°C) results. This temperature is sufficiently high to ensure the prompt ignition of all fuels in general use, even when the engine is working at not more than 30 per cent of the designed speed. It will be appreciated that the lower the piston speed the nearer will the compression approach the isothermal condition, since the longer the time taken for the process to be completed, the greater will be the amount of heat that will pass through the surrounding cylinder liner into the cooling water.

Combustion and expansion stroke

The only part of the combustion process with which we need concern ourselves here is the change in temperature of the air in the cylinder, the exact determination of which is far too complex to be dealt with in a work of this nature. It is, however, possible to arrive at the approximate temperature of combustion by means of a simple calculation.

When injection of fuel into the dense hot air begins, the temperature of the air increases at a uniform rate and reaches a maximum when the last particle of fuel enters the cylinder, assuming, of course, that the fuel begins to burn instantly and that the process is completed the moment the fuel valve closes. Generally, the greater the amount of fuel injected into a cylinder containing a given weight of air, the greater will be the combustion temperature. Supercharging permits a greater quantity of fuel to be burnt without increasing the temperature.

Since in the true diesel cycle the pressure remains constant during the combustion process, and as the gases in the cylinder remain constant also as regards quantity and obey the laws of a perfect gas, it might be expected that the rise in temperature will be in proportion to the increase in volume, or in accordance with the law: $\frac{V_1}{T_1} = \frac{V_2}{T_2}$. This is not the case, however, since the quantity of the cylinder contents is increased by the addition of the fuel and the gases undergo other changes, such as increase in specific heat, which affect the estimation of the exact temperature.

In order to ascertain the approximate value, we will assume that the gases do obey the law: $\frac{V_1}{T_1} = \frac{V_2}{T_2}$, and that injection and combustion of fuel terminate when the piston has travelled one-fifteenth of its stroke. The volume at the end of injection would then be about twice that at the beginning of injection, and consequently the maximum temperature would be twice the final compression temperature. If the final compression temperature is 1,525°F Absolute, then the maximum temperature of combustion would be 3,050°F Absolute or 2,591°F (1,442°C) on the thermometer scale.

In practice the combustion process is not completed until after the fuel valve closes, the actual point on the stroke depending chiefly upon the characteristics of the fuel. The temperature of the cylinder contents, therefore, continues to increase, but at a reduced rate due to the increasing volume of the combustion space during the early part of the expansion period, and the temperature at the end of this period will be greater than it would have been if the maximum temperature were reached earlier in the stroke. Consequently, although the whole of the heat in the fuel may be liberated before the exhausting process begins, so long as the maximum combustion temperature is not reached until comparatively late on the stroke, a proportion of the heat will be wasted. A colourless exhaust is not, therefore, a true indication that all the heat in the fuel is being used to the greatest advantage.

That the first particles of fuel to be injected into the cylinder burn more or less instantaneously is probable, but the same cannot be said of the last of the fuel particles which do not meet pure air upon entry, so that the maximum combustion temperature is probably never reached, in practice, until at some point during the early part of the expansion period. However, it is near enough for all practical purposes to assume that the fuel burns instantaneously, in which case the contents of the cylinder will behave more or less as a perfect gas during the expansion period and follow the same general law as governs the compression process. That is to say, expansion of the burnt gases will take place according to the formula:

$$P_1 \times V_1^n = P_2 \times V_2^n$$

Taking the case already given, then:

$623 \times 2^{1 \cdot 35} = P_2 \times 16^{1 \cdot 35}$

Therefore $P_2 = 623 \times \left(\frac{2}{16}\right)^{1\cdot35}$

$= 623 \times 0\cdot0603$

$= 37\cdot6$ lb/sq.in. Absolute

And since $T_2 = T_1 \times \left(\frac{P_2}{P_1}\right)^{0\cdot259}$

then $T_2 = 3{,}050 \times \left(\frac{37\cdot6}{623}\right)^{0\cdot259}$

$= 3{,}050 \times 0\cdot470$

$= 1{,}432$°F Absolute.

This is the absolute temperature of the gases at the end of the expansion stroke, so that the temperature on the thermometer scale will be 973°F (523°C).

Exhaust stroke

The exhausting process begins before the piston reaches the end of the working stroke; the changes which take place during this part of the cycle are generally known and relatively unimportant, excepting that the temperature of the expelled gases has a great influence upon the maintenance of the exhaust valves of four-stroke engines and the bars dividing the exhaust ports of two-stroke engines. At the moment when the burnt gases are released, the pressure of the gases in the cylinder is in the neighbourhood of 40 lb/sq.in. absolute and the temperature 1,000°F (538°C).

When release of gases takes place, the pressure falls rapidly to that of the atmosphere and the temperature falls also to about 800°F (427°C). The pressure and the temperature of the gases remain practically constant at these values during the whole of the exhaust stroke.

Scavenging

The only part of the two-stroke cycle of operations which is essentially different from the four-stroke cycle is the operation of expelling the burnt gases and recharging the cylinder with pure air.

The scavenging air is supplied at about 2 lb and 15°F (8·3°C) above atmospheric pressure and temperature, respectively, but upon passing through the openings in the heated cylinder walls and making direct contact with the hot burnt gases in the cylinder, its temperature will be increased. As, however, only a small proportion of the air makes contact with the hot cylinder walls and burnt gases, and since it is the first of the air to be admitted to the cylinder which receives the most heat, the rise in temperature will be slight, especially since the air which receives the most heat passes straight through the cylinder into the exhaust passage, leaving comparatively cool air in the cylinder. Therefore, when the compression stroke begins, the pressure and temperature of the air in a two-stroke engine cylinder will not differ materially from those in a four-stroke engine. Actually if the scavenging process is efficiently carried out, less burnt gases will be left in the cylinder and the temperature will be slightly lower in the case of two-stroke engines.

After the exhaust ports are closed, air continues to flow until the scavenging ports close, so that the pressure of the air in the cylinder is from 1 to 2 lb/sq.in. when compression begins, and the same general law as given for four-stroke engines is followed.

CHAPTER 4

General description of the marine diesel engine

The engine invented by Dr. Diesel was intended to work by drawing air into a cylinder, the flow of air from the atmosphere being induced by the outward or suction stroke of the piston. During the first part of the compression stroke the air was to be compressed isothermally, i.e. at constant temperature, by spraying water into the cylinder, the heat of compression being absorbed by the evaporation of the water.

At a certain point during the compression stroke of the piston the water spray was to be stopped and, during the remaining portion of the stroke the air compressed adiabatically with the object of producing a rapid rise of temperature in the cylinder, heavily insulated to prevent loss of heat.

When the piston reached the end of the compression stroke powdered coal was to be injected into the cylinder and, meeting the hot compressed air therein, ignited immediately. After the piston had travelled a certain distance on the outward or working stroke, the injection of fuel was to be stopped and the hot gases were to be expanded to atmospheric pressure and temperature. A thermal efficiency of 50 per cent, it was claimed, would be obtained with such an engine.

After experiments it was found that the ratio of compression and expansion was too great, while water injection into the cylinder had to be abandoned owing to mechanical difficulties with the reciprocating piston. A jacket had to be provided around the cylinder to permit it being water-cooled and so prevent seizure of the piston, while liquid hydrocarbons of low ash content had to be used instead of powdered coal as fuel. Most of these modifications meant a loss in thermal efficiency, but ultimately resulted in a commercially successful engine.

Although the compression ignition engine has become generally known as the " Diesel " engine, Herbert Akroyd Stuart, a Yorkshireman (1864–1927), contributed more than is generally known to its development. He began experimental work at Fenny Stratford in 1886 and by about 1890 actually had two compression ignition engines working, in both of which were first applied the principles now accepted as fundamental in modern diesel engine design.

Although the processes occurring in the cylinders of modern engines remain practically the same, yet the construction of such engines, particularly marine engines, differs very materially from the early designs. No particular person or company of engine builders can claim to have invented and introduced the many and varied improvements that have made the present-day efficient and reliable engine, the change having come about gradually, by the help of many, between the years 1910 and 1930. The improvements effected since that time have been mainly concerned with reducing the weight per unit power developed and making the engine less selective as regards quality of fuel.

Two-stroke v. four-stroke engines

At first most of the engines constructed were of the two-stroke type, but after a few years engines working on the four-stroke principle were mostly favoured, chiefly because the power output requirements for ship propulsion were moderate and the operating conditions in this type less severe. The demand for higher powers and the discovery of materials of construction capable of resisting the more severe operating conditions have, however, brought the two-stroke principle back into favour.

Until 1926 the supremacy of the four-stroke single-acting engine was not seriously threatened, yet while it retained its popularity, the two-stroke was making such steady headway that the advocates of the four-stroke principle introduced double-acting engines with the object of reducing the weight per unit power developed and so minimising the advantage held in this respect by the two-stroke engine.

The four-stroke double-acting engine did not hold favour very long, however, owing to the inaccessibility of the parts—air-inlet, exhaust and other valves—required for the lower end of the cylinders, and the two-stroke single-acting engine took the lead. About this time serious attention was also being given to double-acting engines operating on the two-stroke principle.

The advantages of supercharging were then demonstrated and recognised, and as this improvement resulted in about 30 per cent increase in power output for the same weight, the four-stroke engine again came into favour, the two-stroke double-acting engine remaining a serious competitor. After further experience had been gained with this latest improvement, the original atmospheric four-stroke engine disappeared from the builders' yards, while the supercharged four-stroke single-acting engine and the two-stroke single-acting engine were equally popular for the tramp class of ship. For passenger ships the double-acting two-stroke engine led all others because of the high power required on a line of shafting.

Until this time most engines operated on the air injection system, i.e. the fuel was blown into the cylinder by compressed air at 1,000 lb/sq.in. pressure, but by 1934 all mechanical and combustion difficulties previously experienced with the airless (direct injection) system of fuel injection had been overcome. This mainly resulted from the remarkable accuracy of modern machine tools used for the construction of high-pressure fuel pumps and valves. As, however, this improvement was applicable to both types of engines, with equal advantages, it had no effect upon the race for supremacy.

The present position regarding the types is that the four-stroke is disappearing and is unlikely to return to popularity unless it can be developed to employ a supercharge air-pressure greatly in excess of its rival. The present indications are that the supercharge air pressure will be greatly increased but that this improvement will be applicable to both types. And in recent years the opposed piston two-stroke engine has entered the field to the disadvantage of the four-stroke and single-piston two-stroke engines.

The fuel consumption of the four-stroke engine is roughly 0·3 lb per hour per i.h.p., and that of the two-stroke the same per i.h.p., but slightly greater per b.h.p. to the extent of from 5 to 8 per cent, due to the extra load of the scavenging air pump when this is directly coupled to the engine. The scavenging pump, which is an essential part of this type, as previously described, is required to supply low-pressure air to expel the burnt gases and leave the cylinder full of pure air, since the exhaust and air-inlet strokes are eliminated. The modern four-stroke engine drives its supercharge pump mechanically, though the latter is not essential for its operation, since the most recent development is to supply the low-pressure air in either type by means of blowers driven by the exhaust gases from the engine.

Cross-sections of Sulzer and Burmeister and Wain single-acting two-stroke engines are shown in Fig. 7, at (*A*) and (*B*), respectively. Fig. 8 shows the Burmeister and Wain double-acting two-stroke engine. This works on the opposed piston principle: a main, double-acting piston working between two short-stroke pistons

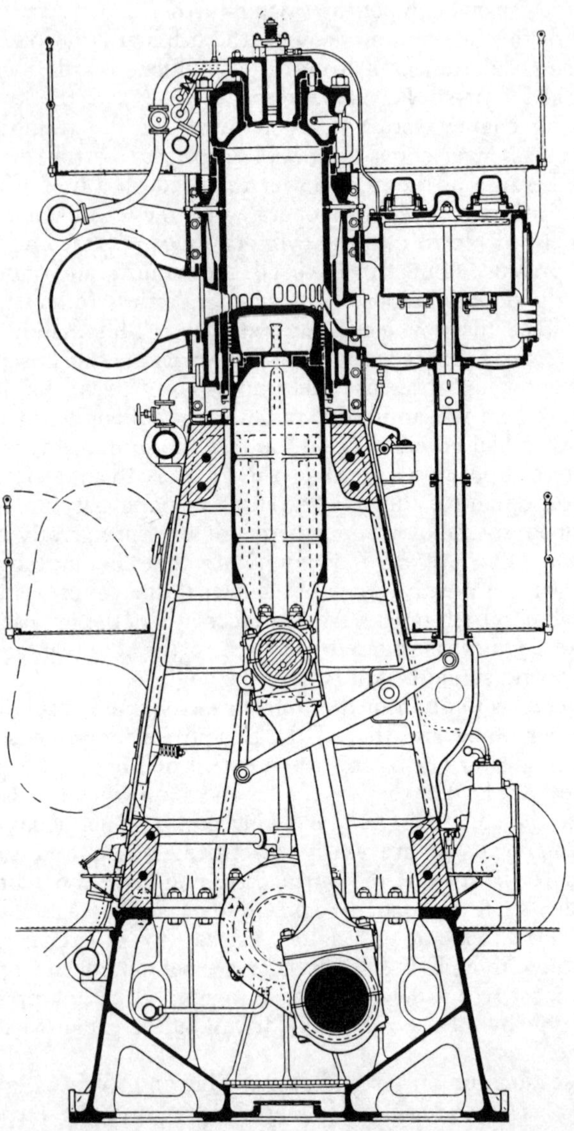

Fig. 7(A)—Cross-section through a Sulzer 2-stroke single-acting engine

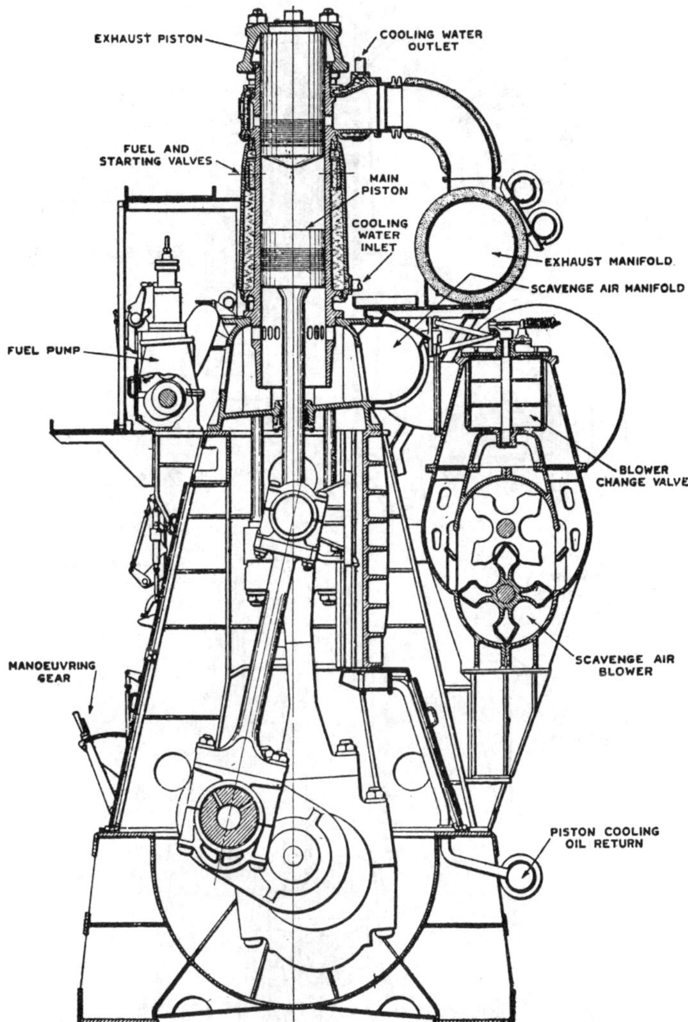

Fig. 7(B)—Cross-section through a Burmeister & Wain 2-stroke single-acting engine

reciprocating in the ends of the cylinder and taking the place of rigid covers. The lower exhaust piston accommodates the piston rod packing.

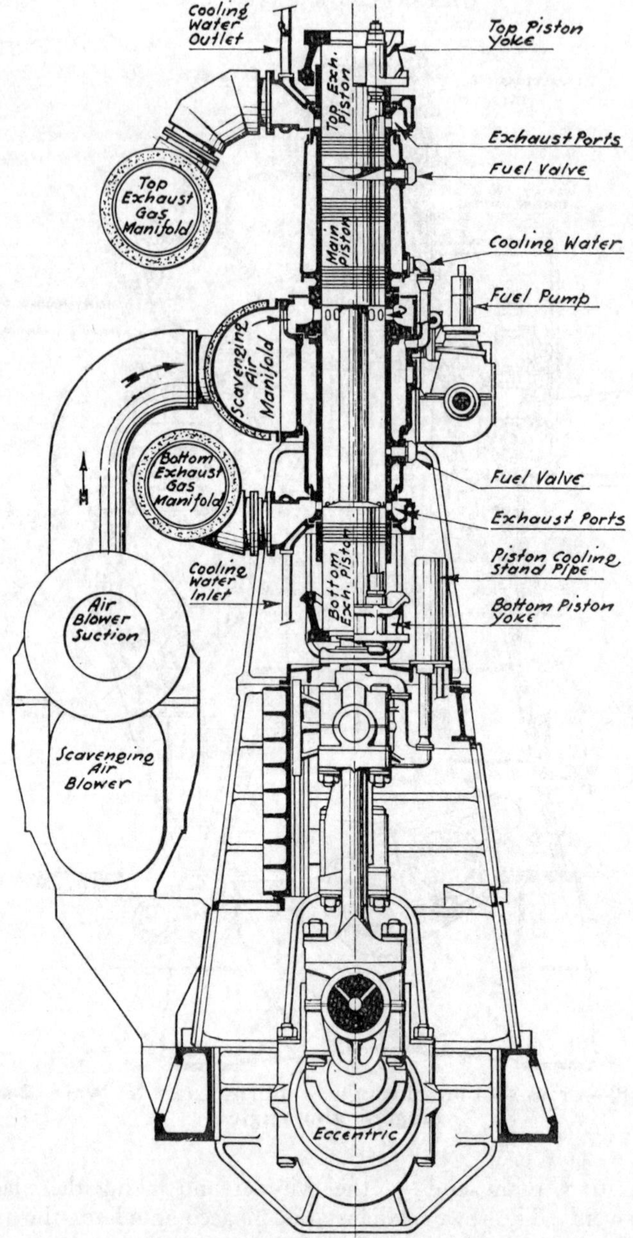

Fig. 8—Cross-section through Burmeister & Wain double-acting 2-stroke engine

Cylinders

The cylinders of engines similar to that shown in Fig. 7(*A*) consist of three main parts, namely, the liner, cooling water jacket, and head or cover, all of which are generally made of cast iron. The jacket of the cylinders, shown in Figs. 9 and 10 may accommodate one liner only, or it can be rectangular in plan and large enough to accommodate as many as four liners, in line. The liners are secured at the top to or by the cylinder head, in which case they must be free to expand longitudinally at the lower end, since the liner works at a much higher temperature and expands to a greater extent than the cylinder jacket. A space is provided between the liner and the jacket through which water is constantly circulated to prevent the liner becoming excessively hot. Rubber rings are used at the point where the liner is slidable in the jacket in order to prevent external leakage of cooling water. The cooling water enters at the bottom and leaves at the top of the jacket.

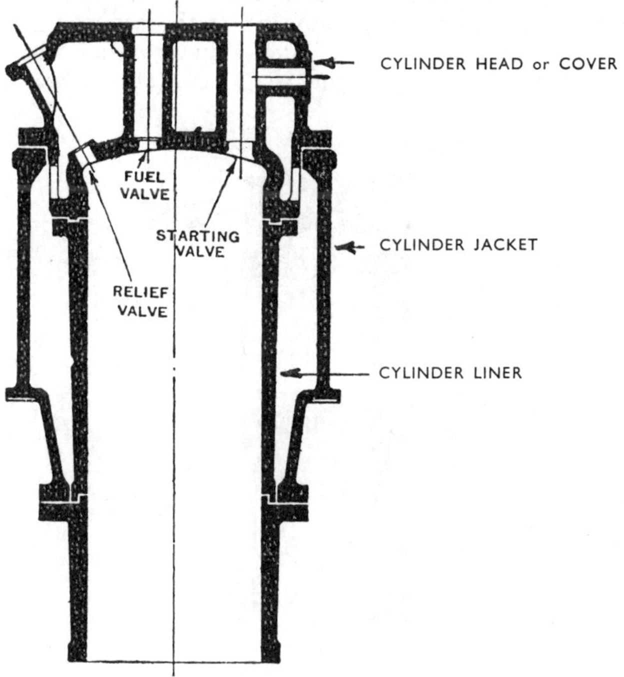

Fig. 9—Cylinder liner, jacket, and head of 4-stroke single-acting engine (Werkspoor)

The cylinder heads are made of cast iron, though cast steel is occasionally used, and are either circular in shape or are square castings of box section which, when a number are bolted together, form the cylinder beam. The heads are generally made very deep as, in the case of most four-stroke engines, they must accommodate the fuel, exhaust, air-inlet, starting, and relief valves, and spaces through which cooling water can freely circulate must be provided around the pockets accommodating these valves.

The cylinder liner shown in Fig. 9 is fastened to its respective cylinder head by stainless steel bolts and nuts in such a way that gas cannot leak outward nor cooling water inward between the two parts, the joint being made by a spigot on the head which fits into a recess in the cylinder liner flange, the surfaces being made gas-tight by grinding them together. The cooling water is prevented from attacking the ground surfaces and eventually causing them to leak by a rubber ring sandwiched between the outer portion of the connecting flanges. The important advantage of connecting the cylinder head and liner in this way is that the connecting flanges, which are hotter than the adjoining, thinner metal, are wholly immersed in the circulating cooling water, and internal heat stresses

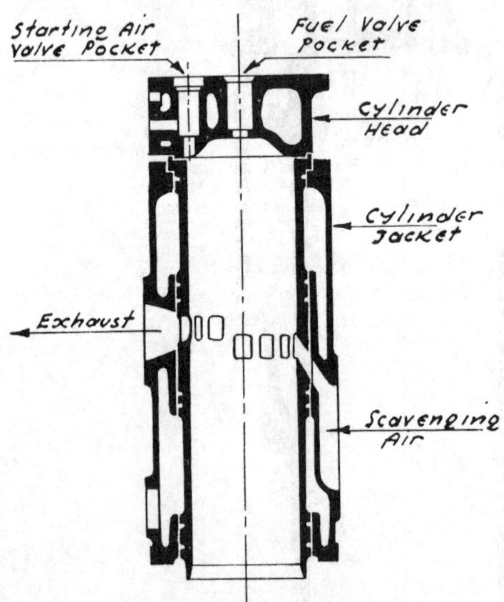

Fig. 10—Cylinder liner, jacket, and head of 2-stroke single-acting engine (Sulzer)

are consequently reduced. Another method of attaching the cylinder liner to the cylinder head is shown in Fig. 10.

Pistons of two-stroke engines are necessarily very deep and cannot be conveniently taken out of the cylinder except from the upper end. The cylinder head is, therefore, made so that it can be disconnected readily from the cylinder liner. The flange of the liner is firmly sandwiched between the head and the jacket or beam (Fig. 10). Rubber sealing rings are provided at the lower end and at each side of the exhaust ports, in order to prevent leakage of cooling water. Slight vertical movement of the liners of four-stroke engines due to the pressure in the cylinders causing the head to " breathe " is not detrimental, but in two-stroke engines the liners must be quite rigid, otherwise the rubber rings at each side of the hot exhaust ports would be affected and leakage of cooling water into the exhaust passages occur.

Pistons

All diesel engine pistons are hollow and are generally made of cast iron. Those above a certain diameter are cooled internally with fresh water or lubricating oil. The pistons of four-stroke crosshead-type engines are only long enough to carry the piston rings, whereas the pistons of two-stroke engines have to be very long, because they must cover the exhaust ports near the lower end of the cylinder liner when the crank is on the top dead centre. Owing to its relatively great length the lower portion of the piston usually passes through the top of the crankcase, otherwise, if the cylinder was made long enough to accommodate the whole of the piston at all positions of the crank, the engine would be appreciably higher than a four-stroke engine of the same power. The pistons of four-stroke engines without piston rods and crossheads are also very long, but the object in this case is to provide a large bearing surface to take the side thrust due to the obliquity of the connecting rods. The tops of pistons are either concave or convex, to increase their strength and resist the distorting effect of heat stresses.

Bedplate

The bedplates are made of cast iron or fabricated steel, and are usually mounted directly upon and bolted to the ship's double-bottom tank top. The lubricating oil which falls from the various bearings collects in the bedplate and flows either into a double-bottom tank or to the pump that circulates the oil. The bedplate must, therefore, be perfectly oil-tight.

As the double-bottom tank is always used for fuel or lubricating oil, the securing bolts are screwed through the tank top to form a fluid-tight joint and prevent water that may flow over the tank top from finding its way into the tank. At each holding-down bolt a cast-iron chock is hand-fitted between the bedplate and tank top to compensate for irregularities of the tank top. Nuts are provided on each end of the bolts and when tightened bind the bedplate, chocks and tank top firmly together.

The propeller-shaft thrust block either forms part of the engine structure or is mounted upon a cast-iron stool bolted to the after end of the bedplate and secured to the double-bottom tank top by studs, with fitted cast-iron chocks between, as described for bedplates.

Crankcase

The main framework consists of A-shaped cast iron or fabricated steel columns mounted on the bedplate, astride the crankshaft between each adjacent pair of cranks and at each side of the outer cranks. The lower ends of the columns are bolted to the bedplate and to the cylinder beam at the upper ends, but are relieved of all tensile loads resulting from gas pressure in the cylinders by long steel tie bolts of heavy cross-section. These tie-bolts pass from the underside of the bedplate to the top of the cylinder beam, thus binding the three main parts of the engine structure, namely, the bedplate, columns and cylinder beam, firmly together. The columns carry the crosshead guide bars, and the spaces between them are filled in and made oil-tight by sheet-iron or aluminium doors that are easily removable, enabling the internal running gear to be overhauled.

The spaces between the tops of the columns are closed by cast-iron covers, the piston rods working through stuffing boxes carried by the covers. The object of the stuffing boxes is to prevent lubricating oil being lifted out of the crankcase by the reciprocating piston rods or pistons if these extend into the crankcase. Between the underside of the cylinders and the top of the crankcase a space is provided to permit examination of the pistons. Separating the crankcase and cylinders in this way also prevents lubricating oil which drips from the cylinders from entering the crankcase and contaminating the bearing lubricating oil.

Crankshaft

The crankshaft is generally of the built-up or semi-built-up type, i.e. either the crankpins, journals, and webs are separate mild steel forgings, or each crankpin and pair of webs are machined out of a single forging, the journals being separate forgings. Webs are sometimes made of cast steel. When the number of cylinders exceeds four, the crankshaft is divided into convenient lengths, connected together by tight-fitting bolts passing through flanges forged on the various lengths at the points where they join. The spur gear, or chain sprocket wheel for transmitting motion to the camshaft, is generally mounted on the coupling connecting two sections.

Passages are bored through the journals, webs and crankpins to allow lubricating oil, normally under a pressure of about 20 lb/sq.in., admitted at the crankshaft bearings, to pass through to the crankpin bearings, after which it passes up a hole bored in the connecting rod and lubricates the crosshead bearings and crosshead guides. In some two-stroke single-acting engines the crosshead bearings are lubricated by an independent supply working at many times the normal pressure, as in this type of engine the load on the bearings is always in a downward direction, and thus the conditions under which these bearings operate are much more severe than in a four-stroke engine.

A flywheel is provided to ensure a uniform turning moment. It is secured to the crankshaft generally between the engine and the thrust block, and by means of teeth on the periphery is used to turn the crankshaft by hand or auxiliary power. Flywheels have the degrees of rotation marked upon them for the purpose of setting the various cylinder valves and fuel pumps which must operate at certain positions of the crankshaft.

The size of flywheel necessary to ensure even turning depends upon the number of cylinders in line, the type of engine—i.e. two-stroke or four-stroke, single-acting or double-acting—and whether the crankshaft is of the balanced or unbalanced type. The greater the number of impulses per revolution the smaller the flywheel need be. In some engines having balanced cranks a flywheel is not provided. Large flywheels are generally cast in two pieces and carefully tested for balance after the two halves have been bolted together and before the flywheel is connected to the crankshaft.

Cylinder-head valves

The air-inlet, exhaust, and starting valves located at the ends of the cylinder are opened by revolving cams through the medium of rocking levers, and closed by means of springs when the force which opens them is removed. The fuel valve of some airless injection engines is opened and closed in the same way, while such valves of the modern direct-injection engines are opened by fluid pressure built up by the fuel pump and closed by springs when the pressure falls.

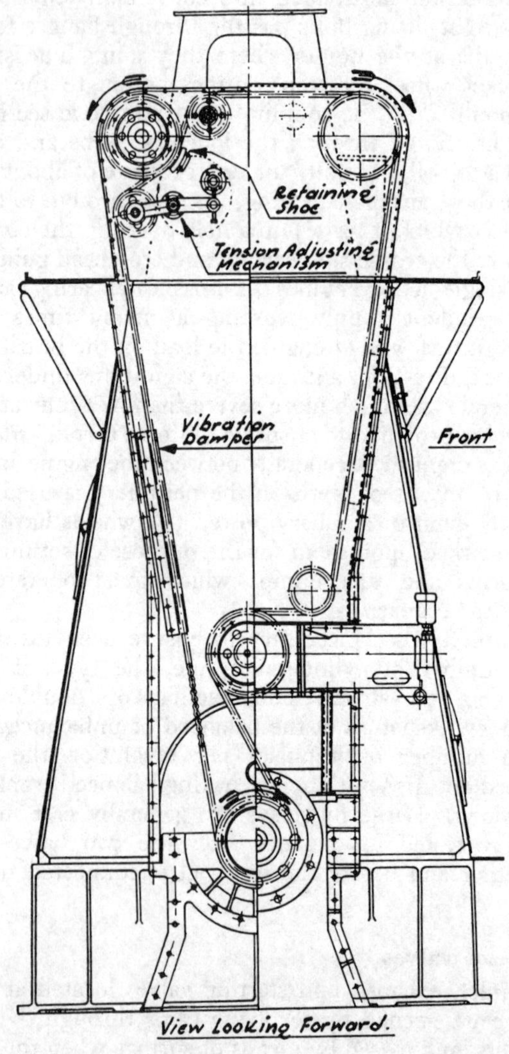

Fig. 11—Crankshaft chain drive of an engine employing two camshafts (Doxford)

All valves, with the exception of the fuel injection and the relief valves, are of the mushroom type and open into the cylinder. The relief valves are automatically opened when the pressure in the cylinder overcomes the spring or compressed-air load, as the case may be. The exhaust and fuel valves of all types of engine are provided with jackets through which either oil or water is circulated in order to prevent overheating. Fresh water is generally used for these valves, but oil is sometimes used for the fuel valves.

The cams which operate the various valves are rigidly secured to a shaft extending the whole length of the engine. This camshaft rotates in fixed relationship with the crankshaft and is driven by the latter, usually by chain and sprocket wheels (see Fig. 11), or in some cases by spur or helical gearwheels.

Usually each valve is provided with two cams, one for ahead and one for astern running. Reversal of direction of crankshaft rotation is effected by moving the camshaft endwise. (Fig. 11.)

Starting gear

Marine engines are set in motion by admitting compressed air, usually at about 350 lb/sq.in., into the cylinders at the right moment. In the cylinder head is a spring-loaded starting valve which is operated by a cam driven from, and timed with, the crankshaft. When the crank of one cylinder is over the dead centre position in the desired direction of rotation, the starting valve in this cylinder is opened and the compressed air admitted acts on the piston and sets the engine in motion. As the other cranks reach this position the respective starting valves are opened and each piston is acted upon in turn. The engine quickly gains sufficient speed to compress the combustion air to a temperature high enough to ignite the fuel when injected in an atomised form. When this occurs the starting air is shut off and the engine begins working on fuel only.

Fuel injection

The fuel is delivered into the fuel valves by small plunger-type pumps, and injected into the cylinders by the pumps themselves, working at from 4,000 to 8,000 lb/sq.in. Before the fuel enters the cylinder it is atomised so that it immediately ignites and burns upon coming into contact with the hot compressed air in the cylinders.

In the now obsolescent air-injection system the exact quantity of fuel is delivered into the fuel valve, containing only compressed air at 1,000 lb/sq.in. At the correct moment the valve is opened mechanically and the fuel charge injected into the cylinder by the high-pressure air.

Low-pressure air pumps

Scavenging and supercharge air pumps are single-stage machines and are of either the reciprocating or rotary type. When of the latter type they are termed " rotary blowers." When of the reciprocating type they are generally driven by means of a connecting rod, cross-head, and piston rod; while rotary blowers are driven either by the main engine through chain and sprocket wheels, or are independently driven, the power being provided by an exhaust gas turbine, electric motor, or a small high-speed diesel engine.

In the Werkspoor four-stroke supercharged engine the whole of the combustion air is supplied by reciprocating pumps located underneath the main engine cylinders; formed by enclosing the space between the bottom of the working cylinders and the top of the crankcase, and utilising the underside of the main engine piston on its downward stroke to compress the air. Each pump is provided with a suction and delivery valve and all pumps deliver into a common receiver which is maintained at a pressure of approximately 4 lb/sq.in.

Running gear

Marine propelling engines have a large stroke/bore ratio and consequently are provided with piston rods. They are therefore of the crosshead type, the side thrust at the crosshead being taken by a slipper working in guide bars attached to the framing. The upper end of the connecting rod is forked and carries two identical bearings in which the two crosshead pins oscillate.

The whitemetal linings of the crankshaft, crankpin, and crosshead bearings are provided with circumferential grooves which allow the lubricating oil to spread over the rubbing surfaces and—after lubricating the crankshaft bearing—the remainder passes from the crankpin bearing into a hole bored through the centre of the connecting rod, and thus to the crosshead bearings. A hole is sometimes bored through the centre of the piston rod also, in order to convey oil or water, as the case may be, to the piston for cooling purposes.

Small stroke/bore ratio engines running at 300/500 r.p.m. are sometimes used for ship propulsion, the power being transmitted through electrical or mechanical reduction gearing to the propeller. Such engines are always of the trunk piston type, the connecting rod being directly connected to the piston.

Engine weights

The average weights of the various types of unsupercharged diesel engines developing about 8,000 i.h.p. are as follows:—

Four-stroke single-acting	250 lb per i.h.p.
Two-stroke „ „	150 „ „ „
Two-stroke double-acting	115 „ „ „
Two-stroke single-acting opposed piston .	130 „ „ „

The direct-coupled marine diesel engine is, in proportion to the power developed, a heavy engine when compared with a steam engine or gas turbine. Recent developments have, therefore, been chiefly concerned with obtaining a greater power output for a given weight. An important contribution has been the substitution of welded, fabricated steel for heavy cast iron for bedplates and framing. Present efforts are directed towards developing a greater power for a given size and number of cylinders by supercharging the cylinders to a greater degree. The larger the weight of air in a cylinder at the end of the compression stroke, the greater will be the fuel charge that can be efficiently burnt therein.

In the case of a certain 11,250 b.h.p. two-stroke engine the saving in weight by adopting welded steel as against cast iron bedplate, framing and beam was 110 tons, the respective weights being 400 tons and 510 tons. The total weight of an engine of similar construction and of a given power output, however, depends mainly upon its revolutions and supercharge pressure. For example, in the case of two engines produced by the same manufacturer, one running at 110 r.p.m. and the other at 225 r.p.m., the weight of the former was 149 lb/b.h.p. and that of the latter 110 lb/b.h.p. As regards the effect of supercharging upon the weight, an engine recently constructed had a weight of only 30 lb/b.h.p. when the cylinders were supercharged to approximately 220 m.i.p. and operating at 375 r.p.m.

Two engines recently built by the same manufacturer illustrate how the weight per unit power output is affected by the total power output. The 4,000 b.h.p. engine had a weight of 140 lb/b.h.p. and that of the 8,000 b.h.p. engine was 115 lb/b.h.p.

CHAPTER 5

Bedplates and framing

Bedplates

The bedplate is one of the most important, if not the most important part, of a marine engine. Satisfactory operation of an engine cannot be expected if the crankshaft and other moving parts are not maintained in proper alignment at all times, and alignment of such parts depends mainly upon the rigidity of the bedplate. Even under fine-weather conditions the bedplate must, in addition to carrying the weight of the engine, resist the torque reaction forces emanating from the propeller, which tends to rotate the engine around the crankshaft. When, to these duties, are added the stresses and strains produced when a ship is rolling and pitching heavily in a seaway, the truth of the opening remark will be appreciated.

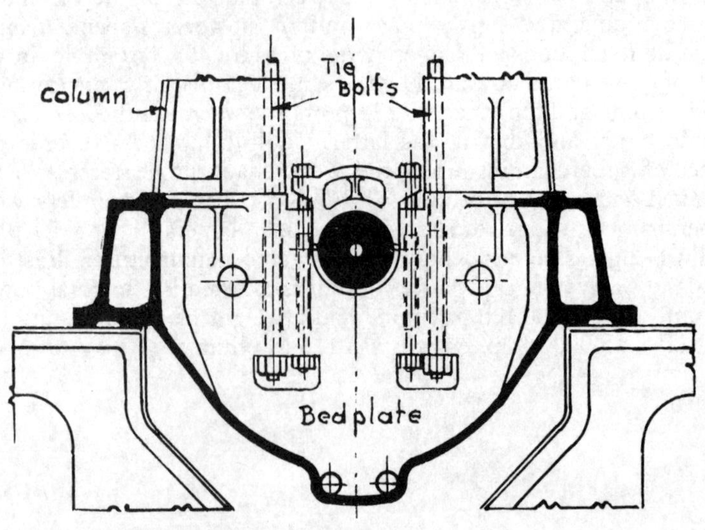

Fig. 12—Trestle-type engine bedplate

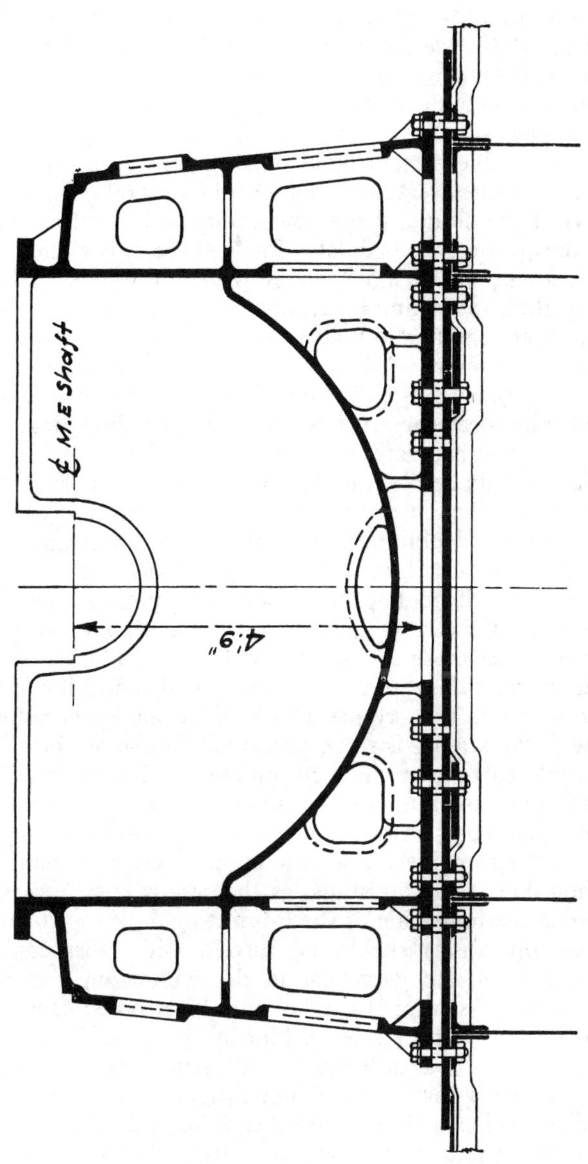

Fig. 13—Box-type engine bedplate

The two types of bedplates in general use are shown in Figs. 12, the trestle, and 13, the flat-bottomed, or box form. Although the former, mostly favoured by engine builders, is satisfactory for a well-balanced engine of moderate length, the type shown in Fig. 13 has its advantages. The box form enables the engine to be bolted direct to the double-bottom tank top, thus obviating the necessity to provide an elevated seating which must be very robust and soundly constructed if the desired degree of rigidity is to be obtained. The stools of the trestle-type bedplate (Fig. 12) are either made of iron or steel castings, or are built up of plates and angles riveted or welded together. Sometimes the double-bottom tank top is stepped to accommodate the trestle-type bedplate, and then stools become unnecessary and a more solid foundation for the bedplate is provided.

The present practice is to make bedplates of large marine engines of welded mild steel construction in order to reduce financial loss in the event of cast bedplates turning out to be defective. Fabricated steel bedplates may be of either the box or trestle type.

With the introduction of the box or flat-bottom type of bedplate and the stepped double-bottom tank top arrangement bedplate troubles can become a thing of the past, provided the design allows of easy access to all holding-down bolts. Judging by the difficulty sometimes experienced in getting at the holding-down bolts, it would appear that there are still a few designers who do not realise that weather conditions at sea can be such that the holding-down bolts are strained, and require to be tightened up occasionally if trouble with the seating is to be prevented. In some ships it is not even possible to tighten the nuts of the outside bolts unless the engine is stopped and numerous oil and water pipes are first removed.

With bedplates of the types illustrated, and properly proportioned, all the operating engineer is called upon to do is to hammer-test the holding-down bolts or studs, as the case may be, occasionally, and examine the underside of the lubricating oil sump for leakages. Both these operations should be carried out whilst engines are operating, as then any weakness in the foundation will be more easily detected. As regards the holding-down bolts, ordinary mild steel is better than high-tensile steel for this purpose if slight working occurs at the seating, as although the ultimate strength of mild steel may be less, such material will not fatigue so rapidly under the conditions to which such bolts are then being subjected.

The most common practice of fitting holding-down studs, commonly referred to as bolts, consists of screw-cutting the holes in the tank-top and screwing down the studs until the conical face at the lower end of the enlarged plain part of the stud seats on the tank-top and forms a watertight joint, as shown at *A* (Fig. 14).

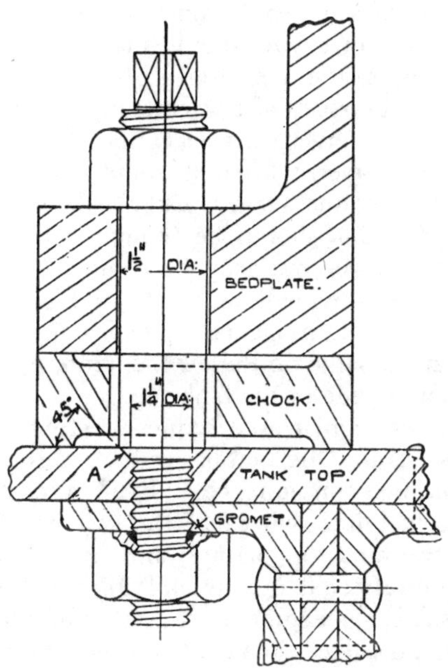

Fig. 14—One design of bedplate holding-down bolt

The lower nut is then tightened up, and the final operation is the tightening down of the upper nut. This is the correct order of operations, but as it is much more convenient to fit a number of studs and tighten down the upper nuts before proceeding into the double-bottom tank to fit the grommets and tighten up the lower nuts, the practice in some yards is to do this—with the result that the holding-down studs do not fully serve the purpose intended, and water eventually leaks into the double-bottom tank in which fuel or lubricating oil is usually kept, and the finding of slack and broken studs is not an infrequent occurrence.

When a stud is screwed into the tank-top and the upper nut tightened first, the few threads in the tank-top plate are strained and the conical face at the lower end of the plain part of the stud is pulled away from the tank-top plate and may not, therefore, prevent water leaking through the stud holes. The function of these lower nuts should be to resist the pull exerted when tightening the upper nuts and so bind the engine bedplate and the tank-top plate firmly together. Therefore, to ensure the most rigid attachment between these two parts, not only must the correct order of fitting be observed, but the lower nuts should make hard metallic contact with the underside of the tank-top. Moreover, the lower nuts should be locked to the studs after tightening, by means of a heavy punch, in order to counteract the slackening effect of vibration.

If the studs are properly fitted it should not be necessary to provide further precautions against water leaking into the double-bottom tanks, but if this should be thought advisable, the upper inside edge of each lower nut may be chamfered and a grommet inserted in the space provided, as shown in Fig. 14. This would serve as an extra precaution against water leaking into the double-bottom tank and at the same time allow the nut to make hard metallic contact with the underside of the tank-top.

The importance of regular and frequent testing of holding-down nuts for slackness cannot be emphasized too strongly, in view of the inevitable serious consequences. Even almost imperceptible movement of the bedplate will cause the cast-iron chocks to wear themselves into the tank-top plating, and in such an event satisfactory repair can be effected only by building-up with welded metal. Before this is possible the engine must first be lifted out of the ship, an operation which involves considerable time and expense.

When a chock is found slack it is no use trying to insert pieces of tin between the chock and the bedplate. The only effective temporary repair is to remove the respective bolt and withdraw the chock, which should be reduced in thickness by about half-an-inch. As a slack chock generally means that it has made an impression in the tank-top plating, the lower edges of the chock should then be well rounded to ensure that when the chock is refitted it sits within the impression or recess worn in the plating. Having procured a make-up piece of steel plate a few thousandths of an inch thicker than the gauged distance between the chock and the underside of the bedplate, the nuts of the adjacent bolts should be slackened and the plate driven in. In certain instances steel wedges will facilitate the operation, but these must be used very carefully, otherwise the bedplate can be damaged.

When the chock is ringed around the bolt and the double-bottom tank cannot be entered in order to remove the bolt, it is usually possible to find pieces of cast iron which can be shaped to the required size and then driven in on each side of the slack chock.

This will prevent matters becoming worse until the bolt can be removed and a more effective repair carried out. It will, of course, be necessary to secure the temporary chocks in some way to stop them working out, but this should not afford any difficulty to a resourceful engineer.

Adequate provision is not always made to cause the lubricating oil to flow freely from the bedplate to the ship's double-bottom tank, with the result that when the oil is cold and viscous, or for other reasons not so fluid as new oil, it accumulates in the bedplate, and the surface of the oil is struck by the crankpin bearings as the cranks pass over the bottom dead centre. This sometimes occurs with oil of normal fluidity if the ship is by the head—or even on an even keel should insufficient thought have been given to this matter by the engine builders.

Such a state of affairs must not be allowed to continue a moment longer than necessary, as the stresses produced may be sufficient to fracture the comparatively thin portion of the bedplate which holds the oil. If the cause of the oil not flowing freely cannot be removed at once, the speed of the engine should be reduced meanwhile and a careful examination made for oil leakages as soon as normal conditions are restored. Particularly is this necessary in cases where the oil sump is formed by bolting a steel plate on the underside of the bedplate. With such construction very few revolutions of the crankshaft will suffice to slacken the bolts and cause the loss of a large quantity of oil in a very short time.

Framing

The portion of the structure between the bedplate and the cylinders is made either of cast iron or fabricated steel. The structure usually comprises a number of A-frames positioned astride the crankshaft which, when the space between them is filled in, forms the crankcase. One frame is situated in line with each crankshaft bearing so that the number of frames is equal to the number of such bearings.

A cast-iron frame, or columns as they are usually called when made in this material, is shown in Fig. 15. Cast iron is strong in compression and the columns are made hollow in order to obtain the highest degree of rigidity for minimum weight. They are flanged at both ends and, although they are attached to the cylinder beam and bedplate by bolts, such bolts merely serve to hold the parts together when aligning during erection and to prevent side movement when the engine is working; the steel tie-bolts described later resist the upward movement due to the gas pressure in the cylinders. The

Fig. 15—Cast iron bedplate and frames of 4-stroke engine
(Note tie-bolts at upper end ready to receive the cylinder beam)

columns carry the crosshead guide bars, to which they are attached by bolts, so that it is essential that the correct alignment of the columns be maintained. In order to prevent these parts getting out of line, the practice is to make a number of the bolts which connect the column to the cylinder beam and bedplate a tight fit, or to employ dowel pins.

The importance of the dowel pins or the tight-fitting bolts at the end of each column is not always fully realised, as occasionally it is found when such parts have been dismantled, the dowel pins have been left out or the fitting bolts replaced by slack bolts. Not only is it the duty of these dowel pins or fitting bolts to resist the thrust of the crosshead guide-bar resulting from the angularity of the connecting rod, but it must be remembered that this thrust is applied when the pressure in the cylinder is at a maximum and, consequently, the compression stress in the columns due to the tension in the tie-bolts relieved. Unless, therefore, the tie-bolts are exceedingly tight, the tendency will be for the columns to be moved in the direction of the thrust on the crosshead guides, and the internal working parts such as the piston rod and crosshead shoes to be thrown out of line. When the bolts at each end of the columns break, it is usually due to the tie-bolts requiring to be tightened up, but if this is the cause of the trouble, movement between the top of the column and the cylinder beam will be observable.

It is the practice of some makers to run lubricating-oil and piston cooling-water pipes through the columns. As such pipes are liable to become defective and may leak without this being at once noticed, this is not good practice. In such cases it is wise to drill a small hole near the base of each column in such a position that in the event of oil or water leaking from the pipes it will flow out of the hole and be noticed. If water pipes corrode and water finds its way into the bedplate the consequences may be serious.

Fig. 16 shows a fabricated steel bedplate and frames for a 10,000 h.p. engine. The total weight is 81 tons and the length 45 feet.

Fig. 16—Fabricated steel bedplate and frames for 10,000 h.p. engine

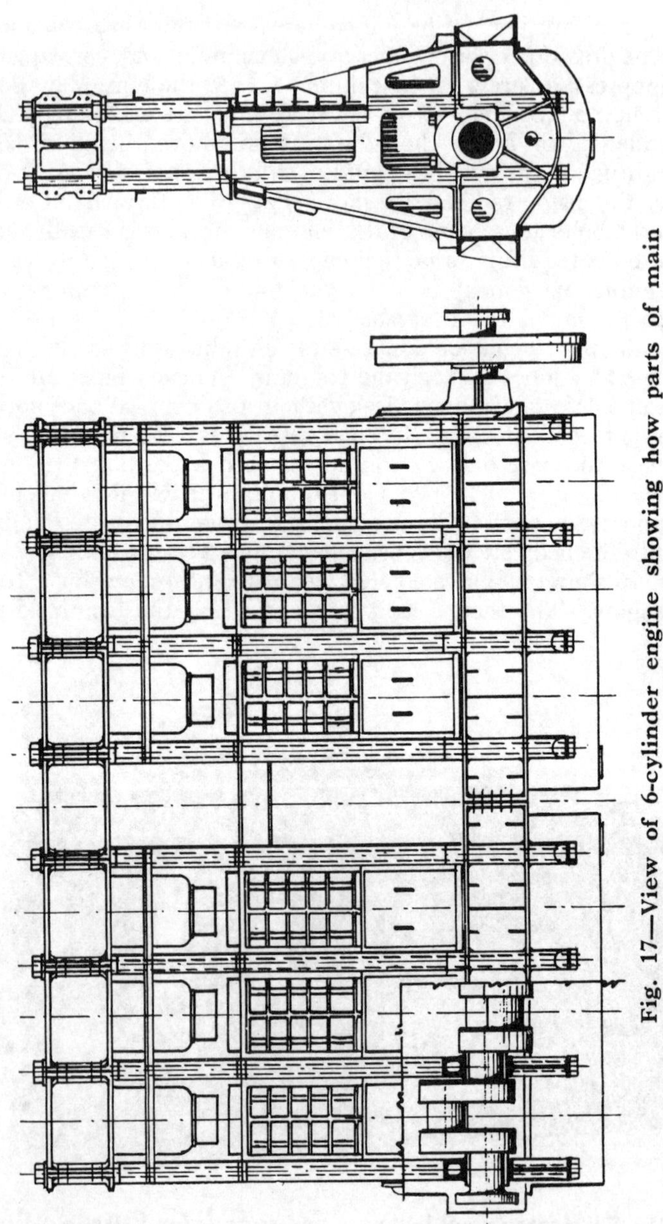

Fig. 17—View of 6-cylinder engine showing how parts of main structure are bound together

The bedplate is of the trestle type and the lubricating oil sump, or crankpit, is formed by bolting semicircular steel plates to the underside of the bedplate between each pair of frames.

Tie-bolts

As mentioned earlier, it is the common practice to bind the cylinder entablature in which the liners are fitted, columns, and bedplate firmly together by means of long steel tie-bolts which pass through the hollow columns, in which they are an easy fit. One such tie-bolt is located at an equal distance on each side of each crankshaft bearing, so that there are two tie-bolts for each column. The tie-bolts are generally made of ordinary mild steel and quite plain, excepting that they are screwed at each end to take nuts. The portion between the screwed ends is reduced in diameter. The lower nut is sometimes square and fits into an opening of similar shape cast in the bedplate, with the object of preventing the nut turning when the bolt is screwed into it and the upper nut tightened. Fig. 17 illustrates how the various parts of the main structure are bound together.

The diameter of the steel tie-bolts and the thickness of the cast-iron columns are so proportioned that when the former are tightened the bolts are slightly stretched and the cast-iron parts compressed a small amount. The object is to ensure that at the moment when the full working pressure in the cylinder occurs and the long tie-bolts are stretched, the cast-iron parts expand and maintain firm contact with the inside faces of the nuts at each end of the tie-bolts. The cast-iron parts of an engine 30 feet high are compressed from 0·5 to 0·75 mm by tightening the tie-bolts.

As time goes on, the tie-bolts may require to be tightened up owing to slight permanent stretch of the bolts and " give " in the screwed portions. When this is necessary, slight movement will be observed between the top of the column and the cylinder entablature during the working stroke of the cycle, and unless such movement is stopped, something serious may happen, as the proper working of many parts of the engine depend upon the tie-bolts properly binding the main structure firmly together under conditions of greatest stress.

The operation of tightening the tie-bolts must be done very carefully, otherwise certain parts may be distorted and strained. The bolts are so long that it is quite easy to stretch them more than necessary and, as the lower ends of each pair of bolts usually take hold of the bedplate in the vicinity of a crankshaft bearing, it is not impossible to distort some bedplates to the extent of throwing a bearing a few thousandths of an inch out of line. This will result if an attempt is made to tighten the nuts until it is impossible to tighten them any further, or if one bolt only is tightened. Whenever it is necessary to tighten one bolt, the nut of the other bolt in line athwartships should always be slackened and then the two nuts tightened evenly to make sure that at the end of the operation the same stress exists in both bolts.

It is difficult to describe in words just how tight these tie-bolt nuts should be, as the degree of tightness is gauged by a combination of factors common to each particular make of engine, but as a guide, and when makers' definite instructions are not available, it may be useful to know that the author's practice for many years has been to use a spanner having a leverage of about 12 inches and a 50-lb ram swung by two men for a distance of 4 feet. When the nut is sufficiently tight, the blows give a solid ring and the nut is moved 2° or so at every blow. In order that the sound of the blows will give a true indication of the tightness of a nut, the spanner should, of course, be pulled firmly by means of a set of rope blocks in the direction in which it is being driven.

Whenever it is necessary to tighten up tie-bolts, it is advisable first to mark the position of the nut and then unscrew it for the

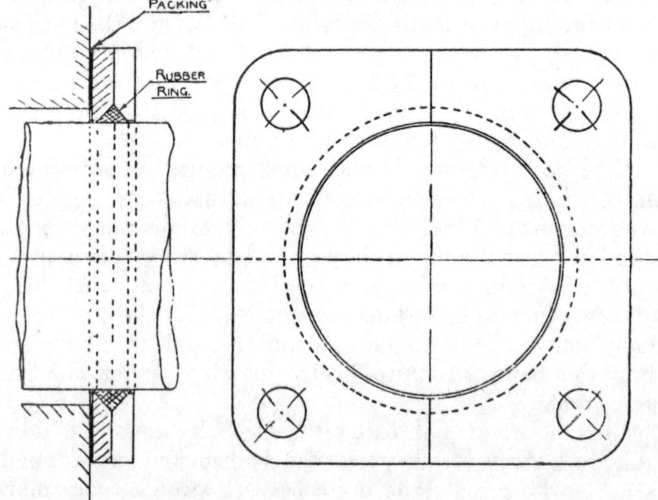

Fig. 18—Method of sealing space around tie-bolts at the points where they pass through cylinder entablature

purpose of applying lubricant to the threads, as if such nuts jam it is sometimes difficult to free them owing to the bolt turning with the nut. Grease applied to the threads and to the bottom face of the nuts will prevent jamming in the threads and undue friction between the nuts and the cylinder entablature. After the nuts have been tightened they should be securely locked in position.

In some engines the combustion air passes through the cylinder entablature before entering the working cylinders, and if the tie-bolts pass through the air space and the crankcase there is a risk of lubricating oil being drawn from the crankcase into the working cylinders. Many gallons of lubricating oil may be lost from the crankcase every day in this way. It is therefore necessary in such cases to prevent the oil mist from passing upwards around the tie-bolts by filling the spaces between the bolts and the holes in the columns with packing. Ordinary steam packing tightly stemmed into the openings may meet the case, but where the design of the columns permits, a more satisfactory arrangement is to bolt two split flanges to the column and sandwich between them a turn of packing, as shown in Fig. 18. If the inside edges of the flanges are bevelled as illustrated and the size of the packing is large enough, the packing will be pressed against the tie-bolt as the flanges are pulled together.

CHAPTER 6

Cylinder construction

Each unit of multiple-cylinder marine engines is provided with a cylinder liner and head as separate parts. The cylinder water-jacket is sometimes a separate part, but generally the jacket is made large enough to accommodate two, three, or four cylinder liners, and when the engine has four or more units the cylinder jackets are bolted together to form an entablature or beam. All three parts are generally made of cast iron but sometimes the head is made of cast steel.

Cylinder liners

A general idea of the construction of four- and two-stroke single-acting engine liners will be obtained by referring to Figs. 9 and 10, from which it will be observed that they are symmetrical about the vertical centre-line. Such liners do not break as a result of gas pressure: nor do they fail due to heat stresses provided the casting is properly made and the engine operated under normal conditions. The only difficulty yet to be overcome is abrasion by the piston rings. Special cast iron is used, but there is not yet unanimity of opinion regarding the most suitable composition or physical characteristics. As, however, cylinder-liner wear is not entirely dependent upon the composition and physical properties of the material, resistance to wear will be dealt with in a later chapter.

So far as the influence which design has upon the wear rate of liners, experience has shown that a low surface temperature, i.e. temperature of the surface in contact with the piston rings, is conducive to minimum wear. The practice is, therefore, to keep the thickness of the metal at a minimum compatible with strength in order to reduce the temperature difference in the metal. Some makers adopt methods which ensure a high cooling-water velocity, which makes for a more rapid transfer of heat and, consequently, a low surface temperature.

Sometimes a comparatively thin cast-iron liner is made sufficiently strong to resist the internal gas pressure by casting ribs on the upper portion surrounding the combustion space. When these ribs are made a good fit in the jacket, as is sometimes the case in small engines, the latter helps to resist the bursting pressure inside the liner. Such a practice, however, causes difficulties when it becomes necessary to fit a new cylinder liner. In other makes these ribs, when the liner and jacket are fitted together, form a spiral channel for the cooling water, the velocity of which is consequently increased. Such a liner is illustrated in Fig. 19. In other, and extremely rare, cases the liners are made much thicker than normal, the object being that as wear takes place they may be rebored and a

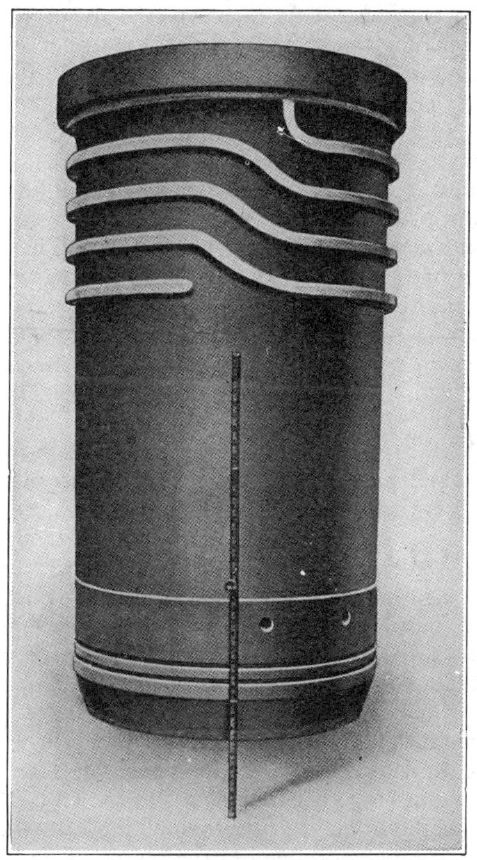

Fig. 19—Cylinder liner showing spiral passage for directing flow of cooling water

thin wearing liner fitted. The practice of one Continental maker is to fit a cast-iron liner into a comparatively thin cast-steel cylinder, the latter providing the strength and the former the bearing surface for the piston rings. The soundness of such a practice, however, is questionable, but it is a good plan where a channel on the liner is provided whereby the cooling water is constrained to move in an orderly circular path.

The reinforced cylinder liner, first used in the Still steam/oil engine, consists of a comparatively thin liner strengthened by stainless steel hoops. By this means a cylinder liner which would normally have a thickness of 1¾ inch can be reduced to about ¾ inch thick. With such a thickness of liner the inner surface would operate at a mean temperature of about 200°F (93°C), against about 300°F in the case of a liner 1¾ inch thick—assuming a cooling-water outlet temperature of 120°F (49°C) and, of course, normal running conditions.

The temperature stress in the relatively thin Still liner is considerably less than in ordinary liners, while the pressure stress is entirely eliminated, this being taken by the steel hoops. The heat stress in a 1¾ inch thick liner is about 6,500 lb/sq.in. tensile, while the stress due to gas pressure amounts to about 3,000 lb/sq.in., so that the total tensile stress in the metal of such a liner is 9,500 lb/sq.in. The heat stress in a liner ¾ inch thick is in the neighbourhood of 3,000 lb/sq.in. and, since there is no pressure stress, this is the total in a reinforced liner.

The outer surface of cylinder liners is always tapered downwards to a smaller diameter because the bursting pressure at the lower end is very much less than that at the upper end, and because much of the heat picked up by the upper end of the liner is conducted to the lower and cooler end. The thinner the lower end the lower will be its working temperature, and the lower its working temperature the greater will be the flow of heat from the upper end of the liner. The chief reason, therefore, for tapering cylinder liners towards the bottom is to reduce the working temperature of the upper, and more difficult, part to lubricate, and not merely to reduce weight of the casting or facilitate fitting.

It is almost universal practice to connect the liner and head of single-acting engines together in the manner shown in Figs. 9 and 10. The only undesirable feature of either of these methods is that it necessitates a large mass of metal in the region of the flanges, which owing to its size cannot be maintained at the same temperature as the remainder of the liner, with the result that heat stresses are set up. Provided, however, the connection is properly designed and the parts carefully fitted together, no trouble arises from this. The ideal arrangement would be for the head and liner to be made in one piece, and this was done by one manufacturer at least for a time, but the practice was abandoned owing to the difficulty of obtaining sound and homogeneous castings. Although the design shown in Fig. 9 has the undesirable feature mentioned, it has a great advantage over the design shown in Fig. 10 in that the necessary heavy mass of metal is completely surrounded on the outside by circulating water, so that the heat stresses are low in comparison.

Details of the two common methods of connecting the cylinder

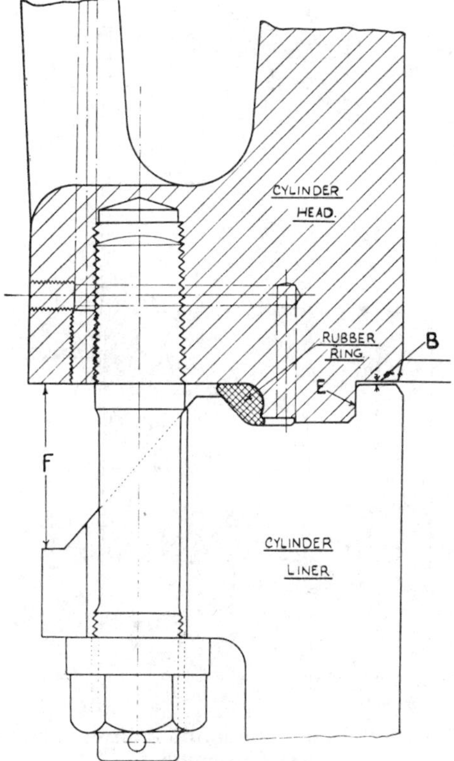

Fig. 20—One method of connecting cylinder liners and heads of 4-stroke engines

heads and liners of four-stroke engines are shown in Figs. 20 and 21. It will be appreciated that not only must provision be made to prevent the high-pressure gas in the cylinder from leaking between the parts into the water space, but that it is necessary also to prevent the water from making contact with the gas joint, otherwise the ground cast-iron surfaces will corrode and leakage of gas eventually occur. It has been proved over and over again that no matter how carefully cast-iron or steel parts are ground together, water, if in contact with the point where they join, will find its way between the surfaces and eventually corrode them. The rubber rings employed to prevent the water reaching the ground surfaces therefore perform a very important duty.

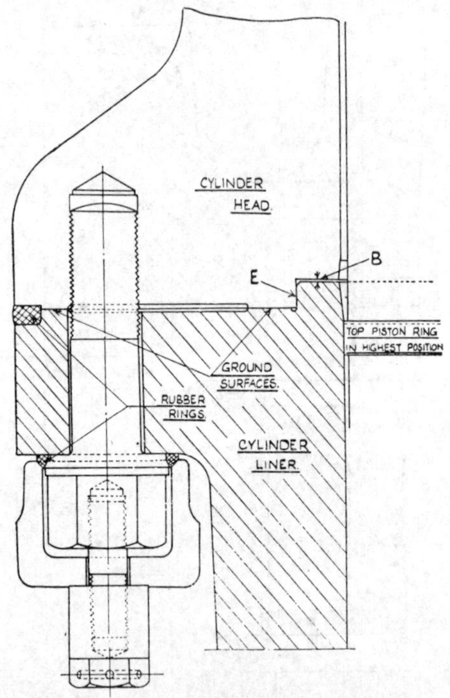

Fig. 21—Another method of connecting cylinder liners and heads of 4-stroke engines

Fitting liners and heads together

When cylinder liners and heads have been separated, the joining surfaces must be perfectly clean before they are connected together again. A thin film of boiled oil will protect the ground surfaces against moisture. If the parts have been ground together, the amount of opening at *B*, Figs. 20 and 21, must be ascertained after the operation. This opening should measure about 0·5 mm when the parts are in their correct relative position, while the vertical surfaces *E* adjoining should have no measurable clearance. Stepping the castings in the manner illustrated protects the ground joint from the intense heat in the cylinder if the clearance just recommended is maintained.

A small clearance at *B* is essential in order to make quite sure that the ground surfaces are not kept apart. If the clearance *B* is measured after the grinding operation, and the head and liner placed together without the rubber sealing ring in position, it will be at once evident if the rubber ring is so big as to prevent the ground surfaces making proper contact when the parts are finally bolted together. In marine engines the weights of the cylinder head and liner are such that either will be sufficient to distort the rubber ring the requisite amount, so that unless the clearance before and after fitting the rubber ring and before tightening the connecting bolts is the same, the cross-sectional diameter of the rubber ring is too large.

Bolting the head and liner together is an important operation, particularly in the case of joints of the form shown in Fig. 20. The nuts must be tightened up evenly, and the distance between the outer edges of the parts indicated checked whilst doing so. Owing to the comparatively great distance of the bolts from the ground joint, excessive weight applied to the nuts will distort the liner and set up an initial stress in the metal immediately below the flange. Distortion of the liner at this point will also tend to separate the ground surfaces on the inner side. The distance *F* between the head and liner should therefore be accurately gauged before and after the nuts are tightened, and the dimension after the operation should not be reduced by more than 0·3 mm.

In the more usual form of joint shown in Fig. 21 the cylinder head and liner make hard contact at two points. Both points are indicated as ground surfaces, but the inner surface only is required to prevent leakage, the outer surface serving merely to ensure a more solid connection between the two parts. The usual practice is to grind the two surfaces at the same time, but the author prefers to have the outer surfaces from 0·1 to 0·2 mm apart when the inner surfaces are ground to the required finish and before the bolts are tightened. Springing the liner flange this small amount during the operation of tightening up the securing bolts will ensure a good contact pressure between the ground surfaces required to prevent leakage of gas.

When finally fitting a cylinder head and liner together, particular care must be taken to see that part of the rubber sealing ring is not forced between the ground surfaces and so prevent them from making hard metallic contact. This is obviated by making the centre line of the groove provided for the rubber ring either above the joining surfaces or below them, as shown in Fig. 21. A brief study of the diagrams, Fig. 22, will clearly illustrate the advantage of the above suggestion. If the groove is arranged as shown in diagram (a), part of the rubber ring is very liable to be nipped as the cylinder head and liner are brought together.

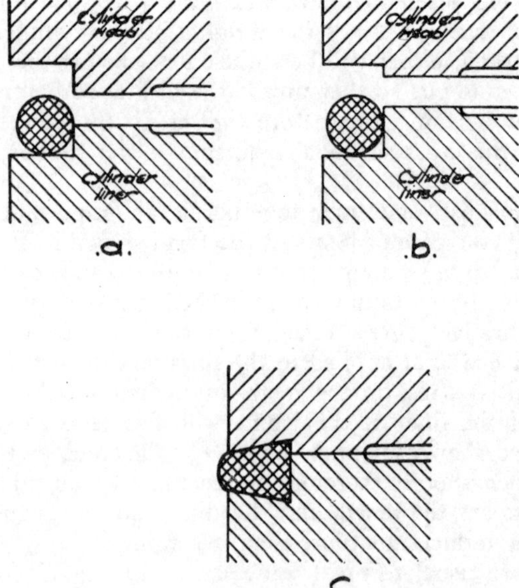

Fig. 22—Methods of locating rubber sealing rings between flanges of cylinder liner and heads

When cylinder heads and liners are bolted together, the spaces between the rubber ring and inner ground surface where the parts are undercut, as well as the clearance spaces around the bolts, are filled with air which becomes heated and expands when the engine attains normal working temperature. This was held to be responsible in a few cases for forcing the rubber ring out of the groove at one and sometimes two places, and allowing cooling water to reach the inner ground surface. By calculation the pressure reached by the air in these spaces is from 5 to 7 lb/sq.in., and as it was only in some of the cylinders that this occurred, it would appear that the cause was that the rubber rings were too small in cross-section and insufficiently nipped. However, to prevent a recurrence of the trouble the grooves were afterwards shaped as shown at (c) in Fig. 22, and no further trouble due to the rings being forced out by the pressure of air unavoidably left in the clearance spaces was experienced.

It is the practice of some engine builders to inject a thin mixture of white lead and boiled oil into these clearance spaces. The connection for doing so is shown in Fig. 20. This practice expels the air from the spaces, through a similar hole, and may prevent water that might leak past the rubber ring from reaching the ground surfaces. As, however, leakage and corrosion may unknowingly be going on, the author prefers to leave the spaces empty and the passage open to the atmosphere, as then not only will leakage of water past the rubber ring be at once apparent, but the trapped air will be free to expand into the atmosphere and prevent a pressure being created.

In the type of joints shown in Figs. 20 and 21, the studs and nuts connecting the parts together must either be made of non-corrodible steel or be prevented from making contact with the cooling water. When ordinary mild steel studs and nuts or bolts are employed the practice is to cover the nuts or the heads of the bolts by a brass, cast iron, or galvanised iron cap as shown in Fig. 21. After examining the arrangement it will be appreciated that the rubber rings which are fitted between the liner flange and the caps are just as important as the rubber rings provided between the cylinder liner and head, so that very great care must be taken when fitting the caps to ensure fluid-tightness.

When cylinder liners and heads are separate castings bolted together and the contact surfaces become defective, the first indication of such a fault is water dripping from the bottom of the cylinder when the engine is at rest. An engine cannot, of course, be run with such leakage taking place without seriously damaging the cylinder liner and piston rings, and to remake the joint or fit a spare cylinder requires a great deal of time. If the leakage occurs at sea or in a port where it is not advisable or convenient to make a permanent repair, the leakage, which will be slight, may be temporarily stopped by removing the piston for access to the inside of the cylinder and stemming round iron wire into the space *B*, Figs. 20 and 21. The diameter of the iron wire should be such that it requires to be driven into the opening. The ends of the wire should be the last to be inserted and should be driven in together after having been cut to a length that will ensure their butting closely when in place. The wire being of iron of the correct diameter and the ends joined as suggested, such a repair will serve the purpose until the ship reaches a port where a permanent repair can be effected. As, however, corrosion of the joining surfaces will continue, the matter should be properly dealt with at the first opportunity, otherwise the cylinder head or liner may have to be put into a lathe to be re-machined.

Originally all liners of two-stroke engines were held in position by sandwiching the upper flange of the liner between the upper part of the jacket and the cylinder cover as shown in Fig. 10. This design has certain disadvantages, chief amongst which is that it necessitates a large mass of metal which cannot be properly cooled at the hottest part of the liner. Also, with this design, it is difficult to arrange for the flow of cooling water to be in a continuous upward direction—so necessary in order to eliminate spaces in which air can accumulate—with the result that cases of serious corrosion of the upper part of such cylinder jackets have occurred.

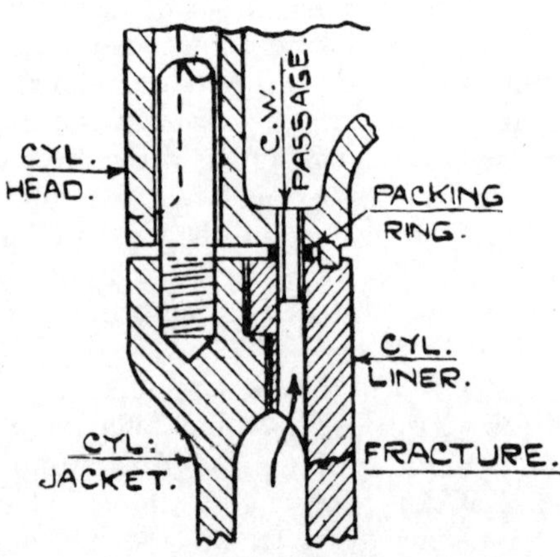

Fig. 23—Method of ensuring effective cooling of cylinder liner flanges of 2-stroke engines

In some engines continuous upward flow of cooling water is obtained by providing a number of holes through the flange of the liner as shown in Fig. 23. The disadvantage of this design is that the presence of the cooling-water holes results in the ground joint between the cylinder head and liner being too great a distance from the face of the cylinder jacket upon which the liner lands, so that unless care is taken when tightening down the cylinder head the part of the liner below the flange will be severely stressed. Cases are known where the liners have actually broken at the point indicated in Fig. 23 owing to excessive tightening of the cylinder-head bolts. In each of these instances the liner did not break until after the engine had been operating for several hours, but the evidence proved beyond doubt that the primary cause was as stated.

The means adopted by one maker to prevent the liner flange becoming sufficiently hot to set up undesirable heat stresses will be noted in Fig. 24. The cylinder liner and jacket are made longer

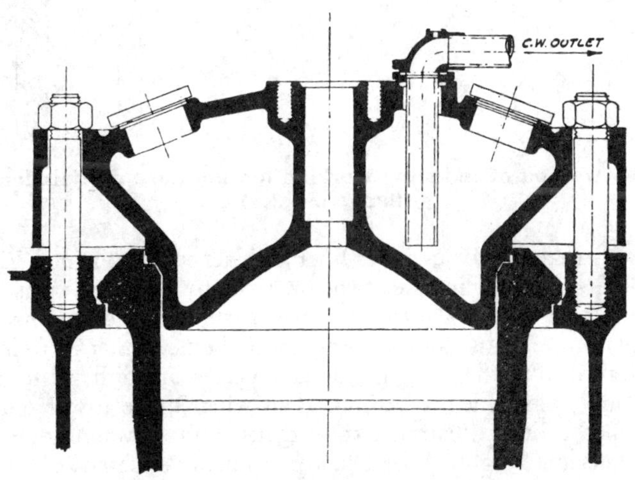

Fig. 24—Section of cylinder head (Fiat)

and the cylinder head extends well into the cylinder liner. This arrangement locates the liner flange well away from the burning gases, and the part of the liner surrounding the combustion chamber is thoroughly circulated by the cooling water.

Fig. 25 illustrates another method of overcoming the difficulty referred to. As will be seen, the cylinder liner extends upwards beyond the cylinder jacket proper, and circumferential divisions are cast on the upper end of the liner to cause rapid circulation of cooling water at this point. The firing ring at the upper end of the liner will be noted. This ring, which is made of special heat-resisting steel, is intended to reduce the flow of heat to the liner flange.

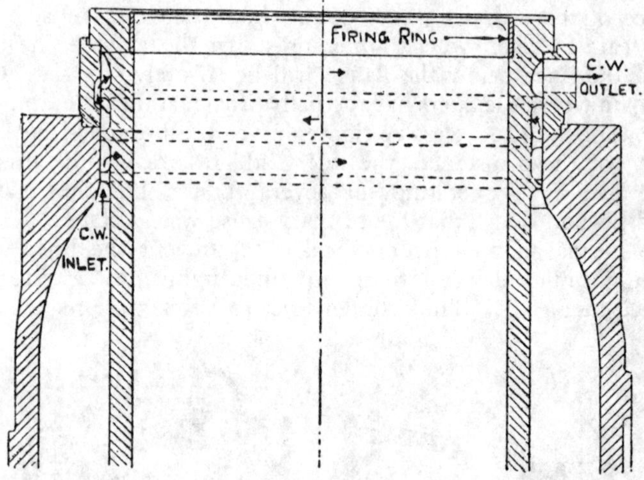

Fig. 25—Method of reducing working temperature of cylinder liner flange (Sulzer)

A two-stroke-engine cylinder liner and jacket are shown in Fig. 26. Such liners may be in one, two, or as many as three parts. The usual practice is to make them in two parts owing to the necessity for providing exhaust and scavenging-air belts, which introduces a complication into the design and renders it more difficult to obtain sound and homogeneous castings than when made up of one part only. In the liner illustrated the exhaust and scavenging-air ports are at the same height, the exhaust ports being situated on the right of the centre-line. The copper rings let into the cylinder liner above and below the exhaust and scavenging-air passages will be observed. The object of these rings, which are a good fit in the jacket and made of soft copper, is to protect the rubber rings against the deleterious action of hot gases in the exhaust, and the oil in the scavenging-air passage. If these copper rings are not a good fit the rubber rings may perish and cooling water leak into the exhaust and scavenging-air passages. Copper is used for this purpose because it has a greater coefficient of expansion than cast iron, and when

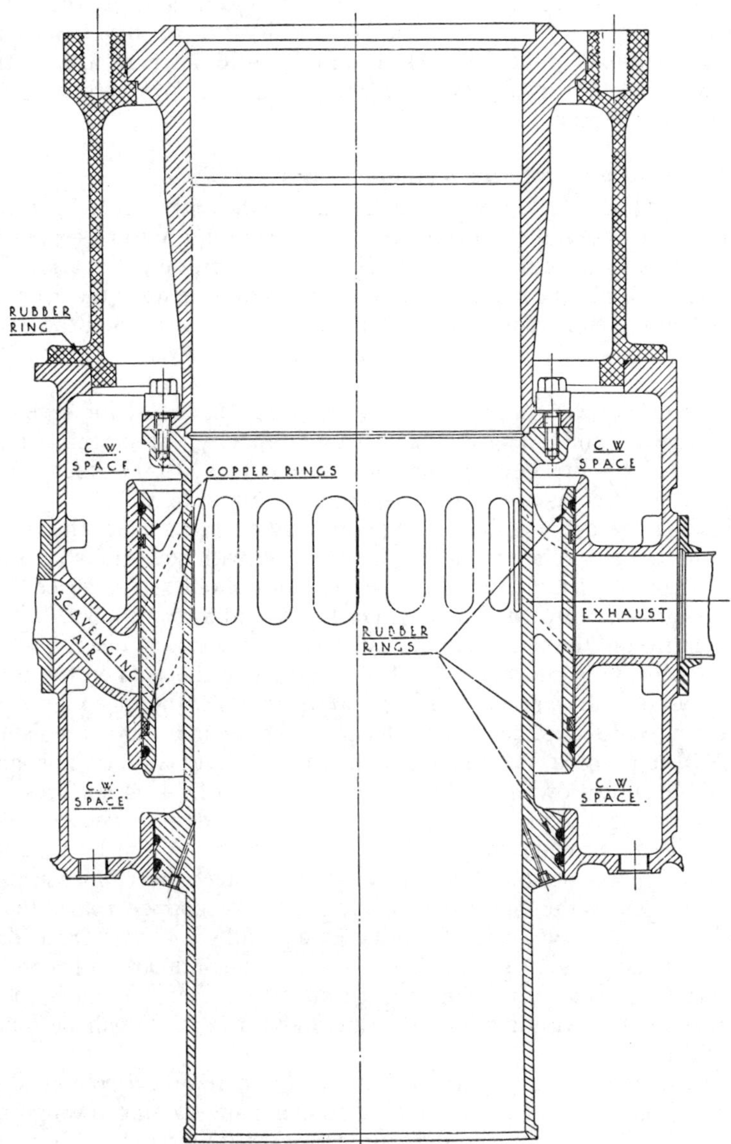

Fig. 26—Section of a 2-stroke cylinder liner and jacket

the engine is working will consequently expand and fill the small clearance space necessary to allow the liner to be fitted into the jacket without difficulty. More will be said later regarding the operation of fitting the two parts together, and the clearances it is necessary to allow.

Removing and refitting cylinder liners

As cylinder cooling-water spaces can be efficiently cleaned without dismantling any of the main parts, the liners require to be separated from their jackets only when the liners are worn out. Occasionally, however, it may be necessary to remake the joint between the cylinder head and liner or renew the rubber rings at the lower end of the liner, either of which operation necessitates the withdrawal of the cylinder liner.

As a rule even liners that have not been disturbed for seven or eight years can be removed without any difficulty, the starting screws provided by the builders being sufficient to start the liner. The usual practice is to provide acorn-ended tap bolts which screw through the cylinder-head flange until they come against the flange of the jacket. When trouble is experienced with such bolts bending or becoming strained at the threads, studs should be screwed well into the holes provided in the liner flange and a strong plate, with a hole through the centre for the stud, laid on the two connecting studs on each side of the starting holes. Tightening the nuts on the three or four equally spaced starting screws will be found to give far better results than acorn-ended tap bolts passing through the flange.

Greater force is usually required to start two-stroke-engine cylinder liners owing to the greater number of bearing surfaces and rubber rings employed. As already mentioned, it is the common practice to provide copper rings above and below the level of the exhaust ports of such liners in order to protect the rubber sealing rings against the hot exhaust gases. These copper rings, to be effective, must be a good fit in the jacket, and sometimes great force is necessary to start such liners owing to scale and carbon becoming jammed between the copper rings and the jacket. In most cases, however, the withdrawing gear illustrated in Fig. 27 will be found sufficient.

In some cases the desired result may be more quickly obtained by the employment of two $1\frac{1}{2}$-inch diameter bolts passing through the liner instead of one through the centre as illustrated. When two bolts are used they should be located diametrically opposite each other and within an inch or so of the liner walls. The first essential in starting a tight liner is to get a direct pull with the chain blocks. If this is not sufficient, screw down the nut *a*, Fig. 27. If a greater force is required, screw down the tap bolts *b*; and if still greater force is necessary, place a screw jack underneath the liner and, after putting a good strain on the different parts of the withdrawing gear, give the bars across the top of the cylinder some sharp blows with a heavy hammer.

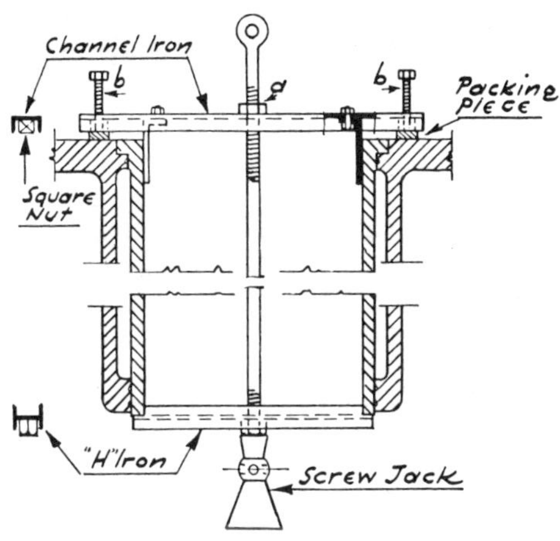

Fig. 27—Cylinder liner withdrawing gear

If a liner is to be refitted, every part of it must be thoroughly cleaned in order that difficulties will not be encountered when refitting owing to pieces of dirt or scale becoming jammed between the close-fitting parts. The same applies, of course, to the inside of the jacket. The usual practice is to chip and afterwards wire-brush the parts in contact with the cooling water, and to clean the fitting parts with an old file. The landing surfaces for the lubricating-oil fittings should be given special attention, and any carbon deposit in the holes likely to prevent the fittings from being screwed down on to their landing surfaces should be removed. The grooves for the rubber sealing rings should be cleaned with an old round file or some other suitable tool that will clean down to the bare metal. Some engineers paint the liners and all other parts in contact with the cooling water, but as properly designed liners rarely corrode, the author prefers merely to clean the surfaces of these parts and give the inside of the jackets only a coat of anti-corrosive paint.

Before a liner is lowered into position all sharp edges inside the jacket over which the rubber rings must pass should be chamfered slightly in order to prevent cutting of the rubber rings, while soft soap, tallow, or other similar lubricant should be liberally applied to the rubber rings and the fitting surfaces so that they will slip easily into the reduced bore of the jacket.

When a new liner is to be fitted, it is advisable first to lower it into position without the rubber rings to check the fitting clearances. A liner should not only drop freely into position by its own weight, but there should be slight diametrical clearance between it and the jacket to allow for the greater expansion of the liner. The lower end radial clearance for engine cylinders of about 30 inches diameter should be not less than 0·2 mm. The clearance may be as great as 0·5 mm without ill-effects, but clearances greater than this will permit excessive lateral movement of the liner when the engine is working, and the rubber rings may consequently not remain effective so long. The radial clearance at the top or "firing" end of certain two-stroke engine liners should not be less than $\frac{1}{1000}$ inch per inch diameter of cylinder, as this part of the liner attains a high temperature and jackets of the type shown in Fig. 10 have been broken beyond repair owing to insufficient diametrical clearance.

Assuming that the clearances are correct, the liner should now be withdrawn and the rubber rings placed in position. The rubber rings should be of such a length that they grip firmly around the liner. If the rings are too slack or do not grip with sufficient pressure they may be rolled out of the groove as the liner is lowered into position. As a rule a 10-per-cent stretch will be found to meet the case. When in position around the liner the rubber rings should project from 1 to 2 mm; the greater the radial clearance between the liner and the jacket the greater must the rubber rings project. If the cross-sectional diameter of the rubber rings is too great and projects too far beyond the machined surface of the liner and a ring of smaller diameter is not available, the cross-sectional diameter may be reduced by shortening the ring and giving it a greater amount of stretch. It is not wise to attempt to reduce the amount projecting by paring off with a sharp knife. If treating the ring in this way will meet the case, better results will be obtained by holding the ring lightly against a high-speed emery wheel.

The question whether or not a rubber ring is good enough to put back often arises; the answer in most cases is just guesswork, and often means a great amount of labour lost if the old rings are put back and should fail to seal the space when the water test is carried out. In most cases the cost of the rubber ring is so small and the amount of extra work involved so great, should the old ring be ineffective, that it is wise to fit a new ring every time a part is disturbed. The effect of working conditions on these rings is rather peculiar. They set cross-sectionally to the shape of the groove into which they are fitted, and stretch as is to be expected, yet their elasticity increases. When a ring takes the shape of the groove the chances are that it will not make a fluid-tight joint if refitted.

If a liner will not drop freely into place by its own weight it is a sure sign that the rubber rings are too large, and if an attempt is made to force the liner down there is a grave danger of the rings being cut and the whole of the operation having to be done over again. Even when the liner drops freely into place it is wise to test the rubber rings for fluid-tightness, before any connecting up is begun, by pouring a couple of buckets of water into the jackets.

In some makes of engine it is advisable to screw the cylinder lubricating-oil fittings into position before the lifting tackle is removed, as it sometimes happens that the position of the liner must be altered slightly to enable this to be done.

When two-stroke-engine cylinder liners are out of their jackets the copper rings at either side of the exhaust ports should be protected against accidental damage by chipping hammers and chain blocks. To be effective these copper rings must be a close fit. If the rings have been burnt or otherwise damaged they must be repaired before the liner is refitted, otherwise the hot gases will attack the rubber rings and leakage of water from the jacket will occur. Damage done by a chipping hammer or chain blocks can usually be repaired by drilling and tapping a $\frac{1}{4}$- to $\frac{3}{8}$-inch diameter hole in the ring and screwing in a copper or brass plug. If the ring is burnt or extensively damaged it will be necessary to chain-plug the damaged portion.

Cylinder jackets

The only attention required by jackets, apart from the removal of deposits, is to examine the internal surfaces for corrosion whenever the cylinder liners are withdrawn. The part most likely to corrode is the machined surface at the point where the lower part of the liner makes contact with it, and it so happens that corrosion is most objectionable at this point as it reduces the effectiveness of the rubber rings in preventing leakage of cooling water from between the jacket and liner. Corrosion should therefore be dealt with at once, or the only alternative may be a new section of cylinder beam, which is a costly item. The affected part must be scrubbed clean with a wire brush and afterwards given two or three coats of Bitumastic solution, the first of which should be applied warm. Galvex and Apexior paints will also be found suitable.

If a small part of the surface is corroded so badly that leakage of cooling water past the rubber ring occurs, the part should be chain-drilled and cast-iron or stainless steel plugs screwed in to make an unbroken surface for the rubber ring to bear against. If, then,

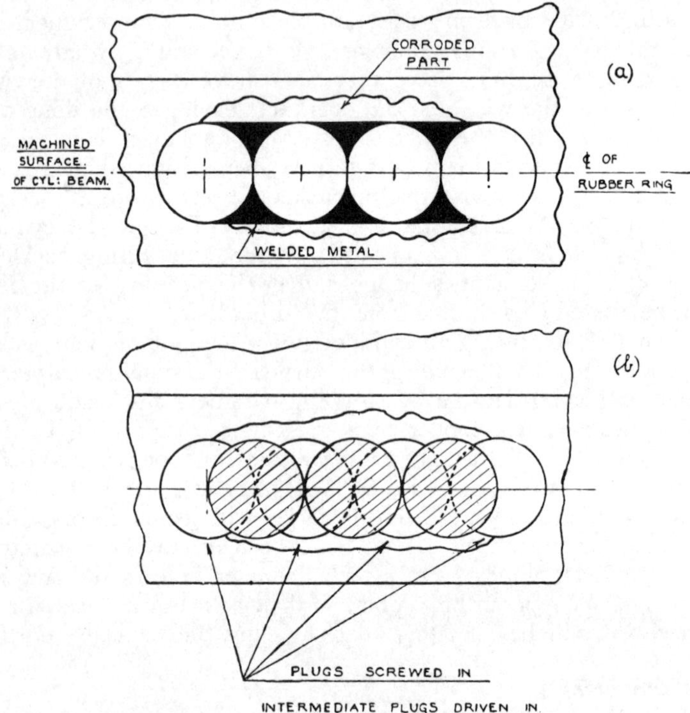

Fig. 28—Method of repairing corroded cylinder water-jacket in way of rubber sealing ring

spaces between the plugs can be filled by welded metal, as shown at (a), Fig. 28, a very satisfactory repair will result. As there is always a danger of the welded metal corroding in time, an even more satisfactory repair would be to drill and fit additional stainless steel plugs at the points where the plugs in the first row join, as shown at (b), Fig. 28. Such a repair, if carefully carried out, will last indefinitely. It is not necessary to screw in the second row of plugs, and the operation will be simplified considerably if these plugs are made a good fit and driven in. The middle plug should be the last to be driven in as, if this plug is made an extra good driving fit, it will tighten all other plugs and make it impossible for water to leak past them. All plugs should be coated with a mixture of red lead and boiled oil before being fitted, and finally dressed up to the curvature of the beam by an emery wheel or hand filing. In the event of it being impossible to withdraw the liner and make a permanent repair, an expedient is to drain the water from the defective cylinder jacket and, after the surfaces have become quite dry, to pour through the opening provided for inspection and cleaning, sufficient celluloid varnish to fill the cooling water space to a depth of about one inch. This will stop leakage of the cooling water until such time as the defect can be dealt with properly.

Cylinder lubricating-oil fittings

In some engines the cylinder liner projects from the bottom of the jacket, and the lubricating-oil fitting is screwed into the uncooled part of the liner. Generally, however, the fitting conveying the lubricating oil from the supply pipe to the cylinder passes through the water jacket.

Passing the lubricating-oil fitting through the cylinder cooling-water space complicates the design of such fittings, as the fitting is exposed to corrosive elements and particular care must be taken to preclude the possibility of water leaking into the cylinder. The design of fitting shown in Fig. 29 is very sound, as not only is the part conveying the oil prevented from making contact with the cooling water, but any leakage of cooling water is readily noticed as it will flow outward.

In the case of one ship the outer tubes were made of galvanised iron which corroded very badly after two years' service. The tubes were machined down and provided with slidable cast-iron sleeves, as shown in Fig. 29, and no further trouble in this direction was experienced. In most cases the whole outer tube is made of stainless steel, but good quality cast iron is equally suitable and, of course, much less costly.

It will be observed that should the outer tube corrode through, or should the joint between the tube and the cylinder liner be improperly made, water will flow outward. When this occurs the fitting should be removed and the leakage stopped at the first opportunity, otherwise the threaded portion of the part conveying the oil will be attacked, and the two parts may become "frozen" together. When this occurs it is often impossible to remove the deposits and separate the parts, and if the threads of the two parts are of different pitch, as is generally the case, it is very difficult to remove the fitting in one piece without damaging the threads in the cylinder liner. The threads in the liner must, of course, be preserved at all costs. The solution to this difficulty is to make the threads of each part of the same pitch, when it would be an easy matter to remove the fitting as a whole and free the two parts.

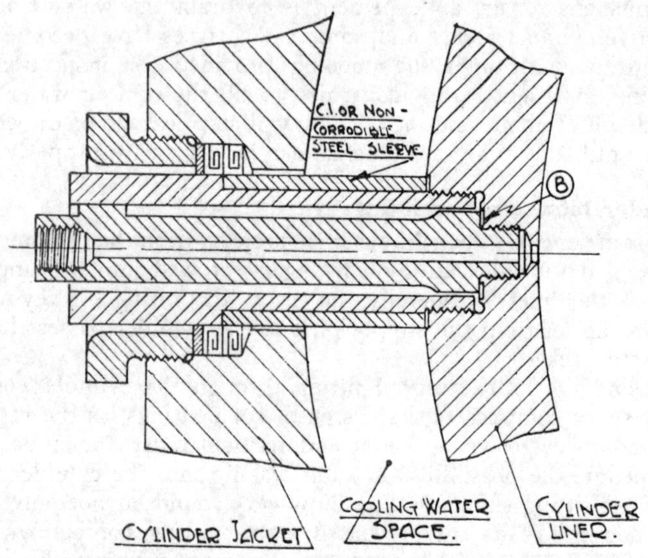

Fig. 29—Lubricating-oil fitting designed to prevent cooling water leaking into cylinder liner

If for some reason the pitch of the threads on the part conveying the oil must be finer than the threads on the outer tube, then the outside diameter of the oil tube should be greater at the ends, as shown in Fig. 29, so that the deposit accumulates around the reduced part. Otherwise it is quite impossible to free the parts in place.

When refitting these parts particular care must be taken to ensure that the various joints are perfectly fluid-tight. A thin mixture of red lead and boiled oil should be applied to the screwed portions. Tests should be made to ensure that both parts land properly and are not being prevented from doing so by the screwed portions bottoming. If some form of packing is necessary between the fitting and the cylinder liner, a soft copper ring (B) will be found suitable. Should the surfaces be too uneven for such packing, a grommet made of a single strand of asbestos will be found to meet the case.

Cylinder heads

Such parts are made either circular or square in shape. When of the latter form they are usually bolted together athwartships to increase the rigidity of the main structure, and held down at each corner by the large-diameter bolt which extends right from the head to the bedplate, as shown in Fig. 17. Circular-shaped heads are held down by a large number of studs screwed into the cylinder-jacket flange and nuts equally spaced near the periphery of the head.

Cylinder heads are made very deep, deeper perhaps than would at first appear necessary. In designing them, however, there are several factors which determine their depth, the chief in the case of some four-stroke engines being the passage leading the exhaust gases from the exhaust-valve pocket to the outer wall. The area of this passage must be sufficiently great to allow unrestricted flow of the gases, and the cooling water must circulate all round the passage if undesirable heat stresses are to be avoided. The exhaust-gas passage could be made wider on the horizontal axis, and not so deep, but as the passage must pass between two holding-down studs its width in circular-shaped heads is limited.

In a few cases the passages through the cylinder head are eliminated by passing the combustion air and exhaust gas through the centre of the respective valve casings. This has the effect of reducing the depth of the cylinder head but necessitates the valves being larger, which is rather a disadvantage, particularly in the case of the exhaust valve which has to be handled more frequently than any other part of a four-stroke engine.

The strength of the cylinder head is not dependent entirely upon the thickness of the lower wall, i.e. the wall of metal in contact with the gases inside the cylinder. The upper wall, besides enclosing the cooling-water space, assists greatly in resisting the gas pressure inside the cylinder, the load being transmitted through the side or outer vertical wall and the walls forming the various valve pockets. Were this not the case the lower wall would be found much thicker and, in consequence, more liable to crack owing to the greater heat stresses that would result.

The cylinder head was the last of the three parts enclosing the combustion chamber to be made positively reliable. Even now cracked cylinder heads are not altogether unknown, but on the rare occasions when they do crack the cause is ineffective cooling or improper fitting of the valves which they contain. The cylinder head of any engine deserves the greatest respect, not only because it is a most intricate casting, in view of the numerous valve pockets which it must contain and which necessitate uneven thickness of metal, but it is subjected to the maximum pressure and temperature conditions. It is also, in most cases, rigidly secured to the main structure and, therefore, not free to expand as is the piston, which is subjected to similar stringent conditions.

When cylinder heads crack the cracks generally occur between the fuel valve and the exhaust-valve pockets—the weakest part of

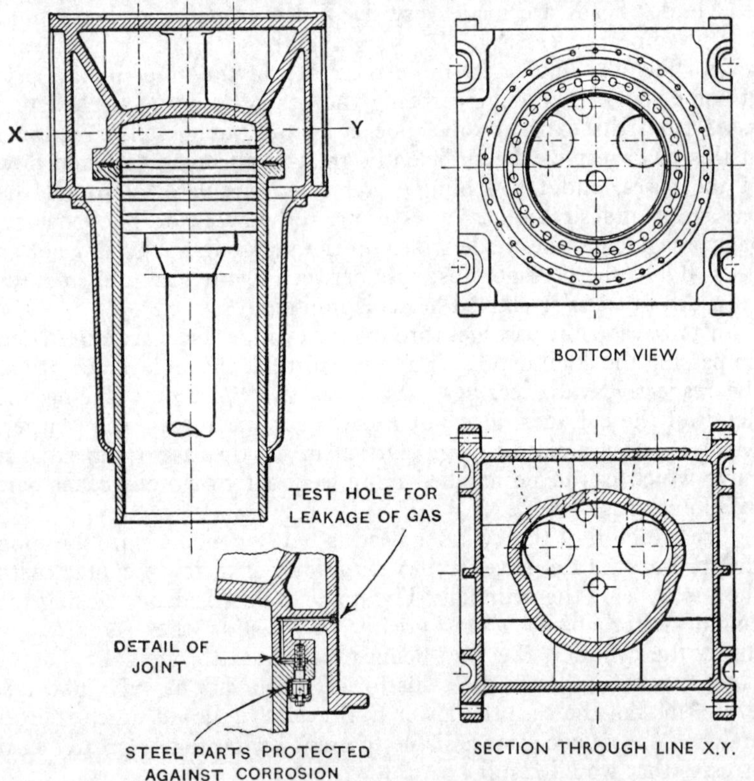

Fig. 30—Box-shaped cylinder head and liner of a 4-stroke single-acting engine (Burmeister & Wain)

four-stroke engine cylinder heads. The spaces between the pockets of the fuel valve and the exhaust and air-inlet valves were in the early engines so narrow that it was difficult to ensure good circulation of the cooling water. To eliminate this weakness a common practice is to offset the fuel valve in order to increase the space between these pockets.

Fig. 30 shows Burmeister and Wain's method of providing the necessary space to ensure efficient circulation of the cooling water. It will be seen that when the piston is at its highest position the upper portion of it is within the cylinder head. The lower part of the head in this case, therefore, forms the upper part of the cylinder, and the cooling water is allowed unrestricted flow to all parts. The air-inlet and exhaust valves, it will be observed, are situated on one side of the fore-and-aft centre-line, and the fuel valve is arranged on the opposite side. In this way a fairly wide space between any two of the three pockets is obtained. The upper portion of the combustion space formed by the cylinder head into which the valves open is shaped as shown in the lower right-hand illustration, while the lower portion in way of the flange is circular to meet the flange of the liner.

Fig. 31 shows one type of two-stroke-engine cylinder head in section. As will be observed, the head is in two parts, the lower

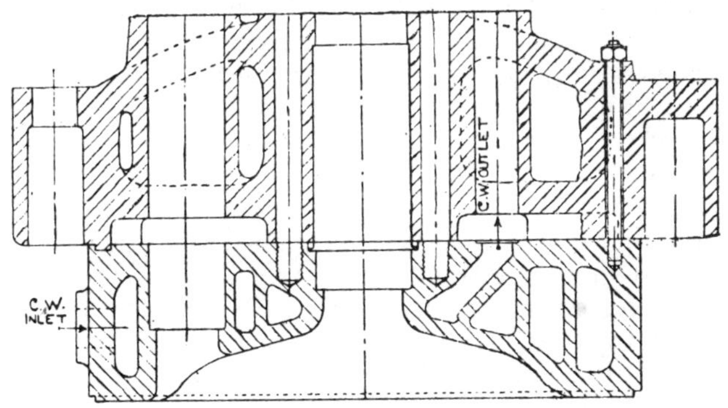

Fig. 31—Cylinder head of 2-stroke single-acting engine (Sulzer)

being made of cast iron and the upper of cast steel. The cast-iron part is exposed to the heat while the outer part forms a bridge to transmit the gas load in the cylinder to the holding-down studs. In this way the part of the head in which heat stresses are set up is relieved of bending stresses produced by tightening the holding-down bolts. Heat stresses in the lower part are reduced by giving the cooling-water space a spiral form, which increases the velocity of the cooling water. The cooling water enters at the left-hand side and after going three times round the head passes into the upper part.

A point sometimes overlooked by designers of double-acting engines is the possibility of corrosion due to the accumulation of water in the parts which form the bottom cylinders. For instance, the bottom cylinder covers of such engines are generally held in position by studs screwed into the cylinder jacket or beam, and nuts on the underside of the cover. As there must be clearance between the outer part of the cover and the jacket to ensure that the ground surfaces are making proper contact, any water running down the jacket is liable to find its way into the stud holes and corrode the studs unless they are made of non-corrodible material, which is not usual practice.

In one such case with which the author had to deal, not only were the covers most difficult to remove, but more than half the securing studs were found badly corroded, the reduction in area in some cases being as much as 30 per cent. As it is impossible to eliminate entirely water from leaking joints or test cocks running down the jackets and finding its way into spaces where it may cause difficulties, provision should be made to allow the water to flow out as fast as it enters. Usually it is possible to fit a rubber ring or other soft packing to keep out the water, but in the case mentioned this was not practicable owing to the irregular shape of the castings, and provision had to be made to allow the water which ran into the bolt holes to escape. This was accomplished by cutting slots across the face of the securing nuts which, being on the underside of the cover, allowed the water to run out of the stud holes as quickly as it entered.

Whenever a cylinder is opened the opportunity should be taken to make a thorough examination of the underside of the cylinder head. Cracks, when they occur, usually begin at the bottom of one of the valve pockets. The crack usually starts when the parts are being cooled, and are mostly produced owing to a greater area, per unit mass, being exposed to the comparatively cold starting air admitted to the cylinder whilst manoeuvring. The metal at these points contracts more rapidly and tensile stresses sufficient to start a crack are set up. For this reason the lower ends of all pockets should be well rounded and any cracks, no matter how small, removed by chipping and filing, otherwise they will extend and may eventually penetrate right through into the cooling-water space.

When a surface crack occurs this does not necessarily mean that it cannot be prevented from extending and that the casting is doomed. In many cases if the crack is caught in time and the metal in the vicinity of it chipped away, the casting may last for many years, and sometimes even indefinitely. Whether this treatment is successful or not depends, of course, upon the design of the casting and the quality of the cast iron of which it is made, but this treatment has been successful in so many cases that it should always be tried before a casting is condemned. No harm can result from such treatment if the casting is already weakened by a crack; chipping the metal away in the vicinity of the crack will not weaken it further. For a successful repair, however, the crack must be completely removed.

Cracks in metal which are too fine to be seen by the naked eye can be detected by first thoroughly cleaning the suspected part and then applying a thin mixture of red lead and petrol. The petrol will have evaporated after a few minutes, leaving the red lead on the surface of the metal, from which it should be wiped off with a dry cloth. The surface should then be examined through a magnifying glass. If a crack exists a thin red streak will indicate the length and width. This streak is due to some of the red lead being carried into the crack by the petrol. If paraffin is used to clean the surface of the casting prior to the above test, the part should be heated before the thin mixture of red lead and petrol is applied in order to evaporate the paraffin, otherwise the mixture of red lead and petrol may not readily enter the crack.

Welding large cast-iron parts such as cylinder heads is not generally successful, and in some cases the intense local heat produced when welding makes matters worse instead of better. Before attempting to weld, therefore, one should be quite sure that something quite so drastic must be done to prevent the crack from extending. It is certain that many castings slightly cracked through casting strain, but which would have lasted as long as other parts of the engine, have been completely destroyed by attempts to repair them by welding. When endeavouring to come to a decision as to what is best to be done with a fractured casting, the age-old method of drilling and plugging at the ends of the cracks, used so successfully in connection with boilers, should be considered.

The author had to repair a cylinder head which had cracked in the outer vertical wall. The crack began near to the exhaust-gas outlet and extended in a circumferential direction through a cooling-water space inspection hole for a distance of 11 inches. The ends of the crack were located by the petrol and red lead method just described and, after drilling and plugging at the ends of the crack, heavy brackets were fitted as shown in Fig. 32. This cylinder head, and several others repaired in the same way, remained in service for many years. When drilling and plugging to prevent a crack

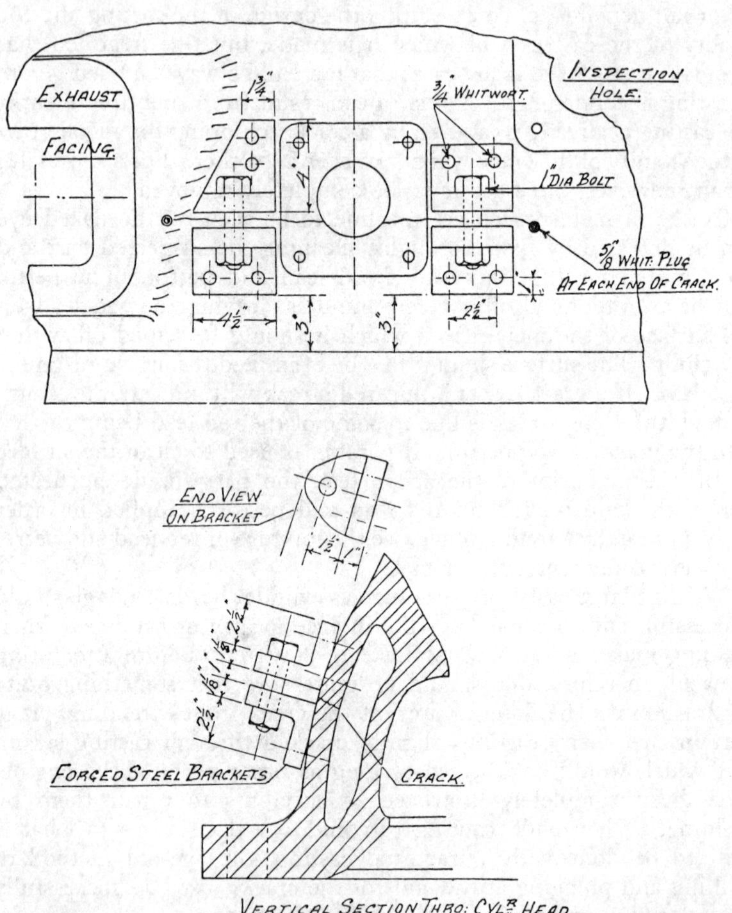

Fig. 32—One method of repairing a cracked cylinder head

extending, it is advisable to locate the holes half-an-inch or so beyond the visible ends of the crack in order to be quite sure that the crack has not already extended beyond the holes.

Fig. 33—Cylinder head broken as a result of fuel valve explosion

There are castings, of course, which can be saved only by welding, and some such repairs have been successful. There is never any difficulty in welding steel parts, and some cast-iron parts can be successfully welded by experts, provided the part to be welded is free to expand when the heat is applied. The difficulty arises when the design of the castings is such that the part being welded cannot expand freely, as, for instance, the spoke of a flywheel, to mention an extreme case. In any case the metal in the vicinity of the crack must be cut out in a V-form to the bottom of the crack. The whole of the casting must then be heated to about 1,000°F (538°C) and, after welding, the casting should again be heated to relieve as far as possible any internal strains produced by the welding operation. The casting should then be completely covered to protect it from cold air-currents and allowed to cool out very slowly. To ensure any degree of success it is essential to heat the casting to a high temperature, but unfortunately it is this part of the operation which introduces grave risks of distortion. Small castings distort to a greater extent than larger castings, so that it is generally necessary to re-machine any surfaces that must be perfectly true.

Fig. 33 illustrates an extreme case of cylinder head failure due to an explosion in the fuel valve of an air-injection engine.

Double-acting engine cylinders

The double-acting principle introduces complications into cylinder liner design, since provision must be made for the liner to expand endwise. If the bottom of the cylinder must be enclosed in the same way as the top and as described for single-acting engines, this allowance for endwise expansion can only be achieved by making the liner in two parts and providing an expansion space between the inner ends of the two liners. The top half of the liner will then be free to expand downwards and the bottom half upwards.

One such construction is illustrated in Fig. 34, from which it will be seen that the bottom half of the liner complete with water jacket can be removed sideways after the piston and piston rod have been withdrawn from the top of the cylinder jacket. Before this can be accomplished the top half of the liner must be removed. Whilst this form of construction has been found entirely satisfactory from an operational point of view it will be appreciated that considerable time and effort are required to carry out certain repairs. The piston can be exposed and piston rings given attention fairly easily, it being necessary only to lower the bottom half of the cylinder on to the top of the crankcase with the special gear provided and raise the piston by rotating the main crankshaft about a quarter of a revolution.

With this type of liner, divided into two parts, it is necessary to prevent gases from leaking outward, and cooling water inward, at the points where the two parts almost join. One method of achieving this is shown in Fig. 35. Leakage of gas is prevented by stepping the ends of the liners and making one a good sliding fit in the other. This provision suffices, as when this part of the liner is uncovered

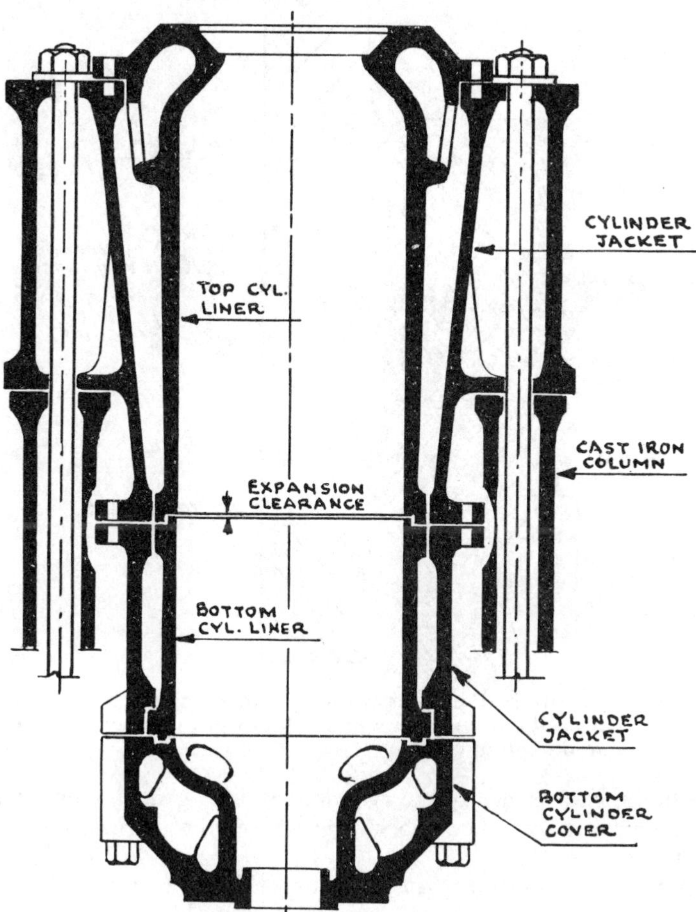

Fig. 34—Double-acting cylinder showing one method of providing for expansion of liner

by the piston the pressure in the cylinder is only slightly above atmospheric.

The provision made to prevent cooling water from leaking into the cylinder comprises a simple steel ring, the two inner ends of which are chamfered, and two rubber rings, one on each side of the steel ring. When the steel ring and rubber rings have been put into

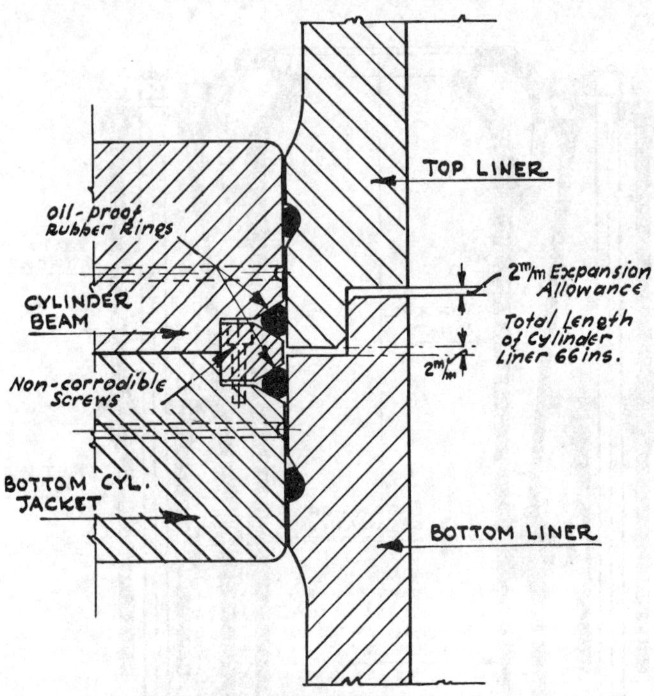

Fig. 35—One method of preventing leakage of gases and cooling water at point where upper and lower cylinder liners join in double-acting engine

position the lower half of the cylinder is raised, generally by rotating the crankshaft, and the rubber rings squeezed to form a watertight joint.

With this arrangement the important thing is to make quite sure that the rubber rings are of the correct size. If they are too small they will, of course, be ineffective, while if they are too large the two halves of the cylinder will be prevented from making contact no matter what force is used to tighten the nuts holding the two halves together. If undue force is used in an endeavour to accomplish this it is possible to break the cylinder-jacket flange even when this is two or more inches thick. Notes upon how rubber rings can be prevented from causing this accident will be given in the next chapter.

Harland and Wolff overcome the difficulties referred to above in a unique way. A section of one cylinder of their two-stroke double-acting engine is shown in Fig. 36, from which it will be seen that the ends of the cylinders are closed by slidable pistons instead of fixed covers. These pistons, called exhaust pistons, not only take the

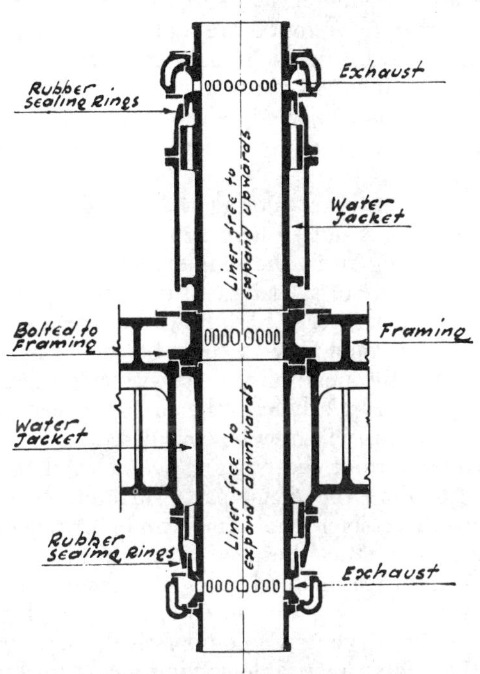

Fig. 36—Method of providing for expansion of liner in 2-stroke double-acting engine (Harland & Wolff)

reaction of the main piston load, but serve to control the release of the exhaust gases. The cylinder liner is in two parts, but instead of being firmly held at the outer ends, the two parts are flanged at their inner ends and bolted to a rigid part which accommodates the scavenging-air ports. Thus the top portion of the liner is free to expand upwards and the bottom portion downwards.

CHAPTER 7

Cylinder cooling

In some engines the cylinder heads are made extra deep, as shown in Fig. 30, and when a number are bolted together a continuous entablature is formed. In such cases the jackets are of relatively light construction, since their only purpose is to enclose the cooling-water space, which is subjected to a pressure of about 30 lb/sq.in. The more usual practice is for the cylinder entablature to serve as a water jacket.

Fresh water is used for cooling the cylinder liners of modern engines, although it is not so long ago that it was realised to what extent scale resulting from the employment of sea-water was responsible for the failure of cylinder castings, and a portion of cylinder liner and piston ring wear. As, however, the cylinder liners of older ships will for some time to come be cooled by sea-water, and as there is always the possibility of sea-water getting into a fresh-water cooling system by accident, the action of heat upon sea-water under such conditions will now be considered.

As the temperature of the burning fuel is in the neighbourhood of 3,000°F (1,650°C), the metal parts surrounding such hot gases would become excessively hot and trouble result unless means were provided to conduct the heat away and keep the temperature of the metal within reasonable limits. All parts of the cylinders are, therefore, surrounded by an enclosed space through which a liquid or gaseous cooling agent of comparatively low temperature is circulated. The only practicable cooling media for engines of large power output are fresh water, sea-water, and lubricating oil, which have low boiling-points, so that providing the cooling medium is not allowed to boil and evaporate away, the maximum possible temperature of the metal in contact with the burning fuel is very low compared with the temperature of the gases inside the cylinders.

It has been found that the piston cooling medium receives about 40 per cent of the heat flow to the entire cooling system, and that about half this amount passes through the cylinder liner. The piston and cylinder head receive approximately the same amount of heat. The reason why such a comparatively small amount of heat passes through the cylinder liner is that only a small portion of this particular part is exposed to the maximum temperature reached in the cylinder. Another reason is that the surfaces of the cylinder head and piston exposed to the burning gases are dry, while the cylinder-liner surface is covered by a film of oil which resists the flow of heat to the metal.

Although the foregoing facts are considered when deciding upon the most suitable cooling medium to employ for the various parts, the choice will depend mainly upon the design and arrangement of certain parts of individual engines. For instance, if the cooling medium for the cylinder liners has to pass through narrow passages liable to become choked with mud or scale, it would be unwise to use sea-water, while if the arrangement of the mechanism conveying the cooling medium to and from the pistons is such that slight leakage into the crankcase is unavoidable, lubricating oil is the only satisfactory medium to employ.

Without a doubt, the best arrangement is to use fresh water for cylinder cooling, its great advantage over sea-water being that it is relatively free from impurities liable to settle out and deposit in the cooling-water spaces. Moreover, higher temperatures can be carried than are possible with sea-water without fear of substances depositing on the cooled surfaces, which would interfere with the flow of heat from the metal to the cooling medium Lubricating oil is, however, an ideal cooling medium since, providing a copious supply is maintained, not only will the cooled surfaces remain free from deposits, but the medium will not attack and corrode the metal as fresh water is liable to do. The adoption of either fresh water or lubricating oil as cooling medium, however, involves additional equipment, such as tanks and coolers.

Doxford's recommend adding potassium bichromate to the distilled cooling water in order to prevent corrosion of the steel parts in contact with the water. This treatment is effective provided no less than the quantity recommended is added. The purpose is to cover the corrodible metal surfaces with a rust-resisting skin, and when sufficient of the chemical has been added to the cooling water a yellow tinge is produced. The weakness of this method of preventing corrosion is that the reverse effect is produced if even a small quantity of sea-water finds its way into the cooling water. Sea-water gives the cooling water a green tinge in daylight.

As there are many ways in which sea-water may reach cooling water to which potassium bichromate has been added, this chemical is not entirely satisfactory. For instance, should a leak develop in one of the fresh-water cooler tubes active corrosion may be started in cylinder cooling-water spaces. In regard to the piston cooling water, should water containing this chemical leak from the conveying mechanism and find its way into the crankcase, the consequences may be serious as the complete exclusion of sea-water from crankcases is not always possible in some makes of engines. The admixture of lubricating oil with even a small quantity of sea-water is most undesirable and must be avoided if at all possible, but if to such a mixture is added water containing potassium bichromate the consequences may be disastrous. It is with a view to eliminating the disadvantages of this chemical that the oil industry has produced an anti-corrosion oil, which if added to the cooling water in proper proportions produces on the metal parts a rust-resisting skin which is not affected by the entry of sea-water into the cooling system. One of the best-known additives is named " Dromus D " oil.

Calcium and magnesium sulphates and calcium carbonate are the ordinary scale-forming substances in sea-water. Common salt is soluble at all temperatures and does not deposit, since the normal concentration is never exceeded in the cylinder jackets of engines. The scale generally found on properly cooled surfaces is principally composed of carbonate and sulphate of lime, and has such poor adhesive properties that, if it is deposited on a curved surface that expands and contracts, it cracks and falls off when a thickness of about $\frac{1}{8}$-inch is reached. But should the temperature of the water in the jackets be allowed to get too high, owing to the flow being obstructed or to the design of the cooling-water spaces being such that part of the water moves very slowly or becomes stagnant, the remaining sulphates, which form a harder scale and adhere more firmly to cast iron, will deposit.

Such scales cannot be dissolved by any known scale-dissolving fluid, and are very difficult to remove by chipping, so that every precaution must be taken to prevent the formation of such scales by carefully feeling every part of the cylinders when the engine is working, in order to ascertain if any particular part works at an abnormally high temperature. Any such part of the cooling-water space should be examined at the first opportunity, and if there is a tendency for excessive quantities of scale to deposit, the circulation of cooling water at this point must be improved by providing a leak-off. It will generally be found that quite a small bore pipe, i.e. about $\frac{1}{2}$-inch, with regulating cock, will be sufficient to give the required circulation and prevent local overheating.

In cases where the stagnant water is not in the vicinity of a part of the jacket where a leak-off hole can be drilled, the overheated water can generally be reached by employing an internal pipe made of copper and brazed to the regulating cock screwed into the water jacket. As hot sea-water is an active corrosive agent it should, if possible, be led into one of the overboard pipes and not be allowed to drain on to the double-bottom tank-top. To ensure a uniform rate of flow, the pressure at the outlet must, of course, be several pounds less than the pressure in the cylinder jacket, so that the desired results are not always obtained by leading the leak-off into the main engine overboard discharge In such cases a good plan is to lead it into the bilge-pump discharge pipe.

It will be appreciated that for the heat to flow from the gas side to the water side of any of the parts forming the cylinder, the temperature of the wall in contact with the gases must vary, it being hottest on the gas side. Published data regarding the actual variation of temperature are scanty, but when the surfaces are free from scale it is unlikely that the inner layers of metal ever exceed 300°F (150°C), and the maximum temperature reached on the cooled side may be taken as 150°F (66°C) when the temperature of the cooling medium as it leaves the cylinder jacket is in the neighbourhood of 120°F (49°C). When scale deposits on the cooled surface of the wall, the temperature of the outer layers of the metal will, of course, be higher, and as the temperature-difference between the inside and outside of the wall remains practically the same, the temperature of the inner surface will be increased by an accumulation of scale on the outer surface.

Owing to it being necessary to cool engine cylinders, complications arise due to the varying temperatures in the same casting causing uneven expansion. Moreover, some of the castings have to be made to varying thickness owing to the necessity to provide for rapid heat transfer from the inner wall of the casting to the cooling water, so that certain parts may be under stress before they are fitted. Because of this the question of effective cooling was one of the greatest obstacles to the development of the diesel engine; but the difficulty of designing and making castings that will withstand, without risk of fracturing, the casting strains and heat stresses set up by unequal expansion when in operation has been overcome.

When cylinder castings of modern engines fracture, the cause is nearly always either faulty workmanship, resulting in an unsound casting, or improper operating conditions. In addition to casting strains and heat stresses, certain of the castings are severely stressed when being attached to the main structure, and if this operation is not thoughtfully carried out the stresses produced may be many times greater than the stresses set up by the pressure of gas in the cylinder. To eliminate casting strains as far as possible, the common practice during manufacture is to anneal the various castings subjected to varying temperatures when in use by heating them in an oven to about 1,300°F (704°C) and letting them gradually cool to atmospheric temperature.

The lower the temperature of the cooling water as it leaves the cylinder jackets, the greater will be the flow of heat to the cooling water and the lower will be the thermal efficiency of the engine. Even though this heat passes into a closed fresh-water cooling system it is eventually discharged overboard with the sea-water used to cool the fresh water. Moreover, the greater the temperature gradient in the metal parts the more severe will be the heat stresses produced in the castings.

This suggests that the hotter the water leaving the cylinder jackets, the better would be the results as regards fuel economy and life of the various castings. This is indeed the case, but there is a practical limit. The limit is imposed by the rubber rings employed to prevent leakage of cooling water at various points between the three principal parts forming the cylinder. Should these rubber rings be subjected to a temperature higher than they are capable of withstanding they will perish and fail to serve their purpose. Failure of a rubber ring may mean a shut-down and much hard work to renew it, so the question of cylinder jacket temperature requires careful consideration.

The reliability of rubber rings depends upon the heat- and oil-resisting qualities of the material used and upon their location. More will be said later about these essential qualities; and as regards location, those in the cylinder head are probably subjected to the greatest heat and are most likely to suffer deterioration, because not only is the cylinder head the hottest part, but the cooling water reaches its maximum temperature at this point. The location of rubber rings in relation to temperature, however, varies so much in different makes of engines that it is not possible to suggest a maximum cooling-water temperature which would cover all, but there are very few engines where a temperature of 150°F (66°C) cannot be safely adopted and many where the temperature could be run up to 180°F (82°C) without ill-effect.

The cylinder cooling-water system of a large marine engine comprises the main supply pipe running the full length of the engine and located below the bottom of the cylinders, with branches leading the water to the lower part of each cylinder jacket. After circulating around each cylinder liner, the water passes to the cylinder head and then into the common pipe that leads into drain tanks, usually situated in the ship's double bottom.

Although not necessary, it is advisable in order to avoid air-locks to give the water a continual upward movement once it leaves the pump. Air in such places may not only interfere with the free flow of the water, but with warm water it will form an active corrosive agent. An arrangement that works well, but is not very popular owing to the additional expense, is for the pumps to deliver into the top of a four/six-ton capacity tank, situated on deck well above the cylinder head level, from which the water flows to the engine. The provision of such a tank not only causes a great deal of the air to separate from the water before it enters the cylinder jackets, but any sediment in the water will settle out in the tank if the water enters at the bottom of one end and leaves at about mid-height at the other end.

It is not now customary to water-cool the "ahead" crosshead guide-bars, as such a practice has been proved unnecessary where pressure lubrication is employed, the copious supply of lubricating oil acting as an effective cooling medium. When these parts are water-cooled, their jackets should be examined occasionally if the practice is for the cooling water direct from the pump to pass through them on its way to the cylinder jackets, as sediment tends to deposit in them. This may in time accumulate to such an extent

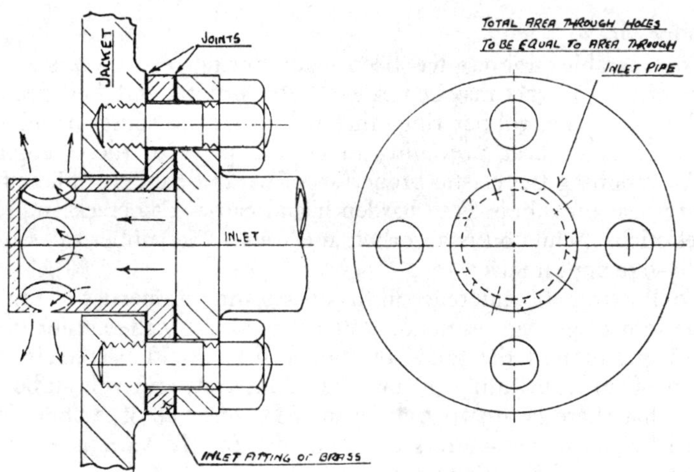

Fig. 37—Deflector for cooling-water inlet to cylinder jackets

that the supply of cooling water to the cylinders is restricted. The surface of the guide-bar opposite the cooling-water inlet should also be examined for wastage, as owing to the jacket being narrow there is a tendency for the ingoing water to erode the surface it strikes against. This can be prevented by employing a deflector, as shown in Fig. 37.

In very cold climates it is advisable, although not necessary, to preheat the cylinders so as to effect starting on a minimum amount of starting air and to reduce heat stresses in the metal parts resulting from sudden heating and consequent unequal expansion of the parts surrounding the combustion space. To warm up an engine's cylinders prior to starting, steam is sometimes led into the lower part of each cylinder jacket. The most common practice is to heat the cooling water by steam whilst it is in the drain tank and afterwards circulate it through the cylinder jackets; or, again, the cooling water leaving the working auxiliary oil-engines may be diverted to the main engines or to the drain tank.

Any of the foregoing methods works quite satisfactorily, although the last two methods are the most suitable, since it is impossible to overheat one or more cylinders, as may be done when a separate steam jet into each cylinder jacket is employed. Excessive preheating must be avoided as it will damage the rubber rings sealing the lower end of the cylinder jackets and at other points, and cause leakage of cooling water.

Rubber rings

Considerable progress has been made during recent years in the manufacture of what may be termed " heat-proof " and " oil-proof " rubber rings, i.e. rubber rings that will resist the action of oil and the degrees of heat prevailing in certain parts of diesel engines whilst retaining the elastic properties of natural rubber. The effect of dry heat on rubber is to harden it and cause it to crack and lose its elasticity, while oil is absorbed and causes the rubber to assume a jelly-like appearance.

To illustrate the difference in the oil-resisting properties of rubber made into rings, the results of tests carried out by the author in an endeavour to find the grade of rubber that would best resist the action of hot lubricating oil may be of interest, and will suffice to show that there is great variation in the properties of rubber rings stated by the manufacturers to be suitable for the various exacting requirements of diesel engines.

With a view to ascertaining the effect of oil upon the natural rubber rings ordinarily used, samples of rings from different sources were obtained and tested by immersion in heated oil. Preliminary tests showed that the effect of lubricating oil was similar to that of fuel oil, excepting that it was slower. Therefore, to accelerate the tests, fuel oil was used, the method of testing being as follows: A 2-inch length of each ring was carefully measured and weighed and afterwards immersed in fuel oil for 48 hours, including two 9-hour periods during which the temperature of the oil was maintained at 212°F (100°C). The samples were then removed from the oil and again weighed and measured.

The effect of this treatment was that each sample of rubber increased both in volume and weight due to absorption of oil, while continuous immersion resulted in the production of a jelly-like mass having practically no cohesion The following table gives the results of tests made on five samples in respect of increase in volume and weight, together with the amounts of sulphur and inorganic matter present in each case:

	No. 1	No. 2	No. 3	No. 4	No. 5
Increase in weight, per cent	124	74	150	40	99
,, ,, volume, per cent	271	143	343	56	92
Sulphur, per cent	2·1	9·4	7·2	3·7	7·1
Inorganic matter, per cent	62·1	59·9	15·0	49·3	4·5

From the above results it was apparent that although the increases in weight and volume were widely different, the effect of the oil did not depend upon the sulphur content of the rubber or upon the amount of inorganic matter, i.e. the substance used by the different makers as a " filler." Examination of these " fillers " showed that they consisted of various substances, including zinc oxide, barium sulphate, silica, etc., none of which appeared to bear any relation to the effect of the oil upon the rubber.

As it was not possible to undertake a research into the quality and properties of the various samples, as distinct from the " fillers," attention was directed to means of treating the samples so as to increase their resistance to the action of oil. Most brands of commercial rubber are vulcanised to a varying extent, which depends not only upon the amount of sulphur present, but chiefly upon the treatment to which the material is subjected. It was apparent that further vulcanising would result in increasing the resistance of the samples to the action of oil, and in the tests which followed one piece each of samples Nos. 1, 2 and 3 was given a vulcanising treatment of half-an-hour and a second piece of each was treated similarly for a period of 2 hours.

The effect of vulcanising is to render the rubber progressively harder and less flexible, according to the temperature and length of time treated. Ultimately, vulcanite is produced which is quite hard and practically inflexible. It should be stated, however, that in these particular tests the degree of vulcanisation produced by the same treatments was not the same with the various samples on account of differences in their compositions. Thus, after two hours' treatment sample No. 1 was converted into vulcanite while samples Nos. 2 and 3 were comparatively flexible.

The following table shows the increase in volume after 48 hours' oil-immersion of vulcanised samples of Nos. 1, 2, and 3, the results of the original test being repeated for purposes of comparison.

	No. 1	No. 2	No. 3
Original test, increase in volume, per cent	271	143	343
Samples vulcanised ½ hour, increase in volume, per cent	92	63	199
Samples vulcanised two hours, increase in volume, per cent	Nil	6	64

The above results clearly show that the resistance of rubber to oil and heat is greatly increased by vulcanisation, but it should be borne in mind that at the same time the rubber becomes less flexible and therefore not so suitable as a jointing material. Thus it is necessary to compromise between flexibility and resistance to heat and oil.

Rubber sealing rings for the lower end of cylinder jackets require to be vulcanised only to a small degree as the temperatures reached are very moderate owing to the cool water entering at this point, but rings employed in cylinder heads require to have greater heat-resisting properties. As, however, it is advisable to have a similar quality of rubber for both ends of the cylinders the degree of vulcanisation is governed by the flexibility necessary to allow the cylinder liners to be fitted into the jackets. If the rubber is too hard, difficulty in this direction will be experienced.

Rubber sealing rings are always of round cross-section, but the spaces or grooves into which they are fitted are never so, except in special cases. The grooves are either square, rectangular or oval in cross-section, or may be any other shape except that of the rubber ring. The reason for this is that, contrary to general belief, the sealing property of these rings depends not upon their being compressed, as is necessary with other forms of jointing, but simply upon the amount they are deformed from their moulded shape. A rubber ring may not completely fill the space provided for it, but if when fitting the metal parts together it is distorted from its true shape sufficiently, it will effectively prevent leakage of water under pressure many times greater than the maximum pressures reached in the cooling system of an engine. A test was made with a rubber ring fitted in a groove of the shape shown at the left of Fig. 38, and between two slidable surfaces, maintained stationary, of course; the pressure of water in contact with the rubber ring was put up to 500 lb/sq.in. without leakage occurring.

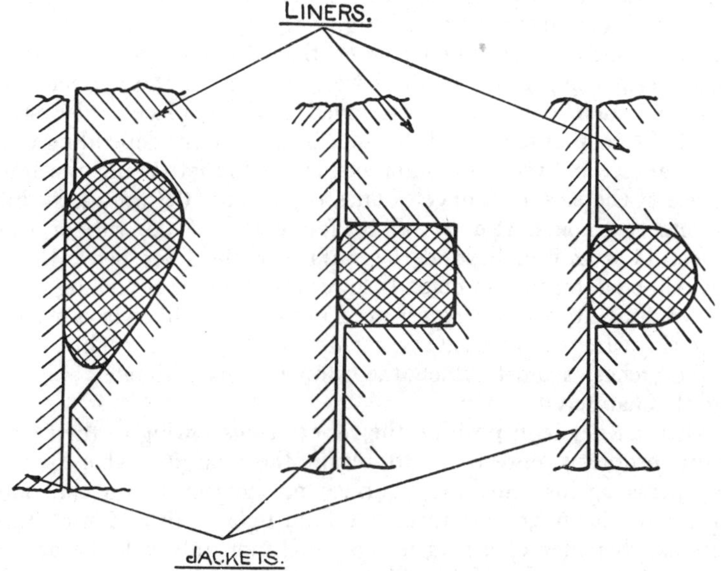

Fig. 38—Types of rubber ring grooves at lower ends of cylinders

Rubber, fully confined, is practically incompressible. The cross-sectional area of a rubber ring, therefore, must never be greater than the cross-sectional area of the groove provided for it, unless the construction of the metal parts between which it is fitted is such that there is an adjacent space into which part of the ring can "overflow," as it were, when great mechanical pressure is put upon it. Since it is the great resilient property of rubber that is depended upon to make an effective seal, and in order to ensure that the metal parts will not be prevented from being assembled in their correct relative position by the rubber ring, which no force applied by means of a hammer or spanner can compress, the cross-sectional area of the rubber ring should be 10 per cent less than the cross-sectional area of the groove. There will then be no difficulty in fitting the parts together and the ring will be deformed by an amount sufficient to prevent leakage. These proportions are based on the assumption that when the metal parts are in their correct position the whole of the rubber ring will be forced into the groove provided for it. In considering this matter of rings and grooves an appreciation of the interesting fact that rubber in compression, when confined, is obeying the laws of hydraulics, is of help.

The different forms of grooves generally cut in the lower part of cylinder liners are shown in Fig. 38. As cylinder jackets are machined out to a size slightly larger than the liner to allow for the greater radial expansion of the latter, the size of the rubber rings must be such that, when stretched and in place, they stand proud of the outer surface of the liner by an amount depending upon the clearance between the outer surface of the latter and the inner surface of the jacket. This clearance is generally 0·2 mm in 30-inch diameter cylinders, and it will be found that if the rubber rings project 1½ to 2 mm beyond the surface of the liner before fitting they will be deformed sufficiently to prevent leakage of cooling water, and no difficulty will be experienced in fitting the liner into position if the rings are well greased and the upper edge of the machined part of the jacket, against which the rubber rings ultimately bear, is slightly chamfered.

When a liner is in position the rubber rings, owing to their great elastic property, endeavour to regain their original shape; thus they press against the inner surface of the jacket and the outer surface of the liner and form the fluid-tight joint. If the cross-sectional diameter of a ring is too small, not only will the area of contact between the ring and the jacket, and consequently the pressure between these parts, be insufficient, but the wedge-shaped space formed immediately above the ring will help the water to pass them. Moreover, owing to "breathing," i.e. the slight upward movement of cylinder heads at the moment of maximum cylinder pressure, slight vertical and lateral movement of the lower end of the cylinder liners of some engines takes place, and the initial pressure with which the rings bear against the cylinder jacket is alternately increased and decreased. If, therefore, the leakage occurs only after an engine begins operating, it is a sure sign that the rubber rings are too small. If the rubber rings have been damaged owing to careless fitting of the liner or to the rings being too large, leakage generally occurs immediately the water enters the jackets.

Rubber rings deteriorate if exposed to the atmosphere for long periods. To preserve them they should be completely buried in French chalk and kept in a cool place.

Joining rubber rings

Make quite sure that an adequate quantity of rubber sealing rings of the various sizes required are always on board. Moulded rings made to the correct free diameter and of the exact cross-section when in the position for which they are intended and slightly stretched are, of course, the most suitable. On occasions, however, it may be necessary to cut a piece out of a ring to reduce its free diameter or to permit a greater amount of stretch in order to reduce its cross-section, after which the ends are re-joined by an adhesive substance usually referred to as rubber solution.

To re-join the ends successfully the cut must be made in a U-shaped piece of wood usually referred to as a mitre block. The width of the groove or channel should be exactly equal to the full cross-sectional diameter of the ring. Also the angle of cut should be 30° measured from the surface of the ring to ensure a reasonably good joining area. A sharp safety razor blade is the most suitable cutting tool and, if the blade is dipped in water, a clean cut is ensured. Oil should never be used for this purpose. The ends should then be slightly roughened by rubbing them on glasspaper, after which they require to be wiped with a clean cloth. Even an oily film such as might be produced by rubbing the ends with the tip of a finger will prevent proper adhesion.

To join the ends first cover each with a thin film of rubber solution and when the film becomes tacky press the ends together until the solution has set, making sure that they mate properly. Only ends which have been cut in exactly the same way should be joined. The setting process takes time, depending upon the properties of the solution used, but if this is unduly long the re-joined portion of the ring may be nipped lightly in a vice while pressing the ends together. When nipped in the vice the scarphed joint should be located vertically.

Rubber rings supplied to ships are made from either natural or synthetic rubber. The latter is generally used in machinery as it can be given superior oil- and heat-resisting properties. To re-join synthetic rubber rings a synthetic solution should for preference be used, as a solution made from natural rubber, besides being less effective as a sticking agent, would deteriorate in the presence of oil or under conditions of temperature. There are a number of suitable solutions available but the writer has found that Bostik No. 1430 is the best for rings intended for cylinder liners and other parts of diesel engines.

CHAPTER 8

Fuel-injection pump construction

As the diesel engine depends for its operation upon the temperature of the combustible air being sufficiently high to ignite the fuel injected into it, and since the heat necessary to start the combustion process is obtained by compressing the combustion air to a high pressure, the air is in a very dense state when the fuel charge is injected These very closely packed molecules of air offer considerable resistance to the passage through them of the finely atomised fuel sprays, so that if the particles of fuel are to penetrate far enough into the cylinder to ensure thorough mixing of the air and fuel, the injection pressure must be very much greater than the pressure of the air into which the fuel is injected. In view of this and the requirement that exactly the same amount of fuel must be injected regularly a hundred or more times a minute for periods of as long as one month, the importance of reliable fuel-injection pumps will be appreciated. In addition to delivering the exact amount of fuel every cycle at a pressure of anything between 1,000 and 8,000 lb/sq.in., the construction of these pumps must be such that the amount of fuel delivered can be varied instantly and within very fine limits.

Although the fuel pumps of all marine diesel engines are of the reciprocating plunger type, they present a variety of forms, the form depending in the main upon the system of fuel injection employed. Some pumps are provided with suction and delivery valves to control the flow of the fuel, while in others the plunger takes the place of the valves by covering and uncovering openings in the side of the cylinder in which the plunger reciprocates. Sometimes, in the former type of pump, the opening and closing of the suction valve is mechanical, while in others the action of the valve is automatic.

The fuel pumps of diesel engines will operate equally well in a horizontal, vertical, or any other position so long as they are designed for the intended position, but in marine practice they are generally placed vertically. The advantage of this position is that the pumps can be more easily freed from air prior to starting, and there is less possibility of trouble due to the pumps becoming air-locked whilst the engine is working, in the event of a little air reaching the pump with the fuel when changing over from one supply tank to another.

Fuel pumps may be attached to any part of the engine so long as they are below the level of the cylinder fuel valve supplied, in order to ensure a continuous upward flow to the fuel discharged and so obviate pockets in which air will accumulate and be trapped. Owing to the very high pressures pumped against, some engine-builders place the pumps as near their respective fuel valves as conveniently possible, so as to reduce to a minimum the length of connecting pipe, which expands slightly during the discharge period and causes an interval of time to elapse between the beginning of discharge by the pump and commencement of opening of the fuel valve. More will be said about this later.

The pumps of the more or less obsolete air-injection engine are generally operated by eccentrics, while those of airless injection engines are operated by cams. The eccentric drive is to be preferred because it gives smoother motion with consequent less wear and tear, but the beginning of the reciprocating motion transmitted by an eccentric is much too slow for airless injection engines, in which the operation of the fuel valve depends upon the sudden building up of pressure by the pump at the very beginning of its discharge stroke. Because of this, not only must each cylinder of an airless injection engine have its own pump, but each pump must be operated by a separate cam with a fixed relative position to the crank. Each cylinder of an air-injection engine must have its own fuel pump—unless distributors, referred to later, are used—but all pumps may if desired be driven by one eccentric. The more usual practice with air-injection engines, however, is to employ two eccentrics, each operating half the total number of pumps.

Airless injection fuel pumps

The function of the fuel pump as applied to airless injection engines is first of all to build up a pressure in the fuel valve sufficient to open it at the right moment, and then inject into the cylinder the exact amount of fuel required to develop the necessary power.

The pumps take a variety of forms, but, as has been explained, all are of the plunger type and with few exceptions discharge to the cylinder during the first part of the in-stroke, the amount of fuel discharged into the cylinder being varied by suddenly by-passing the fuel when sufficient has been injected to meet load requirements. The most common form of fuel pump found on airless injection engines is shown diagrammatically in Fig. 39, from which it will be observed that the action of the suction valve as well as that of the delivery valve is automatic, so that the pump must discharge its full capacity past the delivery valve every discharge stroke. In

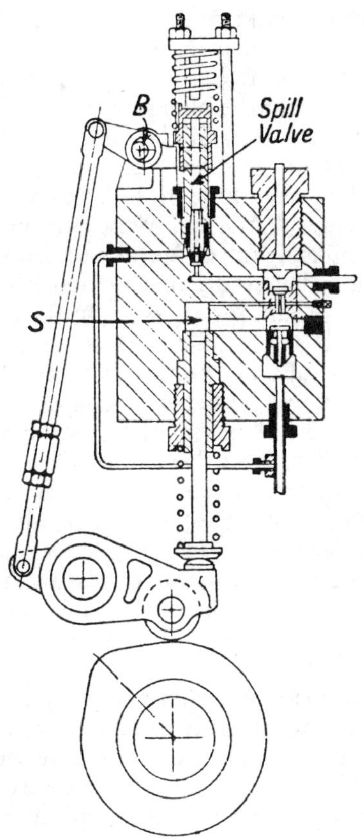

Fig. 39—A simple form of airless injection engine fuel pump

order to ensure that a certain proportion only of the quantity discharged is injected into the cylinder a mechanically operated valve, commonly called a " spill " valve, is provided, which allows the surplus fuel to return to the pump section.

The fuel valves adopted with the airless injection system are fully described in Chapter 10, but in order to make the action of the pump in question clear it would be as well to mention here that the fuel valve consists of a spring-loaded spindle valve (needle), the portion of the spindle above the fuel inlet being larger in diameter than the portion below the fuel inlet, with the result that when the pump builds up a pressure in the fuel valve great enough to overcome the pressure of the spring holding the spindle on its seat, the valve opens and fuel is injected into the cylinder.

The action of this fuel-injection system is as follows. At the end of the discharge stroke of the plunger the space *S*, Fig. 39, is full of fuel under slight pressure, and the compressed spring around the plunger causes the latter to move outward on its suction stroke and fuel to flow into the pump through the suction valve when permitted by the revolving cam. At the end of the suction stroke the increased space *S* is still completely full of fuel at a pressure of about 5 lb/sq.in. Consequently, immediately the plunger motion is reversed and the discharge stroke is begun, the pressure in the space *S* rises quickly and fuel is forced past the discharge valve, thereby increasing the pressure in the fuel valve and connecting pipe.

For reasons which will be stated in Chapter 10 the spring loading of the fuel valve is fairly heavy, with the result that a great pressure must be built up before the valve is forced open and fuel allowed to escape into the cylinder. These high discharge pressures result in the fuel being compressed slightly, the amount depending upon the volume of fuel under pressure. It is for this reason that the general practice is to locate the fuel pump as near to the fuel valve as conveniently possible in this system of fuel injection, since by so doing the length of connecting pipe, and thus its capacity is kept low.

Injection of fuel into the cylinder, therefore, begins very soon after the commencement of the discharge stroke of the plunger, and is continued until the quantity of fuel necessary to develop the power required has been injected. When the necessary quantity of fuel has been injected a spill valve situated on the discharge side of the pump is opened mechanically, the effect of which is to put the discharge side of the pump into communication with the suction side. This sudden release of pressure causes the fuel valve to re-seat smartly and the flow of fuel into the cylinder to be cut off. The spill valve remains open during the remainder of the discharge stroke and an equal portion of the suction stroke, so that after the spill valve opens, the fuel discharged passes back into the pump suction.

To vary the quantity of fuel injected into the cylinder with this form of fuel pump it will be clear that it is only necessary to advance or retard the opening of the spill valve, and this can be easily arranged for by partial rotation of the eccentric fulcrum pin *B*, Fig. 39.

The Bosch fuel pump

Although this particular type of pump is chiefly employed on high-speed engines, it is being successfully used on some propelling engines In view of this and its great popularity because of its simplicity and reliability, this chapter would not be complete without a description of it.

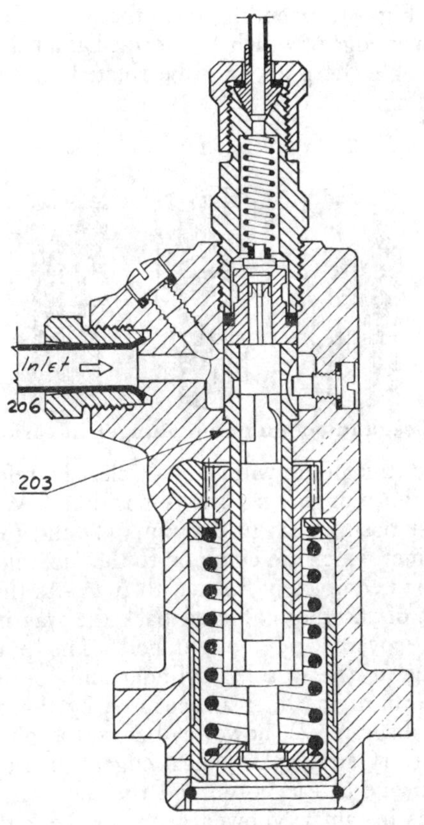

Fig. 40—The Bosch fuel-injection pump

The Bosch pump is of the cam-operated spring return plunger type, as shown in Fig. 40. The plunger has a constant stroke, and one element supplies one cylinder only. Each pump element is provided with only one valve, namely, a delivery valve, the suction being controlled by the movement of the plunger. Fuel flows by gravity, or under slight pressure, to the pump inlet (206) and into the pump through suitably arranged holes in the liner (203); thus the pump is completely filled each cycle and the plunger displaces its full capacity during each delivery stroke, as in the pump already described. To enable the quantity of fuel discharged to the working cylinder to be varied according to the power output required, the plunger is provided with a vertical channel, as shown more clearly in (3) and (4), Fig. 41, extending from the top edge *A* to an annular groove, the upper edge of which *B* is formed as a helix, and means are provided to enable the plunger to be rotated on its axis while the engine is working.

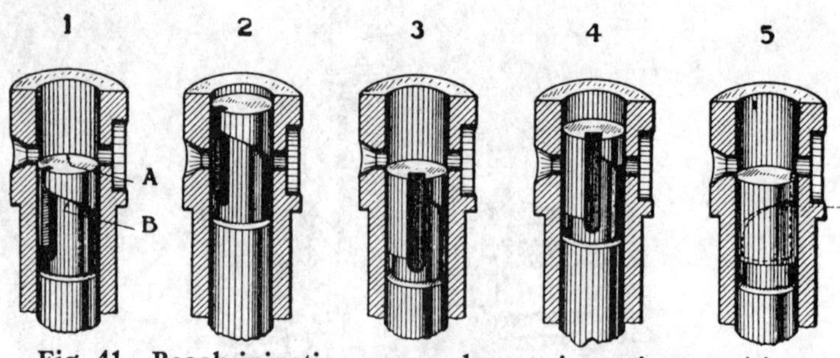

Fig. 41—Bosch injection pump plunger in various positions

The action of this pump will be made clear by referring to Fig. 41, which shows the plunger in various positions. When the plunger is at its lowest position, as in diagrams (1) and (3), the two ports in the pump liner which are common to the fuel inlet are uncovered, and the pump is completely filled with fuel. As the plunger moves upwards, part of the fuel is forced back the way it has come until the ports are covered by the plunger. The pump then begins discharging fuel to the working cylinder and continues to do so as long as the ports in the liner are covered by the plunger. As will be seen from diagram (2), however, before the plunger reaches the end of its delivery stroke the helical edge *B* of the annular groove has uncovered one of the ports, and the fuel remaining above the plunger at this instant is allowed to escape back through this port to the pump inlet. Injection of fuel into the working cylinder begins, therefore, when the plunger completely covers the ports and ends when the upper helical edge of the groove cut in the plunger uncovers the right-hand port.

The position of the plunger when the edge *B* uncovers the port can be varied by rotating the plunger through an angle by means of the toothed control rod shown in Fig. 40, which meshes with the sleeve connected to the collar of the plunger. By moving the control rod endwise in the direction of the arrow engraved on the pump body towards the " Stop " position the plunger will be rotated to the position shown in diagram (5), Fig. 41, when the space above the plunger will be in communication with the right-hand port during the whole of the delivery stroke, and no fuel will be discharged through the delivery valve. By moving the control rod in the opposite direction the release of fuel takes place later, as shown in diagrams (3) and (4), and more fuel is discharged to the working cylinders, the maximum output being reached when the plunger is as shown in diagrams (1) and (2).

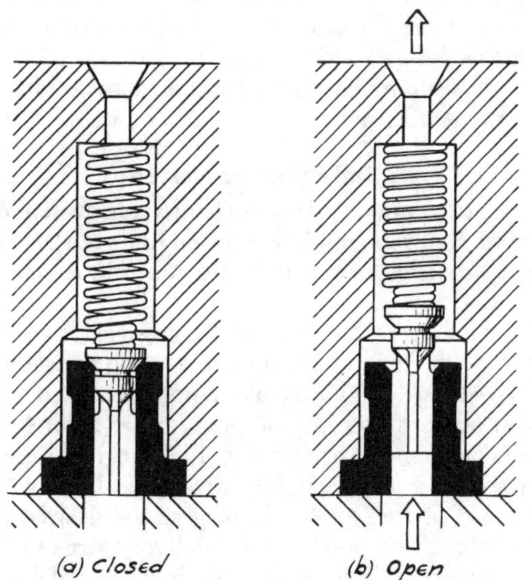

Fig. 42—Bosch injection pump discharge valve

When the helical edge *B* of the plunger uncovers the port in the liner near the end of the delivery stroke, the pressure on the fuel above the plunger is at once reduced to the pressure at the inlet, and the discharge valve re-seats smartly under the action of the spring upon it and the difference in the pressures prevailing at that moment in the pump and delivery pipe. In addition to acting as a non-return valve, this valve is designed to prevent the formation of drops on the end of the fuel-injection valve nozzle after the injection period. The valve is shown in the closed and open positions in Fig. 42 at (a) and (b).

It will be observed that the discharge valve is an ordinary mitre-faced lid guided in the usual way, and that a small piston, which is made a snug fit in the passage, is formed between the lid and the guide. When the inlet ports are covered and the pump begins discharging, the delivery valve must be lifted high enough for the small piston to clear the seat before the fuel will flow as indicated by the arrow heads in (b), Fig. 42. At the end of the injection period the delivery valve re-seats; in doing so the small piston enters the passage and cuts off communication between the pump and the fuel valve. The further downward movement of the valve increases the volume of the space occupied by the fuel between the pump and the fuel valve, and the pressure on the fuel is consequently reduced. The effect of this sudden reduction in pressure in the system is that the fuel valve re-seats more smartly and a more sudden termination of the fuel spray is obtained.

Burmeister and Wain fuel-injection system

The general arrangement of the fuel-injection system employed on Burmeister and Wain airless injection engines is shown in Fig. 43, while an enlarged view of the pump and control mechanism is shown in Figs. 44 and 45.

The plunger is operated on its discharge stroke by a cam through a rocking lever which is connected to the plunger operating rods shown in Fig. 44, the suction stroke being produced by the spring. As in most pumps of this type the plunger has a constant stroke for all engine speeds, and injection of fuel begins immediately the plunger commences its discharge stroke, and is continued until the exact amount of fuel necessary to give the desired engine speed has been injected. The point on the delivery stroke of the plunger at which cut-off or spilling takes place is governed by a regulating plunger of special design which has a constant stroke for all engine speeds, and which reciprocates in a fixed liner in unison with the main plunger.

Referring to Fig. 45, it will be seen that as the fuel is forced out of the chamber by the plunger it is in communication with the discharge on the right and the spill connection hole on the left. This spill connection hole is on both sides of the regulating chamber,

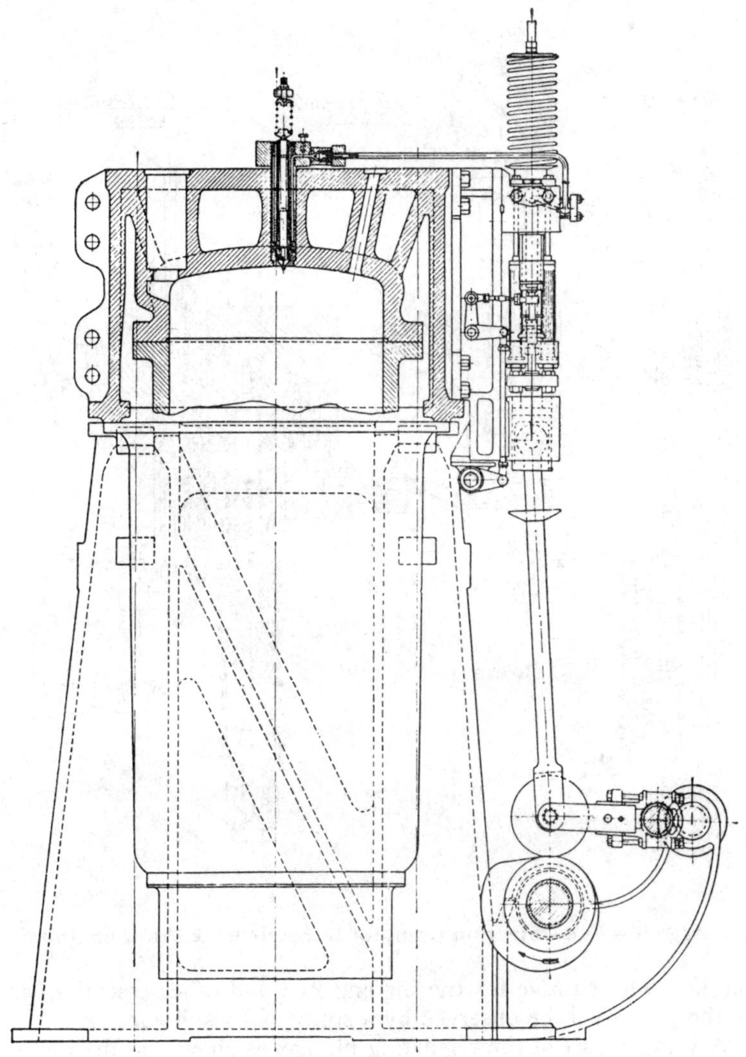

Fig. 43—Fuel-injection equipment of Burmeister & Wain engine

as the scroll on the regulating plunger is double, but there is only one set of three holes for spillage, communication with these being by way of the small diameter of the regulating plunger below the

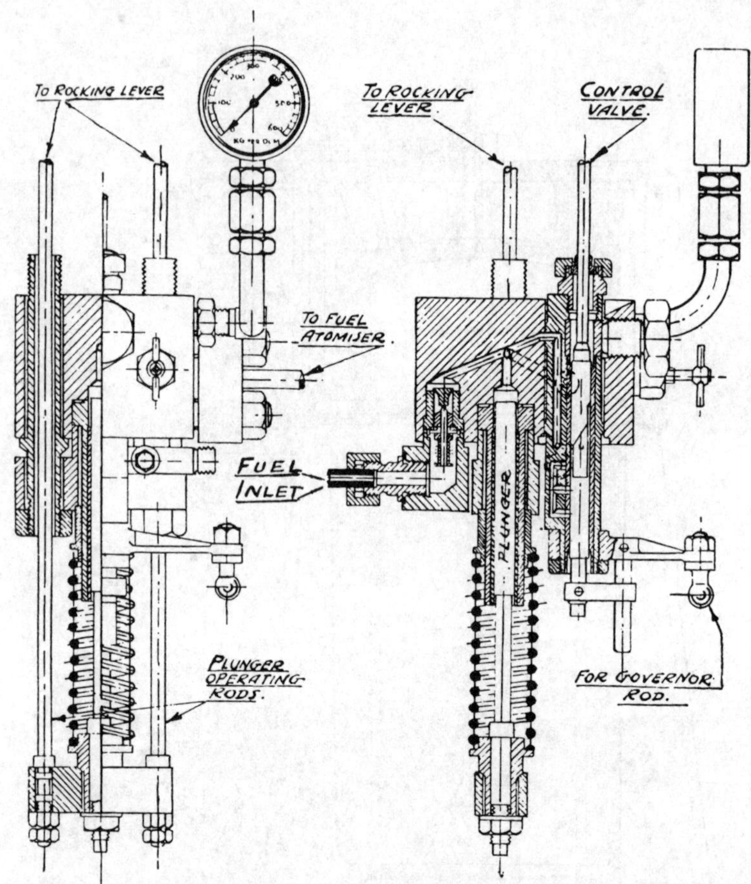

Fig. 44—Fuel-injection pump of Burmeister & Wain engine

scrolls. The passage for the ingoing fuel and other essential parts of the pump will be observed by a study of Figs. 44 and 45.

A view of part of the regulating plunger is shown on the right of Fig. 46, while a developed view is shown on the left of this illustration. The shaded portion of the developed view represents the part of the

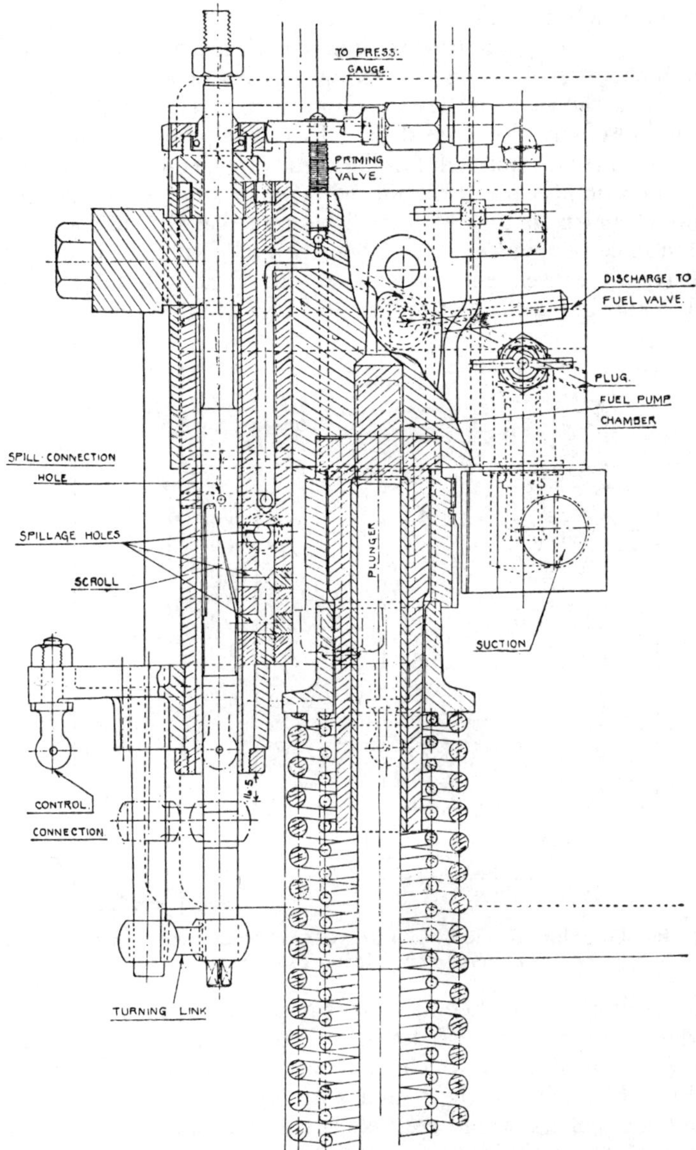

Fig. 45—Control mechanism of Burmeister & Wain fuel-injection pump

plunger which is a fluid-tight fit against the liner in which it reciprocates, while the plain part is undercut sufficiently to permit free movement of fuel between openings in this area. The regulating plunger is shown in its lowest position, which corresponds to the beginning of the discharge stroke of the pump, and the position of the discharge and spill holes in the regulating chamber will be noted.

If the pump is set in motion with the regulating plunger in the position shown in Fig. 46, it will be seen that the discharge holes will at once be uncovered, and that the fuel displaced by the pump plunger will consequently pass to and out of the spill holes; thus no fuel would be discharged to the working cylinder. Suppose, now,

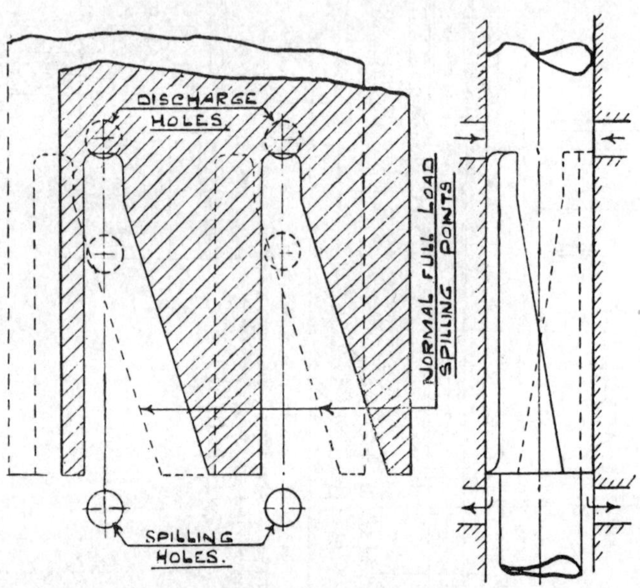

Fig. 46—Developed view of control mechanism of Burmeister & Wain fuel-injection pump

that the pump is brought back to its original position, i.e. the beginning of the discharge stroke, and that the regulating plunger is partially rotated in the direction which would cause the developed view shown in Fig. 46 to take up the dotted position. If now the pump is set in motion spillage would not take place until the plunger had completed about one-third of its stroke, when the relative position of the scrolls and discharge holes would be as shown by the dotted lines. To illustrate this the discharge holes have been moved down instead of showing the regulating plunger in the position occupied when about one-third of the stroke has been completed. A moment's study will sufice to show that the further the regulating plunger is

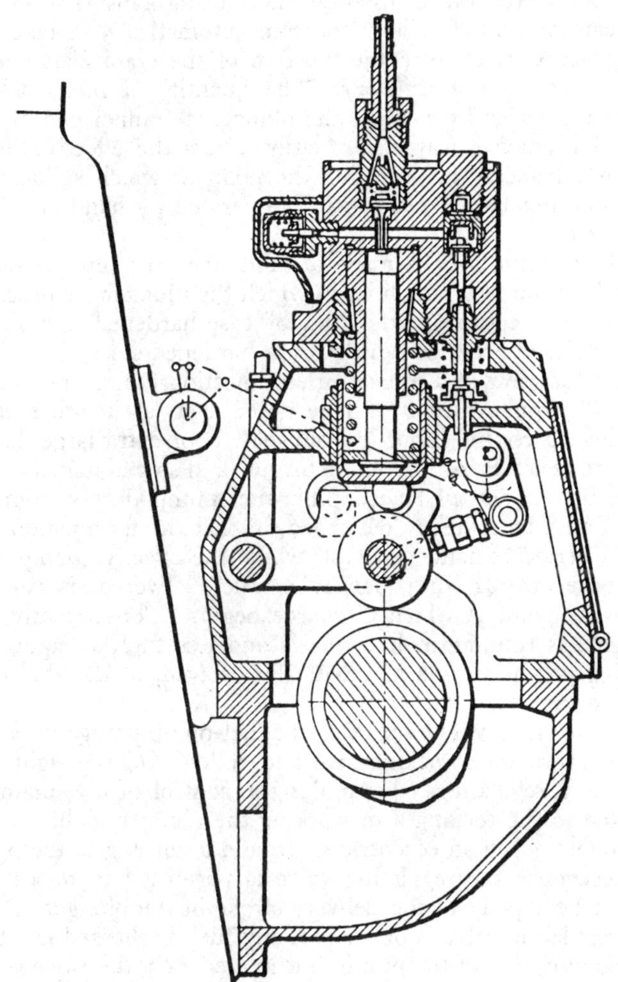

Fig. 47—Fuel-injection pump of a Sulzer engine

rotated the later in the stroke will spillage occur, and the greater will be the amount of fuel discharged to the working cylinder.

In recently constructed engines of this make the fuel-injection pumps operate on the principle just described, but the construction has been modified. The pump plunger is reciprocated by the same cam for both directions of rotation, there being a lost motion clutch on the camshaft which allows the cam automatically to take up its proper position relative to the position of the crankshaft once the engine revolves on starting air. The quantity of fuel discharged per stroke is varied by rotating the plunger, the inner end of which is shaped in such a way that rotation alters the effective plunger stroke by advancing or retarding the point at which spillage takes place. The regulating mechanism is operated by hand and by the speed governor.

The fuel pump body is made of mild steel, the plunger of case-hardened carbon steel, the liner in which the plunger reciprocates of special quality cast iron, the cam of case-hardened carbon steel, and the roller of 3 per cent nickel case-hardened steel.

A sectional view of a Sulzer airless-injection fuel pump is shown in Fig. 47, from which it will be noted that, as in other engines employing airless injection, the camshaft is of extra large diameter in order to resist distortion due to torque, and so maintain a constant valve setting under all loads. This fuel pump differs from those usually found and already described, in that the termination of the injection period remains constant, whilst the effective pump stroke, or, in other words, the quantity of fuel delivered, is varied by altering the point at which discharge begins. Consequently, when the engine is running at low speeds and less fuel is required, the beginning of injection is automatically delayed, a desirable feature in marine engines.

From Fig. 47 it will be seen that the fuel-pump plunger is actuated by a cam through a rocking arm and roller. On the right of the plunger is a regulating valve under the control of a swinging link connected to the rocking arm working the plunger. This swinging link is mounted on an eccentric shaft, and according to the position of the eccentric the regulating valve is permitted to re-seat at an earlier or later point of the delivery stroke of the plunger. As long as the regulating valve is off its seat any fuel discharged is returned to the suction side of the pump, but immediately the valve re-seats, fuel flows past the discharge valve and injection into the working cylinder begins. When the engine is operating, the position of the eccentric controlling the regulating valve can be altered by moving a hand lever at the control platform. This eccentric is under the control of the governor also.

It will be seen from the description on pages 121–2 that the Sulzer engine fuel pump is similar to the pumps found on practically all air-injection engines. The main advantage when applied to airless-injection engines is that as the point at which injection finishes remains unaltered, the fuel pump operation is symmetrical for both ahead and astern running. A single fuel cam therefore serves for both directions of rotation.

The common rail fuel-injection system

The earliest marine engines to operate on the airless-injection principle employed what is generally known as the common rail system, or, sometimes as the accumulator system. This system was invented and developed by Vickers, of Barrow-in-Furness, who are really the pioneers of airless injection of fuel. A few engines still employ the common rail system, the most notable example being Doxford until quite recently.

In the common rail system the fuel pump maintains a pressure of about 6,000 lb/sq.in. in the fuel valve and the pipe connecting it with the pump, while the fuel valve is operated by a cam and rocking lever as in the case of air-injection engines. The construction and operation of the fuel pumps are similar to those applied to air-injection engines, and to be described later, excepting that the construction is more robust to meet the higher pressures.

Any number of pumps may be employed since all pumps discharge into a comparatively large bore pipe called the fuel rail, from which the fuel flows through smaller bore pipes to the fuel valve of each cylinder, the number of pumps being only a matter of convenience and having no direct relationship to the number of cylinders supplied. Such an arrangement, however, permits a defective pump being put out of action without interfering in any way with the working of the engine, as in such an event it is only necessary to increase the output of the remaining pumps. In the case of earlier Doxford engines a separate pump for each cylinder is provided, which either delivers into its own cylinder or into a rail which is common to all cylinders.

When operating an engine provided with the common rail system at varying speeds, the fuel pressure must be maintained at the fuel valves at approximately the normal working pressure. As the quantity of fuel injected into the cylinder varies with the speed of the engine, so the quantity of fuel discharged by the fuel pumps must be regulated in conjunction with the quantity of fuel injected.

Independently driven fuel pumps are always provided to prime and produce a pressure on the system prior to starting from cold, but after the engine begins working, further use of the independent pumps is unnecessary. Although no pressure may exist in the fuel rail when a warm engine is at rest, the few strokes that the fuel pumps make when the engine revolves on starting air are sufficient to produce the pressure necessary to start working on fuel, provided, of course, that all air has been expelled from the pumps and other parts of the fuel system.

The construction of pumps incorporated in the common rail fuel injection system is similar to that of the air-injection engine fuel pumps. Control of the quantity of fuel discharged is effected by varying the timing of the mechanically operated suction valve, which is held off its seat for a portion of the discharge stroke. The non-return discharge valve is automatic, i.e. it opens when the pressure in the pump is sufficient to overcome the fluid pressure acting upon it and closes when the plunger reaches the end of its discharge stroke.

Although the common rail system of fuel injection operates satisfactorily, it is no longer justified because a complicated, mechanically operated fuel valve must be employed. The automatic or hydraulically operated fuel valve works equally well and is of much more simple construction. It is not surprising, therefore, that the common rail system has become obsolete.

The Archaouloff system of fuel injection

As the air compressors of an air-injection engine absorb from 6 to 8 per cent of the total output of the engine, fuel consumption would be reduced if the airless injection of fuel system was substituted. In addition to this the cost of maintaining the air compressors in proper order, and the cost of lubricating them, would be eliminated. The advantages of airless injection of fuel when compared with the older air-injection system are therefore so great that not only do all new engines employ airless injection, but attention is being given to converting the few remaining air-injection engines in service. To do this with some air-injection engines it is necessary only to disconnect the air-compressors and provide special means for injecting the fuel in order to obtain the above reduction in fuel consumption. In others, the shape of the cylinder combustion space is not suitable for airless injection and it is then necessary to provide pistons having a differently shaped head.

The power required to drive airless injection fuel pumps is much greater than that required to drive the pumps of air-injection engines, consequently the former type of pumps give rise to much higher stresses in the operating gear. Therefore, to convert an engine from air injection to airless injection by merely changing the pumps is, except in rare cases, impossible, as the camshaft and driving gear are not usually strong enough to transmit the necessary motion to pumps which discharge at a much greater pressure. This will be appreciated when it is remembered that air-injection engine pumps operate comparatively slowly against a steady pressure of about 1,000 lb/sq.in., whereas airless injection pumps must produce a sudden rise of pressure from a few pounds to about 8,000 lb/sq.in.

These difficulties in converting an engine from air injection to airless injection can be overcome by the employment of the Archaouloff system of fuel injection, in which the force necessary to operate the fuel pump is obtained from a small air-impulse cylinder connected to the combustion space of the engine cylinder. From the arrangement diagram shown in Fig. 48 it will be seen that the pumping unit, of which there is one for each working cylinder, is located near the fuel-injection valve in order to reduce to a minimum the volume of fuel between the pump and the fuel-injection valve. As it happens, there is no real advantage in locating the pumping unit in any other position, as the drive is not mechanical.

The pumping unit, simply, consists of a differential plunger reciprocating in a suitably bored water-cooled cylinder, the larger part of the plunger being in communication with the engine cylinder, and the smaller part serving as the fuel pump. It will be appreciated that in view of the very small diameter of the plunger required to inject the fuel, the diameter of the impulse plunger has not to be very great to give injection pressures in the neighbourhood of 6,000 lb/sq.in.

The action of the fuel-injection system is as follows. Referring to Fig. 48, which shows the plunger in its highest position or at the end of its discharge stroke, assume that the piston of the engine begins to move downward. When this occurs the pressure in the working cylinder and, consequently, the pressure in the air-impulse cylinder, begin to fall and the spring is allowed to return the pump plunger to its lowest position and so completes the pump suction stroke. The pump is then filled with the correct quantity of fuel, from an external source (to be described later), and the plunger remains at rest in this position until the working piston begins its compression stroke. As the compression pressure in the working cylinder increases, a corresponding pressure rise occurs in the air-impulse cylinder, but no appreciable movement of the plunger takes place until the pressure in the pump is sufficient to overcome the spring load on the fuel valve in the cylinder head, which is of the differential type. Thus at a certain point of the compression stroke the fuel valve is automatically opened and the fuel charge injected into the cylinder.

A brief study of Figs. 48 and 49, and the above description, will suffice to reveal the one weakness of this system of fuel injection,

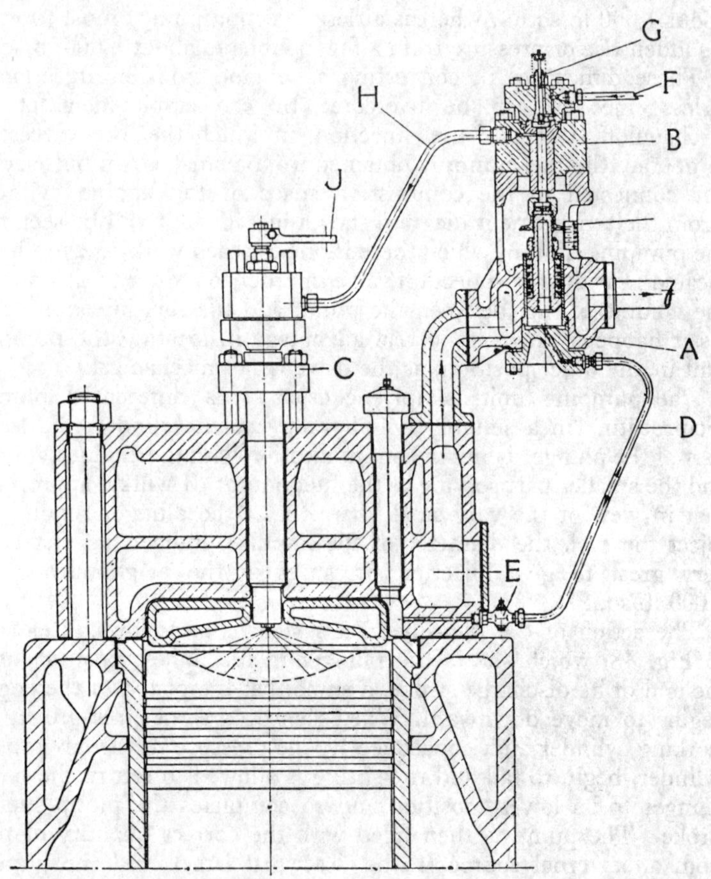

Fig. 48—The Archaouloff system of fuel injection

which is that the pump is, in itself, incapable of varying the amount of fuel injected into the cylinder, and consequently an adjunct is necessary to vary the power developed by an engine fitted with this system. To effect this the practice in the case of converted engines is to utilise the original air-injection system fuel-measuring

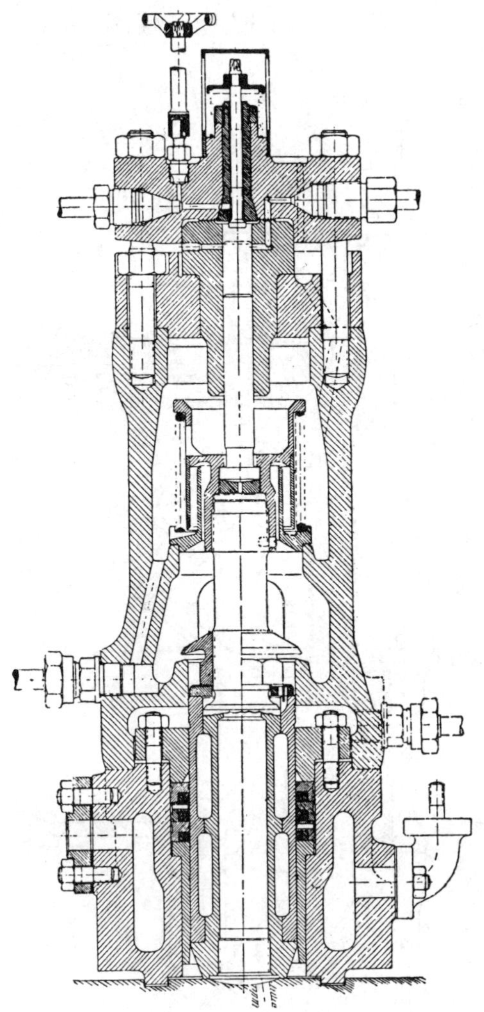

Fig. 49—The Archaouloff fuel-injection pump

pumps, which then discharge to the Archaouloff fuel pump, during the period of low cylinder pressure, the exact quantity of fuel required for any particular power output. The original fuel pumps thus become low-pressure pumps. Future development will doubtless

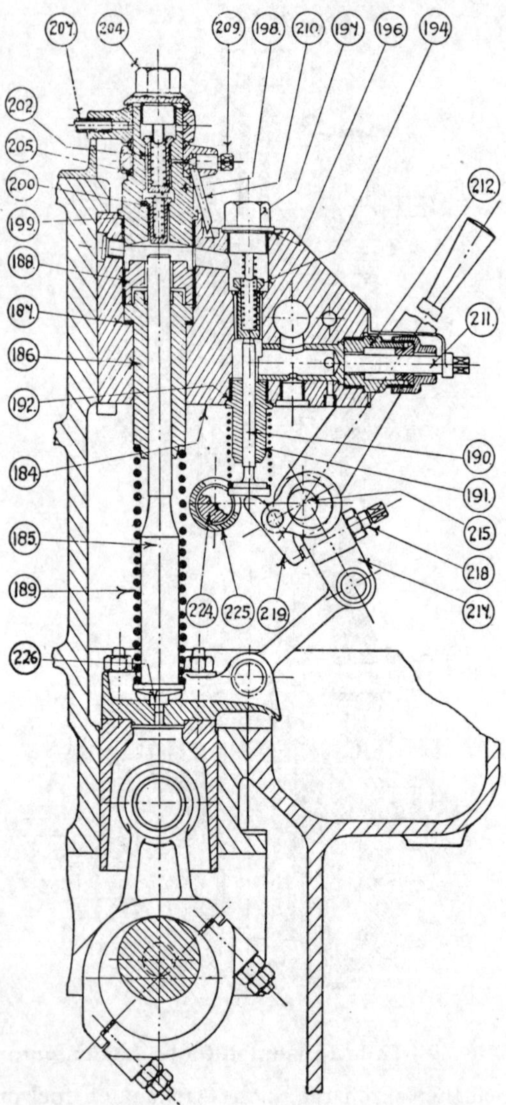

Fig. 50—An air-injection engine fuel pump

eliminate the low-pressure pumps and use in their place an injection pump which is itself capable of regulation, either by varying the stroke of the plunger or by-passing the fuel at an adjustable point on the discharge stroke.

As the Archaouloff fuel-injection pump is actuated by the cylinder compression pressure, injection of fuel occurs near the end of each compression stroke of the piston, consequently the timing of injection is altered automatically when the rotational direction of the engine is reversed. This results in a simplification of the driving gear and reversing mechanism, although so long as low-pressure fuel measuring pumps are employed to supply the fuel to the Archaouloff pumps, the mechanism of the measuring pumps will have to be so arranged that delivery takes place only during the period of low cylinder pressure.

Air-injection fuel pumps

The function of the fuel pump as applied to air-injection engines is to deliver every cycle against a pressure of about 1,000 lb/sq.in., the exact quantity of fuel to meet load requirements into the fuel valve, there to await the opening of the latter, when it is injected through the open valve into the cylinder by highly compressed air. Actually the pressure at the pump is about 30 per cent greater than the pressure in the fuel valve. The almost universal practice is for each cylinder of a multiple-cylinder engine to have an independent pump, but in a few instances one pump supplies all cylinders through a distribution valve box which, as the name implies, divides the fuel up into equal parts and distributes it to the various cylinders.

---

184. Fuel-pump body
185. Plunger
186. Plunger bush
187. Copper sealing ring
188. Gland nut for plunger bush
189. Plunger return spring
190. Suction-valve tappet spindle
191. Suction-valve tappet spindle guide
192. Copper sealing ring
194. Suction valve
196. Whitemetal sealing ring
197. Plug guide for suction valve
198. Delivery valve housing
199. Copper sealing ring
200. Delivery valve.
202. Non-return valve
204. Plug guide for non-return valve
205. Whitemetal sealing ring
207. Discharge connection
209. Priming valve
210. Fuel drain pipe
211. Plug valve for priming
212. Stuffing-box for above
215. Regulating shaft
217. Suction-valve operating lever
218. Suction-valve lift adjusting screw
219. Suction-valve rocking lever
224. Speed governor shaft
225. Starting gear connection
226. Pivot pin for plunger

Although air-injection engine fuel pumps differ in appearance they operate on precisely the same principle, so that a description of the working of the typical example illustrated in Fig. 50, with numbered list of parts, will apply to all.

The pump plunger is given a reciprocating motion by the revolving eccentric keyed to the camshaft or other part of the engine moving at the desired speed. During each in-stroke the plunger displaces a quantity of fuel equal to the displacement of the plunger, but a portion only of this amount is delivered to the fuel valve. The quantity delivered depends upon the point of the stroke at which the suction valve is permitted to re-seat. As will be observed, the re-seating of the suction is controlled by the tappet spindle (190), which reciprocates in unison with the plunger but has, of course, a much shorter travel. It will be seen from the way the plunger and tappet spindle are connected that the height of this tappet spindle, which is adjustable, determines the point on the discharge stroke at which the suction valve re-seats and discharge of fuel to the fuel valve begins.

The speed-control lever of the engine is connected to a light shaft, upon which is mounted and attached one eccentric sheave (215) for each pump. The governor is connected to and operates this shaft also. Should the speed-control lever be moved in a direction which causes the eccentric to rotate clockwise the tappet will be lowered, and if moved in the opposite direction the tappet will be raised. Thus in this simple way is the quantity of fuel discharged to the cylinders—and consequently, the speed of the engine—varied.

Air-injection engine fuel pumps are generally designed to begin discharge when the plunger has completed about one-half of its stroke, so that one-half only of the discharge stroke is effective under normal full load conditions. In this way better control over the fuel discharged and the operation of varying the quantity discharged is obtained than would be the case were discharge to begin earlier when the plunger and, consequently, the suction valve are travelling comparatively slowly.

Speed governors

As is well known, an engine racing causes very severe stresses to be set up and, although apparent damage may not result at the time, yet the foundations of a serious breakdown may have been laid. Not infrequently crankshafts and tail-end shafts have broken when the engines were working under ideal sea conditions. In such cases failure is generally attributed to defective material, but there is no doubt that in some cases the trouble began many months before by allowing the engine to race unduly in a seaway. The entire prevention of racing of slow-running reciprocating steam engines is a difficult matter, owing to the energy contained in the steam which fills the large receivers and passages after the throttle valve has been closed. Diesel engines do not race to the same extent, as the motive power can be wholly, simply, and instantly stopped.

A simple, effective and reliable governor is the Aspinall inertia governor shown in Figs. 51 and 52. This governor consists of a hinged weight *W*, Fig. 52, operating two pawls *PP*, carried on a

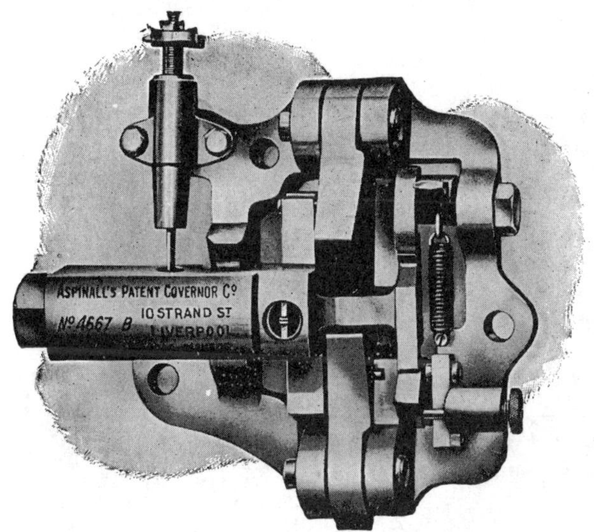

Fig. 51—The Aspinall speed governor

frame which is bolted to some reciprocating part of the engine. Generally, it is necessary to provide a special rocking lever which is driven from the camshaft operating gear. When the revolutions of the engine are increased by about 10 per cent above the normal speed, the weight *W* which is held down in its lowest position by a spring-loaded plunger *B*, is left behind as the lever begins its downward movement and reverses the position of the pawls *PP*, causing the bottom one to engage with the arm *H* controlling the motive power and to lift it throughout the whole upward stroke. This lever is connected to the valves controlling the fuel pump output in such a way that when it is moved upwards the speed of the engine is at once reduced.

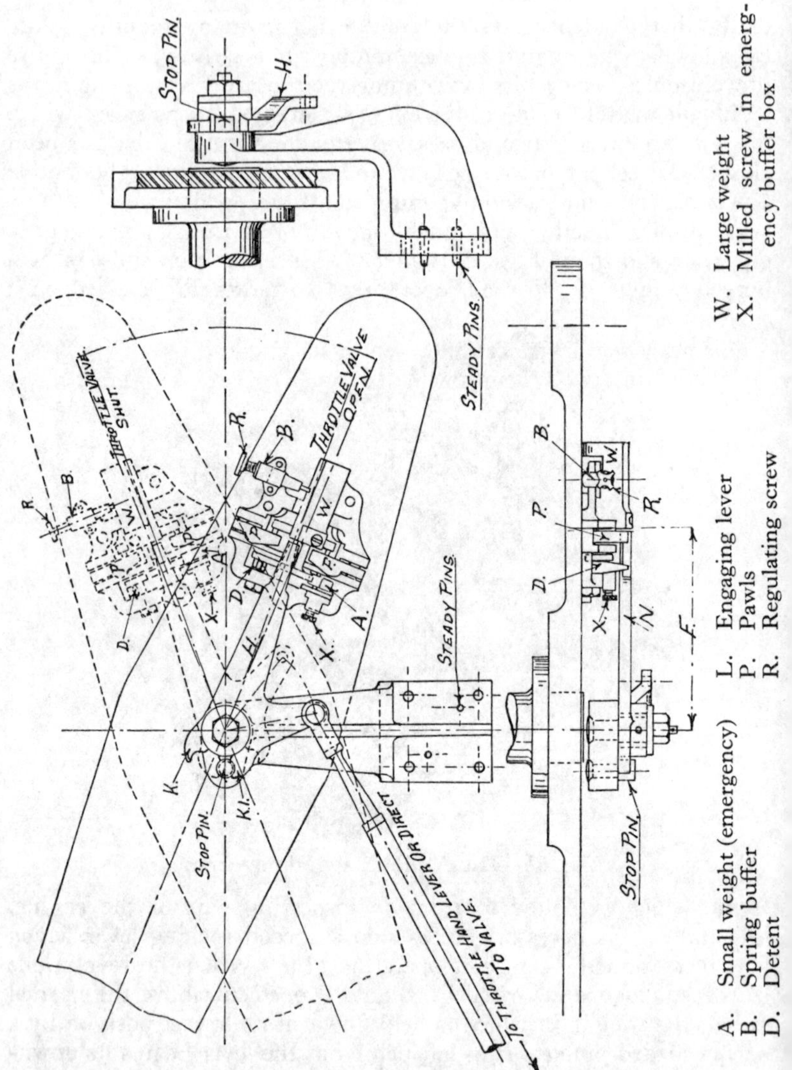

Fig. 52—The Aspinall speed governor operating mechanism

On the return stroke of the rocking lever the detent *D* is lifted. This has the effect of releasing the weight *W*, and if by this time the cause of the engine racing has been removed and the speed has moderated, the position of the pawls *PP* is again altered, the top pawl now engaging with the arm *H* and returning it to its original position.

The Aspinall governor is also provided with an emergency device which only operates when the engine attains an excessive speed, such as would occur in the event of a broken shaft or loss of propeller. In such an event the small weight *A* overcomes the friction of the thrust pin shown in the illustrations and is left behind when the rocking lever begins to move downward at a greatly increased speed. This has the effect of locking the weight *W* in its highest or " shut-off " position and the engine is brought to rest. The emergency device can be disengaged only by pressing the large weight *W* upward by hand, when the small weight *A* will fall out of gear.

To make the Aspinall speed governor more sensitive, i.e. to make it " cut-in " at a lower speed, the spring load on the weight *W* must be reduced. This is effected by screwing back or outward the regulating screw *R*. In order to make the governor less sensitive the regulating screw *R* must be screwed down or inward. To re-set the emergency device depress the small locking plunger through the hole in the milled head of screwed plug *X* and screw the plug inward or outward as required. Screwing the plug inward increases the friction between the small weight and the thrust pin and causes the device to act at a higher speed, while screwing the plug outward has the opposite effect.

This type of governor requires no attention apart from being kept clean and occasionally lubricated. A rag soaked in paraffin should be used for cleaning purposes, and not cotton waste, as bits of cotton are liable to become detached and be left in the working parts. Any good quality mineral lubricating oil is a suitable lubricant. The governor should be examined every month or so for slack nuts and loose pins, and the large weight moved by hand to make sure that it is free to function.

The speed of some marine engines is controlled by a governor of the centrifugal type, of which there are a variety of forms, all of which operate on the same principle. Fig. 53 shows how the fuel-pump output of an air-injection engine is automatically varied to maintain a constant speed of revolution. The governor consists of a sleeve *S* slidable on, but rotating with, a shaft connected to and driven by the engine. Usually the camshaft or the shaft which transmits the motion from the crankshaft to the camshaft is extended to take the governor.

Two weights *WW*, which are connected to a housing which revolves with the shaft, are pivoted in such a way that when they are acted upon by centrifugal force they tilt, and through suitable

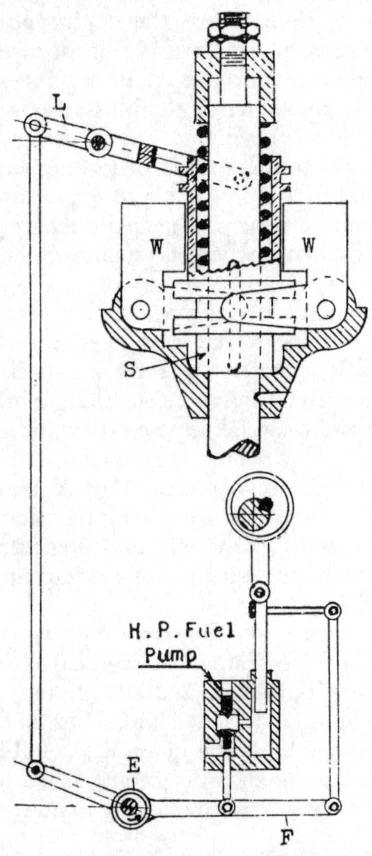

Fig. 53—Centrifugal speed governor, showing how fuel-injection pump output is controlled

levers cause the sleeve *S* to move upwards along the shaft. This outward movement of the weights is resisted by a spring which tends to hold the sleeve in its lowest position, as shown in the diagram, or by two smaller springs located horizontally and connected to the weights in such a way that they offer resistance to the tilting movement of the weights.

Thus the amount the weights tilt depends upon the strength of the spring or springs. From the sliding sleeve *S* connection is made to the fuel-pump suction valves by means of suitable levers and rods—shown in simplified form in Fig. 53. In airless injection engines the connection is made to the spill valve. Regulation of the amount of fuel injected into the working cylinders of the engine is generally effected by the partial rotation of a small eccentric shaft on which are pivoted the levers which operate the fuel-pump suction valves or spill valves as the case may be.

As the position of the weights *WW*, Fig. 53, when the engine is working is controlled by the spring, it will be clear that to re-adjust the governor, to control the engine between certain ranges of speed, the compression of the spring must be increased for higher speeds and decreased when lower speeds are required.

Centrifugal governors are usually wholly enclosed, and since many of the parts are subject to wear and tear they require to be opened up periodically and the parts examined. Cleanliness and efficient lubrication are essential to ensure sensitivity and minimum wear. With low-speed marine engines it is not usually necessary to provide damping devices to prevent hunting. If unnecessary movement takes place it is generally due to tightness or excessive slackness in the parts transmitting the motion of the sliding sleeve of the governor to the fuel-injection pump control mechanism.

After new engines have been working some time it is generally necessary to give the governor spring less compression, owing to the increased mechanical efficiency of the engine and the freer action of the governor. When readjusting the spring load the new position of the adjusting screws should be clearly marked, and all other marks except the makers' original setting marks obliterated.

CHAPTER 9

Fuel-injection pump operation and maintenance

Priming

In nine cases in every ten the cause of an engine failing to begin working readily on fuel when the control is put into the " on fuel " position is inefficient priming of the fuel-injection pumps and fuel valves. The importance of thorough priming cannot be too strongly emphasised, as unlike a steam engine a diesel engine cannot always be " turned-over ' prior to leaving a wharf to make sure that the working fluid is ready to enter the cylinders and do its work immediately. Repeated attempts to start an engine working on fuel will soon use up the starting air, without which a ship is helpless and may suffer or cause damage.

If an engine operates on high-viscosity fuels, as most now do, the fuel must be heated before priming is attempted. The usual injection temperature for such fuels is around 175°F (79·5°C) and in most cases this temperature will be correct for priming. Higher temperatures may cause " gassing " and make priming difficult. With fuels of less than 1,000 secs viscosity, Redwood No. 1, at 100°F (37·8°C) a lower temperature, say 150°F (66°C), may be advisable. When determining the correct priming temperature of any particular grade of fuel it must be remembered that freedom from " gassing " at the normal injection pressure does not necessarily mean that " gassing " will not result at atmospheric pressure, i.e. the pressure at which priming takes place.

The fuel-injection pumps of some engines can be primed very easily and will remain primed with the engine at rest for hours, and sometimes days. In others it is difficult to expel the air, and if the pumps are not in operation for even half-an-hour or less it is necessary to prime again to make sure that the engine will begin working on fuel when required to do so. When the pumps of an engine at rest fail to hold the fuel it is generally due to the valves not being fluid-tight, and the remedy is obvious.

The trouble may, however, be due to other causes. For instance, if the fuel supply tank is located too low and slight leakage occurs from any part of the pump, the leakage does not require to be very great for the fuel to drain from the pump and air sufficient to prevent the pump from functioning properly to take its place. Sometimes the cause is insufficient spring load on the delivery valves, as a result of weak springs or repeated grinding of the valves. If, because of external leakages at the pumps or, from a safety point of view, communication between the supply tank and fuel pumps is closed when a ship is in port, the fuel system must always be thoroughly primed before attempting to start an engine, as no fuel system can be expected to hold the fuel for long when the static head is removed from the suction.

In most cases it is necessary only to open the vent at the fuel valve and give the priming pump a few strokes. To make quite sure of the engine starting first time after the pumps have been opened up for overhaul, attention must first be given to the expulsion of every particle of air from the fuel pumps. The best way to accomplish this depends upon the design of the pump, i.e. the location of the valves in relation to the plunger, and whether the plunger moves downward or upward on its discharge stroke. If the plunger moves downward then it ought to be at the end of its discharge stroke during the priming operation, otherwise it will not be possible to expel the air immediately under the plunger.

Some fuel pumps are provided with vent valves for the release of air, but if the pump is known to contain air the only sure way to expel it is to take out the discharge valve and flood through slowly by gravity or by means of the priming pump until air bubbles can no longer be seen. In some cases it is not necessary to remove the delivery valves, the complete expulsion of air being effected simply by screwing back the plug over the valves and operating the priming pump until fuel alone flows.

The air vents on the fuel valves should then be opened fully, and after all the joints on the fuel pump have been made fluid-tight the fuel should be forced up to the fuel valves, and pumping continued until all air has been expelled from the top of the pipe connecting the fuel pump and fuel valve. The air vents should be shut only after the fuel begins to issue in its natural colour, as discoloration generally indicates the presence of air which, in the interval between priming and starting the engine, will separate from the fuel. The level of the column of fuel standing in the pipe connecting the fuel pump and fuel valve will consequently be lowered appreciably, with the result that the engine must make several revolutions on starting air before the fuel has been forced to the point where it should be.

The air vents on airless injection fuel valves are located in such a position that the fuel must pass through and fill the valve before reaching the air vent, so that to prime the system of such engines properly the air must be expelled from both the fuel-injection pumps and the fuel valves.

With air-injection engines care must be taken not to discharge too much fuel into the fuel valve, as this will have the effect of producing abnormally high pressures in the cylinders upon starting. This cannot, of course, happen if the air vent on the fuel valve is fully open during the operation. Sometimes these air vent valves are of the double-seated type, and when screwed to their full extent in one direction the fuel pumps are put into communication with the atmosphere, while when in the same position but in the opposite direction the fuel must pass into the fuel valve. Care must therefore be taken to see that such valves are not midway between these two positions when operating the priming pump, otherwise fuel may unknowingly be pumped into the fuel valve.

Fuel-pump operation

The plungers must of necessity be a free sliding fit without measurable clearance in their liners in order to prevent leakage of fuel during the high-pressure period. A spring alone is relied upon to return the plunger to the position it must occupy ready for the next discharge stroke. As this must be accomplished in a fraction of a second, even sluggish return of the plunger due to insufficient freedom must be avoided. Before starting an engine, therefore, it is wise to test all pump plungers for freedom by means of a crowbar.

Once an engine is started and the outputs have been adjusted in accordance with indicator diagrams or the exhaust gas temperatures, fuel pumps require no attention apart from lubricating the driving gear and keeping the fuel filters clean so that the flow of fuel to the pumps is not impeded. The fuel is generally sufficient to lubricate the plunger, but fuel is not the best lubricant, so that if it is possible to put a few drops of lubricating oil on the plungers regularly it is wise to do so. Nipples are sometimes provided through which grease can be injected by means of a grease gun. Such means of lubricating the fine-fitting pump plungers is advisable and sometimes necessary, particularly when the liners are made of steel instead of the more usual cast iron. When the liners are made of steel, a little good-quality grease should be injected prior to the engine being started after being idle for a day or more.

Occasionally it is necessary to stop discharge of fuel to one cylinder in order to make some adjustment to the fuel valve or remake a joint in the connecting pipe. In air-injection engines this is arranged for by providing ready means to hold open the fuel-pump suction valve during the whole of the discharge stroke, which allows fuel to flow freely in and out of the pump with the reciprocation of the plunger. When the pump is kept flooded in this way the pump may be kept in motion indefinitely without any ill-effect. In airless injection engines, however, the suction valves are generally of the automatic type and it is not possible to stop delivery of fuel whilst at the same time keeping the pump flooded in order to lubricate the close-fitting parts.

So long as such a pump is in motion it must be flooded with fuel, otherwise the plunger will seize or the liner will at least be badly worn. Since for this reason it is unwise to shut the fuel off at the suction, the pump should either be put out of action or the discharged fuel by-passed. In the majority of engines it is possible to put the pump out of action by preventing the spring from returning the plunger on its suction stroke. This operation must be carried out carefully and the roller raised sufficient only to clear the revolving cam and bring the plunger to rest.

When a plunger working in a close-fitting liner is being insufficiently lubricated it produces a grunting noise, and unless the surfaces can be lubricated it is advisable to put the pump out of action at once and rub down the plunger in the lathe with fine emery paper and lubricating oil in order to let a little more fuel find its way between the sliding surfaces. When a thumping noise is heard, increased pressure pumped against is indicated. This may be due to a choked spray nozzle, or choked strainer when these are fitted at the point where the fuel enters the fuel valve. In some engines the spilling process causes a similar noise, but it is easy to determine the cause, since if the noise is due to abnormally high pumping pressures it is produced at the moment discharge of fuel begins, whereas the noise of the spilling process takes place when discharge of fuel terminates.

The sudden release of fuel during the spilling process and the almost instantaneous drop in pressure from about 6,000 lb/sq.in. to a little above atmospheric pressure is bound to subject certain parts to shock and, consequently, produce noise unless special provision is made to prevent it. In some cases the only provision made is to release the fuel into a comparatively large-diameter pipe, while in others a shock absorber is provided in the form of a cylinder in which is fitted a spring-loaded piston open to the chamber near to the point where the fuel is released. As the fuel is released it acts on the piston and moves it outward against the pressure of the spring, thereby automatically increasing the volume of the space into which the fuel is released.

The power output and, consequently, the temperature of the exhausted gases may be affected in many ways, as pointed out in other parts of this book, but when the drop is sudden it may be due to a piece of grit becoming jammed under one of the pump valves. When the reduction in temperature is gradual, the cause may be accumulation of air in the pump or deterioration of valve faces. Whenever a fault of this nature occurs, the air vents should always be opened to see if accumulation of air is the cause before going to the trouble to take out the valves for examination, while it is advisable to be satisfied that the valves are in proper order before readjusting the timing of the suction valve or spill valve, as the case may be, with the object of increasing the pump output. The danger of increasing the pump output without first ascertaining the cause of the reduction in exhaust temperature is that if air in the pump or a piece of grit under one of the valves is the cause and output is increased, the pump may right itself and the cylinder concerned then be seriously overloaded before being noticed.

Fuel-pump driving cams

The cams and rollers operating the fuel pumps of airless injection engines are made of case-hardened steel, usually nickel-chrome, hardened and tempered to a degree that will increase their wear-

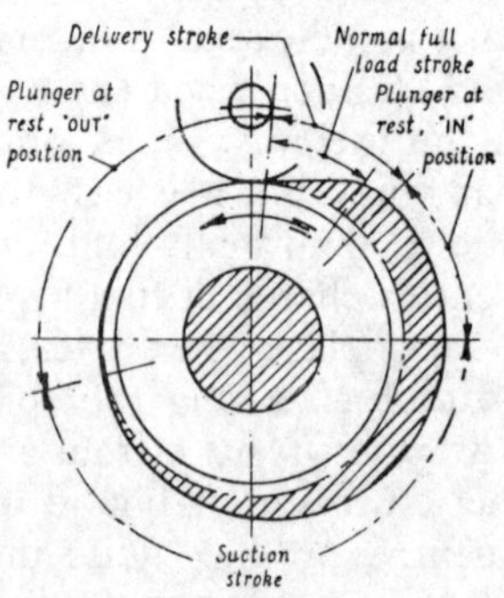

Fig. 54—Airless injection fuel-pump cam

resisting qualities. A typical airless-injection engine fuel-pump cam is shown in Fig. 54, from which it will be seen that the discharge angle is short and steep, while the movement of the plunger during the suction stroke is very slow in comparison.

The discharge stroke of the pump plunger must, of course, be performed in the shortest time possible consistent with smooth running, because to obtain proper combustion of the injected fuel charge the pump must suddenly build up the pressure necessary to open the fuel valve almost instantaneously. It has been found by experience that the best results are obtained when the leading side of the cam peak is tangential to the plain part of the cam, as shown in Fig. 54. A more abrupt opening would build up the pressure more quickly, but the roller would not strictly follow the cam profile and would strike the cam peak with great force and cause wear of a vital part. The roller rides on the cam all the way round, since it is not necessary to have clearance when it is over the plain part of the cam; there is therefore no shock and very little noise when the roller makes contact with the cam peak, and if copiously lubricated and made of suitable material practically no wear takes place.

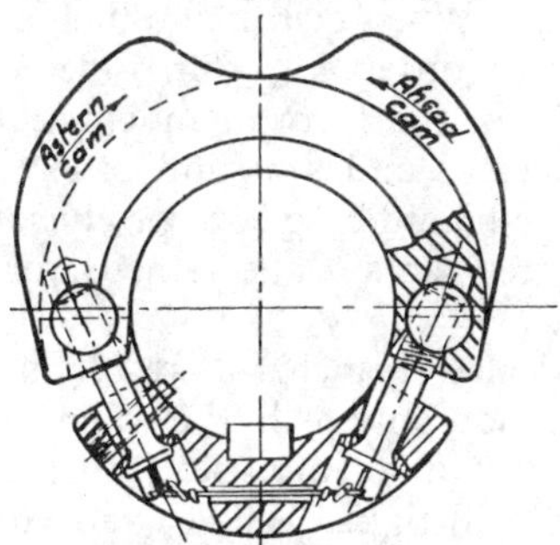

Fig. 55—Airless injection fuel-pump cam, showing method of adjusting timing of discharge

Fig. 55 illustrates a simple method of adjusting the position of the fuel-pump cam relative to the crankshaft and so altering the point at which the fuel pump begins discharging. A disadvantage is that owing to the side-by-side ahead and astern cam peaks being in one piece, the astern cam is retarded when the ahead cam is advanced, and vice versa.

Maintenance of fuel-injection pumps

Fuel pumps of modern design and materials, although working

under exacting conditions of very high and widely varying pressures, are a most reliable piece of mechanism, provided the valves are kept perfectly fluid-tight, the working parts efficiently lubricated, all air excluded from the fuel spaces, and the fuel kept free from pieces of grit or other matter likely to interfere with the proper working of the valves and plungers.

Proper results cannot possibly be obtained unless the valves are absolutely fluid-tight at full working pressure when in the closed position. Springs are generally used to assist the prompt closing of these valves. It so happens that the greater the pressure tending to separate a valve from its seat and cause leakage, the greater is the pressure holding the valve on its seat, so that the valves of pumps working at 10,000 lb pressure should require no more attention than when the pressure is 1,000 lb only. The only difference is that should leakage occur the trouble will increase in proportion to the working pressure, since the greater the pressure the higher the velocity of the escaping fuel and the greater the scoring action.

Fuel-pump valves may begin to leak owing to fine grit or corrosive acids in the fuel, hammering, excessive working clearances, distortion, or unsuitable material. When grit in the fuel is the cause, grooving across the faces will be observed. Corrosive acids in the fuel will cause irregular marks in the form of indentations of minute depth on the faces of the valve and seat and other parts of the valves. The effect of the valve hammering is to produce highly polished and maybe slightly distorted faces. The remedy for this last fault is to reduce the valve lift.

Excessive diametrical clearance will result in constant trouble in this direction, since not only will the valve not re-seat squarely each time it closes, but it is impossible to grind in such a valve properly and make it fluid-tight. When a valve distorts it is generally due to its being too thin as a result of repeated grinding. Sometimes the valves are made of unsuitable material, generally too soft, and begin to spread around the outside of the faces. This spreading is apt to create the impression that the valve has been hammering.

In order to obtain the desired good results with valves made of suitable materials, not only must they be perfectly fluid-tight and be a free working fit without measurable clearance, but the guide in which the valve works must be absolutely square with the faces of the valve and seat, so that in the event of the valve rotating its free movement will not be restricted. Should a valve be found free in one position but tend to jam when rotated to another position, slight easing is permissible, provided the amount removed does not make the valve slack, sideways, in any position. In such an event it is advisable to true-up the defective valve in the lathe or fit a new valve.

When the pumps are provided with removable valve seats, the seat must be firmly secured in its working position before the valve is finally ground in, as there is always a danger of the shape of the seat being altered slightly when this is secured in position. If the faces are in a very bad condition and require a great deal of grinding, the work is more easily accomplished by removing the seat from the pump, but the final grinding should always be done with the seat firmly secured in its working position. After grinding with fine carborundum the surfaces should be cleaned and finished off with polishing paste to ensure that the faces are quite free from scratches. Finally, the valve pocket should be washed through with paraffin or hot fuel oil to remove all trace of grinding paste. The object of heating the fuel is to thin it down and give it greater cleansing properties.

Before fuel-pump valves of any type are refitted after overhaul, the pump suction should be opened and the pump flooded in order to expel all air. Only after all signs of air cease should the valves be dropped through the fuel into position.

As the faces of valves wear and are repeatedly ground-in they tend to become shrouded, as shown in Fig. 56, and the metal around the seats must be cut away. Such a defect in the suction valves of air-injection engines will cause erratic running, while if a delivery valve is shrouded the distance the valve is lifted during the discharge period will be increased, causing hammering and increasing the rate of wear. Whether valves are automatically or mechanically operated it is important that the fuel should begin to flow immediately the valve leaves its seat. Restriction of flow in this way is bound to have an adverse effect on timing or the quantity discharged.

The strength of the springs loading these small valves is very carefully determined, so that the original initial compression should be maintained. When thimble valves, as shown in the upper part of Fig. 56, become greatly worn, it will be necessary to pack up the spring to increase the initial compression. In the case of mushroom valves the lid would probably become so thin that the valve would be discarded before the initial compression of the spring would be materially affected. Insufficient initial compression causes sluggish closing at the end of the discharge period. On the other hand, should the spring load be too great or the lift of discharge valves too small the delivery pressure will be abnormally high, and the valve faces may be scored by the greater velocity of the fuel; also the pump may become overheated.

A suitable material for fuel-pump springs, whether for valves or plungers, is silicon manganese steel. After being bent into shape the springs are specially heat-treated to give them the necessary elastic properties.

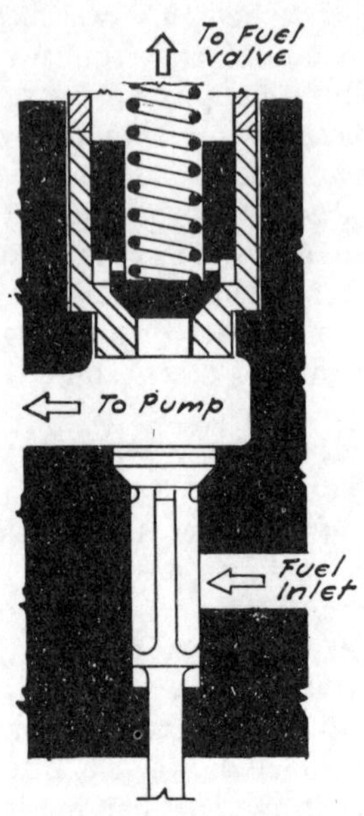

Fig. 56—Fuel-pump valve showing effect of repeated grinding

Grinding the suction valves of air-injection engines, or spill valves of airless injection engines, alters the point at which the valve re-seats on the delivery stroke, as such valves are mechanically operated. It is therefore necessary to readjust the operating gear after each overhaul. The links and pins of the mechanism should be a good free fit without slackness, otherwise the pump discharge, as regards quantities will be erratic. In most air-injection engines the tappet spindle which holds the suction valve off its seat for the desired period is a free working fit through a bored plug, leakage being prevented by the total absence of slackness. In some of the older engines, however, the spindle passes through a small stuffing-box in order to prevent leakage of fuel. In such cases care must be taken to see that the spring is strong enough to overcome gland friction, otherwise if there is any slackness in the operating gear the timing of the valve will be erratic and the quantity of fuel discharged will vary. These stuffing-boxes require to be lightly packed with soft cotton packing well soaked in lubricating oil.

The operation of examining fuel-pump valves and grinding them in if necessary should be carried out at regular intervals and not left until the exhaust gas temperatures are affected or the engine fails to start working on fuel. When it is necessary to readjust the timing of the spill valve of an airless injection engine, or the suction valve of an air-injection engine, while the engine is operating, the cause should be investigated at the first opportunity, as it is quite possible for an engine to appear to work normally with the fuel-pump valves in such a bad condition that when the engine is stopped it is impossible to start it again until the valves have been ground in and made fluid-tight.

In air-injection engines a frequent source of air-locking of the fuel pumps is leaky discharge valves. Because of this two such valves, in tandem, are sometimes provided. The reason why a defective discharge valve leads to air-locking is that when starting an engine the injection air is always admitted to the fuel valve before the fuel pumps are permitted to begin discharging, and upon stopping the engine the fuel pumps are always caused to stop discharging before the injection air is shut off. The high-pressure injection air is thus free to push back the fuel past the leaky valves, and if even a little air enters the pump the engine will fail to start working when the next attempt is made.

In regard to the expulsion of air from fuel pumps, the effect of altering any parts, such as valve cages and plunger sleeves, which are inserted vertically downwards should always be carefully considered before the alteration is carried out, no matter how unimportant the part may appear to be. For instance, suppose a new discharge-valve cage similar to that shown in Fig. 56 is being fitted, and it is found that the part of the cage below the landing edge is too large in diameter for the pocket : indiscriminate filing of this apparently unimportant part of the cage will produce a space which will fill with air when the pump is empty. This air will be difficult to displace, no matter how well the pump is flooded and primed, unless the valve cage is removed and refitted after the pump has been flooded with fuel.

Plungers

Fuel-pump plungers are always made of special material, such as nickel or nickel-chrome steel, and case-hardened; what is called Aircraft S.15 steel being particularly suitable for this purpose. It is highly desirable that the plungers be free from side thrust, and as very little force is required to operate them on the suction stroke they are not usually connected to the part operating them, a spring being sufficient to return them ready for the next discharge stroke. This arrangement allows the plunger to find its own working position and eliminates all forces likely to produce side thrust. Moreover, such an arrangement allows any irregularity in the working of the plunger to be detected at once, since should the plunger begin to jam the spring will fail to operate it on its suction stroke.

Now that suitable materials are available the present practice is to provide in the pump body a liner or sleeve in which the plunger is a perfect working fit, thus obviating the necessity for a stuffing-box and gland. The liners are generally made of good quality cast iron, and if cast iron such as " Perlit " is used many years' service will be required to produce measurable wear or the slightest leakage of fuel. To obtain the necessary very fine fitting, the plungers are ground down to size and the liners lapped out.

When securing liners in position in the pump body the plunger should be inserted and kept moving during the operation. If the plunger jams before the liner is properly secured it means that the landing surfaces are not true, and require to be machined or ground in. On no account should hard spots be ground off a plunger which is perfectly round and parallel. If the plunger is slightly oversize it should be put in the lathe, and whilst revolving at high speed ground down with a fine emery paper and lubricating oil. And if slight distortion of the liner cannot be avoided when securing in position, the liner should be lapped out in place with a lead rod and carborundum paste.

As the plungers must be made such a close fit, fine grit contained in some fuels will not be able to penetrate between the plunger and the liner and damage the surfaces if the inner end of the plunger is left perfectly square. Since, however, a square edge is easily damaged when inserting a plunger, it is advisable to chamfer the end at about a 45° angle. Such an angle will not assist the fine grit in the fuel to find its way between the plunger and the liner, and at the same time will prevent the end of the parallel part of the plunger from being burred when carelessly handled.

Before fuel-pump plungers and other fine-fitting parts are finally put into position they should be given a thin coating of good-quality grease. Inferior quality greases should be avoided as they become dry and tacky. In the absence of suitable grease a good mineral lubricating oil should be used.

Fuel-pump adjustments

Adjusting the mechanism which controls the quantity of fuel delivered is a most important operation and therefore requires great care. Not only must the adjustment be such that the desired speed of rotation is obtained with the control lever or wheel, as the case may be, in normal working position, and such that the engine stops when the gear is put over to the " Stop " position, but the amount of fuel delivered by each pump must be the same to within reasonable limits, so that undue strains are not put upon any part of the engine before the opportunity to balance the power output properly presents itself. It frequently happens that to work a ship out of port a number of full-power movements are necessary, and if the fuel-pump adjustments are not reasonably correct as regards output some of the cylinders will be overloaded. To overload cylinders when all parts are at normal working temperatures may have ill-effects, but to do so when all parts are cold is dangerous, since the excessive temperature-differences produced in the castings surrounding the burning gases may overstress the parts to the point of fracture.

Engine builders have their own particular method of readily adjusting the fuel pumps when the engine is at rest so that the correct amount of fuel will be discharged when the engine begins working. In the main, this consists of putting the engine crankshaft—really the fuel-pump plunger—and the speed-control lever in a certain position and applying a gauge, the dimension of which determines the point on the pump stroke at which the spill valve opens or the suction valve re-seats, respectively, depending upon whether the engine is of the airless or air-injection type.

To adjust the output of the fuel pumps of airless injection engines is a much simpler matter, as all that is necessary is to turn the engine crankshaft until the plunger is beginning its discharge stroke, and to vary the length of the rod or other part of the gear operating the spill valve until the spill valve is slightly open, with the speed-control lever in the " Stop " position. Under these conditions the spill valve will be open for the whole of the delivery stroke, so that no fuel will be discharged by the fuel pump, and consequently the engine will stop when the speed-control lever is brought to the " Stop " position.

To adjust the suction valves of an air-injection engine when no gauges are available, proceed in the following manner. Put the speed-control lever or wheel, as the case may be, in the " Stop " position and turn the crankshaft until the plunger of the pump under consideration is at the end of its discharge stroke. With the pump plunger in this position the length of the suction-valve tappet spindle should be adjusted until the suction valve is just clear of its seat. Small movements of the speed-control lever whilst touching the top of the suction valve with a finger, or a rod held in the hand if the pocket is too deep for the finger, will readily indicate if the tappet spindle is making contact with and lifting the suction valve.

As the suction valve is connected to the plunger in such a way that as the plunger travels on its discharge stroke the suction valve moves nearer to its seat (see Fig. 50), it means that if the plunger reaches the end of its delivery stroke before the suction valve is in its closed position no fuel will be discharged by the pump. If, therefore, the length of the suction-valve tappet spindle is adjusted as described in the preceding paragraph, not only will the engine stop when the speed-control lever is brought to the " Stop " position, but sufficient fuel to ensure full power being developed will be discharged when the speed-control lever is moved to the normal working position.

Having adjusted the suction-valve tappet spindle to the required length and locked same to prevent accidental alteration, the speed-control lever should be put in the normal working position, which is usually a few notches from the extreme position. This will have the effect of first allowing the suction valve to re-seat and then increasing the distance between the underside of the suction valve and the end of the tappet spindle. With the speed-control lever in the working position, the crankshaft should be rotated in the " Ahead " direction until the end of the suction-valve tappet spindle is within, say, $\frac{3}{1000}$ inch of the underside of the suction valve, when the position of the crank in relation to the top dead centre should be noted.

To adjust the remainder of the fuel pumps and ensure that each cylinder is developing approximately the same power when the engine is started up, it only remains to put each successive crank in the position found, and adjust the clearance between the underside of the corresponding suction valve and the end of the tappet spindle to $\frac{3}{1000}$ inch.

To adjust accurately the timing of fuel-pump suction valves, all wear in the links and pins operating the tappet spindle must be taken up by exerting pressure on the tappet spindle in such a direction as to cause it to move away from the suction valve.

If for some reason it is not possible to adjust the timing of spill or suction valves in the manner just described, it is quite a simple matter to find by calculation the point on the discharge stroke of the plunger at which the suction valve should re-seat or the spill valve open, since the effective stroke of the plunger is equal to—

$$\frac{\text{Volume of fuel discharged per stroke}}{\text{Area of fuel-pump plunger}}$$

As an example, suppose it is necessary to find the effective fuel-pump stroke of a two-stroke engine of which the following particulars are known:—

Horse-power per cylinder	500
Fuel pump strokes per minute	100
Fuel consumption per h.p.hr. (assumed)	0·3 lb
Diameter of pump plunger	1 in.
Volumetric efficiency of pump (assumed)	80 per cent
Specific gravity of fuel	0·9
Density of water	0·036 lb/cu.in.
π	3·1416

The quantity of fuel injected into the cylinder at each stroke of the pump is—

$$\frac{500 \times 0{\cdot}3}{60 \times 100} = 0{\cdot}025 \text{ lb,}$$

or $$\frac{0{\cdot}025}{0{\cdot}036 \times 0{\cdot}9} = 0{\cdot}77 \text{ cubic inch.}$$

As, however, the pump is only 80 per cent efficient the actual displacement of the plunger during the period of discharge is:

$$\frac{0{\cdot}77 \times 100}{80} = 0{\cdot}96 \text{ cubic inch.}$$

The effective stroke of the pump is therefore—

$$\frac{0{\cdot}96}{0{\cdot}25 \times 3{\cdot}1416} = 1{\cdot}22 \text{ inch.}$$

This is to say that, in the case of air-injection engines, the suction valve should re-seat when the plunger is 1·22 inches from the end of the discharge stroke, and that in airless injection engines the spill valve should open after the plunger has completed 1·22 inches of its delivery stroke.

Regarding the number of pump strokes per minute used in such calculations, it must be remembered that in air-injection four-stroke engines the fuel pumps do not necessarily work at half the speed of the crankshaft. In some engines of this type the fuel pumps work at the same speed as the crankshaft, while cases may be found where the fuel pumps work at twice the speed of the crankshaft. It all depends upon the general arrangement of the engine and the desire to drive the fuel pumps in the most direct way. Generally, however, the pumps of four-stroke engines work at half the speed of the crankshaft, and at the same speed of the crankshaft in two-stroke engines, the whole of each fuel charge being delivered into the fuel valve at one stroke. The whole of the fuel charge must, of course, be delivered at one stroke in airless injection engines, so that with this system of fuel injection the pumps of four-stroke engines always work at half the speed of the crankshaft, and at the same speed as the crankshaft in two-stroke engines.

CHAPTER 10

Fuel valves

In the preceding chapters dealing with fuel-injection pumps mention was made of the pumps used on air-injection engines. As all diesel engines now being built, and the vast majority now in service, operate on the airless injection system this may appear a little strange. The reason is that there are still a number of engines of the air-injection type in service, and, moreover, it is not unlikely that the Archaouloff system of fuel injection will be more widely adopted in future, in which event the fuel pump used for air injection—or one operating on the same principle—will be required to measure the charge of fuel to be injected into the cylinder by the Archaouloff pump. This is not likely to occur with air-injection fuel valves, but for the benefit of those responsible for the older type of valve and in order to complete the picture of this method of injection, notes on these valves will be included in this chapter.

The function of fuel valves, sometimes referred to as the fuel spray valve, depends upon whether the engine is of the air- or airless injection type. In the former type its purpose is to admit the fuel at the correct time and at the correct rate, whereas in the airless injection engine the rate at which the fuel is injected and the moment of injection are determined by the fuel pump. In both types the valve is responsible for the atomisation of the fuel, so necessary in order that it will readily ignite and burn upon entering the cylinder. The air-injection fuel valve is always mechanically operated, while in airless injection engines it is operated hydraulically by the fuel itself, except when the common rail system is adopted, when it is mechanically operated.

The ideal location for the fuel valve is at the centre of the cylinder head, so that the fuel charge will be distributed evenly throughout the combustion space, and it is generally found in or as near to this position as the design of the cylinder head will permit. In the bottom cylinders of double-acting engines, however, such a location is not possible owing to the presence of the piston rod, and this end of the cylinder is generally provided with two fuel valves, one on each side of the piston rod. When two fuel valves are employed and located in the bottom cylinder cover diametrically opposite each other with the piston rod between, the holes in the fuel spray nozzle are arranged so that the fuel is prevented from striking the piston rod.

Typical examples of the three distinct types of fuel valves are illustrated in Figs. 57, 58 and 59. The first is employed with the

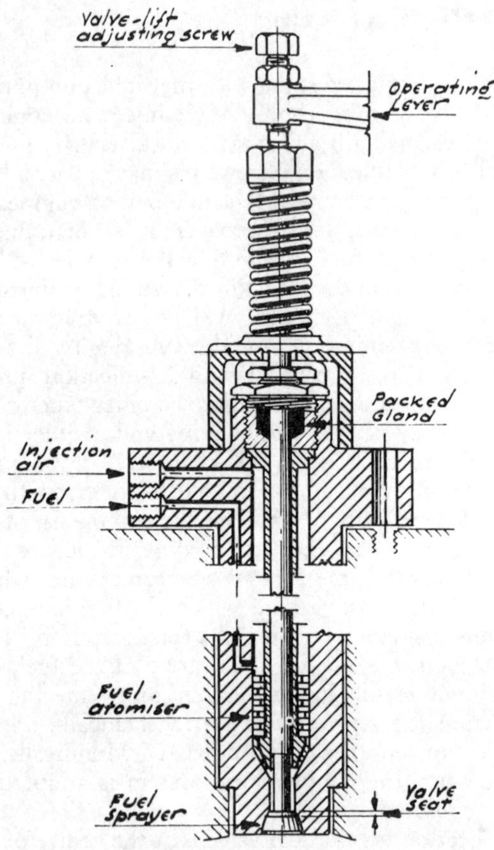

Fig. 57—Fuel valve for an air-injection engine

air-injection system, the second with the common rail airless injection system, and the third with the almost universally used system of airless injection in which the valve is opened by the hydraulic pressure produced by the fuel pump. The first two types are mechanically operated and the third is hydraulically operated.

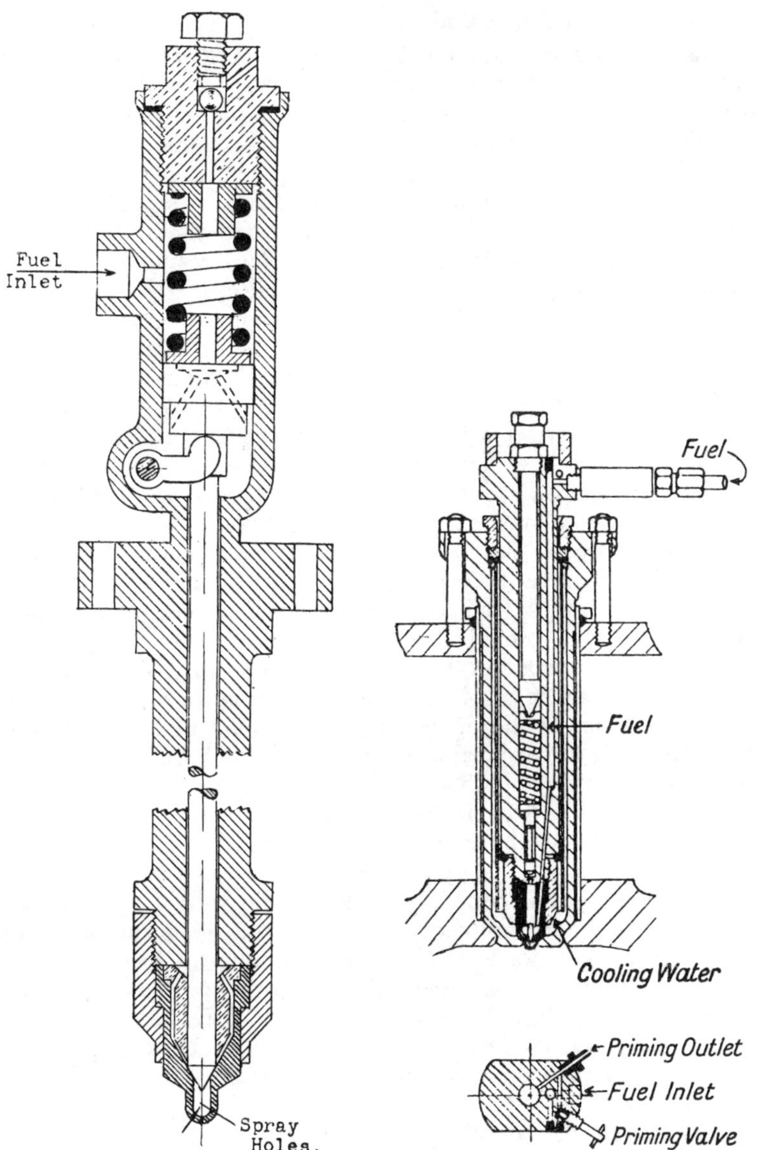

Fig. 58—Fuel valve for common-rail system of fuel injection

Fig. 59—Fuel valve for an airless injection engine

Airless injection fuel valves

Small land-type engines have operated on this system of fuel injection for a great many years, but it was not until about 1930 that it was universally adopted for large marine engines. Prior to this the air-injection engine could burn a wide range of distilled fuels and achieve a higher brake mean pressure in the cylinders, even though its mechanical efficiency was lower by some 8 per cent, due to the power required to drive the air compressor. This superiority over the airless injection system resulted from two factors, the first being the supercharging effect of the injection air which increased the available oxygen by about 5 per cent, and secondly the action of the air in promoting turbulence, and consequently better mixing, of the atomised fuel and air.

Technical improvements in the fuel pumps and fuel valves of airless injection systems have eliminated the advantages possessed by the air-injection system, and has shown the former system to be no less superior on all grades of fuel commonly used Now that it is usual to employ the heaviest grade of boiler fuel, which must be heated to obtain the desired degree of atomisation, the absence of injection air is an advantage, because in expanding down from 1,000 to 500 lb/sq.in. the resulting refrigerant effect would tend to cool the fuel as it entered the cylinder.

As will be seen from Fig. 59, the airless injection fuel valve contains a small spring-loaded needle seating close to the spray nozzle. The lower end of the needle is reduced in diameter, while the upper and larger portion fits snugly in the bored hole through the centre of the valve body, thus providing an unbalanced area. As the fuel pump delivers fuel to the lower end, the pressure acts on the underside of the enlarged portion and lifts the needle against the spring pressure.

The valve body is generally made of mild steel, the needle and spray nozzle of non-shrink steel, and the spring of silicon-manganese steel. Provision is made to circulate fresh water or fuel around the fuel-valve nozzle as it is essential to keep this particular part at a temperature which will prevent the minute particles of fuel from being carbonised as they enter the cylinder. Such a precaution is not necessary with air injection as the expanding injection air has a cooling effect.

The success of the airless injection system is mainly due to the great amount of research work carried out on spray nozzles Combustion efficiency depends largely on the degree of atomisation and the uniform distribution of the fuel in the engine cylinder. Too low

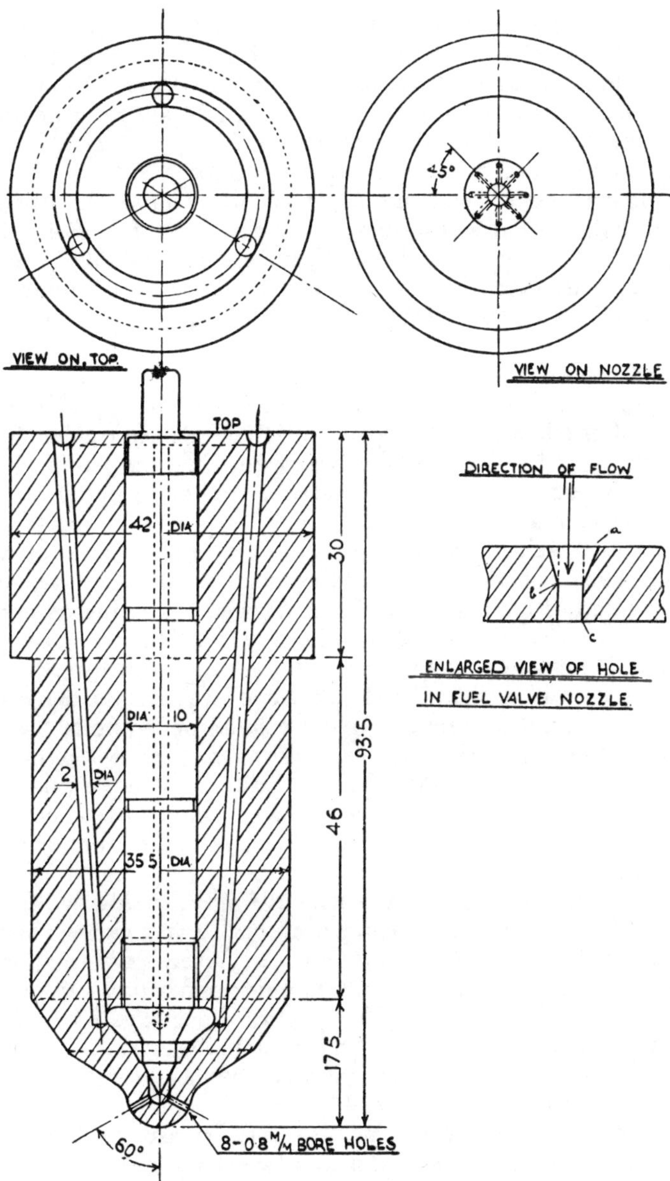

Fig. 60—Airless injection fuel-valve nozzle

a degree of atomisation leads to slow combustion and consequently carbonisation, which may be due to the fuel striking the walls surrounding the combustion space. Too high a degree of atomisation results in the fuel not penetrating far enough into the combustion space and causing undue concentration of fuel in the neighbourhood of the nozzle. The best results are obtained by a condition between these two extremes, and this depends mainly upon the diameter, length and location of the spray holes in the nozzle. For a 1,000 b.h.p. single-acting cylinder there may be eight holes 0·047 inch in diameter with a length of three times the diameter. A typical fuel valve nozzle is shown in Fig. 60.

Airless injection fuel-valve timing

As mentioned in the preceding chapter, the opening and closing points of the hydraulically operated valves are determined by the fuel pump, and generally the valves open when the pump plunger begins its in-stroke and close when the spill valve opens on some point of the in-stroke.

The point, relative to the position of the engine crank, at which a fuel valve opens depends upon the rotational speed of the engine, it being earlier for higher speeds, and whether the fuel is injected pneumatically (Fig. 57) or hydraulically (Fig. 59). In marine type air-injection engines running at about 100 r.p.m. it is usual to begin injection not earlier than 5° before the crank reaches the dead centre position, whereas in airless injection engines operating at the same rotational speed injection may begin as much as 15° before the dead centre. The reason for this difference is that combustion takes place more rapidly in the former type of engine due to the injection air producing a greater degree of turbulence and more intimate mixing of the atomised fuel and air.

In many Doxford airless (mechanical) injection engines the fuel valve opens at about 28° before dead centre and closes some 22° after, but this engine operates on a relatively low compression pressure. This results in the maximum cylinder pressure being in the region of the normal 600 lb/sq.in. Generally, however, the pressure rise upon injection of fuel is 50 lb in the case of air-injection, and 100 lb/sq.in. in airless injection engines, the compression pressure in each case being from 450 to 500 lb/sq.in. The fact that an engine is of the four-stroke or two-stroke type makes no difference to the compression pressure or the point at which injection of fuel begins.

Builders of engines always provide the information required to correctly adjust the fuel-injection system of their particular engine, and whilst the point of injection may vary slightly in different makes of engines it is important that the builders' instructions should be carried out if the best results, both as regards fuel consumption and freedom from combustion troubles, are to be obtained.

Fig. 61* shows the mechanically operated fuel valve of a Doxford opposed-piston airless injection engine. As the fuel pressure in this type of valve is constantly maintained at about 6,000 lb/sq.in. it is used to keep the valve spindle firmly on its seat during the inoperative periods.

Airless injection fuel-valve operation

These valves with their very small spray holes run a long time without requiring attention, but they should not be neglected on that account. It is wise to remove the valves once every three months and test the needles for leakage and the holes for spraying. Ships are usually provided with a test pump for this purpose. When testing, make quite sure that the fuel delivered by the test pump is free from dirt, otherwise a nozzle that was spraying properly before the test may not do so when returned to service.

The spray holes must not be larger than the designed size as a result of wear, nor smaller due to a lining of carbon, while the needle must be absolutely fluid-tight at its seat and must work freely without measurable clearance in its guide. If too free a fit, the opening action of the valve will be sluggish due to slow build-up of pressure as a result of leakage past the enlarged part of the needle, and there will be difficulty in maintaining it fluid-tight at its seat. To test for clearance around the needle, connect the valve to the test pump and fill with thin fuel to the working pressure. If it takes ten seconds or longer for the pressure to fall 1,000 lb the needle can be assumed to be in good order so far as clearance in the guide is concerned. A more rapid fall means that the needle is too free a fit. Before making such tests be sure that the valves of the test pump are perfectly fluid-tight, otherwise an inaccurate result will be obtained.

As the spray holes in fuel-valve nozzles are so small in diameter it is essential for the fuel to be free from solid impurities likely to become jammed in the holes. When spray holes choke, the cause is nearly always pieces of grit entering with the fuel. The holes may, on rare occasions, become lined with carbon when combustion is not so good as it ought to be, but the high pressures employed usually prevent them from becoming completely choked even when carbon deposits on the nozzle. Consequently, not only must the fuel

* See page 723

storage tanks be cleaned out regularly and frequently, but whenever pipes or any other fittings in the fuel system are disconnected all openings must be covered to prevent entry of dirt.

When any of the spray holes become choked the pump delivery pressure rises and the pump begins to hammer. The choking of even one hole out of a total of six will cause the injection pressure to be increased 2,000 lb/sq.in. On some engines pressure gauges are provided to indicate the injection pressure, but any appreciable increase in the pressure will be at once apparent by the sound the pump makes during the discharge period.

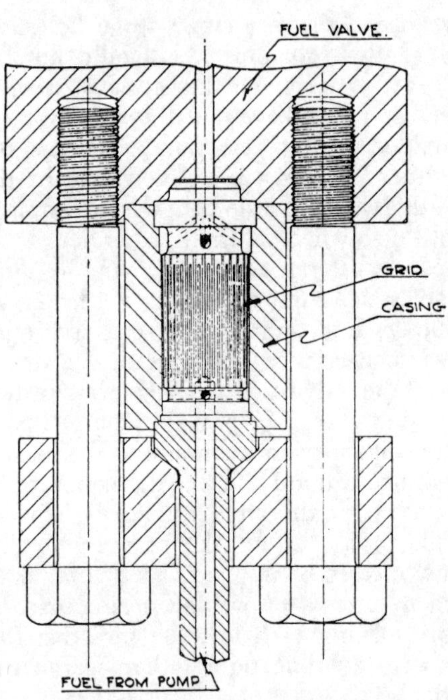

Fig. 62—Airless injection fuel-valve strainer

As it is common practice to provide strainers at the point where the fuel enters the fuel valve, partial choking of the strainer will also cause the fuel pump to hammer. When, therefore, an excessive discharge pressure is indicated in this manner, the strainer should be examined before withdrawing the fuel valve for examination of spray holes. An indicator " draw " diagram (see p. 550) will reveal the exact cause of the hammering, since if the strainer is partly choked the beginning of injection will be later and there will be a slight reduction in the combustion pressure owing to the pump having to build up a higher pressure before the fuel valve opens; whereas if a choked spray hole is the cause the fuel valve will open at the correct time, and the combustion pressure will be more or less normal.

Fuel-valve strainers are made in a great variety of forms, one of which is shown in Fig. 62, but in nearly every case separation of the grit is effected by causing the fuel to pass through small openings by which any particles large enough to become jammed in the spray holes are trapped. The strainer shown consists of a tough steel plug, or grid as it is called, in a steel casing, the outside of the grid being 0·2 mm less in diameter than the inside of the casing. Recesses are provided at the upper and lower ends of the grid, the former being in communication with the fuel valve and the latter wth the fuel pump. Grooves 1 mm wide and 1 mm deep are cut in the surface of the grid, and, as will be observed, half the number of grooves are in communication with the upper recess and the remainder with the lower recess. For the fuel to pass from the lower to the upper recess and thence to the fuel valve it must therefore pass from one set of grooves into the other set, and the only passage for it is between the outside of the grid and the casing—through a space 0·1 mm wide.

Accumulation of carbon on fuel-valve nozzles may be due either to the needle valve leaking, to imperfect combustion as a result of too low an injection pressure, to enlargement of the spray holes, or to inefficient cooling of the fuel valve.

A needle that is not perfectly fluid-tight will not cause pre-ignition, or even affect to any marked extent the combustion or maximum pressure in the cylinder, because in hydraulically operated airless injection systems the pressure in the fuel valve is for the greater part of the cycle less than the pressure in the cylinder until the moment the fuel pump begins delivering. Therefore no fuel in quantities of any consequence will enter the cylinder before its proper time. As a matter of fact, if the leakage is great the combustion pressure is actually reduced, as is proved by the indicator diagrams shown in Figs. 63 and 64.

The former diagram was taken from an engine soon after all the fuel valves had been changed, and as it was known that the timing of the fuel pump was correct and the fuel-valve nozzle clean, the engine was stopped and the fuel valve examined to ascertain the cause of the reduced combustion pressure and power output of a particular cylinder. The cause was found to be due to the internal parts having been reassembled in such a way that the needle valve was jammed and prevented from re-seating. This was put right, the valve refitted, and the indicator diagram shown in Fig. 64 obtained without the slightest alteration to any other part. Other effects on the engine of the valve leaking were a reduction of about 15 per cent in the power output, an increase of 18°F (10°C) in the exhaust temperature, and discoloration of the gases. The difference in the combustion pressure, it will be observed, is as great as 90 lb/sq.in.

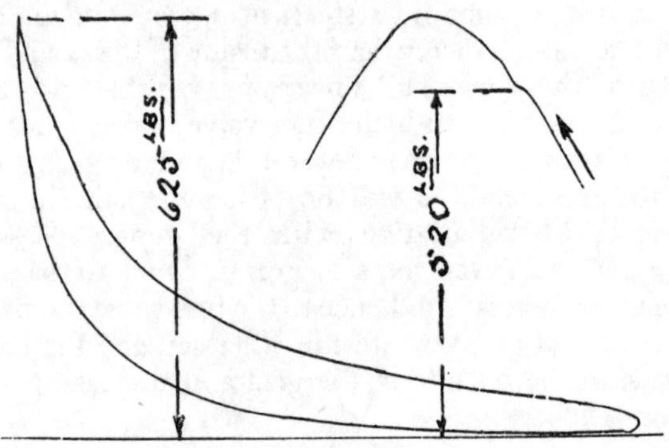

Fig. 63—Indicator diagram showing effect of needle not re-seating

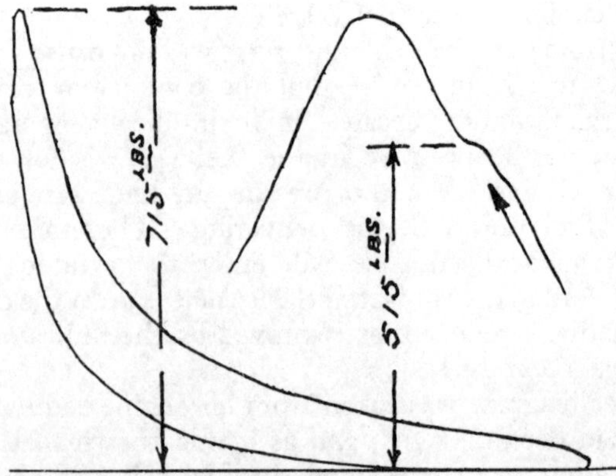

Fig. 64—Normal indicator diagram of an airless injection 4-stroke engine

The cause of reduced combustion pressure and power output when an airless injection fuel valve leaks badly would appear to be due to the valve being partly emptied of fuel during the high-pressure period of the cycle, with the result that the fuel pump must deliver a certain quantity of fuel before the valve is completely filled, and consequently injection of fuel is delayed.

In engines where the fuel-injection pumps are not provided with a discharge valve or an intermediate non-return valve somewhere between the fuel pump and the fuel valve, a needle which is leaking badly at the conical end may stop the cylinder concerned working. This is due to the pressure of air in the cylinder during the compression stroke passing from the cylinder through the spray holes in the fuel-valve nozzle into the fuel valve. If the leakage is very bad the rate at which the fuel is pushed back during the suction stroke of the pump may be greater than the discharge rate of the pump, and the cylinder will stop working.

This fault is more prevalent in high-speed engines where the pump discharges a very small quantity of fuel at each stroke, but has been known to occur in low-speed engines where the quantity discharged is relatively large. In high-speed engines with this particular kind of valveless fuel pump a non-return valve in the line between the pump and the fuel valve is essential.

If the fuel pump is provided with a suction valve, one cylinder only will be affected by a faulty needle, but if, as in the case of some engines, no suction valve is provided, the air or gas from the cylinder whose needle is defective may pass into the suction pipe, which is usually common to all fuel pumps, and " gas " all pumps, in which event the engine will stop and it will not be possible to start it again until the defective needle has been put right. The presence of a suction valve will prevent the air or gas being forced beyond this point, but if there is pressure in the pump during the suction stroke no fuel will flow through the suction valve into the pump.

Leaking fuel-valve needles can, therefore, have very serious consequences in certain makes of engines. To avoid this happening the upkeep of the fuel valves must be given special attention. The effect of a needle leaking and the symptoms have already been mentioned, and when such a fault is detected the priming valve of the cylinder concerned should be opened and the fuel pump made inoperative until the fault has been remedied. Opening the priming valve will allow any gas passing the faulty needle to escape to atmosphere and prevent it from reaching the fuel-pump suction pipe.

When carbon accumulates on the tip of a fuel-valve nozzle it rarely extends into the spray holes sufficiently to choke them, unless the cooling is ineffective and the nozzle is allowed to become excessively hot. Though the flow of fuel is not likely to be restricted by carbon depositing on the nozzle, the fuel sprays will be affected to the extent that imperfect combustion will result. This in turn may reduce the power output quite considerably and bring about all the mechanical troubles usually associated with after-burning. Fig. 65 shows the effect of so much carbon depositing on a fuel-valve nozzle that the direction of the fuel sprays was greatly interfered with. By comparing this with a normal diagram, shown in Fig. 64, taken from the same engine, it will be seen that the combustion pressure and power output are greatly reduced by this fault. The first outward indication of accumulation of carbon is an increase in the exhaust temperature, due to the fuel not mixing properly with the air and consequently not burning completely in the allotted time.

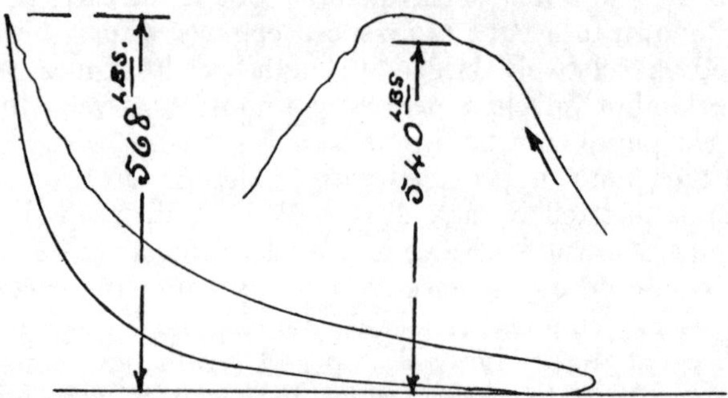

Fig. 65—Indicator diagram showing effect of carbon build-up on fuel-valve nozzle

Overhauling airless injection fuel valves

The spray holes in airless injection engine fuel valves have an important duty to perform, and it is therefore essential that the holes be quite clean and the original size and shape rigorously maintained. Not only does the degree to which the fuel is atomised depend upon the size of the spray holes, but the shape of the holes is of equal importance, since it influences the shape and direction of the fuel sprays, upon which the combustion efficiency of an engine so largely depends. The spray holes, therefore, must be cleaned only by means of the special tools, usually small twist drills $\frac{2}{1000}$ inch less than the original diameter of the holes provided by the engine-builders, and even with the proper tools the operation must be done very carefully.

The drill and nozzle should always be held in the hands. It is most unwise, to say the least, to allow the operation to be done by the employment of a machine in which either the drill or the nozzle is gripped and rotated. The drill should be gripped in a suitable holder and given a semi-rotary movement by the forefinger and thumb whilst holding the nozzle in the other hand. If the carbon is difficult to remove in this way the nozzle should be laid aside for a few days, immersed in a solvent such as paraffin.

In order to illustrate the vital effect which the shape of the spray holes has upon the fuel spray as it enters the cylinder, the abbreviated results of certain experiments carried out may be of interest and value. The object of the experiments was to ascertain the effect upon the coefficient of discharge of altering the shape of an orifice 0·5 mm in diameter through which fuel was forced at a constant pressure. The coefficient of discharge, by the way, is the ratio of the cross-sectional area of the jet immediately after it passes through the orifice, to the area of the orifice itself. As is well known, the area of the jet is always less than the area of the orifice it passes through.

When the single hole in the experimental nozzle was parallel and had sharp edges at each end, the coefficient of discharge was 0·65. The inside edge was then rounded to give 0·5 mm radius, and this had the effect of increasing the coefficient of discharge to 0·80, while a 1 mm radius raised the coefficient of discharge only slightly to 0·88. The inside part of the hole was then countersunk as shown on the right in Fig. 60, and the effect was to reduce the coefficient of discharge, but when all three edges, *a*, *b* and *c*, of this hole were slightly rounded the coefficient of discharge was raised to 0·94.

It has also been proved that the length of the holes in spray nozzles has a great effect upon the penetrability and shape of the spray, the greater the ratio of length to diameter the greater the degree of penetration. With higher length: diameter ratios, the angle of spray is less and consequently the jet maintains a more compact stream and penetrates for a greater distance into the cylinder combustion space.

The results of these experiments will suffice to show how necessary it is to take the greatest possible care of fuel-valve nozzles and not allow the holes in them to be tampered with or roughly handled when being cleaned.

The fuel-valve needle acts as a piston and it is essential that it responds instantly when the injection pressure has been built up. It must therefore be a free sliding fit, but without measurable clearance. If it should be a slack fit the opening action will be delayed slightly, the valve will not be certain to re-seat squarely, and leakage of fuel will occur at the fuel-valve overflow.

Particular care is necessary when reassembling these valves. Not only must every internal part be perfectly clean, but the parts should, if possible, be assembled in the same relative position. As the working clearances are so small, even a quarter of a turn of any one part may interfere with the free working of the needle and adversely affect the spraying action. For instance, the spring must sit perfectly squarely and evenly on the valve needle, otherwise, in spite of the long bearing surfaces provided, the needle may be tilted and sluggish closing result. Before an attempt is made to remove hard places from a needle, or any distance-pieces are fitted between the spring and needle with the object of compensating for wear-down or a weak spring, the spring should be tested by a square when standing on end on a face-plate, and the end of the spring trued up if necessary, so that when in position it bears evenly all round.

When parts of the fuel system have been dismantled they should, in addition to being thoroughly washed in clean paraffin, be blown through with dry compressed air to ensure that the various passages are quite clear. The parts should then be reassembled without attempting to dry them with rags of any description, as fibrous matter too small to be readily seen may be left on some of the parts and be the cause of operating troubles. Instead, lubricating oil should be applied with the tips of the fingers.

To ensure the proper combustion of the fuel charge the whole of it must ignite and burn whilst suspended in air. This can only result if every particle is driven into the cylinder with the requisite force. It is at the beginning and the end of the injection process that this is least likely to occur and produce conditions conducive to the formation of deposit on the fuel-valve nozzles.

As regards the beginning of injection, insufficient injection pressure is most likely to result from a worn fuel-pump cam peak or to the needle being shrouded as a result of hammering or repeated grinding. The former fault will increase the period during which the pressure required to open the fuel valve is built up, and the first of the fuel charge may not, in consequence, be driven into the cylinder with sufficient force; while in the case of the second fault the needle will require to be lifted clear of the shrouding before injection proper begins. Before this occurs a portion of the fuel charge will have escaped past the parallel part of the needle immediately above the conical end, and due to wire-drawing will enter the cylinder at a pressure well below the normal injection pressure. How this might occur is shown, exaggerated, in Fig. 66, on the right, while a photograph of a faulty fuel-valve nozzle after it had been cut to disclose the fault is reproduced in Fig. 67.

The closing action of the valve, which must also be prompt and positive, is not likely to be affected by normal wear of the fuel-pump cam peak, but a shrouded needle would have a serious effect and result in the formation of droplets on the nozzle, which would be quickly carbonised. The fault may not be serious enough to cause

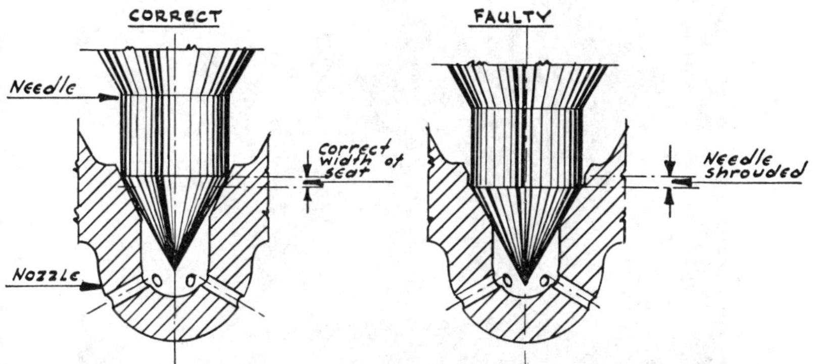

Fig. 66—Correct and faulty seating of fuel-valve needle

trouble when operating on diesel fuel, but it will become more apparent on higher-viscosity fuels, and the fuel rather than the valve may be held responsible. To function properly these valves must, as already stated, be a free sliding fit in their guides without measurable clearance, and the employment of more viscous fuel may result in the closing action being slightly less positive.

Nothing effective can be done on board ship to remedy either of these faults, so the fuel-valve nozzle and needle should be returned to the makers for attention. A worn fuel-pump cam cannot be made good, even by the makers, and the wisest course is to fit a new cam. At the same time all other fuel-pump cams should be checked with a contour template as it is not unlikely that they too will require renewing. Should these cams wear rapidly it means that either the material is unsuitable or the cams have not been copiously lubricated.

In order that the whole of the fuel charge will be injected at a pressure which will ensure every particle of it burning completely in the allotted time, the width of the needle-valve seat is also important: the narrower the point of contact between the needle valve when in the closed position and the nozzle, the more likely will prompt opening and closing result. This is important when

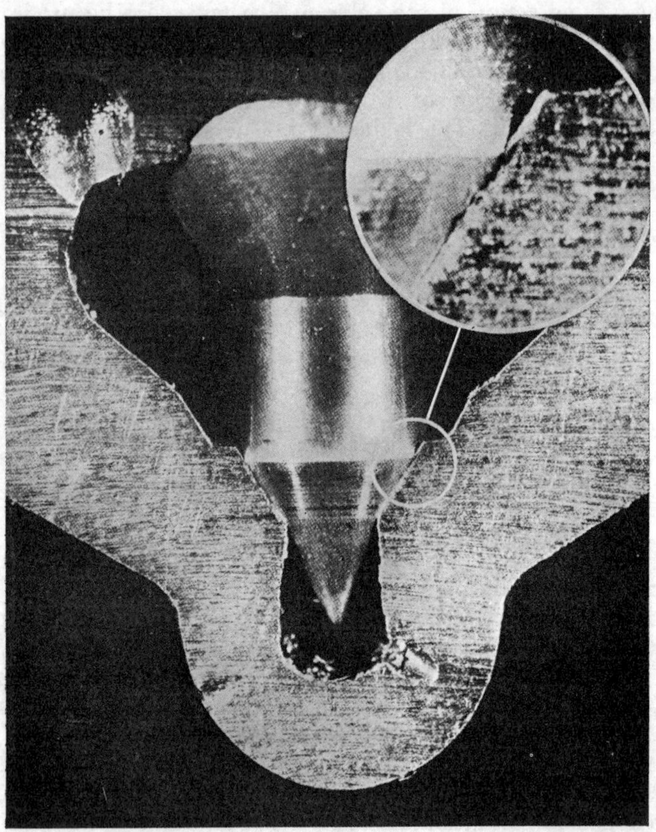

Fig. 67—Fuel-valve nozzle after being cut to disclose fault

burning low-viscosity diesel fuel but it is much more important when burning high-viscosity boiler fuels. With the latter grade there will be a greater degree of wire-drawing at the instant the needle breaks and makes contact with its seat at the beginning and end of the injection period and, consequently, the greater will be the drop in pressure driving the fuel into the cylinder at these points of the process.

At the present time it is the practice for ships' engineers to grind-in needles when they begin to leak, and although the abrasive material used is usually far from satisfactory, with due care the desired result as regards fluid-tightness is obtained. The effect, however, is to increase the width of the seat and remove one cause of improper combustion by introducing another of the same order, since the effect of each is to cause a portion of the fuel to enter the cylinder at a pressure much less than that necessary to ensure proper atomisation, penetration, and, consequently, combustion.

The wear-resisting properties of the materials used in the manufacture of fuel-valve needles and nozzles have improved so much in recent years that it is now usual for such parts to operate for well over 2,000 hours without showing any appreciable increase in the width of seat. It would seem, therefore, that the time has now come when the practice of grinding-in on board should be discouraged and the needles and nozzles sent back to the makers for reconditioning at regular intervals. As the desirable narrow seat is obtained by making the angle of seat slightly different from the angle of the needle valve, the damaging effect of grinding-in, even with the finest abrasive paste procurable, will be understood.

To ensure proper injection of fuel the conical end of the needle should make contact with the nozzle seat, as shown on the left in Fig. 66. As time goes on, the contact surface tends to spread downwards and, when it reaches the condition shown in Fig. 68, prompt and positive start and finish of the injection process will not result. It will be appreciated that so far as the cut-off of the fuel is concerned the wider the seat the greater will be the quantity of fuel between the conical surfaces, which must be displaced by the re-seating needle before actual cut-off takes place.

Before refitting fuel valves in the working position care must be taken to see that the pocket in the cylinder head and the faces which form the joint between casing and cylinder head are quite clean, otherwise if the joint is not properly gas-tight the landing faces will burn and further damage may be done. The valves should drop freely on to their landings, and an examination should be made to see that there is plenty of clearance between the underside of the casing flange and the cylinder head. The fillet at the point where the flange joins the body of the casing sometimes makes contact with the upper edge of the valve pocket and prevents the valve from landing properly. When in doubt regarding this, the amount of clearance, which should not be less than 1 mm, should be checked by lead wire.

Fig. 68—Conical end of fuel-valve needle showing how wear takes place

The best practice is to grind the casings on to their landings in the cylinder heads. Once this has been done the joining surfaces require only to be cleaned whenever a valve is removed. When copper rings are employed they should not exceed 1 mm in thickness, as rings thicker than this expand when heated and take a permanent set, with the result that when they are again cold the pressure on them is relieved, and leakage of gas will quickly burn them. When these rings burn there is a grave possibility of seriously damaging the cast-iron parts. Copper rings should be a good fit on the valve casing, and the outside diameter slightly less than the diameter of the valve pocket, to permit removal without damaging the ring, as such rings tend to spread. A landing has often been damaged by attempting to remove copper rings which have become jammed at the bottom of a valve pocket, by the employment of files and similar tools. During overhaul it is advisable to remove these rings, whether they appear to be in good order or not, and thoroughly clean all contact surfaces. The rings should always be softened by heating, followed by quenching in water, before they are refitted.

Fuel valves that tend to jam in their pockets should be smeared with mercurial ointment before being fitted. Should the joint between the casing and cylinder head leak when the engine is working, difficulty will doubtless be experienced in removing the valve owing to carbon depositing in the clearance space between the casing and the wall of the pocket. In such cases, rather than risk breaking the casing by driving in wedges under the flange, it is wise to remove one of the other valves and push the valve out by holding a pipe against the end of the valve and slowly raising the engine piston up to it, or lift the head.

Air-injection fuel valves

These valves (Fig. 57) consist essentially of three parts, namely a casing, a needle or mushroom valve, and an atomiser. The casing houses the valve and atomiser, and forms a receptacle for the fuel charge and injection air; the valve, which is operated by a cam through a rocking lever, admits the fuel into the cylinder at the correct time; while the atomiser restricts the flow of fuel and breaks it up into small particles.

The casing has two passages opening into it, the smaller from the fuel pump leading the fuel charge to the lower part of the casing immediately above the atomiser, and the other from the injection air-bottle admits the injection air at the upper part of the casing. At the points where the fuel and injection air enter the casing small non-return valves are usually provided, their object being to prevent injection air which has already passed into the fuel valve from entering the fuel pipe connecting the fuel pump and fuel valve and causing air-lock, and also to prevent fuel from entering the injection air-pipe in the event of the fuel-valve casing being flooded owing to carelessness in making certain adjustments to the fuel-valve operating gear. For instance, if the fuel valve remains closed owing to too much clearance between the rocking-lever roller and plain part of the cam, or to some defect in the operating gear occurring, the fuel-valve casing will quickly fill with fuel.

As a safeguard against pressures sufficient to cause damage occurring in the fuel valves, a bursting-tube is provided on each valve. Such a bursting-tube is shown in Fig. 69 and, as will be seen from the diagram, it is surrounded by a cage, so that should the

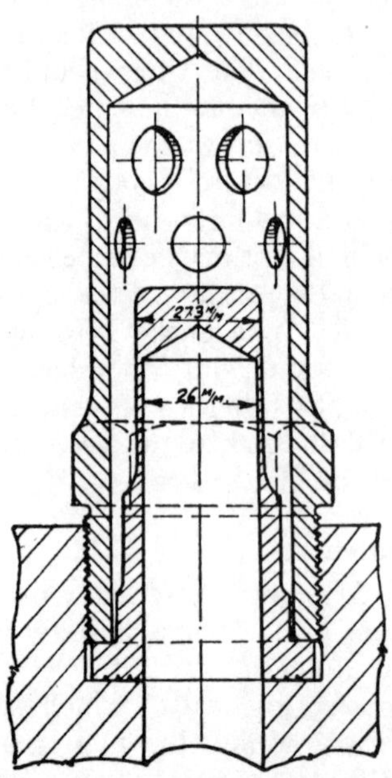

Fig. 69—Bursting-tube for air-injection engine fuel valve

tube burst operators in the vicinity are not injured. The tubes should always be located in an upright position as shown, otherwise moisture will collect in them and in a very short time cause them to corrode and rupture at normal working pressure. When one of these safety devices acts, the injection-air pressure will be rapidly reduced, and if the valve controlling the air to the cylinder on which the escape of air takes place is not closed almost immediately, the engine will stop.

The functions of the atomiser are: (1) to break up the fuel into small particles, (2) to cause the small particles of fuel and injection air to mix together, and (3) to regulate the rate at which the fuel enters the cylinder when the valve opens. If the atomisers do not perform each of these duties correctly, not only will the combustion efficiency of the engine be greatly reduced, but mechanical troubles will ultimately result. This part of the fuel valve has, therefore, a very important duty to perform, and it is essential for those in charge of an engine to make a thorough study of the particular type of atomiser used, and to become fully conversant with the effect which various adjustments have upon the duties referred to before attempting to carry out any alterations.

As stated in a preceding chapter, the fuel pump of an air-injection engine delivers the exact amount of fuel, necessary to develop the required power, into the fuel-valve casing every cycle, where it awaits the opening of the valve. When the valve opens, the whole of the fuel in the casing is forced into the cylinder by the injection air, the pressure of which is greater than the pressure prevailing in the cylinder. Therefore, when the valve closes, the casing contains only injection air at 1,000 lb/sq.in., and when the next charge of fuel is delivered into the casing it will lie on top of the uppermost atomising ring with compressed air above and below it. Thus, when the valve opens, the air below the fuel charge escapes into the cylinder, and the resulting sudden reduction of pressure will cause the air above the fuel charge to begin moving towards the cylinder at a high velocity. As the only way for the air to reach the cylinder is through the slots or holes, as the case may be, in the atomising rings, it chops the fuel up into small pieces, as it were, and carries the "pieces" with it into the cylinder. The operation of atomising and injecting the fuel charge is, therefore, comparatively gradual. It will thus be seen that the fuel and injection air enter the cylinder together, and not the fuel first followed by the injection air as might be supposed.

The fuel valve begins to open and admission of the mixture of fuel and injection air commences, irrespective of whether the engine is of the two- or four-stroke type, when the crank is from 1° to 5° before the end of the compression stroke, the actual point depending upon the rotational speed of the engine and the shape of the fuel cam toe-piece employed to open the valve. The object of starting injection slightly before the piston reaches the end of the compression stroke is to ensure that the combustion process has begun immediately the piston begins its working stroke. If the beginning of the combustion process is delayed until after the piston begins to move on its working stroke the thermal efficiency will be reduced.

The fuel valve remains open only long enough to ensure the whole of the fuel charge being injected. If the valve remains open longer than this no harm will result, but the consumption of injection air will be very much greater than it need be, and the overall efficiency of the plant will be reduced, since it is not possible to regain the whole of the work expended in compressing the air. If, on the other hand, the period the fuel valve remains open is insufficient, a little of the fuel charge will be left in the valve each cycle, and eventually the engine will stop owing to unatomised fuel only being injected into the cylinders. Such a state of affairs will result in any engine if the lift of the fuel valve is very much less than it ought to be, or if the obstruction to the flow of fuel through the atomiser is excessive.

In all air-injection engines the fuel valve closes when the crank is round about 40° beyond the top firing dead centre, which gives a period of opening in the neighbourhood of 45°, but the maximum lift of the valve varies according to the size of cylinder. The valve lift of a 30-inch diameter cylinder is about 5 mm, and it is most important that the correct lift be maintained, as the shape of all fuel cam toe-pieces is such that a reduction of lift means a corresponding reduction in the period the valve remains open.

Air-injection fuel-valve operation

When preparing an engine for service care must be taken to see that the injection air has a free passage to every fuel valve, otherwise damage may be done. For instance, suppose the injection air stop-valve to one cylinder is overlooked, and the engine is started: the fuel will be delivered into the fuel valve but when the valve opens it will not be injected into the cylinder. Moreover, as there will be no pressure in the fuel valve, some of the hot compressed air in the cylinder will flow into the fuel valve when the valve opens and may ignite the fuel therein, with the consequences shown in Fig. 70. Should the fuel ignite, dangerous pressures may result in the fuel valve, since by the time the fuel has started to burn, the fuel valve will have closed and the burning of fuel will take place in a confined space. The same, or even more serious consequences, may result if an engine is started up with too low an injection air pressure, as the enormous pressure will be produced in the injection air pipes also. The injection air pressure must, therefore, never be less than about 200 lb/sq.in. greater than the compression pressure in the cylinder.

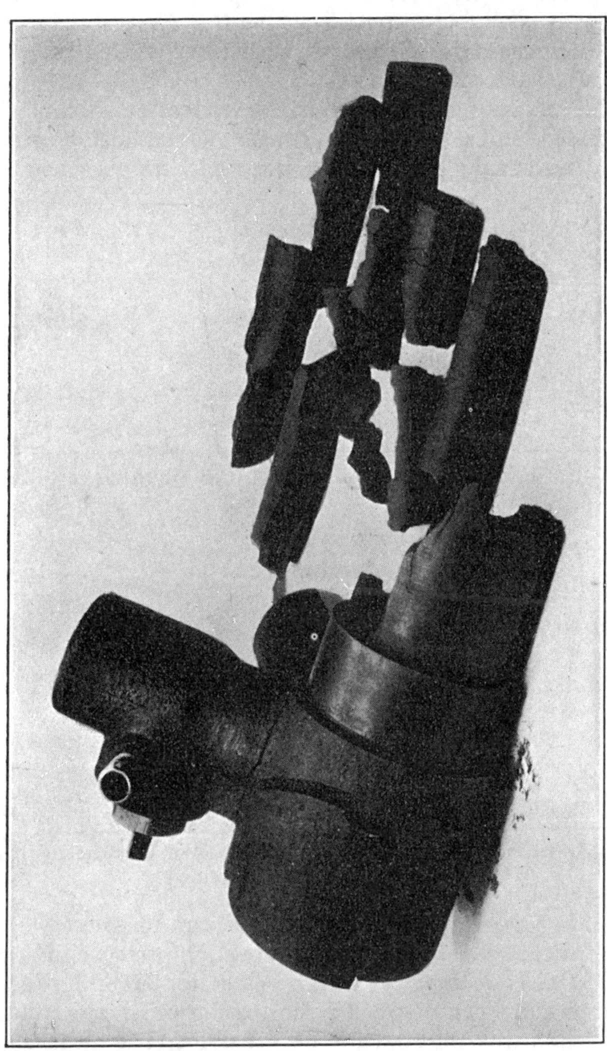

Fig. 70—Result of ignition taking place in fuel-valve casing

Before attempting to start an engine which has been stopped for more than a week, it is wise to be quite satisfied that the packing is not gripping the fuel-valve spindles to such an extent that when the valves are opened they will remain open owing to excessive gland friction. When a ship has been laid up for more than, say, three months, it is advisable to repack all the fuel-valve stuffing-boxes to ensure that when the engine is started the valves will function properly.

The lift of the fuel valves must be correct at all times, as has been stressed, and any readjustment of the combustion pressure is made by advancing or retarding the fuel cam toe-piece. If the

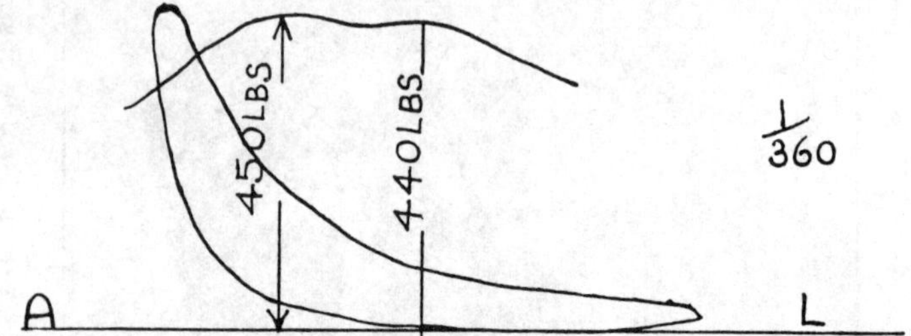

Fig. 71—Indicator diagram showing late opening of fuel valve (air injection)

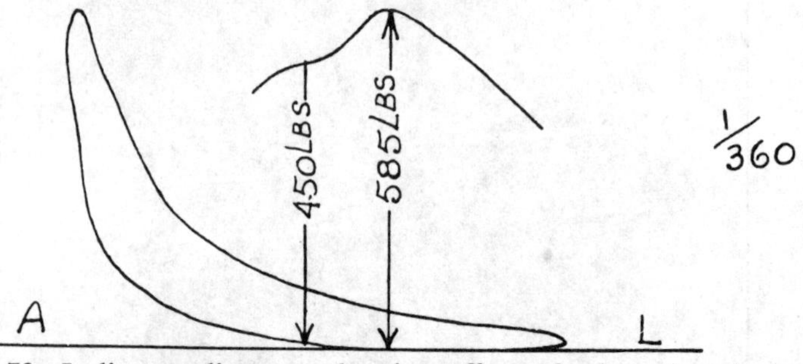

Fig. 72—Indicator diagram showing effect of advancing timing of fuel valve (air injection)

combustion pressure is too low, the fuel cam toe-piece will require to be advanced, while too high a combustion pressure indicates that the fuel valve is opening too early. When it is necessary to alter the position of a fuel cam toe-piece, the amount of alteration which will meet requirements must be carefully considered before any alterations are carried out, as it is not always convenient to stop the engine to correct errors made. The indicator diagrams shown in Figs. 71 and 72 will serve as a guide to the amount necessary. The first diagram clearly indicates a case of late opening of the fuel valve, due either to the cam toe-piece being in its wrong position or to the lift of the fuel valve being too small. The lift of the fuel valve was checked whilst the engine was working, and found to be correct, so the engine was stopped and the fuel cam toe-piece advanced 5°, measured on the crankshaft. An indicator diagram taken from an engine when working normally is shown in Fig. 73.

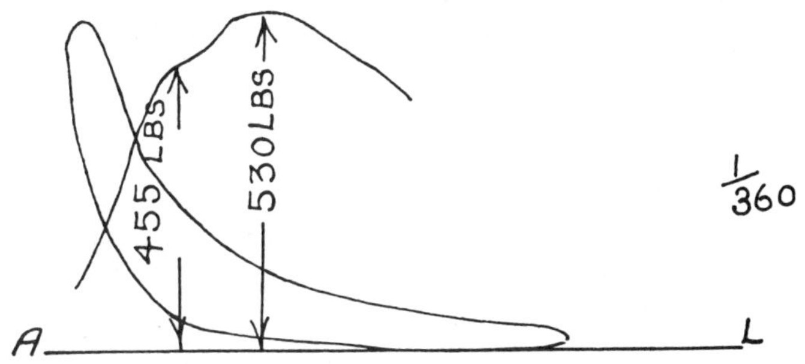

Fig. 73—Normal indicator diagram (air injection)

When for some reason it is necessary to stop the fuel and injection air entering one cylinder of a multi-cylinder engine, the fuel should always be shut off first, and it is advisable to allow injection air to enter for a minute or so after the fuel has been shut off in order to make sure that the fuel-valve casing is free of fuel. On no account must the injection air be shut off before the fuel, otherwise fuel will accumulate in the valve, and very high pressures may be produced in the cylinder when next the cylinder is brought into operation.

When bringing a cylinder into action again the injection air—when this has been shut off also—should always be admitted a minute or so before the fuel pump is made to discharge, and the closing of the priming valve should be the last operation of all.

Adjusting air-injection fuel-valve timing

The first essential in setting this and every other cylinder-head valve is to adjust the operating gear so that the rocking-lever roller makes contact with the cam peak only, i.e. the projecting part of the cam toe-piece. The usual clearance between the roller and the remaining or plain part of the cam is 0·5 mm. The clearance may be slightly greater than this without ill effect, provided, of course, that such a clearance will give the correct period of opening, but it must never be less than this amount, since although all cams are supposed to be concentric with the camshaft, it sometimes happens that the cams become slightly slack on the camshaft and when a new key is fitted the concentricity of the cam is affected. Then again, there is the question of expansion of the operating gear when the engine attains normal working temperatures, which may or may not have the effect of reducing the roller clearance, according to design,

From this it will be appreciated that as the consequences of a roller riding on the plain part of the cam and easing the fuel valve off its seat at the wrong time are so serious, 0·5 mm is little enough clearance. If a clearance less than this is necessary to give the desired open period, then the position of the toe-piece should be raised by fitting packing under it until new toe-pieces of the correct dimensions can be obtained.

Having taken up all slackness in the operating gear by the judicious use of a crowbar inserted under the roller end of the rocking lever, and adjusted the roller clearance to 0·5 mm, the crankshaft should be turned in the " ahead " direction until the rocking-lever roller just makes firm contact with the cam toe-piece. The position of the crank when this takes place should be noted, since it is the opening point of the fuel valve. Rotation of the crankshaft in the same direction should now be continued until the roller begins to leave the cam peak and it is just possible to move the roller with the fingers. As this is the point at which the fuel valve closes, the position of the crank should again be noted. As already stated, fuel valves of this type should begin to open from 1° to 5° before top dead centre, and close from 30° to 40° after top dead centre of the crank, depending upon the rotational speed of the engines and other factors.

If a fuel valve opens too late and closes an equal amount too late, the cam toe-piece will require to be advanced the requisite amount. Should, however, the opening point be too late and the closing point correct, the roller clearance will require to be reduced until the correct angular opening is obtained, and the cam toe-piece afterwards advanced to give the correct opening and closing positions. Conversely, if the opening point is too early and the closing point correct, the roller clearance will require to be increased and the cam toe-piece put back.

CHAPTER 11

Cylinder-head valves

Air-inlet and exhaust valves of the mushroom type are always used in four-stroke engines and sometimes in two-stroke engines. In the latter type the air (scavenging) used for expulsion of the burnt gases and re-charging the cylinder is sometimes admitted through an air-inlet valve in the cylinder head, and the burnt gases are driven out through a row of ports around the lower end of the cylinders. In other makes of two-stroke engines the air is admitted through the row of ports and the burnt gases driven out through an exhaust valve in the cylinder head, similar to those used in four-stroke engines. In yet other types the air is admitted through a row of ports and the burnt gases driven out through a similar row of ports located at the opposite end of the cylinder.

As air-inlet and exhaust valves must pass a very large volume of low-pressure air and burnt gas in a short time they are of large size. They can be opened pneumatically but are generally opened mechanically and closed by a spring after the opening force has been removed. Both open into the cylinder, so that the greater the gas pressure in the cylinder the more firmly are the lids pressed against their seats. Therefore the springs employed to close the valves require to be only strong enough to keep the lid on its seat during the low-pressure period of the cycle, which in four-stroke supercharged and two-stroke engines is always but a few pounds per sq. in. above atmospheric pressure. Only in unsupercharged four-stroke engines does the cylinder pressure fall below that of the atmosphere, and then only very slightly.

Typical examples of the more widely used type of air-inlet and exhaust valves are illustrated in Figs. 74 and 75, from which it will be observed that the only difference is that the latter are provided with renewable seats, and jackets through which fresh water is circulated. The provision of a water jacket is necessary because gases at a temperature in the neighbourhood of 900°F (483°C) pass through the exhaust valve, while the air-inlet valve deals with air at, or only slightly above, atmospheric temperature. The conditions under which exhaust valves work are severe, as they are constantly in contact with high-temperature gases, and if some of the heat picked up were not carried away by the circulating water the housing would distort, the valve and seating faces burn, and the spindle become unworkable.

In the days before the materials now used for exhaust-valve lids and seats were available, and the urgent need was for more power output per unit weight, considerable trouble was experienced owing to the lids and seats becoming overheated and burning away. This

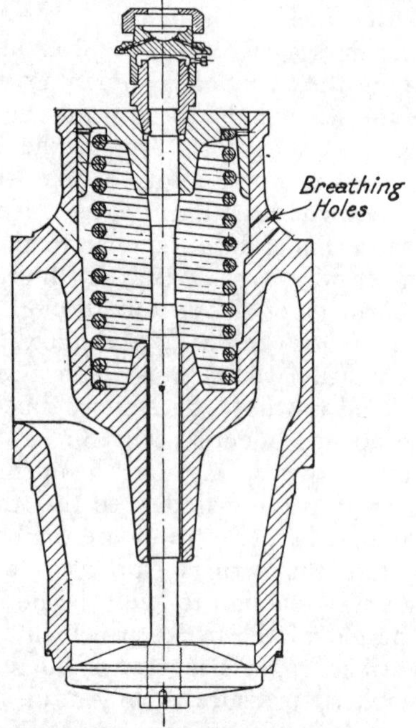

Fig. 74—Typical air-inlet valve

was overcome to a large extent by circulating water through the lid and spindle as well as the housing, as shown in Fig. 76, the cooling water being conveyed by a flexible hose to a fitting secured to the top of the spindle, the water passing down to the lid through a space provided between the stem and an outer casing. After circulating the lid, the water returns up the centre of the spindle and leaves through another flexible hose which leads it to the jacket incorporated in the housing. Such valve spindles and lids are generally made of stainless steel, and provision is made to enable the cooling-water space to be cleaned and examined.

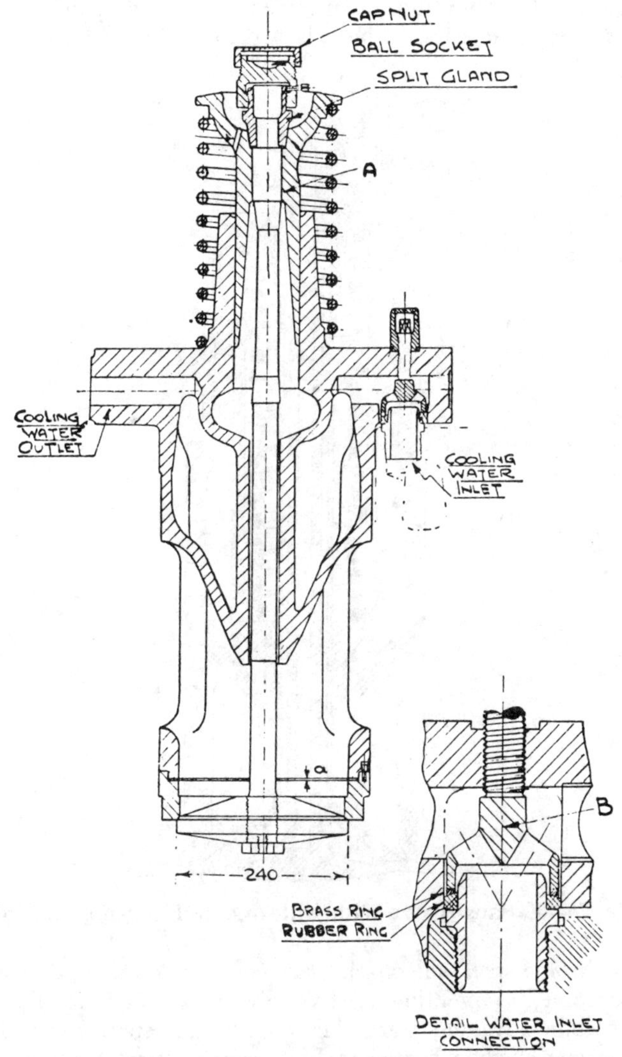

Fig. 75—Exhaust valve with water-cooled housing

The exhaust-valve housings are always made of ordinary good-quality cast iron, but such material is not suitable for the lids and seats that are exposed to the hot high-velocity exhaust gases. Although the superior grades of cast iron such as " Perlit " give very good results, attention has in recent years been paid to special steels for these purposes. There is a great variety of such steels,

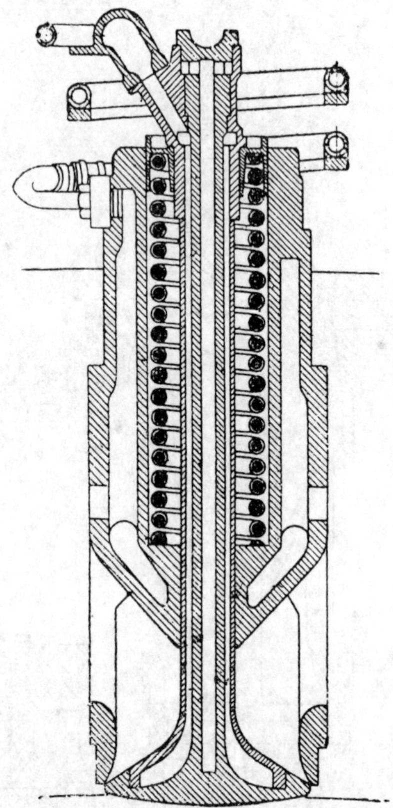

Fig. 76—Exhaust valve with water-cooled housing and lid

such as chrome steel, silicon-chrome, cobalt-chrome, and austenitic nickel-chrome, to mention a few only, now available, for all of which certain advantages are claimed. Some retain more of their tensile strength when heated to high temperatures than others, or retain their ductility better under working conditions and, therefore, are better able to withstand the shock produced as the valve re-seats; while others offer more resistance to oxidation, and scaling is consequently less pronounced at very high temperatures. No doubt steel will eventually be proved to be the most suitable material for exhaust-valve lids and seats, but at the present time, for low-speed engines, the higher grades of cast iron are just as suitable as the best steels.

It has been found that for both two- and four-stroke engines there seems to be little to choose between the special heat-resisting steels and the special grades of cast iron such as "Perlit." One advantage, however, that the high-grade steels possess is that when leakage of gas occurs they do not burn away as quickly as cast iron, with the result that it very rarely happens that so much of the compression pressure is lost that the fuel fails to ignite, whereas when a cast-iron valve begins to leak it quickly burns away, and in a very short time the compression will become so much reduced that the fuel will fail to ignite, and the valve must be changed before the cylinder concerned can be set to work again. In some cases where trouble has been experienced, improved results have been obtained by fitting steel lids and cast-iron seats.

The initial cause of properly fitted exhaust-valve lids and seats burning away is always either a crack across the ground faces, or distortion of the lid or seat due to heat stresses. The temperature of the exhaust gases is not high enough to burn either cast iron or steel, so that burning results only after an opening has been provided between the faces for the gases to pass through at very high velocity during the combustion period. The temperature of the exhaust gases as they pass out of the cylinder is about 900°F (483°C), whereas the temperature of the burning gases is in the neighbourhood of 3,000°F (1,649°C).

In addition to the material and other factors already mentioned, there is no doubt that the shape of the valve lid has a great influence upon the attention required by these valves. It is well-known that all metals in an overstressed state are more susceptible to corrosion and erosion than when in the normal state. It is, therefore, quite logical to suppose that the faces of valve lids in an overstressed condition will be attacked more readily by, which is to say will offer less resistance to the scouring action of, the hot high-velocity exhaust gases. The shape of the lids should, therefore, be such that all parts work at as near the same temperature as possible. If the temperatures at different parts of the lid are uneven, the stresses set up will be uneven also, and the parts in tension will be in a greatly weakened condition. From this it is evident that the best results will be obtained from lids that are as thin as possible and of as even a thickness as practicable. That this is the case has been proved over and over again in practice.

As the common practice is to make the spindles of mild steel and the lids of special heat-resisting steel or high-grade cast iron, it is impracticable to make the lids of uniform thickness because the two parts have to be firmly connected together, and the metal of the lid in the vicinity of the spindle must consequently be fairly thick in order to provide sufficient strength. If the lid is made the same thickness throughout, i.e. equal to the thickness necessary around the hole for the spindle, the lid would be so thick that it would become overheated and distort to such an extent that leakage between the lid and seat would soon occur.

Exhaust-valve lids are of various shapes, but in every case the metal in the vicinity of the hole for the spindle is thicker than at the periphery. Owing to this, the outer part of the lid loses some of its heat to the air passing into the cylinder during the air-inlet stroke, so that the larger mass of metal at the centre of the lid works at a higher temperature. The greater expansion of the centre portion must, therefore, produce tensile stresses in the layers of metal at the periphery of the lid. If the difference in the working temperature is not very great the thinner part of the lid will resist the forces tending to crack or distort it, and no unusual trouble will be experienced. But, if on the other hand, the temperature difference is great, the metal forming the outside of the lid will be overstressed and either crack or distort.

The apparent effect which overstress of this nature has varies with different materials. It may either strain the outer layers of metal forming the ground face, in which condition they are more susceptible to heat, or produce radial cracks across the face. When cracks occur in cast iron, the sharp edges formed quickly burn away, and consequently it is seldom that cracks are found in lids made of this material. When lids are made of heat-resisting steel, radial cracks are occasionally found across the ground face.

In one case which came under the writer's notice, in which heat-resisting steel lids and special cast-iron seats were employed, all the exhaust valves required to be overhauled after about 400 hours; if they had been left in place longer than this the seats would have been damaged beyond repair. When the valves were removed, the ground faces of the steel lids were always found cracked radially all round. The cracks had practically no width but were fairly deep. The ground surfaces of the cast-iron seats were, in some cases, very badly burnt for a distance of from 2 to 4 inches of the circumference.

A cross-sectional view of the steel lids in question is shown in Fig. 77, from which it will be seen that the metal around the spindle is very much thicker than the metal at the periphery, and the conclusion reached was that the cracking was due to tensile stresses

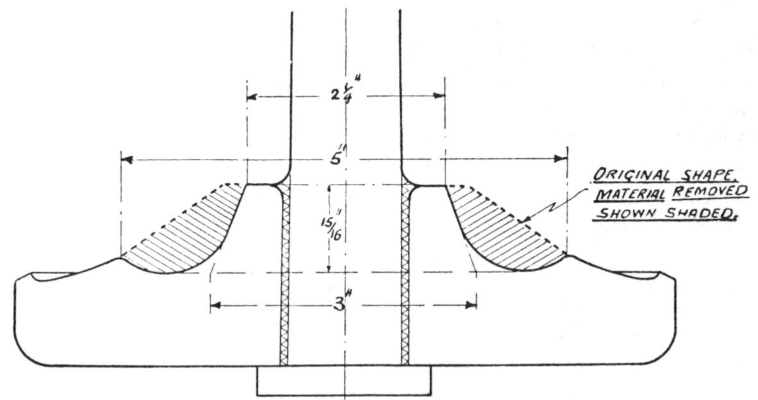

Fig. 77—Modification to steel exhaust-valve lid to minimise distortion

being set up by the greater expansion of the centre portion, especially as the engine was of the supercharged type and the outer part of the valve lids would consequently work at a much lower temperature than the larger mass of metal in the vicinity of the spindle, since in this type of engine cool air follows the hot burnt gases during the exhausting process.

In an endeavour to reduce the temperature difference in the lids and so eliminate the tensile stresses set up at the periphery, the shape of the lids was altered as shown, which clearly shows the amount and position of the metal removed. The effect of this simple alteration was to increase the running period from 400 hours to 1,200 hours, before grinding in became necessary.

The obvious solution to the difficulty is to make the parts of special heat-resisting steel and machine them out of a single forging, i.e. make the spindle and lid in one piece. Such a practice, however, is not favoured by either engine-builders or shipowners owing to the very high cost. The lids are generally screwed on to the spindle, as shown in Figs. 74 and 75, and, to ensure that they will remain firmly connected together, the hole in the lid is of such a size that the lid must be heated before it can be screwed on the spindle. The usual practice is to heat the lid in boiling oil. If a temperature greater than this is required to enable the parts to be fitted together, the lid will be overstressed when it cools, while if the screwing is such that the parts can be fitted together without first heating the lid, the lid will soon become slack.

A point in the manufacture of cast-iron exhaust-valve lids and seats that greatly affects results is the amount of metal that must be machined off the rough casting to bring the parts to the correct dimensions. As the metal near the surface of the casting is harder and more serviceable, the parts should be cast to as near as practicable the finished size, so that an absolute minimum requires to be machined off. Another important point is the release of all casting strains by careful annealing.

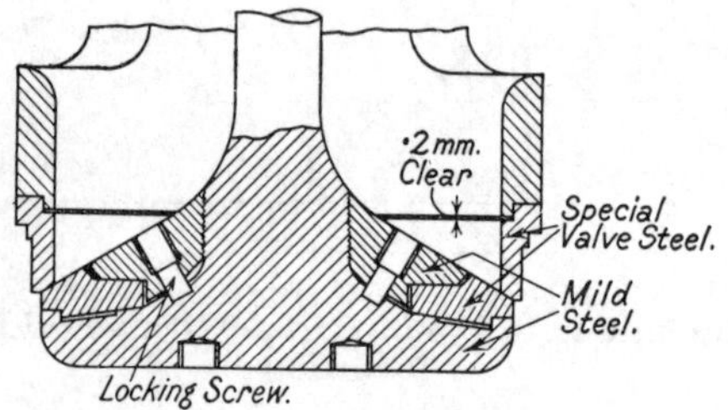

Fig. 78—Exhaust valve with separate detachable seat and portion of lid

In an endeavour to overcome the troubles referred to in the preceding pages and reduce the cost of renewals, some engine-builders adopt an arrangement similar to that shown in Fig. 78. The one illustrated consists of a renewable wearing ring which is held in position by a conical-shaped nut that screws down on to it. Such an arrangement works very well, provided the various parts are properly fitted together. Much time and trouble will be saved during the overhaul of such valves if a liberal amount of thick graphite paste is applied to the threads of the nuts and pinching screws whenever the parts are being reassembled, as this form of lubricant prevents the parts from becoming "frozen" together.

Air-inlet and exhaust-valve springs

The springs of air-inlet and exhaust valves are always of round cross-section, as this shape has been found superior to any other.

Round bars are made into coils more easily than square section bars, which tend to crack at the outside corners during the operation; or if they do not crack during manufacture, they are very liable to do so in service. Various high-grade steels are used in the manufacture of these springs, but silicon manganese is one of the most suitable.

When springs break, a surprisingly rare occurrence considering the duty performed, the cause is generally unsuitable material or improper heat-treatment. It is important, however, to avoid any part of the spring under stress from making hard contact with other parts of the valve. The spigots on the housing and spring cap used for centring purposes should not, therefore, be longer than half the cross-sectional diameter of the stock from which the spring is made, and if it should be necessary for them to be longer than this, the ends of the spigots should be well rounded off, in order to eliminate all likelihood of hard contact between the spring and the spigot when the spring is under compressive stress. Should any part of a spring become damaged and the surface broken either in this way, or by other accident, the affected part should be ground to produce a perfectly smooth surface, otherwise the spring will soon break.

If it is desired to ensure a perfectly reliable spring, the stock from which it is made must have first been " reeled." This manufacturing operation has the effect of producing an exceedingly smooth surface, the advantage of which is that the smallest defects can be readily detected during or after coiling.

A test that will ensure as far as possible a new spring not breaking in service is to compress it until all coils are in hard contact, and let the spring remain in this condition for six hours. After this period, and before the spring is released, the bolt used to hold the spring in a compressed condition should be given several blows with a 14-lb hammer and the spring then carefully examined for cracks. If no cracks are found it may safely be assumed that the spring is free from defects.

Supplies of spare springs are usually carried to meet any emergency, but in the event of no spare springs being available it is generally possible to effect repairs that will enable a ship to reach port safely. When a spring breaks near either end it is not usually necessary to take any action until a convenient opportunity occurs to change the spring, as springs broken in this way have functioned, more or less correctly, for hundreds of hours. When the break occurs about mid-length, however, action must be taken at once, otherwise the two halves will begin to screw into one another and the closing of the valve may be delayed to such an extent that the piston will strike the valve lid and seriously damage it. If a complete spare valve or a spare spring is available, it is best to stop the engine and renew the broken part, but if such a course is undesirable and a suitable spring for a replacement is available, the valve can be kept working by suspending a pair of light rope blocks over the valve and connecting up suitably to the valve spindle with a sound spare spring interposed between the blocks and the valve spindle.

On one occasion during the writer's sea experience, a spring that had broken in two places about mid-length was made to function for over three months when no spare springs were available, in the following manner. The smallest broken part of the spring, consisting of about three-quarters of one coil, was removed, and both halves of the remainder of the spring turned end to end to bring the flat ends of the spring together. A circular piece of $\frac{1}{4}$-inch thick sheet iron, equal in diameter to the outside diameter of the spring and with a hole in the centre for the valve spindle to pass through, was interposed between the two halves of the spring after four equally spaced pins had been screwed into the iron plate in such a position that when the plate was sandwiched between the two halves of the spring they could not work out of alignment. For the ends of the spring it was necessary to make discs out of hardwood, one side of each of these discs being specially shaped to ensure an even pressure being exerted on the spring during the opening of the valve. With the compression of the spring reduced to a minimum, i.e. until the valve began bouncing slightly at the moment it re-seated, this broken spring functioned properly until new springs were received on board.

When it is desired to change a spring without first removing the valve, the spindle must be prevented from falling into the cylinder, and the valve lid held against its seat in order to permit the nut being screwed on to the end of the spindle. In some designs it is possible to hold the spindle in position whilst this is being done. Where this is not possible the spindle may be held in the desired position by injecting low-pressure air through the indicator cock, all other valves being, of course, closed. Should a low-pressure air supply not be available, the crank may be placed on the bottom dead centre and the starting air valve eased sufficiently to allow a little air to enter the cylinder, care being taken to see that compressed air is prevented from reaching any other cylinder and thereby setting the engine in motion. It will be found that a very small

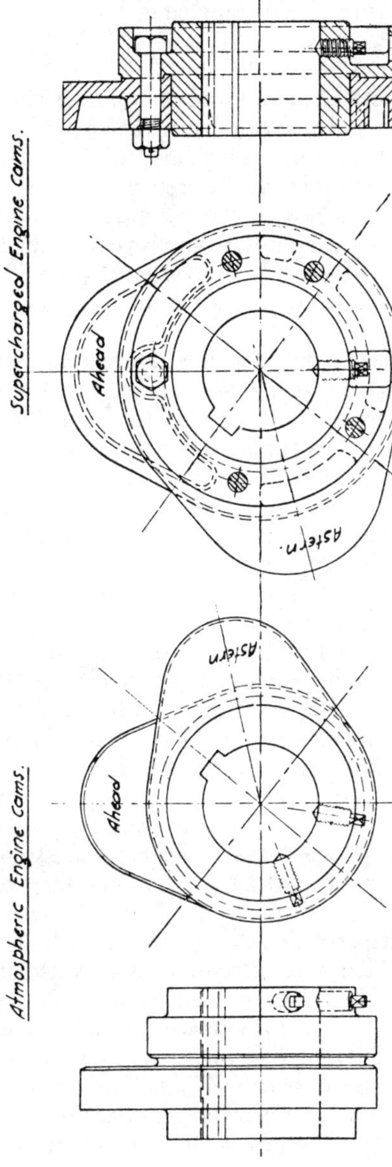

Fig. 79—Exhaust-valve cams of an unsupercharged and a supercharged 4-stroke engine

pressure in the cylinder is sufficient to hold the valve firmly against its seat whilst the springs are being changed.

Air-inlet and exhaust-valve cams

There are two methods employed to operate the air-inlet and exhaust valves. One is by a cam, and the other by an eccentric. The cam drive has been universally adopted because cams can be made in shapes that will give the desired rapid opening and closing of the valves not possible with the eccentric. Another advantage of the cam drive is that it simplifies the reversing mechanism, since to reverse the direction of rotation of a four-stroke engine the common practice is to move the camshaft a certain distance in an endwise direction.

The efficiency of an engine depends to a certain extent upon the design of the cams operating the air-inlet and exhaust valves, which must allow the air and burnt gases an unrestricted flow to and from the cylinder. In the case of the exhaust valve, the open period must not begin too early, otherwise high-pressure gas capable of doing useful work will be released and power will be lost; while if the operation begins too late, back pressure on the piston during the exhaust stroke will result and power will be lost in this way also. The aim in designing cams is to retain the gas pressure on the piston for as long as possible and then open the exhaust valve with sufficient rapidity to avoid undue back pressure on the piston. The ideal cam, from the point of view of efficiency, would have a very square peak, and the valve would have to be provided with a very strong spring to ensure the rocking lever roller following the cam profile. The most efficient cam would, therefore, be very noisy, and wear and tear of the rubbing parts would be excessive, so that the design of cam usually found is a compromise between the ideal and the practical. Typical exhaust-valve cams are shown in Fig. 79, from which it will be noted that the corners are well rounded in order to obtain smooth and, as far as practicable, noiseless working.

Air-inlet and exhaust-valve cams are generally made of good-quality cast iron, and as a rule will run for years without any apparent wear taking place. The most frequent source of trouble is due to their becoming slack on the shaft when made in one piece and secured by keys. To avoid this the cams must be a good tapping fit on the shaft, the securing key well fitted and two pinching screws provided on each side of the centre-line opposite the key as shown on the left of Fig. 79. (The best form of pinching screw for this or any other purpose is cup-ended and case-hardened. When fitted in cams such screws are chiefly intended to prevent end movement of the cam, but in addition there is no doubt that they play a very important part in preventing the cam from becoming slack on the shaft.) In regard to the fitting of the key, the cam should bear heavily on the sides and lightly on the top of the key. A more satisfactory arrangement is to provide a collar as part of the camshaft and attach the cam to it by means of fitted bolts, as is shown at the right-hand side of Fig. 79.

The most common method of operating air-inlet and exhaust valves is shown in Fig. 80, from which it will be seen that one end of the rocking lever is provided with a roller that runs on the cam, and that the other end carries an adjusting screw, the purpose of which is to enable the correct working clearance between the roller and the cam to be maintained. The ends of these adjusting screws, which make contact with the valve spindles, are case-hardened and require to be lubricated. The rocking levers are generally made of

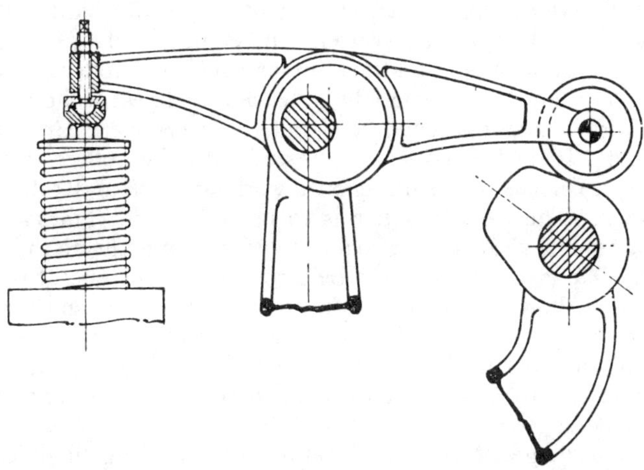

Fig. 80—Rocking lever for operating air-inlet and exhaust valves

cast steel and are mounted on what is termed the fulcrum shaft. In some engines the rocking levers are mounted eccentrically on the shaft, the object being to cause the roller ends of the levers to be lifted clear of the cams during the reversing operation when the camshaft is moved endwise. This operation will be fully explained in Chapter 17.

The fulcrum shaft is carried in pedestal bearings in which it should be a good fit. When the shaft is used merely to carry the rocking levers it should be jammed in the bearings, but when the shaft must be rotated to effect reversal it must be a free but fine fit in the bearings. Although these shafts remain stationary all the time the engine is working, the bearings wear a surprising amount, and it is necessary to readjust the diametrical clearances from time to time, as slackness in these parts is very undesirable.

Cam rollers are made of either hard cast iron or case-hardened steel, and revolve on the case-hardened steel pin fixed in the end of the rocking lever. An alternative to the plain roller is a roller bearing, and this is, of course, by far the superior arrangement; if given a little lubricant occasionally such bearings last indefinitely without wear taking place.

With the normal design of cam profile as fitted on atmospheric engines, the wear rate of the pins and rollers is negligible if properly lubricated and provided the pins are made of case-hardened steel, and the rollers of chilled cast iron or other equally hard material. In supercharged engines, however, where the speed of opening is much more rapid, the conditions under which the rollers work are more severe, and it is generally necessary to line the hole in the rollers with a case-hardened steel bush if excessive wear is to be prevented. If such bushes are pressed into the rollers it is not necessary to make provision against working loose and rotating in the rollers. The usual practice is to use oil for the lubrication of these parts, but wear will be reduced and a saving effected if grease is used. The grease cup should be screwed into one end of the pin, and passages bored through the pin to ensure the lubricant reaching the point where it is needed. The roller pins require to be securely locked in the rocking levers, and the locking arrangements tested from time to time, as a pin working loose may have very serious consequences.

A disadvantage of the cam method of operating air-inlet and exhaust valves is that, on account of the clearance which must be provided between the cam and rocking-lever roller to allow for expansion when the parts become heated, and to ensure that the valve is not prevented from re-seating properly, there is a certain amount of noise produced. This noise, and the wear and tear which generally accompanies noise, can be reduced to a minimum by maintaining just sufficient roller clearance and keeping the parts properly lubricated. It is the practice of some makers to enclose the camshaft and lubricate the bearings by oil from the main pressure system, the oil afterwards flowing into baths in which the cams dip as they revolve. In such cases the oil in the baths is maintained at the correct level by arranging the entry to the pipe returning the oil to the engine sump, to be about one half-inch above the lowest point reached by the exhaust and air-inlet cams.

A great deal of noise is produced when the rollers are not perfectly square with the cam faces, as when this is the case the roller is knocked against the lever at the instant the valve begins to open. In such instances all one can do, apart from re-setting the rocking levers, to cause the whole of the faces to make contact with even pressure, is to reduce the side play of the rollers until they are free without measurable clearance. An obvious source of noise is the levers themselves—if they are allowed movement during the idle period. The least noise is produced when the levers never break contact with the valve, as when the clearance is at the roller end the oil on the cam deadens somewhat the noise caused by the necessary clearance that the rocking lever must have.

In most four-stroke engines there is but little variety in the design of the cylinder-charging and exhausting process, but a novel

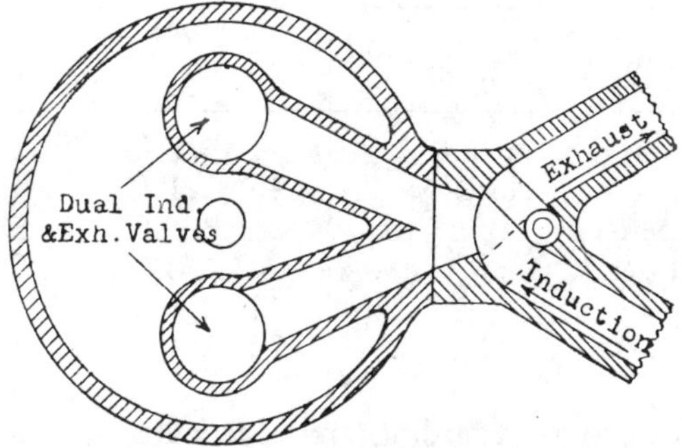

Fig. 81—Combined air-inlet and exhaust valves, with director valve

variation is shown in Fig. 81. There are two valves in the cylinder head similar to the air-inlet and exhaust valves of the ordinary type, but both valves are used for the dual purpose of admitting air during the air-inlet stroke and allowing exit of the burnt gases during the exhaust stroke. These valves are operated by cams and rocking levers in the usual way but open simultaneously about the beginning of the exhaust stroke, and remain open until after the end of the air-inlet stroke. In addition to these valves, and situated within the cylinder-head casting, is a semi-rotary valve operated by an eccentric, the function of which is to give the combined air-inlet and exhaust valves communication alternately with the air-inlet passage and the exhaust passage.

Since both valves are utilised for the admission of air and exit of the burnt gases, the valves, and consequently the holes to accommodate them in the cylinder head, need only be half the total area of those used in the ordinary way, which is the greatest advantage of this arrangement. A further advantage is that the working temperature of the valves will be much lower than that of the ordinary exhaust valve, due to their smaller size and because of the cooling effect of the ingoing air.

Timing of air-inlet and exhaust valves

The positions of the crank when the valves open and close vary slightly in different makes of engines, and those given hereafter are a fair average. The readings are of a four-stroke engine converted to the supercharge principle after working successfully for many years as an atmospheric engine, so that a comparison between the two types can be made.

Valve	Before conversion	After conversion
Fuel injection (air) opens ..	4° B.T.C.	5° B.T.C.
,, ,, ,, closes ..	40° A.T.C.	45° A.T.C.
Air inlet opens	26° B.T.C.	55° B.T.C.
,, ,, closes	26° A.B.C.	28° A.B.C.
Exhaust opens	42° B.B.C.	42° B.B.C.
,, closes	12° A.T.C.	35° A.T.C.

Other information regarding this particular engine after conversion is as follows:—

i.h.p. per hour	5,300
Revolutions per minute	135
Diameter of cylinders, mm	630
Stroke of piston, mm	1,100
Mean indicated pressure, lb/sq.in. ..	120
Supercharge air pressure, lb/sq.in. ..	3
Exhaust-gas temperature	698°F (370°C)

It will be noted that the only important change in the opening and closing points of the air-inlet and exhaust valves when an engine is made to work on the supercharged principle is that the air-inlet valve opens 29° earlier and closes 2° later, and the exhaust valve closes 23° later. The overlap, therefore, of these two valves is increased from 38° to 90°.

Theoretically, as pointed out in an earlier chapter, the air-inlet and exhaust valves should open and close when the crank is on the top and bottom dead centres respectively, but in practice it is necessary to deviate from what is theoretically correct. The air-inlet valve, for instance, opens before the crank reaches the top centre, or before the piston has begun to move on its suction stroke, because the opening process must be more or less gradual to prevent shock and noise, and the valve must be open sufficiently to ensure the air following up the piston immediately it begins to move. If the valve did not begin to open until the crank had reached the top centre, the flow of air into the cylinder during the early part of the air-inlet stroke would be restricted and a partial vacuum created in the cylinder. The effect of this would be to increase what are termed the pumping losses and so reduce the effective work done by the engine, besides reducing the weight of air in the cylinder at the end of the air-inlet stroke, the detrimental effect of which will be obvious.

Closing of the air-inlet valve is delayed until the crank passes over the bottom centre and the compression stroke has begun, to ensure the cylinder being completely filled with air at not less than atmospheric pressure before the compression process begins. If the valve begins to open at 26° B.T.C. and closes at 26° A.B.C., the point of maximum opening is reached when the piston has completed about half of the air-inlet stroke. There is no rest at the point of maximum opening in the case of atmospheric type engines, with the result that the closing operation begins when the piston is at mid-stroke. In supercharged engines there is a longer full-open period, but although the closing operation begins later in this type of engine, the valve closes at a greater rate and re-seats at about the same time.

Delaying the closing of the air-inlet valve until the piston has started the compression stroke might suggest that part of the air would be pumped back into the atmosphere. This is not the case, however, as 26°–28° movement of the crank on either side of the dead centre positions results in only a small movement of the piston. As a matter of fact, it is probable that the delaying of the closing point results in a greater weight of air being available for combustion, owing to the piston moving out of the cylinder at high speed, setting in motion air which has definite weight. The flowing air naturally gathers momentum, and when the piston comes to rest at the end of the air-inlet stroke the air continues flowing into the cylinder until its momentum is expended.

As will be noted from the particulars of an engine given earlier, the exhaust valve begins to open well before the crank reaches bottom centre. The reason for this is that when the piston reaches a point about 42° B.B.C., the pressure of gas in the cylinder is in the neighbourhood of 40 lb/sq.in., and time must be allowed for this pressure to be got rid of, otherwise there would be very considerable back pressure on the piston during the exhaust stroke. When the piston reverses its direction of motion and begins the exhaust stroke, not only must all pressure in the cylinder be released but the exhaust valve must be open an amount sufficient to ensure that when the piston begins expelling the burnt gases there will be least resistance to their flow.

The closing of the exhaust valve is delayed until after the piston has completed the exhaust stroke so as to ensure that there is no resistance offered to the flow of the gases by a rapidly closing valve, and that as much as possible of the burnt gases has been expelled. During the expulsion of the burnt gases the speed of the gases reaches a maximum when the piston is about mid-stroke; after this point the speed of the piston decreases, but the burnt gases have by that time gathered momentum and continue to flow at a greater speed than the piston, with the result that when the piston reaches the end of the exhaust stroke, the pressure in the cylinder is slightly less than the pressure pumped against, i.e. that of the atmosphere.

A light spring indicator diagram taken after conversion of the four-stroke engine referred to above, is shown in Fig. 82, in order to illustrate the effect of the opening and closing processes of air-inlet and exhaust valves.

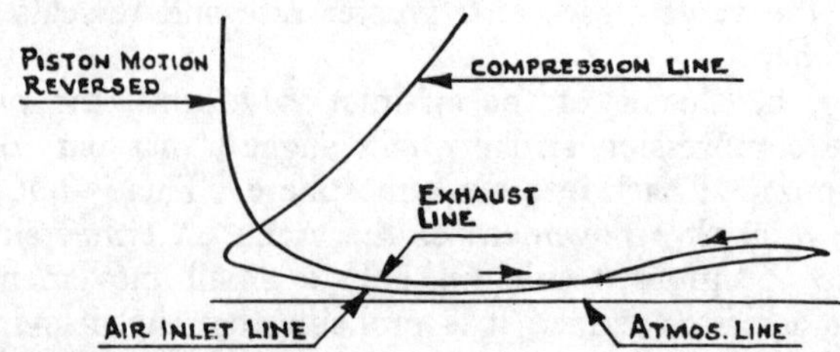

Fig. 82—Light spring indicator diagram of supercharged 4-stroke engine

The above diagram was taken with the valves opening and closing at the new crank positions given in the table on page 184. From this diagram it will be seen that the pressure in the cylinder falls very rapidly during the latter part of the working stroke, the fall being so rapid that it is represented by an almost vertical line. This is to be expected, because the exhaust valve begins to open when the piston is still travelling outward and the volume of the space in which the gases are contained is, consequently, increasing. The rapid fall in pressure at this period of the cycle is, therefore, mainly due to the exhaust valve opening and allowing the burnt gases, at a pressure of about 40 lb/sq.in., to escape into the atmosphere, and partly due to the piston still travelling out of the cylinder when release occurs.

Even though the exhaust valve begins to open well before the end of the working stroke, at which point it is at about the half open position and continuing to open very rapidly, the pressure in the cylinder is still high, i.e. 10 lb/sq.in., when the piston reverses its direction of motion and begins the exhaust stroke. Consequently, the pressure in the cylinder during the exhausting process does not reach a minimum until the piston has completed about 20 per cent of the exhaust stroke, the minimum pressure in this case being 1 lb/sq.in. From this it will be appreciated that if the start of opening of an exhaust valve is delayed owing to incorrect adjustment, or the speed of opening reduced owing to wear of the cam profile, the pressure in the cylinder during the early part of the exhaust stroke will be very much more than that shown on the diagram in Fig. 82 and power will consequently be lost, because the greater the pressure of the gases at this point the greater will be the resistance to the movement of the piston, or, in other words, the pumping losses will be proportionately increased.

For the next 45 per cent of the piston's travel the pressure in the cylinder remains practically constant at the minimum pressure during the cycle, i.e. 1 lb/sq.in. During this period the piston is travelling at its maximum speed, but as the exhaust valve is at or about its full-open position no increase in pressure results.

When the piston has completed about two-thirds of the exhaust stroke, the exhaust valve is rapidly closing and the pressure in the cylinder, it will be observed from Fig. 82, begins to increase. The increase in pressure, however, is not very great, because although the exit for the burnt gases is getting smaller, the speed of the piston is being rapidly reduced. In this particular engine the increase in pressure is from 1 to 2 lb/sq.in.

Just before the end of the exhaust stroke is reached the pressure rises 0·5 lb/sq.in. or so. This is due to the air-inlet valve opening and admitting supercharge air, the gauge pressure of which is 3 lb/sq.in. During the first part of the air-inlet stroke the pressure in the cylinder is maintained at approximately the supercharge air pressure, but as the piston gathers speed, restriction at the air-inlet valve results and the pressure is reduced from 3 lb to less than 0·5 lb/sq.in. As the piston approaches the end of the air-inlet line, however, its speed is again reduced and the pressure in the cylinder rises to about 2·5 lb/sq.in., which is the pressure of air in the cylinder when the piston begins the compression stroke.

Apart from illustrating why it is necessary to cause the air-inlet and exhaust valves to open before the piston reaches the end of the exhaust and working strokes respectively, the foregoing will serve to emphasise the importance of maintaining the correct rocking-lever roller clearance of these valves.

Operation of air-inlet and exhaust valves

The amount of overhauling required by exhaust valves depends to a large extent upon the effective cooling of the valve housing and the cylinder head in the vicinity of the exhaust valve. A good flow of cooling water should, therefore, be maintained not only when the engine is working, but for an hour or so after the engine is stopped in order to carry off the heat left in the castings and eliminate overheating, which causes the parts to distort.

When an engine is started after a change of air-inlet and/or exhaust valves, no time should be lost in making quite sure that the valves are re-seating properly, by endeavouring to hold the rocking-lever rollers stationary between the fingers when they leave the cam peak. If more than finger-tip force is required to do this then the roller clearance should be increased without delay, otherwise the valve faces may be burnt. At the same time a finger should be pressed against the flange joint of each valve housing with its cylinder head in order to make sure that the housing is held firmly on its landing in the head. Should there be relative movement between these two parts, no matter how slight, the holding-down nuts should at once be tightened, otherwise the joining surfaces may be seriously damaged.

The opening and closing action of the valves should be smooth. Jerkiness while closing indicates that the spindle is being gripped unduly and requires to be lubricated. Where possible the valve spindle should be given a rotary movement after the lubricant has been applied, remembering that the best time to apply the force to do this—assuming that it is an exhaust valve that is tending to jam—is when the air-inlet valve is open and there is practically no gas load on the exhaust valve. If excessive force is applied in an attempt to rotate the valve at other points of the cycle, the arrangement for locking the nut on the spindle may be damaged, as it is generally possible only to rotate the spindle by means of a spanner on the nut. Bouncing at the moment of re-seating indicates insufficient spring load. In such an event, however, it is wise to take a light spring indicator diagram before increasing the spring load, as a partial vacuum in the cylinder during the air-inlet stroke owing to restriction in the air passage is sometimes responsible for this fault. It is possible to fit some air-inlet valves the wrong way circumferentially and restrict the ingoing air.

As a rule, if a valve re-seats smartly the spring load may be taken as being sufficient, but it sometimes happens that where an exhaust valve requires more frequent grinding than usual, a little extra spring load will give beneficial results. Care must be taken, however, not to load the valve so much that undue wear of the operating gear takes place.

When the ground faces of either the lid or seat of a well-designed exhaust valve burn away it is generally due to one of the following causes: (1) exhaust-gas temperature too high, causing overheating and, consequently, distortion of the lid; (2) exhaust valve not re-seating properly due to the spindle jamming or insufficient roller clearance; (3) distortion of the valve seat due to uneven or excessive tightening down. In every case the burning away of the metal is caused by gases cutting across the faces at high velocity during the high-pressure period of the cycle.

The exhaust-gas temperature beyond which exhaust-valve trouble may be expected, no matter what kind of material is used for the valve lid and seat, is about 850°F (456°C). If, therefore, the power developed is such that the working temperature is over 850°F (456°C), and constant trouble with the exhaust valves is experienced, the only remedy is to reduce the working temperature by reducing the power output of the engine. In the case of supercharged engines the power output might be maintained and the exhaust temperature reduced by increasing the supercharge air pressure a small amount.

Burning of exhaust-valve faces may also be caused by part of the fuel being sprayed into the cylinder in such a way that intense local heat is produced in the vicinity of the exhaust valve. This may be due to a fault in design, but more often it is due to the fuel-valve nozzle not being in its correct position, or to the holes in the nozzle having become enlarged or distorted and causing one of the fuel sprays to approach too near to the exhaust valve. Fuel-valve nozzles are generally provided with dowel pins to ensure that they will always be refitted in their correct position. The position of the dowel pins is such that the exhaust and air-inlet valves lie between two fuel sprays.

The first indication of an exhaust valve leaking is a whistling noise, but whether it can be heard or not depends upon how near the ear can be placed to the valve. The exhaust temperature will then begin to increase and sparks will be observed at the exhaust-gas test cock. On occasions sparks are observed issuing from around the valve spindle and may lead one to think that the valve faces are leaking. This, however, is the case only when the sparks are seen during the fuel-injection period, since if the valve spindle has too much clearance in the housing, sparks are sometimes discharged at the moment the exhaust valve opens.

When exhaust-valve lids as well as the housing are water-cooled as illustrated in Fig. 76, and the cooling water is discharged direct into a closed system, the proper working of the cooling system is ascertained by feeling the flexible hoses by hand. If working properly the inlet hose will, of course, be at the temperature of the ingoing water, and the outlet hose only slightly warmer. Partial choking of the passages in the valve is indicated by the inlet hose remaining at the same temperature and the outlet hose heating up, while in the case of complete stoppage of the cooling water, both hoses will become hot. Should both hoses become the same temperature as the ingoing water, it indicates—provided, of course, that the cylinder concerned is working at full load—that some of the internal parts of the valve are defective, allowing the water to leave the valve without circulating the head. Partial stoppage of the passages can sometimes be cleared by changing the direction of the cooling water through the valve.

To some engineers, the practice of employing flexible hoses for the purpose of conveying cooling water to and from a moving part may seem undesirable, but nevertheless, such hoses answer the purpose very well, and only give trouble when the water is allowed to get so hot as to cause the rubber to swell and restrict the passage. When this occurs, it is the work of a few minutes only to replace the defective hose. The fuel must, however, be shut off the cylinder concerned whilst doing so, to prevent overheating of the exhaust-valve lid. In the Doxford engine flexible hoses are very successfully employed to convey the cooling water to and from the pistons.

Much that has been written here and in the next chapter regarding the attention required by air-inlet and exhaust valves applies to starting air and relief valves. As, however, starting valves are fully described in a later chapter, only points peculiar to relief valves will be discussed in this chapter.

Cylinder relief valves

These valves ought to receive their share of attention, because though they may be a comparatively inactive member, yet they perform an important duty. When required to operate it is essential that they not only do so promptly, but that they should re-seat properly and be perfectly gas-tight when normal conditions in the cylinder are restored. They should, therefore, be removed periodically, dismantled, the parts cleaned and lubricated, and the lids ground in. A Doxford spring-loaded relief valve is shown in Fig. 83, at *A*.

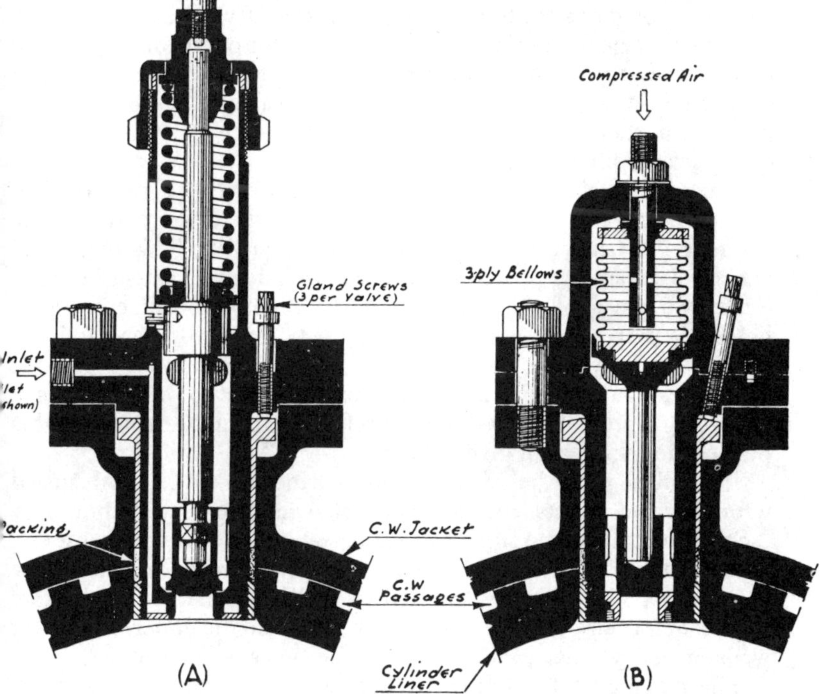

Fig. 83—Cylinder relief valves: (a) spring-loaded type, and (b) compressed air-loaded type

When these valves act, a piece of grit sometimes becomes jammed between the valve lid and seat and prevents it re-seating properly when the cylinder pressure becomes normal again. In such an event the fuel should be shut off from the cylinder concerned, otherwise the valve faces may be burnt. The valve should then be rotated on its seat until the leakage stops. If this does not have the desired effect the cylinder will have to remain out of action and the engine stopped at the first convenient opportunity for the fitting of a spare valve.

Relief valves generally operate when an engine is first started, owing to the injection of an excessive fuel charge or to pre-ignition. Pre-ignition at such times generally results in air-injection engines when the engine is working at low speeds and the injection air pressure is too high for the speed. If the cause cannot be removed at once, the fuel should be shut off the cylinder concerned until the opportunity occurs to remedy the trouble, otherwise the valve faces may be damaged to such an extent that it will be impossible to stop the leakage without taking out the valve for overhaul. Especially is this necessary when rubber rings are employed to prevent leakage of cooling water from around the relief-valve tube forming the pocket for the valve, as the rubber will quickly lose its essential qualities and allow leakage of cooling water.

When the pocket for the relief valve is formed by a tube passing through the water jacket it is usual to screw the lower end into the cylinder and expand the upper end into the jacket. This method is entirely satisfactory, provided there is no relative movement between these two parts of the cylinder head. Should movement occur, however, there is a possibility of the tube being broken, and the only satisfactory arrangement then is to leave the upper end slack in the jacket and provide a stuffing-box and gland to prevent leakage of cooling water. Soft packing is preferable to rubber rings for this purpose for the reason given above.

The tubes must be made of non-corrodible steel. Galvanised wrought iron resists the corrosive elements very well, but only " Staybrite " or other similar special steels will resist them entirely. Some of the special cast irons, such as " Spheroidal," are also quite suitable for the purpose, but when such material is used there must not be any relative movement between the inner and outer walls of the cylinder head, otherwise the tubes will break.

The patented " Lightning " relief valve shown in Fig. 83, at *B*, especially designed for Doxford engines, possesses the following advantages over the spring-loaded type of valve:—

(1) The load is uniform throughout the travel of the valve, i.e. from closed to full-open position, consequently the excess pressure is released promptly and freely.
(2) As the load is not progressively increased as the valve lifts, the gas-tight faces are not cut due to wire-drawing of the hot released gases, and consequently require a minimum of attention.
(3) It will operate with certainty at any predetermined pressure down to 5 per cent above the normal working pressure.
(4) There are no close-fitting parts likely to jam owing to long periods of inaction.
(5) It can be tested for efficient working at any time without stopping the engine or altering the cylinder pressures.

The " Lightning " relief valve is loaded by compressed air taken from the starting air tank, a constant loading pressure being obtained by passing the air through a reducing valve before it reaches the relief valve. The loading pressure is slightly greater than the minimum pressure required to start the engine, so that variation of the starting air pressure has no effect upon the loading of the relief valve. The principle upon which this improved relief valve operates will be clear. It will be observed that instead of the valve being held in closed position by a heavy helical spring, this function is performed by a compressible bellows connected internally to the compressed-air supply.

The bellows is made of three-ply stainless steel which, being extremely flexible and durable, ensures a constant loading pressure irrespective of whether the valve is closed or fully open. When it is remembered that the loading of a valve held down by a strong helical spring increases immediately the valve begins to open, the advantage of air loading in the manner here described will be appreciated.

A spring-loaded valve cannot be tested for load or freedom when in service unless the cylinder pressures are increased to the pressure at which it is set to operate. The " Lightning " relief valve, however, may be tested for efficient working at any time without either stopping the engine or altering the cylinder pressures. It is a matter of merely reducing the loading pressure by the very simple means provided, when the valve will begin to operate at normal working cylinder pressures. When satisfied that the valve is free to act as required, the loading pressure is put back to normal, when the valve will again be loaded to the predetermined pressure and remain closed.

CHAPTER 12

Exhaust and air-inlet valve maintenance

Although the four-stroke engine, which mostly makes use of exhaust valves, is the less in favour of the two types at present, it is not unlikely that it will in time regain some of its lost popularity. One reason for this statement is that if the diesel engine is to remain in the lead for all powers it will require to be highly supercharged, and because of the four-stroke engine's more positive method of ejecting the products of combustion from the cylinders and re-charging them with air, it can be supercharged to a considerably higher degree than the two-stroke. Moreover, some makes of two-stroke engines employ an exhaust valve in the cylinder head, and exhaust valve maintenance remains so important a matter that no apology is needed for devoting an entire chapter to it and the air-inlet valve.

Exhaust valves require more frequent attention than any other part of an engine. The length of time such valves will operate before they should be removed for overhaul varies from three to six months. In some ships the valves are in quite good condition after a much longer period of service but, on the other hand, there are cases where burning of the faces will be found to have taken place in less than three months.

The frequency with which these valves require overhauling depends, apart from the quality of the material used in their manufacture, upon various factors, such as the exhaust-gas temperature, the thought and care with which the valves are overhauled and fitted in working position, and the amount of solid impurities contained in the air and fuel. Purifying the fuel before use by means of centrifugal separators greatly lengthens the period between overhauls. Excessive lubrication of the cylinder has a detrimental effect upon exhaust valves, owing to the particles of unburnt carbon lodging on the ground faces. Imperfect combustion will affect the exhaust valves similarly.

If the gases which pass through the exhaust valves could first be filtered so that all solids, such as particles of earthy matter and partially burnt carbon, were extracted, and if other conditions mentioned earlier in the chapter were normal, the faces of these valves would require considerably less attention. As it is impossible to purify the exhaust gases, some of the particles of partially burnt carbon from the fuel or lubricating oil lodge on the faces during the exhausting process, and are jammed and become firmly attached to one or other of the faces when the valve re-seats. During subsequent exhaust strokes the particles of carbon are made to glow, being combustible, by the hot exhaust gases passing over them, and eventually burn shallow holes, commonly called pits, in the faces.

The amount of overhauling required by exhaust valves can therefore be greatly reduced by purifying the fuel before it enters the cylinders, maintaining the highest possible combustion efficiency, and injecting no more lubricating oil than is necessary to ensure efficient lubrication of the piston rings. From what has been said it will be easy to understand why exhaust valves always require to be overhauled more frequently when certain inferior brands of cylinder lubricating oil are employed.

The best practice is to change and grind the exhaust valves at regular intervals, since if they are left in service too long at a time, the pitting will be so extensive that it will be necessary to machine off a large amount of metal before an unbroken surface is obtained. This is to be avoided if at all possible, as the further the metal is cut into the softer it becomes, and the lower is its resistance to the causes of pitting. If, say, two exhaust valves are removed after two months' continuous service and their condition closely observed, the length of time that the valves of any particular engine will run safely can be gauged and the periodical grinding of the faces regulated accordingly. When, however, a different grade of fuel is shipped, further consideration will be necessary, but if the exhaust gases remain clear and the temperature-increase in the gas does not exceed 2 per cent, the running period of the valves will not, as a rule, be materially affected.

Air-inlet and exhaust valves—generally the former, as they give so little trouble and in consequence are apt to be left in service too long at a time—are sometimes rather difficult to remove owing to accumulation of carbon and dirt between the fitting parts of the housing and the wall of the pocket. Although air-inlet valves operate for many months and even years without requiring any attention whatsoever, yet they should not be neglected on that account. If left in too long they may become " frozen " in and be exceedingly difficult to remove. There have been cases where it was impossible to remove such valves without seriously damaging them. A thin coating of mercurial ointment on the fitting parts of air-inlet valves will prevent them becoming jammed, while it is

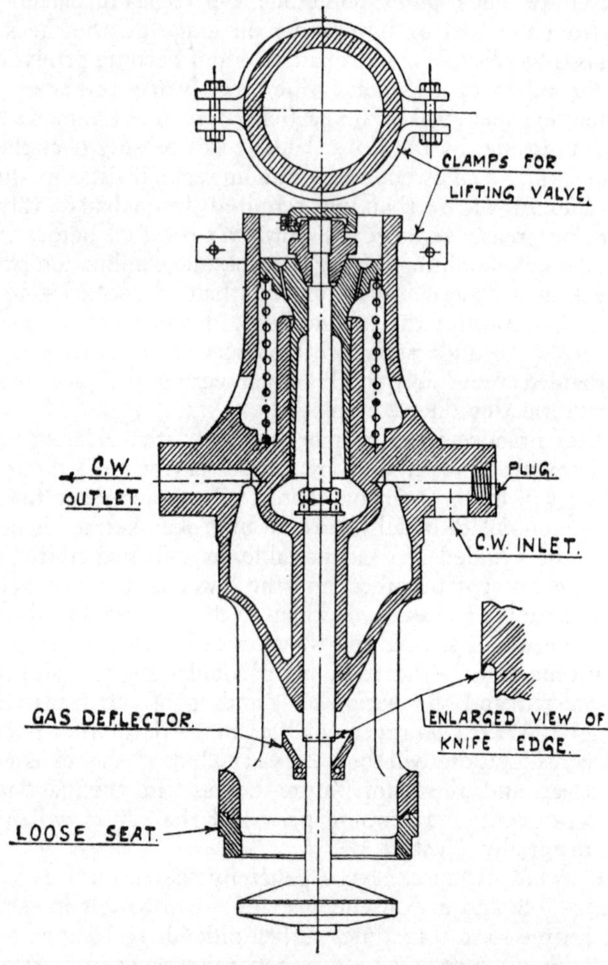

Fig. 84—Air-inlet and exhaust valve withdrawing gear

advisable to sandwich a rubber ring between the underside of the flange and the cylinder head to prevent dirt and water finding their way into the valve pocket. Care must, however, be taken to see that the rubber ring or whatever else is used do not prevent the valve housing from landing properly.

As a rule air-inlet and exhaust valves can be removed by applying only sufficient force to overcome the weight of the valve. When they become jammed in the cylinder head through neglect or some fault in the fitting or operation, however, their removal calls for careful thought if waste of time or damage to the valve is to be avoided. Such valves are generally provided with screwed holes for lifting eye-bolts or starting screws. If not, a clamp around the casing as shown in Fig. 84 should be employed. The lifting tackle must be located exactly in line with the valve spindle, so that a direct pull is obtained. A few inches out of alignment will reduce the effective force of the lifting tackle far more than is realised by many junior engineers.

Should a valve resist a reasonable pull on a set of one-ton chain blocks, tap the housing sharply, first on one side and then on the other, with a hammer, whilst keeping a good strain on the blocks. If it is then necessary to drive fox wedges under the flanges of the housing, this must be very carefully done, as it is an easy matter to break flanges and destroy totally the housing in this way. Two wedges at least must always be used and be driven in diametrically opposite each other, and at points as near to the body of the housing as possible. If greater force than this is necessary to start a valve, a bar can be jammed between the piston top and the underside of the valve and the crankshaft rotated by the *hand* turning gear. Another method, and one that the most stubborn of valves is not likely to resist, is first to take out the valve spindle after the removal of one of the other cylinder-head valves—or even the piston if it cannot be removed in any other way—and make and employ the withdrawing gear shown in Fig. 85, which is self-explanatory. To ensure the desired results, however, it would be as well to mention that the draw bolt and the U-shaped strong back should be of heavy cross-section, and the span between the legs of the latter should be the least possible, for obvious reasons. If a tight valve-housing is given a few blows, first on one side and then on the other with this withdrawing gear in operation, its resistance will soon be overcome.

In large engines the depth of the cylinder head is so great that to remove the valve spindle and insert the draw bolt it will be necessary to attach a piece of wire to the upper end of the spindle before it is lowered into the cylinder. The wire can then be hooked by a rod bent to shape and passed through the air-inlet valve pocket, and the exhaust valve spindle with wire attached withdrawn. The end of the wire is then transferred to the draw bolt which is lowered into the cylinder and pulled through the exhaust-valve housing.

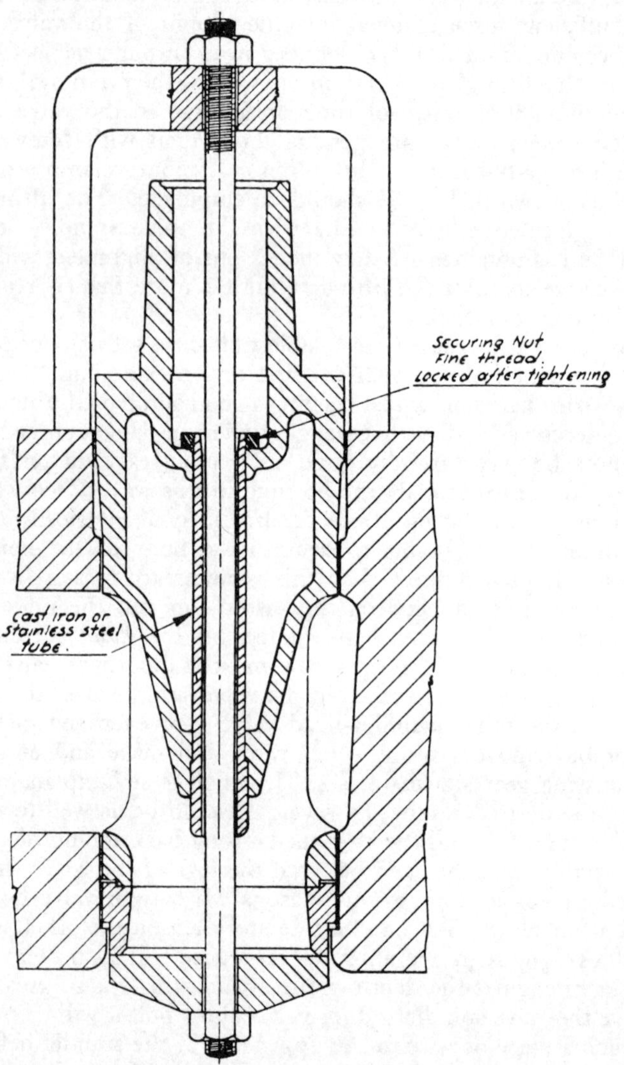

Fig. 85—Cylinder-head valve withdrawing gear: method of repairing housing

In some instances the valve spindle cannot be removed in the manner suggested owing to the lid extending beyond the cylinder bore, as shown in Fig. 30. In such cases it will be necessary to drill and tap two holes in the flange of the housing to take draw studs, if the housing cannot be removed in any other way. If it is not possible or desirable to do this, it is generally wise to remove the piston and drive the valve housing out rather than waste further time trying to draw it out.

Although formerly not uncommon it is now very rare indeed to experience any difficulty in removing the spindle from an exhaust-valve housing owing to accumulation of carbon in the clearance spaces between the spindle and its tubular guide, providing the fuel is burnt properly and the cylinders are not excessively lubricated. Occasionally, however, constituents in certain fuels cause a sticky substance to deposit on these surfaces, and care must be exercised if the valve spindle is to be removed without damaging it. On no account should a spindle be driven out by means of blows delivered on the screwed end by a heavy hammer, as, apart from knocking up the last few threads, the screwed portion may be weakened at the point where it joins the plain part to such an extent that it will break off when in service, with serious consequences. In the event of the valve not being required immediately, a solvent such as paraffin should be applied at regular and frequent intervals for a few days, and the necessary force may be applied by specially made gear, as shown in Fig. 86, without fear of damaging any of the parts.

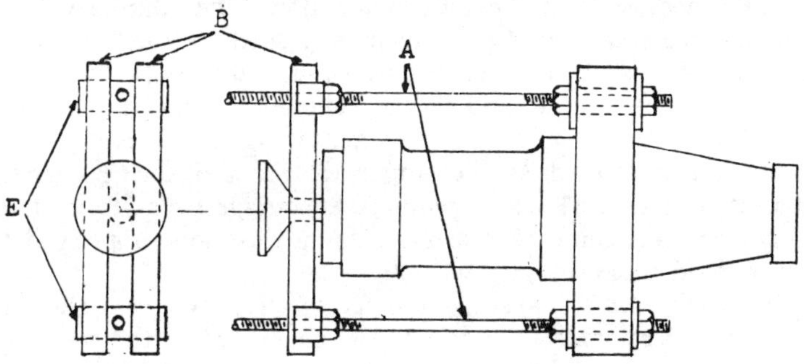

Fig. 86—Method of removing tight exhaust-valve spindle from casing

After an air-inlet or exhaust valve has been dismantled, the various parts should be thoroughly cleaned, particularly the spindle and the bore of the guide in the housing. The fact that the spindle is a free sliding fit should not deter one from examining the sliding surfaces, and scraping off any deposit found there. An old large round or half-round file and a rag soaked in paraffin will do all that is necessary. This work should be looked upon as an important part of the operation of overhauling such valves, as a spindle that is not a perfectly free working fit may prevent the lid re-seating properly without this being readily noticed, and may either prevent an engine from being started owing to the starting air escaping from the cylinder or, if the jamming occurs while the engine is working, the faces of the lid and seat may be quickly damaged beyond repair.

Spindles of exhaust valves should be an easy fit in the housing as, when the parts reach working temperatures, such spindles expand to a greater extent than the guide in the housing, which is surrounded by cooling water. On the other hand, there must not be too much clearance otherwise there will be a greater tendency for solid matter to accumulate around the spindle. The correct diametrical clearance for a $1\frac{1}{2}$-inch diameter spindle is about $\frac{4}{1000}$ inch. Water-cooled exhaust-valve spindles can be made a finer fit, but both types must have clearance in order to allow the lubricant, usually fuel or a mixture of thin fuel and lubricating oil, to penetrate between the sliding surfaces. Many valves work quite well without any lubricant, and lubricant should only be applied if this is not the case.

When difficulties are experienced with exhaust-valve spindles jamming owing to carbonised oil depositing on the sliding surfaces, a deflector attached to the spindle, as illustrated in Fig. 84, might prove beneficial. The upper end of the spindle guide should be bell-mouthed, so that the oil flowing down the spindle will have a better chance of getting where it is needed. When the bearing part of the spindle is enlarged as shown, it should overrun the lower end of the guide, and the end should be shaped as shown so that it will tend to push the solid matter before it. An oil trough is sometimes formed at the upper end of the spring carrier as illustrated in Fig. 84. This tends to encourage over-lubrication, as many engineers think they are not doing their job properly if they do not flood these troughs with oil.

The cooling-water spaces of exhaust-valve housings should be examined occasionally. Owing to the small size of the openings it is not possible to sight the inside of the jackets, and it is not wise to remove the core plugs usually found in the body of the housings more than is absolutely necessary. Normal requirements will be met if the valve is turned upside down and the loose scale and other solid matter removed through the cooling-water openings. Striking the housing with blows from a hammer while in this position will loosen some of the scale and enable it to be removed by means of a piece of wire bent at the end. A simple way to ascertain

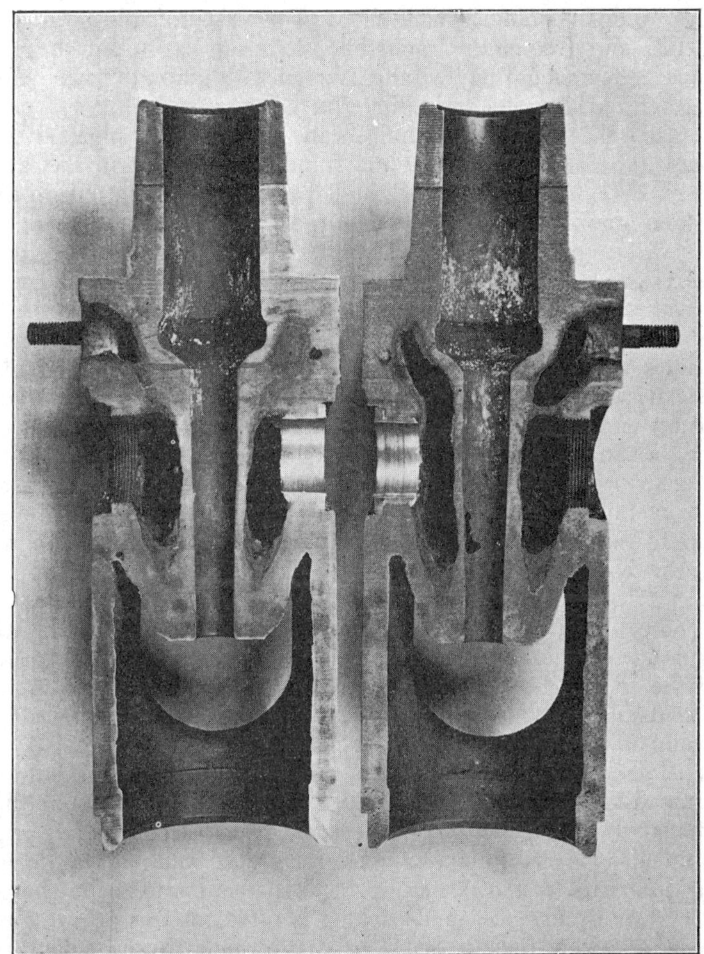

Fig. 87—Exhaust valve cut open to show corrosion and accumulation of deposit

when this is necessary, or in other words to find out how much solid matter is present in the spaces, is to compare the quantity of water the jacket will hold with the quantity required to fill the space in a new valve. The exhaust valve shown in Fig. 87 will be of interest, and serve as a warning against neglect of this part of the overhauling operation.

Core plugs should be made of brass as cast-iron plugs are very difficult, and frequently impossible, to remove. When they are removed they should be liberally covered with graphite paste before being refitted, in order to facilitate further removal.

Usually the valve faces require only to be ground together, but should it be necessary to put the spindle or the seat in the lathe, care must be taken to see that the part is correctly centred, so that the least amount of metal will require to be removed, and that the parts will remain in correct alignment. The angle of the mitre faces is generally 45° to the horizontal. The spindle must be set up in the lathe true to the shank, and not the valve face, as the lid may have had a blow and be bent, or may have become distorted. Spindles are sometimes bent owing to operating the turning gear carelessly with one of the pistons " hung " in the top of the cylinder. In most engines there is sufficient clearance to allow for this being done, but in some instances the valve lid would be jammed against the piston. It is, therefore, advisable always to place the reversing gear in mid-position and open the indicator cocks to prevent accumulation of pressure in the cylinders, when work in progress necessitates hanging-up a piston. If the rocking-lever roller clearance of any of the air-inlet and exhaust valves is found to be more than it ought to be after an overhaul of the nature mentioned, the possibility of the valve lid having been forced against the piston and the spindle bent should be considered. If there is any doubt about damage having been done the valve should be removed for examination.

The point at which the lid is attached to the spindle should be examined for cracks and to make sure that they are firmly connected and that no leakage of gas between them can occur. The spring should also be carefully examined for cracks and its free length compared with that of a new spring. If it is found to be short—a very rare occurrence—and packing is fitted for this or any other reason, take care that the valve is not prevented from opening the normal amount by the spring being compressed solid. Whatever arrangements are provided to prevent the spindle from falling into the cylinder in the event of the screwed end breaking off, these should be examined also. Generally, air-inlet and exhaust valves are, of necessity, located as far away from the centre of the cylinder head as possible, and the upper end of the cylinder liner is, of course, recessed in way of the valves to a depth sufficient to allow them to open fully. In such cases, should a valve spindle break, it would be prevented from falling into the cylinder and causing extensive damage. The arrangements provided to prevent the nut on the end of the spindle from unscrewing should receive careful attention, as should unscrewing occur while the engine is in operation the valve will be prevented from re-seating and the faces will be quickly burnt.

To grind the faces together the valve should be turned upside down and the spindle rotated to and fro by means of a double-handled tool. If a single-handled tool such as a spanner is used, care must be taken not to force the lid to one side when rotating it. The pressure between the surfaces being ground must be the same at all points, otherwise it will be impossible to make a satisfactory job. A coarse grinding powder formed into a thick paste by mixing it with fuel oil, followed by crocus powder, is generally necessary for these valves. After the pitting has been removed in this way, the faces should be lightly wiped and rubbed together again until they are dry and highly polished. If the surfaces tend to tear before this is accomplished, apply a little fuel oil to act as a lubricant. This is a very important part of the operation and should be continued until all scratches made by the grinding powder are completely removed. Moreover, the degree of brightness should be uniform all round. If dull places exist, further grinding is necessary if the best results are to be obtained.

When the surfaces have been properly ground together all parts in the vicinity should be thoroughly cleaned, and the ground surfaces thinly covered with lubricating oil in order to protect them against the corrosive action of moist air. All sliding surfaces should be treated similarly. It usually happens that an air-inlet or exhaust valve is not required for some time after it is overhauled. In such an event the lid and seat should always be separated, i.e. the valve opened sufficiently to permit the whole of the upper surface of the lid to be wiped just prior to the assembled valve being fitted into working position, as dirt generally enters through the ports and deposits on the lid. If this dirt is not removed some of it may become jammed between the faces and cause them to leak when the engine begins working, and those in charge will be at a loss to understand why the valve requires to be changed because it is leaking after only a few days or even hours in service.

Refitting the assembled valve into working position is another very important part of the operation. Careless refitting, or neglect to attend to what might appear to be a minor detail that may be left to the greaser assisting with the work, may be the cause of an involuntary stop at sea to change the valve. In the first place, the outside of the valve and the pocket into which it is to be fitted must be entirely free from dirt and scale. When cleaning the walls of valve pockets, fit a cardboard disc having means of being lifted out, at the bottom of the pocket to catch the dirt and prevent it entering the cylinder. When the valve is lowered into working position all possibility of dirt or scale being dislodged and falling on the ledge in the cylinder head, where it would prevent the valve from landing properly, must be avoided, as, if the surfaces are not properly gas-tight, the flame of combustion will penetrate between them and very soon burn a hole large enough to make the housing seat—and very possibly the cylinder head—of no further use.

Because the gas escaping from a defective housing joint, in the case of exhaust valves, passes direct into the exhaust passage, a slight leak between the housing and the cylinder head cannot be readily detected and the leakage will consequently continue until the joining surfaces are seriously damaged. In air-inlet valves of atmospheric four-stroke engines, leakage between these parts will be indicated by sound at the moment fuel injection takes place. The air systems of four-stroke supercharged engines and two-stroke valve-scavenged engines, however, are entirely enclosed, and not only is it practically impossible to detect slight leakages between the valve and the cylinder head until the parts are seriously damaged, but leakage in such cases is positively dangerous. The containing walls of enclosed air systems, especially in the type of four-stroke engines in which the undersides of the working cylinders are used as supercharger air pumps, generally become covered with greasy matter, and if the air-inlet valves should leak in the manner described there is a grave danger of the flame of combustion causing a fire in the air passages, the serious consequences of which cannot be over-estimated. From this will doubtless be fully realised the vital importance of taking all steps necessary to ensure the joint between the valve housings and the cylinder head being absolutely gas-tight.

The valves should drop freely into position in the cylinder heads. Should a valve not do so there is only one proper thing to do, and that is to take it out and ease by filing the part of the housing that is fouling. If too free—or rather if the fitting parts of the housing are very much less in diameter than the pocket into which it fits—then burnt gases will escape into the engine room in the case of an exhaust valve, and particles of dirt will be drawn into the cylinder if air-inlet valves of atmospheric four-stroke engines are too slack. Air will escape outwards from air-inlet valves of supercharged four-stroke engines or scavenging air valves of two-stroke engines. In such an event leakage can be stopped by fitting a rubber ring or turn of asbestos cord around the body of the valve immediately under the flange. In doing so, however, care must be taken to see that the packing is not so thick that it prevents the housing making good contact with the landing edge at the lower end of the pocket. Because of this possibility packing should be fitted only in extreme cases. No such action should be taken if the leakage is only slight, or if noise is produced at the moment the exhaust valve opens, as the leakage and noise will probably stop when the parts become heated to normal working temperatures.

Before air-inlet and exhaust valves are lowered into position the joining surfaces must be perfectly clean, and one of the surfaces—preferably that of the valve, as the other surface can be more easily sighted when the valve is lifted—given a thin covering of red marking to test the surfaces for bearing evenly all round. If the surfaces are bearing all round but with a varying degree of pressure, it will be necessary to grind the surfaces. The surface in the cylinder head can be ground in the usual way by means of an old valve seat, kept for the purpose, which should periodically be machined true in the lathe. The valve surface can be ground by a cast-iron ring of fairly heavy cross-section made to fit over the reduced end of the housing. This grinding tool also should periodically be machined true in the lathe.

When a valve bears on about one-half of the landing only it indicates that one or other of the surfaces is not quite square with the pocket. This fault is usually found in the cylinder-head surface, and is due to insufficient care being exercised during grinding operations. In such cases it will probably be found that the housing is bearing hard against one side of the pocket, and if filed at this point the surfaces will make proper contact all round. For reasons already given it is not good practice to do this, however, so that when grinding these surfaces care must be taken not to grind them out of proper alignment. As already stated, this fault usually occurs in the cylinder-head surface, so that a gauge should be made to check the alignment after each grinding operation. A suitable gauge consists of a truly machined steel disc, of a size that covers the landing surface, with a round rod fixed exactly in the centre of the disc and perpendicular to it and extending to the top of the valve pocket, so that when resting on the landing the distance between the rod and the side of the pocket can be measured at all points.

The dimensions of the grinding tools should be such that as much of the joining surfaces as possible is covered and ground by them. That is to say, the one for grinding the landing in the cylinder head should be the full diameter of the pocket, and the one used to grind the surface on the housing should be a good fit around the reduced end, so as to ensure that the smallest possible ridges are left at the outside and inside of the cylinder head and housing surfaces respectively. If the tools are of the size recommended it will only be necessary to chamfer slightly the inside edge of the landing in the cylinder head and the outside of the surface on the housing to ensure that the surfaces make proper contact.

Just prior to a valve being finally lowered into working position, the ground surfaces of the housing should be given a covering of boiled oil. White lead and other forms of jointing material are not suitable and are unnecessary if the surfaces are properly ground together.

Sometimes copper rings are found interposed between the joining surfaces. Such rings are effective in cases where the surfaces are only very slightly uneven. Even then they should not be greater than 1 mm thick. The trouble likely to be experienced with thicker copper rings is that owing to the comparatively large expansion properties of copper, the metal is compressed and takes a permanent set when the parts become heated, with the result that when the engine cools off the ring is not jammed with the requisite pressure. During the first few revolutions of the engine when started up again, and whilst the ring is still relatively cool, the gas pressure in the cylinder tends to ease the valve housing off the ring and leakage of the burning gases may occur and quickly destroy the ring, and, maybe, the cast iron at each side of it.

Once cast-iron surfaces are properly ground together they never leak, and require very little attention apart from an occasional rub up as described earlier. If copper rings must be used they should be removed each time the valve is overhauled, the surface underneath cleaned, and the ring softened by heating and quenching in water. The nuts holding the valve in place should be tested for tightness after the engine has cooled down.

If, owing to machining or repeated grinding of the joining surfaces, there is not sufficient clearance between the underside of the flange and the top of the cylinder head to allow the landing surfaces to make hard contact, and it is necessary to raise the position of the valve in relation to the cylinder head, a distance piece should be sandwiched between the housing and the loose seat, and not under the seat. Such packing rings should be made of steel or cast iron. The first impulse is always to fit copper because this metal is softer than iron and will more readily bed itself into an uneven surface. Experience has proved over and over again, however, that it is far better to take a little more time over the repair and fit packing of harder material, which, when once properly fitted, requires no more attention than cast-iron surfaces.

The operation of tightening down the nuts holding the air-inlet and exhaust valves, particularly the latter, in place must be done with particular care. The nuts must be tightened up evenly to ensure an even pressure on the gas-tight joint. Excessive weight on these nuts is quite unnecessary, and may even be the cause of serious trouble, by distorting the valve seat and causing certain parts of the valve faces to make light contact. In some engines it is rather difficult to exert the necessary pressure on the surfaces without distorting the valve seat, owing to its light construction. Deep and moderately thick seats always give the best results, and when an unusual amount of overhauling is necessary to keep the exhaust-valve faces in good order, the question of increasing the depth should be considered.

Distortion of the valve seat results in large measure from the necessity for a large opening in one side of the housing for the passage of the gases. The presence of this opening causes the pressure exerted by the holding-down bolts and the expansion of the housing to be unevenly distributed, it being least at the point immediately under the middle of the opening. Such a large opening is not really necessary, and much better results are obtained by providing a larger number of smaller openings, as shown in Fig. 88.

On occasions the flanges of exhaust valves are broken at the point where they join the housing. This mostly occurs in lightly constructed valves, and happens when tightening the nuts securing the valve in position. Occasionally, however, fracture takes place only after the engine has been working for some time at full power. The cause of this is probably excessive tightening of the holding-down bolts. The initial stress produced in the flanges in this way, added to the stresses resulting from the greater expansion of the lower part of the housing compared with the expansion of the cylinder head, and the gas pressure in the cylinder during the

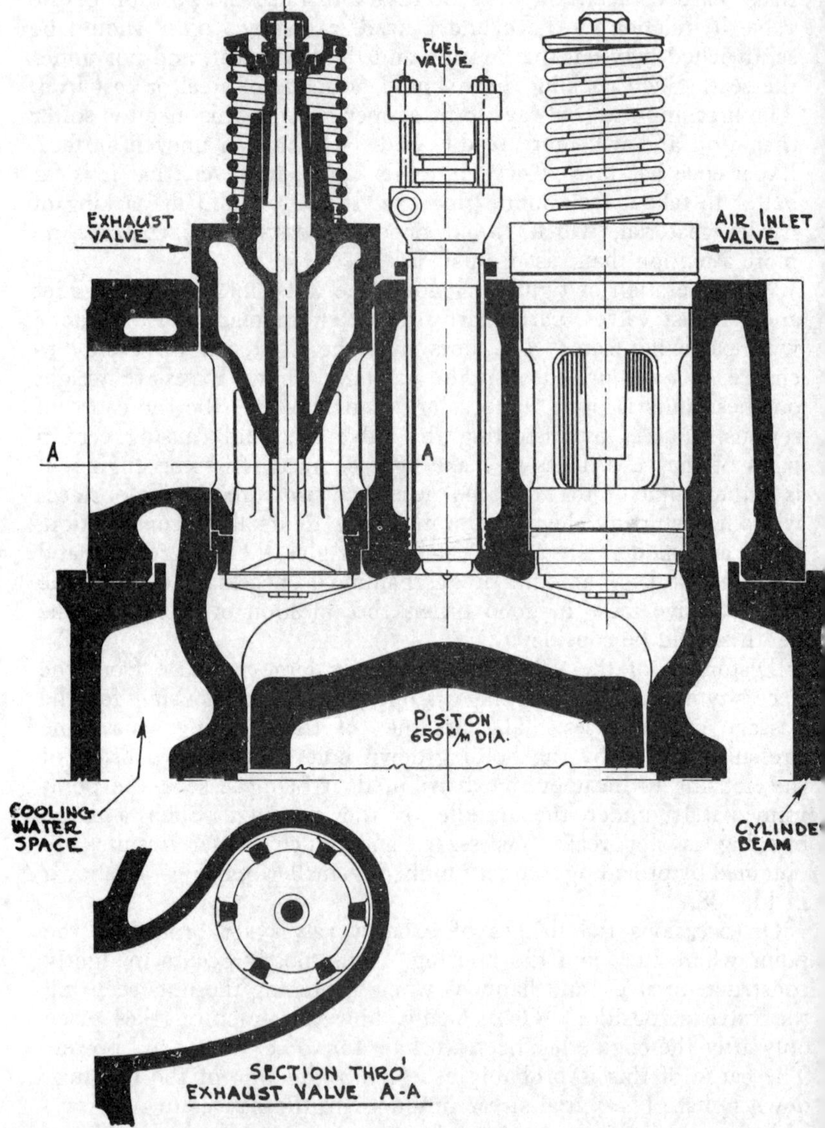

Fig. 88—Modified form of exhaust valve housing to ensure more even pressure on landing in cylinder head

working stroke, is too great, and the valve breaks in the manner described.

It is probably just as well that the valve casing fractures when these conditions prevail, because if it is so strongly constructed that it is able to withstand such enormous stresses there would be a grave possibility of the stresses being too great for the cylinder head, in which case this larger and much more costly part would fracture circumferentially in the wall forming the exhaust-valve pocket. A moment's thought will suffice to convince one that that part of an exhaust-valve housing situated between the landing edge in the cylinder head and the securing nuts is bound to expand more than the wall of the valve pocket, which is surrounded by circulating cooling water.

Excessive weight on these holding-down nuts is quite unnecessary. The leverage offered by a standard spanner followed by a few blows with a 14-lb hammer, is all that is required to ensure the valve being gas-tight. A fact sometimes lost sight of is that if there is " draw " on a metal-to-metal joint it means that the surfaces have not been properly cleaned, or that the parts are not fitting together properly. Excessive tightening of a nut will over-stress a bolt or stud without having real effect upon the joint, but in the case of cylinder-head valves it is the flanges that are strained and, being made of cast iron, it is no wonder that they sometimes break.

Where it is impossible to tighten the nuts with an ordinary spanner, a special form of box spanner should be procured for the purpose. Tube spanners are very suitable for these nuts, being easy to handle and quite strong enough. Where recourse must be made to a heavy hammer and long set chisel, packing pieces should be fitted around each stud between the underside of the flange and the top of the cylinder head to prevent the flanges being broken by injudicious tightening. If the packing pieces are made 0·2 mm smaller than the space into which they are to be fitted, when the valve housing is resting on the landing, the surfaces will make sufficiently hard contact to prevent leakage of gas when the nuts are tightened by the amount that causes the packing pieces to be gripped.

In some makes of large engines the exhaust valves are held down in place by unusually long studs, three or four times longer than they need otherwise be, a tubular distance-piece being interposed between the nut and the flange. The reason for this is that the exhaust-valve housing expands a considerable amount under working temperature conditions. As allowance cannot be conveniently made for expansion when tightening the nuts, since the joint must be gas-tight when the engine is started up and cold, and ordinary short studs would be stretched when the parts become heated and damage done, the studs are therefore made very long, so that as the housing expands the stretch resulting in the studs will take place over a greater length, and consequently the studs will

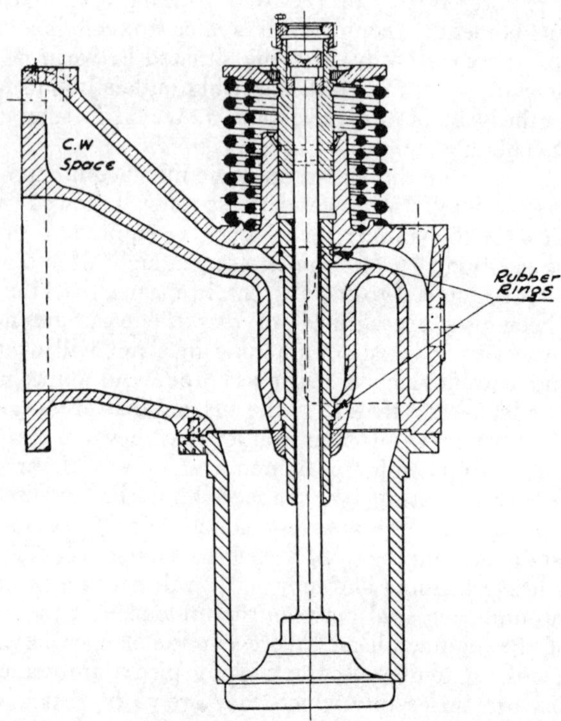

Fig. 89—Exhaust valve, the lower part of housing of which is free to expand (Burmeister & Wain)

not be weakened to the same extent as would be the case if short studs were employed. In other words, the elastic limit of the material would be reached in short studs much sooner than in long studs.

The Burmeister and Wain exhaust valve, illustrated in Fig. 89, solves many of the difficulties referred to in the preceding pages. As will be observed, the gas-tight joint is formed at the top of the pocket instead of at the bottom, as in the more orthodox types, the lower part of the housing hanging in the pocket, as it were. This simple difference eliminates almost entirely the probability of distorting the seat when tightening the securing nuts, and the possibility of damage being done due to the housing expanding to a greater extent than the pocket when the parts become heated. This type of valve requires to be overhauled less frequently than the ordinary type, which proves beyond doubt that distortion of the seat is a contributory cause of exhaust valves leaking. The spindle guide, it will be observed, is a separate part, it being held firmly in position by a nut on the lower end, and leakage of cooling water between the housing and the guide is prevented by rubber rings. If the parts are jointed with Manganisite and the nut properly tightened and locked, no trouble occurs with this arrangement.

Some exhaust-valve housings corrode and allow cooling water to leak into the gas spaces. The corrosion occurs on the water side of the spindle guide or at any point subjected to casting stresses. These points are at the junction of varying thicknesses of metal, and result when the casting is cooling during manufacture, the smaller thicknesses cooling more rapidly and causing the metal at certain places to be over-stressed. These casting stresses cause the metal to be spongy, in which condition it is more susceptible to corrosion.

The first indication of defects of this character is the exhaust spindle running dry and water issuing from around the valve spindle. In some cases the first indication is a fine spray of dirty water being discharged with the exhaust gases and falling on to the deck. In such an event the defective valve will be located by opening the exhaust-gas test cocks and allowing the gases to impinge on a mirror or piece of blotting paper. If the leakage is so bad that water issues from around the spindle, or its presence is indicated by merely holding the hand over the exhaust-gas test cock, it is advisable to stop the engine and change the valve, as the water will corrode the exhaust pipe, and it is not safe to begin manoeuvring an engine with water leaking from these valves, since when the engine is at rest the water will most likely find its way into the cylinder.

A valve that corroded through the spindle guide is shown in Fig. 87 and 91, while one that corroded through an over-stressed part of the casting is shown in Fig. 90. Referring again to Fig. 87, it is interesting to note how the upper part of the bore of the spindle guide has enlarged. This enlargement is due to corrosion and results from the sulphurous gases in the exhaust condensing and forming sulphuric acid, which attacks cast iron. It will be observed that the part of the guide attacked is the part which is surrounded by cooling water and which consequently operates at a lower temperature than the lower part, the temperature of which is too high to condense the sulphurous gases. The spindle of this particular valve had much more clearance than that recommended earlier in the chapter, but as the clearance was not so great as to allow gas to pass when the

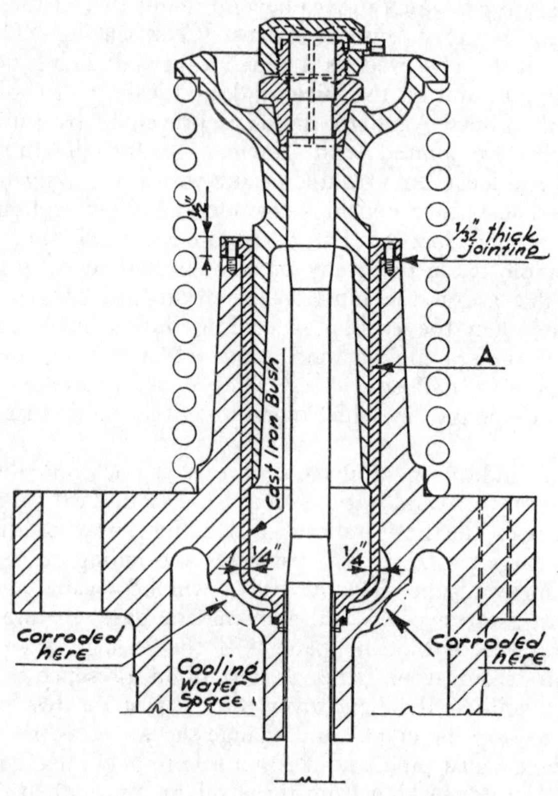

Fig. 90—Repair carried out to a corroded exhaust-valve housing

engine was working, this case will serve to illustrate the necessity of keeping the spindles a reasonably good fit in their housings.

To repair the valve shown in Fig. 87 by boring out the hole for the spindle and fitting a cast-iron or stainless-steel flanged bush with the flange uppermost, as shown in Fig. 91, is a simple matter, and will prove entirely satisfactory if the bush is made a push fit for an inch or so of its length at each end and given a coat of red lead paint before it is fitted. The hole in the housing, and the outside of the bush, should be stepped as shown to facilitate fitting in place. When this part of the housing is too thin to allow this to

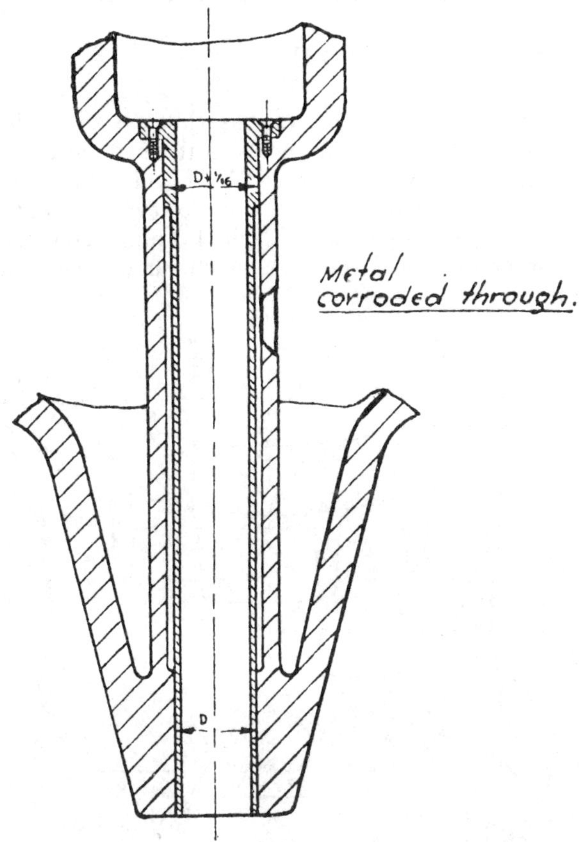

Fig. 91—Enlarged view of repair to exhaust-valve spindle guide

be done, a complete new tubular guide may be fitted as shown in Fig. 85. After the ring nut at the upper end of the tube has been tightened, the end should be riveted over to prevent the nut becoming loose.

CHAPTER 13

Piston materials and construction

Marine engine pistons have at various times been made of cast steel and mild steel, but they are now mostly made of close-grained cast iron. Cast steel pistons proved unreliable, while mild steel pistons are costly to produce. They are, however, sometimes made in two parts, the part in contact with the burning gases being made of heat-resisting steel, and the part which carries the piston rings of cast iron.

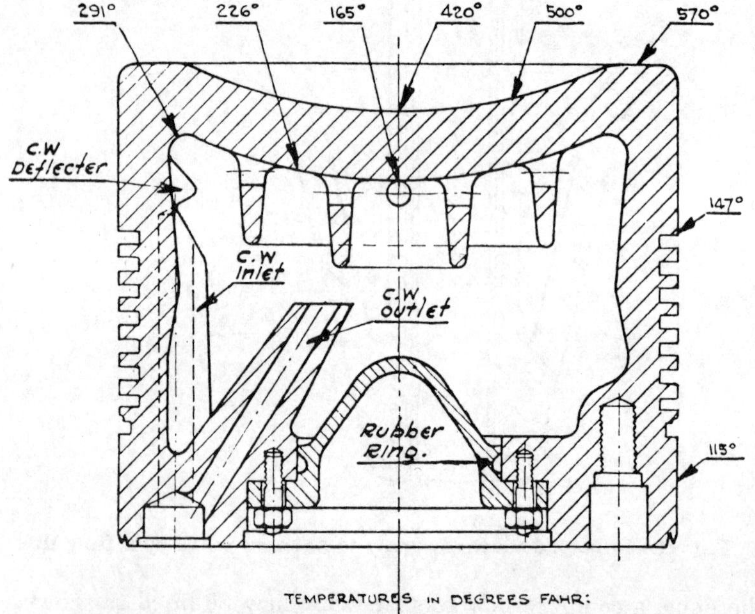

Fig. 92—Example of piston with self-supporting crown; showing also the normal working temperatures at various parts of a 4-stroke engine piston

Whichever material is used, pistons must be hollow, and when the diameter exceeds about 12 inches, water or lubricating oil must be circulated through them in order to carry off some of the heat absorbed from the burning gases and so maintain them at a moderately low temperature.

Pistons are a free fit in the cylinders under normal working temperature conditions, and leakage of gases through the space between the pistons and the cylinder liners is prevented by a number of outward-springing rings carried in grooves in the pistons. Figs. 92 and 100 show typical pistons for a four-stroke single-acting engine. This is the simplest form of piston used in marine practice.

Usually each cylinder is provided with one piston only in engines of both two- and four-stroke types. The fact that they operate on the single- or double-acting principle does not dictate the number of pistons employed. The Doxford engine, for instance, is a single-acting engine employing two pistons per cylinder, while the Sulzer and some other double-acting engines, also of the two-stroke type, employ one piston only per cylinder. In the Burmeister and Wain two-stroke double-acting engine three pistons are provided for each cylinder, one performing the normal function and the other two, one located at each end of the cylinder, serving the dual purpose of transmitting part of the power produced to the engine crankshaft and controlling the admission to the cylinder of scavenging air and egress of the products of combustion.

Two-stroke engine pistons

Fig. 93 illustrates a typical piston of this type of single-acting engine. The piston rod, it will be observed, is first bolted to the piston, as in the case of four-stroke engines, after which an extension, called a trunk or skirt, is bolted to the piston or the piston rod. This skirt is necessary, in port-scavenged engines, to keep the exhaust ports and scavenging air ports covered and so prevent escape of gas and low-pressure air into the engine room when the piston is in the upper part of the cylinder.

As the skirt must be an easy fit in the cylinder, arrangements are provided to prevent leakage of air and burnt gases past these two parts. Two of the methods commonly employed are shown in Figs. 93 and 94. Referring to Fig. 93, it will be seen that this is the more simple of the two, the only addition being two outward-springing rings located near the bottom of the skirt. With this method, however, it is necessary to extend the cylinder liner far enough to contain the rings when the engine crank passes over the bottom dead centre. This means a much longer cylinder, similar to the one illustrated in Fig. 10, and consequently a higher engine.

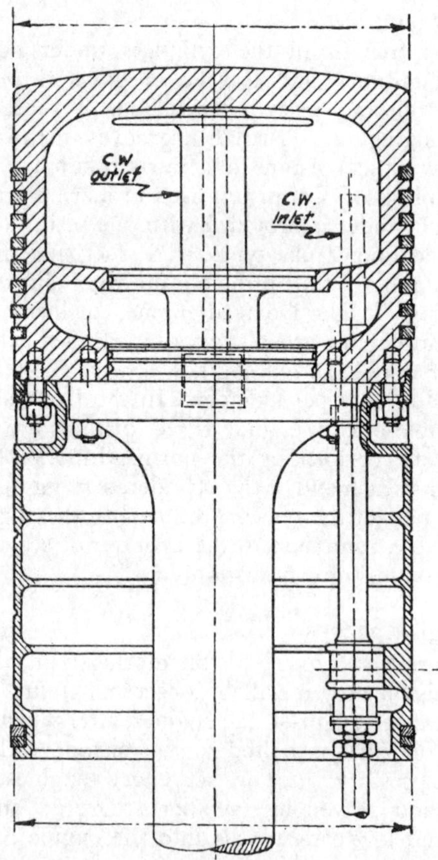

Fig. 93—Piston of 2-stroke single-acting engine

The advantage of the arrangement shown in Fig. 94 over the one just described is that no abnormal length of cylinder is necessary, as the skirt passes out of the cylinder after the crank leaves the top dead centre position. The sealing or oil-scraper rings as they are sometimes called, in this case are made to spring inwards—i.e. to be a spring fit around the skirt. The only disadvantage of this

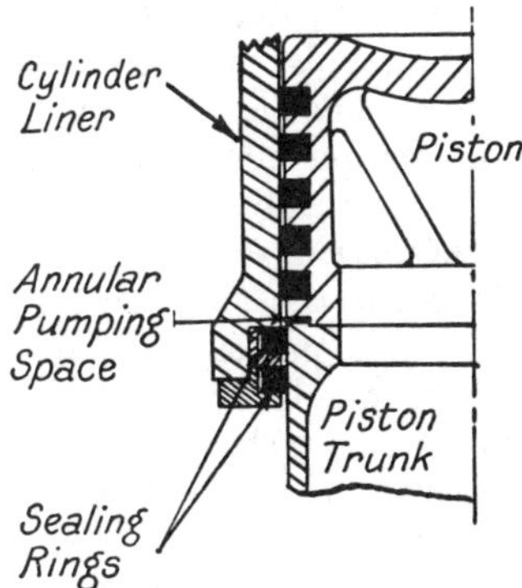

Fig. 94—Method for preventing escape of burnt gases past piston of 2-stroke engine

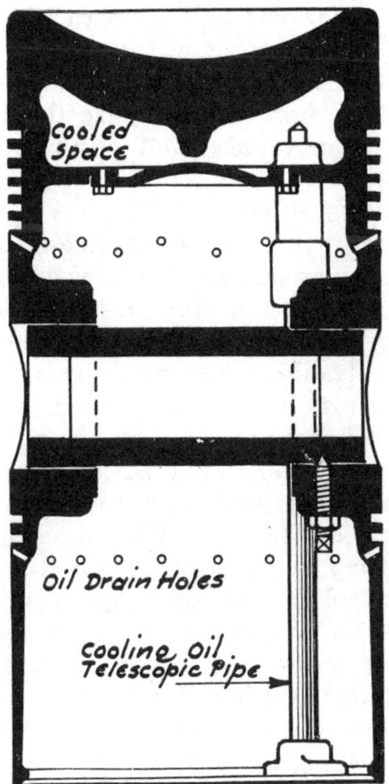

Fig. 95—Oil-cooled piston (trunk type) for engine without crosshead

arrangement is that unless particular care is taken in the design and fitting of the sealing rings the consumption of lubricating oil will be high, owing to a partial vacuum being created between the piston rings and the sealing rings on the up-stroke of the piston, the effect of which is to draw lubricating oil from the crankcase to the upper side of the sealing rings.

As with this arrangement the skirt enters the crankcase where much free lubricating oil is present, the oil-scraper rings in the bottom of the liner and the top of the crankcase must be kept perfectly free and the lower inner edges sharp, so that they will effectively scrape the oil from the skirt as it is withdrawn from the crankcase. Neglect to do so will result in large quantities of oil reaching the cylinders and being wasted. Moreover, this surplus oil will eventually cause the piston rings to jam and carbon to deposit in the exhaust ports.

The pistons of four-stroke engines are only provided with skirts where there is no piston rod and crosshead, the skirt then being necessary to take the thrust caused by the angularity of the connecting rod. A typical example of such a piston is illustrated in Fig. 95. In the case of such pistons of large size the head and skirt are sometimes made separately and bolted together.

Double-acting engine pistons

Fig. 96 illustrates a two-stroke double-acting engine piston. The upper and lower parts, (A) and (C), which make direct contact with the burning gases, are of chrome-steel or other special heat-resisting steel, while the middle portion (B) is made of good-quality cast iron. A feature of this particular make of piston is that the grooves for the piston rings are formed by forcing and afterwards caulking special wear-resisting cast-iron rings, in halves, into grooves cut in the steel ends. The advantage of this arrangement is that the surfaces of the grooves so formed which make contact with the piston rings can be ground before being fitted, and as the corresponding surfaces of piston rings are always ground there is greater resistance to enlargement of the grooves than in the ordinary type of piston. When enlargement does take place, new cast-iron rings, separating the piston rings can be fitted into the piston, and piston rings of normal width utilised. This is a great advantage in such costly pistons as it means that they can be restored to their original condition as regards size of ring grooves at small cost, and obviating the need to machine out the grooves and fit oversize rings.

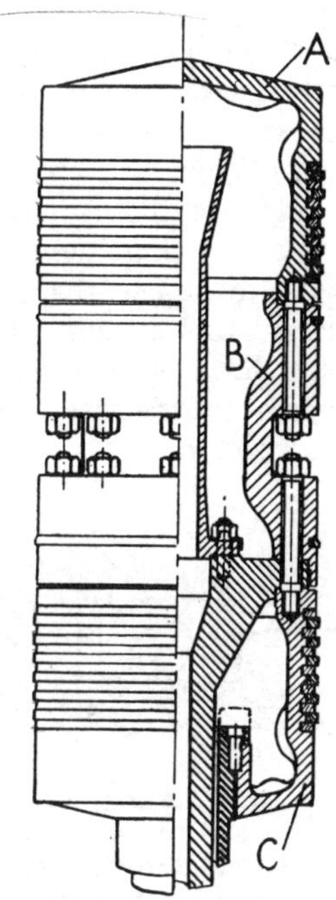

Fig. 96—Piston for double-acting 2-stroke engine

Material for pistons

The two essential properties that pistons must possess are resistance to heat stresses, and resistance to wear. Heat stresses resulting from temperature-differences in the metal can be reduced by skilful design, but not eliminated. From the point of view of heat stresses, cast iron, or forged steel are suitable materials, but greater care must be taken in the design as well as operation of cast-iron pistons if fracture is not to occur. Cast iron, however, resists enlargement of the piston-ring groove resulting from the lateral rubbing action of the rings better than the other materials mentioned, but of the two essential properties which pistons must have, resistance to heat stress is the more important.

In recent years much has been learnt about the design of pistons, and the quality of cast iron used has greatly improved, so that present-day pistons made of this material are better able to withstand heat stress than was the case a few years ago. Steel, on the other hand, has not improved to anything like the same extent in its resistance to wear. Some engine-builders employ composite pistons, the crown, which makes contact with the hot gases in the cylinder, being made of steel and the portion which carries the piston rings of cast iron. When the crowns of such pistons are cast they are generally made of chrome-molybdenum steel.

Cast steel, although allowing a greater latitude in design than forged steel, has the disadvantage that homogeneous castings, entirely free from internal or casting stresses, are not easily procurable, with the result that pistons made of this material and in this way have been known to fracture, and in some cases give inferior results to cast-iron pistons.

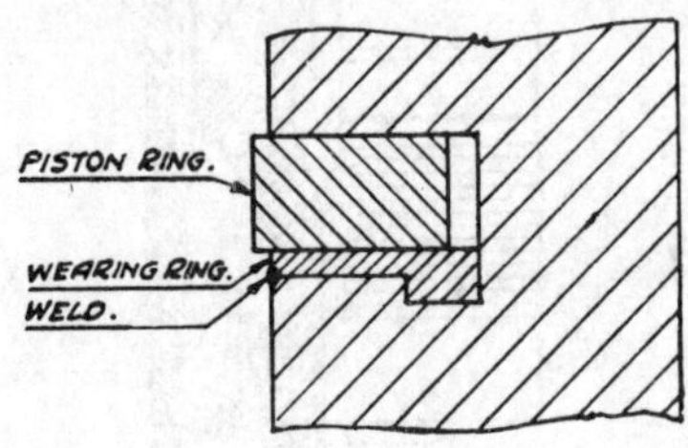

Fig. 97—Piston ring and groove, showing cast-iron wearing ring for forged steel piston

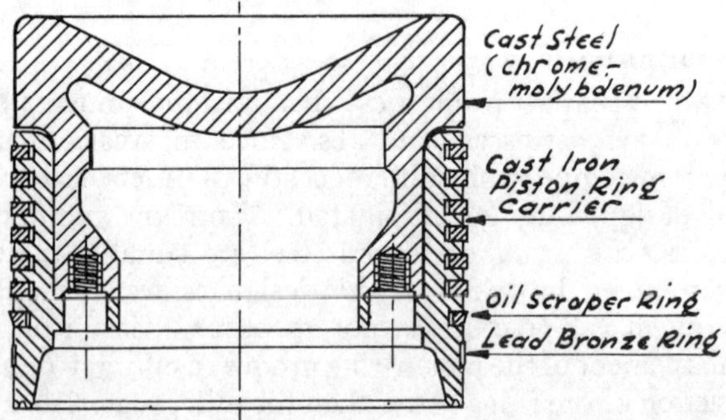

Fig. 98—Composite piston: cast steel crown and cast-iron piston-ring carrier

Forged steel, due to its much greater ductility and its manner of working, which ensures homogeneity, is more reliable than cast steel. As a matter of fact the properties of this material are such that it has never been known to fracture, and is not likely to do so even if a piston is allowed to become overheated and is then quenched with water—treatment which no cast-iron and very few cast-steel

Fig. 99—Piston with cracked crown

pistons will withstand. The disadvantage of making pistons of forged steel is that their first cost is very high because they must be machined out of a solid block.

After many years' experience with cast-iron and steel pistons, the author has found that if forged steel pistons are made of medium carbon steel of 36-40 tons tensile strength and 18 per cent minimum elongation, the enlargement of the piston ring grooves is little greater than in pistons made of good-quality cast iron, provided the maker uses only the lower part only of an ingot. When ordinary mild steel of 28-32 tons tensile strength is used the grooves enlarge rapidly and it is necessary to adopt means to prevent this. One method is to provide a thin cast-iron ring, in halves, in the bottom of each groove, as shown in Fig. 97, the wearing rings being firmly secured to the piston by welding and afterwards machined to size. Another method of getting over the difficulty is to provide a cast-iron or specially tough sleeve over a mild steel or cast steel body, as shown in Fig. 98.

The four main causes of cast-iron pistons cracking are (1) unsuitable material, (2) faulty design, (3) inefficient cooling, and (4) local overheating.

When a piston is properly designed and efficiently cooled but made of unsuitable material, the cause of cracks is due to the inability of the material to withstand the stresses produced by the normal temperature-difference of adjacent and connecting parts of varying thickness, or the normal temperature-gradient in any part one side of which is exposed to the hot gases and the other side to the comparatively cool water. The maximum temperature-difference is produced in the crown, and is in the neighbourhood of 250°F (121°C). Fig. 99 shows a piston with cracked crown.

Construction of pistons

Marine engine pistons, instead of being flat, are always either concave or convex at the top, as shown in Figs. 92 and 100 respectively, the object being to increase their strength and allow greater freedom during expansion and contraction, which naturally result when an engine is started from cold and stopped after a long run, respectively.

The convex form is better able to withstand the pressure of the gases in the cylinder and probably expands more freely, but the concave form, on the other hand, produces a combustion space nearer the ideal, which, we are told, is spherical in shape. There are, however, many engines with convex pistons giving the desired combustion efficiency. Moreover, with increasing diameters of cylinders and higher combustion pressures the piston crowns must be made thicker to withstand the pressure of the gases in the cylinders.

Increasing the thickness of this part, however, produces a greater temperature-difference and the heat stresses are therefore increased. As the convex form is stronger for a given thickness, and will expand and contract more freely, it follows that the heat stresses will be less in pistons having this shape of crown.

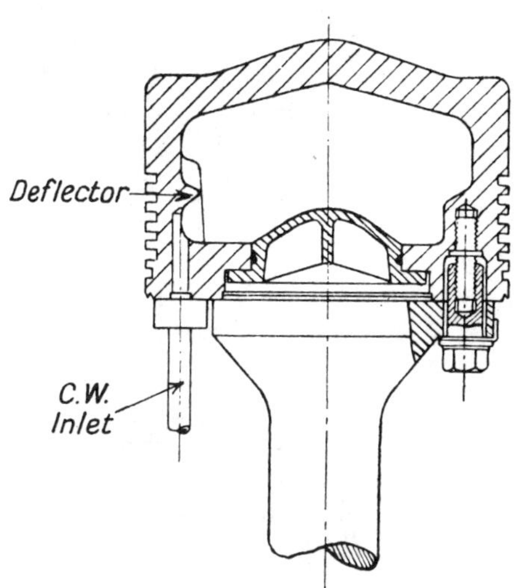

Fig. 100—4-stroke engine piston with convex crown

Originally the crowns of pistons were made comparatively thin in order to reduce as far as possible the heat stresses and, consequently, one main cause of fracture. This necessitated the employment of ribs, webs, or struts cast inside the piston to support the crown and prevent collapse under the gas pressure. Such a piston is illustrated in Fig. 101. These supports did not, in fact, prevent the deformation of the piston when it reached normal working temperature, and the supports were then overstressed and frequently broke, after which the unsupported thin crown would begin to " breathe " and eventually cause the circumferential wall to crack in the vicinity of the top piston-ring groove. Soon after this time the quality of cast iron obtainable was greatly improved, and it became almost general practice to omit all form of support inside the piston, and by thickening up the crown to make it self-supporting. This is shown clearly in Fig. 92, the whole of the piston load being transmitted to the piston rod through the circumferential wall. The two annular ribs shown serve the dual purpose of strengthening the crown and facilitating the flow of heat from the crown to the cooling medium.

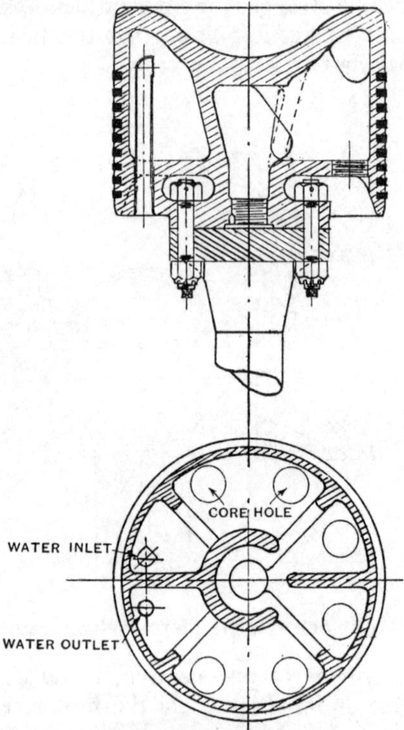

Fig. 101—Early type of piston with internally supported crown

When an engine is working at full power and the piston and other parts have attained normal working temperatures, the approximate temperatures at different parts of the piston are as shown in Fig. 92. From the values given it will be seen that the hottest part of the piston crown is at the periphery, and that there is quite an appreciable difference between the outside and inside surfaces of the crown. This difference in temperature, as already stated, depends upon the thickness of the metal at this point—the greater the thickness the higher will be the working temperature of the outer surface and, as the temperature of the inner surface is independent of the thickness of metal, the greater will be the difference in temperature and consequently the greater the stresses produced.

As the temperature of a concave-shaped piston increases, the crown expands and tends to lift or straighten out as shown by the dotted lines in Fig. 102. As the inner surface is at a lower temperature and therefore expands to a lesser extent than the outer surface, the lifting of the crown due to temperature-increase relative to other parts of the piston reduces the tensile stresses set up at the inner surface and there will be less liability to fracture.

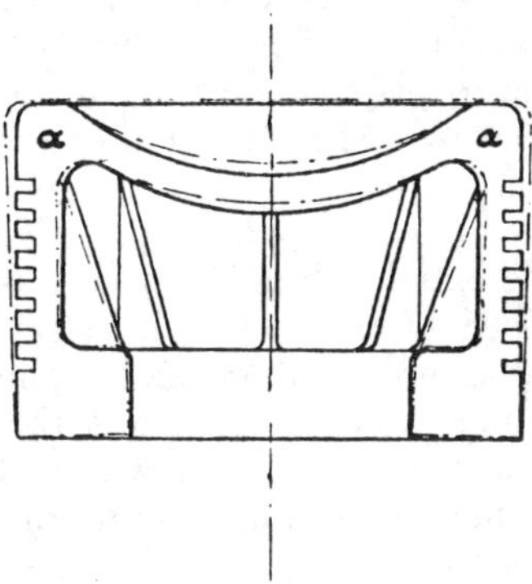

Fig. 102—Dotted lines showing, exaggeratedly, how a piston deforms under working conditions

If, therefore, the crown is made thicker, not only will the temperature-difference between the inside and outside surfaces be increased, but the greater rigidity will reduce the amount of deformation and augment the heat stresses. The foregoing may suffice to show (1) the advantage to be gained by the adoption of a curved crown, and (2) that there is a limit to the thickness of the crown.

As the crown of a concave-shaped piston lifts in its efforts to expand, the circumferential wall is forced outward from the top, as shown exaggerated in Fig. 102. If no ribs are provided inside the piston and the shape of the corners is as indicated by *a* in the illustration, the deformation stops at the top piston-ring groove and a bending stress is set up at this point. This was a common fault in the past and resulted in the upper piston rings being jammed and serving no useful purpose, and when after a time these particular rings were found stuck fast and covered with carbonised oil, the fuel or lubricating oil was invariably held responsible.

This bending stress was very often the cause of pistons cracking circumferentially in the vicinity of the top piston-ring groove, the crack starting on the inside and working outwards. This is a rather serious weakness, as apart from the cost of replacement, the crack is not usually discovered until the casting is almost in two pieces and large quantities of water begin leaking into the cylinder. Pistons have been known actually to divide into two pieces while an engine was working, and as can be imagined, very serious damage resulted.

In an endeavour to transfer the bending stress to a stronger part of the piston the upper inside corners are sometimes shaped as shown in Fig. 98. Increasing the flexibility at this point has solved some difficulties due to pistons cracking in the vicinity of the top groove, but in other cases where the reduction in the thickness of the metal at this point has been too great, the only effect has been to cause the cracks to occur higher up. The provision of webs binding the circumferential wall to the flange, as shown in Fig. 102, has the effect of distributing the bending stress over a greater part of the circumferential wall and generally eliminates cracking in the vicinity of the top groove, but unless the parts are correctly proportioned the flange is lifted, as shown by the dotted lines, and trouble will result due to the bolts connecting the piston to the piston rod breaking.

Apart from the correct proportioning of the various parts of cast-iron concave-type pistons, the solution of several of the difficulties mentioned would appear for the length to be not less than three-quarters the diameter, as cracking occurs much more frequently in short stiff pistons. As the crowns of convex-type pistons expand more freely, the circumferential wall is not forced outward to the same extent, and cracks of the nature just described occur less frequently.

From the temperatures given in Fig. 92, which were obtained by careful and elaborate tests carried out by Messrs. Sulzer Bros., it will be seen that the temperatures of the crowns of pistons vary in both directions. That is to say, the temperature of the outer surface at the centre is different from the temperature at the periphery, while the temperature of the outer surface is, of course, different from the temperature of the inner surface. The temperature-difference at various points between the inside and the outside is fairly regular, i.e. 250°F (121°C), but the temperature of the outer surface at the centre is very much lower than the temperature at the periphery. This is due partly to the presence of a greater mass of metal at the periphery, in which heat is accumulated, and partly to the cooling medium being more effective at the centre than at the sides.

If the metal near the periphery is hotter than the metal at the centre it will, of course, expand to a greater extent and put the metal at the centre in a state of tension. This, then, may explain why some pistons crack at the centre of the outer surface, in star formation, as shown in Fig. 99, since in all such cases it is obvious that the metal has been torn apart by tensile stress. A piston cracked in this way is not immediately dangerous as the cracks take a long time to develop, but they will eventually extend right through into the cooling space.

It occasionally happens that a ship suddenly develops piston trouble after running satisfactorily for a year or even longer. When the cracks occur in the circumferential wall the cause is nearly always due to weak design or unsuitable material, while if the cracks occur in the crown and begin on the inside, temporary stoppage of the cooling medium is often the cause.

It would appear that the working temperature at the periphery of pistons would be less, and the temperature-difference in the outer surface of the crown correspondingly reduced if the heat were allowed to flow more freely to the circumferential wall, which, it will be observed from Fig. 92, works at a much lower temperature than the crown. The obvious way to accomplish this would be to make the upper part of the circumferential wall thicker than is the present general practice. The tendency of some designers is to reduce the thickness of metal at this point with the object of producing greater flexibility between the crown and the circumferential wall, also to keep as low as possible the weight of a moving mass. Experience with various shapes of pistons suggests that the effect of this practice is not only to weaken the piston at a vital point, but to restrict the flow of heat also, and cause heat to be " banked-up," as it were, at the point where the crown joins the circumferential wall. On the other hand, the thicker the circumferential wall, the greater will be its working temperature, which is not to the good of the piston rings. But in view of the great advances made in other directions, such as more efficient lubrication and better combustion of fuel (to mention two only), and the fact that it is now very rare to find even the top ring stuck in its groove, it would seem that many pistons could be made thicker at this point without any detrimental effect upon the piston rings.

Piston repairs

Pistons crack so infrequently now that on the rare occasions when failure occurs the practice is to fit a spare piston and scrap the old one. The reason for this is that in most cases repair can only be effected by welding, and whilst welding technique has made considerable progress in recent years, successful repair of large marine-engine pistons cannot be guaranteed.

Cracks in the circumferential wall always begin on the inside, and before there is any outward indication of the defect the crack has generally extended for at least half the circumference. In such cases it is not usually worth the time spent and cost incurred to attempt a repair, as the apparently sound metal holding the crown to the circumferential wall will be so weakened that further cracking may be expected to occur at any time. Should, however, it be a case of holding up a ship because no spare pistons are available and the engine cannot be operated satisfactorily with this particular cylinder cut out, a few months further service may be assured by breaking off, or separating completely, the crown from the remainder of the piston, and repairing as shown in Fig. 103.

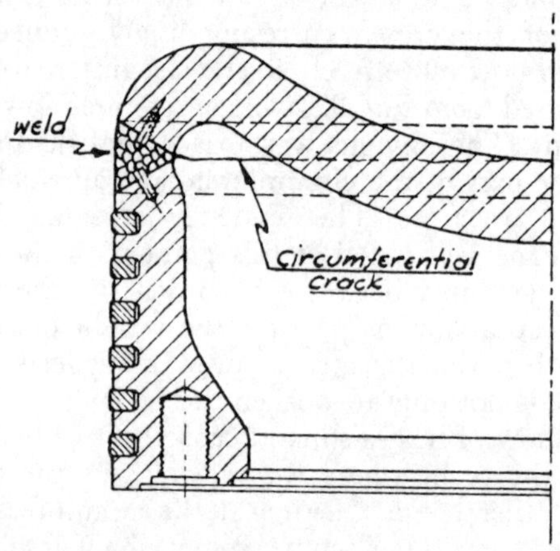

Fig. 103—Repair to piston cracked through circumferential wall

The two parts are machined in a lathe at each side of the fracture to form a 45° " V," and after fitting one-inch diameter mild steel studs spaced four inch apart as illustrated, the space made by machining is welded up. The steel studs are necessary in order to increase the strength of the weld. The best way to break off the crown prior to repairing is to drill an inch-diameter hole through the crack and drive in a drifting tool. If the circumferential wall is very thick it may be necessary to make two or three such holes and drive drifting tools into each simultaneously. The holes are afterwards filled when the parts are welded together. An internal water-pressure test of about 50 lb/sq.in. will be necessary after the repair has been carried out.

When the crown of a piston cracks, good results are obtained by machining out the metal in way of the cracks and fitting a special cast-iron or heat-resisting steel plug, as illustrated in Fig. 104.

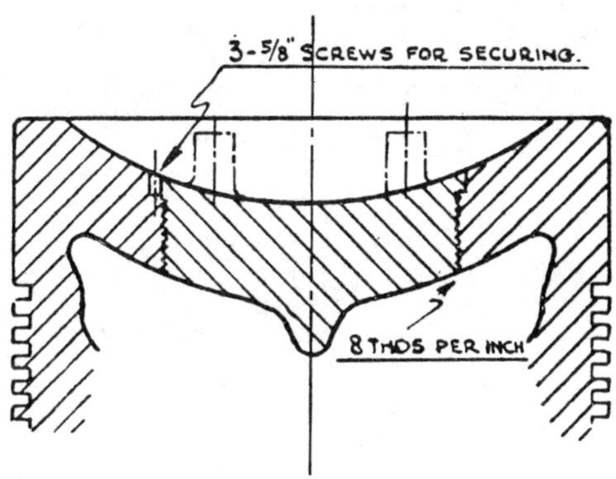

Fig. 104—Repair (No. 1) to piston cracked in crown

Such a repair will prove satisfactory in cases where the crown is very thick and a good portion of the plug can be screw-cut. The corners of the hole and plug, however, should be well rounded, and the locking-screws provided, to prevent the plug unscrewing, would be less likely to cause trouble if fitted from the inside, as square corners in any part subjected to such intense heat must be avoided.

Fig. 105 illustrates a successful repair carried out to several 32-inch diameter oil-cooled pistons. Numerous fine cracks were found about the centre of the crowns and, although the cracks did not look serious, they were found to extend well into the metal. The hole in the centre of the crown was increased until all trace of the cracks had been machined out, and a nickel-chrome steel plug fitted as shown in the illustration, which is self-explanatory.

The plug must, of course, be a good screw fit and well tightened. An important point in connection with such a repair is to chamfer the upper end of the hole in the piston and the corresponding end of the plug, especially if the plug is made of cast iron, since if a sharp corner of cast iron is exposed to the heat it quickly cracks and the crack is liable to extend. The extension provided for screwing in the plug should not be cut off unless it is necessary. If it does have to be removed and the piston cannot be put in a lathe, it should be drilled and finally lightly dressed by means of a chisel, as heavy hammer blows are liable to slacken the plug.

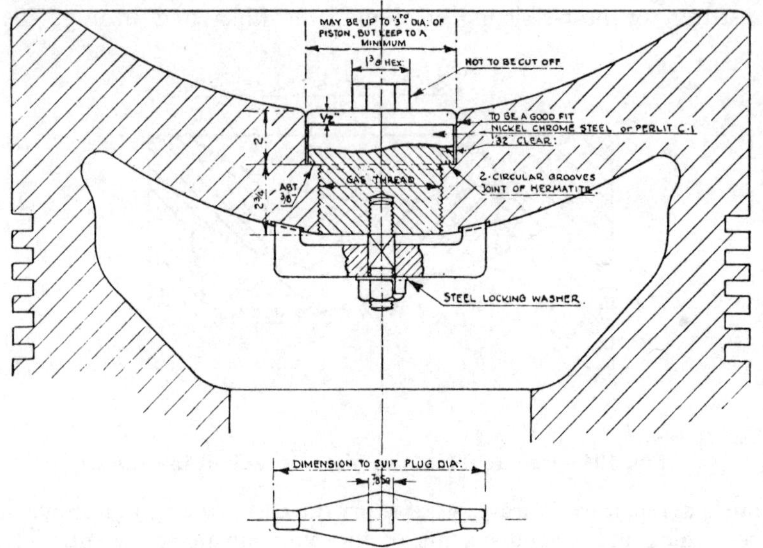

Fig. 105—Repair (No. 2) to piston cracked in crown

This type of plug and method of securing same in the piston are preferable to those shown in Fig. 104, because owing to the provision of a dog to hold the plug firmly in position, the screwed portion is relieved of all strain, due to inertia, and need not occupy such a great proportion of the length of the plug. The advantage of this is that the landing for the plug can be kept well away from the hot gases and there is, therefore, less risk of distortion and, consequently, leakage taking place of piston-cooling medium into the cylinder.

The screwed portion of the plug shown in Fig. 104 is depended upon not only to resist the inertia forces, but to form a fluid and gas joint also, as the thin flange becomes distorted by the heat and cannot be relied upon to prevent leakage. In regard to the repair shown in Fig. 105, care must be taken to secure the dog firmly. If the plug diameter is in the neighbourhood of two-thirds the

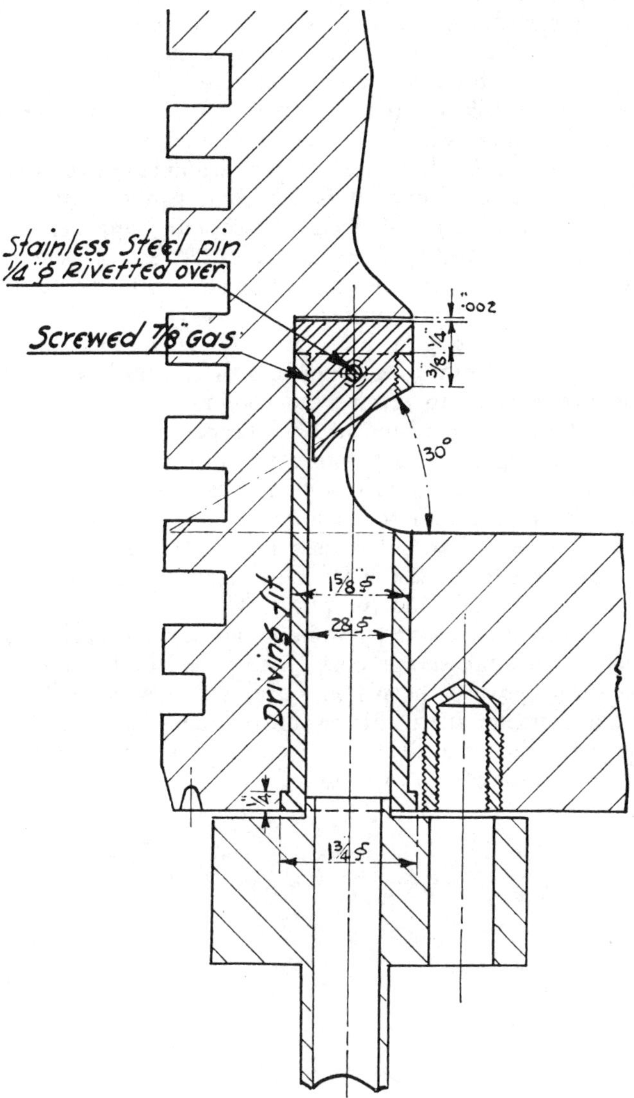

Fig. 106—Repair to cooling-water inlet passage in piston

piston diameter, it will be advisable to secure the dog by two studs. If Hermatite or other similar jointing solution is not available for the landing surfaces, white lead will serve the purpose.

The piston illustrated in Fig. 106 was cooled by means of a water jet forced through a telescopic pipe. The water impinged on a deflector similar to that shown in Fig. 100, and after a time most of the water was thrown back around the telescopic pipe instead of flowing to the outlet. Upon examination the cause was found to be that the deflector had become badly eroded; instead of the water striking an inclined surface and being deflected into the piston it was striking a surface more or less perpendicular to the jet. The repair, which is fully illustrated in Fig. 106, consisted of boring out the cooling-water inlet passage to a slightly larger diameter and inserting a Staybrite (non-corrodible) steel bush. The method of closing the upper end of the bush and providing the inclined surface to ensure the cooling water being deflected into the interior of the piston will be observed.

The projecting metal separating the piston rings of pistons is sometimes broken owing to insufficient care being exercised when refitting the piston into the cylinders. As the amount of metal generally broken off in such cases is rarely more than 10 inches of the circumference, the most satisfactory repair is to screw a number of steel studs into the piston where broken and build up to the finished dimensions by welding, and finally machining. The diameter of the studs should be a $\frac{1}{4}$ inch or so less than the thickness of the metal between the piston rings, and they should be spaced about one diameter apart. Moreover, the holes for the studs should not be more than one diameter deep, as this, or too many studs, might weaken the piston too much.

CHAPTER 14

Piston operation and maintenance

Operation of pistons

The main points which come under this heading are cooling and lubrication, which are dealt with in Chapters 15 and 21, respectively. If the pistons are effectively cooled and efficiently lubricated, therefore, they require no further attention whilst operating, apart from the engineer listening, during routine inspections, for anything that may go wrong with the parts connecting the pistons to the piston rods. Such defects are indicated by sound, and if any sound that cannot be accounted for is heard, prompt action is necessary because such defects become rapidly worse.

The only trouble likely to be experienced whilst operating is leakage of gases past the piston rings as the cylinder liners and/or piston rings become worn. When this occurs the only thing that can be done apart from renewing the parts is to increase slightly the cylinder lubricating-oil supply and use an oil of higher viscosity, in this way endeavouring to seal the spaces through which the gases leak. It is now very rare for leakage to be caused by the piston rings being jammed in their grooves, but when this is the case, owing to the employment of unsuitable lubricating oil or bad combustion of fuel, with a single-acting engine, it is possible, while running, to free the lower rings and reduce the gas leakage temporarily, provided action is taken in time. Nothing can, however, be done about the upper rings. The following procedure should be followed:

Shut off the fuel to the cylinder concerned for two hours or so, and during that time constantly spray the cylinder walls with warm soapy distilled water, and occasionally work the cylinder lubricator by hand to increase the amount of lubricating oil injected. If this does not have the desired effect then there is nothing for it but to expose the piston and free the rings by hand.

Overheating of a piston and cylinder liner due to friction between these two parts seldom occurs, but on the rare occasions when this does happen the cause is often put down to inferior quality of the lubricating oil or fuel. Such a conclusion is perhaps only natural, because the surfaces are always found dry. This dryness, however, is due to the heat generated by the friction vaporising the oil which was on the surfaces before the excessive heat began to be generated. Should the trouble occur soon after an engine has been working with new piston rings, the cause is most likely due to one or more of the new rings not having been given sufficient end clearance. This fault has been known not only to cause overheating but to fracture the lower end of a cylinder liner.

Misalignment of the piston rod or excessive slackness in the crosshead guide may produce sufficient friction between the piston and cylinder liner to cause overheating, especially in two-stroke engines where the piston is of great length. Insufficient cooling of the piston will, of course, cause it to expand and so reduce the working clearance. The designed clearances, however, are such that nothing short of a complete stoppage of cooling medium when the engine is working at full power would reduce the clearances around the piston so much as to cause the parts to make hard contact, unless, of course, owing to misalignment of the running gear, the clearances at certain points are very much less than they ought to be when temperatures are normal.

The most likely cause of a piston running hot after it has been working satisfactorily for some time is insufficient lubrication, or leakage of cooling water from a part that will adversely affect the oil film. A not infrequent cause is water leakage at the cylinder lubricating-oil fittings. It is wise therefore to test these fittings occasionally to make sure that they are bearing hard against the liner.

The first indication of a hot piston is smoke, in the case of single-acting engines, and a grunting noise in the case of double-acting engines. Prompt action is necessary in both cases, but less risks should be taken with double-acting engines as naturally the piston in this type of engine must be much hotter when the first symptoms are observed. In all cases the engine speed should be at once reduced to dead-slow, the fuel shut off from the cylinder concerned, the maximum quantity of cooling medium circulated through the piston, and the output of the cylinder lubricator increased.

It is not advisable to stop the engine unless there are indications that the piston is getting hotter, as such action may cause the piston to seize. If the engine must be stopped, the turning gear should be engaged as quickly as possible and the engine kept moving until the excess heat has been carried off. This is not likely to happen in under half-an-hour. The engine should be re-started with the fuel shut-off to the cylinder concerned, and the engine speed increased very gradually from dead-slow. If after an hour or so there are no indications of overheating the cylinder may be put on light load for the next 24 hours.

If it is possible to keep the engine running slowly under conditions previously recommended, cooling of the overheated piston may be expedited by injecting soapy distilled water through the lubricating-oil fittings by means of a syringe. It was not suggested, it will be observed, that the flow of cooling water through the cylinder jacket should be increased. The reason is that to restore normal conditions nothing should be done which would have the effect of making the cylinder liner close in on the overheated and expanded piston. Cutting off the fuel will in itself cause a general reduction in the temperature of the liner and result in it closing in on the piston, and it is not considered wise to reduce the working clearance between the piston and liner still further by increasing the flow of jacket cooling-water.

When a piston becomes overheated the first act of many engineers is to pump the maximum quantity of lubricating oil into the cylinder in the shortest possible time. A moment's thought will suffice to reveal the error of such a practice. The normal running temperature of the piston rings is in the neighbourhood of 200°F (93°C), and when the rubbing surfaces become overheated to the extent that smoke is given off, the temperature must be nearer 600°F (316°C). Lubricating oil, therefore, which has a flash-point of about 400°F (204°C) is of very little use and, applied under such conditions, will simply vaporise.

In some engines cylinder liners are in two parts, either with the object of facilitating the removal of the piston from the bottom of the cylinder or for some other reason in connection with the design. When knocking occurs in a cylinder the possibility of the two parts of the liner not being perfectly fair with one another should be considered, as only a few thousandths of an inch misalignment will produce knocking as the piston passes over the joint. There is sometimes a space between the inner ends of the two parts to allow for expansion of the liners in an endwise direction. Under certain conditions this space between the liners will cause a tapping noise. The noise is produced by gases trapped between the piston rings during the high-pressure period of the cycle being suddenly released into the space. Generally the noise gets less and less and finally disappears altogether as the space between the liners becomes filled with carbonaceous matter.

Piston connecting-bolts

A great deal of trouble has been experienced in the past due to these bolts breaking and, although matters have greatly improved, instances of trouble in this direction still occasionally occur. As the trouble was not confined to engines of the four-stroke type, the original theory that the cause was due to the inertia load put upon the bolts at the end of the exhaust stroke had to be ruled out. The greatest contribution to the solution of the difficulty was the provision of larger piston-rod flanges, larger in diameter and of a greater thickness, while considerable improvement resulted from the adoption of longer connecting bolts, which allowed piston flanges to distort a small amount upon attaining working temperature, without unduly straining the bolts. In well-designed pistons of modern engines no such distortion takes place—but all pistons are not well designed.

The diameter of piston-rod flanges in modern engines is only slightly less than the diameter of the cylinders, so that the pistons are now well supported and the bolts are located nearer the periphery, where the deformation of the piston flange is least (see Fig. 100). Furthermore, a greater number of bolts can be accommodated in flanges of larger diameter.

Even though the factors which affect the piston connecting-bolts have been very successfully dealt with, the design and material of the bolts—or studs and nuts as the case may be—still require careful consideration. The best material for the purpose is steel with an ultimate tensile strength of 32-38 ton/sq.in., an elongation of not less than 25 per cent, and a yield point of between 17 and 19 ton/sq.in. Material of lower tensile strength stretches to too great an extent, and if of higher tensile strength it fatigues more readily and may break.

Where studs and nuts are employed it is advisable to use materials of slightly different properties to obviate the possibility of seizure. If, therefore, the studs are made of the same material as recommended for bolts, the nuts should be made of ordinary mild steel of 28-32 ton/sq.in. ultimate strength. It is the practice of some engine-builders to make nuts of very soft steel having an ultimate strength in the neighbourhood of 26 ton/sq.in. Such steels are too ductile for this purpose, especially if, as illustrated in Fig. 100, the nuts are of the cap or box type, because the threads " give " under working conditions and the nuts become slack.

The screw-cutting of piston connecting-bolts and nuts must be of the highest standard also, otherwise the pressure on the joining surfaces of the piston and piston rod will be relieved and serious trouble may develop. When piston connecting-nuts are a slack fit on the studs, either new good-fitting nuts should be procured or an attempt made to improve the fit of the existing nuts. The following operation will be found to have the desired effect upon old slack nuts. Heat the nut to be shrunk to a dull red and, holding it flat in a pair of tongs, slowly dip it into water until about one-third is immersed. When the red colour has disappeared, gradually lower the nut into the water until the whole of it is immersed, taking about three minutes over the operation. This will be found to make the nuts close-in an appreciable amount without unduly hardening them or affecting the properties of the material in any other way. After this treatment it will probably be found necessary to run a tap through the nuts, that is, of course, assuming that the threads of the studs are of the correct size and that the fault lies in the nuts. It is not necessary that these nuts should be so tight that they have to be screwed all the way by means of a spanner, but complete freedom from trouble cannot be expected if the nuts are slack on the studs when all the threads are engaged.

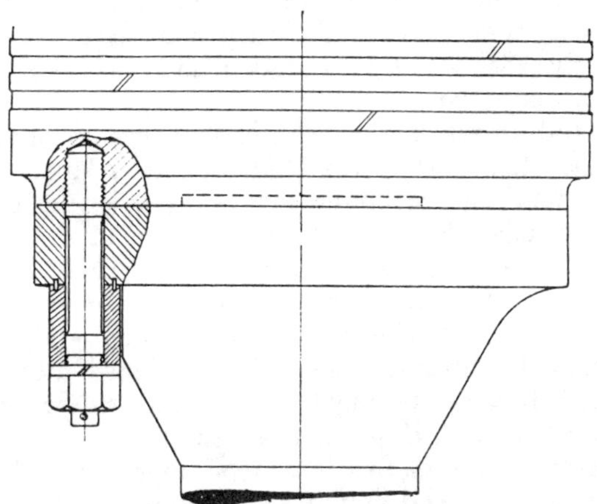

Fig. 107—Modified form of piston connecting-stud

In a few cases where the piston connecting-bolts or studs have broken, the trouble has been cured by fitting new studs of larger diameter. In other cases the trouble has been overcome by replacing the short studs by longer studs, as shown in Fig. 107. When tap bolts are employed, the holes in cast-iron pistons should be provided with tough steel bushes with fine threads, screwed tightly into the piston, dowel pins being provided to prevent them being unscrewed when removing the tap bolts. The bushes should be coated with a mixture of red lead and boiled oil before being screwed into place, and when in place should be slightly below the surface of the piston, so that the joining surfaces of the piston and piston rod will not be prevented from making proper contact.

Cases there are, however, where these connecting studs or bolts break, and the known stresses due to heat and inertia cannot be held responsible. The trouble in one case investigated was found to be caused by excessive tightening of the nuts. It transpired that the nuts occasionally became slack, and the practice of hardening up at each port of call was instituted to prevent involuntary stoppages at sea to tighten up slack nuts. As a result of this practice the initial stress in the studs was increased at each port by, possibly, injudicious tightening until—when this was added to the heat and inertia stresses—the elastic limit of the material was reached and the inevitable happened while the engine was working. The cause of the nuts becoming slack was found to be due to too soft a steel having been used in the manufacture of the nuts, while examination of the broken studs showed that they had been stretched at the disengaged threads, which in a stud of even diameter form, is of course, the weakest part.

When a stud or bolt is stressed a certain amount of stretch takes place. If the plain part of the stud or bolt is larger in diameter than the diameter at the bottom of the threads, the total amount of stretch will take place in the small portion of the stud's length occupied by the disengaged threads. What is more, the stretch is not distributed evenly over the whole of this portion of the studs, but chiefly at the bottom of the threads, which is a mere fraction of the pitch of the threads. This will be evident if a bolt is stressed to destruction, because the angle of the thread will be found to have increased very slightly, if at all, while the pitch of the threads has increased greatly. From this it will be appreciated that the total stretch in such studs and bolts takes place in a much smaller proportion of their length than would appear likely at first sight.

The smaller the proportion of length in which a certain amount of stretch takes place, the sooner will the elastic limit of the material be reached, so that the obvious remedy would be to distribute the stretch over a greater part of the stud's length by reducing the diameter of the plain part to the diameter at the bottom of the threads, as shown in Fig. 107. When tap-bolts of this length are employed, the distance-piece between the head of the bolt and the piston-rod flange will require to fit into a recess $\frac{1}{4}$-inch or so deep in the piston-rod flange, otherwise there will be too much spring in the bolts when tightening, and the good solid connection that is so necessary will be difficult to obtain, with the result that the bolts are likely to be found loose after a short time.

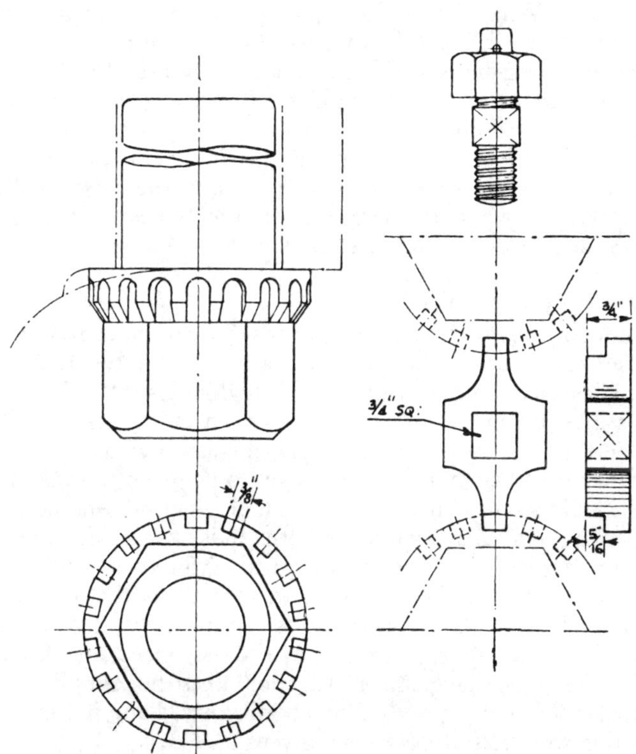

Fig. 108—Locking plate for piston connecting-nut

Something more effective than split pins should be provided to lock piston connecting-bolts and nuts in position. Spring-locking washers have proved quite effective, but the consequences of these nuts and bolts becoming loose are so serious that a more positive arrangement should be provided. The matter is of sufficient importance to justify an arrangement the same or similar to that illustrated in Fig. 108. Locking-plates that fit over the cants of the nuts are not advisable, as they encourage either excessive or insufficient tightening to enable the plate to be fitted.

The practice of some engine-builders is to drill the parts and thread brass or iron wire through two or more bolts. Such a practice is positively dangerous, as it has been proved over and over again that wire up to $\frac{3}{16}$-inch diameter will not prevent a loose nut from unscrewing. Wire of this size is quickly sheared, and if made of a larger diameter it is almost impossible to thread it through the holes. If the connecting-bolts and nuts are a proper fit and well tightened, the locking device is not likely to be called upon, but in view of the ever-present possibility of the nuts becoming loose, and the serious consequences of a nut falling and getting jammed between the piston and the top of the crankcase, where there is usually very little clearance when the crank is on the bottom dead centre, a positive locking device for these nuts is very necessary.

Maintenance of pistons

Although properly operated pistons do not now require to be removed more often than is necessary to meet the requirements of the Classification Societies, yet it is highly desirable that it should be possible to remove them without much effort. In the Doxford and Werkspoor engines, for example, this is possible, but in certain other makes sufficient attention has yet to be given to this important matter. Generally speaking, the double-acting engine is at a disadvantage in this respect as both ends of the cylinder are of necessity enclosed by heavy castings. Moreover, the piston is usually connected to the piston rod in such a way that it is necessary to remove both parts. This involves the dismantling of the piston-rod packing also, but as time goes on the operation of removing double-acting engine pistons will doubtless be simplified. In a few makes of such engines sympathetic regard for those who have to do this work has already been given.

The easiest way to remove a single-acting engine piston is to take it out of the bottom of the cylinder. This is practicable in four-stroke crosshead-type engines, but more difficult to arrange in two-stroke engines owing to the much greater length of piston. Taking the piston out of the top of the cylinder necessitates the dismantling of all the valve-operating gear and disconnecting and lifting the cylinder head, an operation that requires a great deal of time and effort in engines of the size that we are concerned with, as marine operating engineers.

The Werkspoor method of removing the pistons of their four-stroke single-acting engines is a good example of what can be done in this direction by designers who appreciate the difficulties the men at sea may have to contend with. Of two-stroke engines the Doxford must be given the highest marks for accessibility. In the Werkspoor engine it will be observed, from Fig. 109, that the cylinder liner is in two parts, and that the lower part, called the extension liner, is bolted to the underside of the cylinder beam and is therefore detachable. When this detachable part of the liner is disconnected and lowered on to the top of the crankcase, and if the crank is on the bottom dead centre, the external parts of the

Fig. 109—Method of removing piston and piston rod of 4-stroke single-acting engine (Werkspoor)

piston and rings are fully accessible for inspection, cleaning and renewal of piston rings. Should it be required to remove the piston for complete examination, this can be done by simply disconnecting the piston from the piston rod and sliding the piston out on rails provided for the purpose, and shown in the illustration. The extension liner in the larger engines is provided with a water jacket, and both the extension liner and the piston are landed on the rails and withdrawn together, the extension liner being afterwards taken off the piston when it is required to get at the piston rings or to examine the piston thoroughly.

One method of removing the pistons of four-stroke single-acting engines is illustrated in Fig. 110, which will be found to be self-explanatory. It would be as well to mention, however, that the nuts connecting the piston to the piston rod should be slackened before the piston is taken right out of the cylinder, and when refitting the parts, the final hardening up of these nuts should be done after

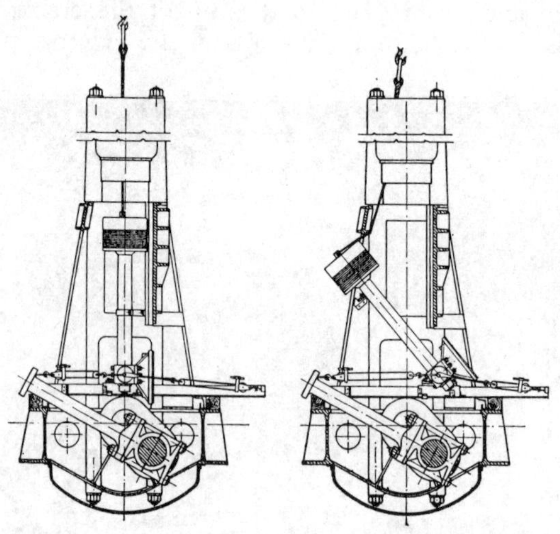

Fig. 110—Method of exposing piston of (Burmeister & Wain) 4-stroke engine

the upper end of the piston has been entered in the cylinder. It will be found that this part of the operation can be done more easily and more satisfactorily in this way than when the piston and piston rod are in the position shown at the right of the illustration.

It is also possible to expose the pistons in this make of engine by raising the cylinders clear of the pistons. The nuts holding the cylinder down are first removed, and tubes are screwed on to the exposed ends of the tie-bolts. These tubes act as a guide as the heavy cylinder is lifted by means of the overhead crane.

Whenever it is considered advisable to remove the pistons of an engine for examination, all piston rings should be removed as soon as possible and the grooves thoroughly cleaned. Piston rings are rarely found jammed in their grooves nowadays, but carbon and other solid matter still accumulate behind them and must be removed periodically if the rings are to function properly and damage is to be prevented. More will be said later regarding this and other points in connection with piston rings. The piston should then be cleaned and every part of the external surface examined, particularly the crown and the circumferential wall in the vicinity of the top groove, not forgetting the bottom of this and the next groove.

If the pistons are cooled by water it is not usually necessary to examine the inside of the pistons on each of these occasions, but the door on the underside which encloses the water space should always be examined for slack nuts and leakages past the joint. The strain put upon these doors by the mass of water in the pistons is not always realised, and occasionally leakage occurs and corrosion of the piston and piston-rod joining surfaces eventually results. Packing not thicker than $\frac{1}{32}$-inch should be interposed between the piston and the door, and the nuts must be thoroughly tightened and afterwards locked in some way. Split pins do not offer sufficient security, and if no better means are provided it is advisable to lock the nuts by lightly centre-punching between the nut and the stud.

When lubricating oil is the cooling medium the opportunity should be taken to inspect the inside of the pistons for carbon deposit. The inlet and outlet passages should not be overlooked as pieces of hard carbon sometimes become jammed in them and, of course, restrict the flow.

Before a piston is refitted, the joining surfaces of the piston and piston rod and the landing for the connecting bolts or nuts must be thoroughly cleaned, and the former rubbed over with boiled oil. In the event of the piston and/or piston-rod surfaces being slightly corroded, as sometimes happens when the pistons are cooled by water, the affected part should be levelled up to the unaffected part by Manganisite, or some such hard-setting substance, otherwise the corroded area will enlarge and may result in the connecting bolts becoming slack. When Manganisite is used the piston should be at once placed in position on the piston rod and the connecting-bolts lightly tightened, and finally hardened up after the Manganisite has set hard.

When the piston and piston-rod joining surfaces are badly corroded, it would be advisable to fit a spare part and have the corroded surfaces machined at the first opportunity. If spare parts are not available or it is not possible to fit them in the time, sheet packing, such as Acme, of a thickness not greater than $\frac{1}{32}$-inch may be fitted with advantage between the surfaces. When packing is interposed between the surfaces in this manner the connecting-bolts should be hammer-tested for tightness at every opportunity as, not unnaturally, they are more likely to become loose then when the surfaces are metal-to-metal.

While pistons are out, the cylinder lubricating-oil holes should be inspected from inside the cylinder and cleared of semi-solid matter which tends to accumulate in them. The piston rings should be well oiled and centralised on the piston with the gaps in their proper position in relation to one another. When a piston is entered from the top of the cylinder no difficulty is experienced nor special precaution necessary to enter the piston rings if the top of the liner is bell-mouthed sufficiently, or if an adapter of the type shown

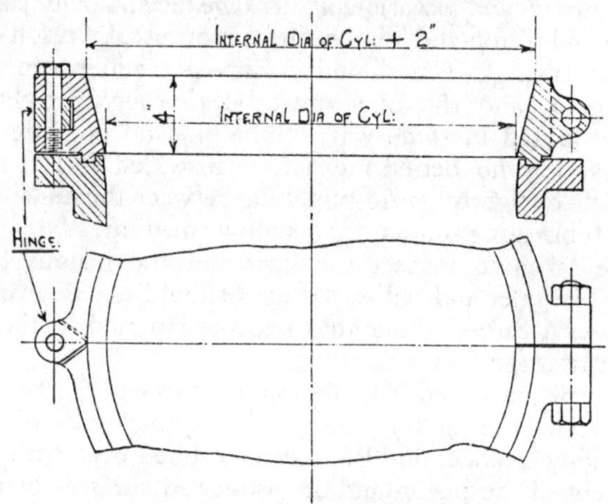

Fig. 111—Piston-ring adapter

in Fig. 111 is employed. If the liner is not bell-mouthed sufficiently, or if no such tool is available, the best way to enter the piston rings is to lower the piston very slowly until the first ring is just nipped and, beginning at one side of the gap, push the ring into the groove with a piece of hardwood until it springs into the cylinder. If the weight on the ring is too great the ring may be broken, so that the success of the operation depends upon the ability to manipulate correctly the lifting tackle suspending the piston.

The piston-ring adapter recommended above should preferably be in halves, hinged at one side, and the two parts held together at the other side by a bolt. The advantage of such an adapter over a solid one is that it can be placed in position after the piston rod or the connecting-rod, as the case may be, has entered the cylinder. Also, it often happens when refitting pistons that it is necessary to raise the parts a little after some of the piston rings have entered the cylinder, with the result that the last ring to enter would spring out, unless great care is taken to prevent it doing so, which would mean starting all over again: whereas with a split adapter it could easily be placed over the ring that had sprung out of the cylinder, and after screwing the two parts of the adapter together, the piston is again ready to be lowered further into the cylinder.

When pistons are refitted through the bottom of the cylinder, it is usual to land the piston on the piston rod and, by means of the turning gear, raise the piston into the cylinder. This operation must be carefully carried out, even when a piston-ring adaptor is employed, as it is so easy for a piston ring to become jammed and break the metal of the piston separating the piston rings.

Before a new piston is fitted its diameter should be measured to make quite sure that it will have the necessary working clearance. These dimensions will doubtless be correct if the new part has been supplied by the engine-builders, but it should never be taken for granted, in view of the very serious consequences that would result from insufficient working clearance, and the small effort required to compare the old and new pistons in this respect. In addition to checking the top, middle and bottom external diameters, the radial depth of the piston-ring grooves should be measured in order to make sure that there will be sufficient clearance behind the rings to allow them to expand freely. One cylinder liner has, to the writer's knowledge, been very seriously damaged within a few hours of a new piston being fitted owing to the manufacturer making a mistake with the radial depth of the piston-ring grooves.

The overall length of the piston, and the distance from the joining surface to the top piston-ring groove, should be checked also, to make sure that the cylinder compression-pressure will be correct and that the top of the piston or the top piston ring will not foul some part of the cylinder. A ridge is sometimes formed at the upper end of a cylinder liner after a period of service, and if the top ring on the new piston is located higher it will strike the ridge and break, or do more serious damage.

The diametrical working clearances necessary between the parallel part of two- and four-stroke engine cast-iron pistons and the smallest part of the cylinder liner are shown by the curves in Fig. 112. Similar curves for the clearances necessary for that part of the piston above the piston rings cannot very well be given, as they depend upon the design of the piston, and the design of pistons varies so widely. Generally, however, the tapering begins at a point between the top and second piston-ring grooves, and the diametrical clearance at the top of the piston should be about five times the diametrical clearance at the parallel part. The clearance at the parallel part must be the least possible in order to prevent "piston slap," but the clearance above the rings is not so important so long as it is

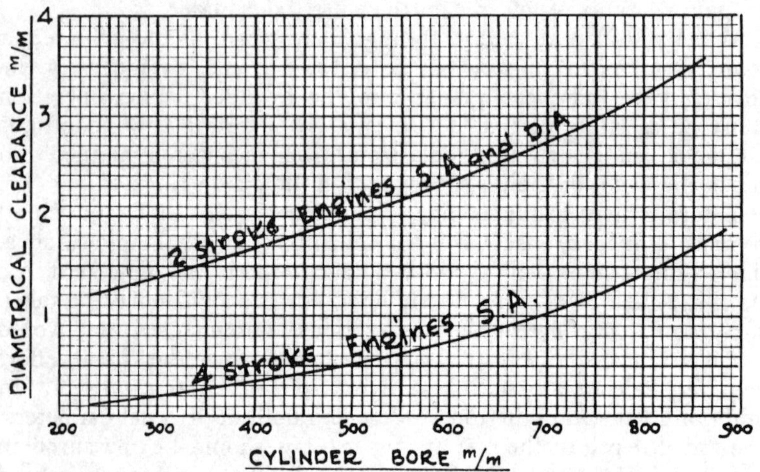

Fig. 112—Diametrical clearance curves for cast-iron pistons

sufficient to allow the piston to expand without making contact with the cylinder. Excessive diametrical clearance at the parallel part will reduce the bearing surface in the piston grooves, and by exposing a greater proportion of the rings to the gas pressure in the cylinder the stresses produced in them, particularly the uppermost ring, will be increased, and the working conditions generally made more severe.

Piston rings

The efficiency and proper working of any engine depend in a large measure upon the effective sealing of the working clearances between the pistons and cylinders. This is more necessary in the internal combustion engine than in any other, since if leakage of gases occurs the compression pressure will be reduced; power will be lost; the cylinder liner and piston rings will wear excessively;

after-burning will result, and the exhaust valves will begin to leak. To the above formidable list is to be added rapid deterioration in general, so that nothing further need be said about the important part played by piston rings.

The material from which piston rings are made must possess strength to stand up to the stresses and shocks to which they are subjected by the high gas pressures and sudden reversal of motion. It must also have good wear-resisting properties, and have a high degree of elasticity so that the rings made from it will retain their spring and maintain contact with the cylinder at all times, even when the cylinder bore is not parallel. Moreover, the rings must withstand distortion due to their having to be forced over the end of the piston in order to get them into their working position. Any tendency to take a permanent set will reduce their effectiveness very considerably. All are agreed that at the present time cast iron is the most suitable material for the purpose. The cast iron used, however, should be close-grained, homogeneous, and, for cast iron, extremely tough and elastic. The making of piston rings is a specialised business.

Piston rings are made in two qualities, namely soft and hard, having Brinell hardness figures of 150–160 and 175–185 respectively. This test for hardness is described in Chapter 25. It is not a reliable guide to the wear-resisting properties of cast iron, but as there is no other test in general use to indicate this property, and in view of the fact that, generally speaking, rings of a high Brinell figure do not wear away to the same extent as rings made of softer material, it can be used as a rough guide. The hard cast-iron is generally used, but some favour the softer material so that the piston rings rather than the cylinder liner will wear. Such rings will certainly wear more rapidly than the harder rings, but as the metal wears away and mixes with the lubricating oil it must make a good grinding paste, so that it is very questionable whether the liner wear rate is reduced or increased by the employment of soft piston rings.

It is difficult to obtain reliable information at sea regarding the wear rate of piston rings made of different grades of cast iron, and their effect upon cylinder-liner wear, as the influencing factors are so varied and numerous, but the author holds the view that there is nothing to be gained by the use of the softer grades of cast iron for piston rings, and that the metal used should be the hardest possible consistent with ductility and the other necessary properties.

Each piston is provided with from five to seven piston rings, generally of the Ramsbottom type—a type of piston ring which dates back to 1855 and was the ingenious invention of an engineer of that name. Very soon after these piston rings came into general use it was found that if rings which had lost their " spring " were hammered on the inside, their quality was restored, and thus originated the modern hammered piston ring, the only difference being that the hammering is now done automatically and more scientifically. The Standard Piston Ring Company, which has studied this question thoroughly, first machine the rings to the correct diameter of the cylinder, then by a special automatic machine they are hammered round the internal surface in such a way that the heaviest blow is made and, therefore, the greatest stress set up at the point in the ring diametrically opposite the point where the ring will be cut. The blow of the hammer decreases uniformly on each side of this point until the joint is reached, where it is zero. The result of this automatic and graduated hammering is that, in addition to the ring becoming self-expanding, a uniform tension is set up in the ring which prevents it from wearing unevenly.

Piston rings are made concentric and are self-expanding, that is to say, they exert sufficient spring of themselves, without external aid, to press against the cylinder and prevent leakage of gases past the piston. They are designed to exert a pressure of from 3 to 5 lb/sq.in. against the cylinder wall. From this it will be appreciated that properly made piston rings prevent leakage of gases, and thereby maintain a high mechanical efficiency of the engine.

The joints of Ramsbottom piston rings take various forms, the three types most commonly adopted for marine work being shown in Fig. 113. *A* is the plain joint, *B* and *C* the bevel, and *D* the stepped joint. (*C* is included to show how, with *B*, alternate rings in a piston can have opposing slopes of bevel to avoid joints becoming in direct line.)

Since a piston ring has to stand up to such severe conditions of pressure, heat, and sudden reversal of motion, it is only to be expected that of the three types illustrated the simpler and stronger types, indicated at *A* and *B* (and *C*), have become the most popular. From the point of view of leakage and strength there is nothing to choose between these two types, though the simplest type, shown at *A* may cause a ridge to be worn on the cylinder liner, this would no doubt occur if the joints of all rings are fitted, or work into, line.

The type of joint shown at *D*, which is still favoured by some engineers, is costly to make because a piece must be milled out of the ring to make the joint. The ring is first roughly machined to a diameter larger than that of the cylinder for which it is intended, and then cut and shaped as shown. The ends of the ring are then drawn together and the ring afterwards truly machined to the required diameter. The contention that the lap form of joint, i.e. type *D* in the diagram, is more effective in preventing leakage of gases than the other types is a fallacy, since when the ring is in position the gases obtain easy access to the back of the ring through the top

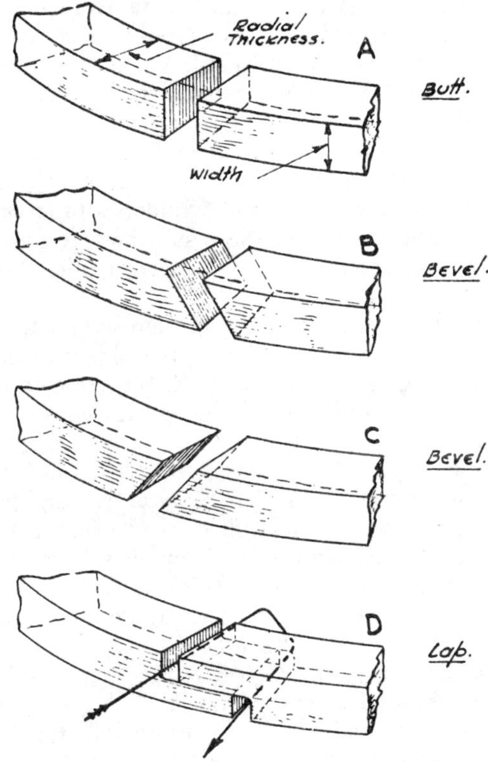

Fig. 113—Types of piston-ring joints

half of the joint, and pass out again to the other side of the ring through the lower half of the joint, as indicated by the arrow and dotted lines. The earliest marine diesel engines were provided with piston rings having lap joints, but experience has definitely proved this and other fancy forms of joint to be quite unnecessary. When leakage of gases occurs with the bevel type of joint, the cause is more likely due to inefficient lubrication, a subject which will be dealt with fully in a later chapter.

A serious objection to the lap type of joint is that the thin and greatly weakened ends frequently break off. When this occurs not only is the piston ring suddenly made ineffective, but the small pieces of broken metal are liable to become jammed between the piston and the cylinder liner. Many cylinder liners have been seriously damaged in this way. Another disadvantage is that when in position in a new cylinder this type of ring does not exert uniform pressure against the surrounding wall, with the result that ring wear is uneven. As already explained, the spring in this form of ring is produced by first making it of larger diameter and then cutting a piece out so that when the ends are joined the ring tends to spring outward. As can doubtless be visualised, the act of closing the gap so that the ring will fit the cylinder is to stress the ring at a point opposite the joint, with the result that the greatest outward pressure, and consequently wear, take place in the vicinity of the joint.

At one time piston rings were occasionally made thinner near the joint, or bored eccentrically, with the object of equalising the outward spring pressure all round. The objection to this was that the reduction of the radial thickness at the ends caused greater wear to take place in a vertical direction, and such rings soon became slack in their grooves. The best practice is undoubtedly to make the rings of uniform radial thickness (concentric) and hammer them as already described, so that they will exert an even pressure all round.

The cross-section of piston rings is either square or rectangular; when of the latter form the radial thickness is always greater than the width. The radial thickness has an important influence not only upon the pressure with which the rings bear against the cylinder wall, but also on the stress to which the ring is subjected when forcing it over the end of the piston, and in springing it into the cylinder. The stress set up is proportional to the square of the thickness, and also to the amount the rings must open and close when operating in a cylinder having a tapered bore. The advantage of rings having comparatively large radial thicknesses is that they offer greater bearing surface on the top and bottom surfaces of the grooves, and the wear in this direction is less; but from what has been stated it will be appreciated that there is a limit to the radial thickness of piston rings. In a 30-inch-diameter cylinder engine the limit seems to be about 1¼ inches, and the width of the rings is half the radial thickness.

The best results as regards piston ring and cylinder-liner wear are obtained with rings of reasonably small width. This is explained by the fact that the friction between the outer surface of a ring and the cylinder liner is proportional to the total pressure, and as the total pressure is equal to the pressure per square inch multiplied by the area of contact, the smaller the area the less the total pressure, hence the narrower the rings the less the friction. In practice a certain amount of additional friction is caused by gases getting behind the rings and forcing them outward against the cylinder liner, the amount being proportional to the area occurring for the passage of the gases between the ends of the rings and the upper surface of the rings and the grooves. As gases acting in this way increase the total pressure between the rings and the cylinder and, consequently, the friction, narrow rings have the advantage also.

A further advantage of narrow rings over wide ones is that the rate of enlargement of the piston grooves is very noticeably less. This may be due to their smaller weight, since the inertia force due to their weight during the reciprocation of the piston will be less. Furthermore, narrow rings bed themselves to the curvature of the cylinder more quickly than wide rings, but if the bearing surface is made too small they will, of course, wear more rapidly. Judging by results, the best proportion for piston rings appears to be for the radial thickness to be one and a half times the width.

As piston rings are subjected to severe conditions they require to be very carefully fitted. They must be sufficiently free in their grooves to ensure that they will function properly when heated to working temperature, and that the ends of each ring will be almost, but not quite, touching. The piston rings expand cross-sectionally to a slightly greater extent than the corresponding part of the much heavier and more rigid piston, so that due allowance must be made for this extra expansion both in a vertical and radial direction.

When deciding upon the working clearances to be given to piston rings, it must be remembered that the piston expands outward and that the piston rings expand inward, both deformations tending to reduce the clearance between the bottom of the grooves and the inner surface of the piston rings; and furthermore, that in some cases the expansion of the piston crown deforms the circumferential wall in such a way that the width of the upper grooves is reduced slightly. Whilst the vertical clearances must not be so small that the rings are jammed upon working temperatures being attained, they must not, on the other hand, be too great, otherwise the rings will flutter radially, due to the gas pressure acting upon them, or hammer and destroy the oil film when the motion of the piston is reversed, both of which will enlarge the grooves.

The upper rings, being subjected to the greatest degree of heat, require to have the greatest amount of clearance. For the more common sizes of cylinders satisfactory results have been obtained with the following differences between the widths of groove and piston ring, No. 1 being counted the top ring:—

Cylinders 15 to 25 inches diameter	Nos. 1 and 2 rings, 0·003 inch
	,, 3 ,, 4 ,, 0·002 ,,
	,, 5 ,, 6 ,, 0·001 ,,
Cylinders 25 to 35 inches diameter	Nos. 1 and 2 rings, 0·005 inch
	,, 3 ,, 4 ,, 0·003 ,,
	,, 5 ,, 6 ,, 0·001 ,,

All additional rings, if any, should be an easy fit without measurable clearance.

When ordering new piston rings the exact width required should be stated, so that they will go into place without having to be filed, as filing is most harmful. The top and bottom surfaces must be ground perfectly smooth and even. If they are merely machined or filed, the ridges that will remain after such operations, no matter how carefully the work is carried out, will soon wear off, and when this occurs the ring will be slack and begin to hammer and enlarge the groove.

As the grooves wear it is necessary to machine them and fit new oversize rings. This operation is advisable when the grooves have widened by 0·75 mm, so that the new rings will be 1 mm greater in width than the old rings. If the rings are allowed to work with a slackness greater than this, the rate of enlargement will be greatly increased and, consequently, the useful life of the piston will be reduced.

Some grooves, usually the upper ones, are generally found worn to a greater extent than others, but to avoid confusion it is wise to machine all grooves out to the same size and to a round figure, such as 15, 16, or 17 mm. Apart from being absolutely parallel the sides of the grooves must be perfectly smooth, as the interval between the machining operations depends very largely upon the time which elapses before the initial slackness occurs.

Now that carbon and other substances resulting from imperfect combustion or inefficient cylinder lubrication rarely deposit on the piston rings, the rings require only sufficient clearance to allow a thin film of lubricating oil to form between the surfaces. Lubrication of these surfaces is just as essential as that of the surface that bears against the cylinder liner, because the piston rings are constantly altering their position relative to the piston when an engine is in operation. This movement is caused by the opening and closing of the rings when the cylinders become worn and assume a tapered form. This explains why the rate of enlargement of the piston-ring grooves is always greater the more a cylinder liner is worn.

Should the end clearance—or gap between the ends of piston rings—when in position in the cylinders be too small, the rings will expand and break. This is the least that will happen as they are quite capable of causing the liner to heat up or even of fracturing the lower end of the liner before they themselves break. On the other hand, if the gap is too great the annular space at the back of the rings will be in open and free communication with the combustion space, and the high-pressure gases thus permitted to get behind the rings will force them against the cylinder wall and cause rapid wear of both parts.

The minimum amount of clearance necessary at the joints of piston rings depends, of course, upon the working temperature of the piston and the position any particular ring is to occupy, since the upper rings are subjected to the highest temperature. The amount of clearance depends also upon the position of the rings on the piston relative to the cooling-water spaces. In some old engines they are placed much higher on the piston than is the practice to-day, with the result that the top ring is located at an uncooled part of the piston. The piston rings of some two-stroke engines are located as near to the ends of the piston as practicable, since the piston rings in this type of engine determine the point at which the scavenging air or exhaust ports open and close. For instance, the lower the rings are located on the piston the earlier in the stroke will the ports open and the later will the ports close.

Two-stroke engine pistons work at a higher temperature than those of four-stroke engines, so that the clearance allowed in the former type must be greater. If, when calculating the amount of end clearance to be given to piston rings of four-stroke engines (when this information is not stated on the manufacturer's drawings) the following temperatures are assumed, the clearances will be approximately correct (for two-stroke engines the temperatures should be increased 50°F):—

Working temperature of Nos. 1 and 2 piston rings, 200°F (93°C)
„ „ „ „ 3 „ 4 „ „ 175°F (79°C)
„ „ „ „ 5 „ 6 „ „ 150°F (66°C)

If one of the above temperatures is substituted in the following formula the minimum amount of end clearance necessary for the various rings (having any form of joint) will be found:—

$$\text{Clearance} = \left(D_1 \times \frac{D_2 - D_1}{2}\right) \times 3{\cdot}1416 \times x \times (T_2 - T_1)$$

where D_1 = inside diameter of piston ring;
D_2 = outside diameter of piston ring;

and $D_1 + \dfrac{D_2 - D_1}{2}$ = mean diameter of piston ring;

x = coefficient of expansion of ordinary high-grade cast iron = 0·000006 for each degree (Fahr.) increase in temperature;

T_1 = initial temperature of piston ring, i.e. atmospheric temperature;

T_2 = working temperature of piston ring.

There is no doubt that in many instances the best results are not obtained from piston rings because the engineer who decides upon the amount of clearance to be given is afraid the amount is insufficient, and gives a little more to be on the safe side. Those who give a little more than is stated on the manufacturer's drawing just because it doesn't look very much, overlook the fact that the cylinder liner also becomes heated and expands. It is, of course, a serious matter if the rings butt and break, but there is not the slightest doubt that a great deal of the initial wear of piston rings and cylinder liners is due to the rings being given too much end clearance and allowing high-pressure gas to get behind the rings. Once cylinder liners have begun to wear it is impossible to arrest the wear by careful attention to the fitting of piston rings, since the clearance to be given is determined by the diameter of the least worn part of the cylinder, and consequently, when the piston is at the position where it is subjected to the high pressures of the cycle, the gap at the ends of the piston rings is many times greater than is necessary for that particular part of the cylinder.

Piston-ring stopper pins

For a piston provided with a great number of piston rings, stopper pins to prevent the rings turning on the piston are not really necessary.

They are certainly responsible for many damaged cylinder-liner surfaces and broken piston rings, and because of this and the fact that they are apt to be troublesome when re-fitting a piston into its cylinder, they are not recommended. At one time stopper pins were generally believed to be essential in all cases, and some engineers still consider that if stopper pins are not fitted, the joints of the rings tend to work into line while the engine is in operation, and leakage of gases will occur as a result. Another argument advanced in favour of stopper pins in the case of two-stroke engines is that unless the rings are anchored in this way there is a danger of the ends of the piston rings springing outward and fouling the edges of the scavenging-air and exhaust ports, and damaging either the ring or the liner.

Considering the small width of ports in even the largest cylinders it is difficult to accept this view, nor is it confirmed in practice. When rings having the stepped form of joint (*D*, Fig. 113) were much used, broken ends were not unusual, and when such damage occurred in a two-stroke engine it was assumed that the end of the ring had sprung out and got caught on one of the ports. The author's view is that the ring would have broken in any case, even in a four-stroke engine cylinder—which they did do very frequently—moreover, this is proved by the fact that bevel-cut, unanchored rings very rarely break at the ends, even in two-stroke engines.

The advocates of stopper pins also raise the question of rings "wandering" and causing undue wear of the rings and, perhaps, the cylinder liner. As is well known, the cylinder liners generally wear more in one direction than another, or in other words, become oval, and if perfectly round piston rings are fitted into such a cylinder the outer surfaces of the rings will quickly wear to the curvature of the upper end of the cylinder, since it is at this end of single-acting engine cylinders that the greatest outward pressure is exerted behind the rings, and lubrication is least efficient. Should, then, rings begin to "wander," it means that they will be constantly riding on the high parts of the cylinder, i.e. the smallest diameter, and consequently greater wear will result than would be the case if the rings were "anchored" and bearing with equal pressure all round after they had worn to the curvature of the cylinder.

The forces tending to cause piston rings to rotate on the piston whilst an engine is operating can only be the pressure of the gases to which they are subjected, and the unevenness of the cylinder bore. The clearance in a vertical direction also seems to have an influence upon their rotational movement—the greater the clearance the greater the tendency for the rings to rotate. From observations made it has been found that the rotational movement varies according to the position of the ring on the piston, it being greatest in the case of the top ring, while the bottom ring moves but little. This would suggest that the principal force tending to cause "wandering" is the gas pressure in the cylinder.

The gas pressure in the cylinder will have a greater effect in this direction on the bevel type of joint than on any other, due to the sudden pressure rise upon injection of fuel. To those who object to piston rings wandering it is suggested that better results will be obtained by the employment of the form of joint shown at *A* or *D* in Fig. 113. The only objection that can be made against the former—the simplest possible form of joint—is (as already mentioned) that a vertical ridge may be formed on the liner, but in view of the large number of rings used on a piston and the fact that piston rings do "wander" slightly due to the peculiar way in which cylinder liners wear, and do not tend to work into line, no ill-effects will result from the use of this type of joint. A common practice when rings having the bevel type of joint are used is to alternate the right- and left-hand rings as shown at *B* and *C*, Fig. 113, so that if there is a tendency for the rings to rotate due to gas pressure they will rotate in opposite directions.

One advantage of the bevel type of joint is that in the event of the end clearance being a few thousandths of an inch less than it ought to be, there is less danger of the ring breaking than would be the case in the butt type of joint, because the surfaces that make contact are inclined and a ring will be free to close in a little more after the ends make contact, and the amount depending upon the vertical clearance in the groove.

When ordinary stopper pins screwed into the piston are used they may be square or rectangular, but not round, so that when the piston ring is fitted over them they cannot unscrew. The recess in the rings for the stopper pins should be near the joint, so that the rings will not be weakened or possibly broken when they are being sprung over the piston. Although the stopper pins should be a sufficiently good fit in the recesses to preclude the possibility of the pins unscrewing, they must not be too good a fit otherwise the ring will jam on the pin and wear unevenly, besides having its effectiveness as a sealing agent reduced.

Special piston rings

The only disadvantage of the simple Ramsbottom piston ring,

no matter which type of joint is employed, is that as all cylinder liners wear unevenly and develop a tapered form, the piston rings become less effective in preventing leakage of gases. The clearance allowed between the ends of such rings fitted into worn cylinders must, of course, be sufficient to allow for expansion of the rings when in the least worn part of the cylinder, with the result that when the piston is at the greatest worn part, the gap between the ends of the rings is very much more than it ought to be, and leakage occurs.

In an endeavour to overcome this disadvantage various special types of piston rings, generally referred to as " double-" or " triple-seal " piston rings, have been introduced. A triple-seal ring manufactured by the Standard Piston Ring Company, is illustrated in Fig. 114. The term triple-seal is derived from the claim that

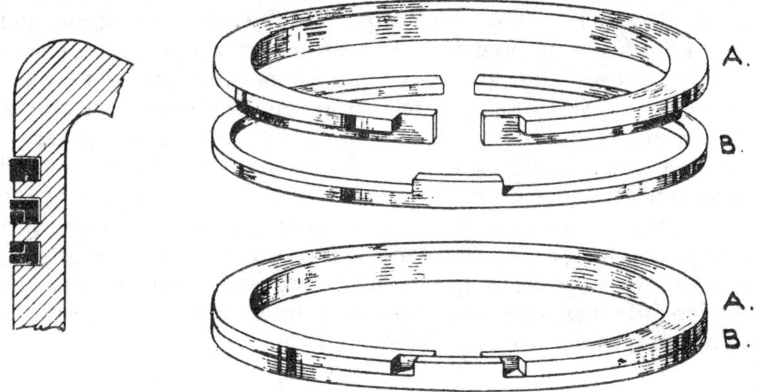

Fig. 114—Triple-seal piston ring

such rings seal the ring faces and the cylinder wall, the bottom face of the piston-ring groove on the compression stroke and the top face on the working stroke. After an examination of the ring illustrated the claim that the space between the ring and the cylinder is completely sealed even when the cylinders are badly worn will not be disputed, but should such rings have vertical clearance in the grooves the gases will, of course, reach the annular space behind the rings, as in the case of the more common Ramsbottom ring.

In order to obtain improved sealing effect, special piston rings must be made up of two or more parts, consequently they are not so strong as the Ramsbottom type, even when the width of the grooves is increased a reasonable amount to allow the cross-sectional area of the parts to be increased. For instance, in a 30-inch-diameter cylinder the width of Ramsbottom rings would be about 12 mm, and that of triple-seal rings 16 mm, in order that the parts should not be too frail. The width cannot be increased indiscriminately because the weight and consequently the inertia forces increase in proportion, and rapid enlargement of the piston grooves would take place. Breakages seldom occur, however, if the cylinder-liner surface is perfectly plain, but where the liner is divided into two or more parts, the parts must be absolutely in line, otherwise the rings will break.

None of the special types of piston rings are able to withstand the stresses and shocks of the cylinder pressures as well as Ramsbottom rings, so that when special rings are used it is often advisable to protect them somewhat by fitting a Ramsbottom ring in the uppermost groove, the special rings being fitted in the second and third grooves. It is unfortunate that breakages do occur, and that this practice is necessary because it is the uppermost piston ring that causes most of the cylinder-liner wear owing to gases getting behind and forcing it outwards, and the uppermost groove is therefore the position where, if they could be fitted satisfactorily, triple-seal rings would be most useful. When one of these special piston rings is fitted in the uppermost groove, the wear rate of the cylinder liner is less than when a Ramsbottom ring is fitted in this position. When a Ramsbottom ring occupies the top groove, however, with special rings in the second and third grooves, the cylinder-liner wear rate is not materially different from that resulting when Ramsbottom rings are fitted throughout.

Fitting piston rings

The operation of fitting piston rings on the piston is a very important one, and there are many points to observe if the best results are to be obtained. Before springing a ring over the piston it should be tried in the groove for which it is intended, to make sure that it has the necessary clearance in a vertical direction, and that it is free to make contact with the bottom or back of the groove. It must also be tried in the smallest part of the cylinder to check the end clearance.

In regard to groove radial depth, the rings at this trial fitting should enter freely until their inner surface is below the piston surface. If they are prevented from doing so by ridges having formed near the bottom of the groove, the inner edges of the ring must be well chamfered, so that when the ring is in its working position and in a heated and expanded condition it will not be jammed between the cylinder wall and the ridges. Pistons have become overheated and cylinder liners even broken by this fault.

Because an old piston ring worked satisfactorily as regards clearance in this direction, it must not be taken for granted that a new ring will do so. The old ring will be of less width and radial thickness than the new ring, consequently the ridges will be formed on part of the groove surfaces abutted by the new ring. In other words, the inside diameter of the new ring will be less than that of the old ring when sprung into the cylinder, and if ridges have been formed in the sides of the groove by the old ring they will in all probability reduce the radial clearance of the new ring to a serious extent.

Not only should a piston ring make contact with the bottom of the groove when in the working position, but the surfaces, particularly the lower surface, should make good contact with the corresponding side of the groove, otherwise the ring will eventually break due to the bending stress produced in it by the gas pressure. If a ring rests on a ridge it is not possible for the surfaces to make proper contact, and as it is very difficult to remove the ridges by hand, the inner edges of the new ring must be chamfered until the surfaces do make good contact. The rings must not be chamfered too much, however, as it has the effect of reducing the bearing surface of a vital part. If this is likely to occur an attempt should be made to remove the ridges by chipping. A side-cutting chisel will be found the most suitable tool for the purpose.

In the light of past experience it is difficult to understand why undercutting the bottoms of piston-ring grooves is not a more usual practice. For steel pistons this is doubtless good practice, as the objection that it may weaken and cause the projecting parts of the piston between the rings to break cannot be raised. Many hundreds of cast-iron pistons have the grooves undercut near the bottom, and it is rare indeed to hear of ill-effects due to this, while if there is a reasonable thickness of metal provided between the rings, fracture never occurs.

When the radial thickness of a piston ring becomes reduced to the extent that the end clearance is about equal to the width when the ring is squarely fitted into the least worn part of the cylinder, it should either be fitted into one of the lower grooves or be scrapped. This is on the assumption that the unworn part of the cylinder is very little greater than the original diameter of the cylinder, as is generally the case.

Another point to watch in regard to the fitting of rings on to new pistons is to make quite sure that the grooves have been properly cut, and are not as shown (exaggerated) at (a), Fig. 115. Such a serious fault is not noticeable until the ring is sprung into place on the piston, unless a plate gauge, as shown at (b) is available. If such a gauge is made it must be remembered that pistons are nearly always tapered from the second groove upward: and should

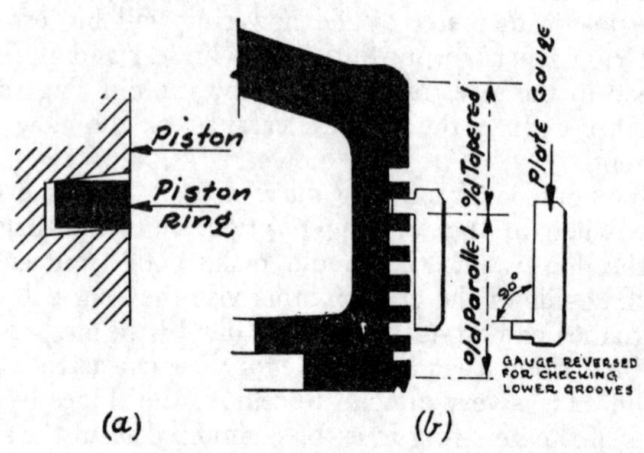

Fig. 115—Part view of piston showing serious wear in ring grooves and use of plate gauge for checking

the grooves be cut at an angle, even though only very slightly, this will cause the rings to jam. This is only to be expected, for, supposing that, when fitting, the ring is given 0·004 inch clearance in a vertical direction, and in the depth of the groove the latter is inclined 0·003 inch, this will mean that when in the working position the ring will have only 0·001 inch clearance, and trouble due to the rings jamming in their grooves is almost sure to follow.

If a piston has been in service for some time the vertical clearance of the piston rings will be greater than is necessary. Should the grooves be enlarged to the extent that there is more than 0·75 mm clearance it is wise to fit a spare piston until the grooves can be machined out and oversize piston rings obtained and fitted.

Stopper pins, when they are fitted, should be carefully examined to make sure that they are firm and not cracked, and when the piston rings are of the lap joint type the reduced ends of old rings should be well cleaned and searched for cracks. Before the rings, whether they be new or old, are fitted in the working position, the outer edges require to be slightly chamfered in order to ensure efficient lubrication.

The common method of springing rings over pistons is open to the serious objection that their concentricity may be permanently affected thereby. Piston rings distorted in this way will not only have their effectiveness as a sealing agent reduced, but will be the cause of undue wear of the rings and cylinder liners. Piston rings should be sprung outward the least amount necessary to allow the rings to pass over the end of the piston, and with as even a pressure as possible. This can only be done if an expanding tool similar to that shown in Fig. 116 is employed. Each end of a piston

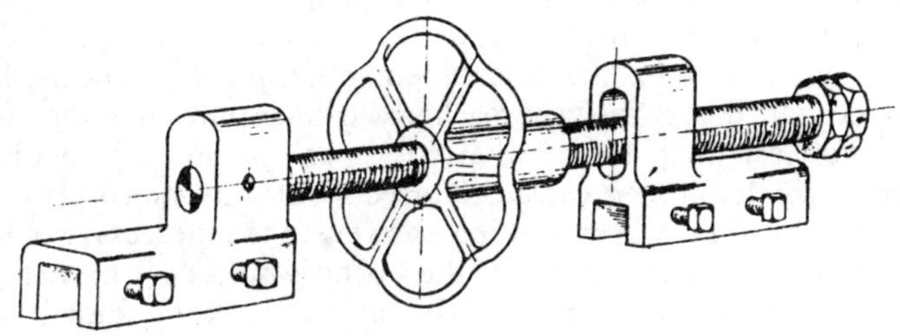

Fig. 116—Piston ring expanding tool

ring is firmly gripped by the square-headed screws shown, after which the ring is laid on the top of the piston and is sprung open by rotating the wheel until the ring is opened just sufficiently to pass over the piston. The rings can be taken out of their grooves and off the piston by this tool with equal ease and with no more risk of affecting their concentricity.

CHAPTER 15

Piston cooling

As diesel-engine pistons are exposed to the burning fuel in the cylinders they absorb a great deal of heat. If the pistons consisted merely of a solid block of metal, the heat absorbed would make them red hot and cause them to expand. Such pistons would expand freely enough (neglecting any question of fit in the cylinders), since when heating up the outside would get hot first and be in an expanded state before the heat reached the inner portion of the piston.

It would seem, therefore, that so far as the heating-up process is concerned the heat stresses produced would not be so very great in a solid piston. When cooling, however, the process would be reversed, because the outside of the piston would cool first and the contraction of this portion over the still hot and expanded centre portion would produce such enormous tensile stresses in the outer layers of metal, that they would crack in a very short time.

Apart from this, solid pistons would become so hot that efficient lubrication of the piston rings would be quite impossible, and, in addition, the inertia forces, especially in the case of four-stroke engines, would be unduly great; moreover, not only would power be lost but the attachment of the piston to the piston rod would present serious difficulties. After reaching a certain temperature the heat absorbed by pistons, irrespective of size, must therefore be conducted away as fast as it is absorbed, and the only practicable way of doing this is to make the pistons hollow and cause a liquid or gas to flow through them.

The cooling media employed are air, water or oil. Air is not very effective and can only be applied to small engines of low power output. In such engines the air in the crankcase automatically circulates the inside of the pistons and carries off the excess heat, which is conducted through the crankcase to the surrounding atmosphere.

The cooling of pistons by a liquid becomes necessary in two-stroke engines when the cylinder diameter reaches about 10 inches, and 15 inches in the case of four-stroke engines. The reason why it becomes necessary in the former type of engine first will be understood when it is remembered that the temperature of combustion is in the neighbourhood of 3,000°F (1,650°C), and that the pistons of such engines are subjected to this intense heat every revolution, as against once every two revolutions in four-stroke engines.

In some engines the cooling liquid is led into a large hollow space formed in the piston, and the reciprocation of the piston is relied upon to bring the liquid into contact with the hottest parts. In others a higher rate of heat transfer is obtained by providing for more positive circulation, the cooling liquid being compelled to flow through a channel and over the hot surfaces at high velocity.

Sea-water would be the most convenient cooling medium in ships, as any other medium, apart from air, necessitates the employment of coolers and storage tanks, with reserves to make up for leakages and evaporation. An objection to the use of sea-water is that it leads to the deposit of a hard, non-conducting scale on the inner surface of the pistons. It has, however, been found that the amount of scale thus formed is small, provided a sufficient quantity of water is circulated to prevent undue rise in temperature. Excessive scale deposit is more likely to be formed after shutting down the engine, if the water circulation is stopped too soon; the heat then remaining in the piston walls raising the stagnant water to a high temperature.

If an engine operating at full power is suddenly stopped, the water left in the pistons will quickly approach boiling-point unless the circulation is continued. It is, therefore, very necessary to continue circulating the cooling medium, no matter whether sea or fresh water or lubricating oil is used, for an hour or so after an engine has been stopped. The real reason why sea-water for piston cooling has become unpopular is that leakage from the mechanism which conveys the cooling medium to and from the pistons is difficult to prevent, and sea-water, even in small quantities, in the crankcases or near the cylinder liners and piston rods is most objectionable.

Cooling pistons by fresh water

Fresh water is widely used for cooling pistons. Because most rivers are contaminated it is rarely wise to replenish the system from them, while water supplied in barges at some foreign ports may contain a proportion of river and even sea-water. Unless, therefore, water is drawn from a town supply it should be subjected to close examination.

The advantage of fresh water over lubricating oil is that the interior of the pistons remains clean even when the system is not properly operated. Pistons may crack under such conditions, as with other media, but no non-conducting matter will be deposited. Slight leakages from the systems are sometimes unavoidable, but generally the means provided to convey the water to and from the pistons are of such a design that the leakages are confined to places outside the crankcase. The loss due to evaporation is negligible if the temperature is not allowed to exceed 150°F (66°C), and, provided the water is free from air and is not allowed to develop acidity, no trouble due to corrosion occurs.

Whenever a piston is in need of attention and allows gases to be blown out of the bottoms of the cylinders, any exposed part of the piston-cooling medium conveying mechanism that makes contact with the oil or water, as the case may be, should be protected, in order to exclude corrosive acids. The same applies, of course, to gas issuing from defective piston-rod glands of double-acting engines. Air in the cooling water will cause copper pipes and certain steel parts to corrode also, so that when the cooling water is supplied by reciprocating pumps, as little air as possible should be admitted. There is much to be said for the yet too uncommon practice of delivering cooling water to a tank located well above the level of the engine before it reaches the pistons, as a great deal of air is separated from the water in this way.

When fresh water containing a more than usual proportion of solid impurities in suspension has to be used, there is a tendency for acidity to develop and for gradual silting-up to occur, due to the water being constantly circulated in a closed system and the addition of impurities in the make-up water. In order to prevent this, potassium bichromate may be added to the water. About one pound of commercial bichromate of potash in crystal form per ton of water is dissolved in hot water, and then added to the system. This treatment causes the water to become a yellow colour, and if upon inspection of the water flowing from the pistons it is found that the water has not become discoloured or that the colour fades after a time, more bichromate of potash should be added.

In order that this treatment should have the desired effect it is essential that the yellow colour should be maintained, but as piston cooling water generally becomes slightly discoloured in other ways, a more reliable guide as to whether enough bichromate of potash has been added is to keep a highly polished mild steel rod immersed in the piston cooling-water tank. This rod should be examined every day, and when rusting of the surface occurs more bichromate of potash should be added.

As the addition of bichromate of potash to piston cooling water has the effect of producing a corrosion-resisting skin on the metal surfaces in contact with the water, its use is not advisable where the screw type of piston cooling pump is employed, as it tends to cause jamming. Nor must sea-water be allowed to mix with piston cooling water treated in this way, as the result will be the formation of hydrochloric acid which, needless to say, will cause more corrosion in a day than pure water will cause in a month. When, therefore, bichromate of potash is added to piston cooling water, every precaution must be taken to prevent the piston coolers leaking.

The Shell Group market an anti-corrosive fluid called " Dromus D." A small quantity of this fluid, which has the appearance of lubricating oil, added to the piston cooling water causes a thin oily film to be deposited upon all metal surfaces and thus protects them against any corrosive elements present. This fluid is most effective, but in piston-cooling conveying mechanisms employing packed glands, such as when a pipe reciprocates in a stand-pipe, care must be taken to use a packing resistant to oil, of which there are a great variety. " Dromus D " contains an acid-neutralising component as well as a medium capable of forming a protective film on metals. It is not suitable as a lubricant.

Cooling pistons by oil

Lubricating oil is being more frequently used to cool the pistons, particularly when glands or other parts of the conveying mechanism liable to leak are located inside the crankcase so that leakage of the cooling medium will not contaminate the bearing lubricating oil. Another advantage claimed for this form of cooling medium is that it improves slightly the engine efficiency. This is explained by the fact that the specific heat of oil, or its capacity for absorbing heat, is lower than that of water, and consequently the inner surface of the pistons operates at a slightly higher temperature.

It is also claimed that the higher working temperatures of the inner surfaces of the pistons reduce the temperature range in the metal, and that the heat stresses are reduced when oil is used. The only practical advantage, however, is, as already stated, that slight leakages from the system when certain parts are in need of attention are not detrimental to the bearing lubricating oil. This is certainly a great advantage, as very considerable and serious trouble has resulted in the past owing to contamination of bearing lubricating oil by piston cooling water.

As lubricating oil is a comparatively expensive cooling medium, loss by evaporation must be reduced to a minimum. It has been found that the amount lost in this way is of little account if the temperature is not allowed to exceed 140°F (60°C).

When properly designed pistons are cooled by lubricating oil, no difficulties of any kind will be experienced, provided the oil used is of suitable quality and the pistons are not allowed to get overheated due to shortage of cooling oil. If allowed to become overheated, even the most suitable oil for the purpose will carbonise. Should the oil become overheated and carbon deposit on the surfaces, the transfer of heat to the cooling oil will be restricted, and certain parts of the piston will be overheated and stressed even to the point of fracture.

The qualities of oil used for piston cooling are of utmost importance if the pistons are to be effectively cooled and carbonisation of oil prevented, even in engines where particular care has been taken in the design stage to obviate the oil reaching too high a temperature. It should be a wholly mineral oil, such as Shell "Talpa Oil 30," which conforms to the following general specification:—

Specific gravity	0·903 to 0·907
Flash-point (closed)	not less than 415°F (212·8°C)
Pour-point	about 0°F
Viscosity Red. No. 1 at 70°F (21°C)	about 1,850 sec.
,, ,, ,, ,, 100°F (37·8°C)	,, 550 ,,
,, ,, ,, ,, 140°F (60°C)	,, 170 ,,
,, ,, ,, ,, 200°F (93·3°C)	,, 60 ,,

"Talpa Oil 30" is suitable for both piston cooling and bearing lubrication, so that it can be used separately for either duty, or in systems where the bearing oil is used for piston-cooling purposes. Some oils contain an anti-oxidant additive as well as an additive to prevent the formation of carbon, but so far it has not been found necessary to employ such additives in straight mineral oils having properties as given in the above specification, provided, of course, that the design of pistons conforms with the best current practice and that the piston-cooling system is properly operated. Notes as to how these conditions are achieved are given later.

The deposit found inside oil-cooled pistons is of either a hard or a soft nature. The hard deposit is generally caused by the inner surfaces of the piston being allowed to become overheated, and the soft deposit by the employment of unsuitable cooling oil. If, however, unsuitable cooling oil is circulated through an overheated piston the resulting deposit will be of a hard nature.

The hard deposit usually accumulates on the hottest part of the piston until a thickness of $\frac{1}{8}$-inch or so is reached, when, owing to the expansion and contraction of the piston, it cracks and falls off—while the soft deposit remains attached to the hottest part and must be removed by hand. Although a piston is more likely to be fractured by the accumulation of soft deposit because the hard kind never reaches great thicknesses, yet the hard deposit is none the less objectionable, because the loose pieces may choke the oil outlet passages and reduce or stop circulation.

Overheating of pistons may occur after an engine is stopped, due to heat travelling from the hot outer surface of the crown to the cooler inner surface, thus increasing the temperature of that part of the piston with which the cooling oil makes contact to a degree well above the temperature which occurs when the engine is operating normally. To avoid carbonisation it is essential, therefore, that an adequate quantity of cooling oil should be circulated whenever the pistons contain heat.

Just how long cooling oil requires to be circulated after an engine is stopped depends upon the arrangement provided inside the pistons to ensure the oil reaching the crowns, but in a great many instances an even greater pressure on the system is necessary immediately after the engine has stopped than when it is working at normal speed. In any case, the normal working pressure at least should be maintained until some time after the temperature of the oil leaving the pistons is no greater than the temperature of the oil entering.

When an engine is working at normal speed, any oil in the pistons is constantly being thrown against the hot crown, so that pressure in the system alone is not depended upon to bring the oil into contact with the hot surfaces. When an engine is stopped, however, a pressure sufficient to ensure the pistons being completely filled with oil must be applied, otherwise the whole or part of the crown will become overheated and the oil in the vicinity will be carbonised.

In some engines the bearing lubricating oil is used for cooling the pistons, the oil after leaving the bearings being caused to circulate the pistons. The usual arrangement is for the pump to draw from a double-bottom tank and deliver the oil through a strainer and then a cooler to the cap of each crankshaft bearing. A little of the oil lubricates these bearings, the remainder passing to the crankpin bearings through holes drilled in the crankshaft pins, journals and webs. Here again a little is used to lubricate the crankpin bearings, the remainder passing to the crosshead bearings through a hole bored through the centre of the connecting rod. From the crosshead bearings the oil passes through holes drilled in the crosshead and piston rod to the piston, whence it is discharged back to the crankcase. The holes in the crankshaft and the annular grooves in the bearings are unusually large for the size of such parts in order to allow a sufficient quantity of oil to reach the pistons.

A common practice when the pistons are cooled in this way is to provide a non-return valve at the bottom of the central hole in the connecting rod. The purpose of this valve is to prevent the oil draining from the passages situated above the valve when the engine is stopped. Generally this valve serves the intended purpose and gives no trouble, but it will be appreciated that the valve is constantly on the move when the engine is working and may break or become so badly worn that it may interfere with the free passage of the oil. Because of this possibility, which may have serious consequences, the valve should be examined whenever the crankpin bearing is separated from the foot of the connecting rod. The author prefers not to rely upon this most inaccessible valve to prevent draining of the oil, but rather to keep the stand-by pump operating when manoeuvring in and out of port. When an engine must be stopped without notice, the first act should be to start the stand-by piston cooling-pump, or take what other steps are necessary to avoid interruption of flow of the coolant through the piston.

Summing up; cooling the pistons by the bearing lubricating oil, which is the simplest possible method of cooling pistons by a liquid, works very well and is entirely suitable where comparatively small quantities of oil are required to maintain the pistons at the working temperature. The disadvantage is that owing to evaporation, and consequently deterioration through contact with parts at such high temperatures, the lubricating properties of the oil are in time somewhat reduced, and the wear rate of the bearings becomes greater than when the oil is used for lubricating purposes only. When this method of cooling pistons is employed, particular attention must be given to the coolers, as, even though the oil first passes through a strainer, carbon particles from the inner surfaces of the pistons find their way into them, and they must be cleaned frequently.

In one ship where the pistons were cooled in this way the question of replacing the main engines by new ones was being considered because of constant piston failures, crankshaft breakages, and excessive bearing wear. Upon a specialist investigating the matter the seat of the whole trouble was found to be at the oil coolers, which had not been cleaned sufficiently often, with the result that the oil was supplied to the engine at too high a temperature and at far too low a pressure. The consequences of this were that the bearings were unevenly and excessively worn, the crankshaft alignment was affected and the pistons became overheated and cracked because a great proportion of the oil which should have been delivered to the pistons leaked from the ends of the badly worn bearings. Long hours and much energy spent in trying to keep the bearings properly adjusted could have been avoided, as they were in the years that followed, if a fraction of the time and energy had been expended in regularly cleaning the coolers at frequent intervals. Apart from installing a more efficient oil strainer no alteration was made to the machinery.

When pistons exceed about 20 inches in diameter the quantity of lubricating oil required to keep the temperature of the pistons within moderate range is such that the lubrication and cooling systems must be separate. This entails the employment of special mechanism to convey the oil to and from the pistons, so that the greatest advantage of oil cooling—namely, mechanical simplicity—is sacrificed.

Cooling-medium conveying mechanism

The piston-cooling mechanism presented considerable difficulty at the beginning of the motorship era, owing to the medium having to be led from a stationary to a rapidly moving part of the engine and vice-versa, and in many instances it was either directly or indirectly the cause of engines being taken out of a ship. Unavoidable leakages causing contamination of the bearing lubricating oil, and breaking of some part of the mechanism owing to the severe conditions under which it worked, were the chief causes of failure. In most present-day engines the design eliminates the risk of leakage of the cooling medium into the crankcase, and if the mechanism now provided is properly maintained and given the necessary attention whilst operating it is perfectly reliable.

The conveying mechanism is always of either the swinging link or the telescopic type, examples of which are shown in Figs. 117 and 118, respectively. The former type can be applied equally well to either single- or double-acting engines, but the telescopic-pipe type shown can only be employed on single-acting engines, since the inlet and outlet pipes must be directly connected to the piston. For double-acting engines the pipes must be connected direct to the crosshead.

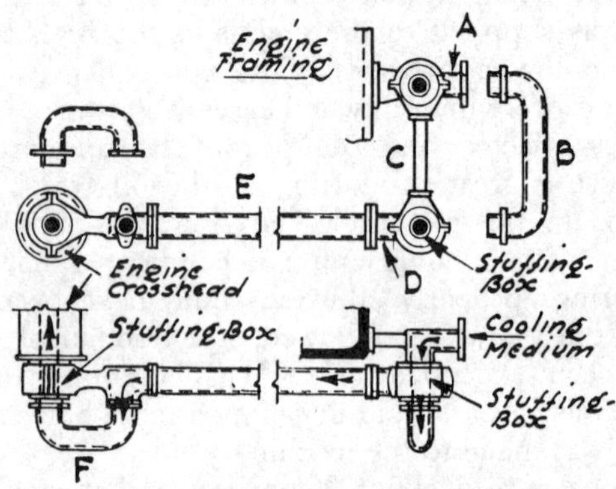

Fig. 117—Swinging link method of conveying cooling medium to and from piston via engine crosshead and piston rod

In the swinging link type shown in Fig. 117 the water is delivered under a pressure of about 25 lb/sq.in. to the hollow fitting *A* securely bolted to the engine structure. The outlet branch of this fitting is bored to form a stuffing-box and receive one end of the U-shaped pipe *B*. It is also machined externally to form a journal for the top bearing of the swinging link *C*. The hollow two-way casting *D* is bored internally and machined externally similarly to *A* in order to take the other end of the U-shaped pipe *B* and the lower bearing of the swinging link *C*. The water then passes through a pipe *E* to one end of the engine crosshead, as indicated by the arrowheads. A reduced extension of the crosshead serves as a journal for the bearing at the crosshead end of the conveying mechanism, a stuffing-box being provided at the point where the U-shaped pipe *F* enters the crosshead. The cooling medium returns through similar mechanism attached to the other end of the engine crosshead.

The difficulty in preventing leakage at the glands constituted the greatest drawback of this system when water was used as the cooling medium. Not only did the water that leaked mix with the bearing oil, but it washed the lubricating oil out of the swinging links and crosshead bearing, causing excessive wear of these parts. For fresh-water cooling such a conveying mechanism is thus not entirely suitable, but it is satisfactory where lubricating oil is used as the cooling medium.

Fig. 119 shows an arrangement sometimes adopted to enable the cooling medium to pass from the engine crosshead to the centre of

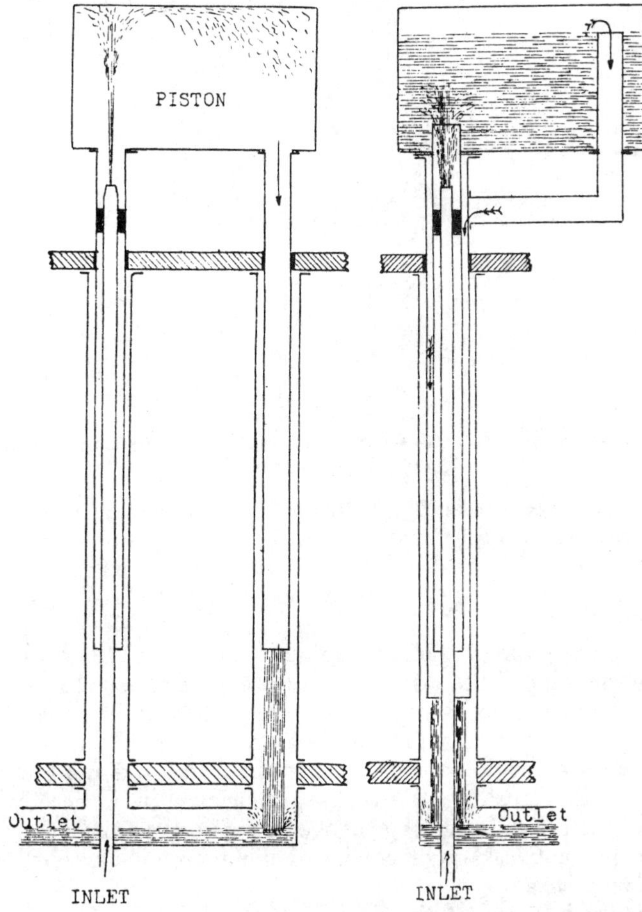

Fig. 118—Telescopic pipe method of conveying cooling medium direct to and from piston

the piston rod, thence to the piston. As there must be entirely separate inlet and outlet passages the whole length of the piston rod, and in order to avoid having to bore two holes, which would weaken a rod of a given diameter, the general practice is to fit an internal pipe of either bronze or stainless steel. The hole in the piston rod is made much larger in diameter than the diameter of the internal pipe, except for a short distance at the bottom where it is counterbored, or reduced, to fit the pipe. In this way two

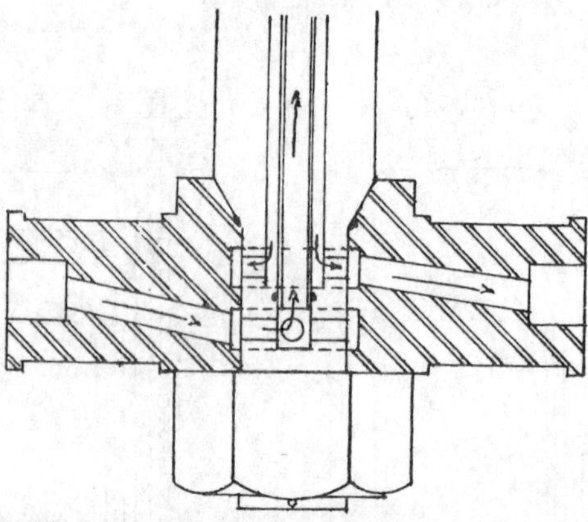

Fig. 119—Passages in crosshead and piston rod to convey cooling medium to piston

entirely separate passages are formed with one hole only in the piston rod, the cooling medium passing to the piston through the pipe and returning through the annular space outside it, to the opposite hollow crosshead pin, as shown by the arrow heads in Fig. 119.

The free passage of cooling medium to and from the crosshead to the internal pipe in the piston rod is made possible by the provision of two annular grooves registering with two rows of holes drilled in the piston rod as shown in Fig. 119, the lower row communicating with the inside of the internal pipe in the piston rod and the upper row with the outside. With this arrangement it is necessary to chamfer the upper inside edge of the piston-rod nut and fit a rubber ring to prevent leakage of cooling medium from between the nut and the crosshead.

The disadvantage of the foregoing arrangement of passing the cooling medium through the crosshead is that unless lubricating oil is used for cooling purposes, or all the parts in contact with the cooling medium are non-corrodible, corrosion occurs and, apart from the wastage of such vital parts, they become " frozen " together and it is sometimes very difficult indeed to separate the piston rods and crossheads. (To make this less difficult all such parts should be liberally coated with a thin mixture of white lead and tallow before they are fitted together.) To overcome this difficulty the cooling water is sometimes admitted to the centre of

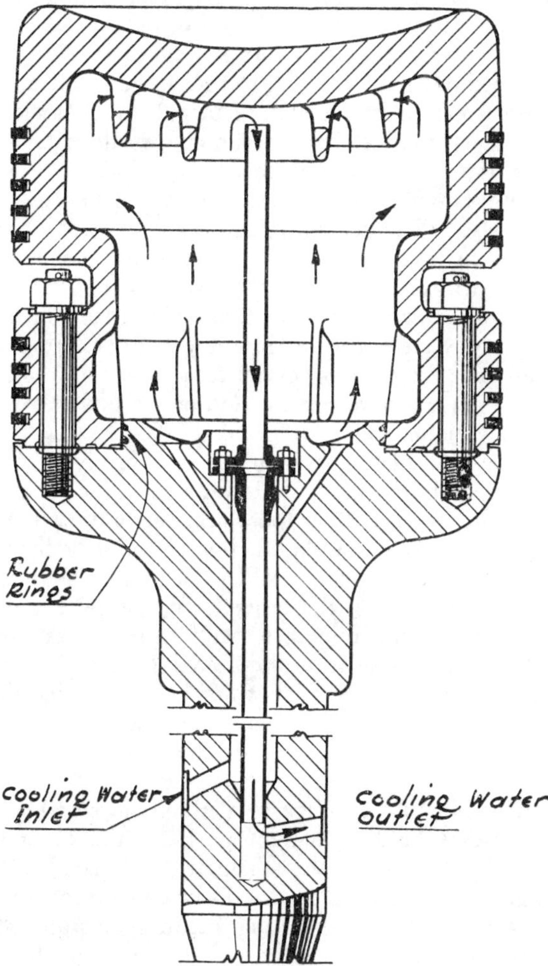

Fig. 120—Double-acting engine piston and piston rod, showing passages for cooling medium

the piston rod through radial holes, as shown in Fig. 120. Boring holes through the piston rod in this way naturally weakens it; even so, of the double-acting engine piston rods known to the writer, in only two instances did fracture begin at the radial cooling-water holes. Moreover, investigation carried out at the time proved beyond doubt that the presence of the radial holes had nothing whatever to do with the failure of these two piston rods.

A great deal of trouble with internal pipes in piston rods has been experienced in the past owing to the employment of unsuitable materials, incorrect methods of securing, and careless fitting. " Staybrite " steel or steel having similar excellent non-corroding properties is the best material for these pipes, but manganese bronze is quite suitable, provided the cooling medium is either oil or distilled water. Should, however, there be any possibility of sea-water entering the system through defective coolers or tanks, galvanic action will be set up and corrosion of the piston rod and other steel parts may be expected. Even piston rods made of 3 per cent nickel-chrome steel are not immune to this action, and such rods have had to be taken out of service for this reason. The corrosion generally takes place at the extreme end of the pipe where it makes contact with the piston rod.

Internal pipes for piston rods are always firmly secured at the upper end and a sliding fit at the lower end. The fit at the lower end is important, since if it is too slack not only will part of the cooling medium be short-circuited, but the pipe will vibrate and will either itself become worn or will enlarge the hole in the piston rod in which it fits. If, on the other hand, the pipe is too tight it may jam and, not being free to expand and contract, may suffer strain at the point where it is connected to the securing flange. These pipes sometimes reach a length of 12 feet, so that the amount of expansion and contraction is quite considerable, even allowing for the expansion and contraction of the piston rod in the same direction.

Bronze pipes should be a free fit without measurable clearance, while steel pipes should be a light push fit, the difference being necessary owing to the greater diametrical expansion of bronze pipes for a given rise in temperature of the cooling medium. Sometimes the part of the internal pipe that fits in the piston-rod counter-bore, i.e. the lower end, is smaller in diameter than the remainder of the pipe. In such cases the length of the parts should be checked when fitting a new pipe, so as to ensure that the pipe is free to expand for $\frac{1}{4}$-inch or so in an endwise direction, as on one occasion when sufficient allowance was not made for expansion, the pipe was strained at the point where it was attached to the flange, and it eventually broke away from the flange.

The upper ends of internal pipes are normally secured to piston and rods in two ways, either by screwing or expanding. In Fig. 120 the pipe is shown expanded into a flange and in Fig. 121 the pipe is shown screwed into a special fitting. Bronze pipes are

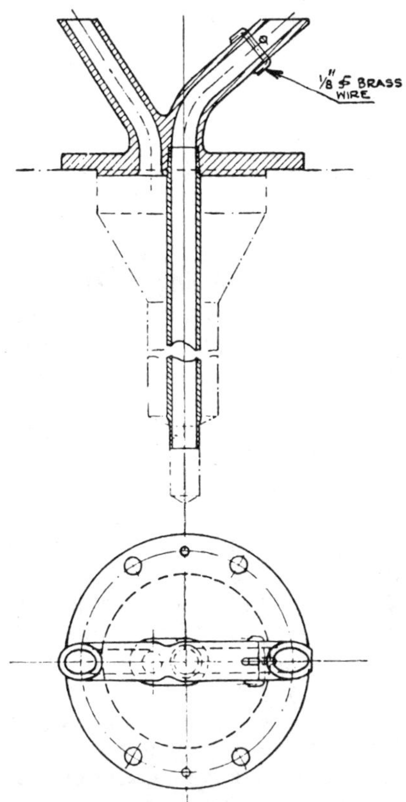

Fig. 121—Internal fitting for piston for entry and exit of cooling medium

afterwards brazed and steel pipes welded. Particular care is necessary when welding pipes made of certain steels, as on occasions when pipes have broken at the point where they are attached to the flange, the cause has been attributed to the physical properties of the material of which the pipes were made having been changed by the intense local heat set up during the welding operation. Heating in this way certainly hardens some of the special steels and makes them brittle. To avoid affecting the pipes in this way it is wise whenever possible to weld or braze the extreme end of the pipe to the flange instead of at the point where the pipe joins the flange. More will be said regarding this important matter later in this chapter in connection with piston-cooling telescopic pipes, which work under similar conditions.

Telescopic pipes

It is practically impossible to design a connection of the stuffing-box and gland type which will remain absolutely fluid-tight indefinitely, and since part of the piston-cooling medium conveying mechanism must always be located inside the engine crankcase, the attention of the advocates of fresh-water cooling has been directed towards perfecting a cooling system the success of which is independent of fluid-tightness at the various moving joints. The result is that the telescopic-pipe system is now greatly favoured, the principle adopted by the leading manufacturers differing only in details.

Fig. 118, *ante*, shows telescopic-pipe arrangements, in both of which it will be noted that a system of open pipes is adopted and that no glands of any importance are necessary. Leakage can only take place near to the end of the inner pipe, and water leaking at this point will simply fall back into the drain and join the water returning from the pistons.

In the type illustrated on the left of Fig. 118, a system now obsolescent, a comparatively small jet of water under high pressure is directed against the crown of the piston, and the water, under atmospheric pressure only, escapes freely through a separate pipe, the height of the end of which ensures that the piston remains more or less empty. When such small quantities of water are used, part is evaporated and a relatively large amount of heat is absorbed and carried away by the steam in latent form. The advantage of this method of cooling pistons is that an empty piston means a smaller unbalanced mass, and as a comparatively small quantity of water is required the capacity of the supply pumps, and the power to operate them, are correspondingly reduced. On the other hand, the consumption of water is high owing to evaporation.

While this method of cooling pistons may be theoretically sound, it was found in practice that efficient cooling depended largely upon the small quantity of water lying at the bottom of the space at the moment the crank passed over the top dead centre, the water

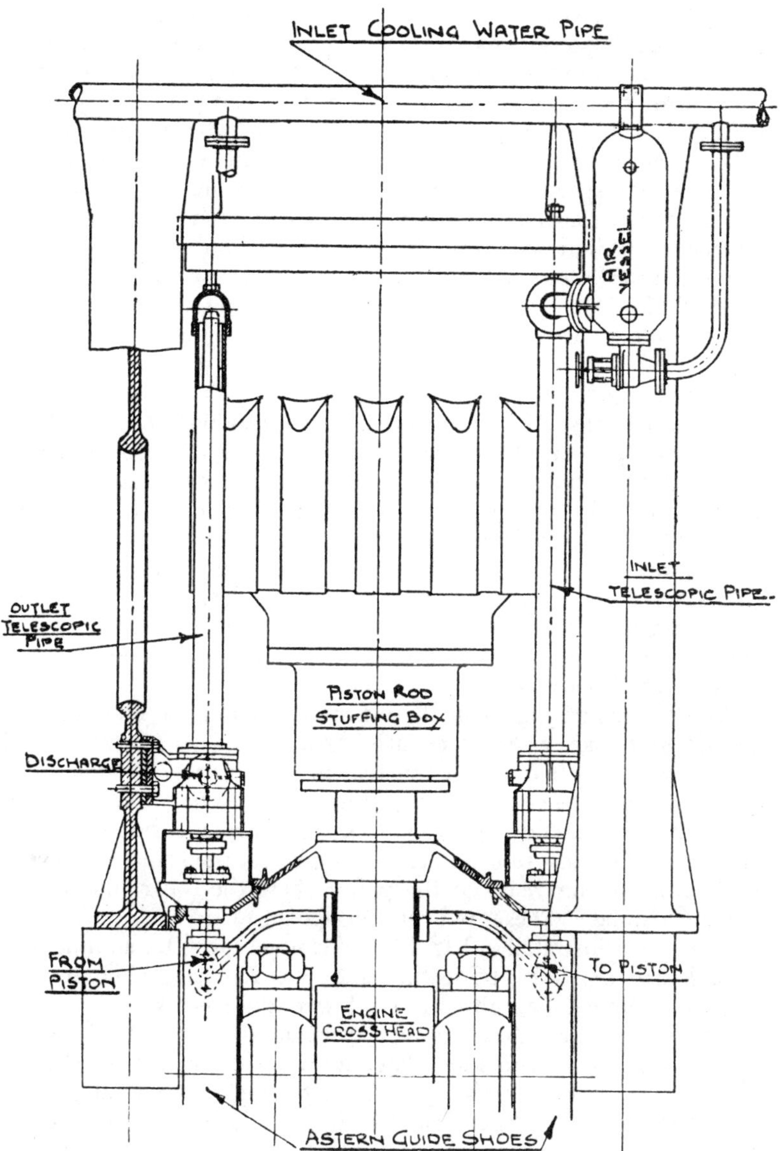

Fig. 122—Piston-cooling telescopic pipes, suitable for either single- or double-acting engines

being splashed against the hot piston crown when the direction of the piston's motion was reversed. From this it will be apparent that there is a limit to the minimum revolutions at which an engine fitted with this system may be run with safety. If the speed is reduced until the water lying at the bottom of the space is not splashed against the piston crown the piston will become overheated, and when the speed is again increased the comparatively cold water will be thrown against the overheated crown and the piston may be fractured. This did actually occur on a few occasions, with the result that the " drowned " piston as shown diagrammatically on the right of Fig. 118, is now almost universally adopted, excepting that separate pipes for the inlet and outlet are now generally provided.

Fig. 122 shows one method of arranging the piston-cooling telescopic pipes on a double-acting engine. The inner pipes in this case are attached to the astern crosshead guide shoes, and the cooling water to and from the piston rod passes through bronze or copper pipes connected to the piston rod and astern guide shoes. As the inlet telescopic pipe is always full of water it is equivalent to a solid ram, and a decided pumping action takes place as the pipe reciprocates. It is necessary, therefore, to provide the inlet with an air vessel to prevent hammering, while unless the arrangement of the pipes is such that the water has a free passage from the outlet pipe, it is generally necessary to provide the outlet pipe with an air vessel also.

As with this arrangement the inner pipes enter the crankcase on the down stroke where they are exposed to the lubricating oil splashing about therein, and on the up stroke pass into the outer or stand-pipe, which contains piston-cooling water, two stuffing-boxes must be provided for each pipe, one to scrape the lubricating oil off the pipe and return it to the crankcase, the other to prevent leakage of cooling water at the point where the inner pipe enters the stand-pipe. These two stuffing-boxes with their respective packings are illustrated in Fig. 123. The upper or water stuffing-box is packed with U-shaped leather and S.E.A. rings, while scraper rings of whitemetal are fitted in the lower stuffing-box.

The success of telescopic-pipe packing depends chiefly upon the rings being free to move laterally a small amount, so that in the event of the inner telescopic pipe not being in proper alignment the pipe will not bear against and wear one side of the packing only. In the case of the oil scraper packing special care is necessary when fitting to make sure that each ring is free to follow any slight lateral movement of the pipe, and that the flow of oil back to the crankcase is not restricted. If the oil cannot flow away as quickly as it is scraped off the pipes, a pumping action will occur and the oil will find its way past the packing no matter how well it is adjusted. When difficulty has been experienced in stopping leakage of oil

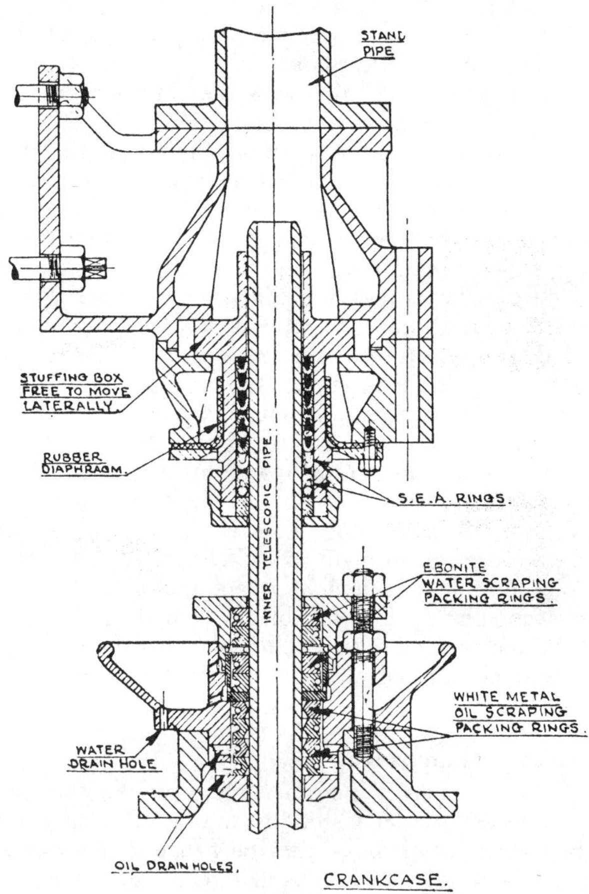

Fig. 123—Stuffing-boxes and packing for piston-cooling telescopic pipes

past such packing, the strength of the garter springs has sometimes been increased. The effect in all cases was to cause rapid wear of the packing and pipes and merely reduce the amount of leakage, the leakage being stopped entirely only after the drain holes behind the packing had been either increased in number or diameter. When the rings are mounted one upon the other, as shown in the lower stuffing-box in Fig. 123, radial grooves must be provided in one of each pair of joining surfaces to allow the oil scraped off. the pipe by each ring to flow freely to the space behind the packing rings, and thence to the drain holes.

As the cooling water or oil leaves the conveying mechanism it generally flows into open troughs or hoppers situated at the front of the engine and connected to pipes that lead the medium to the double-bottom tanks. The flow through each piston is, therefore, under constant observation, as it ought to be, since only a very short time elapses between stoppage of the cooling medium and something serious happening. Sometimes the system is wholly enclosed, the flow being observed through a window. This arrangement is very neat in appearance, but accidents are less likely to happen if the temperature of the medium can be felt by hand as well as observed on a thermometer.

Splashing at the troughs will not take place if the main return pipe to the double-bottom tank is free from pressure. The pressure results from accumulation of air or vapour in the main pipe, which naturally rises and tries to escape at the open troughs. One or more air outlets, comprising 1-inch diameter pipes extending above the level of the troughs, should therefore be connected to the top of the main return pipe at points where the gas is most likely to accumulate. The trouble is sometimes caused by the location of the main return pipe being such that the cooling medium cannot flow freely through it under certain conditions of the ship's trim.

Operation and maintenance

In single-acting engines the inner telescopic pipes are sometimes directly connected to the piston by means of flanges and studs, a piece being cut out of the piston-rod flange to allow this in cases where the piston-rod flange is equal to, or almost equal to, the diameter of the piston. The outer telescopic pipes, or what are called the stand-pipes, are located inside the crankcase and bolted to the underside of the crankcase top. There are thus no joints which are likely to leak, and water may be used without fear of admixture with the bearing lubricating oil unless, of course, the stand-pipes fracture or the castings are porous.

The inlet and outlet stand-pipes are generally separate, but sometimes they form a single casting as shown in Fig. 124. The casting in such cases is rather complicated and not always free from defects, which on occasions reveal themselves only after

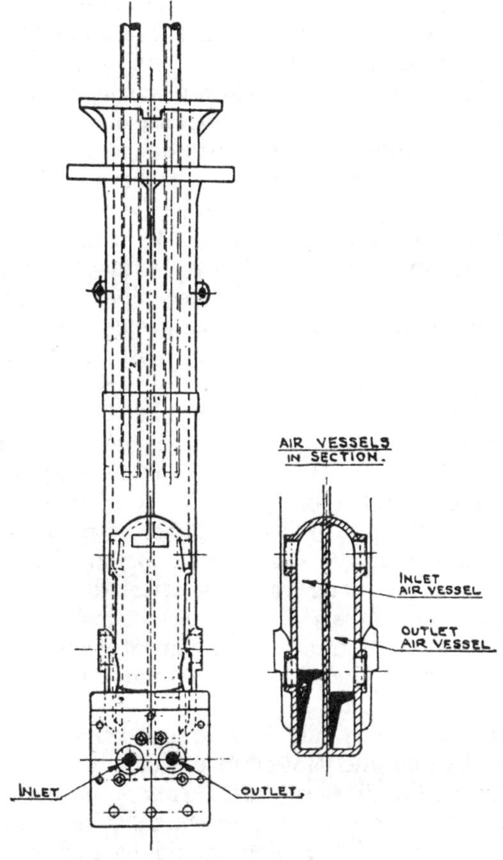

Fig. 124—Piston-cooling telescopic pipes with air vessel shown in section

months and even years of service, the first indication in many instances being a large amount of water mixed with the bearing lubricating oil. In one case the defect, in the form of a porous area, occurred at the top of the air vessel. The first indication of something being wrong was heavy hammering. Examination revealed the hammering to be not of a mechanical nature, so that it was assumed to be due to water-hammer. Admitting extra air through the pump's snifting valves improved matters slightly but did not stop the hammering completely, and later the stand-pipe fractured and allowed much water to enter the crankcase. Tests afterwards carried out revealed the metal at the top of the air vessel to be sufficiently porous to allow the air to escape. Such intricate castings should, therefore, be viewed with suspicion and be examined under pressure whenever the crankcases are opened up.

Inner telescopic pipes, as mentioned already, are made of either bronze or stainless steel; Firth's "Staybrite" and one or two other similar steels have been found to be the most suitable. Bronze pipes wear and require to be skimmed after a time, but pipes made of the steel named operate for years without measurable wear taking place. Negligible wear of these pipes is highly desirable since, apart from the leakage of cooling medium that takes place as they wear, the whole of the packing must be renewed when the pipes are skimmed.

The pipes are either screwed or expanded into flanges suitable for attaching them to the part of the engine operating them, as shown in Fig. 125. As with piston-rod internal pipes, the practice of afterwards welding, or brazing in the case of bronze pipes, at the point where the pipe joins the flange is questionable, as the intense local heat produced during such operations has an undesirable effect upon some materials, i.e. it makes them hard and brittle and liable to break in service. Screw-cutting the parts with a vanishing thread makes the best attachment, though, of course, it leaves a weakness at the point where the thread finishes; but breakages are uncommon.

Where pipes have been pulled out of their flanges when in service, the material of which the flanges were made was on occasion found to be the cause. The flanges must, therefore, be made of specially tough steel, and unless perfect meshing of the threads can be guaranteed, the end of the pipe should be lightly expanded by means of a roller-type tube expander. Expanding the pipe into shallow recesses cut in the flange, as shown at the top of Fig. 125, gives the best results, provided the proper material is used for the flange as well as the pipe, and that the expanding operation is carefully done.

If the flange is made of one of the softer steels the threads in the flange strip after a time and the pipe separates from it. If welding is thought advisable, the upper surface of the flange should be recessed around the hole for a distance of about $\frac{1}{4}$-inch and the flange and pipe welded together at this point, as shown, rather

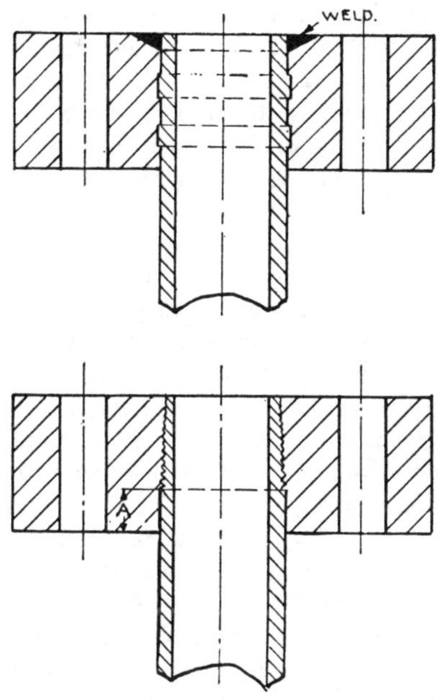

Fig. 125—Methods of attaching inner telescopic pipes to flanges

than at the point where the pipe joins the flange. Welding at the end ensures that the physical properties of a vital part of the pipe are unaffected.

The breaking of telescopic pipes is still all too common, and although this is sometimes due to bad design or to the use of unsuitable materials, lack of attention in the fitting together of the pipes and flanges is often responsible. The pipes nearly always break at the end of the threaded portion, which is only to be expected as this is the weakest part of the pipe. Therefore any strain that may be put upon the pipe due to bad alignment must not be allowed to reach this part, and as such strains are bound to occur at the point where the pipe joins the flange the screw-cutting must not finish at this point. The most obvious way to prevent the weakest part of the pipe from being subjected to this strain is to allow a certain proportion of the plain part of the pipe to enter the flange as shown in the lower sketch, Fig. 125.

Most makers adopt this practice, but what a great many overlook is the absolute necessity for the plain part of the pipe, indicated by *A* in the illustration, to be a perfect fit in the flange. If this is not the case it requires very little imagination to realise that the strain will occur inside the flange where the connection proper to the flange begins, namely, the point where the thread finishes—the weakest part of the pipe. The same applies to pipes expanded into their flanges, since the expanding process may make the material brittle.

Although the telescopic-pipes in modern engines work at a high speed, breakages cannot be attributed to this unless there is something wrong with the design or the material. But if such were the case all the pipes would be expected to break because they are working under exactly similar conditions. In one ship where breakage occurred the trouble was completely overcome by increasing the thickness of the pipes from 3 to 5 mm, which, judging by the results obtained in other ships, would appear to be the minimum thickness if breaking is to be avoided, all other conditions being equal.

Generally, however, it is only an occasional pipe that breaks, and if the points already mentioned that bear upon this matter have had attention, the cause of the trouble will probably be found in the adjustment of the packing in the stuffing-boxes. Apart from the faults already mentioned, the only thing that may cause the pipes to break or pull out of their flanges is if the packing grips the pipes too tightly, causing undue friction. This generally occurs when the packing rings have been left in too long, or the pipes are not properly lubricated. When, therefore, excessive force on the gland nuts is required to stop leakage at the glands when an engine is working normally, the cause should be ascertained and the packing rings renewed if found necessary. The possibility of screwed glands binding on the threads and failing to compress the packing should not be overlooked.

Although the design of telescopic-pipe packing generally allows for slight misalignment of the pipes, it is nevertheless essential for them to be in good alignment if the best results are to be obtained. Misalignment can generally be observed when an engine is working, but when fitting a new pipe, or re-fitting an old one, the piston should always be moved from the top to the bottom of the cylinder and the pipe checked for being central in the stuffing-box before the packing is fitted. The possibility of a pipe being bent should not be overlooked, as rough handling will easily bend these pipes. Slight misalignment can be corrected by fitting sheet-packing up to $\frac{1}{32}$-inch in thickness between the telescopic-pipe flange and the piston, and tightening the securing nuts so as to bring the pipe into line. Finally all nuts must of course be quite tight. If this is not sufficient to correct the error, the surface of the telescopic-pipe flange that joins the piston must be filed, or machined if filing does not suffice.

As a rule telescopic-pipe glands leak when an engine is first started up, and the leakage gradually diminishes and finally stops when the cooling medium and the parts concerned attain normal working temperatures. It is possible, therefore, that undue strain is often put upon the telescopic-pipe connections when an attempt is made to stop the leakage before the parts become heated, with the result that when the parts do become heated the packing grips the pipes unduly and damage to the pipe connections ultimately results. When, therefore, it is necessary to tighten the glands when the parts are cold to stop excessive leakage, they should be slackened as the parts become heated until a little leakage occurs, and then tightened just the requisite amount and no more. This will ensure the pipes being gripped with the minimum pressure necessary to prevent leakage. If water is the cooling medium the pipes will require to be lubricated during this operation.

The practice is to provide means to force grease to the centre of the packing, but although grease is a good lubricant and effectively seals small openings and prevents leakage, regular swabbing of the pipes with lubricating oil ensures efficient lubrication also. When fresh water in a closed system is employed to cool the pistons, excessive quantities of grease forced into the telescopic-pipe stuffing-boxes will find their way into the water, where the grease mixes with the solid impurities brought in with the water and forms a thick sticky substance, which is anything but a lubricant. The effect of this particular substance is most harmful when cold, it being responsible for much friction between the telescopic pipes and the packing when an engine is first started. A further effect of this sticky substance when the cooling water is supplied by screw pumps is to cause the screws to jam when standing for any length of time. Such pumps must, therefore, always be moved by hand to make sure that they are free before the driving power is applied, otherwise some part of the driving gear may be broken.

From the foregoing it will be appreciated that the tightening of the glands and lubrication of the telescopic pipes call for special care. Lubricant should always be applied to a pipe when the gland is being tightened, and only sufficient grease to cause the pipe to feel slightly greasy should be injected when this form of lubricant is employed. If the resistance to the entry of grease is less than it ought to be, the packing should be examined at the first opportunity, as it suggests that the bottom turns of packing are not fitting properly around the pipe.

Leakage of water from telescopic-pipe glands must be prevented, as apart from the waste of water it will have a serious effect upon certain vital parts. Its effect upon the piston rods of double-acting engines will be apparent, while the parts affected in single-acting engines are the piston and piston-rod joining surfaces. No matter how well these parts are bedded together, water splashing from the telescopic-pipe glands will eventually find its way between the surfaces and corrode them.

Position of inlet and outlet

When an engine is working at full speed it is immaterial whether the cooling medium enters at the bottom and leaves at the top of the piston-cooling space, or vice versa, since, as already mentioned, any liquid entering the piston is violently thrown against the walls of the piston before it passes through the exit ; but in order to obtain the best cooling effect when the engine is operating at very low speeds, or is stopped suddenly with all parts at normal working temperature, the exit for oil or water, as the case may be, should always be at the top of the space. This will ensure the pistons being full, irrespective of the quantity of oil or water discharged by the pump. If the outlet is situated at the bottom of the cooling space, the piston would be emptied if the pump output was reduced to any great extent, and although the cooling medium would be circulating and perhaps showing no excessive rise in temperature, the upper part of the piston would become dangerously hot and fracture might occur. It is general practice to locate the outlet for the cooling medium at the upper part of the cooling space, but in some cases it is not high enough.

From the various illustrations of concave-type pistons shown in the preceding chapter it will be noted that the highest part of the cooling space is at the sides, and it is this part of the piston that will become overheated when an engine is stopped with all parts at normal working temperature. Under such conditions steam or oil vapour will be produced and accumulate at the highest point of the space so that the most vital part of the piston will be uncooled. To minimise the adverse effect of an improperly located outlet on such occasions all one can do is to increase the flow of coolant through the pistons to the maximum capacity of the piston-cooling pump. The area of the outlet is generally larger than the area of the inlet, so that it is not possible to create sufficient pressure in the pistons to compress the gas and raise the level of the liquid.

As, even under working conditions, the periphery of the crown is hotter than the centre, the difference in temperature will be even greater if the pistons are not completely filled, and consequently the tensile stresses produced at the centre of the outer surface of the crown will be of a higher order than when the engine is working normally at full power. It will thus be seen that the heat stresses in the crowns may be greater when an engine is stopped after a run than when working normally at full power.

For this reason the practice, whenever possible, of allowing an engine to operate at reduced power output for half-an-hour or so until most of the heat has been conducted away from the pistons is commendable. This, however, is not always possible, so that it is necessary to circulate an adequate quantity of coolant immediately the engine is stopped. It is not unusual to find that where 25 to 30 lb/sq.in. pressure is thought to be necessary when the engine is working at normal speed, 10 lb/sq.in. is considered sufficient when the engine is stopped, whereas more effective cooling of the pistons under all conditions would doubtless be obtained if 10 lb were maintained whilst the engine was working and 25 lb when stopped with the parts at normal working temperatures.

A fact very often overlooked is that the position of the gauge registering the pressure on the piston-cooling system is generally such that the actual pressure in any piston that may happen to come to rest in the top of the cylinder is very much less than that shown on the pressure gauge. Apart from the pressure on the gauge due to static head, a certain amount of the pressure registered on the gauge is lost in overcoming friction in the tortuous passages to the pistons. It is, therefore, safe to say that in a large marine engine the pressure in some of the pistons will be practically nil when the pressure showing on the gauge is 15 lb/sq.in.

The fact that a steady stream of liquid at normal, or less than normal, working temperature issues from each piston after stopping an engine should not be taken to mean that the pistons are being properly cooled. If the pressure in the pistons is not reasonably high, and the outlet is located several inches from the top of the space, as is sometimes the case, the piston crowns will become overheated although the temperature of the circulating liquid does not rise to any great extent.

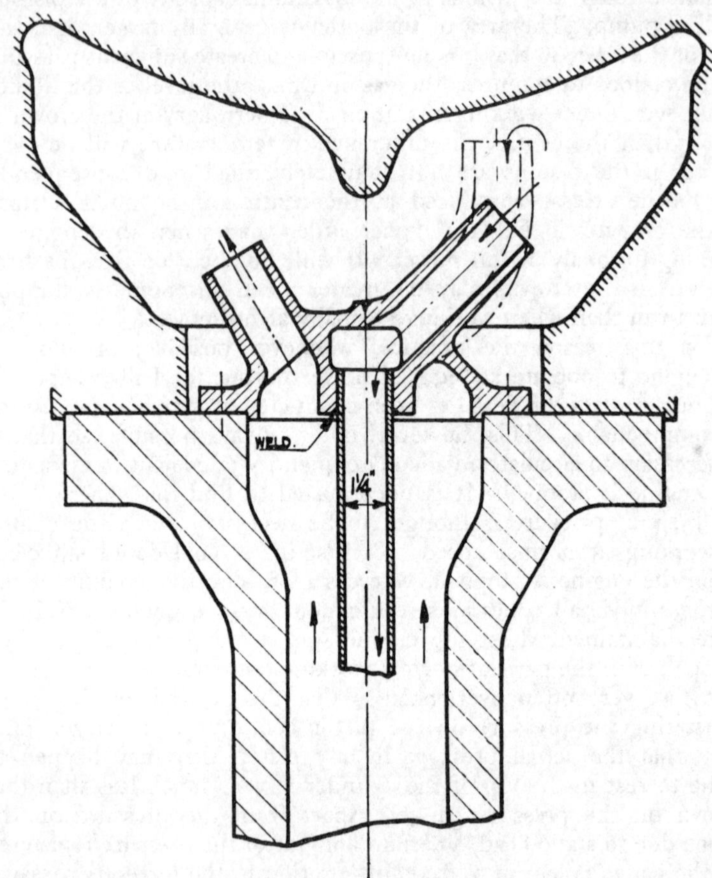

Fig. 126—Modification to internal fitting in piston to raise level of cooling medium

Where the outlet for the cooling medium is cast in the piston and located too low, it is generally possible to bore out the hole to a larger diameter and fit a stainless-steel pipe of the desired length. In Fig. 126 is shown an alteration carried out to a piston internal fitting with the object of raising the level of liquid in the piston. The original position of the outlet is indicated by the full lines. Raising the outlet in this way had the effect of ensuring more effective cooling after the engine was stopped, and overcame the trouble due to pistons cracking. The importance now attached to keeping the cooling medium well up to the piston crowns will be apparent upon examination of the illustrations of modern engines included in this book.

Where unsuitable cooling oil is used, or carbonisation in the pistons cannot be prevented for some other reason, steps must be taken to prevent pieces of carbon jamming in the outlet passages in the piston or piston rod and restricting the flow of cooling medium. The simplest way to do this is to rivet two pieces of round brass or stainless-steel wire, at right angles to each other, in the outlet, as shown in Fig. 127. When the passages become choked it is usually

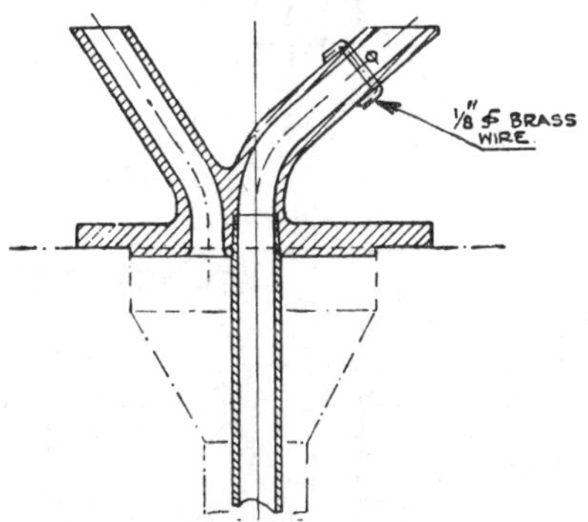

Fig. 127—Simple method of preventing carbonised oil from entering and choking piston-cooling passages

necessary to dismantle the parts completely, but before going to such a length an attempt should be made to remove, or rather displace, the obstruction by injecting compressed air into the outlet, until the opportunity occurs to dismantle the parts completely and remove the deposit. Displacing the obstruction in this way has on several occasions permitted a cylinder to be worked until port was reached, but in such cases the flow must be constantly observed as stoppage may occur at any moment.

In one particular ship which came under the author's notice, a great deal of trouble had been experienced with the piston-cooling system, in which lubricating oil was used, owing to obstructions restricting the flow of oil through the pistons. On occasions the stoppage was complete, and it was necessary to cut out the cylinder concerned until the opportunity occurred to clear the passages. In some instances it had been possible to displace the obstructions by blowing through compressed air, but in others this was not possible. When the pistons and piston rods were removed and the

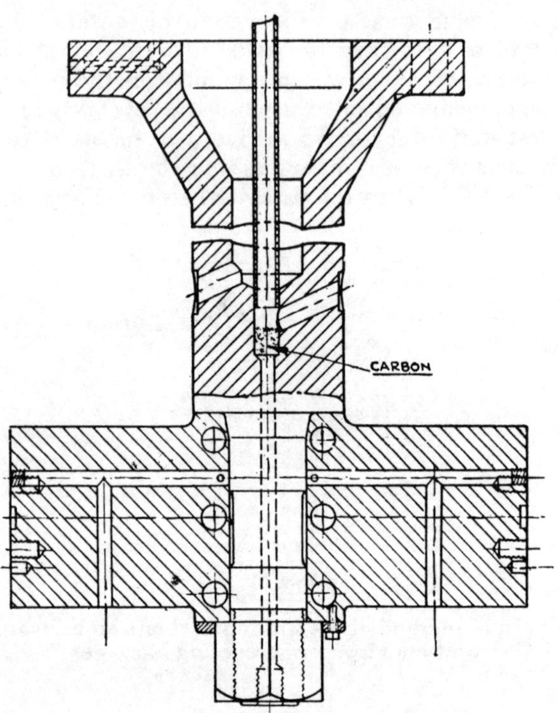

Fig. 128—Method of removing carbonised oil from bottom of central hole in piston rod

internal pipe in the latter was withdrawn, some of the pipes were found to contain pieces of hard carbon, while the obstruction in others occurred at the bottom of the central hole in the piston rod, as shown in Fig. 128. This part of the passage had become choked owing to small pieces of carbonised oil from the internal surfaces of the piston accumulating at the bottom of the central hole and restricting and eventually stopping the flow of oil through the radial hole. The pounding action to which these fine particles of carbon were subjected by the slack column of oil above caused them to be bound together into a hard solid mass.

The design of the pistons and other parts in this ship was such that a certain amount of carbonisation in the piston could not be prevented without large and costly alterations, so that easy means had to be adopted to clear the passage at the lower end of the piston rod every year or so without going to the trouble of removing the pistons and piston rods. The larger pieces of carbon were prevented from leaving the piston and entering the outlet pipe, in the manner already described and illustrated in Fig. 127, while a hole was drilled from the bottom of the central hole to the end of the piston rod, as shown in Fig. 128, to allow a rod to be inserted to break up the carbon deposited there, the broken particles then being removed by flushing through with the piston-cooling pump.

The general arrangement of a piston-cooling system which gives satisfactory results with either water or oil as the cooling medium is shown diagrammatically in Fig. 129.* This diagram shows how the cooling medium is first delivered to a tank, situated well above the cylinder heads of the engine supplied, before it is delivered to the pistons. This enables any vapour present in the warm water or oil delivered by the pump to separate, and ensures a more uniform flow through the pistons and, consequently, more effective cooling, particularly when cooling the pistons with the engine at rest after a long run.

The tank is enclosed and worked under pressure which is readily controllable from any convenient position. The air or oil vapour which separates from the cooling medium rises to the top of the tank and is driven out through the overflow pipe. Manipulation of a screw-down valve attached to the end of the overflow pipe regulates the pressure in the tank, and consequently the pressure of the cooling medium supplied to the pistons.

Whilst the foregoing arrangement has proved most effective in preventing corrosion when water is used as the cooling medium, and the elimination of cavitation in the pistons when either water or oil is used, the general practice is, none the less, for the pumps to deliver direct to the pistons, presumably with the object of keeping down initial costs.

Coolers

A sectional view of a Serck cooler is shown in Fig. 130. These coolers are suitable for cooling either oil or water by means of

* See pages 724/5

sea-water, the sea-water passing through the tubes. The provision made to allow the stack of tubes to expand freely will be noted.

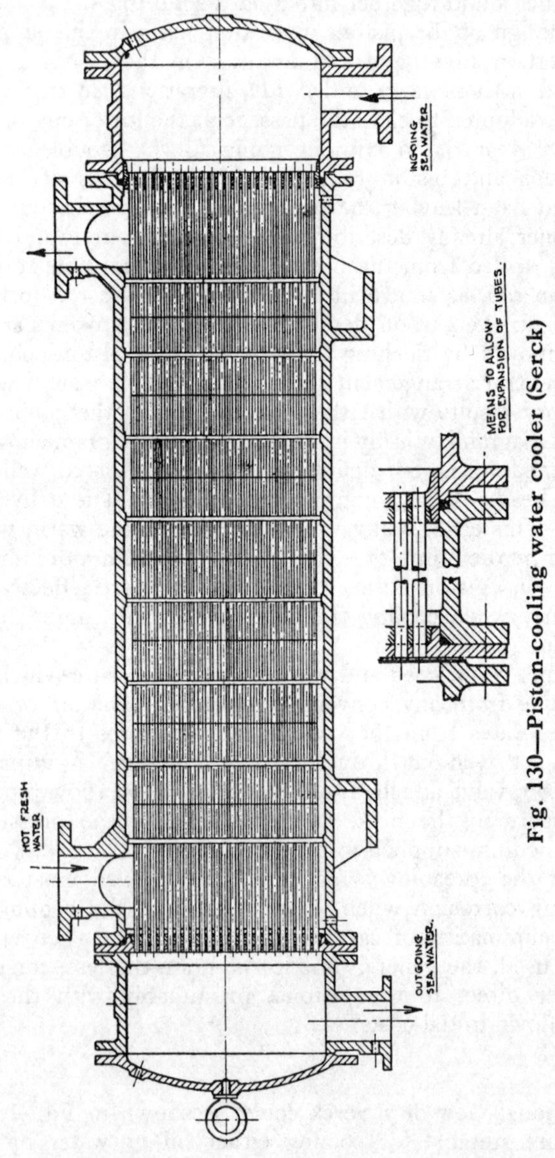

Fig. 130—Piston-cooling water cooler (Serck)

When re-assembling such coolers particular care must be taken to see that the rubber ring at the slidable end does not jam the tube stack, the effect of which would be to strain the tubes at the point where they enter the tube plates and might cause sea-water to leak and mix with the cooling water or oil, as the case may be. The seriousness of such a fault will be appreciated.

Considerable trouble has been experienced in the past owing to corrosion of cooler tubes. Much of this was due to the employment of unsuitable material, and a little to accumulation of air. Cupro-nickel has been found to be a suitable material, and air brought in with the water will have no ill-effect if the coolers are located vertically and a constant leak-off is provided from the uppermost point. The leak-offs should preferably be led direct overboard, as the hot aerated sea-water is very corrosive and will damage tank tops or other steel parts with which it makes contact. In any case the leak-off pipes should be made of stainless steel, as copper and other metals quickly corrode away.

Coolers must, of course, be cleaned periodically if their efficiency is to be maintained. For the side of the tubes in contact with sea-water the treatment is to fill the space with a scale-dissolving fluid—which is simply hydrochloric acid with an inhibitor added to protect the metals against the acid—and allow it to remain for about 24 hours, after which it should be thoroughly washed out. When, as is usual, the sea-water passes through the tubes, all dissolved matter will be removed by running the pump at maximum output, but when the sea-water circulates around the outside of the tubes it will be necessary to wash out thoroughly with a strong jet of water.

Although the fresh-water side of coolers rarely requires to be cleaned, yet the surfaces should be examined occasionally, as deposit due to the use of water containing a comparatively high proportion of impurities, or oil leaking into a closed fresh-water system, sometimes occurs. When greasy matter has to be removed from the outside of the tubes, the desired results can only be obtained by removing the tube stack and dislodging the deposit by a strong jet of steam, unless a trichlorethylene apparatus is installed.

Where oil coolers are employed this apparatus should be provided, as it enables the coolers to be cleaned without dismantling any part of the cooler. This is a great advantage as tubes are very often damaged when the tube stack must be removed for cleaning. The apparatus consists of a 5- to 10-gallon vessel, depending upon the size of coolers, containing the solvent trichlorethylene, in which is fitted a tubular coil that may be connected to both a steam and sea-water supply. A pipe connects the vessel, called the vaporiser, to the cooler so that when the steam is admitted to the coil the solvent is vaporised and the vapour rises into the cooler. After two or three hours all greasy matter will have been dissolved, and if then the cooling water is turned on to the coil in the vaporiser, the solvent will condense and return to the vaporiser, bringing the greasy matter with it.

After the coolers are cleaned they should always be subjected to a pressure test, as the removal of scale and dirt sometimes uncovers a defect and leakage occurs. When a tube leaks between the tube plates all that is necessary is to plug the tube by driving pieces of softwood into each end. It is not usually advisable to go to the trouble of fitting one or two new tubes if corrosion is the cause, as many of the others will be on the point of giving out and the time for re-tubing throughout is not far away. Re-tubing should be considered when about 10 per cent of the tubes have been plugged.

When the piston-cooling medium is oil, the coolers require more frequent cleaning attention as the prolonged use of oil results in the formation of sludge. Lubricating oil invariably contains hydrocarbon compounds which are liable to undergo chemical change and form asphaltic sludges, through oxidation, at even moderately high temperatures.

Since asphaltic sludge becomes less soluble in oil as the temperature of the oil is reduced, deposition takes place in the coldest part of the circulating system, which is between the oil-cooler tubes, assuming that the cooling water passes through the tubes. Moreover, at this point of the system the velocity of the flowing oil is relatively low, and this is conducive to a build-up of sludge which will seriously reduce the efficiency of the cooler. As the cooler becomes less efficient the working temperature of the oil rises and this accelerates the formation of sludge, which in turn raises the temperature of the oil until a point is reached at which the cooler becomes so obstructed that the deposited sludge is detached and enters the oil stream. The sludge then appears in other parts of the system and may settle in pistons or may choke small pipes or other restricted passages.

From this it will be seen that if oil coolers, used either for piston cooling, or bearing oil, are not given proper attention the conditions produced give rise to a vicious circle of cause and effect. Actually the accumulation of sludge in coolers is in one way helpful, since it makes essential the periodic removal of such matter from the circulating system. Regular centrifuging will also get rid of a portion of the sludge and extend the life of the oil, but centrifugal separators deal only with the sludge in circulation, so that if the best results are to be obtained the sludge deposited in the coolers must also be removed at intervals.

CHAPTER 16

Starting gears

During the development of the diesel engine the starting gears were outstanding in that even in the first marine engines to be constructed these parts operated quickly and reliably. On the occasions when an engine failed to respond to the starting lever the cause was not likely to be found in the starting gear but in some other part, as, for instance, one of the cylinder-head valves jamming in the open position and allowing starting air to escape. The same reliability was given by reversing gears, although in recent years the tendency has been to replace the positive but robust mechanical gears by more complicated pneumatically-operated gears.

The almost universal method of starting a marine diesel engine is by admitting highly-compressed air into the working cylinders. The compressed air, called the starting air, is admitted by either a mechanically or pneumatically operated valve, one of which is located in each cylinder head and timed to open and close when the respective crank is in such a position that when starting air acts upon the piston attached to it, the crankshaft will be rotated in the desired direction. This is sufficient to set the engine in motion and compress the air in another cylinder to a temperature high enough to ignite the fuel when injected.

At one time the admission of comparatively cold starting air into the working cylinders for this purpose was considered by some to be the cause of undue wear of the cylinder liners and piston rings, and other methods of setting the engine in motion, such as enclosing the bottoms of the cylinders and causing the compressed air to act on the underside of the piston, were adopted.

There was doubtless just cause, in the early days, for the objection to effecting starting in the first mentioned way, because the starting air delivered by the compressors of that time contained a great deal of moisture, and owing to the fuel pumps also not being so efficient as they are to-day, engines had to run " on air " longer than is now necessary before they could be expected to begin working on fuel—with the result that the lubricating-oil film was washed off the cylinder walls and greater wear of these parts took place.

Modern engines in proper condition can be set to work on fuel almost as quickly as the starting gear can be put over, while starting air rarely enters more than two cylinders for each start. As so little starting air is now used for this operation the moisture has ample time to settle out in the starting-air tanks before it reaches the engine cylinders.

Even with modern engines, however, it is always wise to give the working cylinder extra lubricating oil when a lot of manoeuvring is called for ; and after the ship is moored the turning gear should at once be engaged and the pistons run up and down the cylinders a few times, in order that the lubricating oil left between the piston rings is spread over the surface of the liners to prevent rusting while the engine is not in use. Moreover, the reversing gear should be put into mid-position so that while the engine is standing the cylinder valves will be closed and outside air, which is partly responsible for the rusting, excluded from the cylinders.

Although the compression pressure necessary to produce a temperature sufficiently high to ignite the fuel is in the neighbourhood of 500 lb/sq.in., the starting-air pressure usually employed is less than the compression pressure. The pressure generally employed varies from 350 to 600 lb/sq.in., but most engines can be set in motion with starting-air pressures down to 150 lb/sq.in.

At first sight this may appear rather strange because the area of the piston in the starting cylinder acted upon by the starting air is, of course, the same as the area of the piston compressing the combustion air in the cylinder which will start the engine working on fuel. The explanation is, of course, that a compression pressure stated to be 500 lb/sq.in. is the terminal compression pressure, and is only such for a very small proportion of the compression stroke, whereas the full starting-air pressure is applied for a much longer period. In other words, so long as the work done in the starting cylinder (starting-air pressure multiplied by the area of piston multiplied by the distance travelled by the piston before the starting air is shut off) is greater than the work expended in the cylinder in which the air is being compressed (mean compression pressure multiplied by the area of piston multiplied by the stroke of piston), the engine will be set in motion.

Suppose, for example, that in a two-cylinder engine working at 500 lb compression pressure, the starting air is admitted throughout the whole of one stroke instead of, as is usual, for a part of the stroke only, the starting-air pressure necessary to set the engine in motion and compress the air in the other cylinder, neglecting frictional and other resistances, will be—

$$\frac{\text{Mean compression pressure in lb/sq.in.} \times \text{area of piston in sq. in.} \times \text{stroke in feet}}{\text{Area of piston in sq. in.} \times \text{stroke in feet}}$$

From this it will be seen that if the starting-air pressure is greater than the mean compression pressure the engine will be set in motion, and as the mean compression pressure in this hypothetical case is 250 lb/sq.in., the minimum theoretical starting-air pressure necessary will need to be greater by an amount sufficient only to overcome friction and other mechanical resistances.

Even this proportion of the compression pressure is greater than that necessary in practice owing to the momentum of the flywheel and other revolving parts. When starting air is first applied to a working cylinder the only resistance to be overcome is due to friction, the crankshaft having to be rotated through a certain angle before the resistance due to compression of air in other cylinders is felt. By the time this occurs the flywheel and other moving parts have gained a certain amount of momentum, and this force acts in unison with the starting air and assists in the starting operation. There are, in fact, quite a number of small engines which depend entirely upon the momentum put into the moving parts to compress the air to the requisite pressure and temperature. The engine is first set in motion by the starting air, which is then shut off at the same time as the fuel pumps are brought into operation, and the momentum of the moving parts alone compresses the air to the necessary pressure and temperature.

Crank starting angles

In all marine engines coupled direct to the propeller shaft the starting air is admitted successively to each of the cylinders for a proportion of what is under normal working conditions the power stroke. Admission begins when the crank is over top dead centre and is continued for a period depending upon whether the engine is of the two- or four-stroke type, and the number of cylinders arranged to receive starting air, since in order that an engine will start from any position of the crankshaft one cylinder at least must always be in communication with the starting-air supply. Moreover, the crank of that cylinder must be in a starting position, i.e. not too near the top or bottom dead centre positions.

As a two-stroke engine has two working strokes in every two revolutions of the crankshaft, against one in the case of four-stroke engines, the former type of engine for an equal number of cylinders has double the number of strokes available for the starting operation ; consequently, for a given number of cylinders the period during which the starting air is admitted need only be half that necessary in four-stroke engines. Furthermore, the greater the number of cylinders available for starting, irrespective of the type of engine, the smaller will be the angle between the cranks and the shorter may be the period during which starting air need be supplied to the individual cylinders.

In two-stroke engines starting air is admitted to the cylinders for a period equal to the angle between the cranks plus a certain amount of overlap, while in engines of the four-stroke type, starting air is admitted for a period equal to twice the angle between the cranks, plus overlap. Overlap is the period during which starting air is admitted to two cylinders at the same time, and is essential in marine engines directly coupled to the propeller shaft in order to ensure prompt starting, no matter what the position of the crankshaft may be. The amount of overlap necessary to ensure this depends, apart from the factors already mentioned, upon the speed with which the admission valve in the cylinder head opens, and to a certain extent upon the point at which admission of starting air into the cylinders begins.

Starting valves that are operated by cams are made to open and close comparatively slowly in order to prevent shock to, and wear and tear of, the operating gear, and consequently during the first and last part of the open period the valve is not open sufficiently to allow the necessary amount of air to pass into the cylinder. To be really effective the amount of starting air entering the cylinders must be sufficient to follow up the moving piston and maintain the full starting-air pressure in the cylinders, otherwise the speed of rotation will not be great enough to compress the air in the other cylinders to a temperature high enough to ignite the fuel. It will be appreciated that there is a minimum piston speed below which the requisite compression pressure and consequently temperature will not be produced. If the speed is too low a greater proportion of air will leak past the pistons, and of the air that remains in the cylinder and is compressed, a greater proportion of the heat will be absorbed by the surrounding walls and therefore less will be available for the ignition of fuel.

As already stated, the amount of overlap to ensure prompt starting from any position depends also upon the point at which admission of starting air into the cylinders begins : the earlier the commencement of admission the greater must be the amount of overlap.

Take, for example, a six-cylinder two-stroke engine, the cranks of which will be 60° apart, and to the cylinders of which starting air is admitted when the crank has travelled 20° beyond the top dead centre. Further, we will assume that admission of starting air is continued until the crank is 90° beyond the top centre, so that when one crank is 80° beyond the top centre (from which position the starting valve will remain open for another 10°), the following crank will be 20° beyond—which is the point at which admission of starting air begins. Thus, in this case the amount of overlap is 10°, which is sufficient to ensure prompt starting from all positions, assuming, of course, that the rate at which the starting valve opens is not unduly slow, since anywhere between 20° and 90° beyond the top dead centre is a good starting angle.

We will now suppose that starting air is admitted at the top dead centre position instead of 20° after, with the same admission period of 70° and the same amount of overlap, i.e. 10°. With the valves timed in this way, one crank would be only 10° beyond the top centre when starting air is cut off the cylinder of the preceding crank. Ten degrees over the top centre is obviously a poor starting angle, and it would, therefore, be necessary to increase the amount of overlap so that the admission of starting air would be continued beyond 70° over the top centre position.

In practice, the starting-air valves are usually timed in a way that will ensure their being full open when the crank reaches a point 45° over the top centre, and the number of cylinders is generally sufficient to permit the starting air being shut off before the crank reaches 45° before the bottom dead centre position, so that if a marine engine does not start instantly from any position of the crankshaft it means that some part is not in proper order.

When making adjustments to the timing of the starting-air valves or operating gear, it must be remembered that such valves must be closed before the exhaust valves or exhaust ports, as the case may be, open, otherwise starting air will be wasted. In regard to the opening point of these starting-air valves, they may, if desired, begin to open on the top dead centre if the operating gear is of the type that opens the valves comparatively slowly, as the crank will be well beyond the centre before the quantity of starting air admitted to the cylinder will be really effective.

The admission point must in no case be earlier than this, however, as with some types of fuel-injection systems it is possible for the engine to be set working in the wrong direction ; and if the reversing gear is set for the opposite direction of rotation something serious may happen, especially in the case of four-stroke engines, since in this type the combustion air is then drawn through the exhaust valve and the burnt gases are discharged through the air-inlet valve. On one occasion, when a four-stroke unsupercharged airless injection engine was set in motion with the reversing gear set for the opposite direction of rotation, the pressure of the exhaust gases caused the air silencers to burst and the pieces to be thrown in all directions.

Starting-air valve construction and maintenance

One such valve is located in each cylinder head of either single- or double-acting engines. The valves are operated mechanically by cams and rocking levers in the same way as air-inlet and exhaust valves of four-stroke engines, or by compressed air acting on a piston or bellows attached to the valve spindle. Like the air-inlet and exhaust valves, starting-air valves are generally of the mushroom type, are contained in cast-iron or bronze housings, and open into the cylinder.

The internal parts are made of non-corrodible materials such as bronze or stainless steel in order to obviate jamming as a result of the corrosive action of the moist starting air. Examples of the two types of starting valve in general use are shown in Figs. 131 and 132. Valves may be found which differ in detail from those illustrated, but they are always opened either mechanically or pneumatically and are returned to their closed position by a spring when the activating force is removed.

The total time these valves are in use is so short compared with other cylinder-head valves—relief valves excepted—that they require comparatively little attention beyond making sure that all moving parts are quite free, and that the valve lid seats with the requisite pressure when in the closed position. It is of course necessary occasionally to grind the lid and seat together, as unless these are perfectly gas-tight the parts will be quickly burnt and put beyond repair by the escaping hot gases during the combustion or working stroke of the piston.

The sluggish working of one starting-air valve only may prevent an engine from being set in motion, so that each and every valve must be given periodical attention and not left until the inevitable happens. The work of re-assembling and refitting these valves in the working position requires the same care as with air-inlet and exhaust valves, and the various hints already given in connection with these valves apply also to starting valves.

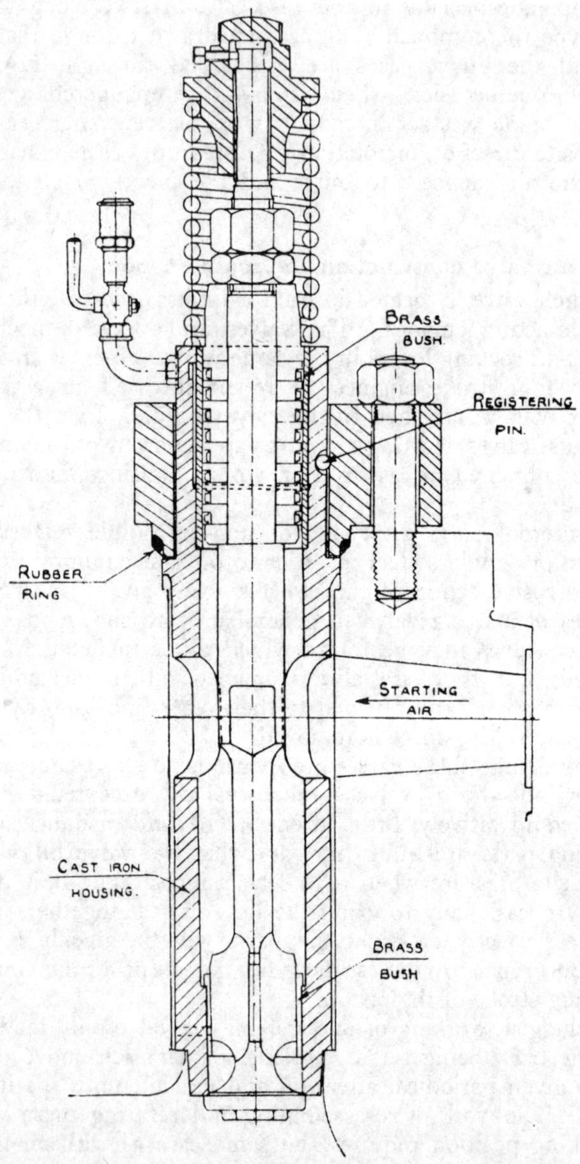

Fig. 131—Typical mechanically operated starting valve

Most starting valves would remain in good order indefinitely were it not for the moisture contained in all air that has been compressed. The amount of attention these valves require will therefore be reduced if proper use is made of the means generally provided to drain off from the compressor and starting-air tank moisture condensed during and after compression. As in the case of other cylinder-head valve housings, they tend to become "frozen in" if left in too long, so that it is wise to remove them at least once every year to clean and grease the outside of the housing and the inside of the pocket.

The housings generally rest on a landing near the bottom of the pocket where they must be perfectly gas-tight, and leakage of air into the engine room should be prevented by a rubber ring as shown in Figs. 131 and 132. When refitting these valves particular care must be taken to see that the cross-section of the rubber ring is not too great, otherwise the housing will be prevented from landing properly, the consequences of which may be serious. If in doubt, a ring of small cross-section should be fitted in preference to one that is too large, as the leakage of air will be of little account, because in most designs the pressure of air would tend to jam a slack rubber ring into the opening.

The moving parts of starting valves require to be sparingly lubricated occasionally. A good plan is to lubricate them at every port just prior to the engine being put into operation again, the valves being worked by hand while the lubricating oil is being applied to ensure that it reaches all parts. When a valve is not working freely it generally jams in the open position, and the cause of the engine failing to start is not in doubt very long. Should it so happen that the crankshaft is in such a position that the cylinder in which the defective valve is situated is not required to set the engine in motion, the burning gases will have free entry into the starting-air supply pipe, and if this should contain greasy matter an explosion may occur.

It occasionally happens that the friction between the rubbing surfaces is sufficient to keep the valve open during the low-pressure period of the cycle. In such an event a large quantity of starting air will be wasted during the exhaust and air-inlet strokes and dangerously high-compression pressures may be reached. From this it will be seen that failure to start is not the most serious consequence of neglecting to keep the starting valves in proper working order.

The correct spring load on these valves must be maintained in order to ensure prompt closing. The load must not be increased,

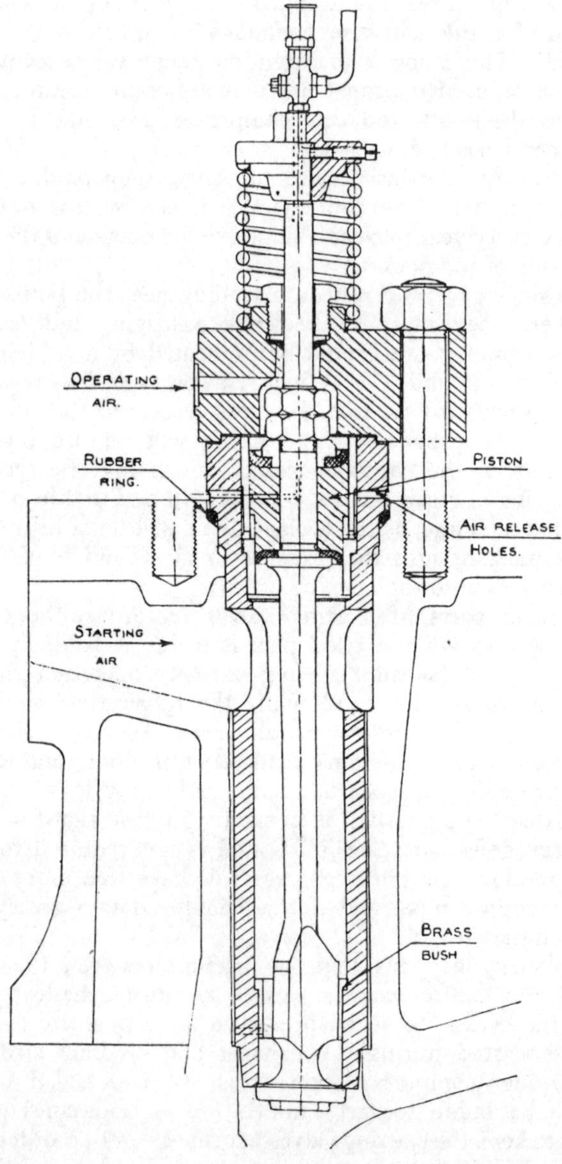

Fig. 132—Typical pneumatically operated starting valve

however, for the sole purpose of overcoming undue friction, as apart from subjecting the operating gear to unduly severe working conditions, excessive spring load in the case of some starting valves will mean that an engine will not start so readily when the starting-air pressure has been reduced by more than the usual amount of manoeuvring.

As starting-air valves are of the type that open into the cylinder, and as the pressure of the starting air tending to open them is counterbalanced by enlarging the upper part of the spindle as illustrated in Fig. 131 (on page 302), the spring load requires to be sufficient only to hold the valve firmly on its seat during the low-pressure period of the cycle. Should the spring load be insufficient to ensure this, and it be necessary to increase the compression load by fitting packing washers, care must be taken to see that the valve lift is not reduced owing to the spring now having insufficient compression clearance, otherwise the rocking lever or some other part of the operating gear will be broken when an attempt is made to set the engine in motion.

Another important point to be observed in connection with mechanically operated starting valves is to maintain the correct cam-roller clearances, otherwise an engine may fail to start if the clearance is too great, and starting air will be wasted if too small. If the roller rides on the plain part of the cam and prevents the valve from seating, the starting air leaking into the cylinder during the compression stroke may increase the terminal compression pressure so much that the turning effort of the starting air in the active cylinder will be unduly resisted; consequently, when the cylinder begins working on fuel the valve faces will quickly become burnt.

It is generally sufficient to adjust the roller clearance to about 0·5 mm, but it sometimes happens that the clearance varies even for different cylinders of the same engine, so that the timing should occasionally be verified by placing the crank in the position where the valve should begin to open, and setting the adjusting screw so that it is just possible to move the roller with the fingers. The cam-shaft should then be rotated in the " ahead " direction, if it is the " ahead " cam that is being checked, until it is again just possible to move the roller, at which instant the position of the crankshaft should be noted. This will, of course, be the closing point of the valve. The closing point should then be compared with the opening point of the exhaust valve or ports, as the case may be, to make sure that the starting valve closes before the exhausting process begins, and the amount of overlap of the successive starting-air valves ascertained.

Any adjustments necessary will require to be made by varying the rocking-lever roller clearance, as starting-air cams are generally made in one piece and are rigidly secured to the camshaft since they do not wear and it is rarely necessary to have to alter their angular position. The only time that the cams, rollers, or other parts of the starting-air valve operating gear are liable to wear is when the parts are allowed to vibrate or are allowed movement owing to slackness when the engine is working on fuel. Springs or other devices are usually provided to hold these parts when not in operation, and care should be taken to see that such parts serve the purpose intended.

When refitting starting-air valves, care must be taken to see that they are not prevented from opening to their fullest extent. As these valves open into the cylinder and the lids are sometimes inside the pockets, it is as well to be sure that the lids do not foul the sides of the pockets. The clearance at this point is not always great owing to the desire of designers to make the diameter of the pockets as small as possible, for reasons already explained in a previous chapter. Owing to this, cases are known where the valve lid, when cold, was clear of the side of the pocket, but when heated to working temperature the clearance was not sufficient to allow for expansion, and the valve jammed lightly but sufficiently to prevent its functioning properly.

Before an engine is set in motion after a period of inaction, no matter whether the starting valves have been out for attention or access to other parts or not, each valve should be opened to its fullest extent by hand a few times and the operating gear tested to make sure that it is free, as these parts, owing to their long periods of inaction, may not work freely when required to do so.

Starting gears

In addition to a starting valve in each cylinder head the starting equipment or system of an engine includes (1) a relay valve, sometimes called the automatic valve or the master valve, (2) a pilot valve, and (3) a distributor. The pilot valve is operated by the engine control lever or wheel, as the case may be, and when opened allows air to flow to the piston-operated relay valve. Opening of the relay valve permits starting air to pass to the starting valve of each engine cylinder. The distributor controls the admission and cut-off of the starting air to the cylinders.

Each engine designer has his own particular ideas about starting equipment, and while modern engines differ widely in detail they operate on one of two basic principles, depending upon whether mechanically or pneumatically operated starting valves are favoured.

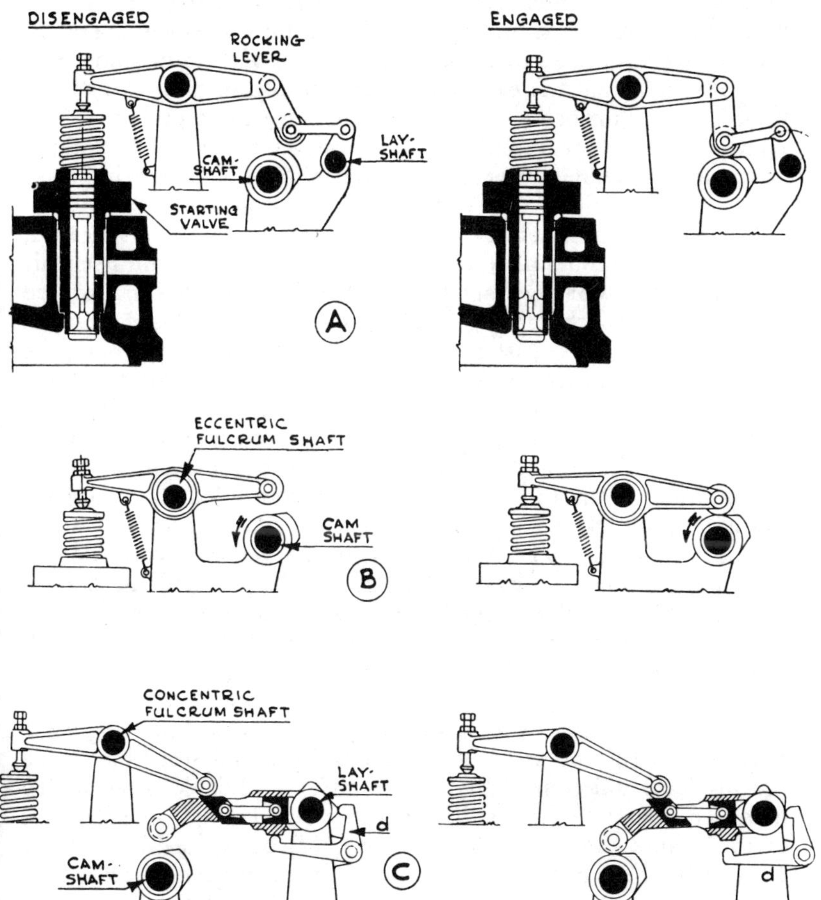

Fig. 133—Starting gears suitable for mechanically operated starting valves

To understand any of the various starting gears that are now in use it is necessary to have knowledge of the two basic principles, and these reduced to their simplest form are shown in Figs. 133 and 134.

Fig. 133 shows three ways by which the mechanically operated starting valve can be engaged and disengaged quickly and positively as required. In each case the valve is provided with two cams mounted side by side on the camshaft, one for starting in an ahead direction and the other astern. To change from one cam to the other the camshaft is moved endwise, prior to which operation the rocking-lever roller must be lifted well clear of the cams, otherwise the roller will foul the cam it is desired to use in the event of the peak of that cam being in or about the uppermost position. The final operation is to return the rocking-lever roller to its working or engaged position. After the engine has started, the rocking-lever rollers are lifted clear of the cams and the starting valves disengaged.

When an engine is at rest the starting gear is, of course, disengaged, and although nothing undesirable will result in the case of mechanically operated starting valves if starting air is admitted to the valves, provided the spring holding them in the closed position is strong enough to resist the effort of the starting air to open the valves, it is usual to provide a relay valve in the starting-air line. A relay valve and its function will be described on a later page.

The three methods employed to engage the starting valves shown in Fig. 133 will be understood without much explanation. In (a) the position of the rocking-lever roller is controlled by a layshaft. Partial rotation of this layshaft in an anti-clockwise direction swings the rocking-lever roller into line with the vertical centre-line of the cam, in which position it will be acted upon and the corresponding starting valve opened as the cam peak makes contact with it. Should the cam peak be uppermost when the layshaft is rotated, indicating that the crank of the corresponding cylinder is in a starting position, the roller and the end of the rocking lever to which it is connected will be forced upwards and the starting valve opened. In (b) the same effect results by partial rotation of the rocking-lever fulcrum shaft, while in (c) a slidable steel wedge is moved in and out of position by a cam on a layshaft, the function of the second cam and bell-crank lever (d) being to lift the roller clear while the camshaft is being moved in an endwise direction.

When an engine fitted with this type of starting gear begins working on fuel, the rocking-lever rollers are lifted into the position occupied when the camshaft is being moved endwise. Thus, not only are the starting valves inoperative, but the rocking levers remain stationary and needless wear is avoided.

Fig. 134 shows an outline of a typical starting system when pneumatically operated starting valves are employed. As this

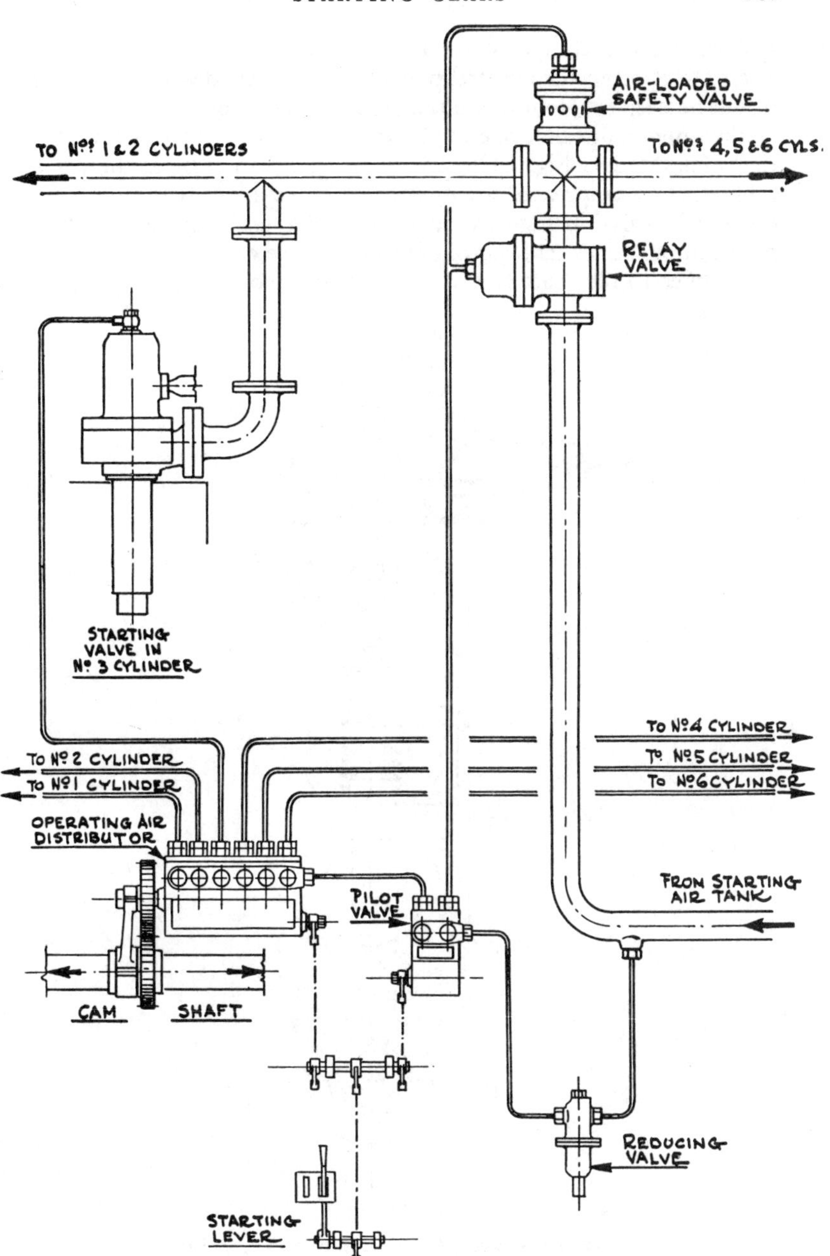

Fig. 134—Starting gear suitable for pneumatically operated starting valves

system is more complicated than the one just referred to we will revert to it after certain components have been described, as then it will be easier to follow the sequence of operations.

The pneumatically operated type of starting valve, similar to that illustrated in Fig. 132, is made to open and close at the correct moment by compressed air controlled by small distribution valves, one such valve being provided for each starting valve. These distribution valves take various forms, but the one shown in Fig. 135 will suffice to illustrate the working principle of this part.

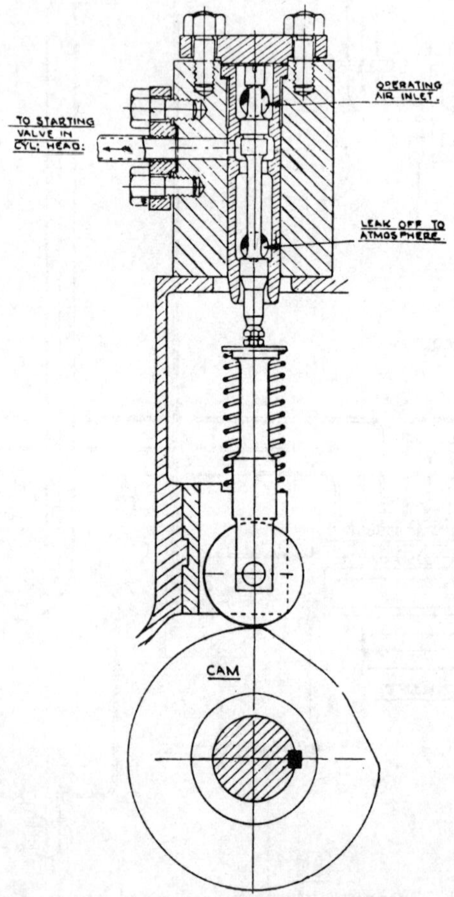

Fig. 135—Starting-air distribution valve

From an examination of the starting valve shown in Fig. 132 it will be seen that when the starting air is admitted to the valve, no movement of the valve will take place because the pressure tending to open the valve is counterbalanced by the pressure acting on the underside of the piston, which, it will be noted, is of the differential type. In addition to this the spring tends to keep the valve closed, so that there is no fear of the valve opening unless the force intended to make it do so is present. This force, referred to in the illustration as operating air, acts on the top of the piston and opens the valve, allowing starting air to enter the cylinder.

The pressure of the operating air is usually less than the pressure of the starting air, but the area of the piston acted upon and the strength of the spring are so proportioned that admission of the operating air causes the starting valve to open quickly, and when the supply of operating air is cut off the spring returns the valve smartly to its seat. Leakage of compressed air past the piston is, in this case, prevented by cup leathers, while the space between the ends of the piston is in communication with the atmosphere. This open communication with the atmosphere is necessary, not only to get rid of any air that might leak past the pistons, but to prevent air being trapped and compressed in the space underneath the larger diameter of the piston. Restriction of this opening would cause the valve to open and close sluggishly.

The admission and release of the compressed air operating the starting valve is controlled in the first place by a pilot valve operated mechanically by the engine control lever or wheel. When in the " stop " position the operating air is cut off, and when moved to the " start " position the operating air is permitted to flow to the distribution valves, of which there is one for each cylinder.

When the control valve permits the operating air to flow, it enters the distribution valves, one of which is shown in Fig. 135. Should the cam be in the position indicated, the small piston valve will be in its highest position and the flow of operating air in this particular distribution valve will stop. The cam being in this position indicates that the crank of the cylinder supplied by this distribution valve is not in a starting position, so that the starting valve must remain closed until the crank is rotated into its appropriate position.

Judging by the position of the cam the engine crank is on top dead centre. Assume then that the cam is moved in an anti-clockwise direction so that the piston valve is allowed to take up a lower position. The pressure of operating air acting on the upper piston will overcome the spring and allow operating air to pass to the starting valve and open it. At the same time the middle piston will close the opening and prevent the operating air passing to the atmosphere.

After 90° or so of crankshaft rotation the piston valve will be forced upwards and the flow of operating air to its respective starting valve stopped. To ensure that the starting valve closes smartly it will be put into communication with the atmosphere when the valve reaches the position shown in Fig. 135.

The cams operating the distribution valves are mounted on the main cam or other shaft having a fixed angular relationship with the crankshaft, and the overlap of the cams is such that no matter what the position of the crankshaft may be there will always be one at least of these valves that will open. Operating air at full pressure will therefore pass to this particular starting valve and open it. The starting valve will remain open and starting air will continue to be admitted to the working cylinder until the cam peak closes the valve. Before this valve closes another valve will have been acted upon by its respective cam, and operating air allowed to pass to the starting valve of the unit whose crank is next over the top dead centre and commencing the working stroke. Thus each cylinder receives in turn its charge of starting air as its respective crank passes over the firing top dead centre.

Reversal with this type of starting gear is usually effected by providing each distribution valve with two cams keyed side by side on a shaft which is arranged to move endwise in order to bring the " ahead " or " astern " cam, as desired, in line with the valve. During the reversing operation the distribution valves open automatically, so that, as the camshaft is moved endwise, the peaks of the reverse cams will not foul any of the rollers ; also the rollers should be clear of the cams when the engine is working on fuel, in order to prevent unnecessary wear and tear. A spring is therefore usually provided as shown, which withdraws the rollers after communication between the starting-air tanks and the distribution valves has been closed by the starting gear.

Relay valves

When an engine is at rest or working on fuel, means are always provided to release the pressure of air in the starting valves so that starting air reaches these valves only when they are required to open. The usual arrangement is to provide a valve which is operated in some cases mechanically but more often pneumatically, by the starting gear. The valve can be closed by hand also (see Fig. 136) to enable the starting air to be shut off when it is necessary to operate the starting gear without setting the engine in motion, as, for instance, when the starting-valve roller clearances are being adjusted. A mechanically operated valve in its simplest form is shown diagrammatically in Fig. 137, while a pneumatically operated valve is shown in Fig. 136.

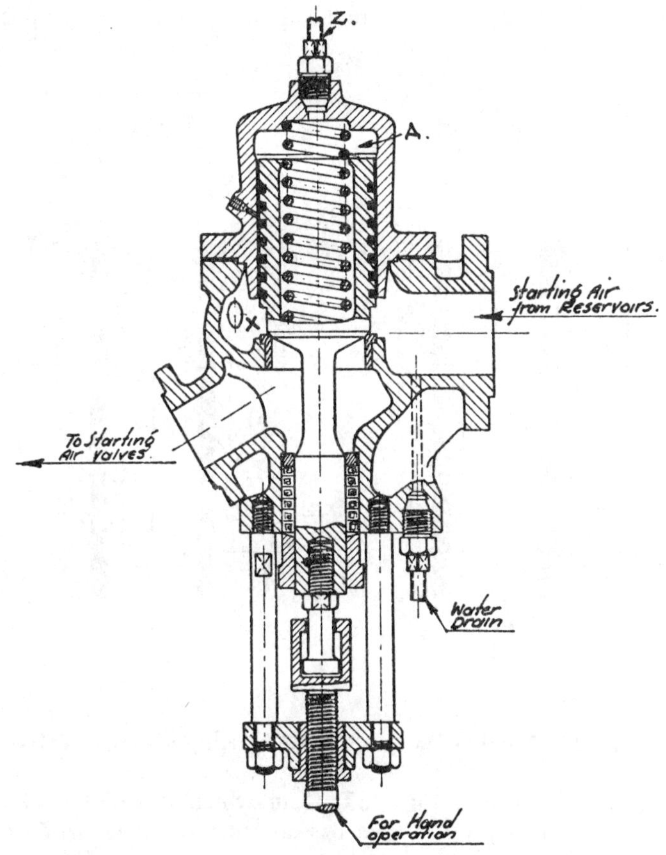

Fig. 136—Pneumatically operated starting-air relay valve

The relay valve shown in Fig. 137 consists of a piston slidable in a cylinder in which ports are arranged. When the piston or slide, which is connected to the starting gear in such a way that it is given a quick upward movement, is in the position shown in the left-hand sketch, the inlet ports are closed so that starting air cannot pass to the engine. The pipe connecting the valve to the starting valves in the cylinder heads is, however, in communication with the atmosphere, so that when the valve is in this position there will be a total absence of operating air pressure in the starting valves.

When the starting gear is operated the beginning of the movement causes the slide of the valve to be quickly raised to the position

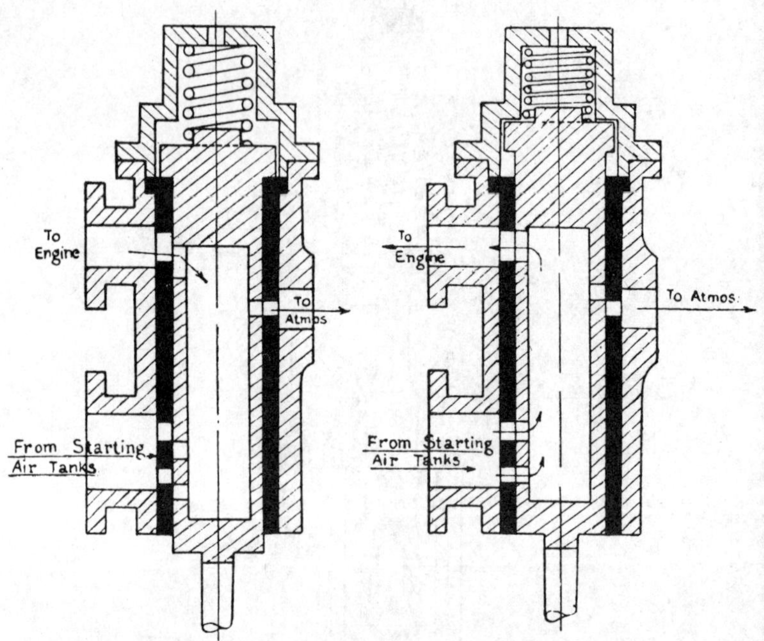

Fig. 137—Mechanically operated starting-air relay valve

shown at the right of Fig. 137, from which it will be seen that the starting air is given a free passage to the engine while at the same time the opening to the atmosphere is closed. The starting gear is usually stopped momentarily when the valve is in this position, and then put over into the normal working position. When the gear is put over to the normal working position a trip gear automatically operates, and the spring mounted on the slide returns the valve smartly to its closed position, i.e. the position shown at the left of Fig. 137.

A pneumatically operated starting relay valve is shown in Fig. 136, and its action is as follows. When the starting gear is in the "stop" position and starting air from the tank is allowed to pass to the valve through the opening indicated, compressed air at the same pressure is allowed to enter the space *A* through the connection *Z*. This will have the effect of forcing the valve against its seat, because although the pressure at both ends of the piston is the same, the air in the space *A* is acting on a much larger area. When, therefore, the starting gear is put into operation, the first movement causes the supply of compressed air to the space *A* to be shut off and immediately afterwards put into communication with the atmosphere. Releasing the air pressure on the top of the piston allows the starting air acting on the underside to raise the piston and open the valve, when the starting air will have a free passage to the starting-air valves in the cylinder heads. As the starting gear reaches the "on fuel" position compressed air is again admitted to the space *A*, and the supply of starting air to the cylinder is cut off.

When an engine is at rest or working on fuel, the relay valve is in the closed position and no starting air passes to the cylinder-head starting valves. Between the relay valve and the starting-air tank it is customary to provide an ordinary screw-down stop valve, the purpose of which is to enable maintenance work to be carried out upon the relay valve without first having to blow-down the starting tank.

When manoeuvring, this stop valve must of course be full open, as it ought to be when a ship is in fog or in narrow waters, as a stop and re-start may be required at any moment. When clear of land and shipping a not uncommon practice is to shut the stop valve, the idea being, presumably, to prevent leakage of compressed air from the starting tanks. If the relay valve is in proper order no such leakage will take place, and the practice of shutting the stop valve is questionable even when an emergency stop and re-start is most unlikely. After all, men do occasionally fall overboard when a ship is well clear of land and other shipping.

If starting-air stop valves must be closed then it should not be necessary for the engineer-on-watch to run up two or three ladders and cross gratings before the stop valve can be opened. The situation of these valves is such that it is usually a simple matter to fit an extension rod so that the valve can be opened or closed from a point over the manoeuvring platform.

After what has been written regarding certain components of pneumatically operated starting systems, we are in a better position

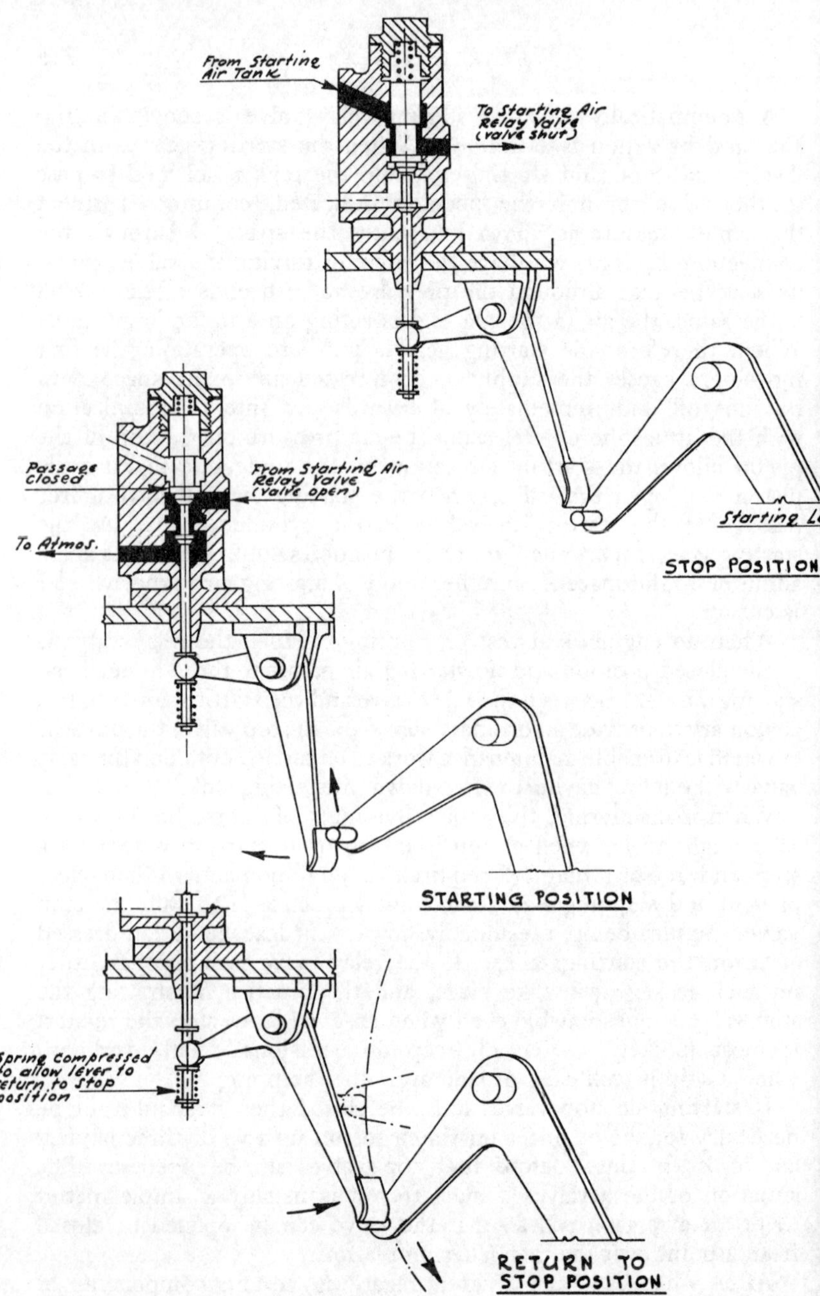

Fig. 138—Section of pilot valve controlling operating air to relay valve and distributor

to follow the starting operation from beginning to end, and for the purpose will refer back to Fig. 134.

The starting air is usually contained at a pressure of 600 lb/sq.in. and the capacity of the starting-air tank is large enough, without replenishment, to enable the engine to be started twelve times at least. The pressure in the tank varies according to the number of starts required in a given time and the capacity of the air-compressor, but generally it is possible to ensure a good start when the pressure in the tank has been reduced to half the normal full pressure. Although a varying starting-air pressure is permissible within certain limits, the pressure of the air operating the relay valve and starting valves requires to be constant. It is for this reason that if the operating air is taken from the starting-air tank a reducing valve is employed. The pressure of the operating air must be less than the minimum pressure in the tank at which the engine will start with certainty, so that the full designed operating air-pressure will be available when there is only sufficient starting air left in the tank to ensure one more start.

When the stop valve on the starting-air tank is opened, compressed air flows through the large-bore pipe direct to the relay valve (Fig. 134), and via the reducing valve and small-bore pipe to the pilot valve. No air can pass through the relay valve, however, until the pilot valve is operated by the engine control lever. The first effect of moving that lever from the " stop " position is to open the right-hand pilot valve, and operating air then flows to both the safety valve and the relay valve—the former shutting and the latter opening. When the relay valve opens, starting air flows to the starting valves of all cylinders, but the engine remains at rest as these valves are closed. The right-hand pilot valve and operating gear is similar to that shown in Fig. 138 but, unlike the relay valve shown in Fig. 136, admission and not release of the operating air opens the valve.

The effect of further movement of the engine control lever away from the " stop " position is to open the left-hand pilot valve and allow operating air to pass to the distributor. This distributor contains a pair of valves (Fig. 139), a pressure valve *A* and an exhaust valve *B*, for each cylinder, operated by cams which have a fixed angular relationship to the engine crankshaft. The function of the pressure valve is to allow operating air to pass to and open the starting valve, and that of the exhaust valve to release to atmosphere the compressed air in the starting valve and connecting pipe when the starting valve is required to close. Fig. 139 shows a section through one pair of valves in the distributor.

Whatever the position of the engine crankshaft may be, one pressure valve will be open and the exhaust valve will be in closed position as shown in Fig. 139. As the crank of the cylinder served by this particular pair of valves is evidently in the starting position

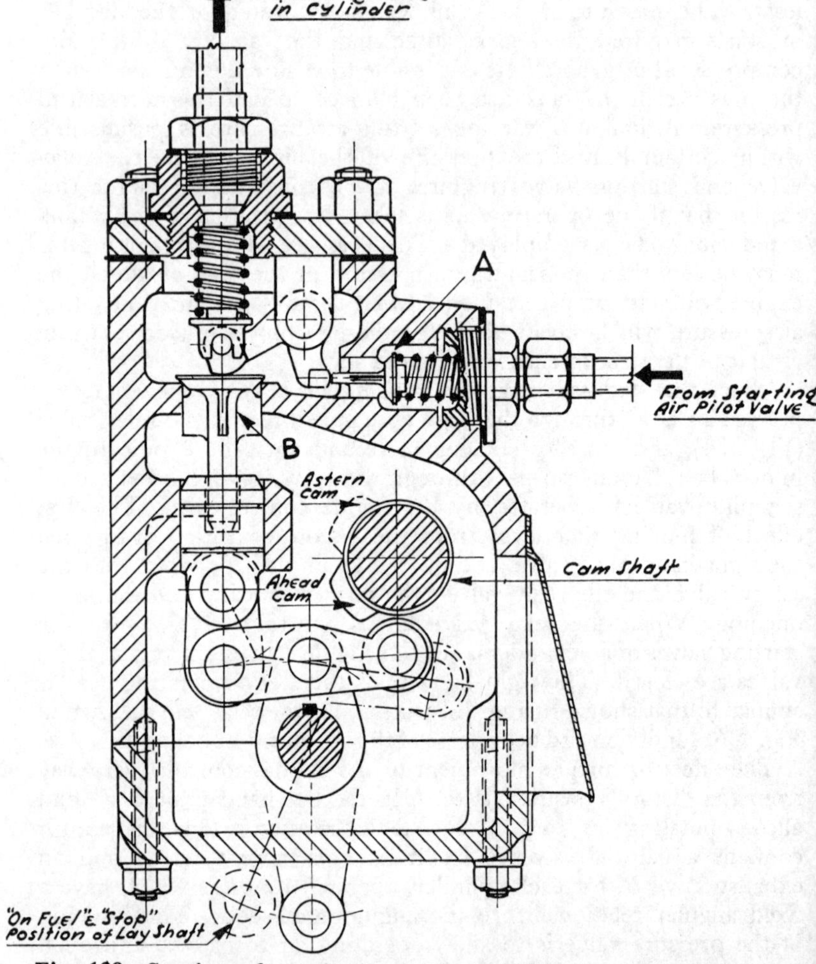

Fig. 139—Section of starting operating-air distributor, showing one pair of valves

the starting valve will be opened and the engine set in motion. As the crankshaft and consequently the camshaft operating the distribution valves revolves, each cylinder will receive starting air as the corresponding crank reaches the starting angle. At the end of the starting angle the distributor pressure-valve closes and the exhaust valve opens. The operating air left in a particular starting valve and the pipe connecting it to the distributor is therefore released to the atmosphere, causing the starting valve to close smartly.

When the engine control lever is moved to the " on fuel " position the pilot valves are returned to the position occupied when the engine is at rest, the effect of which is to unload the safety valve and close the relay valve. At the same time the operating air in the distributor is exhausted so that the entire starting system is freed of compressed air. The starting air trapped between the relay valve and the starting valves in the cylinder heads is released to atmosphere by the unloading of the safety valve, the construction of which is illustrated in Fig. 142 and a fuller description appears on page 327. A further advantage of this particular form of safety valve is that the valve being unloaded when the engine is at rest or working on fuel, a build-up of pressure due to a leaking relay valve cannot occur.

When it is required to start the engine in the opposite direction with this form of starting gear, it will be seen from Fig. 139 that all that is necessary is to move endwise the camshaft operating the distributor valves so that the reverse cams will engage the rockers operating the pressure and exhaust valves.

Another starting arrangement sometimes found consists of a centralised starting-air distribution chest containing a number (the number depending upon the number of cylinders) of mushroom or sleeve valves operated by cams mounted upon the camshaft, or some part of the camshaft driving gear, and of a size that will allow the requisite quantity of starting air to pass. Each of these distribution valves is connected to its respective cylinder by a pipe, and when the engine is working normally on fuel the hot gases are prevented from reaching the distribution valve by a simple spring-loaded non-return valve located in the cylinder head. These non-return valves are, of course, necessary with this form of starting gear to confine the air to the cylinder during the high-pressure period of the cycle. This scheme must not be confused with the more generally used arrangement shown diagrammatically in Fig. 134, in which the comparatively small quantity of compressed air, entirely separate from the starting air, is distributed to pneumatically operated starting valves in the cylinder heads which are supplied with starting air from a common " rail."

Combined mechanical and pneumatic starting valve

The ingenious starting valve used for many years with considerable success by Burmeister and Wain, shown in Fig. 140, simplifies the starting gear very considerably, as it eliminates the mechanism which in other cam-operated valves must be provided for the purpose of disengaging the valve when the starting gear is put over to the "on fuel" position.

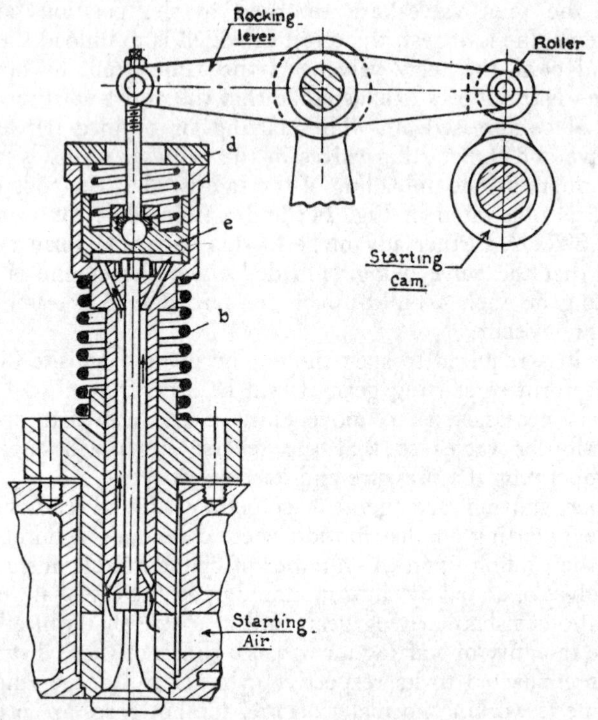

Fig. 140—Combined pneumatic and mechanical starting valve (Burmeister and Wain)

The action of this type of valve is as follows. When the valve is in the position shown in the illustration, the engine is at rest or working normally on fuel—we will assume the former condition—and the rocking-lever roller will be out of reach of the cam when it revolves. Assume now that the starting air is turned on and that it enters the lower part of the valve as shown by the arrowhead. Part of the air passes to the small cylinder at the upper end of the valve through holes and acts on the underside of the small piston *e*.

The compressed air acting on the piston *e* overcomes the light spring located above it and forces the piston to the top of the cylinder. As one end of the rocking lever is attached to this piston, the effect of raising the position of the piston is to move the opposite end of the rocking lever nearer the cam and consequently into the working position.

If the crank of this particular cylinder, and consequently the starting cam, are not in a starting position there will be no further movement of the valve, but the rocking-lever roller will be in such a position that it will be acted upon by the cam-peak when it does revolve. But suppose the crank to be in a starting position—the cam in the position shown—the rocking-lever roller would come into contact with the cam-peak before the piston *e* is hard up against the ring *d*. The result of this would be that the pressure of air acting upon the bottom of the small cylinder would overcome the spring *b* and force the whole " cylinder " down, and consequently open the valve, admitting starting air to the working cylinder of the engine. So long as the starting air is in communication with the starting valve the valve remains operative, since the parts are so proportioned that the mechanical force required to open the starting valve is less than the difference between the air-pressure load on the bottom of the small cylinder and the spring load on the piston *e*.

After the engine begins working on fuel the supply of starting air is shut off, and the compressed air left in the starting valves and connecting pipes is allowed to pass into the exhaust pipe or the atmosphere direct by a relay valve similar to the one shown in Fig. 137. In the absence of air pressure in the starting valve, the spring located above the piston *e*, Fig. 140, is sufficiently strong to keep the piston at the bottom of the cylinder, thus raising the rocking-lever roller clear of the revolving cam-peak whilst the engine is working normally on fuel.

Maintenance of starting gears

The fact that this part of an engine is in use for a very small proportion of the engine's life does not mean that attention is unnecessary. The actual amount of maintenance work required to make good wear-and-tear may be small, but regular attention is necessary to ensure that the gear is always ready to operate promptly when required. Such an occasion may arise at any time, and if the gear is not in proper order the consequences may be serious, as, for instance, when entering or leaving a port and an emergency " full astern " movement is required when, or for some reason, it is necessary to stop and re-start the engine in heavy weather.

The most likely cause of the starting gear failing to operate is jamming of some part owing to dryness. The dryness results from the moisture generally contained in compressed air carrying off the lubricant on its passage through the system when the gear is brought into operation. The best lubricant for relay valves, pilot valves, and distribution valves is a thin film of good-quality grease. Excessive oiling of these valves is inadvisable for reasons to be given presently, so that the aim should be to make the compressed air as dry as possible. This, of course, is effected by frequent drawing-off of the condensed moisture when the air compressor is operating and not allowing water to accumulate in the starting-air tanks. For information regarding this part of air-compressor operation see Chapter 21.

Frequent draining of the air compressors is necessary, not only to get rid of the condensed moisture, but also to prevent surplus lubricating oil passing into the starting system along with the compressed air. If this is not done, or if the compressor cylinders are given too much oil, the atomised oil will settle out in the starting-air manifold or supply pipe during the periods the air is not in motion and produce a greasy lining in the pipe.

Whenever possible the starting-air pipes should be examined internally for accumulation of greasy matter, since should a blow-back occur due to a jammed starting valve, the presence of oil and grease may have serious consequences. The pipes should also be examined internally for corrosion, particularly where bent, as the bending process seems to make the material more susceptible to corrosion. Also, if the pipes are connected in a strained condition or are allowed to vibrate they are more likely to corrode. The thickness of pipes that cannot be examined internally should be tested by tapping with a lightweight hammer or piece of iron rod. If a seriously wasted part of the pipe is tapped with the rod it will at once be revealed by the sound produced.

In most installations the various parts comprising the starting system can be opened up for examination whilst the engine is operating normally. Needless to say, such work should be done only when the ship is well clear of land and other shipping and after consultation with the navigating officer. As a rule the only attention required is to see that the parts are free and lightly lubricated, at the same time rubbing the valve lids on their seats to make sure that they are airtight.

The relay valve with its pilot valve, as well as the distribution valves, are generally made of non-corrodible materials, such as bronze and stainless steel, and as they are inoperative most of the time they require to be ground-in only occasionally to make them airtight. Each valve must, of course, be perfectly airtight when in the closed position if the gear is to operate satisfactorily, and tests should be made every six months or so to prove that such is the case.

Particular care must be taken when carrying out any tests which require admission of compressed air to the starting-air system. On no account may starting air reach the engine cylinders. Just how to test the various valves and at the same time obviate the possibility of this occurring it is not possible to say here, as details in different ships vary so much, but generally it will be found sufficient to lash the engine control lever in the "stop" position in cases where the cylinder starting valves are mechanically operated. Where the valves are pneumatically operated it is a wise precaution to uncouple the operating air-pipes at the starting valves.

The valves which determine the starting-air admission period must be correctly timed, otherwise the period may be too short, when the engine may fail to start, or too long, resulting in wasteful use of starting air. Grinding-in mechanically operated valves in the cylinder head, or distribution valves which control pneumatically operated valves, has the effect of reducing the clearance between the valves and the cams operating them, and consequently lengthening the starting-air admission period. After grinding-in, therefore, the timing should be checked, otherwise the air compressor may have difficulty in maintaining the requisite starting-air pressure when a ship is passing through a waterway such as the Manchester Ship Canal, where much stopping and re-starting is required.

In particular it is most essential to make sure that when the engine control lever is in the "stop" position the clearances recommended by the engine-builders exist between the pilot valve, the distribution valves and the mechanism which operates them, so that there is no doubt about their being seated. For instance, if the pilot valve controlling the relay valve has insufficient clearance, the relay valve may open immediately the starting-air tank stop valve is opened when preparing an engine for service. This premature opening of the relay valve may not have any adverse effect with some forms of starting gears, but with others the effect may be to admit starting air to the cylinders, with serious consequences. Such a fault has been responsible for damage to the engine turning gear.

If one or more of the distribution valves is held off its seat due to insufficient clearance when it ought to be in the closed position, starting air will enter cylinders whose cranks are not in the starting position and the engine will either fail to start or will move a few degrees only and then stop. When an engine starts, stops, and then moves ahead and astern for a few seconds before coming to rest, it is a sure sign that the distribution valves are not properly set. The clearances recommended vary in different makes of engine but are generally between 0·5 mm and 1·0 mm for both the pilot and distribution valves.

The rocking-lever roller clearance of mechanically operated starting valves is also particularly important. If the clearance is incorrect the operative period will be too long or too short and have the same adverse effect as a similar fault in distribution valves. Moreover, if the clearance is so small that the valve is prevented from re-seating properly, the lid and seat will quickly burn away and put the valve beyond repair.

Safety devices on starting-air systems

It has been shown in the foregoing pages how pressures greatly in excess of the normal starting-air pressure can be attained in the starting-air system. As a matter of fact, explosions due to ignition of the greasy matter in the pipes have occurred, with resulting serious damage to the engine. A very rapid increase in pressure is a possibility to be guarded against, and the safety device provided must offer an immediate and sufficiently large area of escape for the excess pressure.

The ordinary form of spring-loaded relief valve is not suitable for this purpose because it would require to be of such a large size to be effective, so that other devices are adopted. One is to provide a copper, steel, or bronze bursting-diaphragm constructed to rupture at a predetermined pressure—generally three times the maximum starting-air pressure. Two diaphragms of different construction are shown in Fig. 141, both of which offer a large and immediate exit for the excess gases when they rupture. One such diaphragm is usually provided at each end of the starting-air manifold. When the length of a manifold exceeds 40 feet more than two safety devices are advisable. In all such cases one in the middle and one at each end is considered sufficient to prevent a dangerous rise in pressure.

The importance of these safety diaphragms will be appreciated when it is realised that the consequences may be very serious, not

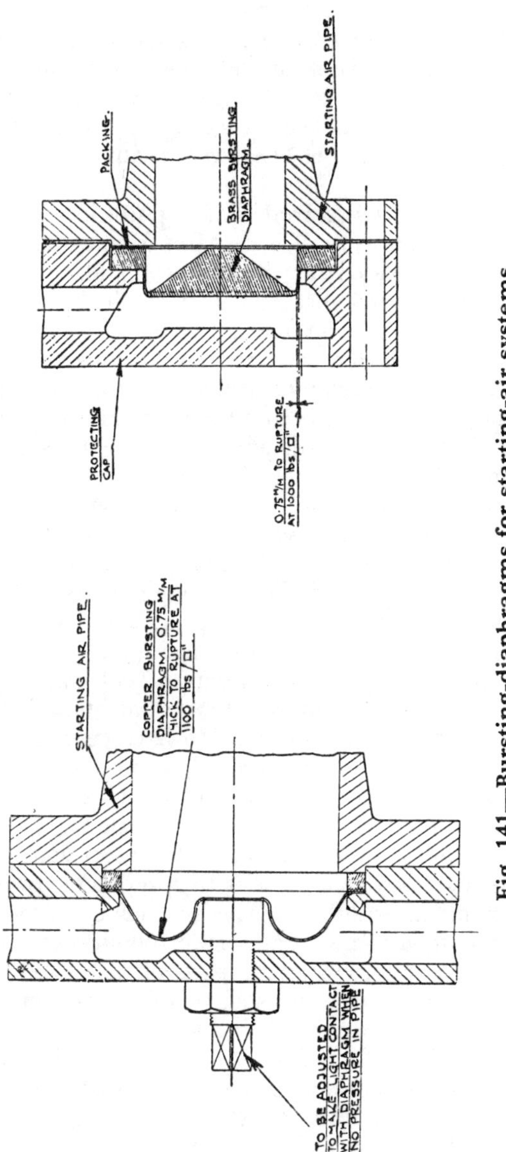

Fig. 141—Bursting-diaphragms for starting-air systems

only in the event of their failing to act when required, but should they act prematurely when manoeuvring a ship in or out of port, as the starting air must be shut off and a new diaphragm fitted before the engine can again be started. These diaphragms may rupture prematurely owing to fatigue or corrosion, and since they are generally a small and inexpensive part it is advisable to renew them frequently.

Safety diaphragms will corrode and rupture in a very short time unless the starting-air manifold is kept free from condensed moisture. Drain cocks are provided for this purpose and, as a further precaution against the water making contact with the diaphragms, the ends of the starting-air manifold are sometimes inclined upwards. The ends of the pipe, however, must be inclined only sufficiently to prevent the water reaching the diaphragms, because if inclined too much and an explosion occurs the maximum pressure resulting may not reach the nearest diaphragm before damage is done to some other part.

On one occasion a copper safety diaphragm failed at normal pressure after only 10 days' service. The three other diaphragms made of the same material and fitted at the same time were in perfect order when examined after as many months. The diaphragm that failed had corroded, and the appearance of the inner surface suggested that a very active corrosive agent had made contact with this particular diaphragm. As sulphuric acid was suspected, the starting-air valves were removed for examination, and one near to the affected diaphragm was found to have been leaking between the housing and the landing surface in the cylinder head.

As this is a possibility to be guarded against, the diaphragms, if not made of absolutely non-corrodible material, must be treated in a way that will protect them in the event of starting-air valves leaking. The best way to do this is to spray the surface in contact with the starting air with lead. The best solution would doubtless be to make the diaphragms from non-corrodible steel, but there are certain difficulties in making these parts of this material, and until these difficulties are overcome such diaphragms cannot be relied upon to function within the desirable narrow limits of the predetermined pressure. The design shown at the left-hand side of Fig. 141 gives the best results, as these diaphragms are spun out of sheet copper, which ensures an even thickness and greater reliability.

Spring-loaded safety valves open and close automatically, but they are not often fitted because they are rightly considered unsuitable for the rapid release of excess pressure. Such valves must be heavily loaded to prevent leakage under normal working conditions, and the employment of heavy springs to ensure this naturally restricts the opening for the quick release of excess pressure in the event of an explosion occurring in the starting-air manifold. That this is true is proved by the serious damage done on numerous occasions when spring-loaded safety valves have been employed.

The bursting-diaphragm type of safety device is more suitable, as immediately the diaphragm ruptures an unrestricted opening equal to the full area of the starting-air manifold is immediately available for the release of excess pressure. The disadvantage of bursting-diaphragms is, however, that when they rupture, the engine cannot be re-started until new diaphragms have been fitted, and as this operation takes about half-an-hour a ship may get into a serious position before the engines are again available.

The ideal safety device for this important part of diesel engines should therefore be one that would have the advantages of both types and the disadvantages of neither. In other words, it should act instantly upon a predetermined pressure being reached and offer an unrestricted opening for the release of the excess pressure so large that it would be impossible for dangerously high pressures to be reached. Furthermore, the device should be automatic in its action, so that not only will the system be protected from damage, but the engine will be available for duty immediately the excess pressure has been released.

Such a patented safety device, called the " Lightning " Full-Bore Relief Valve is illustrated in Fig. 142. This device comprises three parts only, namely, the body, the cover, and an internal part which is free to move endwise in the body. The movable internal part is cylindrical and provided with two mitred faces, one at each end. This part is, in fact, a double-seated valve. The area of the inner (smaller mitre) end, however, is smaller than the outer (mitred) end, with the result that if the compressed air admitted at *A* is at the same pressure as the starting air in the manifold, the pressure tending to hold the valve in the closed position will be equal to the difference in the cross-sectional areas.

Assuming that an abnormally high pressure has been produced in the starting-air manifold and that the pressure is sufficient to overcome the pressure acting on the loaded end of the movable part, this part will immediately be raised off the two seats and in doing so will close the small holes *B* and cut off communication between the compressed air entering at *A* and the chamber *C*. The air in chamber *C* will then be able to escape freely to atmosphere through the exit holes *D*. The loading air pressure being suddenly reduced in this way, will cause the valve to open instantly to its fullest extent and release the excess pressure in the starting-air manifold—also through the holes *D*. When excess pressure has been released, the compressed air acting on the inside of the movable part will immediately and automatically close the valve, uncover the holes *B*, and give the valve its normal loading.

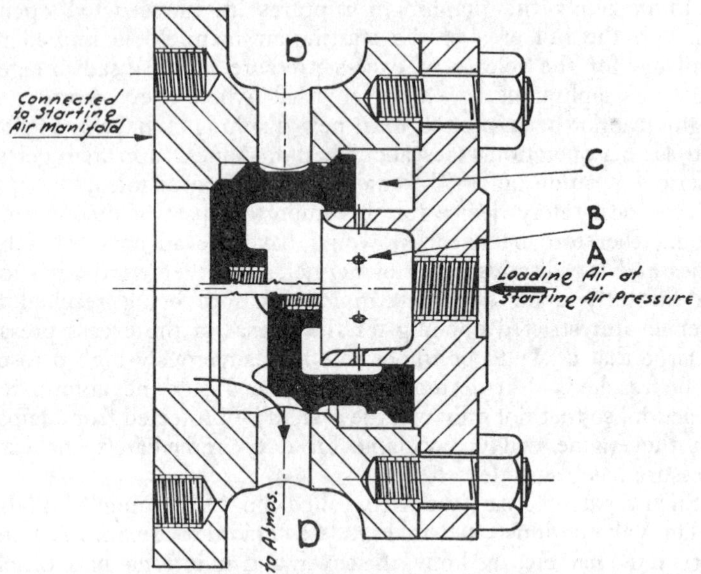

Fig. 142—Compressed-air loaded safety valve for starting-air systems (" Lightning ") (*Trewent & Proctor Ltd.*)
Upper half-section shows valve closed.

Generally the difference in areas of the two ends of the movable part is 1 to 1·5, so that if the normal starting-air pressure is 600 lb/sq.in. the valve will operate when the pressure in the manifold reaches 900 lb/sq.in. The pressure necessary to open the valve may be anything designed—down to 5 per cent above the normal working starting-air pressure: it is only a question of proportion between the areas of the part in way of the two mitred faces.

The advantages of this device over bursting-diaphragms will be evident, while the main advantage over the ordinary spring-loaded safety valve is that it cannot be overloaded either by accident or intention. A further desirable feature is that there are no close-fitting parts liable to jam, no matter how long the inactive periods may be.

CHAPTER 17

Reversing Gears

In the preceding chapter it was shown that in order to start an engine in the direction opposite from that of the previous run all that was necessary was to move a camshaft (the main if the starting valves in the cylinder head are mechanically operated, or a smaller auxiliary camshaft if the valves are operated pneumatically) in an endwise direction so as to bring the appropriate cam in line with the valve. In either case the cams may, of course, be mounted on any shaft so long as that shaft has at all times a fixed angular relationship to the engine crankshaft.

A reversible engine having no reversing gear in the generally accepted sense could be constructed. For such an engine to be capable of developing power in relation to its size in either direction it would have to operate on the two-stroke principle, the fuel-injection process would have to begin and end about the same number of degrees on either side of the top dead centre of the engine crank, and the air-inlet (scavenging) and exhaust ports would require to be at the same distance from the top of the cylinder so that both sets of ports would be opened and closed by the piston at the same time. To reverse such an engine all that would be required would be to stop it by cutting-off the fuel and then start it in the opposite direction. Such an engine would develop the same power in either direction of rotation, but it would have a high fuel-consumption rate.

As will be seen from Fig. 143, the cylinder processes of a modern two-stroke engine are not so simple. The exhausting process is the only one which begins and finishes at the same time for either direction of rotation, so that separate cams must be provided for mechanical starting and fuel injection, while the admission of scavenging air must be controlled in some way to suit the desired direction of rotation. The reason for this will be fully explained in the next chapter. In some modern engines fuel injection begins and ends at the same point on either side of the top dead centre, in which case one fuel-pump cam serves for both directions of rotation.

The gear required to reverse a two-stroke engine is nevertheless relatively simple compared with that necessary for four-stroke engines; this will be apparent from the sequence diagrams of the cylinder processes shown in Figs. 143 and 144. Not only are there two additional valves in the cylinder head, i.e. the air-inlet and exhaust valves, but in no instance do the opening and closing points of any valve occur at the same point on either side of a dead centre position.

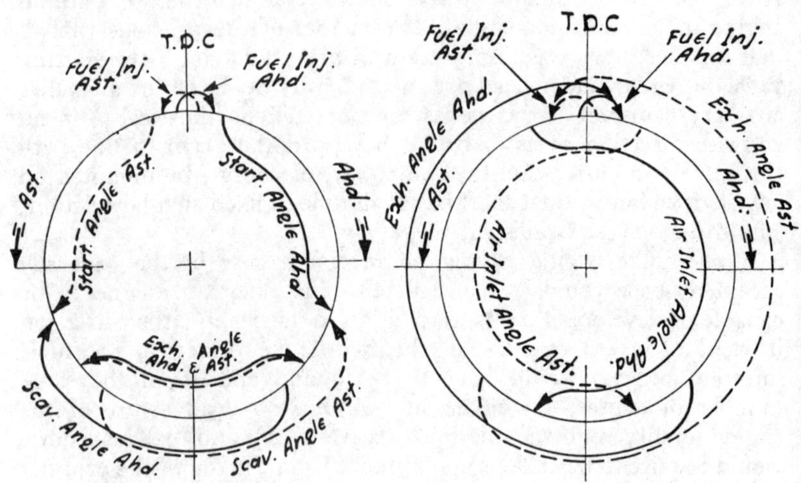

Fig. 143—Sequence diagram of the cylinder processes of a 2-stroke reversible engine

Fig. 144—Sequence diagram of the cylinder processes of a 4-stroke reversible engine

The question is sometimes asked, can a diesel engine run in an ahead direction with the reversing gear in the astern position, and vice versa ? The answer is that it can do so in both two- and four-stroke types. Neither engine can be started in the wrong direction with the reversing gear in its correct position, but if owing to some disarrangement of interlocking gear the reversing gear is put over to the astern position when an engine is being driven in the ahead direction by the propeller, the engine will continue to operate in the ahead direction if the fuel-injection pumps are operating. This, however, is most improbable as it should not be possible to put over the reversing gear until the engine control lever is brought to the " stop " position, and this has the effect of making the fuel-injection pumps inoperative.

Stopping an engine

When an engine is to be stopped and its direction reversed, it should be allowed to come to rest before the reversing gear is "put over" and the starting lever operated. In some cases no ill-effect will result by not doing so, or an engine may even be brought to rest and started in the opposite direction more quickly, but generally it is an unwise practice. Most marine engines come to rest within one or two revolutions of the control lever being put into the "stop" position. It is only when a ship is travelling at speed and the engine is being driven by the propeller that the engine may take a relatively long time to stop.

The mechanical efficiency of marine diesel engines has increased quite appreciably during recent years. Doxford, for instance, claim over 91·5 per cent for their latest supercharged engines. The advantage of a high mechanical efficiency in respect of fuel economy will be obvious but it does introduce a difficulty, namely that an engine will not stop so readily when the fuel is shut off, and if a ship is moving through the water it may be minutes before the turning force through the propeller is expended and the reversing gear can be safely "put over."

There are devices for bringing an engine to rest quickly under such conditions. These devices operate in a way which causes the compressed air to be released at the end of the compression stroke of the piston. In an engine not provided with such a device compression of the air tends to bring the engine to rest after the fuel is shut off, but the expansion of the air during the next stroke of the piston has the opposite effect. If, however, the compressed air could be released after it has done its useful work in slowing-up the engine, a partial vacuum would be created during the next stroke of the piston. Both strokes would therefore serve to bring the engine to rest.

Reference to the compressed-air-loaded cylinder-relief valve illustrated in Fig. 83 (at B) will help to show how this is achieved. At the end of the compression stroke the relief valve is suddenly unloaded and the compressed air in the cylinder escapes to the atmosphere. As the piston begins its next (outward) stroke the relief valve automatically closes and communication between the atmosphere and the cylinder cut off. The effect of this is to produce drag, since as the piston moves outward a partial vacuum is created in the cylinder.

De-compressing cylinders

Upon stopping a multiple-cylinder engine at least one of the cranks will come to rest when the corresponding piston has completed part only of the compression stroke, so that this particular cylinder will contain air under pressure. Also it may happen that the engine comes to rest before a piston has completed its working stroke, in which case the cylinder will contain burnt gases under pressure.

In both two- and four-stroke engines the compression stroke for one direction of rotation becomes the working stroke of the opposite direction of rotation, and vice versa, so that, if an engine which is to be reversed stops with air under pressure in a cylinder, it is this cylinder which will receive starting air upon the engine being started in the reverse direction. Such a condition will have no ill-effect upon any part of the engine if the reversing gear is put over. The starting valve will, of course, have to be opened against a pressure, but as it is of small diameter the resistance to be overcome will not be greater than the mechanism operating the starting valve can easily deal with.

Moreover, if the reversing gear of an engine is put over before one of the pistons has completed its working stroke, i.e. before the products of combustion are released, the cylinder will contain burnt gases under pressure, and as explained the working stroke becomes the compression stroke upon the engine being started in the reverse direction, the burnt gases will be compressed. As the pressure in the cylinder may be 40 lb/sq.in. or more when the piston begins to move into the cylinder, it will offer appreciable resistance to the turning effect of the starting air in the starting cylinder.

In four-stroke engines the exhaust stroke for one direction of rotation becomes the air-inlet stroke for the opposite direction of rotation, and vice versa. In the event of the engine being started in the reverse direction with a cylinder partly filled with burnt gases, the only effect would be that the first charge of fuel to be injected may not burn in a sufficiency of air.

At one time all diesel-engine cylinders were provided with decompression gear. This comprised means of automatically easing either the exhaust valve or the relief valve off its seat during the reversing operation and allowing any pressure to escape. As, however, an engine generally makes one or two revolutions after the fuel has been shut off, during which all burnt gases are expelled, many engine-builders do not now consider such provision necessary, although there can be no doubt that the best condition for starting, especially when the starting-air pressure is well below the maximum, is for the cylinders to be entirely free of air, or burnt gases, under pressure.

Reversing gears of four-stroke engines

With most reversing gears it is possible to complete the operation from full ahead to full astern in less than ten seconds, and it is rare indeed to hear of an engine failing to reverse unless the proper maintenance of some part of the gear has been neglected. It is a common thing for upwards of 25 reverse operations to have to be executed in one hour when a ship is passing in or out of some docks.

The cylinder-head valves of four-stroke engines are always operated by two sets of cams, one for " ahead " and the other for " astern " operation. In nearly all designs the two sets of cams are mounted on a single shaft, the " ahead " and " astern " cams for each valve being located as near as practicable to each other in order that the changeover from one set to another can be effected in the shortest time and with the least possible movement of the gear.

An engine must first be stopped, then the valve rocking-levers raised well clear of the cams to allow (a) the levers or (b) the camshaft to be moved in an endwise direction, so that the rollers of the rocking levers will be directly over and in line with the cams that correspond

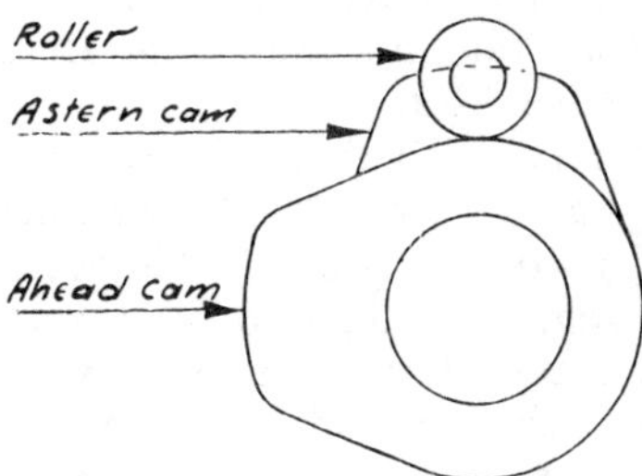

Fig. 145—Possible position of cams when engine stops, illustrating the need to raise rocking-lever roller when camshaft is moved endwise

to the reverse direction of rotation. After the camshaft, or rocking levers, according to type, have been moved to the desired position, the rocking levers are returned to their normal working position when the engine is ready to be started in the reverse direction to that of the preceding run. Fig. 145 shows why it is necessary first to raise the rocking-lever rollers clear of the cams before the camshaft is—or the rocking levers are—moved in an endwise direction, and Fig. 146 shows the positions of the various " ahead " and " astern " cams of a four-stroke engine relative to each other and to the crankshaft when the crank is on the firing top dead centre.

This is the principle upon which practically all four-stroke-engine reversing gears work, though the means adopted to carry out the various stages of the operation vary in different makes of engines. The gears described hereafter are not selected because

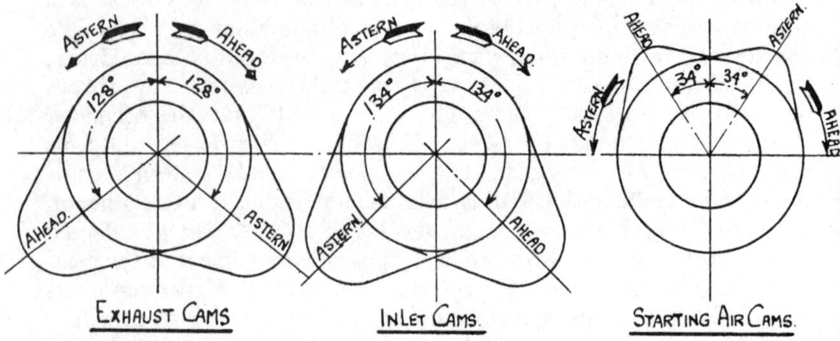

Fig. 146—Position of ahead and astern cams of 4-stroke unsupercharged engine when crank is on firing top dead centre

they are the most commonly used, but because they most resemble several makes and incorporate in some way or other ideas frequently encountered in modern engines.

A very simple and reliable method of reversing which stood the test for a great many years was that adopted by Burmeister and Wain for their original four-stroke engines. This gear, which is shown diagrammatically in Fig. 147, consists of a reversing crankshaft located near the lower end of the cylinders and extending the full length of the engine. The " ahead " and " astern " cams actuate the valve through long tubes, commonly called push rods, and a rocking lever.

The reversing shaft is provided with one small-throw crank for each cylinder. To each of these cranks four short levers are attached by rotatable bearings, one each for the starting-air inlet and exhaust valves. On the camshaft are two cams side by side for each valve, one being for " ahead " and the other for " astern " operation, and to bring the desired cams into line with the rocking-lever rollers, the camshaft is moved in an endwise direction by an amount slightly greater than the width of one cam. While the camshaft is being moved longitudinally it is necessary that the rollers should be quite clear of the cams, for reasons already given. This is effected by rotating the reversing shaft one complete revolution, which, as will be seen, causes the rollers to be swung well clear of the cams before endwise movement of the shaft begins. The endwise movement of the camshaft is effected by a rack operated by the servo

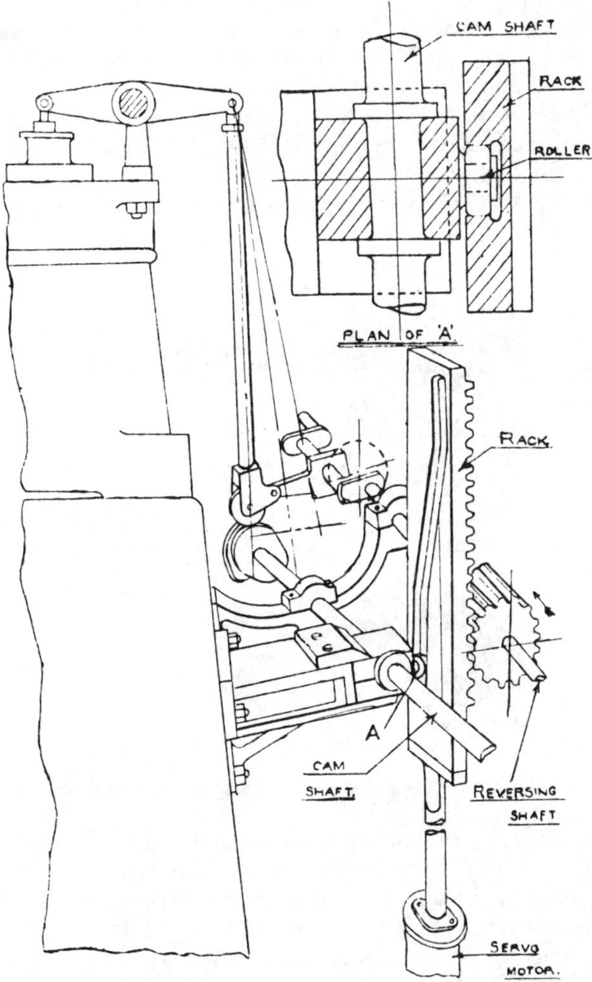

Fig. 147—Original reversing gear of Burmeister and Wain 4-stroke engine

motor which rotates a pinion on the reversing shaft. In the face of the rack is a slanted groove which engages a roller attached to the camshaft bearing, as shown in the top right-hand corner of Fig. 147.

In the case of the well-known Werkspoor four-stroke engine the cams for "ahead" and "astern" operation are mounted side by side, as in the B. & W. reversing gear just described, but instead of moving the camshaft in an endwise direction to engage the reverse cams, the position of the valve rocking-levers is altered in the unique manner illustrated in Fig. 148.

As will be observed, the valve rocking-levers are mounted on eccentrics keyed to the reversing shaft *A*. These eccentrics are keyed at an angle, consequently the rocking levers are slightly askew on the shaft, as shown, when the engine is working in one

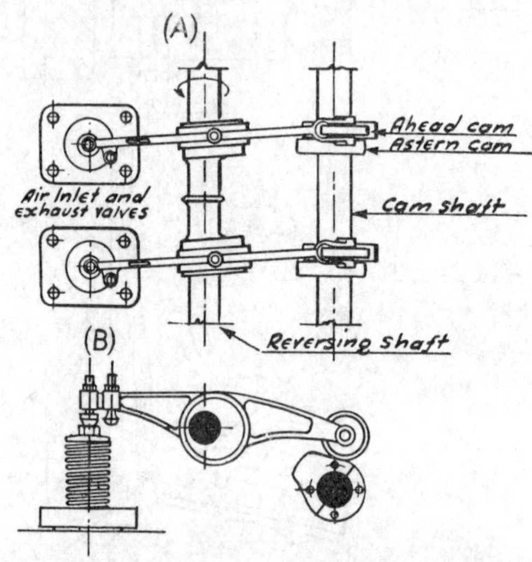

Fig. 148—Reversing gear of Werkspoor 4-stroke engine

direction. During the reversing operation the shaft *A* is rotated in the direction indicated by the arrow; this has the effect, it will be seen, of first lifting the rollers clear of the cams. The rotary movement of the shaft is continued until a point half a revolution from the starting position is reached, when the rocking levers will again be in working position. The rollers, however, will be immediately over the reverse cams, since by rotating the reversing shaft 180°, and consequently the eccentrics upon which the rocking levers are mounted, the position of the rocking levers will have been altered.

It will be seen that during the reversing operation the centres of the eccentrics carrying the rocking levers are moved in a crosswise direction towards the camshaft an amount equal to the throw of the eccentrics. Consequently it is necessary to provide two separate valve strikers or tappets, as shown at *B*.

The effect upon the position of the rocking levers of mounting the eccentrics askew on the reversing shaft will be clearly demonstrated by placing a piece of stiff paper askew on a pencil and rotating the pencil through an angle of 180°.

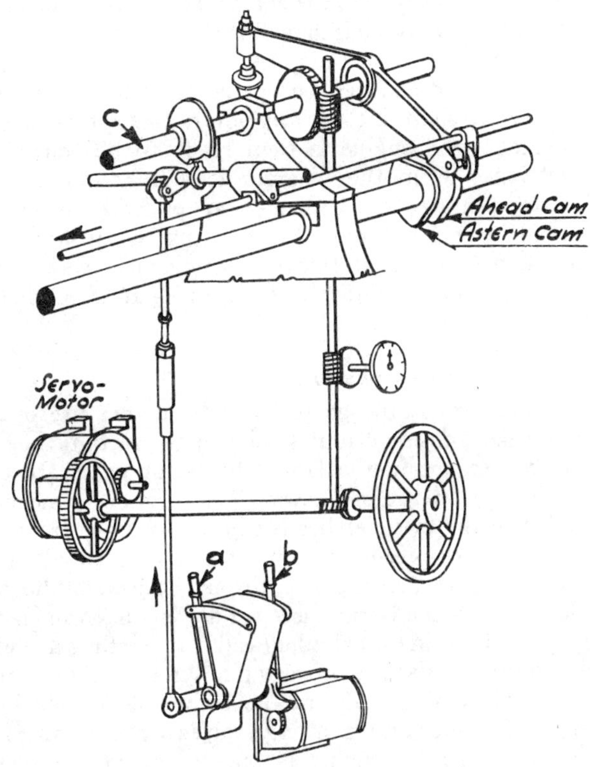

Fig. 149—Reversing gear suitable for a 4-stroke engine

In the reversing gear illustrated in Fig. 149 the " ahead " and " astern " cams are located in the usual way, but the camshaft is not moved in an endwise direction, neither do the valve rocking-levers alter their position; instead, the rocking-lever rollers only are moved longitudinally, this being effected by making the fork end of the rocking levers sufficiently wide to allow for the movement. The rollers are moved by short arms having forked ends which are mounted on a light shaft extending the entire length of the engine. The resistance to be overcome when carrying out this part of the reversing operation is so small that it can quite easily be accomplished by hand, in the manner shown in the illustration.

The rocking-lever rollers are raised clear of the cams by rotating the rocking-lever fulcrum shaft *C* (Fig. 149), the levers being mounted on eccentrics keyed to the shaft. This part of the operation is carried out by a rotary air motor. When the rocking levers are raised so that the rollers clear the cams, the hand lever which moves the rollers is unlocked and can be operated, and by continuing to rotate the fulcrum shaft the rocking levers are returned to their working position; the engine is then ready to be started in the reverse direction. From the diagram it will be noted that the left-hand lever *a* moves the rollers in an endwise direction, and the right-hand lever *b* controls the reversing motor which rotates the fulcrum shaft *C*. The interlocking arrangement which prevents the rollers being moved until the fulcrum shaft is in the proper position will be noted.

Reversing gears of two-stroke engines

As mentioned earlier, the gears of such engines are of simpler construction than those of four-stroke engines, but they are of greater variety because in the latter the burnt gases are expelled from the cylinders in the same way, i.e. through a mechanically operated valve in the cylinder head, whereas in two-stroke engines the burnt gases are expelled in many different ways. In some cases the burnt gases are expelled through ports in the cylinder liner, while in others the burnt gases are driven out through a mechanically operated valve in the cylinder head in much the same way as in four-stroke engines. Also, there are engines in which the burnt gases are driven out through ports around the lower end of the cylinder by the scavenging air which enters through valves in the cylinder head.

The simplest form of engine is one in which the scavenging air enters and the burnt gases leave through ports uncovered by the piston when it nears the end of its down or outward stroke. In the Sulzer engine scavenging air begins to flow into the cylinder only when the pressure in the cylinder has fallen below the scavenging air pressure, as described in the next chapter. As this process occurs automatically for either direction of rotation the reversing gear is extremely simple, and comprises means of controlling merely the starting air and the fuel charge to suit the direction of rotation. Furthermore, in some engines the fuel-injection pump setting is suitable for either direction of rotation.

The cams operating the fuel-injection pumps and starting-air valves are sometimes duplicated as in four-stroke engines, but if the starting-air valves are pneumatically operated the reversing gear is further simplified, since the fuel pumps and the starting-air distributor valves (see Fig. 139) can be grouped together and operated by cams mounted on a short length of shafting having, as in the case of a camshaft extending the full length of the engine, a fixed angular relationship with the engine crankshaft.

It will therefore be seen that the reversing gear of two-stroke engines can be of very simple construction indeed—and could be simplified still further if the Archaouloff system of fuel injection were to be employed. As mentioned in a previous chapter, the fuel-injection pump of this system is operated by the compression pressure in the engine cylinder, and the point at which injection begins will consequently be the same for either direction of rotation. The only part whose setting would then require to be altered to effect reversal of rotation would be confined to the starting-air distributor valves; thus a near approach would be made to a reversible engine without reversing gear.

Servo motors

To alter the position of the valve-operating gear when the direction of rotation must be changed, a reversing motor, or servo motor as it is called, is generally employed, but means are always provided to enable the operation to be carried out by hand power in case the servo motor should be out of order. These servo motors, which are operated either by oil pressure, compressed air, or electricity, take various forms. A compressed-air motor commonly used is shown diagrammatically in Fig. 150.

This servo motor consists of an air cylinder, which is the active agent, and an oil cylinder, called the braking or buffer cylinder, in strict alignment, the purpose of which is to ensure smooth working by reducing the shock that would otherwise result from the employment of an air cylinder only. At the same time the oil cylinder may provide alternative power for altering the position of the engine valve gear.

Referring to Fig. 150 it will be noted that, in the position shown, compressed air from the starting-air tank or reservoir will enter the cylinder and force the piston outward, the opposite side of the piston being in communication with the atmosphere. In doing so, the lubricating oil in the braking cylinder will be discharged through a restricted passage to the other end of the cylinder, thus

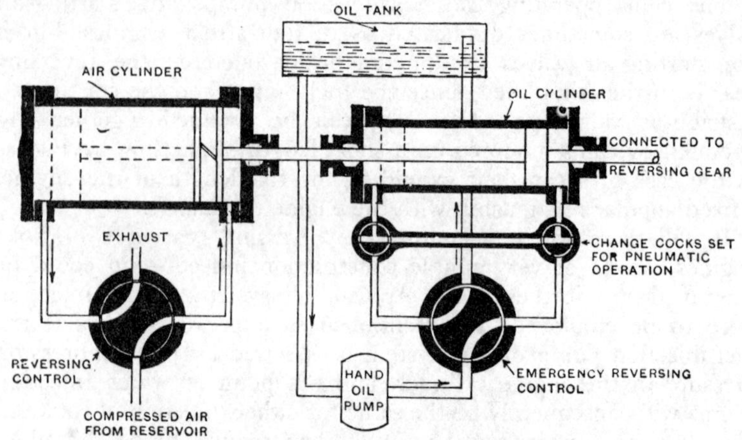

Fig. 150—Servo motor, reciprocating type

ensuring smooth motion at uniform speed. With this type of servo motor complete reversal of the operating gear is effected during one stroke of the piston, so that when the piston is at one end of the cylinder the gear is set for " Ahead " operation, and when at the other end for " Astern."

To reverse the motion of the servo-motor piston, and consequently the valve gear, a movement of the reversing lever causes the rotary valve (reversing control) to be moved through an angle of 90°, thereby admitting compressed air to the opposite end of the air cylinder, and at the same time placing the other end of the cylinder in communication with the atmosphere.

To alter the position of the reversing gear by hand power, the cocks of the oil cylinder are operated to bring it into communication with the emergency reversing mechanism—such as a hand pump with an oil supply tank, and a rotary valve called the emergency reversing control. The latter is operated in a similar manner to the air control valve, and a brief study of Fig. 150 will suffice to show how alteration of the emergency reversing control will allow the oil to be drawn from the tank and discharged at will to either end of the braking cylinder, the oil forced from the opposite end of the cylinder returning to the tank.

The usual method of transmitting the reciprocating motion of the servo-motor piston into a rotary motion at the reversing shaft is to attach a rack to an extension of the servo-motor piston rod which engages with a pinion keyed to the reversing shaft, as shown in Fig. 147, the full stroke of the piston causing the reversing shaft to be rotated one revolution. An exception is the Werkspoor reversing gear shown in Fig. 148, where one stroke of the servo-motor piston rotates the reversing shaft one-half a revolution only when going from " Ahead " to " Astern " or vice versa.

The rotary servo motor shown diagrammatically in Fig. 151 effects reversal of the valve gear through worm gearing. The motor consists of a shallow cylinder in which revolves a rotor with

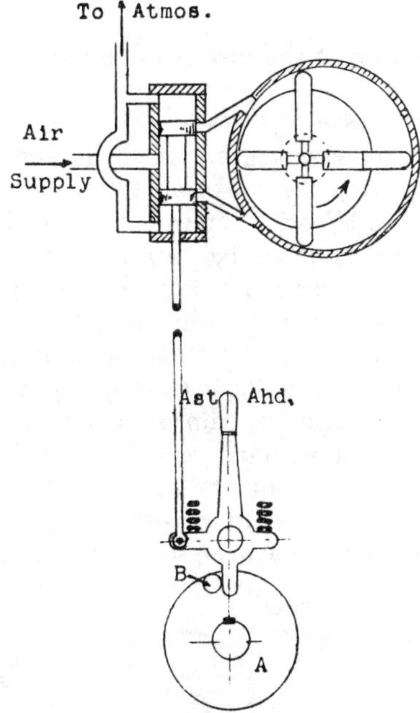

Fig. 151—Servo motor, rotary type

only sufficient side clearance to allow for free movement. Four equally-spaced slots are cut in the rotor, which is off-centre. In each slot is fitted a vane which is free to be pushed outward against the walls of the cylinder when compressed air is admitted to the centre of the rotor. The compressed air that drives the motor is controlled by a piston valve connected to the hand lever in such a way that when the lever is moved in the direction marked " Astern," the position of the piston valve is lowered and compressed air is allowed to pass through the lowest port into the cylinder, where it acts on the partly exposed vane and rotates the rotor in the direction of the arrowhead.

As the rotor revolves each vane is acted upon in turn, and offers an increasing area to the compressed air driving it, owing to the vanes being constantly pushed outward and having to follow the curvature of the cylinder. The compressed air trapped between the vanes as the rotor revolves is carried round and discharged through the upper port over the top of the piston valve into the atmosphere. To stop the motor it is only necessary to return the piston valve to its mid-position, whilst to reverse the direction of rotation the position of the piston valve requires to be raised.

Starting and reverse gear interlocks

The starting and reversing gears of all marine engines are interlocked, that is to say, the valve-operating mechanism must be in the correct " Ahead " or " Astern " position before the starting wheel or lever, as the case may be, can be operated, and conversely, the starting wheel or lever must be in its stop position before the reversing gear can be operated. This interlocking is very necessary because the arrangement of the valve-operating mechanism must be such that if an attempt is made to start an engine with the reversing gear not in its correct position, damage may be done.

To describe all the interlocking gears in general use would require far too much space, and would be of little value, as knowledge of one or two will make the study of others fairly easy. Where the starting gear is operated by a wheel, the interlocking device may take

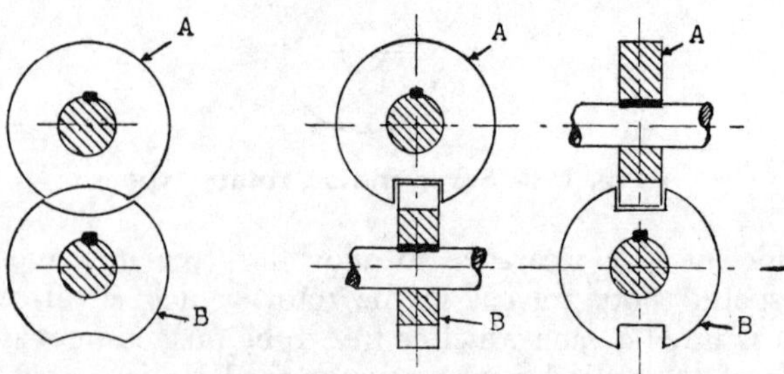

Fig. 152—Interlocking devices for starting and reversing gears

the form of two discs secured to any two spindles that are arranged either parallel or at right-angles to one another, one spindle forming part of the starting gear and the other forming part of the reversing gear.

Referring to Fig. 152 where, at the left, shafts are shown parallel, it will be observed that the disc *A*, which we will assume is attached to the starting gear, can be rotated only when the disc *B*, which is attached to the reversing gear, is in one of the two positions that coincides with either the correct " Ahead " or " Astern " position of the valve gear; likewise, the spindle upon which the disc *B* is mounted cannot be rotated unless the slot in *A* is in the position shown in the illustration, which corresponds to the stop position of the starting wheel. The right-hand portion of Fig. 152 shows the arrangement applied to shafts at right-angles.

Many simple but ingenious devices are to be found to prevent damage resulting from mistakes in handling. One is indicated in Fig. 151. The disc *A* is suitably geared to the reversing gear operated by the servo motor, and during reversal of the valve gear makes nearly one complete revolution. It will be observed that owing to the pin *B* projecting from the disc, it would not be possible to move the lever in any direction but the right one—namely, in the case shown, " Astern." While the servo motor is in operation and the valve gear is being reversed, the lever must be held over until the gear reaches the reverse position, when the pin *B* strikes the lever and forces it to its mid-position, thus causing the supply of compressed air driving the servo motor to be automatically cut off.

Manoeuvring operations

Before concluding this chapter the various stages in the operation of starting and reversing engines will be given. The first to be described will be that found on Burmeister and Wain's four-stroke engines, a pictorial view of which is shown in Fig. 153.*

With this gear the operations of starting, reversing and regulating the speed when working on fuel are carried out by the rotation of a single handwheel (1). A pointer and suitably inscribed dial located above the handwheel indicate the position of the manoeuvring gear. At this stage we will assume the pointer to be at " Stop." When the starting-air stop valve (4) is opened by hand, starting air flows from the starting-air tanks to the relay starting valve (5) in two directions, one being through the pipe (6) and the other through the smaller pipe (7) past the pilot valve (8), which is in the open position whenever the engine is stopped or working on fuel.

* See pages 726/7

The relay valve (5) is pneumatically operated, the compressed air that passes the pilot valve (8) and through the pipe (9) acting on top of the piston attached to the spindle and keeping the valve closed. Consequently, the starting air cannot pass beyond the relay valve (5) unless the air passing to it through the pilot valve (8) is shut off and all pressure in the pipe (7) released. The pilot valve (8) is of the piston type, while ports are arranged in the valve housing in such a way that the pipe (9) and, consequently, the space above the relay-valve piston, can be put into communication with either the compressed air in pipe (7) or the atmosphere.

The engine is now ready to be set in motion by rotating the starting wheel. Since, however, the starting wheel and the telegraph are interlocked, an order must be received from the navigating bridge before the starting wheel can be moved from the " Stop " position. Operating the telegraph from the bridge rotates the small shaft (10) through the chain (11). Mounted on the shaft (10) are two cams placed side by side and with peaks in line, i.e. at 180°, each operating a small lever located underneath, the levers being at the opposite sides of the cams. Consequently, when the shaft (10) is rotated in either direction, one or other of the levers (12), depending upon whether the telegraph has been moved in the " Ahead " or " Astern " direction, is raised clear of the slot in the disc (13) in which the end of the lever fits. As the disc (13) is fixed to the shaft carrying the starting wheel, it follows that the starting wheel can be rotated only in the direction indicated by the telegraph.

Assuming that the telegraph has been operated in the " Ahead " direction, the starting wheel will be free to be moved in this direction to the point marked " Start " on the indicator, assuming that the reversing gear is in the correct position. This movement of the starting wheel rotates the small crank (15), and through a system of rods and levers causes the trigger rod (16) to be moved in a downward direction until a knife-edge fitting attached to it engages one end of the lever (17). This has the effect of raising the pilot valve (8) and closing the passage connecting the starting-air stop valve (4) and the relay starting valve (5) through the pipes (7) and (9).

The same movement of the pilot valve puts the pipe (9) in communication with the atmosphere at (18). The pressure on top of the piston in the relay valve being released in this way allows the valve to open automatically and admit starting air to the starting-air manifold pipe (19) and the small pipe (20). The compressed air that enters the pipe (19) is what passes into the working cylinders and sets the engine in motion, while that passing into the pipe (20) enters the starting-air distributor indicated at (21).

The starting valves in each cylinder head are pneumatically operated, and if the one (22) shown in section is examined it will be seen that the starting air cannot enter the cylinder until the pressure is applied above the piston and the valve opened. The opening and closing of the starting valves are controlled by an equal number of distributor valves (21) of the piston type, which are housed in one or more forged steel blocks. The distributor valves are arranged radially around the camshaft and machined internally to form two passages, one being for the compressed air supplied through the pipe (20) and the other for exhausted air which passes out of the pipe (23) into the atmosphere.

The distributor valves are operated by two cams mounted side by side on the camshaft, one being for " Ahead " operation and the other " Astern." These cams are simply discs having a piece cut out of the periphery, very similar to the interlocking discs shown in Fig. 152, and having a fixed angular relationship to the crankshaft. When the starting wheel is rotated to the position marked " Start " and compressed air passes the relay valve, part of it enters the pipe (20) and then passes to the distributor. The compressed air entering the distributor pushes all piston valves inward until the ends of the spindles attached to them make contact with the cam. In every case but one the projecting spindle attached to the valves will make contact with the plain part of the cam before the valves have travelled far enough to uncover the ports, and the air will be prevented from going further. There will, however, always be one valve at least opposite the piece cut out of the disc, and this valve will travel further than the others and uncover the port in its housing.

Compressed air will therefore pass through the port into the pipe (24) leading to the top of the starting valve (22)—assuming, of course, that the crank of this unit happens to be the one that is in the starting position. The compressed air acting on the top of the piston attached to the starting-valve spindle forces the valve open and allows starting air to enter the working cylinder. The engine is then set in motion, and some time before the working piston of the unit under consideration reaches the end of its stroke, the distributor cam, having a fixed angular relationship to the crankshaft, revolves and the distributor valve is forced outward on to the plain part of the cam. This has the effect of covering the port in the housing, which shuts off the operating air to the starting valve (22), at the same time putting the pipe (24) into communication with the atmosphere. Releasing the pressure in the pipe (24) causes the starting valve to return smartly to its seat, and the supply of starting air to this particular cylinder is cut off. It will thus be seen how each starting valve is made to open and close in turn as the cranks come into starting position.

When the speed of the engine is sufficient to ignite the fuel—actually a slight pause only in the " Start " position is necessary to attain the desired speed—the starting wheel is moved to the " Fuel " position. This further movement of the starting wheel causes the downward movement of the trigger rod (16) to be continued until it strikes the cam plate (25) and disengages the lever (17). The pilot valve (8) then opens and allows the compressed air to flow to the top of the relay valve (5) where it acts on the piston and closes it, thus shutting off the starting air from the starting-air manifold (19).

Upon further examining Fig. 153 it will be seen that any movement of the starting wheel is transmitted through a system of rods and levers to the fuel-pump control shaft (27), which in turn gives a rotary movement to the plungers of the Bosch type fuel pumps indicated by (28). The connection between the starting wheel and the fuel-pump controls is so arranged that when the engine is running " on air " the fuel pumps deliver into the spill pipe, but immediately the starting wheel is moved from the " Start " position the fuel pumps begin delivering into the working cylinders. To vary the speed of the engine when working on fuel it is necessary only to move the starting wheel to the right or left, as required, within the fuel control area marked on the indicator dial.

As previously stated, the reversing operation in this make of engine is also carried out by rotating the starting wheel. The position on the indicator at which the reversing gear can be put over is before the starting position and is distinguished by the word " Reverse " on each side of the " Stop " position, that on the right being to bring the gear " Astern," and that on the left to bring the gear into the " Ahead " position. As is usual, an interlocking device is provided whereby the engine cannot be set in motion until the reversing gear is in its correct " Ahead " or " Astern " position, the arrangement being as follows. A lever (29) is keyed to the starting wheel shaft (14), while a quadrant (30) is mounted on a small shaft and so arranged that its face and the lever (29) are almost touching. The corners of the quadrant are thickened to form stops, and the length of the lever (29) is such that when the reversing gear is in mid-position, the starting wheel can only be moved to the respective reversing positions before coming against the stops on the quadrant (30). The reversing gear going over to the " Ahead " or " Astern " position alters the position of the quadrant by means of the scroll (31) on the reversing shaft (32) (on which the cylinder-head rockers are mounted) and suitable connecting links, so that the lever (29) is free to pass in the desired direction.

Assuming the reversing gear to be in the " Astern " position, and that the starting wheel has been rotated to the position " Reverse " on the indicator in the " Ahead " direction, the cams (33) will raise one of the two valves in the reversing gear control box (34). This valve will allow operating air to enter the air cylinder (36) of the servo motor on the top of the piston and force it to the bottom of the cylinder, which position of the piston corresponds to the " Ahead " position of the reversing gear. The vertical movement of the rack (35) attached to an extension of the servo-motor piston rod rotates the reversing shaft (32) one complete revolution through the gear wheels shown. As the valve rocking-levers are mounted on eccentrics keyed to the reversing shaft, the effect of rotating the latter is to raise the lever rollers clear of the cams whilst the scroll on the back of the rack moves the camshaft in an endwise direction.

Had the reversing gear been in the " Ahead " position when the starting wheel was rotated in the " Ahead " direction, it would have been possible to put the wheel right over to the " Start " position, since the interlocking mechanism already described between the starting and reversing gears would be in a position to allow this, and the operating air passing to the servo motor would have no effect since it would act on the top of the piston when it was already at the bottom of the cylinder. But suppose the engine is now operating in the " Ahead " direction and it is required to go " Astern ": to effect this the starting wheel is brought back to the " Stop " position, and when the engine stops, the wheel is moved further in the same direction until the pointer indicating the position of the gears reaches the " Astern " reverse position. The interlocking mechanism will prevent the wheel from being moved further until the operating air, which by this time has been allowed to pass the servo-motor control valve, acting on the underside of the servo-motor piston, forces it to the top of the cylinder, at which position the starting wheel is unlocked and is free to be rotated to the " Start " position " Astern."

To put the reversing gear into the mid-position, as is usual when the engine is stopped and until the next order from the navigating bridge is received, all that is necessary is to rotate the starting wheel to the reverse position, and when the gear is half over return the wheel to the "Stop" position. This has the effect of merely opening one of the servo-motor control valves, and when the piston has completed half its stroke and the starting wheel

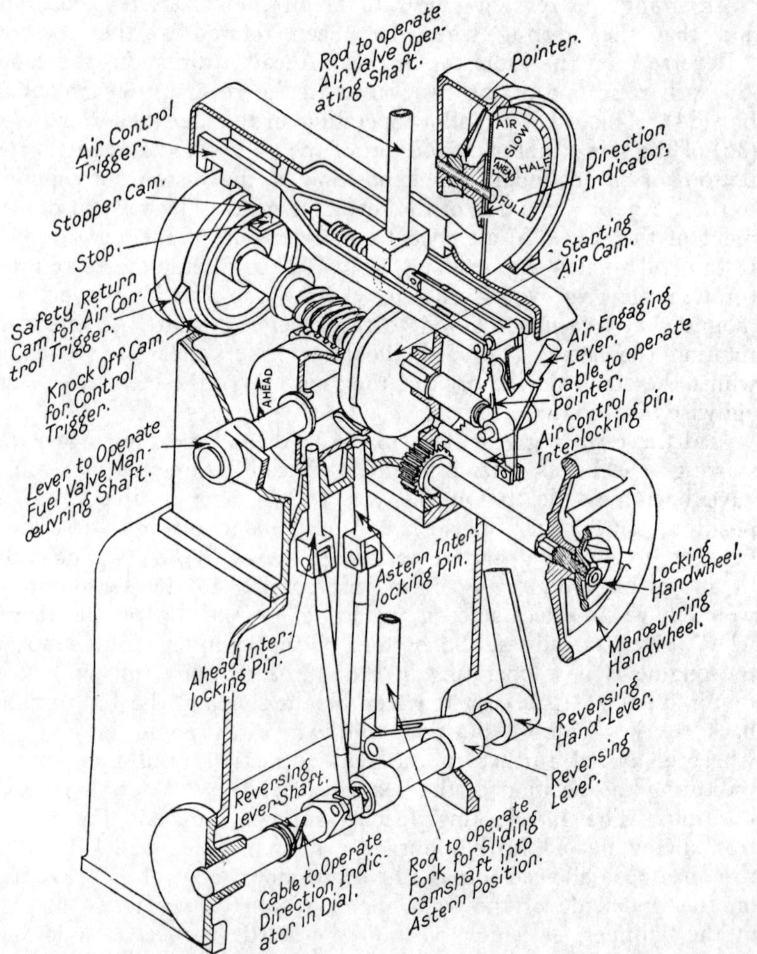

Fig. 154—Manoeuvring gear of Doxford opposed-piston engines built before 1958

is returned to the " Stop " position, the control valve is closed and the operating air shut off.

In the Doxford manoeuvring gear both the starting and reversing operations of this two-stroke opposed-piston engine are effected by hand power, no servo motors being necessary to operate the gears. For a pictorial view of the complete control mechanism employed on this make of engine, built prior to the year 1958, see Fig. 154.

When the indicator pointer showing the position of the gear is at the " Stop " position, the rocking-lever rollers of the fuel and starting valves—the fuel valves of these engines are mechanically operated—are clear of the cams, and the camshaft can be moved endwise into the desired position by operating the lever located beside the manoeuvring wheel. When the reversing lever is moved into either extreme position, the locking pins indicated in the sketch are given a corresponding movement, the effect of which is to put the starting wheel into gear. If now the manoeuvring wheel is rotated, the rod which brings the starting-air distribution valves into operation is lifted and the engine will be set in motion. A further movement of the manoeuvring wheel in the same direction causes the starting-air valves to be disengaged and the fuel valves engaged. Continuing the rotation of the manoeuvring wheel, the lift of the fuel valves is increased and greater power is developed if required.

As described earlier in this book, each cylinder of the Doxford engine is provided with two fuel valves located diametrically opposite each other, and two camshafts are employed, one to operate the valves at the front of the engine and the other the valves at the back. The front camshaft operates the starting valves also. As the front camshaft only is used for manoeuvring, the back camshaft is not made to move in an endwise direction, and the fuel valves operated by this shaft remain inactive until the engine is working in the desired direction and the manoeuvring wheel is rotated further.

In the year of writing this book various parts of the Doxford engine, including the manoeuvring gear, were re-designed. The starting gear was greatly simplified and the fuel system brought more into line with general practice. The modern Doxford engine will be described in a later chapter, but as we are mainly concerned with the engines in service, and there are a great many, this description of the manoeuvring gear previously adopted is essential.

The manoeuvring gear found on some Sulzer two-stroke engines is shown diagrammatically in Fig. 155. It may be divided roughly into three separate mechanisms, namely, the starting system, the fuel control system, and an interlocking system which affects the other two simultaneously and ensures reliable manoeuvring.

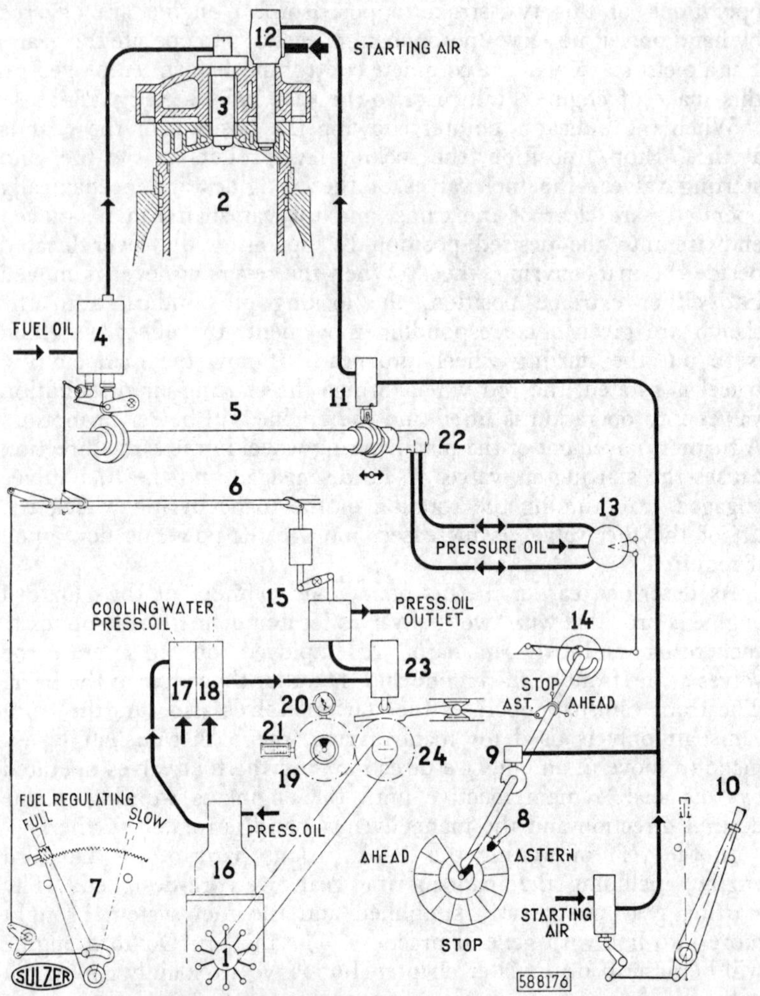

Fig. 155—Control mechanism of a 2-stroke engine (Sulzer)

The fuel control system comprises the fuel pump, fuel valve, levers and rods, which regulate and measure the quantity of fuel to be injected, but do not cut off or open up the fuel supply when the engine is stopped or started. These parts are indicated by 4, 3, and 7, respectively, in the diagram. In this particular type of Sulzer's manoeuvring gear, the fuel pump is operated by a symmetrical cam which serves for running ahead and astern. Consequently, when reversing the engine it is not necessary to alter the controls of the fuel system.

Starting is effected by operating a lever (10) which causes operating air to pass through the control valves (11) to the starting valves (12) and controls their opening and closing. A small plunger (9) is subject to the pressure during the starting operation, with the result that it is impossible to move the reversing control during the starting period. This plunger operates a pin which engages in a slot of the reversing shaft as soon as this shaft is in the stop position, and forms the interlock. The reversing of the engine is effected through the engine-room telegraph lever (8). By moving this lever an operating disc (14) is made to rotate and moves a valve (13) by means of suitable rods. According to the position of the telegraph lever (8), this valve (13) is rotated mechanically into the ahead or astern position, so that pressure oil which is led to the valve acts on the piston of a servo motor (22) in the required direction. This piston moves the ahead or astern starting cams axially, thus bringing the appropriate cams under the control valves (11). The cams are fitted on a sleeve which slides on the camshaft (5).

The interlocking system prevents any wrong movements being carried out, and stops the engine and gives an alarm in case of failure of certain essential services. For example, the apparatus (23) not only shuts off the fuel automatically when the reply signal is given to the order to stop and reverse, but also restores the fuel supply again automatically as soon as the engine is rotating in the desired direction. Since these functions are automatic, there is no danger that the engine might run in the wrong direction.

The apparatus consists essentially of an operating disc (24), which is connected mechanically to the crankshaft (1), and of a valve block (23). Between these two lies a slipper, the position of which depends on that of the reversing mechanism or of the reply lever. If the engine has to be reversed from ahead to astern, the valve (23) is opened by the slipper, and oil under pressure is led to a servo-motor piston (15), thus causing the rod (6) to bring the fuel delivery to zero. When the engine begins to rotate astern, the operating disc also turns astern and, by reversing a pawl, closes the valve (23) so that the servo motor (15) again sets the fuel pump on to delivery. Further safety devices (16), (17) and (18) are provided. The first is a governor which operates when the speed of the engine is too high. The servo motors (17) and (18) are operated by the pressure of the bearing lubricating oil and cylinder cooling-water respectively. When the pressure in either of these services falls below a safe level the fuel regulation comes under the control of the apparatus (23) and (15). The governor (16) also acts on the fuel regulation through this portion of the mechanism.

In addition to the above a locking device is provided which makes it impossible to start the engine unless the engine turning gear is disengaged. This is a very important safety device as disengagement of the turning gear under certain unusual circumstances before operating the starting gear is sometimes overlooked, with the result that the turning gear is completely wrecked. The control pressure-oil system indicated in Fig. 155 can be changed over to compressed air, if required, by simply turning a cock.

Fig. 156* shows in diagrammatic form the manoeuvring gear of a M.A.N. four-stroke engine. A written description has been purposely omitted since the names of the various parts are given and the illustration will be easily understood. Moreover, time spent tracing the sequence of the various stages of the starting and reversing operations will be good practice. Besides, this manoeuvring gear is similar in many respects to those already fully described.

Maintenance of reversing gears

Much of what was written about the maintenance of starting gears at the end of the previous chapter applies to reversing gears. Both are in use for a very small part of the engine's life, and whilst it is not expected that much wear and tear will take place in reversing gears, they may go wrong at a critical moment if not given some attention when all appears to be going well.

As the periods of inaction are of lengthy duration and as some of the parts make contact with moist compressed air, maintenance consists chiefly of keeping the various parts clean, lubricated, and free to function as intended at any moment. Also, it must not be assumed that because the small poppet valves incorporated in the gear are so little used that they will remain air- or oil-tight indefinitely. Infrequent use of such parts may even be more conducive to pitting and corrosion of the faces than would more frequent use. Both oil and compressed air may contain corrosive elements which, being undisturbed for long periods, carry on their destructive work unimpeded.

* See page 728

Valves having stems that project from their housing should be given periodical attention, as the stems may become dry and jam owing to being exposed to the warm engine-room atmosphere. Especially is this necessary if the stems are pointing downwards, as any condensed moisture in the compressed air will run down them and cause dryness and maybe corrosion. If eventual jamming is to be prevented the valves should be removed and lubricated occasionally. A thin covering of good-quality grease is the best lubricant for such parts.

Such parts as reversing shafts must, of course, be perfectly free in their bearings so that the servo motor will change the position of the gear in the shortest time. On the other hand, there should not be measurable clearance in the bearings, otherwise the timing of valves which the reversing shaft operates may be adversely affected. Moreover, any such clearance will increase if the shaft serves as a fulcrum for the rocking levers in motion during the normal running of the engine. A case is on record where the clearance in the reversing-shaft bearings was allowed to become so great that on one occasion when it was necessary to reverse the engine quickly, the rocking levers mounted on eccentrics keyed to the reversing shaft were not lifted high enough, with the result that the rollers fouled the cams as the camshaft was moved endwise. Not only was serious damage done to the rocking levers but, the engine not being immediately available for "Astern" running, way could not be taken off the ship and a collision, involving enormous cost, could not be avoided.

In some manoeuvring gears "lost motion" couplings or clutches are incorporated. Such parts must be perfectly free to rotate through a certain angle, relative to the shaft upon which they are mounted. Even though the bore of such couplings may be lined with a phosphor-bronze bush they tend to jam unless kept clean and lubricated regularly. Attention of this kind is particularly necessary if they have been exposed to water, whether it be rain or sea spray entering through the skylights or water from a "broken" joint during overhaul. It is a simple matter to keep these "lost motion" couplings or clutches free, but generally it requires much time and effort to make them free once they have become jammed.

The servo-motor oil system, when employed, must be kept completely filled with oil, as the presence of only a very small quantity of air will cause an uneven or jerky movement of the reversing gear when it is brought into use. The servo-motor piston-rod stuffing-box packing should be renewed before it becomes so hard that undue pressure must be applied to the gland nuts to stop leakage of oil or compressed air. Steel piston rods that are allowed to rust whilst at sea will quickly make the packing ineffective when the motor is again used.

CHAPTER 18

Cylinder scavenging and supercharging

The earliest engines operated on the four-stroke principle, and this type is still favoured by some designers competent to judge the relative merits of the two types. The chief advantage is what might be termed the straightforward design of the parts that deal with the expulsion of the burnt gases and the re-charging of the cylinders with pure air, which permits the simplest possible form of cylinder liner. It cannot be denied, however, that the utilisation of only half the number of piston strokes is perhaps more than a fair price to pay for this advantage.

In all other respects two- and four-stroke engines are much alike, so that in view of the advantage possessed by the former in regard to weight per unit power developed, it is no wonder that the designs of scavenging systems have varied to an extraordinary degree during recent years in the search for a simple yet reliable and efficient system.

The overall efficiency of a two-stroke engine depends largely upon the design of the scavenging system. Inefficiency in this part reduces the power output per unit weight, because if the cylinders are not fully charged with pure air each cycle the desired mean indicated pressure cannot be produced. Incomplete scavenging also results in increased fuel consumption per unit power developed, because the more burnt gases that are mixed with the combustion air, the lower will be its oxygen content and the maximum combustion efficiency will not be possible. Other effects of incomplete scavenging, and consequently poor combustion, are that the lubricating oil becomes contaminated to a greater extent, thus leading to greater wear of the piston rings and cylinder liners. The mean temperatures in the cylinders and the heat stresses in the metal surfaces surrounding the burning gases will also be greater in an engine with an inefficient scavenging system.

On the other hand, the cylinders of a particular two-stroke engine may be completely scavenged and re-charged with pure air, when none of the foregoing mechanical difficulties would arise, but if this is accomplished with more air than is necessary the mechanical efficiency of the plant would be low, since work must be expended to provide the scavenging air, and the overall fuel consumption per unit power developed would be abnormally high. It will thus be seen that a great deal depends upon the exhausting and re-charging system of a two-stroke engine.

In the two-stroke engine the process of driving out the products of combustion and re-charging the cylinder with pure air is concentrated into about 120° of crank angle, as against about 400° in four-stroke engines. Moreover, these processes take place while the piston is at either side of the bottom dead centre, and consequently only a very small portion of the compression and working strokes is lost.

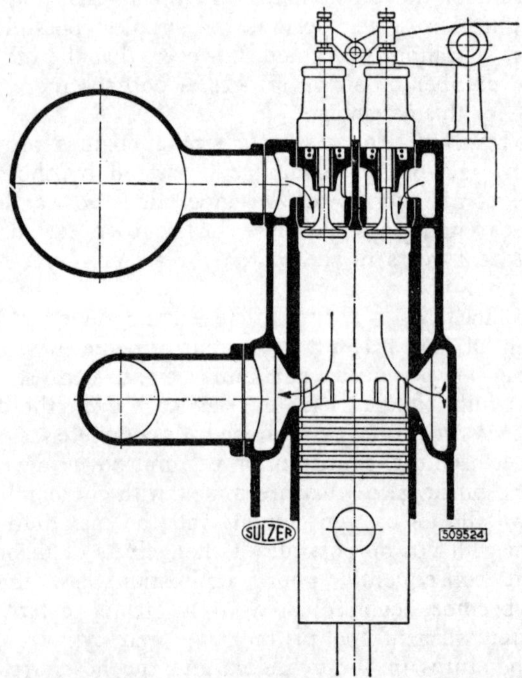

Fig. 157—Uniflow scavenging of 2-stroke engine cylinder (Sulzer)

In most cases the burnt gases are driven out of the cylinder through openings near the bottom, but in the Doxford and B. & W.

opposed-piston engines they are expelled through ports situated at the top of the cylinder. Release of gases begins when the piston has travelled about 80 per cent of its working stroke, and the openings for their exit are always of such a size that the pressure in the cylinder falls rapidly to almost that of the atmosphere.

The scavenging air is admitted through ports or valves, the ports, when used, being located either at the same end of the cylinder, or at the opposite ends. Sometimes the scavenging air entering ports at the lower end of the cylinder drives the burnt gases out through a mechanically operated valve at the opposite end. Admission of scavenging air is timed to begin when the pressure of burnt gases in the cylinder has been reduced to that of the scavenging air or less, and its duty is to sweep the remaining burnt gases out and then fill the cylinder with air by the time the piston has completed roughly 20 per cent of its compression stroke. The difficulties encountered by designers in effecting this are numerous, but in the main consist of preventing as far as possible mixing of the burnt gases and scavenging air, and reducing to a minimum the amount of scavenging air which passes out into the exhaust passages without serving any useful purpose.

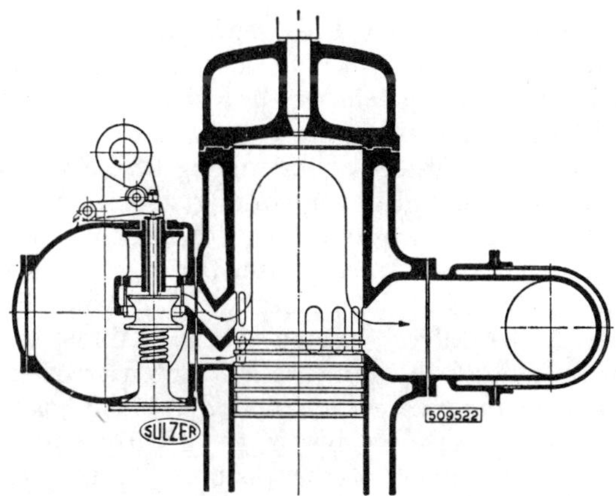

Fig. 158—Loop flow scavenging of 2-stroke engine cylinder (Sulzer)

Scavenging systems are of either the uniflow or loop-flow principle, illustrated in Figs. 157 and 158. The former term is applied to the systems of opposed-piston engines, such as the Doxford, and all engines in which the scavenging air enters at one end of the cylinder and drives the burnt gases out through openings at the opposite end. In loop-flow systems the direction of the flow of scavenging air is reversed whilst in the cylinder, so that scavenging-air enters and the burnt gases leave at the same end of the cylinder. Many two-stroke engines are scavenged in this manner, chief amongst which is that of Sulzer's.

To obtain the best results the pressure, and consequently the velocity, of the scavenging air must not be too low or too high. If too low the burnt gases will not be driven out, and if too high the air will cut through the burnt gases instead of pushing the gases before it, and cause mixing and wasteful use of air, nor will the cylinder be properly scavenged. The scavenging-air pressures employed are in the neighbourhood of 2 lb/sq.in.

The pressure in the working cylinders when release of burnt gases occurs is about 40 lb/sq.in., so that in all two-stroke engines the exhaust passage must first be opened to allow some of the gases to escape and the pressure to fall before the low-pressure scavenging air is admitted; further, to obtain the best results the admission of scavenging air must be continued for a while after the closing of the exhaust passage to ensure that the cylinder is fully charged with air.

It is probable that Sulzer Bros. have done more than any to improve the two-stroke engine, so that it will be instructive to follow briefly the development of the cylinder scavenging system introduced by this enterprising firm.

Fig. 157 shows the system of scavenging first employed. As the piston approached the end of its working stroke a row of ports in the cylinder wall were uncovered by it, through which some of the products of combustion escaped. After the pressure in the cylinder had fallen to about that of the atmosphere, but while the ports were still uncovered, the valves situated in the cylinder head opened, allowing air at about 2 lb/sq.in. pressure to enter the cylinder and begin the scavenging process. When the burnt gases had been expelled and their place taken by air, the exhaust ports were closed by the upward movement of the piston. As the scavenging-air supply was continued, the cylinder received a supplementary charge of air up to the scavenging-air pressure, after which the air-inlet or scavenging valves were allowed to close and the compression process began.

This system gave good results so far as scavenging efficiency was concerned. The system was abandoned, however, because of the large valve pockets required in the cylinder heads weakening these vital parts and causing them to fracture. Metals have been greatly improved since that time, however, so that the same trouble would not be expected with present-day engines employing this method of scavenging.

These and other minor difficulties led to the study of other methods, and Fig. 158 shows the first arrangement of the loop scavenging system introduced by Sulzer's. The cylinder head in this case contained fuel and starting valves only, the scavenging air entering the cylinder through a row of ports arranged opposite the exhaust ports. Actually the scavenging air was admitted to the cylinder through two rows of ports occupying about half the periphery of the cylinder liner, the remaining half being taken up by the exhaust ports.

The reason for employing two rows of scavenging ports was to ensure that the exhaust ports would be opened first and that scavenging air would continue to be admitted after the exhaust ports were closed. To obtain this timing of the exhausting and re-charging process, it will be apparent that the admission of the scavenging air must be controlled other than by the piston, since if on the downward movement of the piston the exhaust ports are the first to be uncovered, they will not be closed by the upward movement of the piston until after the scavenging air ports have been closed.

Referring to Fig. 158, it will be seen that one row of scavenging ports is located immediately above the other, the lower being the scavenging-air ports proper, and the upper the supplementary scavenging-air ports, while the exhaust ports are on the opposite side of the cylinder. It will also be noted that the supplementary scavenging-air ports are cut in the cylinder liner with their upper edges slightly higher than the corresponding edges of the exhaust ports, and that the scavenging air entering through these ports is controlled by a valve. In the earliest engines having this scavenging system, the valve was of the double-beat type, as shown, actuated by eccentrics and rods from the camshaft. This was replaced in later engines by a valve of the rotary type driven through gearing by the camshaft.

The action of this scavenging system is as follows. Assume the piston to be moving downwards under the pressure of the expanding gases. After the piston has completed about four-fifths of its stroke, the supplementary scavenging-air ports are uncovered, but since the valve controlling the flow of air through this row is closed, no scavenging air is admitted to the cylinder. Further downward movement of the piston uncovers the exhaust ports and some of the burnt gases escape.

By the time the piston has travelled far enough to begin uncovering the lower row of scavenging-air ports, the pressure in the cylinder has been reduced to that of the atmosphere, so that when the low-pressure scavenging air is admitted through these ports, the remainder of the burnt gases are driven out of the cylinder. About the same time as the scavenging ports proper are uncovered by the piston, the valve controlling the flow of air through the upper row is opened and scavenging air is permitted to enter the cylinder through the supplementary ports also. This valve remains open until all the ports have been closed by the upward movement of the piston, so that the upward movement of the piston first closes the main scavenging-air ports, then the exhaust ports, and lastly the supplementary scavenging-air ports. In this way the exhaust gases are first released and the cylinder is left full of air under slight pressure; thus the same timing is obtained as with valve-scavenging, but without the large openings in the cylinder head.

A further development of this method of scavenging is illustrated in Fig. 159. Here the mechanically operated double-beat valve

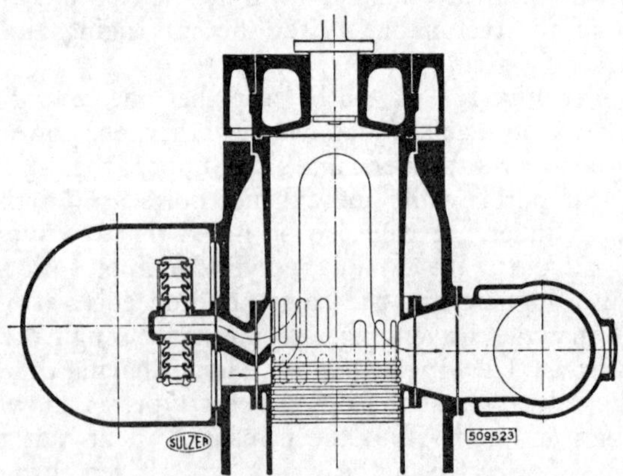

Fig. 159—Loop flow scavenging system having automatic scavenging valves (Sulzer)

controlling the flow of air through the upper row of ports is replaced by groups of automatic multiple-disc valves, the advantage of which is the elimination of the valve operating gear. These valves automatically open on the down-stroke of the piston only—when the pressure in the cylinder has fallen below the pressure in the scavenging-air receiver—and automatically close on the up-stroke of the piston, when the compression pressure in the cylinder exceeds the pressure in the scavenging-air receiver.

Fig. 160 shows the arrangement of the Sulzer scavenging process for double-acting two-stroke engines. As will be observed, three

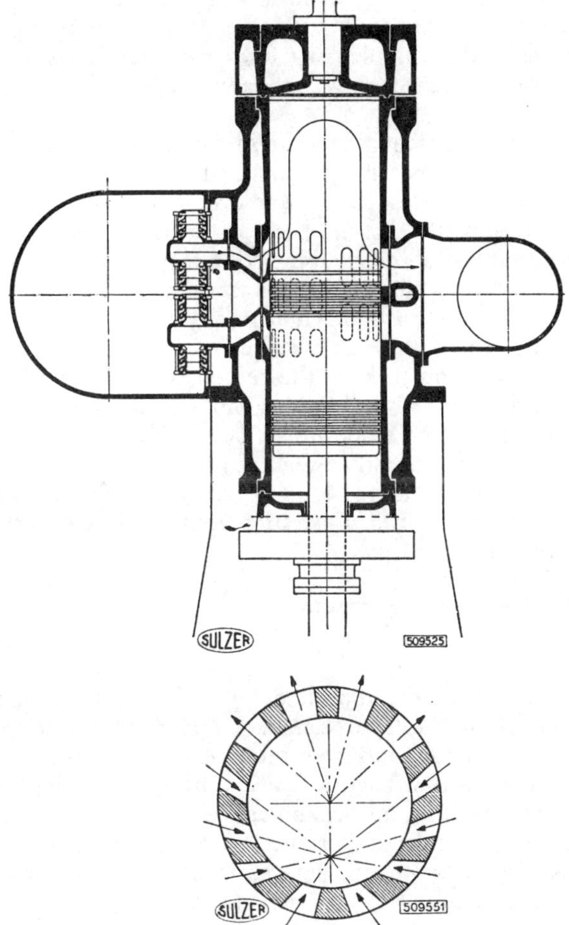

Fig. 160—Loop flow scavenging system having automatic scavenging valves, double-acting engine (Sulzer); and *(below)* cross-section through cylinder liner having backward sloping scavenging ports

rows of ports are provided, one above the other, in addition to the exhaust ports which are on the right-hand side. The middle row of scavenging ports remains permanently in open communication with the scavenging-air receiver, so that scavenging air flows through these ports into the cylinder whenever they are uncovered by the piston. The flow of scavenging air through the top and bottom rows of ports, however, is controlled by the automatic valves in exactly the same manner as described for single-acting engines. In some cases the middle row of scavenging ports is omitted, the whole of the scavenging air passing through the automatic valves.

There are many scavenging systems for two-stroke engines, most of which it has been possible to adapt successfully to double-acting engines, the flow of air in the bottom cylinders of such engines being almost identical with that in the top cylinders, so that nothing further need be said about double-acting engines of this type.

In addition to the point at which scavenging air is admitted, the direction taken by the air upon entering the cylinder is of importance, the aim being to avoid the air sweeping across the cylinder towards the exhaust ports and to keep the scavenging air behind the burnt gases as much as possible. To accomplish this the scavenging-air ports are given a steep slope upwards, as shown in Figs. 158 and 159. In addition to this some makers arrange the outer scavenging ports to turn backwards, as it were, as shown in Fig. 160. The scavenging-air ports in this illustration are those in which the arrow-heads are pointing inwards.

Operation of scavenging systems

All factors affecting the entry of the air have an important effect upon the scavenging process, so that the necessity for preventing the accumulation of carbonised oil in or around scavenging and exhaust ports will be appreciated. Neglect to do so results in imperfect combustion and the innumerable mechanical troubles which inevitably follow such a fault. Carbonaceous deposits result from excessive cylinder lubrication as well as imperfect combustion, so that it is of particular importance to see that no more lubricating oil than is necessary for efficient lubrication is introduced into the cylinders. Under conditions of bad combustion or excessive cylinder lubrication the deposit generally accumulates in the exhaust ports where it restricts the free exit of the burnt gases, but the scavenging-air ports should also be examined whenever a piston is removed from a cylinder, as in some scavenging systems the burnt gases flow momentarily into these ports and carry carbonised oil with them before the exhaust ports are uncovered.

One of the difficulties experienced with the early port-scavenged engines was cracking of the bars between the ports in the cylinder liners due to the heat stresses set up by comparatively cold air entering through one half of the ports and hot burnt gasses passing out through the remainder. In modern engines, however, no serious trouble arises from this, provided the temperature of the burnt gases is not allowed to become excessive, and that this part of the cylinder is properly circulated with cooling water and the cooling-water spaces in the vicinity are kept free from scale and mud.

The fact that the cylinders are cooled by a fresh-water system is no guarantee that scale will not deposit on the water side of cylinder liners. The only way to avoid scale is to use distilled water, and even then the water will be contaminated if a cooler tube leaks. Water received from barges should always be tested and should be rejected if it has had sea-water mixed with it; the seams of such craft are not always as watertight as they ought to be. Drain tanks should also be cleaned out periodically as it is surprising how much sediment accumulates and will be circulated through the cylinder jackets when a ship is unsteady in bad weather.

Restriction of the flow of scavenging air into the cylinders is not always due to carbon deposit. In one engine in which the scavenging air entered through ports arranged at the lower end of the cylinder liner and the exhaust gases were expelled through a mushroom valve in the cylinder head, the abnormally high scavenging-air pressure (3·5 lb/sq.in.) and exhaust temperature (900°F) could not be accounted for until it was found that the pistons did not completely uncover the scavenging-air ports by amounts varying from 4 to 10 mm. The explanation was that the engines had at some time previously been fitted with new pistons which differed in one important respect from the original pistons.

Although the scavenging air is compressed only slightly, heat is generated, and some makers pass the air through coolers of the tubular type on its way to the engine cylinders. The advantage of cooling the air is that its density is restored and the charge of air for combustion is consequently increased to normal weight. The higher the temperature of the scavenging air the greater must be the pressure to ensure the requisite amount being in the working cylinders at the beginning of the compression stroke. In view of the fact that in most systems the best scavenging effect is obtained the lower the pressure of the scavenging air, and since the higher the pressure the greater will be the amount of air that passes to waste through the exhaust ports, any arrangements provided for cooling the scavenging air should be kept in good working order.

The chief reason for the comparatively low exhaust temperatures in two-stroke engines is that in slow-running marine engines the scavenging air is in contact with the hot burnt gases during the scavenging period of the cycle for a relatively long time, during which the scavenging air absorbs some of the heat and the temperature of the exhaust gases is, in consequence, reduced. Moreover, a certain amount of mixing takes place, and if the desired combustion efficiency is to be obtained this mixture of burnt gases and scavenging air must be driven out of the cylinder. This results in a further reduction of the exhaust temperature.

The transfer of heat from the burnt gases to the scavenging air cannot be avoided, but the extent of the mixing which takes place depends upon the efficiency of the scavenging system. It is because of this that there is such a wide variation in the temperature of the exhaust gases from different makes of two-stroke engines. Such temperatures range from 350° to 750°F (177° to 400°C), whereas the exhaust temperatures of four-stroke engines are always in the neighbourhood of 800°F (427°C). Some two-stroke engines are therefore capable of generating more steam in waste heat boilers than others, so that although the thermal efficiencies of the engines may be the same, the overall efficiencies may be different.

Supercharging

The object of supercharging is to force air into the working cylinders during the re-charging portion of the cycle so that at the beginning of the compression stroke the air in the cylinders is under definite pressure instead of being at or only slightly above atmospheric pressure. Consequently, at the end of the compression stroke, or at the moment when fuel injection begins, the cylinders will contain a greater weight of air and will consequently be capable of burning a proportionately greater quantity of fuel. The real object, therefore, of supercharging an engine is to obtain greater power output for the same size of cylinder.

A greater mean effective pressure and, consequently, a greater output of power can be obtained within certain limits from an engine by simply injecting more fuel, but the effect of burning a greater quantity of fuel in the original quantity of air is to increase the cylinder temperatures throughout the cycle. Most unsupercharged engines will carry an overload, i.e. will develop more than the rated power output, for an hour or so without mechanical difficulties arising, but after a time certain parts become overheated and serious mechanical trouble will result. The amount of overload that an engine will carry for an hour or so is about 10 per cent. Should one engine be capable of operating longer than another under such conditions, it indicates that in the normal charge of combustible mixture a greater proportion of air has been allowed, and consequently the cylinders are larger either in diameter or length for a given power output.

It can be shown by means of entropy diagrams that the power output of an engine in which the compression starts from atmospheric pressure can be increased 50 per cent without any increase in the mean temperature of the cylinder contents, provided the weight of air in the cylinders when the fuel is injected is in proportion to the amount of fuel injected. It is indeed claimed by the originators of supercharging, and the claim can be proved theoretically, that the mean temperature of the cycle is even lower than in an unsupercharged engine, and that the fuel consumption per unit power developed is less.

That this is true there is no doubt, because the supercharged engine has available a greater supply of air per pound of fuel burnt than an unsupercharged engine, the cylinders of which, in the case of four-stroke engines, are probably barely full at the beginning of compression; and as in the supercharged engine a proportion of the air is used to rid the clearance spaces of burnt gases at the end of the exhaust stroke, the combustion efficiency of a supercharged engine could be slightly greater. This scavenging process at the end of the exhaust stroke, referred to more fully later, may also be expected to serve as an internal cooling agent, resulting in a lower working temperature of cylinder heads and their valves. The slightly better fuel economy arises from an increase in the mechanical efficiency when an engine is supercharged. This is due to the power output being increased without a proportionate increase in the frictional resistances; consequently a lower proportion of the power developed is absorbed in overcoming friction, or other factors which account for the difference between i.h.p. and b.h.p.

In practice it can be definitely stated after several years' experience with a great number of large supercharged engines, that the wear rates of such parts as cylinder liners, piston rings, exhaust valves and the principal bearings are no greater, while there is no noticeable difference in the amount of lubricating oil required to lubricate the cylinders efficiently. That the results obtained justify the extra initial cost of supercharging there is not the slightest doubt.

SUPERCHARGING FOUR-STROKE ENGINES

Fig. 161 shows indicator diagrams taken from an engine that was built as an unsupercharged engine and afterwards supercharged. This conversion resulted in only a moderate increase in power output, but it clearly illustrated the advantages of supercharging.

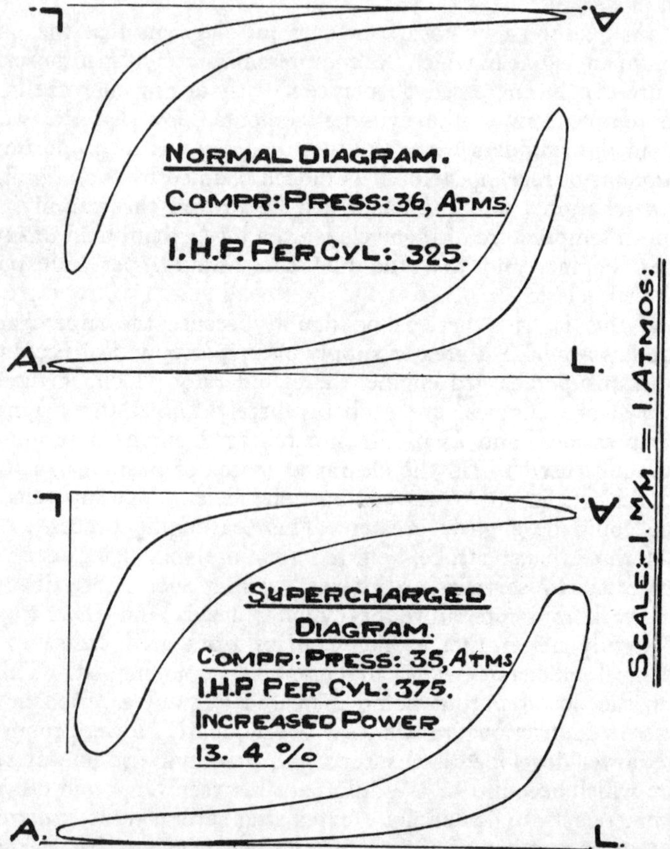

Fig. 161—Indicator diagrams taken from a 6-cylinder 4-stroke engine before and after being supercharged

The piston speed was the same in each case, so that the whole of the extra power obtained is represented in the larger diagram. If no alteration had been made to the compression ratio, the terminal compression pressure would have been increased. As will be seen, the indicator diagrams are approximately the same height, the greater mean indicated pressure being shown by a broadening of the supercharged diagram. Higher maximum cylinder pressures are not desirable since it would mean a heavier and more costly engine, so that the same final compression pressure is obtained by increasing the clearance space and thereby reducing the compression ratio.

As mentioned earlier, a proportion of the air supplied to the working cylinders is employed to scavenge the cylinder clearance space at the end of the exhaust stroke. This process is not an essential part of the supercharging operation, but since the air is available to accomplish this it is generally done, because there are obvious advantages in starting combustion with the cylinder containing no trace of burnt gases from the previous cycle.

Scavenging of the clearance space is effected by increasing the overlap of the air-inlet and exhaust valves, i.e. the period at the end of the exhaust stroke and beginning of the air-inlet stroke when both valves are slightly open. At this period of the cycle the pressure at the air-inlet valve is higher than the pressure in the exhaust manifold, with the result that a quantity of cool air enters the cylinder at a high velocity through the partly open air-inlet valve and expels the hot burnt gases in the clearance space through the partly open exhaust valve.

The effect of this scavenging of the clearance space upon the combustion efficiency is bound to be beneficial, while cool air flowing through the upper part of the cylinder in this way will have an important cooling effect upon the exhaust valves and surfaces exposed to the burning gases. Some claim that the beneficial effect of this cooling process is so great that longer life may be expected from such parts of a supercharged engine than from similar parts of an unsupercharged engine. This view, however, is not borne out in practice, since the cylinder heads and pistons of either type never crack unless there is something wrong with the design or material, or unless improperly operated, while there is no difference in the attention required by the exhaust valves. It is probable, however, that were it not for the cooling effect of this scavenging air, such high mean effective pressures could not be safely developed in supercharged engines. Such engines must therefore be given the same attention as unsupercharged engines.

The opening and closing points, referred to the crank position, of air-inlet and exhaust valves of both supercharged and unsupercharged four-stroke engines are approximately as follows:—

Valve	Supercharged	Unsupercharged
Air inlet opens	55° B.T.C.	20° B.T.C.
,, ,, closes	28° A.B.C.	25° A.B.C.
Exhaust opens	42° B.B.C.	42° B.B.C.
,, closes	35° A.T.C.	14° A.T.C.

Valve settings may be found to vary with the system of supercharging, but from the foregoing, which is a fair average, it will be seen that while the overlap period in the unsupercharged engine is 34°, it is 90° in the supercharged engine. In addition to increasing the period of overlap, the opening and closing speeds of these valves are increased as much as practicable in order to provide a reasonably large area of opening for the entry of air and exit of the burnt gases. Consequently the peaks of air-inlet and exhaust cams of supercharged engines are fuller, i.e. less pointed.

The Buchi system

This, the first supercharging system to be applied to marine engines on a large scale, comprises a turbine driven by the exhaust gases of the engine, driving in turn a turbo-blower which draws air from the atmosphere and delivers it under pressure to a pipe in communication with the air-inlet valves of the engine. The diagrammatic arrangement of a six-cylinder four-stroke engine supercharged by the Buchi system is shown in Fig. 162, from which the main features can be clearly distinguished.

The machine supplying the air consists of a single-stage blower and a single-stage turbine wheel, mounted on the same shaft and revolving in suitable casings, delivering air to the common duct feeding the working cylinders. A bearing is provided on each side of the blower wheel, while the turbine wheel is overhung. The rotational speed under normal full load conditions is in the neighbourhood of 6,000 r.p.m. and the pressure of air delivered about 4·5 lb/sq.in.

As will be observed from Fig. 162, the engine is provided with two separate exhaust-pipes, one receiving the exhaust gases from

Nos. 1, 2 and 3 cylinders and the other from cylinders Nos. 4, 5 and 6; the gases are led by these pipes to the same end of the turbine but pass out of separate nozzles to impinge on the vanes of the turbine. The gases from each group of cylinders do not, therefore, mix until they have passed the turbine wheel. This is a very important feature of the Buchi system, as it is essential that the exhaust pipes be so arranged that interference between the

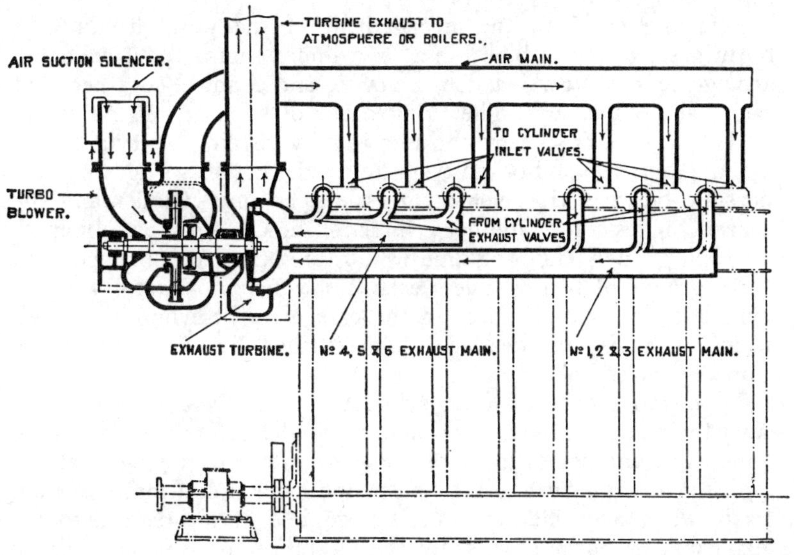

Fig. 162—Diagrammatic arrangement of the Buchi system of supercharging

exhausts of different cylinders is avoided, in order to permit the scavenging of the cylinder clearance spaces to be carried out in the most efficient manner. Upon leaving the turbine the gases enter a common pipe, and after passing through a silencer or waste heat boiler are discharged into the atmosphere.

The burnt gases reach the turbine at a pressure varying from 1 to 4 lb/sq.in. and at varying temperatures up to 800°F (427°C), depending upon the speed of the engine. The drop in temperature of the gases while they pass through the turbine is about 150°F (66°C) at full load. It will be appreciated that when the speed of the engine is reduced, the pressure and temperature of the gases reaching the turbine become less, and the speed of the turbine is consequently reduced. Naturally the pressure of air delivered by the blower is reduced also, but this is as it should be because as the quantity of fuel injected into the cylinders is reduced to effect a reduction in speed, the smaller is the amount of supercharge air required. This variation of the supercharge air pressure, and consequently the amount supplied to the working cylinders at various loads, is quite automatic, no hand regulation of the exhaust turbo blower being necessary.

Referring again to the arrangement of the pipes leading the burnt gases to the turbine: in a six-cylinder engine the usual crank arrangement is Nos. 1 and 6, 2 and 5, and 3 and 4 together, and each pair 120° apart. The firing order of such an engine would be 1, 4, 2, 6, 3, 5, so it will be seen that by forming the cylinders 1, 2 and 3, and 4, 5 and 6 into two groups, the greatest length of time possible between the exhausting process in one cylinder and the scavenging process in another cylinder of the same group is obtained. As even greater length of time would, of course, be obtained with three groups of two cylinders each, but since two groups of three cylinders, or four cylinders in the case of eight-cylinder engines, is found to give the desired results, further division would be an unnecessary complication.

With two groups of three cylinders the crankshaft travels 150° after the release of burnt gases in one cylinder before the scavenging process in another cylinder of the same group begins, so that the pressure in this particular exhaust pipe has ample time to spread, as it were, and offer an almost negligible back pressure to the expulsion of burnt gases from the clearance space of an adjacent cylinder when the piston in that cylinder reaches the end of its exhaust stroke.

The fluctuations of pressure in one working cylinder, the air-inlet manifold, and the exhaust manifold of the Buchi supercharged engine are shown on the crank angle diagram, Fig. 163. It will be observed that the pressure in the exhaust manifold (line *B*) is below the pressure in the air-inlet manifold, except for a period of 70°. This occurs when the exhaust valve opens; and as will be seen from the line *B*, representing the pressure in the exhaust manifold, the pressure rises above the air-inlet pressure of 5·3 lb/sq.in. when the crank reaches a point about 8° beyond the bottom dead centre, and remains so until the crank is nearly 80° beyond the bottom dead centre.

The scavenging process cannot, of course, be performed during this period. As the scavenging process requires a crank angle period in this case of 130°, it is evident that with five or more cylinders exhausting into the same manifold the periods of maximum pressure

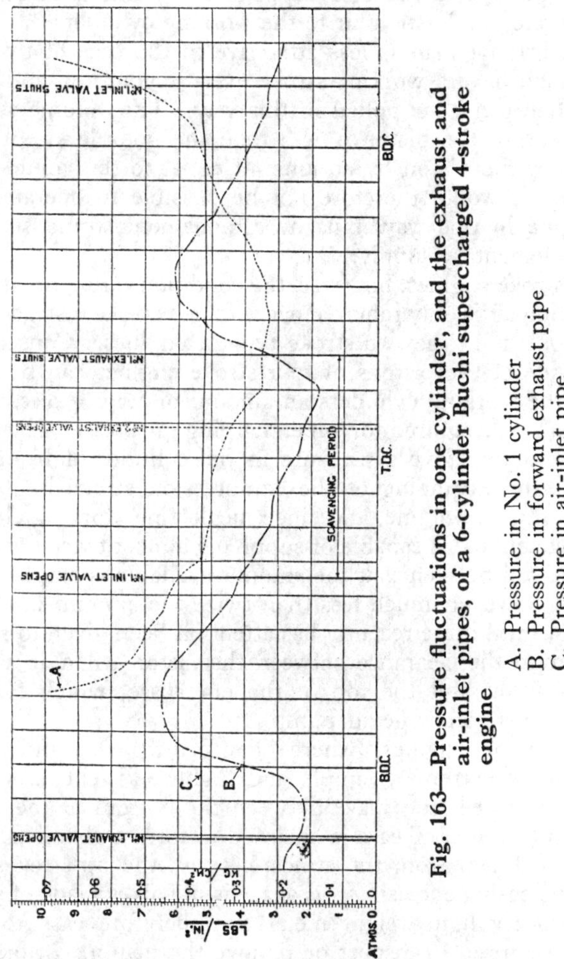

Fig. 163—Pressure fluctuations in one cylinder, and the exhaust and air-inlet pipes, of a 6-cylinder Buchi supercharged 4-stroke engine

A. Pressure in No. 1 cylinder
B. Pressure in forward exhaust pipe
C. Pressure in air-inlet pipe

in the exhaust manifold would overlap and proper scavenging of the cylinder clearance spaces would be impossible.

The Werkspoor system

The employment of the underside of the working pistons of a

crosshead type engine as an air pump dates from the early days of the diesel engine, and the idea has occasionally been revived since that time, either as a main or supplementary means of supplying scavenging and combustion air to the working cylinders.

Such an arrangement is less attractive in the case of two-stroke engines which have a working stroke every revolution, and require more air than can be supplied in this way. The volume swept by the underside of the piston is less than the volume swept by the upper side of the piston by an amount equal to the volume of the piston rod. It would therefore not be possible to operate a two-stroke engine in this way, but the arrangement would serve as a useful supplementary supply.

In four-stroke engines, however, the conditions are quite different, as combustion air is only required every fourth stroke instead of every second stroke as in the two-stroke type of engines. Consequently, the underside of the pistons of four-stroke engines can be used to deliver to the working cylinders an amount of air in excess of their stroke volume as required for supercharging purposes. The amount of air necessary to give a pressure in the cylinder of from 4 to 5 lb/sq.in. at the beginning of the compression stroke is about 1·3 times the cylinder volume, and since, neglecting working clearance, a four-stroke engine is capable of supplying almost twice the amount required, it will be seen that the amount available is ample.

Actually, however, much less than twice the amount is supplied, because not until quite recently has attention been given to reducing to a minimum the clearance between the piston when at its lowest working position and the top of the crankcase, which forms the bottom of the supercharge air pump.

In Werkspoor engines, where this principle is utilised, the arrangement is extremely simple and highly efficient. As will be seen from Fig. 164, the space between the bottom of the cylinder and the top of the crankcase is enclosed to form a chamber, *S*, into which air is drawn from the atmosphere on the up-strokes of the piston. The casing enclosing this space is in halves made of silumin, which is a very light-weight metal and therefore easy to handle when it is required to inspect or remove the piston. In order that the underside of the piston can be kept under observation whilst the engine is working, a window *D* is provided, the inner surface of which can be cleaned by a wiper operated from the outside. Immediately under the bottom of the cylinder liner a lip is formed to catch oil dripping from the cylinder, the oil being led to a point of the casing where a drain cock is provided. As a rule these drain

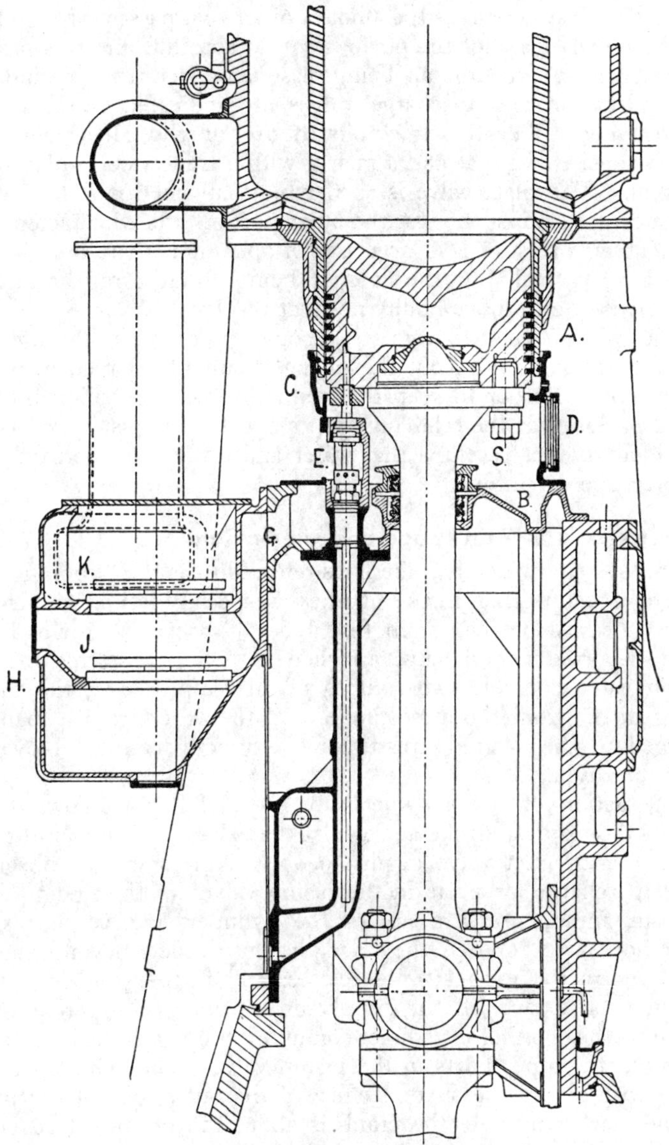

Fig. 164—Under-piston supercharge air pump of 4-stroke engine (Werkspoor)

cocks are always open, as the amount of air that passes through them on the down-stroke of the piston is of no account, and this practice ensures the supercharge air being reasonably free from oil and dirt.

The suction and discharge valves are indicated by *J* and *K*, respectively. The valves employed are of the Hoerbiger type, which consist of a seat and a guard, with a thin circular plate-valve between. The plate-valve is so flexible that when it is held down at the centre against the seat the outer portion lifts when acted upon by small air pressures. A large area of opening is therefore obtained with a very small lift, the amount being about 2 mm, and since the valves do not move bodily no wear results.

The piston cooling-water telescopic pipes pass through the supercharge air pump, but the casing is suitably shaped in way of these pipes in order to keep the glands for same outside. Suitable gland packing for the telescopic pipes and for the piston rod is also provided, as it is essential that water and oil be excluded from the supercharge air pumps.

Burmeister and Wain's supercharging system

This system, which is sometimes referred to as the " topping-up " system of supercharging, embodies a special design of air-inlet valve. As will be seen from Fig. 165, this valve is provided with a multi-ported piston valve attached to the valve stem, and this piston valve controls two sources of air supply—one, the upper, being direct from the atmosphere, and the other from a manifold charged to the desired pressure by a directly coupled blower of the rotary type.

The action of this air-inlet valve is as follows. Towards the end of the exhaust stroke and whilst the exhaust valve is still partly open, the air-inlet valve begins to open, and as will be observed, the supercharge air ports in the piston valve are the first to open, and air under pressure enters the cylinder and scavenges the clearance space. When the crank has proceeded beyond the top dead centre the exhaust valve closes, and further opening of the air-inlet valve cuts off the supply of scavenge or supercharge air and puts the cylinder into direct communication with the atmosphere through the upper ports in the piston valve. The cylinder is then filled with air by the suction effect of the out stroke of the piston in the usual way. As the crank is about the bottom dead centre and the air-inlet valve in the act of closing, the process is reversed and, by the closing action of the air-inlet valve, the cylinder is put into communication with the supercharge air through the lower ports in the piston valve. Consequently, when the air-inlet valve finally closes and compression begins, the cylinder is filled with pure air at a pressure of from 4 to 5 lb/sq.in.

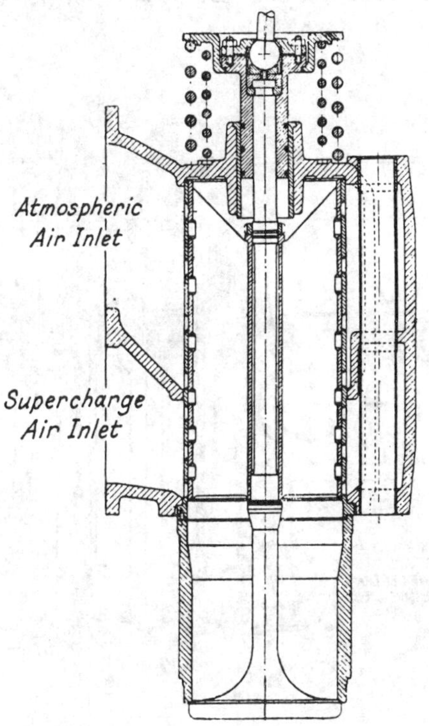

Fig. 165—Air-inlet valve of supercharged 4-stroke engine (Burmeister and Wain)

With this supercharge system the engine-driven blower has to supply about one-half the total quantity of air which passes into the cylinder. Consequently, the blower in such cases is comparatively small.

The characteristic feature of another method of supercharging by the same manufacturers, which is very similar to the Werkspoor system already described, is the means employed to control the air to and from the supercharge air-pump located under the working cylinders. As will be observed from Fig. 166, a rotary valve driven at half the engine speed puts the enclosed space under the working cylinder alternately in communication with the atmosphere and the pipe leading the air to the air-inlet valve. In order to maintain the correct setting of the rotary valve when the engine's direction of rotation is reversed, it is necessary to alter the position of the rotary valve relative to the crankshaft.

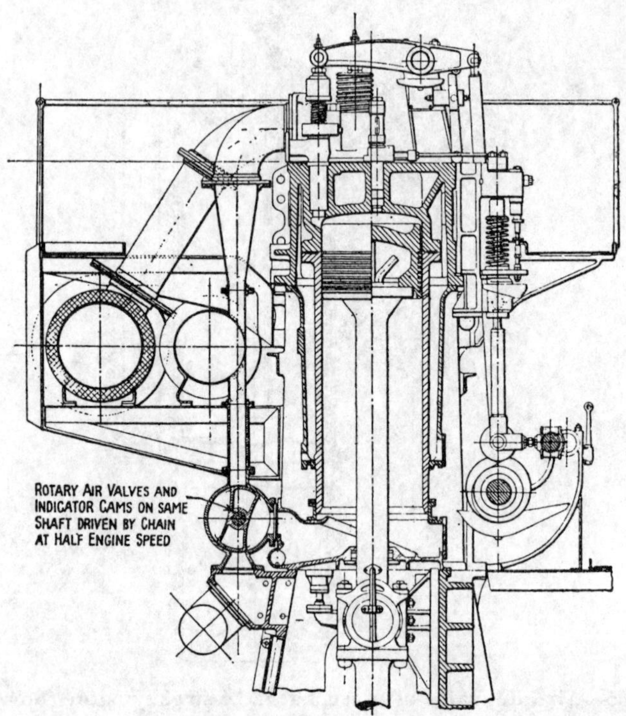

Fig. 166—Under-piston supercharging system for 4-stroke engines, with rotary valve

One minor advantage of the systems not employing an exhaust-gas turbine for the supply of supercharge air that is of special value where steam-driven auxiliaries are desired, is that the temperature of the gases entering the waste-heat boiler is higher, and therefore more effective in generating steam. The temperature drop in an exhaust-gas turbine used in the Buchi system is about 150°F (66°C), but this loss is more or less offset by the higher mechanical efficiency of an engine employing an exhaust-gas turbine.

SUPERCHARGING TWO-STROKE ENGINES

Strictly speaking, two-stroke engines have always been supercharged in that the pistons begin the compression stroke with the air in the cylinders above atmospheric pressure. The pressure at this point of the cycle of operations being equal to or slightly below the scavenging air pressure. As, however, the actual compression process begins later than in four-stroke engines it is questionable whether this initial pressure results in a greater weight of air being present in the cylinders of corresponding size at the end of the compression stroke.

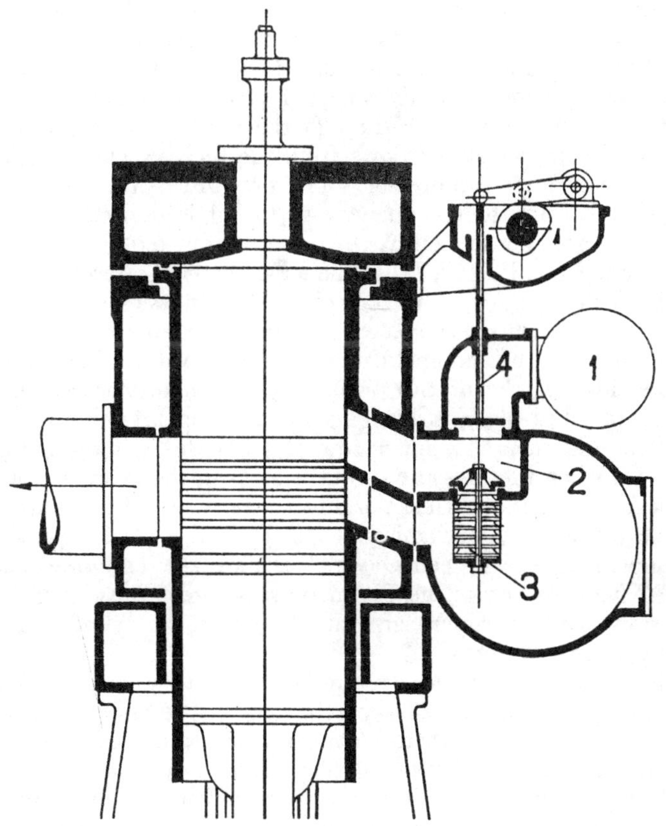

Fig. 167—Simple method of scavenging and supercharging 2-stroke engine cylinder (Sulzer)

Until recently efforts to increase the power output of a given size of cylinder by supercharging were confined to four-stroke engines. One reason for this is that two-stroke engines have twice the number of working strokes in a given number of revolutions and, in consequence, there is a greater transfer of heat to the cylinder liner, head, and piston, which sets a limit to the maximum power output. This development had therefore to wait until a method of supercharging two-stroke engines was found which permitted an increase in the power output whilst still keeping the heat transfer to the cylinder walls within acceptable range.

The simplest possible method of scavenging and supercharging two-stroke engine cylinders is shown in Fig. 167. The first part of the process is the same as the system already described and illustrated, but after the cylinder has been charged with air up to the scavenging air pressure, a mechanically operated valve opens and compressed air flows into the cylinder through the upper row of ports. The supply of compressed air flows from the receiver (1), supplied by a low-pressure air-compressor. The pressure of the air varies, of course, according to the quantity of fuel it is desired to inject at each cycle and, consequently, the power output required.

Referring to Fig. 167, (1) is the supercharge-air receiver, (4) the mechanically operated valve controlling the admission of supercharge air, (2) the chamber connected to the upper row of supercharge ports, and (3) the automatic scavenging-air valve. Near the end of the down-stroke of the piston the scavenging process already described takes place, scavenging air entering first the lower row of ports and then the upper row of ports through the automatic valve (3) when the pressure of burnt gases in the cylinder has been reduced. After the exhaust ports have been closed by the up-stroke of the piston, the mechanically operated valve (4) is opened and the supercharge air in the receiver (1) is allowed to enter the chamber (2). When this occurs the automatic scavenging valve (3) is closed and, as described, supercharge air flows into the cylinder through the upper row of ports.

All two-stroke engines, no matter which system of cylinder scavenging is used, can be supercharged to give about 35 per cent greater power output than a similar unsupercharged engine, and notable developments are taking place in the exhaust turbo-charging of this type of engine notwithstanding the difficult problems involved.

The exhaust-gas temperature of the two-stroke engine is lower than the four-stroke engine because, as already mentioned, the gases are cooled by the cylinder scavenging process. The average temperatures are 800°F (427°C) for the four-stroke and 600°F (316°C) for the two-stroke. The effect of this lower exhaust temperature is to make relatively less energy available for doing work in an exhaust-gas turbine. Even when an engine is operating at full power and maximum exhaust temperature there is insufficient energy available to supply an adequate quantity of supercharge air; and when operating at reduced power there may not be sufficient to scavenge the cylinders effectively. When starting an engine conditions would be even worse, as during the first few revolutions there may not be enough air to expel the burnt gases and leave the cylinders full of air.

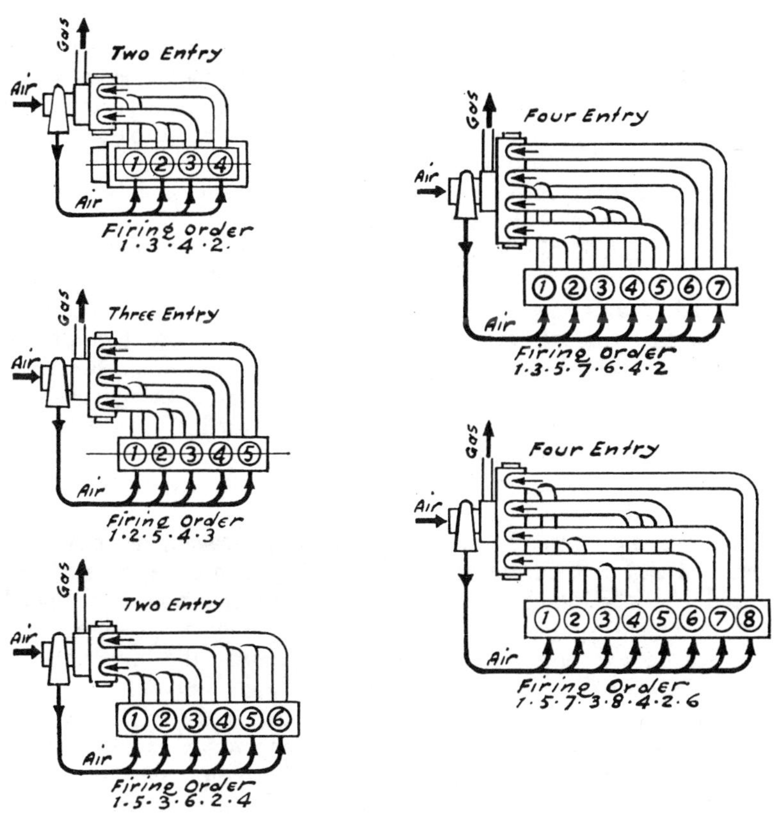

Fig. 168—Arrangement of exhaust pipes of 4- to 8-cylinder supercharged 2-stroke engines, with typical firing orders

To supercharge a two-stroke engine it is necessary, therefore, to supply the air for scavenging as well as supercharging by (a) directly-driven rotary or reciprocating pumps, (b) an independently-driven turbo-charger, or (c) an exhaust-gas turbine in conjunction with (a) or (b). The present trend is to adopt the third arrangement.

Supercharged two-stroke engines employing exhaust-gas turbines operate on one of two distinct systems, one being called the constant-pressure system and the other the pulse system. In the former the normal exhaust-gas manifold is retained, so that all cylinders exhaust into a common pipe which is connected to the turbine inlet. In the pulse system the exhaust manifold is of similar construction to that adopted on Buchi four-stroke turbo-charged engines, described earlier in this chapter. As the name implies, the aim of this system is to obtain the maximum pulse energy for driving the exhaust-gas turbine. In the constant-pressure system the exhaust manifold pressure at full power is about 7 lb/sq.in., and in the pulse system in the region of 4 lb/sq.in.

If consecutively firing cylinders of a diesel engine supercharged by exhaust-gas turbo-blowers are allowed to exhaust into a common pipe or manifold, there is a tendency for the exhaust pulse of one cylinder to adversely affect the scavenging process of the cylinder that had fired previously. This is avoided by employing an exhaust-gas turbine with two or more gas inlets, in which the ducts in the casing segregate the gases right up to the nozzles which direct the gases on to the blades of the turbine. The exhaust manifold arrangement for engines having from four to eight cylinders and typical firing orders are shown in Fig. 168.

The various arrangements of pumps and blowers for supplying the air are shown in Fig. 169.

In (a) the presently used reciprocating scavenging pump is retained and used in the normal manner. When the engine attains speed the additional air required for supercharging is supplied by the exhaust-gas turbine, the blower of which is in series with the scavenging pump. With this arrangement the engine starts and operates at low speeds as an unsupercharged engine.

In the arrangement shown in (b) the deficiency of the exhaust turbo-blower is made up by a small-capacity scavenging pump operating in parallel with the blower. In this case both the scavenging pump and the blower compress the air to the maximum pressure required.

The arrangement shown in (c) is the same as that shown in (b), except that instead of the small scavenging pump directly connected

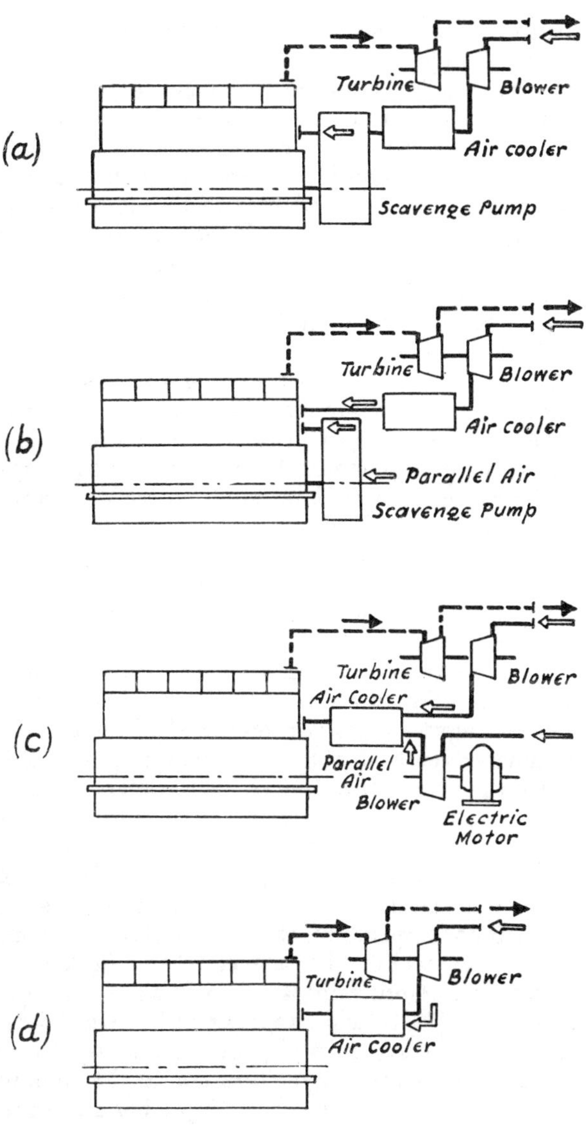

Fig. 169—Various arrangements for supplying supercharge air to 2-stroke engines

to the engine, an independently electrically-driven blower is substituted.

The supercharging of two-stroke engines entails much more complication than four-stroke, and the efforts of designers will no doubt be directed towards the arrangement shown in (d), Fig. 169, and so bring the supercharged two-stroke more into line with the four-stroke engine. The elimination of the large, heavy and costly scavenging pump is highly desirable if the two-stroke engine is to retain the popularity it now enjoys in unsupercharged form. Before an exhaust turbo-blower capable of providing sufficient scavenging air at all engine speeds can be produced, however, many difficulties have to be overcome. In the meantime it is not unlikely that the problem will be partly solved by utilising the lower end of the engine cylinders as scavenging air-pumps as described earlier for four-stroke engines. Such an arrangement eliminates the undesirable separate scavenging pumps or an independently-driven turbo-blower, and enables the engine to start and operate at speeds too low to make the exhaust turbo-blower effective.

Fig. 170 shows one type of Burmeister and Wain two-stroke supercharged engine, in which the scavenging air enters the cylinder through ports uncovered by the piston as it nears the end of its down-stroke, the burnt gases being driven out through a large mechanically operated exhaust valve in the cylinder head. The exhaust gases drive the turbo-blower which delivers air into the large receiver arranged around the lower end of the cylinder. The emergency independently-driven turbo-blower used for starting and slow-speed running will be observed on the left of the illustration.

As explained earlier in this chapter, the increased power output obtained by supercharging is largely the result of the increased weight of air in the cylinder during the compression stroke, consequently more fuel can be burnt. The weight of a given volume of air depends upon its temperature, and as the air must be compressed before it enters the cylinder its temperature is increased and its weight reduced. In compressing air to 5 lb/sq.in. its temperature is raised about 90°F (32°C) and its reduction in weight of the order of 10 per cent. As the supercharging pressure is increased beyond this figure the effect of the temperature rise in the compressor is, of course, more pronounced, so that the higher the supercharge air-pressure the more necessary it is to cool the air before it is delivered to the engine cylinders.

In engines supercharged to a pressure of about 3 lb/sq.in. it is not considered worth while to cool the supercharged air. This

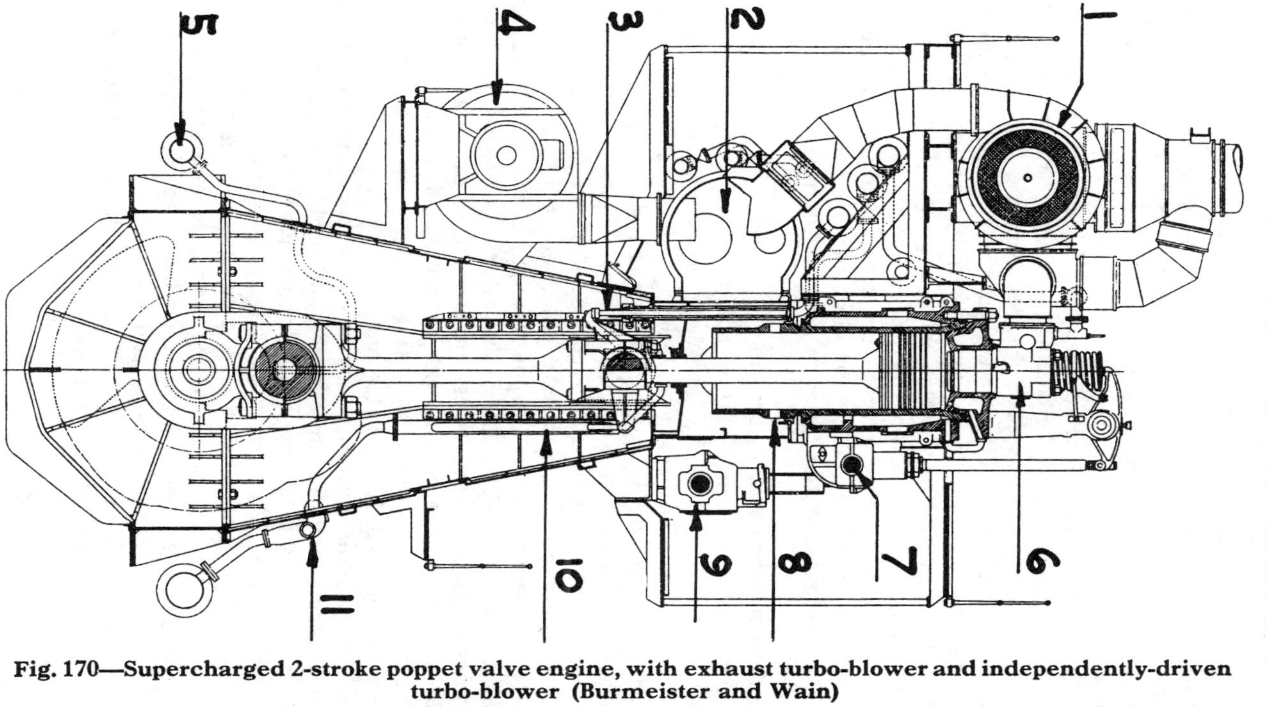

Fig. 170—Supercharged 2-stroke poppet valve engine, with exhaust turbo-blower and independently-driven turbo-blower (Burmeister and Wain)

1. Turbo-blower
2. Scavenge and supercharge air
3. Piston-cooling telescopic pipe inlet
4. Motor-driven scavenge blower
5. Bearing oil supply
6. Exhaust valve
7. Camshaft
8. Scavenge air ports
9. Fuel-injectionpump
10. Piston-cooling telescopic pipe outlet
11 Piston-cooling oil outlet

represents an increase in power output of about 35 per cent over unsupercharged engines. If higher output is required, the supercharge air-pressure will have to be greater than 3 lb/sq.in. and cooling of the air will be necessary if these desired results are to be obtained.

Higher supercharge air-pressures are inevitable and more attention will be given in future to the cooling. Cooling of the air before it enters the engine cylinders has a double advantage. Not only does it enable more fuel to be burnt in a given size of cylinder and result in a proportional increase in power output, but in addition it reduces the temperature of the exhaust gases. Lower exhaust temperatures in supercharged engines are desirable, particularly if the gases are used to drive a turbo-blower, as should the temperature exceed about 800°F (427°C) special heat-resisting materials, which are costly, would have to be used in the gas turbine.

Operation of supercharging system

Being mainly concerned with installations now in service rather than future installations, the following notes refer to experience gained with four-stroke engines. Although considerable thought is, at the time of writing, being given to perfecting a completely satisfactory supercharging system for two-stroke engines, the author is of the opinion that the supercharged four-stroke engine will be with us for a long time yet. This view is prompted by the fact that whilst for a given size of cylinder the power output of the two-stroke may be increased 35 per cent, there is no valid reason why the supercharging of four-stroke engines cannot increase the power output by 100 per cent at less cost and with less complication. Nevertheless, a description of present-day two-stroke engine supercharging systems will be found in Chapter 28.

As supercharging pressures increase, the back pressure in the exhaust manifold will become greater, and further gains can be got only by raising this pressure and having larger exhaust turbines with more stages. The four-stroke engine, by virtue of its simpler and more positive scavenging and re-charging processes, is better able to cope with the more exacting conditions imposed by higher supercharging pressures. The cylinder liner and piston are of the simplest possible construction, and the four-stroke engine has proved itself better able to operate on residual fuels than are engines operating on the two-stroke principle.

In order to derive the greatest benefit from supercharging an important point to observe is that the air/fuel ratio is at all times correct. If the proportion of air is too great no mechanical difficulties will arise, but the overall efficiency of the plant will be reduced because the surplus air will be heated unnecessarily and will carry off heat. Moreover, if the exhaust gases are used to generate steam in boilers, the same quantity of heat will pass through the boilers, but since it will be at a lower temperature less steam will be generated. It is the temperature rather than the mass which governs the amount of steam produced. On the other hand, should the proportion of air be too small, an engine will not run many hours before serious trouble occurs with exhaust valves and other parts surrounding the combustion space.

As a rule the supercharge air-pressure keeps steady, and in the majority of cases the arrangement is so simple that nothing which would cause a fluctuation in pressure is likely to occur; especially is this so when the undersides of the working pistons are used to supply the air. On rare occasions a valve may, of course, break or be prevented from re-seating properly, but the reduction in capacity from such a fault is, owing to the large number of pumps employed, so small that apart from two or three degrees' increase in the exhaust temperature, the working of the engine is unaffected.

In some cases valves of the butterfly type are introduced into the supercharge pump suction-pipe for the purpose of regulating the supply of air to the engine. As such valves, which are usually of light construction, are exposed to comparatively strong intermittent air-currents, it is wise to remove them occasionally to make sure that they remain firmly attached to their spindles. In one case where the valve was attached to its spindle by two taper pins the pins sheared and the valve closed, causing three of the six pumps to be put out of action instantly and without warning. The safest way to connect these parts is to square the hole through the valve and the corresponding part of the spindle.

While a few degrees' difference in the opening and closing points of the air-inlet and exhaust valves of an ordinary engine is not very important, the same cannot be said of supercharged engines, because owing to the difference in the shape of the cam peaks a few thousandths of an inch alteration in the rocking-lever roller clearance has a far greater effect upon these engines.

Fig. 171 shows a normal light-spring indicator diagram taken from a four-stroke Werkspoor supercharged engine, from which it will be seen that when the piston has completed about 70 per cent of the exhaust stroke the pressure in the cylinder rises from that of the atmosphere owing to the rapid closing of the exhaust valve. The pressure reaches a maximum of 2·8 lb when the piston is about 20 per cent from the end of the stroke, which is the point where the air-inlet valve opens. The pressure then begins to fall to the pressure of the supercharge air which, measured from the diagram, is 2·4 lb, the gauge pressure at the time the diagram was taken being 2·7 lb/sq.in.

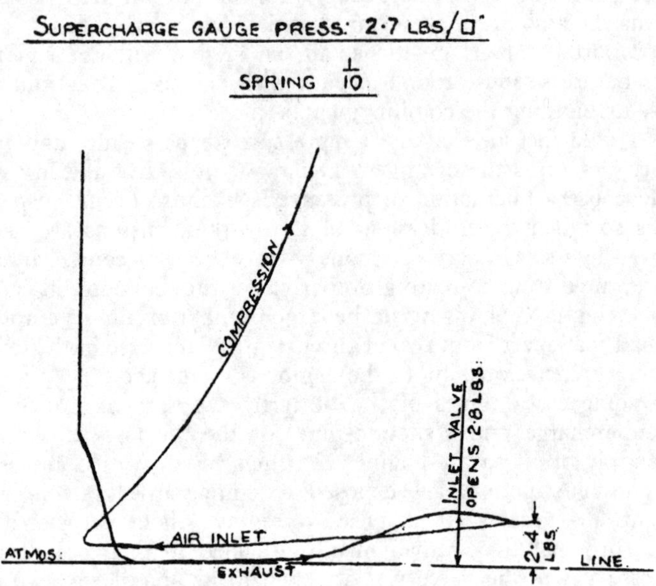

Fig. 171—Light-spring indicator diagram of typical supercharged 4-stroke engine

This rise in pressure towards the end of the exhaust stroke is not a desirable feature since it represents negative work, but the amount is so small that its effect is of little account. Although the pressure of the burnt gases in the cylinder is slightly higher than the supercharge air-pressure when the air-inlet valve opens, the pressures being 2·8 and 2·4 lb respectively, it is doubtful whether this small difference will cause the burnt gases to flow into the air-inlet pipe before the pressures equalise and the air and burnt gases begin to flow in the proper direction.

From close observation of engines employing this system of supercharging there was no evidence of this, but it will be apparent that to obtain the best scavenging of the cylinder clearance space the pressure in the cylinder when the air-inlet valve opens should be the least possible. In any case the pressure in the cylinder should not be higher by an amount greater than that shown in Fig. 171.

To illustrate the effect of the exhaust valve opening too late and closing too early, the exhaust valve rocking-lever roller clearance of the same engine was increased 0·25 mm only and the diagram

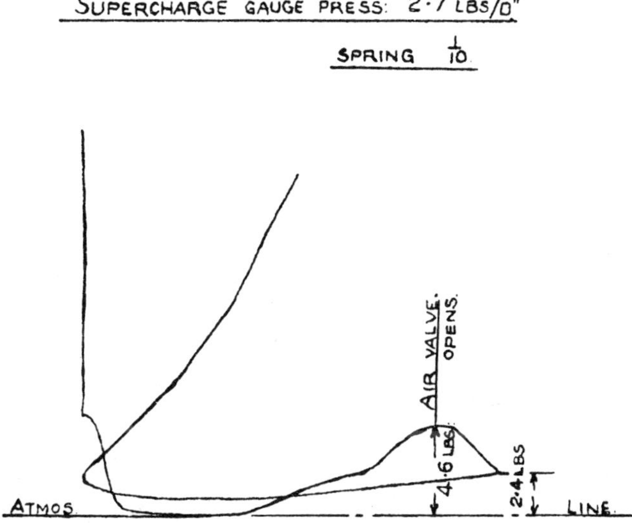

Fig. 172—Light-spring indicator diagram of supercharged 4-stroke engine showing effect of exhaust valve opening too late and closing too early

shown in Fig. 172 taken. This diagram shows clearly how too early closing of this valve causes the pressure in the cylinder during the latter part of the exhaust stroke to begin rising earlier and to a higher pressure.

A light-spring diagram taken from a Buchi supercharged engine is shown in Fig. 173. With this system it will be observed that the pressure in the cylinder during the exhaust stroke is comparatively high and almost the same as the pressure during the air-inlet stroke. The reason for this is that in the Werkspoor system (Figs. 171 and 172) the gases enter an open exhaust pipe, whereas in the Buchi system the exhaust pipes are closed by the exhaust-gas turbine.

As already mentioned the amount of fuel that can be burnt efficiently depends upon the weight of air in the cylinders, and since the weight of a given volume of air depends upon its temperature, it follows that the higher the temperature of the

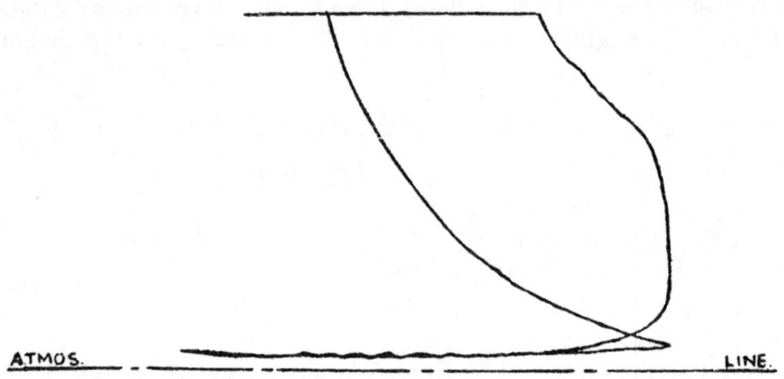

Fig. 173—Light-spring indicator diagram of a Buchi supercharged 4-stroke engine

air in the cylinders at the beginning of the compression stroke, the higher must be its pressure if a constant weight of air, or in other words, the air/fuel ratio, is to be maintained. As the temperature of the air in a ship's engine-room varies very considerably it is, therefore, necessary to adjust the supercharge air-pressure according to the atmospheric temperature. In the event of a ship travelling from a cold to a hot climate and the supercharge air-pressure being maintained constant, the effect would be to increase the exhaust temperature. This increase in temperature is due partly to the higher initial temperature of the cycle. Should the exhaust temperature be maintained constant during such variation in atmospheric temperature by reducing the amount of fuel consumed, then the power output will, of course, be reduced as the atmospheric temperature increases.

As the power output must, of course, be maintained constant it is necessary to vary the supercharge air-pressure. In order to ascertain the extent of this variation close observation was kept on an engine during a period when the temperature of the engine-room atmosphere, from which the supercharge air supply was drawn, increased from 70° to 100°F (21·1° to 37·8°C). The revolutions per minute and the exhaust temperatures were not allowed to vary, and under these conditions the necessary increase in the supercharge air-pressure was found to be as shown in the following table:—

E.R. Temperature °F	E.R. Temperature °C	Supercharge air-temperature, °F	Supercharge air-temperature, °C	Supercharge air-pressure lb/sq. in.
70	21·1	118·4	48·0	2·6
75	23·9	122·3	50·1	2·7
80	26·7	124·2	51·1	2·8
85	29·4	126·5	52·4	2·9
90	32·2	129·8	54·3	3·0
95	35·0	133·2	56·2	3·1
100	37·8	136·0	57·8	3·2

As the object of supercharging is to enable a greater quantity of fuel to be burnt without a corresponding increase in the mean cylinder temperatures, a greater quantity of fuel injected unaccompanied by the appropriate supercharge air-pressure results in an increase in the mean cylinder temperatures and, consequently, the exhaust temperatures.

When working normally any increase in the exhaust temperature due to an insufficient supercharge air-pressure will be readily indicated on the exhaust pyrometers, but when manoeuvring this is not the case, so that it is possible to have an excessively high temperature in the exhaust manifold with the pyrometers registering normal or less than normal temperature. It is necessary, therefore, to see that the supercharge air-pressure is in the neighbourhood of the normal working pressure when the fuel-pump control lever is brought to its normal full-power running position. If for some reason it is not possible or advisable to manoeuvre with the supercharge air at this pressure, then the fuel-pump control lever position must be adjusted accordingly.

When the underside of the working piston is used for the supply of scavenging or supercharge air, particular care is necessary to see that lubricating oil is not lifted from the crankcase and deposited in the air pumps by the piston rods. To obviate this, scraper packing is always provided at the point where the piston rods enter the crankcase. If, however, this packing is not of an efficient type or is not kept properly adjusted, large quantities of oil will leak and frequent cleaning of the pumps and valves will become necessary, or a fire may be started.

A sectional view of a type of oil-scraper packing which has proved entirely satisfactory in service is shown in Fig. 174. The rings are made of cast iron and each consists of six identical segments held in close contact with the piston rod by a garter spring. The inner surface of these rings is shaped as shown so that as wear takes place the scraping edge is retained. A total clearance of 2 mm is allowed between the ends of the segments of each ring to ensure that they are not prevented from making proper contact with the surface to be scraped. The uppermost scraper ring should have a total end clearance of about 6 mm for reasons which will be given later.

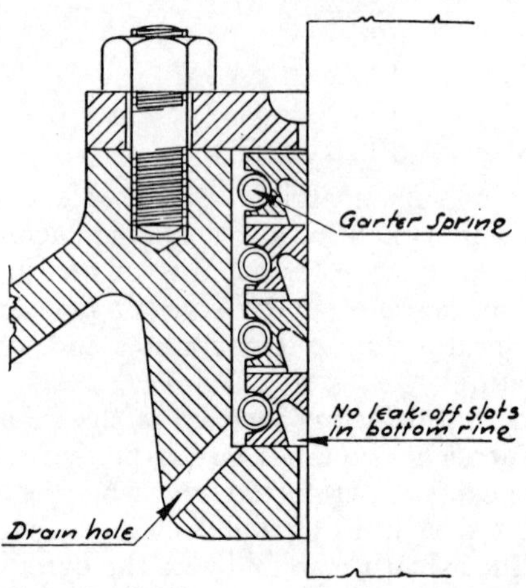

Fig. 174—Piston-rod oil scraper packing in crankcase top

The draining arrangements on the underside of the three upper scraper rings will be noted. The segments forming the lowest ring should not be slotted in this way, as there is generally sufficient clearance between the piston rod and the stuffing-box to enable the oil scraped off by the bottom ring to return directly to the crankcase. The omission of slots in the bottom ring is rather important, as a great deal of oil is collected by the bottom ring, and if this ring is slotted much of the oil will flow to the back of the packing and obstruct the oil collected by the upper rings from flowing freely through the drain-holes at the lower end of the stuffing-box. These drain-holes should be left to deal only with the oil collected by the upper scraper rings.

The scraper rings must, of course, be free to move laterally after the gland is tightened down, otherwise apart from serving no useful purpose they will wear excessively and unevenly. When all parts are in working position and the gland is tightened down, the total clearance in a vertical direction should be about 0·2 mm.

If the clearance is greater than this the packing rings will hammer and wear unduly. If the overall depth of the packing rings is made 0·2 mm less than the depth of the stuffing-box it will generally function satisfactorily, but it is always wise to check the rings for freedom after all parts are assembled, as it is not possible to make observations while the engine is operating. Such a test can generally be made by pushing a finely tapered piece of steel between the piston rod and the uppermost packing ring.

The pressure exerted by the garter springs is important, since, if too small, oil will leak past, and if too great the rings will quickly wear away and, what is even more serious, the piston rod will be worn. The pressure necessary to stop leakage of oil is really quite small. With all segments held around the piston rod by the garter spring it should be possible to grip one segment between finger and thumb and pull it clear of the rod. If leakage occurs with such pressure it means that there is something wrong with the scraping edge of the rings or the fitting of the rings.

The end clearance of the segments forming the top ring must be comparatively large, as, apart from ensuring that the segments make good contact with the piston rod, a gap in the ring is necessary to allow air to gain access to the back of the packing. Should this space fill with oil and communication with the atmosphere be cut off due to the segments butting, the oil will not flow freely from the bottom of the stuffing-box into the crankcase. In such an event a pumping action will take place and oil will find its way past the packing rings irrespective of the pressure exerted by the garter springs. Often when this occurs the tension of the garter springs is increased with the object of stopping the leakage, but the only effect is to reduce it slightly and increase the wear of the rings. If preferred, air can sometimes be given free access to the space behind the packing rings by drilling holes through the gland in line with the space. Such holes must, however, be at least ¼-inch in diameter, otherwise they will simply fill with oil and prevent the air from reaching the space.

If considered necessary, dowel pins may be employed to prevent the gaps of the rings from working into line, but experience has shown that the chances of the gaps in all rings working into line if properly staggered when first fitted, are very remote. If dowel pins are fitted particular care must be taken to see that they do not bind two segments in different rings together and consequently hold one of them clear of the piston rod. Dowel pins should therefore be a reasonably slack fit in the holes of the adjacent ring.

CHAPTER 19

Scavenging air-pumps, turbo-blowers, and exhaust pipes

Scavenging pumps are really low-pressure air-compressors. They may be either of the reciprocating or rotary type, and driven either from the engine to be supplied or independently. Pumps of the reciprocating type are sometimes single-acting and sometimes double-acting, depending upon their location. Those driven from an extension of the main engine crankshaft or by beam levers coupled to one of the piston-rod crossheads are always of the double-acting type, while those situated under each main engine cylinder are of the single-acting type. Wherever possible the double-acting type is used, for obvious reasons.

As scavenging pumps have to supply a large quantity of air at low pressure they are necessarily of large size, especially when driven at the main engine speed. Their capacity is in the neighbourhood of 1·5 times the total volume swept by the working pistons, and they absorb about 5 per cent of the total output of the engine. Although nothing simpler than a slow-running reciprocating pump, one of which is shown diagrammatically in Fig. 175, could be imagined, yet in view of the low mechanical efficiency of such and the desire for reduced weight and a more compact engine, rotary compressors, either directly or independently driven, have been adopted by some engine-builders.

Reciprocating pumps, as already mentioned, are driven either from an extension of the main crankshaft, or from one of the crossheads by means of rocking levers. The advantage of the latter method is that the scavenging pump does not add to the overall length of the engine. It is usual to employ one, and in some cases two double-acting pumps, but some of the largest engines have a separate pump for each cylinder driven from the crossheads, and in some instances from the connecting rods.

Reciprocating scavenging-pump valves are usually automatic in action and of the thin plate type. Sometimes, however, they are of the reciprocating piston, rotary, or semi-rotary type, and mechanically operated, the advantages of which are that they never break and seldom require to be cleaned. Furthermore, the pumping losses with positively operated valves are said to be less, although some of the automatic plate valves are highly efficient in this respect. Mechanically operated valves must be provided with reversing gear in order to alter their setting relative to the pump piston when the direction of the engine is reversed.

Valves of the automatic type are illustrated in the lower part of Fig. 175. The valves are made of special steel, and small springs are sometimes provided between the valve plates and the guards

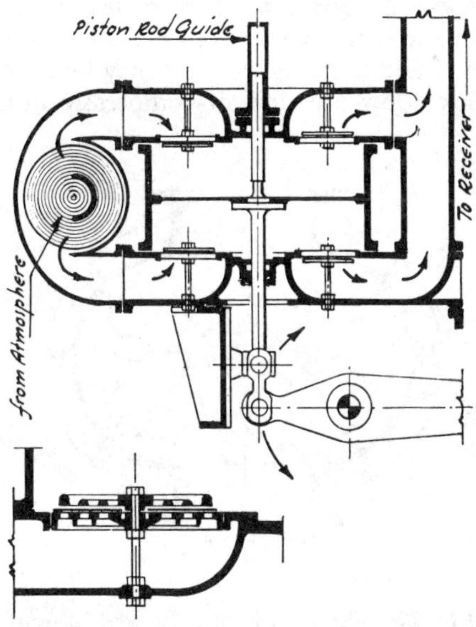

Fig. 175—Diagram of a double-acting scavenging air-pump; (*inset*) showing suction valve

to cause the valves to re-seat promptly—or they may be of the type described in the previous chapter. When the flow of air to and from the pump is controlled by piston or rotary valves, such valves are actuated by eccentrics on a secondary crankshaft driven by the main crankshaft. Altering the timing of the valves for the reverse direction of rotation is sometimes carried out automatically by allowing a certain angle of free play between the main crankshaft and the eccentrics or crank actuating the valves, so that when the engine direction of rotation is reversed the scavenging-pump valves remain stationary until the play in the actuating gear has been taken up.

Reciprocating scavenging air-pumps, as a rule, require no attention whilst operating, apart from lubricating the piston, which requires very little oil. Valves of the automatic type require to be cleaned occasionally and examined for cracks, broken springs, and slack nuts. The slots in the air intake should be kept free from dirt, and the inside of the suction pipes as well as the slots thoroughly cleaned.

Of the total heat energy in the fuel consumed by the average diesel engine, some 30 per cent is contained in the burnt gases when they reach the exhaust manifold. This quantity of heat is a potential source of additional power and may be used to drive a gas turbine coupled to a low-pressure air-compressor of the rotary type.

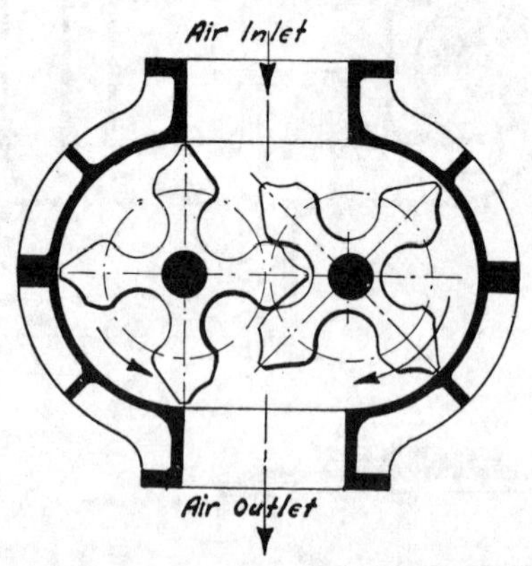

Fig. 176—End view of a Rootes blower

At the present time sufficient heat energy can be recovered from the burnt gases to produce an air pressure of 5 lb/sq.in. in the engine cylinder at the commencement of the compression stroke, but this will no doubt be improved upon when turbines and blowers can be made more efficient. One or more turbo-blowers, each arranged to serve a separate group of cylinders, are usually provided in the case of high-power installations.

Rotary air-compressors used to supply scavenging and supercharge air are either of the positive displacement type or the centrifugal type, shown in Figs. 176 and 177, respectively. As a rule the former is used when the blower requires to be directly connected, usually by a chain drive, to the engine, and the latter when it requires to be driven by the exhaust gases. Either can, of course, be driven by a steam turbine or an electric motor.

The centrifugal compressor, or blower, is almost universally used on supercharged engines where it is desired to take full advantage of the heat energy in the exhaust gases, because it is of extremely simple construction and noiseless at high speeds. There are no valves, the only moving part being the rotor or impeller which, provided the air drawn in is reasonably free from dirt and oil, requires no attention. Moreover, this type of blower compresses air to a given pressure with a minimum rise in temperature.

In the case of the centrifugal compressor it will be readily appreciated that since air is admitted to the centre of the impeller—the only possible point of admission in this type of machine—the

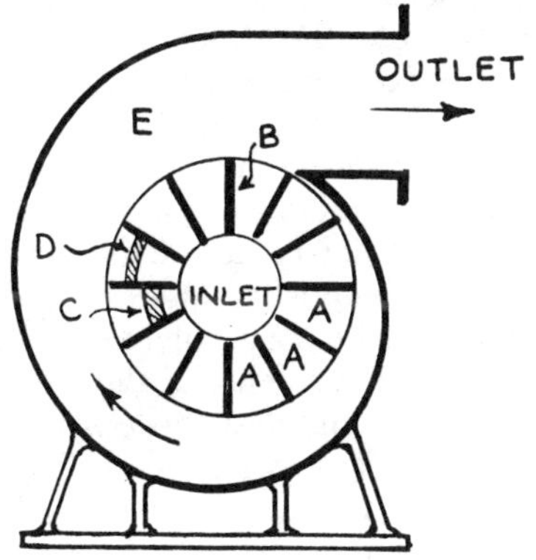

Fig. 177—Diagram showing passage of air between vanes of a centrifugal blower

shape of the vanes should be such that when the air between the adjacent vanes is acted upon by centrifugal force it is caused to flow towards the periphery of the impeller and be thrown off into the annular space around the impeller, thence to the outlet.

Fig. 177 shows how this is effected. As the impeller revolves at high speed in the direction of the arrowhead, a partial vacuum is created at the centre of the impeller and air begins to flow in through the inlet. The air enters the spaces *A* of the impeller, formed by two discs with radial vanes *B* between them. In two of the spaces on the left of the impeller are shown a unit quantity of air at different points in its travel towards the periphery of the impeller. At the position *C* the unit quantity of air is acted upon by centrifugal force of a certain magnitude which causes it to move outward to the position *D*. At the position *D* the air has a greater peripheral speed and consequently will be acted upon by centrifugal force of greater magnitude. Thus as the air moves outward between the vanes, its speed is being constantly accelerated. The air leaving the periphery of the impeller at high velocity exerts a force on the air filling the space *E* and already flowing towards the outlet of the compressor, with the result that the air leaving the outlet is under pressure.

If vanes were not fitted between the discs of the impeller no such movement of the air would take place, and as air has definite weight the vanes must be subjected to a force acting in a direction opposite to the direction of rotation. It is this tangential force which the driving unit must overcome. The greater the speed with which the air between the vanes moves outward the greater will be the tangential force, and consequently the power absorbed by the compressor.

The vanes of a centrifugal compressor may be of three types, i.e. bent forward, radial (straight), or bent backwards. Each type produces a different air velocity at the tip for a given diameter, so the efficiency and characteristics of the compressor would vary considerably according to the shape of the blades. Although each type has advantages and disadvantages, the radial type is the most commonly used as it is the simplest to design and to manufacture.

The centrifugal compressor is basically of the two-dimensional flow type. That is to say, the air leaves the periphery of the impeller with a tangential velocity and a radial velocity. Upon leaving the impeller it has a free vortex motion before it passes into the diffuser or specially-shaped passage which leads the air to the supercharge air-receiver of the engine supplied if the compressor is of the single-stage type, or to the centre of the second-stage impeller if of the multi-stage type. The diffuser throat area and shape are of particular importance as they determine to a great extent the compressor characteristics.

Fig. 178 is a sectional view of a Napier turbo-blower used for supercharging either four- or two-stroke engines. The turbine wheels and compressor impeller are mounted on a steel shaft revolving in two ball-bearings. The one at the compressor end takes the axial thrust, while the bearing at the turbine end is so housed that it can move endwise a small amount to accommodate the difference in the expansion and contraction of the machine when starting up and shutting down.

Fig. 178—Exhaust gas-driven turbo-blower (Napier)

The turbine and compressor casings are made of special cast iron, the turbine wheel of heat-resisting steel, and the impeller of corrosion-resisting aluminium alloy. To prevent heat from the turbine finding its way to the compressor, cooling water is circulated through both the gas inlet and outlet casings of the turbine.

Operation and maintenance

Scavenging pumps require very little attention, apart from occasional examination of the suction and delivery valves and the piston rings. The valves tend to become dirty and the piston rings to jam, so that they should be looked at now and again, particularly as these low-pressure air-compressors are at best of low efficiency and become extremely inefficient should the parts mentioned not be kept in good order.

Scavenging pumps require very little oil for efficient lubrication of the piston if the oil can be delivered to the points where it is required. In pumps of large diameter this is far from easy, as to ensure the whole of the cylinder surface being given a film of oil of even thickness the oil requires to be injected at a large number of points. Multiplication of the number of points means that the quantity entering at each point must be exceedingly small if over-lubrication is to be avoided, and it is often difficult to adjust lubricators to deliver such minute quantities consistently. The author overcame this difficulty in one ship by providing a small-bore pipe and regulating cock which allowed a little oily vapour from the main engine crankcase to be drawn into the scavenge pump-suction.

When scavenge pumps are driven from the engine crankshaft the piston and clearances seldom require to be re-adjusted, but when driven by rocking levers and links the tendency is for the piston to take up a lower position as the bearings wear. With some forms of driving mechanism the position of the piston is raised as the parts attain working temperature, so that when re-adjusting the position of the piston this should be taken into account. When working, the top and bottom piston end-clearances should, of course, be the same, but when the pump is inoperative and the parts at atmospheric temperature it may be found that the clearances ought to vary a certain amount to obtain the maximum output from the pump. The maker's clearances vary between $\frac{1}{8}$-inch and $\frac{1}{4}$-inch, the tendency in design being to keep the clearance as small as possible and so avoid these large, cumbersome pumps being larger than is necessary.

The most important point to observe in the operation and maintenance of exhaust-gas turbo-blowers is the efficient lubrication of the bearings. Ball-bearings provided in the Napier blower are lubricated by an independent auxiliary pump delivering at a pressure of about 45 lb/sq.in. through a filter and a cooler. As the rotor revolves at a speed in the region of 6,000 r.p.m. it is essential that the supply of oil to the bearings be continuous. Lloyds require that the lubrication system should operate satisfactorily when the machine is tilted to an angle of 15° in any direction, such as might be experienced when a ship is rolling. The quantity of oil consumed should be carefully watched. It should be negligible, but if this is not the case the possibility of leakage either into the turbine or the blower should be considered. It is good practice for each of the two bearings to have an independent system, as then the faulty bearing can be readily located.

The turbine blades will remain clean for a considerable time provided the engine exhaust gases are free from unconsumed particles of carbon and other solid matter. Should, for some reason, an engine be operated under poor combustion conditions, carbonaceous matter will deposit on the rotor and stator blades, and if allowed to accumulate the efficiency of the turbine will decline and, consequently, the output of the blower will be reduced.

Fouling of the turbine blades can also result from the employment of fuel having a high ash content, such as occurs in many residual fuels. Most so-called diesel fuels are a mixture of a light distillate and residual, so that even this more costly grade may contain incombustible ash. The universal practice is to centrifuge residual fuels before supplying to the engine, so that the major portion of the ash content is removed and the exhaust gases will then be free from this harmful material. In view of the possible presence of residual oil in diesel fuel it is wise to centrifuge this grade also when the exhaust gases are used to drive an exhaust-gas turbine.

Turbine blades are made of heat-resisting steel. They ought also to be capable of resisting the corrosive elements in the exhaust gases, produced mostly by the sulphur constituent in some fuels, which become active when an engine is operating well below the rated power and the temperature of the exhaust gases is less than the normal figure.

The extent to which some steels expand and contract between the maximum and minimum temperatures to which they are subjected varies greatly. As a rule those which possess the highest coefficient of expansion are more or less self-cleaning, but unfortunately such steels have not the best heat- and corrosion-resisting properties.

Carbonaceous matter, ash and other impurities, when present in the exhaust gases, deposit on the blades when they are in a heated and expanded condition, so that if the coefficient of expansion of the steel used is high, the amount the blades contract will also be high. The result is that with blades made of such material the deposit tends to crack and become detached when the turbine is shut down and the parts cool to engine-room temperature.

Blades made of steel having a low coefficient of expansion are not self-cleaning to the same extent, and the impurities in the exhaust gases will continue to build-up until the turbine becomes so inefficient that it will be necessary to open up the turbine and hand-clean the rotor and stator blades. Should it be inconvenient to do such a major operation the turbine efficiency can be partly restored by injecting steam during the periods the plant is shut down in port. The effect of the steam is to soften the deposit and make it adhere less firmly to the blades, with the result that much of it is thrown off when the turbine begins working again.

The clearance between the tip of the rotor blades and the turbine casing is, for obvious reasons, kept small, the amount varying in different makes of turbine but generally in the region of 1 mm. When, therefore, blades shed their deposit much of it will enter this small annular space. Generally it is quickly broken up by the blades and discharged to the atmosphere when the turbine begins working, but it is wise when possible to make sure that the rotor is free before the engine, and thus the turbine and blower, are started.

As mentioned earlier, if fouling of exhaust-gas turbines is to be avoided the engine should always be operated at maximum combustion efficiency and as much of the ash content as possible removed from the fuel by centrifuging before it is supplied to the engine. Such precautions are necessary in any diesel engine, but neglect in the case of exhaust-gas turbo-charged engines will have additional undesirable effects.

Provided the air drawn into the blower is free from oil- and water-vapour the blower impeller will remain clean and efficient for many years. As a rule attention is not necessary between special classification surveys, and when the blower is opened up for inspection a paraffin-soaked rag will generally remove any matter adhering to the vanes.

Exhaust-gas pipes

Exhaust-gas pipes are necessarily of large diameter in order that a minimum of resistance will be offered to the flow of the burnt gases on their way to the atmosphere, and they are made of either cast iron or mild steel. Cast iron is superior to steel for this purpose as it resists the corrosive sulphuric acid produced with certain fuels when an engine is working at reduced power output, but steel is mostly used because pipes of this material are cheaper and besides being less liable to fracture are lighter in weight.

When the exhaust gases are not required for any other purpose, such as driving a gas turbine for supercharging or the generation of steam in boilers, exhaust pipes are sometimes provided with jackets through which water is circulated, as the reduction in temperature resulting therefrom enables a pipe of smaller diameter to be employed. As, however, it is now the common practice to make use of the heat in the exhaust gases, provision is generally made to retain as much of the heat as possible. Consequently, instead of the pipes being jacketed and water-cooled, they are very often covered thickly with heat-resisting material. A suitable insulation is two layers of asbestos, each of $\frac{1}{4}$-inch thick, covered by one 3-inch-thick layer of magnesia. The reason for not making the whole of the insulation of one or other of these materials is that although both have high heat-resisting properties, magnesia is liable to disintegrate if placed in contact with the pipe, and asbestos, besides being comparatively expensive, is more easily damaged than magnesia.

Uncooled steel exhaust pipes require no attention provided adequate allowance is made for expansion and contraction. Even if such a pipe fractures the matter is not serious as the only effect is to allow a little burnt gas to enter the engine-room, and this can usually be stopped by stemming asbestos into the crack, or fitting a band around the pipe in way of the crack, without having to stop the engine. There is, however, more to go wrong in water-cooled pipes and the consequences may be much more serious. The inner wall of such pipes may be damaged by vibration, insufficient allowance for expansion, sudden contraction due to the pipe being allowed to become overheated and then quenched with water, or corrosion on the outside by water, and on the inside by sulphuric acid. From this it will be seen that leakage of cooling water into the gas space is possible. Such leakage occurring while an engine is working is not immediately harmful, the only effect being to send a fine spray of dirty water over the ship, but may have serious consequences if not detected before the engine is stopped and started again. Especially is this so if that part of the exhaust pipe running along the engine is located above the level of the cylinder heads, for then the water leaking into the gas space will at once flow into combustion spaces of the engine through any exhaust valve or port that happens to be open at the time. When the exhaust manifold is located below the level of the cylinder heads, as it ought to be when water-cooled, the whole pipe must first fill with water before it will reach the cylinders.

The consequences of water reaching the cylinders in this way are so serious that suitable test cocks should be provided at two or three points along the exhaust manifold. When manoeuvring an engine with a doubtful exhaust pipe it is wise to leave the drain cocks open, so that in the event of a leak occurring it will be detected at once and the necessary steps taken to prevent water getting into the cylinders. Even when the exhaust manifold is known to be in perfect order this practice is commendable in cases where it is located above the level of the cylinder heads.

As exhaust-gas pipes, no matter whether they are water-cooled or not, are heavy and must be firmly secured to the engine and ship's structure, provision must be made for the expansion and contraction between every two points of attachment. The number of expansion fittings on this part of the installation is therefore great and, since there is as yet no uniformity of opinion regarding the best method of allowing for unrestricted expansion and contraction, the arrangements found are numerous and vary widely in design. It is, therefore, perhaps not surprising that instances of trouble and expense with this particular part are more common than would appear necessary.

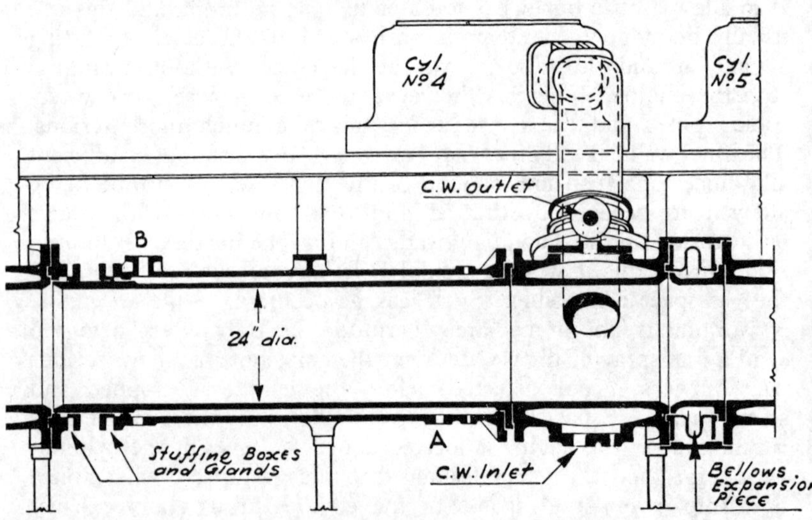

Fig. 179—Portion of water-cooled exhaust-gas manifold of 6-cylinder engine

The expansion of exhaust pipes depends upon the temperature of the wall in contact with the gases. Records of such temperatures are seldom taken, but the temperature of an uncooled pipe may be assumed to be 250°F (121°C) when the temperature of the gases entering the pipe is 800°F (427°C). With a coefficient of expansion for cast iron of 0·0000062 per degree F, a 30-foot length of uncooled piping would expand lengthwise from $\frac{3}{8}$- to $\frac{1}{2}$-inch. The object of this rough calculation is simply to illustrate how necessary it is to provide for the expansion of this part, and to emphasise the importance of keeping whatever arrangements are provided in proper working order.

Part of the exhaust manifold of a six-cylinder engine is shown in Fig. 179. Each section, it will be observed, is water-cooled, and two different methods of providing for expansion are employed. At the end where the sections are short and the amount of expansion consequently small, what are termed bellows pieces are provided, while the long length at the middle of the engine (the left-hand

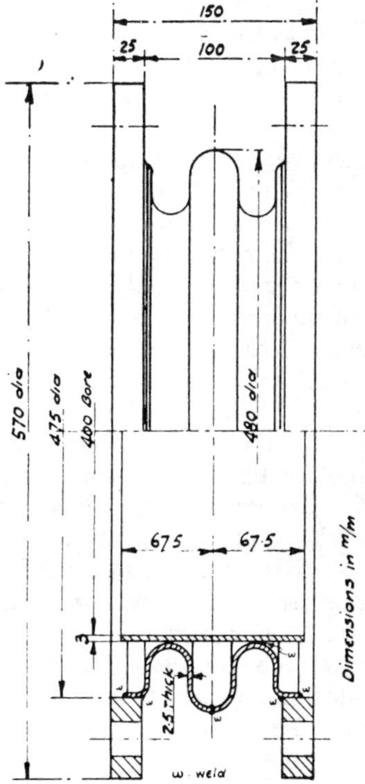

Fig. 180—Bellows expansion piece for exhaust-gas pipe

side of the illustration) is provided with a stuffing-box and gland. One of these bellows pieces is shown in greater detail in Fig. 180. The usual practice is to make the overall length about $\frac{1}{4}$-inch less than the gap into which the piece is to be fitted, and to stretch it by means of the connecting-bolts, with the result that when the parts attain normal working temperature the expansion piece is relieved of practically all strain. The gasket should be placed in position at one end and the bolts tightened before the gasket is inserted at the other end of the bellows piece.

Another method of allowing for the free expansion of an exhaust pipe is shown in Fig. 181. The flanges connecting the various sections, it will be observed, are made extra large in diameter and undercut on the joining surfaces to give flexibility and freedom to move endwise in either direction. The object of the three stay-bolts is to ensure that the two pipes forming each section expand inward and so eliminate all strain at the ends. This arrangement works very well so long as the flanges are large enough in diameter and thin enough to give the necessary degree of flexibility. If this is not the case, fracture at the point where the flange is welded to the pipe is likely to occur.

Fig. 182 illustrates yet another method of allowing for the expansion of exhaust pipes. This telescopic type of expansion piece is very simple in design and robust in construction, allows unlimited expansion of the exhaust pipe, and is reliable. Furthermore, being telescopic it can be fitted or removed with ease. The illustration is self-explanatory.

As it is occasionally necessary to disconnect some part of the exhaust piping to re-make a joint, to gain access to some other part, or to allow for part renewal, the method of connecting the flanges and the material used for the bolts and nuts deserve consideration. Bolts and nuts, both of which are accessible to a spanner, are preferable to tap-bolts. If the design of the pipe makes tap-bolts necessary, then the flange into which the bolts screw should be drilled a larger size and brass-bushed. Brass tap-bolts do not become " frozen-in " to the same extent as steel tap-bolts, but unless made a slack fit they do tend to jam and are easily broken off. Steel may be used for both bolts and nuts on water-cooled pipes, but when the pipes are of the uncooled type the nuts should be made of brass. Needless to say, no bolt or nut should be refitted unless graphite paste has been liberally applied.

When stuffing-boxes and glands are provided to prevent leakage of water and gas from between the sliding surfaces of water-cooled exhaust pipes, the type of packing used and the method of fitting the packing must be given careful thought, otherwise it will be a

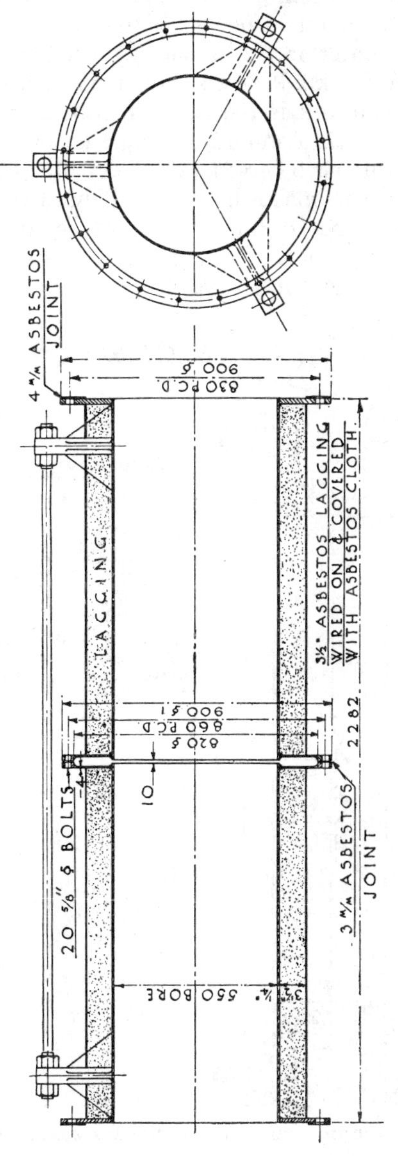

Fig. 181—Flexible-flange type of exhaust-gas manifold

very difficult matter indeed to renew the packing when it becomes necessary to do so. First of all, the gland should be a slack fit on the pipe and in the stuffing-box. There is nothing to gain and much to lose by the gland being just a free fit, when all parts are new and in clean condition. The packing used should be of the loosely-plaited asbestos kind which should be soaked in boiled oil for an hour or so before it is required. Before being inserted into the stuffing-box, each turn should be squeezed between the hands to remove the free oil and be given a thick coating of graphite paste, boiled oil being used to make the paste. If hard packing must be used, then it should be of round and not square cross-section, and each turn thickly coated with graphite paste. This is most important, since although the oil evaporates after a time, the carbon

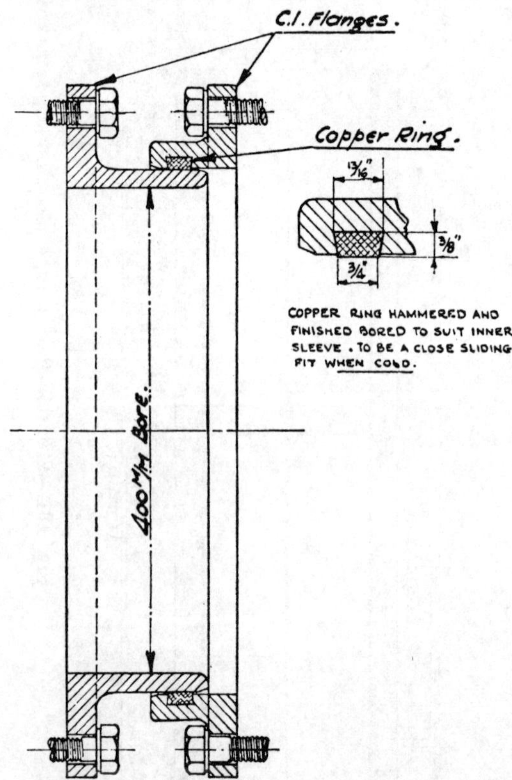

Fig. 182—Telescopic expansion piece for exhaust-gas pipe

remaining facilitates withdrawal of the packing when this becomes necessary. Some engine-builders use hard asbestos packing of square section for these stuffing-boxes, and, unfortunately, often fit it in a dry state.

Asbestos in some form or other is always used as packing between the flanges connecting the various sections of the piping together. Wire-woven asbestos is the most suitable, but any of the good-quality steam jointings answer the purpose very well. Asbestos millboard is widely used because it is inexpensive, and is satisfactory provided the proper initial pressure is put upon it and is maintained. Should this not be the case, however, the packing will disintegrate and leakage of gas will occur. Where such jointing is employed it is wise, therefore, to be quite sure that the bolts are properly tightened, in view of the large amount of work usually entailed in re-making these joints. Especially is this necessary in the case of new installations after the first week or so in service.

Exhaust test cocks

Such fittings are usually provided opposite the branch from each

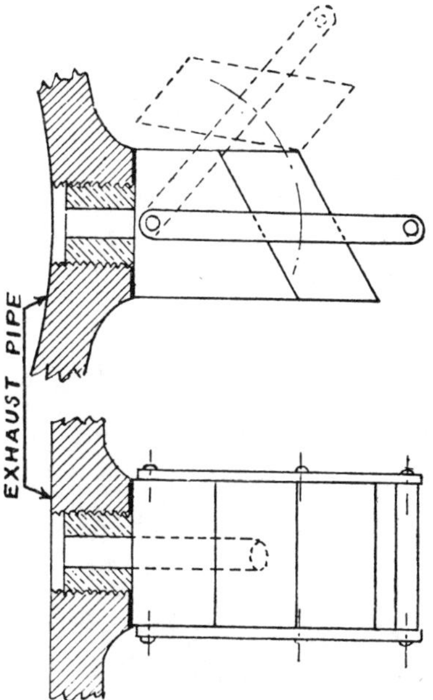

Fig. 183—Exhaust-gas testing device

cylinder, their main object being to enable the engineer to ascertain in which cylinder, if any, imperfect combustion is taking place. Unless they are given frequent attention, these small cocks soon become unworkable owing to the high temperature to which they are subjected, and they break when the occasion to use them arises. When screwed into the pipe they are nearly always troublesome because they get so hot. An extension piece about 6-inches long interposed between the exhaust pipe and the cock will be found to improve matters, without reducing in any way the usefulness of the fitting.

Fig. 183 shows a very simple and reliable exhaust-gas testing device which no amount of heat will affect in any way. The weight of the shutter alone is sufficient to prevent the escape of gas when in the closed position. The dotted lines in the upper sketch represent the shutter in the open position, the shutter being suspended but quite free to rotate between the levers. To those in charge of engines fitted with troublesome cocks, it will be time well spent to make the fittings illustrated.

CHAPTER 20

Lubricating oils

Until about 1939 fuel economy, after reliability, was of first importance in a ship's propelling installation. Next in importance came the weight of an installation per unit of power developed, as upon this and the fuel consumed during a voyage depended the maximum weight of cargo a ship of given dimensions could carry; the less fuel required and the lower the weight of the propelling plant, the greater would be the weight of cargo carried on a given voyage.

These factors are still important, but cost of maintenance rather than fuel economy now takes second place to reliability. This has come about owing to the cost of maintenance work having increased so much recently. The cost of fuel has also increased, but whereas the saving in the fuel bill between an engine of low fuel economy and one of high economy is not to be rejected as of little account, it is small compared with the present cost of maintaining an engine in proper working order.

Apart from making good the ill-effects of corrosion in the cooling-water and (occasionally) lubricating-oil systems, and, of course, the employment of unsuitable materials, the amount of maintenance required on an engine depends upon the rate at which important parts wear, and this in the main depends upon the effectiveness of lubrication. The subject of lubrication is therefore of vital importance, and to understand the principles involved it is necessary to have a knowledge of the physical properties of the lubricants used, whilst an elementary knowledge of how oils are produced will prove useful.

Lubricating oil manufacture

The great bulk of lubricating oil, of which there is a large variety of grades, is manufactured from the higher boiling-point constituents of crude petroleum which are left in the residue after the fuels such as petrol, paraffin and gas oil have been driven off during the distillation process to which all crude petroleum is now subjected. From some crudes the yield of lubricating oil is small, and from others comparatively large, while some crudes are not suitable for working up into lubricants. Moreover, some crudes yield lubricants suitable only for special purposes.

From the point of view of lubricating oil manufacture, crude petroleum may be divided into three general classes, as follows: (1) the paraffinous class, such as Pennsylvanian, which contains paraffin wax but little or no asphaltic matter; (2) the naphthenic or non-paraffinous class, for example, Venezuelan, which contains asphaltic matter but little or no paraffin wax; and (3) the mixed class which contains both paraffin wax and asphaltic matter in fairly large quantities. Examples of this latter class are the crude oils of Borneo and certain crude oils of Mexico.

The first operation in the manufacture of lubricating oil consists of a distillation process whereby the more volatile constituents of the crude petroleum are separated from the heavier ones from which lubricating oil is ultimately obtained by elaborate refining processes. The lubricating oil distillates obtained from paraffinous crudes are known as wax distillates, because they contain paraffin wax in comparatively large quantities. The presence of wax in lubricating oil is in most cases undesirable, because it gives a high pour-point, i.e. the oil will not flow freely at ordinary atmospheric temperatures. Therefore, the wax, which may have lubricating properties, must be removed if a lubricating oil is to meet requirements as regards the pour-point. This is done by chilling down the wax distillates by means of brine from a refrigerating plant, and afterwards filtering it under pressure in a filter press. The low temperature causes the wax to solidify, in which state it readily separates from the more fluid constituents. After this process, which is called de-waxing, the oil is re-distilled into fractions of different viscosities, and each fraction is filtered by percolation through fuller's earth to give it a lighter colour and a more attractive appearance. The products produced in this way from paraffinous crudes are known as " neutral oils " and range from very thin spindle oils to light machine oils having viscosities of from 45 to 85 seconds Red. No. 1 at 140°F (60°C). The residue from the operation has a very high viscosity and is usually termed " black oil " or steam-cylinder oil.

In working up Pennsylvanian crudes, the distillation is sometimes stopped before all the light lubricating-oil fractions have been taken off as distillates. The residue is then de-waxed and refined by filtration and the product is known as a " long residuum," which is a heavy machine oil having a viscosity in the neighbourhood of 200 seconds Red. No. 1 at 140°F (60°C). The de-waxing in this case is generally done by chilling to precipitate the wax, which is then removed by high-speed centrifugal machines.

Non-paraffinous and mixed base crudes do not yield residual lubricants, but by the use of modern methods in which distillation is effected under high vacuum, high-viscosity oils can be distilled from the crude oil with very little cracking. With the old method of distilling in batch stills working at atmospheric pressure, the most viscous distillate which could be obtained without severe cracking taking place was a heavy machine oil with a viscosity of about 200 seconds Red. No. 1 at 140°F (60°C). In a modern high-vacuum plant, distillates of 1,200 seconds are commonly made.

Lubricating oils are generally distilled twice. In the first distillation all the lubricants in the crude oil are removed and collected together as a primary distillate. This primary distillate is then submitted to a second distilling process in which the products are collected as separate fractions such as spindle oil, light and heavy machine oil, and a heavier oil generally known as cylinder oil. This latter fraction is commonly used for steam-engine cylinders, but is unsuitable for diesel-engine cylinders. A small amount of lime or soda is added to the oil before the second distillation in order to neutralise the acids in the oil and prevent them from passing over with the secondary distillates.

A chemical refining is given to each fraction of the second distilling process in order to remove the less stable constituents and to improve its colour. The first part of this treatment consists of adding from 2 to 10 per cent of sulphuric acid according to the class of oil being treated and the requirements of the finished product. The oil and acid are thoroughly mixed by blowing compressed air through the mixture for about half-an-hour, after which it is allowed to settle and the acid tar, a black viscous substance, separates to the bottom of the agitator, which is the name given to the vessel in which this part of the refining process takes place. In some plants the slow settling process is replaced by a centrifugal treatment which removes the acid tar with comparative rapidity.

The acid tar oil, which is dark in colour and dull in appearance, is then treated by stirring it with a soda solution to neutralise the acid. After allowing the soda solution to separate from the oil, the oil is washed with water. Another and more modern method of treating the acid tar oil is to heat it and mix it with a bleaching earth and a small amount of lime which removes all traces of acid from the oil. The mixture is then rapidly circulated by a pump which draws the oil and earth from the bottom of the container and returns it to the top.

In order to remove the bleaching earth and lime the hot oil is pumped under high pressure through filter-presses, in which the oil is forced through filter-paper supported between sheets of coarse canvas. In this way the earth and other solid matter is separated from the oil, but as much oil remains on the filter-paper the substance collected must be treated by solvents to extract the oil from it. After this earth-refining and filtration, the oil is yellow or pale-red in colour, according to the extent of the treatment, and is fully refined.

Whilst the oils produced in the manner described are suitable lubricants, it is usual to blend and clarify the " straight " or " raw " products, as they are called, before they reach the consumer, the qualities of the finished oils depending upon the specific purpose for which they are intended. Blends may be classified under three headings, namely: blends of distillates, blends of distillates and residues, and blends with fatty or fixed oils. The latter class are known as compounded oils.

An oil refinery normally produces three or more distillates which are blended together in varying proportions to produce oils of intermediate viscosities. For instance, the distillates produced may be what are known as a 150 Pale, a 300 Pale and a 1,200 Red., from which the whole range of oils from light spindle to heavy engine may be produced. Blending is usually carried out in steam-heated vessels provided with either paddle agitation or compressed air, and the blending is carried out at the lowest convenient temperature (about 140°F or 60°C) necessary to mix the oils completely.

In regard to the second class of blended oils, most of them consist of distillates and what is called bright stock, which is a refined residue, added for the purpose of increasing the viscosity of the finished oil. For instance, in the case of Pennsylvanian oils the thickest distillate obtained is only 85 seconds Red. No. 1 at 140°F (60°C), and the incorporation of bright stock is necessary if more viscous oils are required. Bright stock is also generally used for introducing high heat-resisting qualities into internal-combustion engine cylinder oils, but as it increases the carbonising tendency of the finished oil its uses in this way are limited.

Vegetable and animal oils are fundamentally different from mineral oils in that they contain oxygen. As a result of their chemical constitution fatty oils, as they are sometimes called, emulsify with water, and are, moreover, less resistant to oxidation than are mineral oils. Thus such oils tend to produce gummy deposits when exposed to heat. Fatty oils, however, have greater powers of adhering to metallic surfaces, and because of this desirable property sometimes improve the lubricating qualities of mineral oils. Although vegetable oils oxidise to a higher degree than animal oils, both have an affinity for oxygen and, if not properly blended, produce sticky substances on the bearings and develop acidity, which may have a corroding effect on metal parts. The formation of acid is accelerated at the higher temperatures and in the presence of moisture or other oxidising agents.

Fatty oils are generally classified according to their behaviour when exposed in thin films to the air, and are known as drying or non-drying oils. Linseed oil is an example of the former, while castor oil is a non-drying oil. It is the latter class that are suitable as lubricants, the drying oils being suitable for paint manufacture because of their property of forming a varnish-like substance on exposure to the air. Certain oils, notably rape and fish oils, which fall in between these two classes and are called semi-drying oils, are used in the manufacture of certain special lubricating oils. Such oils are first subjected to a blowing process with air which oxidises them, thereby increasing their viscosity and emulsifying properties. Blends of mineral oil with blown oils are suitable where water on the bearing surfaces is present, as in air-compressors, and consist of mineral oil blended with from 5 to 25 per cent of either blown fish or blown rape oil, although occasionally other fatty oils such as castor and coconut are used.

There are many substances on the market, the manufacturers of which claim that if a little of such substance is added to a much larger quantity of mineral oil, the lubricating qualities of the latter are improved. These substances are usually certain acids extracted from fatty oils.

Lubricating oil tests

Many of the tests applied to lubricating oils are used in connection with fuels. These tests include specific gravity, flash-point, pour-point, and viscosity. There are many other chemical and physical tests in addition to those given above and those about to be described, but it is proposed to deal in this book only with those generally made use of by consumers of lubricating oils.

Unfortunately, the most important property of a lubricant, namely, its lubricating value, is the most difficult to ascertain and define. No easily applied and reliable test, except that of carefully observing results obtained under actual working conditions, has yet been devised, and unfortunately this test requires months and sometimes years to carry out. Research work by several authorities is being undertaken in this direction, and the day is perhaps not far distant when the lubricating value of an oil will be clearly defined and easily tested. In the meantime, operating engineers must be guided by the results of generally recognised physical and chemical tests the significance of which will now be stated, their own experience, and the practical experience of others.

Carbon residue test

This test is sometimes referred to as the Coke Test. Its object is to evaluate the tendency of a lubricating oil to form carbon when subjected to heat, such as when injected into the cylinders of a diesel engine for the purpose of lubricating the piston rings. The best known test is the Conradson, which will be described, but it should here be stated that the conditions existing in this or any other carbon residue test are not very similar to those prevailing in diesel-engine cylinders, so that the figures obtained from such tests are not always a reliable guide to the coking tendency of an oil.

In the Conradson testing apparatus, a sample of the oil to be tested is heated in an iron crucible, which is enclosed in another and larger crucible. The two crucibles are then covered by a hood provided with a chimney and heated. When vapour appears at the chimney it is ignited and the heating operation is continued until the vapours cease to burn. The weight of coke or carbon left in the crucible per 100 parts of the sample of oil is called the Conradson coke value. In other words, the carbon residue is weighed and the percentage calculated on the weight of the original sample.

The practical value of this or any other coking test is doubtful, as the relation between the figures obtained and the tendency to form carbon in practice holds good only when comparing oils from the same oilfield, while it has been proved in practice that a low Conradson carbon value is not always found in a really good lubricating oil. It is also a fact that the coking figure of oil in continuous circulation in a diesel-engine crankcase increases with use, but that its lubricating properties are not necessarily reduced. It would appear, therefore, that the carbon residue or coking test is of very little value when selecting an oil for bearing lubrication, as in practice it has been found that so long as the Conradson carbon value of an oil for cylinder lubrication is not over 1 per cent, no deposits in the cylinder need be anticipated because of this. For air-compressor cylinders, however, the coking figure should be reasonably low, as the higher the figure the greater the tendency for carbon to deposit on the valves. The usual Conradson carbon values for diesel engine and air-compressor cylinder lubricating oils are 0·6 and 0·2 per cent respectively.

Demulsifying value

The bearing lubricating oil of steam engines is always liable to admixture with water, and that in diesel engine and air-compressor crankcases may occasionally have water mixed with it in various ways, such as through leaking joints in the cylinder-cooling system, or defective packing of piston cooling-water telescopic pipes. Moreover, it occasionally happens that in effecting repairs, water unavoidably enters the crankcases when certain parts of the cooling system are disconnected, and mixes with the bearing lubricating oil.

It is, therefore, extremely important that the lubricating oil used for such purposes should separate from water fairly readily. Should it not have this property and a viscous emulsion be formed by the churning action to which the oil is subjected when in use, not only may the engine be seriously damaged but the whole of the oil in the system will have to be thrown away. When it is remembered that the quantity of oil in continuous circulation in some engines is as much as 2,000 gallons, the importance of the demulsification value will be appreciated. Oils differ in their affinity for water, and a number of tests to determine the rate and extent of the property to separate from water have been devised.

The demulsification tests usually consist of churning samples of the oil with a certain proportion of water, either mechanically or by blowing steam through the mixture. In the former method 20 cubic centimetres of oil is added to double the quantity of water and after raising the temperature to 130°F (54·4°C) violently stirred for five minutes. The mixture is then allowed to settle and a reading taken every minute of the amount of water which separates; these readings are taken every minute for an hour. The amount separated in any given time multiplied by 60 and divided by the number of minutes occurring from the moment the mixing operation is stopped is called the Herschel demulsification value.

In the other method steam it led into 20 cc of oil contained in a graduated vessel until by condensation of steam the total volume of the mixture of oil and water equals 40 cc. The vessel containing the mixture is then transferred to a bath containing water at a temperature of 200°F (93·3°C) and the number of minutes required for complete separation of the water is called the I.P. (Institute of Petroleum) demulsification number. Thus if it takes 2½ minutes for the 20 cc of water to separate from the sample of oil, it is said to have a demulsification number of 2·5. A similar test is in use in America, but there the time for the water to separate is expressed in seconds, and if the 20 cc require 2½ minutes to separate, the oil is said to have an S.E. (steam emulsion) number of 150. The demulsification figure for good oils is from 4 to 6 minutes I.P.

A simple and practical way to form some idea of the demulsification property of samples of oil is to mix violently measured quantities of oil and water at a given temperature, and then allow the mixture to stand and note the time taken for the water to separate from the oil. When, therefore, it is necessary to ship a different grade of lubricating oil, the demulsification value of which is unknown, procure two stoppered bottles and pour into one a quantity of the new oil and double the quantity of fresh water. Into the other bottle should be poured oil and water in the same quantity and proportion, but the oil in this bottle should be a sample of the oil that has proved satisfactory in this respect. The quantity of oil and water should be such that the bottles are not more than half full. The bottles with their contents should then be placed in an oven until the temperature of the mixture is about 120°F (49°C), and then both violently shaken for exactly the same time and in the same way. If the bottles are then allowed to stand undisturbed it will be seen whether the new oil has better or worse demulsification properties than the oil previously used.

Acidity

The acids found in lubricating oils, whether new or used, are one or more of three kinds, namely, petroleum or natural acids, which are indigenous to petroleum oils; a mineral acid, i.e. sulphuric acid, the presence of which indicates careless refining; and fatty acids, found only in compounded oils. The first and third are organic acids and the other an inorganic acid. Natural acids are very weak, and although they tend to increase in amount during the useful life of an oil in continuous circulation they are without appreciable effect upon metals. An excessive amount, however, may reduce the demulsification value of the oil. In the refining process, as already stated, sulphuric acid is generally used in the refining of lubricating oils in order to remove certain undesirable constituents of the crude oil. After this treatment, the oil is washed first with water and then with an alkaline solution to remove all traces of the sulphuric acid. If, therefore, mineral acid is present it means that the oil has not been properly refined.

Lubricating oils must be quite free from mineral acid, which is highly corrosive and may cause pitting of the bearing surfaces, double-bottom tanks and pipes and fittings of the lubricating system. The presence of mineral acid in any of the well-known high-grade mineral oils is unlikely, but as some refining methods are not as perfect as others, small quantities of sulphuric acid may be found in the lesser known brands of lubricating oil. Traces of fatty acids, or in other words organic acids, are sometimes present in lubricating oils whether they are pure mineral oils or compounded with fatty oils. Generally, however, such acids in small amounts are not harmful since thay have no corrosive action upon metals; and when present in small quantities and of the right kind actually improve the lubricating properties of the oils. When they are present in large quantities, however, certain metals are attacked. Lead and zinc are quickly affected by such acids, and on brass verdigris is formed. Tin is the only soft metal that is impervious to fatty acids.

The term "acidity" generally conveys the impression that if certain metals, especially steel, are brought into contact with the oil corrosion will occur. This, however, is not the case in the science of lubrication, as only any quantity of inorganic acids or large quantities of organic acids have this effect. The really harmful inorganic acid in lubricating oils is measured by mixing water with the oil and, after violently agitating the mixture, estimating the acidity of the aqueous extract. It is usually expressed as a percentage in terms of sulphuric acid or sulphuric anhydride. In this country it is usual to express the acidity of fatty oils in terms of oleic acid. Another method of expressing acidity is known as the "acid value," which is the number of milligrammes of potash (KOH) required to neutralise the free acid in one gramme of oil. Again, the acidity is expressed in degrees which are the number of cubic centimetres of normal alkali required to neutralise the acidity of 100 grammes of oil.

Generally speaking, the percentage of acid in a lubricating oil should be as low as possible, but just what the maximum limit should be depends upon the corrosive properties of the acids. In some cases bearing oil in continuous circulation has been found to have an acidity value of 8 per cent, and not only did the oil have excellent lubricating properties, judging by the small amount of wear in the bearings, but neither the bearing surfaces nor any other metal part in contact with the oil showed the least sign of pitting or other forms of corrosion. On the other hand, oils with an acidity value of only 2 per cent have been found to cause pitting of the bearing surfaces, but in such cases it is generally found that sea-water has leaked into the lubricating oil. Moreover, oils differ considerably in their tendency to develop acidity when used in continuous circulation in the bearing and piston-cooling systems of diesel engines.

It would appear, therefore, that while it is wise to determine the acid value of crankcase oil occasionally, the real guide as to whether or not oil is unfit for further use depends upon the condition of the bearing surfaces and other parts. The mere statement of acidity, without due reference to the nature of the acid, is of no practical value if the acidity be considered from the viewpoint of its corrosive properties, and this seems to be the only real ground for objecting to unspecified acidity. As a rule, before any evidence of pitting of the bearing surfaces or corrosion of other parts becomes apparent, the internal parts of centrifugal purifiers, when used to purify the lubricating oil, will have corroded and require attention. Acids in lubricating oils are more active in a centrifugal machine, and on occasions when the thin conical plates have become badly corroded and the bottom of the bowl, when made of mild steel, has been attacked, no evidence of corrosive action on the bearing surfaces of any other part of the lubrication system could be found.

Experience has shown that the bad effect of the acids in the oil passing through centrifugal separators can be mitigated to some extent by introducing a warm-water feed with the oil. The acid content has a greater affinity for water than for oil and is consequently carried out of the bowl with the water. If sufficient fresh water is available, it is preferable to arrange for a continuous feed of about 5 per cent of the quantity of oil treated, but if this is impracticable small quantities of fresh water fed slowly into the separator at intervals will be found to have a beneficial effect. In many instances it is possible to utilise the condensate from the steam heater where this forms part of the lubricating-oil purifying equipment.

Sludge test

As is well known, a certain amount of sludge always accumulates at the bottom of bearing-oil drain tanks, no matter which brand of oil is used or what precautions are taken to keep clean the oil in circulation. This sludge is mainly the result of oxidation, and the extent of this form of deterioration differs widely with different oils. All lubricating oils consist chiefly of compounds of carbon and hydrogen, and when these are violently churned in air, as in the crankcases of diesel engines, chemical combination between the oxygen in the air and the hydrocarbons takes place, resulting in the formation of oxidised hydrocarbons. With some oils excessive oxidation takes place and the colour of the oil quickly becomes darker, the viscosity is increased, acidity is developed and carbonaceous matter is formed. Such oils have a very short life and serious trouble will result if they are kept in use too long.

The importance of the sludge or oxidation test will therefore be appreciated. This test is carried out by placing a known volume of oil in a tube contained in a hot bath at a fixed temperature. A measured quantity of air is then slowly bubbled through the oil for a certain time. This treatment quickly causes the oil to darken and become less fluid, and at the end of the test the changes in viscosity, carbon residue value and other properties are noted. The oil that changes least under these conditions is the oil best able to resist oxidation and from which the least sludge formation may be expected. " Shell," or any of the other well-known brands, resists oxidation, even in hot moisture-laden air, to the desired degree. Oil of the brand mentioned has been known to be in continuous circulation in a diesel-engine crankcase for eight years, at the end of which time the acidity value was less than 3 per cent, and not more than 2 per cent of the oil in the form of sludge was found at the bottom of the double-bottom drain tank, while the bearing wear was negligible and signs of corrosion non-existent.

SELECTION OF LUBRICATING OILS

Bearing oils

Selecting an oil for the bearing system of a diesel engine is not an easy matter for the operating engineer, as any of the physical tests which can be carried out by him, such as specific gravity, flash-point, etc. have no bearing upon the lubricating qualities of an oil. The chemical and other tests mentioned in the foregoing pages are, perhaps, of greater value, but these are out of the province of the operating engineer. The wisest course is for him to take a good brand of oil and observe results carefully. Any of the well-known oil producers can be relied upon to supply a safe, if not entirely suitable, oil for any particular purpose if the exact requirements are given. The Shell Petroleum Co. Ltd. produce a range of lubricating oils called " Shell " Talpa Oils, in appropriate viscosities for cylinder, crankcase, or dual-purpose lubrication.

Cost

Where the selection of oil is left to the operating engineer the question of price will not have an undue influence upon him, because he knows from experience that the suitability of a lubricant for a particular purpose cannot be judged solely by its price. Nevertheless, low-priced oils of unknown brands should be accepted with caution and refused if their adoption entails risks with a ship at sea. The difference in the costs of the least and the most expensive oils is small, whereas the difference in the results obtained may be so considerable as to make the cheapest oil the dearest by far, in the end.

Colour

Some engineers are influenced by the colour of an oil. Colour is no guide to the lubricating value of oils, although if oils from the same source are being compared, the oil having the palest colour is generally the most stable. It is a very difficult matter to describe the exact colour of most oils, and since the colour depends upon the manner in which they are viewed, i.e. by transmitted light or reflected light, tests for colour are only useful in connection with refinery practice.

As many engineers still hold the view that a pale-coloured oil has inferior lubricating properties to oils of darker colour, it should be mentioned that colour as a rule merely indicates the extent to which the oil has been refined, and has no connection whatever with the " oiliness " of a lubricant. Castor oil is an extreme example. This oil is one of the most efficient bearing lubricants obtainable, and yet it is almost colourless.

Specific gravity

Other engineers believe that the higher the specific gravity of an oil, the greater its lubricating properties. This is by no means the case, although the higher-gravity oils have usually, but not always, greater viscosity, which is doubtless one of the fundamentally important physical characteristics of lubricating oils. Nevertheless specific gravity is of little value in selecting an efficient lubricant. Oils of the same specific gravity might be good or bad for any particular purpose. For instance, the poorest Pennsylvanian oils have a high specific gravity, while the best Texas oils have a comparatively low specific gravity.

Viscosity

A knowledge of the viscosity of an oil is no doubt the most valuable single guide as to its suitability for any particular purpose. Yet, although the viscosity is recommended as the best guide, it must be clearly understood that the viscosity, considered apart from certain other properties, does not constitute sufficient information on which to base a selection of a suitable lubricating oil. It has been stated by oil technologists that the lubricating value of oils of high or low viscosity varies but slightly.

The behaviour of a lubricating oil in practice, so far as concerns wear and tear, is largely determined by its viscosity, which is such an important characteristic that most of the large oil-producers grade their oils on the viscosity basis. In addition to having a reasonably high viscosity at atmospheric temperature, it is essential for the oil to have the property of resisting a change in its viscosity under conditions where the temperature varies an appreciable amount. Most liquids become thinner when heated, and with lubricating oils this thinning tendency is very marked.

The thickness of an oil film which must separate the rubbing surfaces of a bearing and ensure a minimum of wear, is proportional to the viscosity of the oil for given conditions of working. Therefore, if the viscosity is too low the oil film will be too thin, the rubbing surfaces of the bearing will not be kept a sufficient distance apart, and wear will take place. All other things being equal, the best lubricant is the one whose viscosity changes least upon variation in temperature. The decrease in viscosity per unit rise in temperature is called the temperature coefficient of viscosity, and as lubricating oils differ widely in this respect, a knowledge of the viscosity at various temperatures is essential.

It is customary to express the viscosity of oils at three or more different temperatures. Given this information, a viscosity–temperature curve can be drawn and the viscosity values for higher, lower, or intermediate temperatures can be ascertained. From such a viscosity–temperature curve it will be found that at temperatures between 70°F and 100°F (21·1° and 37·8°C) the viscosity of all oils changes very rapidly, and that after this point the change is less rapid, until at temperatures of 200°F (93·3°C) and upwards the change in viscosity with rise of temperature is relatively small. The viscosities at different temperatures of a good crankcase lubricating oil are as follows:—

Viscosity Red. No. 1 at	70°F (21·1°C)	1,850 secs.
,, ,, ,, ,,	100°F (37·8°C)	550 ,,
,, ,, ,, ,,	140°F (60°C)	170 ,,
,, ,, ,, ,,	200°F (93·3°C)	60 ,,

To illustrate how widely the different classes of lubricating oil vary in respect of viscosity, it might be mentioned that light spindle oils have a viscosity of 150-300 secs. Red. No. 1, while heavy engine oils reach 5,000 secs. at the same temperature.

The instruments used for determining the viscosity of oils are not available to the operating engineer, but a rough idea of this property can be judged by half-filling a bottle with oil and rolling it in a horizontal position between the fingers. The viscosity of different oils can be compared in various ways. The best, perhaps, is to fill to nearly full two long sample bottles with different oils, cork the bottles, and make sure that the temperature is the same. Then suddenly invert the bottles simultaneously and note the comparative rapidity with which the air bubble rises to the surface. The temperature of each sample should then be raised an exactly equal amount by placing them in an oven to say 100°F (37·8°C), and the operation repeated, when the comparative change in viscosity at the elevated temperature will be apparent. The one in which the air bubble takes longer to reach the surface will, of course, be the more stable.

Flash-point

A knowledge of the flash-point of lubricating oils, especially when used in enclosed crankcases, was at one time considered important, but present-day refining methods are so advanced that lubricating oils possessing what might be termed a dangerous flash-point are now unknown. The flash-point is not, as some believe, a measure of the volatility of an oil, so that a high flash-point does not necessarily mean less loss by evaporation from the crankcases. The flash-point is the flash-point of the most volatile constituent of the oil and is almost independent of the quantity present. For example, the addition of a very small quantity of paraffin will reduce the flash-point of a much larger quantity of lubricating oil to that of paraffin, but have no measurable effect upon the volatility of the oil.

It is only necessary to consider the flash-point of lubricating oils when the temperature of the surfaces to be lubricated is in the neighbourhood of the flash-point, but since the flash-point of such oils generally lies between 400° and 450°F (204° and 232°C), and the temperature of the bearings in enclosed crankcases rarely exceeds 150°F (66°C), there is no possibility of trouble arising because the flash-point temperature is too low. Should a bearing or piston-rod become overheated the temperature will quickly reach 1,500°F (816°C) or even higher temperatures, and the lubricating oil may catch fire, but it is, of course, out of the question to produce an efficient lubricating oil to withstand such a temperature.

Nor has the flash-point of lubricating oil any connection with its ability to resist decomposition by heat, and in no way is it related to the tendency of the oil to be carbonised or oxidised, so that the flash-point is of no value in selecting an oil to be used for piston-cooling purposes, provided it exceeds 415°F (213°C).

From the foregoing it will be seen that, so far as the operating engineer is concerned, the only important test results are the viscosity, the demulsification value, and the power to resist oxidation. The only value possessed by the vast majority of generally accepted tests seems to be to describe a particular oil that has been found suitable in practice, so that exactly similar oil can be supplied subsequently. The composition of lubricating oils is apparently so complex that the knowledge possessed even by the oil chemist is not as yet complete.

Engine cylinder oil

For the lubrication of diesel-engine cylinders an oil is required that will, under extremely severe conditions of pressure and temperature, form a tenacious and unbroken film on the cylinder walls to protect the parts from wear and prevent gases from leaking through the minute spaces between the rubbing surfaces of the cylinder and piston rings. On the other hand, as the oil film is subjected to a shearing action by the piston rings, an oil having low internal friction is necessary in order that the power absorbed in shearing the film of oil should not be unduly great. Furthermore, in view of the desirability of introducing the oil sparingly at a limited number of points—remarks upon this will be made later—the oil must be sufficiently fluid to spread rapidly over the cylinder walls and maintain an oil film of uniform thickness.

The temperature of the burning gases in diesel-engine cylinders is so high, i.e. in the neighbourhood of 3,000°F (1,650°C), that it is quite impossible to produce an efficient lubricant to withstand this temperature. Any oil, therefore, must be partially burnt, irrespective of its flash-point or other properties. This being so, an oil for this purpose must be sufficiently volatile to burn away without leaving behind carbonaceous matter, but at the same time be sufficiently stable—the property of resisting chemical changes—to avoid formation of gummy matter, which results when the oil remains on the rubbing surfaces too long and is oxidised. It will thus be seen that the constituents of the oil must be so balanced as to give certain properties equal value, and that unless the oil producer is fully conversant with the conditions in the engine cylinders one property may be developed at the expense of other equally desirable properties.

It was stated earlier that the oil should be thick enough to form a tenacious and unbroken oil film on the cylinder walls, and yet be thin enough to spread evenly over the whole surface. This property is dependent to a great extent upon the viscosity of the oil. Should it be too viscous it will not spread sufficiently rapidly and a proportion of the oil will be thrown out of the bottom of the cylinder of a single-acting engine on the down-strokes of the piston, while other parts of the cylinder surface will run more or less dry. Thus, a too viscous oil may cause high frictional losses, excessive cylinder-liner and piston-ring wear, and leakage past the piston rings.

At one time it was believed that the employment of a more viscous oil would always reduce wear and prevent leakage of gases past the pistons in the event of these troubles being experienced. In some cases the desired results will doubtless be obtained by substituting a thicker oil, but it is equally true that there are cases where the same results can only be obtained by using an oil of lower viscosity. In other instances it will be found that the consumption of lubricating oil can be reduced without ill-effects by using an oil of lower viscosity. As an example, suppose an engine requires a certain quantity of oil of a certain viscosity to give normal cylinder-liner wear and a proper sealing effect to the piston rings. Should the oil used be too viscous, a greater amount than is really necessary will have to be supplied to cause the oil to spread to the points mid-distant between the injection holes in order to prevent leakage of gas past the piston at these points. As can be imagined, only a proportion of the surplus oil will reach these points. If the oil is so viscous that it will not spread sufficiently and dry spots occur, leakage of gases past the piston and excessive cylinder-liner wear will only be prevented by substituting a less viscous oil.

On the other hand, it is hardly necessary to state that a cylinder oil should not be too thin, otherwise it will run down the cylinder wall immediately upon leaving the injection holes, without being given an opportunity to spread around the cylinder. Oils that have proved themselves suitable for the lubrication of diesel-engine cylinders have the following properties:—

Viscosity Red. No. 1 at	70°F (21·1°C)	from 2,300 to 2,850 secs.	
,, ,, ,, ,,	140°F (60°C)	,, 200 ,,	280 secs.
,, ,, ,, ,,	200°F (93·3°C)	,, 60 ,,	100 secs.

In days gone by, lubrication technologists advocated the use of compounded oils for engine cylinders, the mineral oil having added to it from 5 to 10 per cent of fatty vegetable or animal oil, with a view to improving the " oiliness " of the mineral oil. Compounded oils, however, were not entirely satisfactory, and research during recent years has produced a new diesel-engine cylinder lubricant which has given better results, especially in engines operating on residual fuels.

This new lubricant is known as " Shell " Alexia Oil A, and is an emulsion of 70 per cent of high-grade straight mineral lubricating oil and the remainder pure water. Dissolved in the water during manufacture are special additives; these neutralise the corrosive acids which are formed by combustion and have been proved to be responsible for a proportion of cylinder-liner and piston-ring wear. When the lubricant is injected into the cylinder by the usual force-feed lubricators, the water evaporates and the additives and the oil remain in the cylinder to neutralise the acids and lubricate the piston rings. Because of the water content it is necessary to inject 30 per cent more than the normal quantity of conventional lubricating oil.

Air-compressor cylinder oil

Although air-compressors are now seldom used to supply air for injecting the fuel into diesel-engine cylinders, they are universally used to supply compressed air for starting marine diesel engines, and it is felt that this chapter would not be complete without a reference to the lubricating oils used in these machines.

The object of lubricating the cylinders of air-compressors is to provide an oil film between them and their piston rings and to furnish an effective seal, thereby reducing wear of these parts to the minimum, and preventing leakage of air upon which power has been expended. The requirements of air-compressor cylinders from a lubricating standpoint are similar to those of engine cylinders, the only difference being that the temperatures reached are not nearly so high. The oil is sparingly fed into the cylinders in the same way, and must be capable of spreading evenly over the whole of the rubbing surfaces. In the case of some air-compressors, however, the question of moisture in the cylinders must be taken into consideration when endeavouring to select the most suitable grade of lubricating oil.

As the conditions prevailing in air-compressor cylinders are not so severe as in engine cylinders owing to the lower maximum temperatures (300° and 3,000°F—149° and 1,650°C—respectively), some of the well-known high-grade engine cylinder oils are entirely suitable for the lubrication of air-compressor cylinders. The condition in air-compressor cylinders as regards moisture, however, varies very much, and in some cases the best results are obtained by using an oil containing about 5 per cent of saponifiable matter, which causes it to combine with the water and ensures the formation of a more adhesive oil film.

Compared with engine cylinders, the oil injected into air-compressor cylinders remains on the rubbing surfaces for relatively long periods since it is not subjected to the intense heat prevailing in engine cylinders. Consequently the oil in air-compressor cylinders undergoes long exposure to the strongly oxidising effect of high-temperature air. Unsuitable oils will oxidise readily under these conditions and form gummy deposits that may cause the piston rings to jam in their grooves and make the action of the valves sluggish. The principal considerations influencing the qualities required in a suitable oil are therefore the oxidising effect of the air compressed, and its reaction to the presence of moisture.

As in the case of the engine-cylinder lubricants, air-compressor cylinder oils must be of the correct viscosity. A too viscous oil will not spread readily over the rubbing surfaces, resulting in excessive cylinder wear and leakage of air past the pistons. The fluid friction will be great and cause loss of power through undue piston drag. Moreover, dust and other impurities in the air taken into the cylinders will more readily cling to over-lubricated surfaces and cause the formation of very undesirable paste-like deposits.

The flash-point of air-compressor cylinder oils is not so important as was at one time believed, provided, of course, that it is not unusually low. Many explosions in the past have been attributed to the employment of a lubricating oil having too low a flash-point, but it is now held that in the circumstances where explosive mixtures can be formed, oil-vapour is derivable from the lubricating oil regardless of its flash-point. Furthermore, the amount of vapour liberated at the flash-point temperature is so small and forms such a small proportion of the total quantity of gases in the cylinder, that it is very doubtful whether an explosive mixture can be obtained unless the machine is over-lubricated. It will be remembered that the flash-point of an oil is the flash-point of its most volatile constituent, and that this constituent forms a very small part of the whole. Where explosions have occurred, the cause has no doubt been due to excessive lubrication of the cylinders and abnormally high air temperatures, under which conditions the explosions would have occurred even if the flash-point of the lubricating oil used had been much higher.

It is still a common belief that for the cylinder lubrication of air-compressors a very high flash-point oil is essential, or that the flash-point of the oil used must, at any rate, be much greater than the temperature of the air in the cylinders into which it is introduced, otherwise it will at once vaporise and serve no useful purpose. This, however, is quite erroneous. All petroleum oils, no matter whether they be called petrol, diesel oil or the heaviest lubricating oils, consist of a number of hydrocarbons, most of which vaporise at a different temperature. Therefore, any petroleum oil is really a complex mixture of hydrocarbons, and cannot vaporise completely unless the oil is heated to a temperature high enough to vaporise the least volatile hydrocarbons in the group. This vaporising temperature range is not so marked in the lighter oils, but it is well known that if, say, lubricating oil is heated to a high enough temperature it eventually becomes thicker or more viscous, owing to the lighter hydrocarbons being vaporised and passing off. Such oils, therefore, are still capable of lubricating rubbing metal surfaces, even though the temperature of these surfaces has greatly exceeded the flash-point of the oil.

Comparing petroleum with water may make this more clear. Water is composed of substances in definite proportions, and, therefore, has a definite boiling-point. If water is heated to its boiling-point and maintained at this temperature, the whole of the water will eventually be vaporised. Fuel alcohol also has a definite boiling-point—namely, 173°F (78·3°C)—and if heated and maintained at this temperature, the whole of it will eventually be vaporised and pass off. It has been said that petroleum is composed of substances having different boiling-points, so let us assume for the moment that lubricating oil consists of a mixture of alcohol and water. Now, if such a mixture is heated the alcohol will begin to boil at 173°F, and if a flame is applied an explosion or rather a flash will occur, yet, for purposes of illustration, the residue will have lubricating properties. To vaporise the whole of the mixture, the temperature must be raised to the boiling-point of water, which is in excess of the flash-point of alcohol, its most volatile constituent. Thus it will be seen that while vaporisation of oils in air-compressors is to be avoided, there is no disadvantage in using an oil the flash-point of which is only slightly greater than the air-temperatures.

More time than might appear necessary has been spent in proving this, because there are decided disadvantages in using very high flash-point oils.

The objection to a very high flash-point is that such oils are, as a rule, unsuitable for air-compressor cylinder lubrication because they are too viscous. The flash-points of oils do not vary directly with their viscosities, but generally it may be said that the flash-points of heavy oils are higher than those of light oils. Therefore, apart from other considerations, oils of low flash-point would be of too low a viscosity to satisfy requirements from a lubricating standpoint, and, because of this, most high-grade air-compressor cylinder oils have a fairly high flash-point.

The importance of using a high-grade lubricating oil for air-compressors cannot be emphasised too strongly. It is of even greater importance than the quality of oil used for engine cylinders because the least possible amount must be injected into air-compressor cylinders. The more unsuitable the oil is the greater must be the amount used to maintain an unbroken film of oil on the rubbing surfaces, and the greater the amount used the more trouble there will be with paste-like deposits on the valves and in the air passages. Whether the oil used is a straight mineral or compounded oil, it is more economical to use the best, as not only will the amount of inferior oil required be from twice to four times that of a high-grade oil, but the valves and air-spaces will require to be cleaned much more frequently. From this it will be appreciated that a cheap compressor oil is really the most expensive.

In some multi-stage high-pressure air-compressors, the presence of moisture in the cylinders greatly influences the class of lubricant best suited for the purpose. The quantity of moisture carried into an air-compressor depends chiefly upon the humidity of the atmosphere, but it is also a fact that condensation is greater in some machines than in others, due to differences in the construction of the coolers. To ensure efficient lubrication of air-compressors in which comparatively large quantities of water are carried into the cylinders, it is necessary to use a compounded oil, because moisture in the air tends to wash off the lubricating film when straight mineral oil is used. The cylinder walls and valves will then rust and rapid wear-and-tear will take place.

A straight mineral oil and a compounded oil that have been found suitable for air-compressor cylinder lubrication have the following properties:—

	Mineral	Compounded
Specific gravity	0·902	0·905
Flash-point (closed)	400°F (204°C)	400°F (204°C)
Viscosity Red. No. 1 at 70°F (21·1°C)	1,100 secs.	1,100 secs.
,, ,, ,, ,, 100°F (37·8°C)	360 ,,	360 ,,
,, ,, ,, ,, 140°F (60°C)	120 ,,	125 ,,
,, ,, ,, ,, 200°F (93·3°C)	50 ,,	53 ,,
Fatty matter	Nil	5%

All-purpose oils

Most operating engineers prefer to use the same grade of lubricating oil for bearing systems, engine cylinders and air-compressor cylinders. For marine service there are obvious advantages in using only one grade of oil, but there is no doubt that the friction surface requirements of the parts differ from the lubrication standpoint. For instance, the oil required for the bearings must be one that will remain sufficiently fluid at comparatively low temperatures to flow by gravity, and at the same time not become too fluid at moderately high temperatures. It must not give or throw down any deposits when subjected to the combined action of heat and the violent agitation which takes place in engine crankcases.

Oil for engine-cylinder lubrication must possess heat-resisting properties, and withstand the alternating direction of motion of the piston rings and possible contamination with partially burnt fuel; while in compressor cylinders the lubricant, besides possessing moderate heat-resisting properties, must be free from any tendency to volatilise, and possess high adhesive properties to withstand the action of moisture in the air.

If, therefore, cheap oils are employed it is wise to use those specially prepared for the various purposes, provided one can be quite sure that the different grades will always be used for their respective purposes. If, however, by accident or owing to shortage of one particular grade the bearing oil is used for the engine cylinders, serious harm may be done, while it might be positively dangerous to use some such oils for compressor cylinders. There is not the least doubt that some instances of excessive wear of vital parts and even breakdowns are due to this cause, and for these reasons all-purpose oils, which can be supplied by the leading oil companies, are strongly recommended.

Oil which is to be used for all purposes, including the cooling of pistons, should be wholly mineral, and what oil salesmen call "100 per cent straight distillate." Such oils usually have a specific gravity of between 0·903 and 0·907, a closed flash-point of not less than 415°F (213°C), and conform with the viscosities given on page 421.

Lubricating oil additives

A recent development in the production of lubricating oils is, as has already been mentioned, the inclusion of additives which confer special properties on certain oil blends. These additives, usually supplied as concentrates in mineral oil, contain very small quantities of organo-metallic derivatives and are incorporated during the blending process. The organic compounds used are derived from phenol or salicylic acid combined with such metals as zinc, calcium, or barium. These additives function on account of their anti-oxidant and detergent properties.

In addition to functioning as a lubricant, oil in continuous circulation in an engine crankcase acts as a coolant, since it must carry away frictional heat generated in the bearings, as well as heat conveyed from the cylinders by the piston rods and other parts. Thus the oil not only makes contact with metals at moderately high temperatures, but in addition mixes intimately with air. Under such conditions the oil is susceptible to oxidation, and it is now the practice to include in oil for such a purpose an oxidation inhibitor, incorporated during the blending process at the refinery.

The importance of stability in the viscosity of an oil has already been discussed. Allied with the viscosity is the viscosity index requirement. An oil with a high viscosity index—i.e. one showing least change of viscosity when subjected to varying temperatures—is desirable under most conditions encountered, and a recent development is the introduction of viscosity index improvers. A wide variety of synthetic polymers (produced by a reaction based upon the combination of two or more unsaturated molecules to form one large molecule) are used, and what is called the poly-isobutane type is now widely adopted in viscosity index improvers.

The most important property of oil is its "oiliness," which is closely related to the viscosity. It has been demonstrated that the lubricating property of a mineral oil can be improved by selected "oiliness" agents, and although the development is only in its infancy there is no doubt that more will be heard of it at some future time.

Probably the most widespread development in lubricating oil additives has been in connection with detergents. The present tendency in the marine engineering industry to increase the rated power of a given size of engine, combined with the use of cheaper and more viscous fuels, has resulted in lacquer-like substances being deposited on pistons. Crankcase temperatures are also tending to increase, and as a result oxidation of the circulating oil can be expected to be more rapid.

A lubricating oil containing this type of additive is able to release and disperse carbon deposits in engine cylinders and to keep in suspension the finely-divided oxidation products present in crankcase oil. Many complex chemical compounds have been patented as detergent additives, but generally those used are metallic soaps, and the quantity incorporated may be as little as 1 per cent of the oil containing them.

Calcium phenyl stearate is an effective detergent which also possesses the property of being able to break up large sludge particles into much smaller ones. Detergent additives, however, can adversely affect other desirable properties of a lubricating oil, so that their incorporation requires great skill and only well-known brands should be accepted. Some oils may contain as many as six compounds, each of which serves a particular purpose. A difference between a straight-run oil and a detergent oil is that the latter becomes black and opaque in use more quickly.

To combat excessive cylinder-liner wear in two-stroke engines when operating on certain high-viscosity fuels, a new type of lubricant in emulsion form has been developed. This lubricant was referred to briefly earlier in this chapter. The additive in this case is a basic organic salt whose function is to neutralise the sulphuric acid formed from the sulphur in the fuel under certain operating conditions.

Heavy duty (HD) oils containing alkaline additives, which had proved effective in reducing wear in small high-speed engine cylinders, did not possess sufficient neutralising ability to cope with the conditions occurring in the cylinders of large two-stroke marine engines. Oil technicians of the Royal Dutch/Shell Group then began investigating this problem and found that an emulsion of water and oil was able to carry into the engine cylinders a far greater quantity of neutralising additive than oil alone. The next problem to be solved was to prevent the water settling out when left undisturbed for long periods, and so keep the additive evenly distributed throughout the mixture. A satisfactory solution to this problem has also been found, and this type of lubricant is now extensively used, resulting in an appreciable reduction in cylinder-liner and piston-ring wear.

When marine diesel engines have to operate in very cold climates, the low temperatures may cause the separation of small quantities of wax, a constituent of some lubricating oils, and prevent the oil from flowing freely. To meet such a condition additives called pour-point depressors are introduced by oil-refiners. These additives are mostly alkyl naphthalenes, and by their use the pour-point of an oil can be lowered to temperatures below zero on the Fahr. scale. One explanation of the action of additives of this type is that they prevent the crystallisation of wax by reason of their colloidal nature. In general the effectiveness of pour-point depressors decreases as the viscosity increases.

From this very brief review of the latest developments in lubricating-oil production it will be seen that oil technologists are contributing very materially to the solution of problems that have troubled operating engineers in the past.

CHAPTER 21

Lubrication of bearings and cylinders

Now that we know something of the characteristics of a good lubricant for any particular purpose, we will pass on to a study of how the best use can be made of the oil—and its application is just as important as its quality: it could in fact be argued that it is even more important. For instance, an unsuitable oil properly applied will result in slow but excessive wear of the rubbing metal surfaces, whereas a suitable oil improperly applied will not only have the same adverse effect, but in addition may produce frictional heat so quickly that greater damage is done in a much shorter time. Under such conditions the whitemetal lining of the bearing will melt and run, and the shaft journal may be scored.

In addition to applying a suitable lubricating oil to bearings correctly, the oil must be kept reasonably free from impurities if wear of the metal surfaces is to be the least possible. All oils in continuous circulation change colour, but it is only the presence of certain impurities which reduces their lubricating qualities. If all impurities can be removed from a used high-grade oil its original lubricating qualities will be restored, no matter how long it has been in use. More will be said later in this chapter regarding the effect of various impurities and the purification of used lubricating oil.

Theory of lubrication

Enough time and thought is not always given by operating engineers to the important matter of efficient lubrication. It is not sufficient that a bearing should appear to require no attention when in use, as, in these days of enclosed crankcases and copious supplies of lubricating oil, this is no indication that everything is as it should be. The aim should be to operate bearings with as little frictional resistance as possible and so reduce wear to a minimum. With present-day metals and oils there is no reason why the amount of wear in the principal bearings of a diesel engine should not be negligible after several years' service.

The fact that a bearing works at a low temperature does not always signify that it is working properly. With the pressure system of lubrication overheated bearings are rare, but cases of excessive wear are still far too common. A bearing may be lubricated with water, and provided a sufficient quantity of water is fed into the bearing to carry off the heat as fast as it is generated, the bearing will not, of course, become overheated, but the rubbing surfaces will wear excessively. This is what happens when an engine is lubricated on the pressure system by an unsuitable oil.

From this it must not be inferred that a bearing lubricated with a copious supply of good lubricating oil never becomes overheated. For example, suppose a whitemetal-lined bearing has not been given sufficient working clearance, the whitemetal in contact with the shaft will quickly become overheated and melt. No further damage will result, however, because as soon as the tightness is removed by the melting of a small portion of the whitemetal, the copious supply of oil will quickly carry off the heat and the bearing will assume the normal working temperature—provided, of course, that the whitemetal has not run into the oil grooves and cut off the supply of oil. A bearing damaged in this way is said to have "wiped."

Lubrication is of two kinds, namely fluid lubrication and boundary lubrication. Fluid lubrication occurs when there is a copious supply of suitable oil fed into a bearing, the two surfaces of which are moving relative to one another at moderate speeds, as in the case of the principal bearings in an enclosed crankcase when the engine is operating. Boundary lubrication occurs when a bearing carries a heavy load and the relative movement of the two surfaces is so slow that the journal presses upon the bottom portion of the bearing, and squeezes out the oil from between the surfaces.

It may at first sight appear somewhat strange, but it is nevertheless true, that theoretically the total friction in a perfectly lubricated bearing when operating normally is independent of the load that may be put upon it. It may be argued that this rule does not hold in practice, because if a bearing should become overheated one of the obvious steps to take is to reduce the load. The answer to this, of course, is that an overheated bearing is not perfectly lubricated.

In spite of the above theoretical statement all practical engineers know that there is a limit to the maximum load that can be put upon a bearing, and that if this limit is exceeded the bearing will become overheated. The cause of this is not that the increased load on the bearing increases the friction, but that the greater the load the greater is the tendency for the oil between the rubbing surfaces to be squeezed out and lubrication to be impaired. If the load is such that the oil film is completely destroyed and the metallic surfaces make contact, the bearing will quickly become hot.

Fluid film lubrication

The film of oil between the surfaces is maintained by the oil being drawn in between the surfaces. This is due to the movement between them and depends solely upon the viscosity of the oil and the relative speed of the surfaces: the more viscous the oil and the higher the speed of the journal, the greater is the tendency for the oil to be drawn in between the most heavily loaded portions of the bearing.

It is common knowledge that if two metals are brought into contact, and an attempt is made to move one or both in such a way that the speeds of the surfaces in contact are different, or the surfaces move in opposite directions, resistance will be felt. The amount of resistance varies with different metals, but all will offer resistance to such movement. If force is applied to overcome this resistance to movement, the force expended will be converted into heat, and the metals will eventually become so hot that they will fuse and seize.

This frictional resistance is due mainly to the pressure forcing the metals together, and to the irregularities of their surfaces in contact; the lower the pressure and the smaller the irregularities, the less will be the frictional resistance to relative movement. Even when the contact surfaces are made as smooth as possible and are lightly loaded, the resistance to relative movement will cause dry metals to become so hot that eventually it will be impossible to continue the movement, or even if water or air are circulated to carry off the heat as fast as it is generated, the metals will be ground to powder in a very short time.

When, therefore, certain parts of machinery have to move in opposite directions to, or at different speeds from, other parts to which they are connected or with which they are in contact, the joining surfaces must not be allowed to make metallic contact; in other words, the surfaces must be separated by a medium which offers considerably less resistance to the relative movement of the parts. All gases and most liquids offer very much less frictional resistance than solids, and oils are the most suitable for the purpose.

The common practice, therefore, when one solid must support another in motion, is to furnish means for the production and maintenance of a thin film of oil between the rubbing surfaces. The astonishing fact that an oil film will keep such surfaces apart even when loaded to very high pressures and operated at moderately high speeds, has occupied the attention of oil technologists for years. The thickness of the film varies with the operating conditions of a bearing, but it will be very thin by ordinary standards, probably not more than a thousandth of an inch. This is relatively thick, however, when compared with the size of the molecules of which the oil is composed. If 100,000 oil molecules are placed end to end they will measure about one thousandth of an inch.

In order to help us to understand how the oil forms a film between the metal surfaces, and what are the special properties which cause it to remain between the surfaces even when subjected to great pressure, we will assume that we have before us the commonest type of bearing, namely, a shaft revolving in a stationary bearing. Since an oil film has definite thickness and covers completely the rubbing surfaces, it will be evident that the inside diameter of the bearing must be greater than the diameter of the shaft by an amount equal to at least twice the thickness of the oil film. When, therefore, the shaft is at rest it will make metallic contact with the lowest point of the bearing and the clearance around the shaft will be greatest at a point diametrically opposite.

Immediately the shaft begins to revolve in the direction indicated in Fig. 184, the shaft moves slightly to the left and tends to climb up the bearing (an opposite movement would occur with the shaft revolving in the reverse direction). In doing so the oil in that part

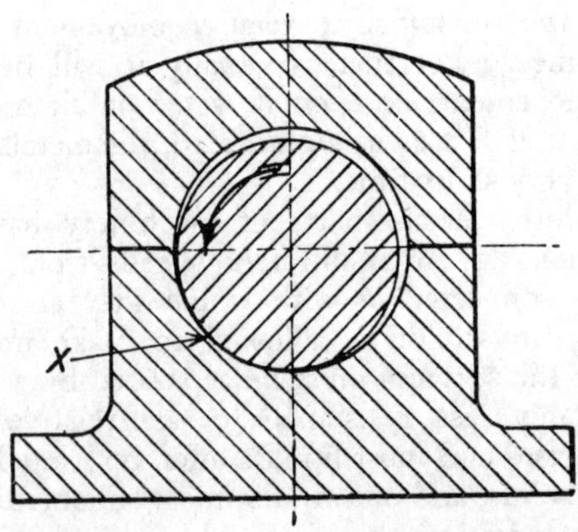

Fig. 184—Position of a revolving shaft in a bearing

of the clearance space on the left of the shaft is squeezed, and if the medium employed were water it would readily be squeezed out of the ends of the bearing and the surfaces would make metallic contact. As, however, oil is used the action is very different. The film is formed by the greater adhesion properties of the oil to the metal surfaces and maintained by the higher viscosity of the oil, which is drawn into that part of the clearance space most heavily loaded, indicated by X in Fig. 184. Thus the motion of the shaft acts like a pump and produces its own oil pressure, the pressure on the oil before it reaches the bearing serving merely to ensure a plentiful supply of oil to that part of the clearance space where no pressure due to load exists.

This pumping action was demonstrated in no uncertain manner in a gravity-lubricated engine which came under the author's observation. Oil was conveyed to a point near the bottom of the crankshaft bearings from boxes situated some 40 feet above the bearings. A little of the oil may have found its way into the bearings, but when the supply from the boxes was supplemented by oil poured into the top of the bearing, the oil would flow upwards into the boxes and cause them to overflow.

All fluids, even gases, will act as lubricants under suitable conditions of speed, load, and bearing clearance. It is well known, for instance, that air will act as a suitable lubricant for spindles running at very high speeds, and that in practice the higher the relative velocity of the rubbing surfaces, the lower must be the viscosity of the lubricant to obtain the best results. This explains why the very lightest of lubricating oils are referred to as spindle oils.

Boundary lubrication

As already stated, in fluid film lubrication the friction between the shaft and the bearing varies according to the viscosity of the lubricant, the speed of the shaft, and the load carried by the bearing. With any given oil the clearance in a bearing at the point of maximum pressure becomes smaller with increased loading, or with reduced speed, and when these reach a certain value the oil film becomes too thin to keep the rubbing surfaces apart and a condition arises which has been called " boundary " lubrication.

Under these conditions the friction between the rubbing surfaces is at least 30 times greater than that which exists with " fluid film " lubrication. Moreover, the friction in this case is independent of the viscosity of the lubricant or the speed of the shaft, but dependent upon the load carried by the bearing and a property that has been termed the " oiliness " of a lubricant. The precise explanation of this peculiar property involves considerable knowledge of molecular physics, but it suffices to state that it is the tendency of the oil molecules to attach themselves to the metal bearing surfaces. This property will be appreciated when it is remembered how difficult it is to remove all trace of lubricating oil from surfaces which have been coated by it.

Although there are these two distinct kinds of lubrication, intermediate states are possible, the conditions which determine the state being the load, speed, and form of motion. For instance, reciprocating parts, such as piston rings, do not produce a fluid film so readily as a shaft revolving in a bearing, and the lubrication of such parts as camshaft driving-chains presents yet further peculiarities which are far too complex to be dealt with here. The principal bearings of an engine operate under fluid film conditions, but as the speed of the engine is reduced the pumping action of the crankshaft journals and crankpins becomes less and less, and the oil film becomes thinner, until, just before the engine stops, lubrication no longer depends upon the viscosity of the oil but upon its peculiar property which has been termed " oiliness," and the resistance of the rubbing surfaces becomes boundary friction lubrication. Inferior oils have a lower degree of oiliness, and are consequently more easily squeezed out. When this occurs the rubbing surfaces make metallic contact and wear takes place.

Under conditions of boundary lubrication, fatty oils and certain fatty acids, owing to their chemical constitution, produce less friction than do straight mineral oils, although the difference is not nearly so great as the difference in friction between fluid film and boundary lubrication, which, as already stated, is about thirty times, whereas the friction with fatty oils is in the neighbourhood of one-third the friction produced when using a mineral oil. Under fluid film conditions the distance the rubbing surfaces are kept apart depends, so far as the lubricant is concerned, upon the viscosity, and as mineral oils may be of the same viscosity as fatty oils it will be seen that compounded oils are only really advantageous under boundary conditions of friction.

As already mentioned, the principal bearings of an engine work under fluid film conditions except at the moment of starting and stopping and when turning an engine by auxiliary power, so that as far as these bearings are concerned the extreme oiliness imparted to mineral oil by the addition of a certain proportion of fatty oil is really superfluous. It might be expected that in the crosshead guides, camshaft driving-chains and gear wheels, where conditions of boundary lubrication exists, compounded oils would be more suitable, but as, in fact, the wear of these parts when lubricated by a good brand of mineral oil is negligible after years of continuous service, the employment of a compounded oil does not appear to be justified.

It has been stated that for fluid film conditions of lubrication an oil having a fairly high viscosity is required, since there is no doubt that the thickness of the oil film, and consequently the distance the rubbing surfaces are kept apart, all other conditions being equal, depends solely upon the viscosity of the oil. The shaft of a bearing which has been properly adjusted and is efficiently lubricated actually floats on a layer of oil which effectually prevents metallic contact, and the frictional resistance to be overcome is simply that due to the resistance of the oil film to shear. Under these ideal conditions no wear of the metal surfaces will take place, so that if wear should take place under fluid film conditions of lubrication, it either means that the viscosity of the oil is too low or that the bearing has not been properly adjusted to ensure the oil being drawn in and the oil film produced.

On the other hand, a bearing oil should not be too viscous, as although a thick oil film offers less resistance than a thin one, a relatively viscous oil sets up high resistance to motion by virtue of the internal friction of the liquid itself. This resistance is transformed into heat and will cause the working temperature of the bearings to be increased. A further disadvantage of using an oil that is too viscous is that in addition to lubricating the bearings it is the duty of an oil in continuous circulation to absorb the heat generated in the bearings and convey it to the sea-water circulating the coolers. A very viscous oil will not absorb heat or give it up in the coolers so readily as an oil of lower viscosity, with the result that the working temperature of the bearings will be greater.

In all bearings heat is generated, due either to fluid or metallic friction, but in properly adjusted and lubricated bearings the heat produced is wholly due to the former, which causes the temperature of the bearing to be increased gradually until what is called the running heat is attained, when it remains constant. At this stage heat is still being generated, but owing to the temperature-difference it flows to the engine framing and the surrounding air, or is carried off by the circulating oil as fast as it is generated, and thus no further increase in temperature results.

The lubricating oils generally supplied to ships have the desired viscosity at the assumed running temperature: they should, therefore, be kept as near the working temperature as possible when in use. The amount of fluid friction in a large marine engine caused by the lubricating oil being too cold and viscous is quite appreciable and should be avoided. The remark that an engine runs freer out East is often heard. The reason is that the lubricating oil has a lower viscosity and is nearer the working temperature for which it was selected. Actually the effect of raising the temperature of the bearing oil from 50° to 105°F (10° to 40·6°C), and the cylinder cooling-water outlets from 70° to 110°F (21·1° to 43·3°C), was, in the case of one 4,000 h.p. engine, to increase the speed by five revolutions per minute for the same amount of fuel consumed. Because of this, some method of heating the oil before it is brought into use should always be provided and made use of. In cold weather the temperature of the bearing oil should always be raised, both to facilitate starting and assist the pumps which must lift the oil and force it through innumerable tortuous passages. Another trouble that may arise due to cold oil being circulated through the system is that the oil side of the cooler tubes will become coated with a heavy, greasy film, which may reduce the efficiency of the cooler when the proper working temperature is reached.

Engine cylinder lubrication

Efficient lubrication of engine cylinders is most important for the following reasons: (1) to reduce friction between the rubbing surfaces and, consequently, wear of the liner and piston rings; (2) to reduce the power absorbed in overcoming the friction of the piston rings and thereby procure a higher mechanical efficiency; and (3) to form an oil film that will effectually seal the minute spaces and prevent leakage of gases past the rubbing surfaces. The fact that piston rings have been " run-in " does not imply that they are bearing evenly all round, as uneven wear and distortion of the cylinder liner owing to temperature variations produce minute spaces through which gases will leak unless they are sealed by oil.

Lubricating oil is injected into the cylinder at from 2 to 6 points around the circumference, the number depending upon the size of the cylinder. Sometimes the various points are fed through an encircling ring of piping with branches to each point. This method was the cause of much uneven liner wear in the past, owing to the oil naturally taking the path of least resistance, resulting in over-lubrication of certain parts of the surface and under-lubrication of the other parts. The present practice is to provide a separate feed from the lubricator to each point, so that the amount of oil injected at each point may be varied at will. If wear of the cylinder liner and piston rings is to be reduced to the minimum, and the most economical use made of the lubricating oil injected, this is by far the best method of introducing the oil.

Opinions differ regarding the number and disposition of the points at which the oil should be injected into cylinders. It is often found that makers of a 32-inch-diameter cylinder engine inject the oil at two points only, while another maker injects the oil at as many as six points. Just how designers arrive at the number of injection points required is difficult to understand, since the factors which mainly determine the number in a given diameter of cylinder are the viscosity of the lubricating oil used, and the working temperature of the cylinder liner. Neither of these factors varies to any appreciable extent, so one would expect to find the distance between the points to be more or less standardised.

In order to obtain the best results as regards wear of the cylinder liners and piston rings and sealing effect, the whole of the cylinder surface must, of course, be covered by an oil film of a certain minimum thickness. This condition would be readily obtained by introducing the oil at a large number of points around the cylinder, but as the desired results must be obtained with a minimum expenditure of lubricating oil, and as there is a limit to the smallest quantity which a lubricator will consistently deliver, it will be appreciated that the oil must be introduced at the least number of points consistent with efficient lubrication of the rubbing surfaces. Were it possible to inject the oil in small enough quantities, the reduction of the number of points to the absolute minimum would not be so important; the points, however, must be spaced as widely as possible in order to reduce the total quantity of oil used in a given time. If, on the other hand, the points are spaced too widely apart, the parts of the cylinder liner in the vicinity of the points of introduction will be excessively lubricated, and the parts midway between the points will be insufficiently lubricated.

The spacing of the points at which the oil should be introduced has been carefully considered and close observation kept upon a large number of ships in which the spacing varied from 15 to 52 inches, and the conclusion arrived at is that, with any of the well-known brands of lubricating oil having the viscosities recommended in the previous chapter, the points of introduction should be not less than 24 and not more than 30 inches apart in order to obtain the minimum cylinder-liner and piston-ring wear with the least possible expenditure of lubricating oil. In a ship in which the points were spaced 52 inches apart, the average cylinder-liner wear was 50 per cent greater than in a ship, having similar engines, where the number of points was increased from two to four and the spacing reduced to 26 inches—while the cylinder-oil consumption in the latter case was slightly less.

As pointed out in the previous chapter, the less viscous an oil at the working temperature, the more readily will it spread over the rubbing surfaces, so that the less viscous the oil used the further apart may be the points at which it is introduced, and vice versa. There is, however, a limit to the minimum viscosity of an oil, since should it be too thin it will readily run down the liner and be swept out of the cylinder of a single-acting engine by the piston on its downward strokes and, consequently, not be given the opportunity to spread. The result of this will be excessive wear and abnormally-high oil consumption.

Oil grooves in cylinders

As the number of points at which the oil is introduced must be the least possible consistent with efficient lubrication, any means adopted to assist the spreading of the oil—provided, of course, they have no ill-effect in other directions—are justified. That the provision of oil grooves in the cylinder-liner surface accomplishes this there is no doubt. The spaces formed by each pair of piston rings, the piston, and the cylinder liner are undoubtedly the greatest distributing agents, but oil grooves in the cylinder-liner surfaces greatly assist in distributing the oil in these annular spaces. The provision of oil grooves is now common practice, but there are still many who hold the opinion that the cylinder liner should have a smooth unbroken surface in order that the oil film shall not be disrupted. This, however, has not been found to be of any great advantage in practice, because in the scores of engines that have come under the author's observation the best results, as regards cylinder-liner and piston-ring wear as well as oil consumption, have been in engines the cylinders of which were not only provided with oil grooves, but whose cylinder liners were in two pieces, so that the oil film on the cylinder walls was broken right round.

The foregoing remarks apply to grooves located near the bottom of the cylinder where the gas pressure is at its lowest value, and, therefore, unlikely to be a source of leakage, the usual location for four-stroke single-acting engines being between the two uppermost piston rings when the piston is at its lowest working position. In engines of comparatively long stroke a proportion of the oil can with advantage be introduced about the middle of the cylinder.

The efficient lubrication of two-stroke engine cylinders is a much more difficult matter than that of four-stroke engines. Not only does the cycle of operation tend to produce higher working temperatures, but openings must be provided at the lower end of the cylinder liner for the admission of scavenging air and in some cases the egress of burnt gases, into which it is difficult to prevent some of the lubricating oil from escaping. When the oil is introduced immediately above or below the scavenging-air or exhaust ports too great a proportion of the oil finds its way into these ports and serves no useful purpose, besides causing objectionable deposits of carbon. The points of introduction in this type of engine should, therefore, be located comparatively high, the position recommended being between the two lower piston rings when the piston is at its highest working position.

When the oil-injection points are located at the uppermost part of the cylinder it is not, of course, wise to cut oil grooves in the cylinder-liner surface as they would naturally be a source of gas leakage past the piston rings. The annular space formed between each pair of piston rings must, in such cases, therefore, be depended upon to distribute the oil over the surface of the cylinder liner.

Oil grooves must incline downwards from the injection holes. If they do not incline sufficiently the oil will overflow from the upper end of the groove, and a large proportion of the oil will be swept to the bottom of the cylinder by the piston and serve no useful purpose. On the other hand, if the oil grooves are inclined too much, most of the oil will flow to the end of the groove and then overflow with the same results. The exact amount the grooves should incline depends, of course, upon various factors, such as the number of piston strokes in a given time, the viscosity of the oil, etc. But if they are made from 15° to 25° from the horizontal axis—the smaller figure being for high-speed engines—the minimum amount of oil will be lost.

Another very important point in connection with the cutting of oil grooves in cylinder liners is that the beginning of the groove should drop vertically from the injection hole for one to two inches, and the radius of the curve joining the vertical and circumferential parts of the groove should be as large as practicable, in order to prevent too much oil overflowing at the point where the direction of flow is changed. There is more likelihood of the oil being retained and distributed gradually over a large area when the grooves are given this form than when the groove takes a circumferential course immediately. When two grooves run from an injection hole particular care must be taken when cutting to ensure that they are exactly similar, so that the whole of the oil will not flow into one groove.

A certain amount of lubricating oil is always thrown out of the bottoms of single-acting engine cylinders. When the quantity is more than a few drops a minute, it means that the cylinder is being over-lubricated, or that the oil grooves, if provided, are unsuitable or require to be re-cut. If the surplus oil drips from all parts of the cylinder it indicates over-lubrication, while if the bulk of the oil drips from a few points only it is a sign that either the grooves are at fault or the oil is of unsuitable viscosity. If the end of the cylinder liner is wiped while an engine is working at normal temperatures, it is an easy matter to ascertain whether the oil is leaving from one or more points or fairly evenly all round.

To ensure that the connecting pipe is always fully charged and that injection of lubricating oil into the cylinder begins immediately the engine—and consequently the mechanical lubricator— is set in motion, a small spring-loaded non-return ball valve is always provided at the cylinder end of each supply pipe. In addition to preventing the oil from draining from the pipe while the engine is at rest, with the lubricators located above the level of the point of injection, these valves prevent solid matter from the cylinders reaching the pipe. The duties of these valves, which, owing to their small size and their location, are apt to be forgotten, are very important, and they should be given periodical attention, the attention required consisting chiefly of washing thoroughly in paraffin and observing if corrosion of the ball or seat has taken place. These parts do sometimes corrode due to their being exposed to the burnt gases, and if they are not properly fluid-tight the connecting pipe may be emptied when the engine is at rest.

The balls should always be free to lift the requisite amount. Should this not be the case there is a possibility of the oil being injected in a more or less atomised state. Oil in this state is more susceptible to the action of the hot oxidising air in the cylinder, and in undergoing chemical change will lose its lubricating properties. The cause of the oil being atomised may be excessive spring load on the balls, partial choking of the hole through the cylinder liner, or air getting into the suction of the lubricator.

In most cases where two metals rub one upon another, lubricating oil liberally applied will reduce the friction set up between the surfaces without having any ill-effects, but the conditions under which engine cylinders and pistons operate are such that a too liberal supply of lubricating oil will cause trouble without giving any real advantage.

As in other machines, the efficient lubrication of these parts depends upon an oil film over the whole of the rubbing surfaces, but in engine cylinders this film is more difficult to maintain, since, as already stated, part of it is burnt away during the working stroke of the cycle and must therefore be renewed after every working stroke. The amount of oil necessary to renew this film is so small that no lubricator can be expected to deliver regularly at each stroke of the plunger such a minute quantity, so that the practice is to cause the lubricator to deliver a greater amount at regular intervals of from 20 to 30 working strokes of the piston. Any oil supplied in excess of the minimum required will not only serve no useful purpose, but will be decomposed or burnt and leave behind carbon and gummy substances which will cause the piston rings to jam in their grooves. This will prove a very serious matter should the cylinders open into the crankcase, as leakage past the pistons will quickly result and will blow the partially burnt carbon and other matter into the crankcase, where it will mix with the bearing lubricating oil and cause rapid deterioration.

Provided the lubricating oil is properly introduced into an engine cylinder it will do one of two things; namely, it will either adhere to a dry surface, or if there are no dry surfaces to adhere to, it will work its way past the piston rings and some will be thrown out of the bottom of the cylinder in a contaminated condition, the remainder finding its way above the piston rings where it will be burnt.

In order to form a better idea of what takes place, let us follow the course of a charge of oil that has been deposited between the piston rings as the crank passes over the bottom dead centre. Assuming that the previous stroke of the piston was a working stroke, the oil will be carried up by the piston and a small part of it will adhere to the more or less dry walls of the cylinder.

All lubricating oils are attracted by metals, some more than others, and when they make contact with metals they cling to them with astonishing tenacity even when the metal surfaces are smooth and highly polished, as are the internal surfaces of cylinder liners. (As an example, suppose a highly-polished piece of steel is dipped into water, most of the water will run off it immediately it is withdrawn, and if it is shaken it will become perfectly dry. If, now, the same piece of steel is dipped into lubricating oil it will emerge completely wetted, and no amount of shaking will free it from the whole of the oil. This simple test proves the superior attraction of oils for metals. As regards the clinging properties of lubricating oil, it will be found that no matter how smooth and highly-polished the piece of steel may be, long and vigorous rubbing is necessary before it loses its taste of oil. This simple experiment proves also that while surplus oil can easily be removed from metal surfaces, the molecules of what we might call the first, i.e. the closest, layer of oil are exceedingly difficult to separate from the metal, and although the thickness of this layer may be only a fraction of the thickness of cigarette paper, it has a definite lubricating value.)

Returning now to the oil that it is assumed has been delivered into the annular spaces between the piston rings as the crank passes over the bottom dead centre, we find that very little of the oil escapes during the early part of the up-stroke of the piston. The reason for this is that the lower part of the cylinder liner, where the temperatures and pressures are comparatively low, is always well covered with oil, and any oil that might adhere to the thin film already on the cylinder surface will be easily scraped off by the upper edge of the piston ring below it, in the same way as the surplus oil can be removed from the piece of polished steel by drawing it between the fingers. During this part of the piston's stroke, however, the oil tends to spread around the piston, so that when the upper and drier part of the cylinder surface is reached, a large area is wetted or oiled; as the oil attaches itself directly to the bare metal, the outward pressure of the piston rings is not nearly sufficient to remove it, even when the piston is completing the compression stroke and the piston rings bear comparatively hard against the cylinder liner.

It will thus be seen that so long as the oil makes contact with the cylinder, the dry parts will be lubricated without any special means being provided for forming an oil film. The oil film, however, will be so thin that boundary friction conditions will occur, and even if the oil used is one of high grade rapid wear may result. Even though a film of suitable oil on the upper part of engine cylinders may be less than one hundred-thousandth of an inch in thickness, and have lost its mobility as a fluid, yet the molecules adhere so strongly to the metal that they become rigid, and no practicable pressure will remove them.

It is not possible to obtain fluid film conditions of lubrication in the cylinders of engines, because it is necessary to introduce the oil very sparingly. It is, however, possible to approach these conditions and so reduce the friction between the surfaces by treating the piston rings in the manner now about to be described. It may be safely assumed that the astonishing results as regards wear in a properly operated engine—roughly 14 million strokes of the piston to wear the cylinder liner one thousandth of an inch—are due mainly to the annular spaces between the piston rings acting as oil reservoirs. It is the common and proper practice to apply lubricating oil liberally to these spaces and the piston rings before a piston is entered into the cylinder, and there is no doubt that most of the oil introduced subsequently finds its way there. As, therefore, these annular spaces between the piston rings contain oil, arrangements should be provided to enable it to enter between the rubbing surfaces, and by so doing to approach as far as possible fluid-film conditions of lubrication.

Formation of oil film

It has been shown that the provision of a wedge-shaped space at the leading edge of the rubbing surfaces greatly facilitates the entry of the particles of oil, even when the surfaces are very heavily loaded. It is reasonable to suppose that if the edges of piston rings are chamfered, the oil in the annular spaces between the rings will more readily escape and produce a thicker oil film on the cylinder liner. The lower part of the cylinder (single-acting) is exposed to a comparatively low temperature, and when the piston is at this part the gas pressure behind the piston rings tending to force them against the cylinder is very much less than when the piston is at the upper part, consequently the oil film at the lower end is much thicker than that at the upper end of the cylinder. Therefore, whatever arrangements are provided to cause the oil to escape from the annular spaces between the piston rings should have for their object the carrying of the oil to the upper part of the cylinder liner.

As most of the oil is contained in the annular grooves formed by the lower piston rings, the oil is more likely to pass to the upper grooves—and, consequently, into the uppermost part of the cylinder where the greatest wear takes place—if the lower edges of the piston rings only are well chamfered, as shown in Fig. 185. The effect of shaping the rings in this way will be as follows. Assuming the piston is beginning the up-stroke, the oil already between the piston rings will be carried upwards owing to the sharp upper edge of the piston rings. Moreover, the surplus oil on the lower part of the cylinder wall will be scraped off by the sharp upper edge and carried to the upper part of the cylinder also. When the piston reaches the upper part of the cylinder where the surface is more or less dry, some of the oil will attach itself to the cylinder wall, in spite of the scraping effect of the sharp upper edge of the piston rings, and lubricate the surfaces to a limited extent. Having carried the oil to the upper part of the cylinder where it is required

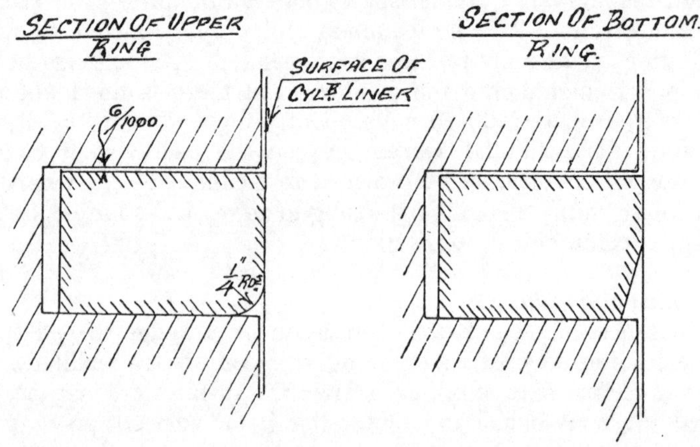

Fig. 185—Piston rings showing chamfered edges to assist the formation of an oil film

most, as much of it as possible should be left there, and this is most likely to be effected by chamfering the lower edges of the piston rings, which will assist the oil to escape from the annular spaces and form an oil film of maximum possible thickness on the cylinder walls, ready for the next up-stroke of the piston. Thus it will be seen that by chamfering the piston rings in this way the piston is made to work as a simple single-acting pump.

As will be noted in Fig. 185, the lower half of the outer surface of the bottom piston ring is bevelled to form a comparatively large wedge-shaped space with the cylinder liner. The object of this is to assist as much as possible of the oil film below the piston to pass the bottom ring on the down-stroke of the piston, instead of being driven before it and thrown out of the bottom of the cylinder, as would be the case if the lower edge of this ring were left sharp. The rubbing surface of this ring can be reduced to the extent illustrated without ill-effect, because the pressure forcing the ring outward is comparatively small and not likely to cause undue wear. In trunk-piston engines, where a relatively large quantity of oil is thrown on to the cylinder walls by the cranks, the bottom ring should be shaped as shown, but inverted in order that the surplus oil will be scraped off the cylinder walls and returned to the crankcase.

The ideal arrangement for the lubrication of cylinders would be for the position of the injection holes around the cylinder to be such that when the crank is on bottom dead centre, the holes are opposite the space between the two upper rings, and injection of oil timed to commence only after the holes have been wholly passed by the bottom piston ring on the downward stroke of the piston. Practically the whole of the oil would then be trapped between the piston rings, where it would be safe from direct contact with the burning gases, and the least amount possible would get under the piston and be thrown out of the bottom of the cylinder and wasted.

Many attempts have been made to time the discharge of oil to take place as the crank passes over the bottom dead centre, but it is very doubtful whether the desired results were ever achieved because of the difficulty of calculating the time-lag in the pipes connecting the lubricator with the cylinder. Even if the lubricators are properly timed, there is the change in viscosity of the oil due to varying temperature to be considered, which would, of course, affect the time-lag, i.e. the interval between the lubricator commencing discharge and the moment injection into the cylinder begins, the delay being mainly due to the friction in the small-bore connecting pipe.

Oil grooves cut in the cylinder-liner surface make timing of the lubricator less necessary, because they change the supply of oil from an intermittent flow into a more or less continuous flow, and from close observation made by the author it would appear that better results are obtained from oil grooves carefully cut in the cylinder-liner surface than from timed lubricators. From the foregoing it will be apparent that if oil grooves are provided, the whole object of timing the lubricators is defeated.

The matter of timing injection of oil relative to the position of the piston is again being seriously considered by some engine-designers. They propose to inject the oil by a pump operated by the cylinder compression pressure, much in the same way as the fuel is injected by the Archaouloff method. Each cylinder would be provided with a separate pump or lubricator situated near the point of injection, so that time-lag in the connecting pipes would be obviated; but as the pump would be operated by the terminal pressure in the cylinder, injection must take place at the end of a compression stroke and when the piston is beginning its working stroke.

In principle the proposal is sound, but there will probably be practical difficulties. Such a lubricator would undoubtedly ensure delivery of the whole of the oil to the desired point, i.e. between the piston rings, a feature which is extremely important in double-acting two-stroke engines. In such engines the oil must not be injected too near the middle of the cylinder, otherwise some of the oil will enter the scavenging air and exhaust ports and be carbonised or start fires. In view of this it is preferable to inject the oil into the space between the two sets of rings when at the ends of the cylinder, and a lubricator operated by the terminal compression pressure would ensure delivery of the oil as desired.

Renewal of cylinder liners

Consideration must be given to the question of renewing cylinder liners when the maximum amount of wear reaches 6 mm in the case of cylinders of 30 inches diameter or over; the smaller the diameter the less will be the permissible maximum wear. Sometimes large-diameter cylinder liners are allowed to run to 8 mm maximum wear, but generally in such cases piston-ring renewals are very frequent, and excessive quantities of lubricating oil are necessary to prevent gases blowing past the piston rings. In view of this, and the fact that the wear rate increases rapidly after the enlargement reaches 6 mm, it is wise to renew the liners then.

If a four-stroke engine is properly operated and the cylinders are lubricated with a sufficient quantity of suitable lubricating oil, the wear rate is in the neighbourhood of $\frac{4}{1000}$-inch per 1,000 hours of full-power operation. In two-stroke engines the wear rate is about 50 per cent greater. The wear rate increases slightly as the cylinders enlarge, but if the average rate is taken as $\frac{7}{1000}$-inch per 1,000 hours, the length of time liners will last can be arrived at with a fair degree of accuracy. The practice of supercharging up to 130 lb/sq.in. mean-indicated pressure has no appreciable effect upon the wear rate of cylinder liners and piston rings. The effect of supercharging to a higher degree has yet to be determined, but there is no apparent reason why the wear rate should be appreciably different from the figure given above.

As actual examples of cylinder-liner wear the following case may be quoted. The engines are of the supercharged four-stroke type, developing 125 lb/sq.in. M.I.P. at 125 r.p.m., the diameter of the cylinders being 29·5 inches. After four years' continuous service the average maximum wear of the six cylinders was 2·64 mm. As the annual running time was just under 6,000 hours, the average maximum wear per 1,000 hours works out at 0·11 mm, or a little over $\frac{4}{1000}$-inch. In the case of another ship the average maximum wear of the six cylinders was 5·80 mm after seven years, the average wear per 1,000 hours being 0·14 mm, or nearly $\frac{6}{1000}$-inch. These figures illustrate how the wear rate increases as the cylinders enlarge—and also shows the excellent results obtainable when careful attention is paid to lubrication.

Cylinder lubricating-oil consumption

The amount of lubricating oil necessary for efficient lubrication depends, of course, upon many factors in addition to the size of cylinder, but it is rarely less than 0·5 gallon or more than 0·75 gallon per cylinder per day in engines having cylinders in the neighbourhood of 30 inches in diameter. To work on statements that diesel engines require so much oil per h.p. developed is most unwise. The best practice is to give an engine the maximum amount stated above, and then, upon close observation of the points mentioned earlier, to reduce gradually the amount used until the best results are obtained with a minimum expenditure of oil.

Air-compressor cylinder lubrication

As no combustion process takes place in the cylinders of air-compressors, the temperatures are fairly low compared with those prevailing in engine cylinders, and consequently very little oil is necessary for efficient lubrication of the piston rings, provided, of course, that full use is made of the oil and that it is of suitable quality.

Over-lubrication has a bad effect upon the working of air-compressors, while on the other hand it is hardly necessary to state that unless sufficient oil is injected to maintain an unbroken film of a certain minimum thickness, excessive wear of the cylinder liners and piston rings will result. The exact amount of oil required can only be determined by trial and close periodical examination of the parts concerned, which should be opened up frequently until the minimum amount of oil necessary for efficient lubrication has been decided upon. The method of introducing the oil, the area of the surface to be lubricated, the piston speed, air temperatures, and the efficiency of the water jackets, which affect the viscosity of the oil, are all variable factors in different sizes and types of air-compressors, so that it is quite impossible to state here how much oil these compressors require.

The greatest wear always takes place in the third stage or H.P. cylinder, due to the pressure forcing the rings against the liner being greatest in this cylinder. In a great many cases the working temperature is higher in this cylinder than in those of the lower stages, but provided the temperature is not abnormally high the heat produced is not responsible for undue wear. Air temperatures rarely exceed 300°F (149°C), and at this temperature a well-refined mineral or compounded oil is practically unaffected. Vaporisation of the oil, providing it is properly injected, is most unlikely at this temperature, as oils of the viscosity suitable for air-compressors do not begin to give off appreciable quantities of vapour at temperatures below 400°F (204°C).

The parts which indicate whether too much or too little oil is being introduced are the cylinder liners and discharge valves. If too little oil is being used, the liner will show excessive wear at the upper end and the discharge valve will be found in a clean and almost dry condition. The piston rings will have worn excessively also. If too much oil is being used the liner wear will be about normal, while the discharge valve will be thickly coated with carbonised oil. If the liner and piston rings are found unduly worn, and the discharge valve is thickly coated with carbonised oil also, the trouble is doubtless due to the employment of an unsuitable oil. Should the oil used be a high-grade mineral oil, better results as regards wear will probably be obtained by using a smaller quantity of compounded oil.

The amount of oil necessary is so small that when the cylinders are opened up, the rubbing surfaces should appear dry, but when a finger-tip is rubbed over the surface and then rubbed against the thumb, the presence of oil should be perceptible. Should the surface actually be wet, over-lubrication is indicated. The two lower piston rings are also a good guide as to whether or not a compressor is being over-lubricated. These rings, when first exposed, should be just wet with oil and no more, while the upper rings should appear to be dry, but would be actually covered with a very thin film of oil. Another guide as to the correct amount of lubricating oil is the condensed moisture blown from the coolers. The water should feel only slightly greasy when the fingers are wetted by it and then rubbed together. Oil floating on the water drained off is a sign of over-lubrication.

Moisture in the air is very largely responsible for compressor cylinder and piston-ring wear, the upper end of the H.P. cylinder being most affected by it. Some compressors make a comparatively large quantity of water, while in others a few drops are all that is ever found when the cooler drain-valves are opened. Contrary to what might be expected, it is in the compressors which produce little or no water that the greatest wear takes place assuming, of course, the cylinders are receiving the normal quantity of lubricant. As two compressors working in the same atmosphere must take in the same quantity of moisture, the only reason why one should eject more water than the other is that the separating arrangements provided in the coolers of the former machine are more efficient. This, then, would explain why, all other conditions being equal, greater wear takes place in what may be termed a dry air-compressor.

The proportion of moisture in a given amount of free air increases during the compression process, and were it not for the rapid rise in the air temperature, part of the water would be liberated in the cylinder. As, however, the capacity of the air for holding moisture increases greatly with rise in temperature, the moisture does not condense in the cylinder. But when the air enters the cooler and its temperature is reduced, its capacity for holding moisture decreases, and all moisture in excess of the saturation value corresponding to the new temperature and pressure of the air, will be condensed and fall to the bottom of the cooler, while the air with its normal quantity of moisture will pass on to the next stage cylinder. This is what happens theoretically, but in practice, unless means are provided to separate the water from the air, the air will carry fine particles of water into the next stage cylinder, when, as water, it will have an adverse effect upon the lubricating-oil film.

This doubtless explains why first stage or L.P. cylinders sometimes show no appreciable wear after ten years' service, while the third stage or H.P. cylinder liner requires to be renewed about every four years. Furthermore, the more efficient the separators are, the greater will be the quantity of water found at the bottoms of the coolers, and the drier will be the air passing to the higher stage cylinders. Thus when little or no water appears at the L.P. and M.P. stage drains of a multiple-stage air-compressor, excessive cylinder-liner and piston-ring wear may, as a rule, be expected in the two higher stages—especially the H.P. When, therefore, a fair amount of water collects in the coolers it indicates that the air going to the higher stage cylinders is comparatively dry and that the oil films are less likely to be adversely affected by water.

In order to assist in forming an oil film over the rubbing surfaces of H.P. cylinders, the outer edges of the piston rings should be chamfered in the manner recommended for engine piston rings. In the lower stages, however, where the piston is generally of the differential type, the best results will be obtained by chamfering the top and bottom edges of all rings an equal amount. As the holes in the M.P./L.P. cylinder liner through which the lubricating oil is introduced are only covered by the piston for a very small proportion of the stroke, and as timing the lubricators to discharge at the instant the piston rings pass over the injection holes is impracticable, short oil grooves cut in the cylinder surface are necessary, otherwise the bulk of the oil will be swept to either end of the cylinder and cause frequent cleaning of the valves to be necessary.

Cylinder lubricators

There are many forms of engine cylinder lubricators, all of the mechanical type, suitable also for lubricating the cylinders of air-compressors, but the design mostly favoured is the differential plunger type similar to the one illustrated in Fig. 186. The advantage of this type of plunger over the simple ram is that small quantities of oil can be discharged per stroke with a relatively large plunger bore.

The essential conditions to be met by a lubricator for the purpose of cylinder lubrication are:—

(1) It must be capable of delivering regularly every stroke a minute quantity of oil against moderate pressure.
(2) It must have a wide range of adjustment, and maintain consistent delivery when the feed is cut down to as low as one bubble per minute.
(3) It must operate equally well with shaft rotation in either direction.
(4) It must be capable of being instantly operated by hand.
(5) The quantity of oil discharged per stroke should be clearly visible.
(6) Each pump unit should be easily removed from the container and replaced by another without having to stop the lubricator or interfere with the working of the other pump units.

With the type of lubricator shown in the illustration, the actual amount of oil passing to the cylinder can be seen as it climbs the guide wire provided (but not shown in the illustration) in the centre of the water column. This, however, is not the amount injected into the cylinder at the moment it is seen, but the total discharge of a number of strokes of the lubricator plunger.

Under normal working conditions there is a considerable interval between the bubbles of oil seen to rise through the water or glycerine, and by some not fully conversant with the construction of this type of lubricator, it might be thought that no oil is being injected into the cylinder during that period. This, however, is not the case, since the discharge side of the lubricator being filled with water or glycerine and oil under slight pressure, the amount of oil discharged per stroke must displace and inject into the cylinder

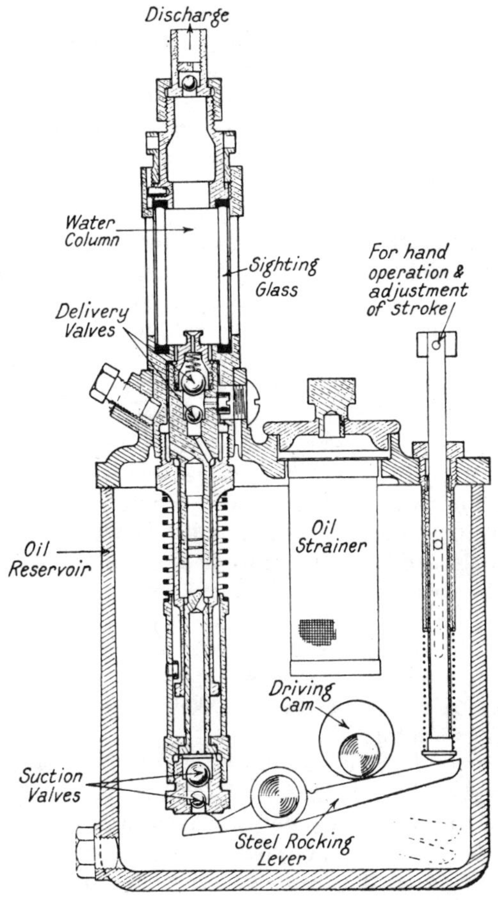

Fig. 186—Lubricator suitable for engine or air-compressor cylinders

an equal amount of oil at the far end of the discharge pipe; therefore, if it takes ten strokes of the plunger to form a bubble of oil sufficiently buoyant to leave the nipple, it follows that an amount of oil equal to one-tenth of that oil-bubble has been injected into the cylinder at each stroke of the plunger. (When glycerine is used instead of water the oil-bubbles are smaller, because of the greater specific gravity of the glycerine.)

Purification of lubricating oil

Lubricating oil in continuous circulation, as in an enclosed crankcase, becomes darker in colour after a time, but does not necessarily deteriorate in lubricating quality. The discoloration is due to the presence of certain foreign matter, and if this is removed the oil regains its original appearance and qualities. Colloidal graphite or carbon is mainly responsible for discoloration, but as the particle size of such matter is considerably smaller than the normal thickness of an oil film, this impurity will not cause wear in bearings unless, of course, the quantity present is so great that it accumulates at certain points of the system and interferes with the free flow of the oil. A very small percentage weight of colloidal carbon can produce a very dark colour, and it is not possible to estimate the quantity present by the appearance of the oil, since a small quantity may make an oil as dark as a large quantity. Because of their very small size, colloidal carbon particles are difficult to separate, and it is not possible to restore oil to its original colour by passing it through filter cloth or even centrifugal separators.

Metallic impurities are the most objectionable as they are responsible for most of the bearing wear which takes place. Such impurities result mainly from corrosion of steel pipes, and as corrosion of such parts is accentuated by the presence of sulphuric acid the system should be tested regularly and any water present removed, particularly if the design of the engine is such that gas from the cylinders may enter the crankcase. Metallic particles also act as catalysts, and oxidation of the oil takes place and, consequently, tarry substances are formed.

Part of the products of combustion consist of sulphur dioxide and water vapour, both of which under normal working conditions are exhausted from the cylinders in a harmless gaseous state. If these gases should, however, be cooled to the condensing temperature of water vapour, as is the case when they leak into the atmosphere past the piston rings, the water formed will absorb comparatively large quantities of the sulphur dioxide and produce sulphurous acid, which readily becomes oxidised to sulphuric acid. Drainings collected from the trays under the cylinders should not, therefore, be mixed with the bearing oil. Even when the leakage of gases is too small to be noticeable these injurious acids are formed with many fuels.

The usual practice is to extract the solid impurities from oil in continuous circulation by means of centrifugal separators. Much, however, can be done towards reducing the work of these machines—and, incidentally, make opening them up for cleaning less frequent—if proper use is made of strainers, and if good attention has been given by the engine-builders to the natural tendency for the larger particles to separate from the oil and settle on the bottom of the drain tank.

Strainers should be of the duplex type and of large size, being provided on each side of the lubricating-oil pump, the one at the pump suction to protect the pump against excessive wear from larger particles, and the one on the discharge side to collect what the larger mesh of the suction strainer allows to pass. The mesh of the gauze used for this purpose is usually No. 40 for the suction side and No. 80 for the delivery.

To maintain the oil in the best possible condition the whole system should be cleaned out once every year and the oil run through a centrifugal separator before it is returned to the system. To do this it is necessary to have a tank in which the oil can be stored whilst the drain tank and other parts of the system are being cleaned. In most ships this can be arranged. Such a practice would result in less attention being required by the suction and delivery strainers and less frequent cleaning of centrifugal separator bowls when the engine is operating—especially when the ship is rolling in a seaway—besides making for less wear in the bearings.

The lubricating oil circulating through a crankcase is not only used for lubrication, but also for carrying off the heat generated in the bearings. In large diesel engines, therefore, it is necessary to have large quantities of oil in continuous circulation, as much as eight tons not being an unusual quantity, and to prevent accumulation of impurities it is necessary to purify on what is termed the continuous by-pass system, during normal working of the engine.

Fig. 187 shows a suggested arrangement of pipes and valves connecting the engine with the oil drain tank and purifying machine; from the diagram it will be noted that the oil flows by gravity from the engine bedplate to the drain tank through a gate-valve. A valve is necessary at this point as occasions may arise when it is an advantage to isolate the engine from the drain tank. One such occasion is when work is going on inside the crankcase and water from disconnected pipes enters the crankcase. A gate-valve is preferable to a globe-valve as there is less chance of solid matter in the oil being caught and held by this type on its way to the drain tank.

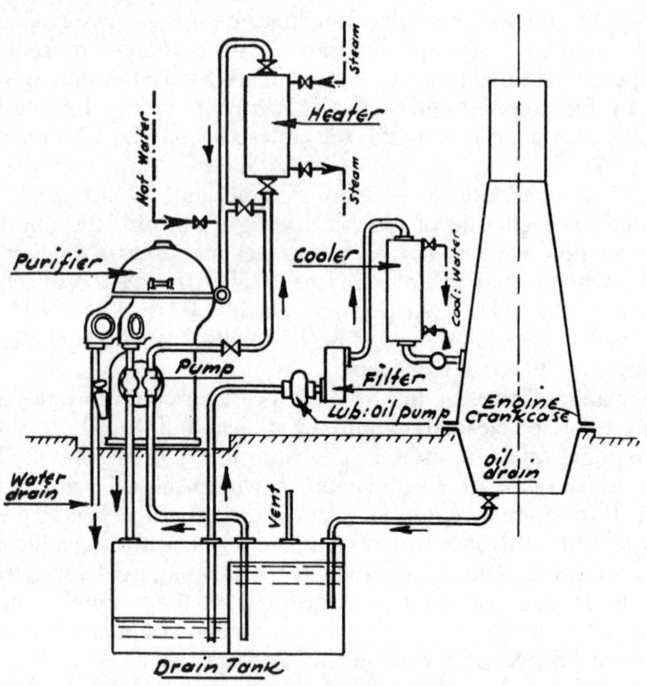

Fig. 187—Lubricating oil purifying system

The oil flowing from the engine is led to a point about half-way down the drain tank. If the oil entered at a higher point, more of the solid particles would pass over the weir into the compartment from which the oil is returned to the engine, and if lower it would disturb any sediment lying at the bottom of the tank. The aim should be to encourage the solid particles to settle out in this compartment of the drain tank so that they can be reached by the pump supplying the purifier, which, it will be observed, draws from this compartment.

The oil should be at 140° to 160°F (60° to 71°C) when it reaches the purifier, and as this is usually the normal working temperature of the circulating oil in hot climates, it is not always necessary to use the heater, and the arrangement of valves and pipes should be such that this component of the purifying system can be by-passed. The purified oil is returned to the system via the compartment from which the main lubricating-oil pump draws for delivery to the filter and cooler, thence to the engine. In some ships the oil passes through the cooler before reaching the filter, but the author prefers the oil to be strained before it enters the cooler. Such a sequence ensures that the coolers will remain efficient for a longer time and require less frequent cleaning.

The purpose of admitting water at about 160°F (71°C) to the purifier is to facilitate priming of the purifier bowl and to enable some of the larger particles of solid matter which collect in the bowl to be washed out occasionally. Water admitted with the oil in the ratio of about 1 to 20 also carries off any acids which may have formed in the oil.

The colour of the oil in circulation can be improved by blowing live steam into the oil before it is purified. This causes some of the colloidal carbon to coagulate, in which condition it is more easily removed from the oil by the purifier.

Needless to say, water, even if fresh, left in crankcase oil is highly undesirable, not only because it reduces the lubricating value of the oil, but because it may form an emulsion and result in the oil in the system having to be replaced by new oil. Once the oil and water become so intimately mixed as to form an emulsion, neither centrifuging nor any other treatment, apart from re-distillation, will separate them. If the oil is purified by the continuous by-pass system, leakage of water into the crankcase can be readily detected at the water outlet of the purifier. If the quantity of water flowing is more than the merest trickle, a search for the leak should be made. If it is not convenient to do this at once, the throughput of the purifier should be increased in the hope that the rate of extraction of the water will be equal to the rate at which it is leaking into the oil system. If the water is fresh, the leak will probably be from the piston-cooling system, and if it is salt, from the oil cooler.

The important point in connection with oil in continuous circulation is that the oil in the drain tank should be as clean as possible, rather than that the purified oil returned to the circulating system should contain the least possible quantity of impurities. To achieve the latter condition only a very small proportion of the oil can be treated in a given time, because the higher the degree of purification, the lower the throughput, and vice versa. The throughput of the purifier should therefore be regulated so that the first condition is obtained.

The correct throughput of a purifier is that which results in the rate of purification being equal to the rate of contamination. To determine this, operate the purifier with a throughput equal to half the rated capacity of the machine for twelve hours and weigh the solid matter collected in the bowl. The throughput should then be reduced to quarter capacity for twelve hours, and then after cleaning, the bowl operated at three-quarters capacity for a similar period. If the quantity of solid matter removed is greater than at

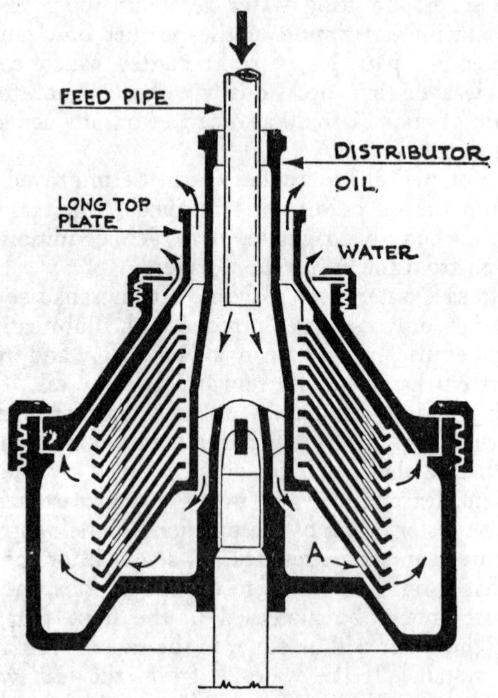

Fig. 188—Centrifugal purifier bowl

the original throughput, it indicates that the new throughput is the most suitable, but if the quantity of solid matter extracted is less, it means that the new throughput results in a greater quantity of solid matter remaining in the circulating oil. By altering the throughput a few times and checking the quantity of solid matter removed, the throughput which gives the cleanest oil in the system can be found.

There are two distinct types of centrifugal purifier. One has a long and relatively small-diameter tubular bowl, and the other a short and relatively large-diameter bowl. Of the two types the latter is more extensively used and, as will be seen from Figs. 188 and 189, the bowl contains a number of conical plates. The centrifugal force acting at the outer edge of the plates, when the bowl is revolving at about 6,000 r.p.m., is about 10,000 times greater than gravity—

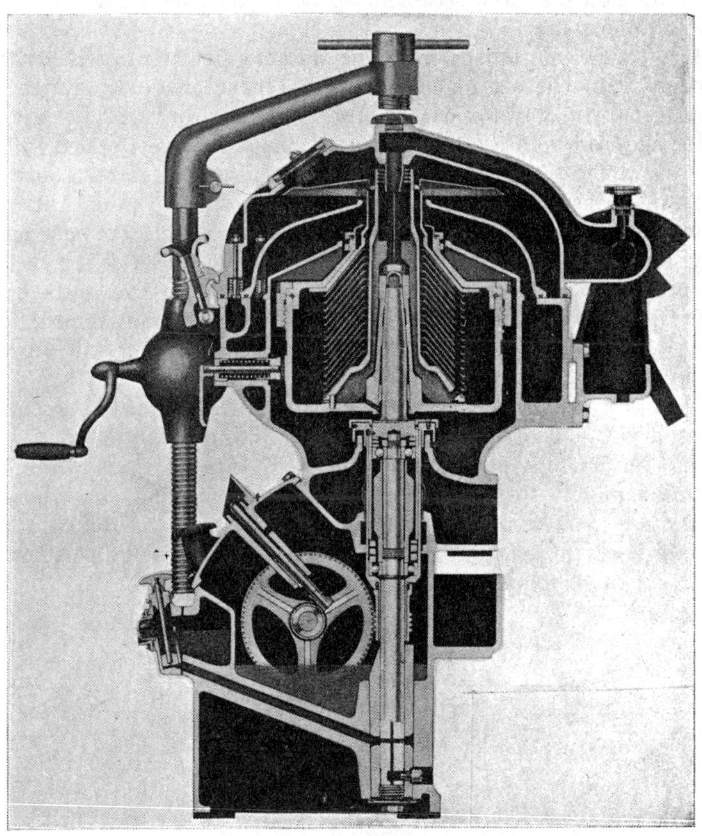

Fig. 189—Centrifugal purifier in section (De Laval)

the larger the diameter of the bowl or the higher the speed, the greater the centrifugal force. The positioning of the conical plates in the manner shown divides up the oil space in the bowl into a number of thin layers of oil about 1 mm thick, in which separation from the oil of the heavier solid particles and water takes place.

The solid particles, and water if present, are thrown off the conical plates into the confines of the bowl, where those particles accumulate which are too heavy to be carried out of the bowl with the separated water. As separation takes place mainly between the conical plates, the high separating efficiency of this type of bowl is maintained until the sediment space beyond the plates is almost full of solid matter.

As oil must not escape from the water outlet of the purifier, the passage from the sediment space must be sealed with water. A small quantity of water is therefore run in after the bowl attains full speed and before oil is admitted. With the bowl sealed in this way any water entering the bowl with the oil will be thrown outward and cause the sediment space to overflow, but the initial quantity of water will remain. The quantity of water in the sediment space may be reduced by evaporation, but the machine will function correctly so long as the vertical line of contact between the oil and water does not extend to the water passage formed between the long top plate and the bowl cover. Should this occur, oil will be seen leaving the water outlet.

Makers of centrifugal separators and other oil-purifying equipment always provide comprehensive working instructions, which should be carefully studied and followed. The foregoing notes are intended merely to supplement the makers' instructions, which to reproduce in a work of this kind would require too much space. Should such information not be on board, the makers will readily supply it upon request.

CHAPTER 22

Bearing adjustment and crankcase explosions

The fact that a bearing has a relatively large bearing surface for the load carried and is copiously supplied with a high-grade oil is no guarantee that it will operate satisfactorily. The adjustment of the bearing and the means adopted to lead the oil to that part of the bearing where it is needed, i.e. the most heavily loaded part, are of equal importance. When bearings operate at too high a temperature or wear excessively, the grade of oil or the quality of the whitemetal used is sometimes held responsible, whereas the cause is incorrect adjustment of the bearing, by which is meant not so much the provision of the correct diametrical clearance, but the shaping of the bearing surface in a way which will enable an oil film to be formed between the surfaces of the bearing and the journal rotating or oscillating in it.

A shaft revolving in a bearing will carry a far greater load per unit area than a flat rubbing surface. This is due to the rotary motion of the shaft causing it to take up a slightly eccentric position in the bearing which, as pointed out in the preceding chapter, greatly facilitates the formation of the oil film—the oil which enters the wedge-shaped clearance being drawn in and carried round with the shaft. A typical example of the immense value of this drawing-in process is to be found in a comparison of the two forms of thrust bearings employed in marine installations. In the now obsolete multi-collar type, which have rigid flat surfaces running in an oil bath, the maximum bearing pressure allowed when designing such parts is 50 lb/sq.in., and the results obtained could not be called satisfactory. In the case of the Michell thrust bearing described in the next chapter, which employs the drawing-in process of lubrication produced by the tilting action of the flat surfaces, the bearing pressure allowed is 300 lb/sq.in., and provided the bath is kept charged with suitable oil such bearings operate for years without any measurable wear taking place.

The early diesel engines were mostly of the two-stroke single-acting open-fronted type and bearings were lubricated on the drip system. Considerable trouble was experienced in those engines, due not so much to the bearings themselves, as to the method of leading the oil to the bearings. For instance, it was quite a common practice with crankpin bearings to lead the oil from an oil-box attached to the upper end of the connecting rod to the centre of the top half, and from the hole drilled through the crown to cut numerous wide oil grooves in the most heavily loaded part. In an engine working on the double-acting principle, where the load on the crankpin and crosshead bearings is reversed every revolution, thereby giving the oil a chance to escape from the grooves, such a practice is less objectionable, even though the bearing surface is reduced at a most vital part. These grooves did not serve the purpose intended in two-stroke single-acting engines however, because, when fitting, the bearings were always carefully bedded to the crankpin in accordance with good practice, thus forming a fluid-tight joint which prevented the oil from leaving the grooves and entering between the contact surfaces.

The following, which occurred in one of these early motorships, is a good example of the uselessness of sharp-edged oil grooves cut in the heavily loaded part of crankshaft bearings. From an oil-box situated well above the level of the cylinder head, pipes conveyed the oil to the centre of the bottom half of each crankshaft bearing, the most heavily loaded part of these particular bearings. From the oil hole in the bearing a wide oil groove running in a fore-and-aft direction was cut in the whitemetal with the object of distributing the oil over the whole of the rubbing surfaces.

What actually took place was the reverse to what was intended; not only was the oil unable to enter the bearing through a fluid-tight joint formed by the journal and bearing, but oil was actually pumped back to the oil-box, causing it to overflow. The cause of this was that owing to the failure of the arrangement the bearings began to warm up, and to prevent a further rise in temperature oil was fed into the bearings by hand through openings in the bearing caps. The oil introduced at this point found its way to the side clearance between the journal and the bearing, and was carried round by the shaft until it reached the sharp-edged oil grooves cut in the bottom of the bearings. These grooves, acting as scrapers, collected the surplus oil, and the pumping action of the shaft caused it to be discharged to the oil-box, which in consequence overflowed.

Such methods of feeding oil to bearings may serve the purpose in the case of crosshead and crankpin bearings of four-stroke single-acting, or double-acting engines of either type, where the load on the bearings is reversed, but in two-stroke single-acting engines, where the pressure is always in a downward direction, it is necessary to make other provision to assist the lubricating oil to enter between the contact surfaces. In four-stroke engines of either single- or double-acting type, or two-stroke double-acting the bearings of which are copiously supplied with oil, oil grooves in any shape or form cut into the crown of the bearings have been found to be quite unnecessary.

Even though there are many diesel engines giving the desired good results without a single oil groove in any of the principal bearings, the old practice of cutting oil grooves in all directions is still greatly overdone. In some cases they are, of course, advisable, or may even be necessary, but when this is so the loaded area of the bearing should always be avoided. The object of an oil groove should be merely to lead the oil to the edge of the loaded area so that it may be drawn into this area by the wedge-shaped formation of the surfaces. When the loaded area cannot be avoided, the grooves should be made narrow, in order to reduce the effective bearing surface as little as possible, and the following edge of the groove should be well rounded to form a wedge-shaped space and allow the oil to leave the groove and enter between the loaded surfaces. The grooves should not, of course, approach too near the ends of the bearing, and afford an easy outlet for the oil. They should be cut fairly deep and with a tool that is well rounded, since grooves of triangular cross-section tend to cause the whitemetal to crack. Furthermore, when the direction of an oil groove must change it should change very gradually, as sharp turns may, besides stopping the oil from flowing freely along the groove, cause dirt to accumulate and eventually stop the flow.

When fitting bearings, the two halves, after being bedded to the journal, should be well scraped at both sides, beginning at the joint and decreasing gradually and evenly the amount of metal removed until a point about 30° from the joint is reached, thus forming the wedge-shaped clearance which has proved so essential for the efficient lubrication of bearings of this type. This side clearance does not reduce the effective bearing surface to any material extent no matter what the size of the bearing may be, so that no harm is done. The extent mentioned, and shown in Fig. 190, should be the minimum if a finely pointed clearance is to be produced. The width of the clearance at the joint should be $\frac{1}{1000}$-inch per inch diameter of the journal, and if the space created is to be of the desired shape it must extend circumferentially, with gradually decreasing width, for at least 30°. Oil-retaining strips must, of course, be left at each end of this clearance space, otherwise leakage of oil from the bearing will occur. If these strips, which should make light contact with the journal, are about 0·5 inch wide, no trouble will be experienced should the bearing tend to close in upon attaining its normal working temperature.

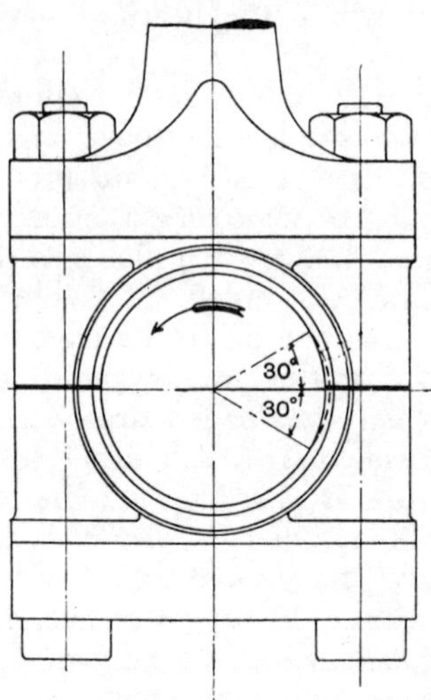

Fig. 190—Crankpin bearing, showing extent of wedge-shaped clearance at sides

The foregoing suggestions apply to engines lubricated on the so-called forced system as well. The idea of forced lubrication is not to force the oil between the rubbing surfaces, but only to provide a good and steady supply. Such bearings operate satisfactorily, not because lubricating oil under a pressure of about 20 lb/sq.in. is forced between surfaces loaded to from 600 to, in some cases, as much as 2,000 lb/sq.in., but simply because a plentiful supply of oil is delivered to the wedge-shaped clearances of the bearings, when it is drawn in and carried round by the revolving journals.

The pressure carried on the bearing-oil system should, of course, be sufficient to preclude any possibility of an ample supply of oil not reaching the crosshead bearings. In most cases a pressure of 30 lb/sq.in. will meet the case. Excessive pressures are unnecessary and, besides giving the pump more work to do they tend to atomise the oil as it escapes from the small openings at the ends of the bearings, thus creating an undue amount of oil mist in the crankcases.

Atomised oil in the heat of engine crankcases is more liable to oxidise. It will thus be seen that excessively high bearing-oil pressures are really harmful and should not, therefore, be employed.

The universal adoption of the enclosed design of crankcase for all types of marine diesel engines has produced a similarity in the

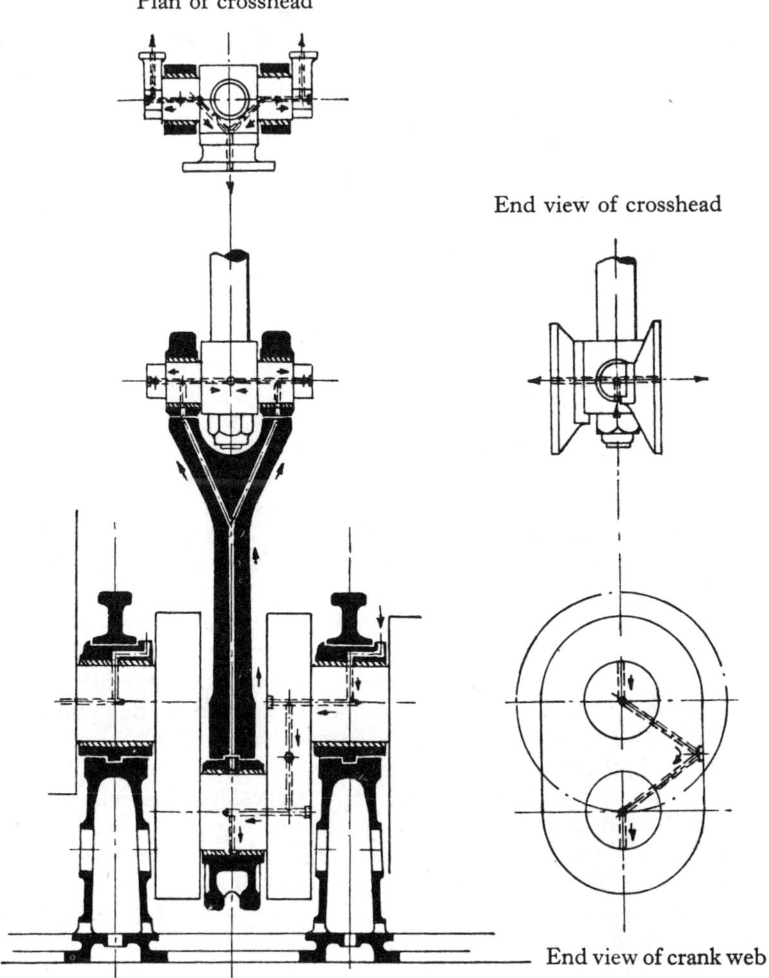

Fig. 191—Method of feeding lubricating oil to principal bearings

method of lubricating the principal bearings, such as crankshaft, crankpin, crosshead bearings and crosshead guides. This method consists of a main supply pipe extending the entire length of the engine, with a branch to each crankshaft bearing-cap, from which bearing the bulk of the oil passes to the crankpin bearing, and then to the crosshead bearings and guide shoes through holes bored in the crank, connecting rod and crossheads, as shown clearly in Fig. 191. The oil escapes out of the ends of the bearings, falls into the crank-pit, then the drain tank, and after passing through strainers and coolers is again delivered to the bearings.

In order to allow the lubricating oil to pass on from one bearing to another, the common practice is to provide an annular groove cut in the whitemetal and extending right round the bearing surface. This groove registers with the radial hole in the crankshaft, crankpin or crosshead journal as the case may be, and ensures a constant flow of oil to all bearing surfaces. As the oil reaches the various bearings, a little of it enters the wedge-shaped clearances provided at the sides of all properly adjusted bearings and is drawn in between the rubbing surfaces. Some of the oil also escapes from the ends of the bearings, so that a quantity of oil greatly in excess of the amount actually required to lubricate the bearings efficiently must be circulated.

At one time it was the practice, and still is to a small extent, to cut the annular groove in the principal bearings parallel to the ends of the bearings. This practice results in a ridge being formed on the pins and journals. These ridges develop very slowly, and are not detrimental from an operating point of view, but they must, nevertheless, be filed off when they stand proud of the bearing surface by more than $\frac{6}{1000}$-inch, otherwise there will be difficulty in adjusting the bearing clearances correctly. Ridges on the crosshead and crankpins can be removed without much trouble, but it is a very long and difficult job to remove ridges from the crankshaft journals, and usually delays other work in hand which necessitates the turning of the crankshaft.

To prevent the formation of these ridges, the annular groove should be cut at an angle and not parallel with the ends of the bearing. To ensure the oil which leaves the radial hole in, say, a crankshaft journal, flowing uninterruptedly into the groove when it is cut askew as suggested, it would be necessary either to elongate the end of the hole in the journal or make the groove so wide that the hole, as it revolves, keeps within range of the groove. This, however, is quite unnecessary judging by the results obtained where no attempt is made to ensure an uninterrupted flow of oil.

Fig. 192 shows crankshaft bearings to be found in some B. & W. type engines. The usual annular groove in the middle of the bearing is omitted, the lubricating oil supplied to the spaces formed above and below the inner bearing shell reaching the rubbing surfaces through the four holes shown. Fairly wide longitudinal grooves, shown in the cross-sectional view, are provided at each side of the

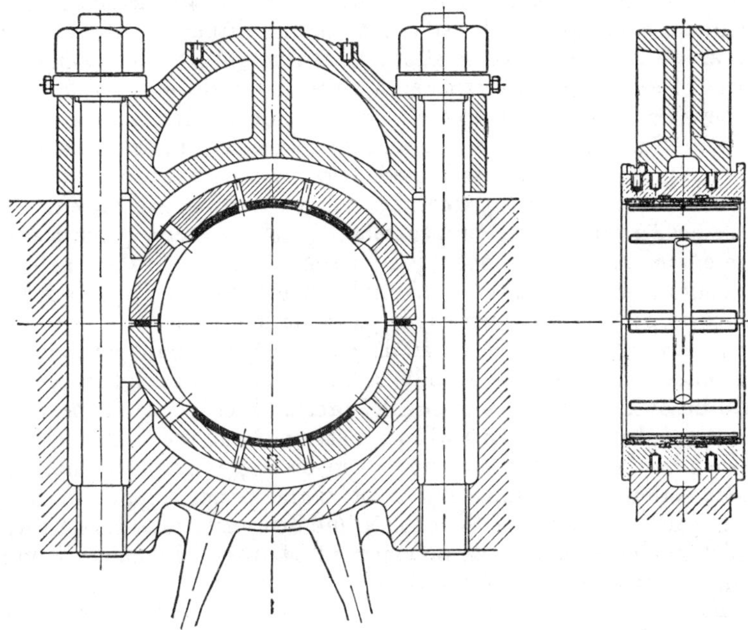

Fig. 192—An unusual type of crankshaft bearing developed by Burmeister and Wain

loaded area. These grooves are given a wedge form in order to assist some of the oil at the sides of the bearing to enter between the rubbing surfaces. The oil enters the crankshaft journal through two radial holes arranged at such an angle to each other that one hole is always in communication with one of the spaces at the top and bottom of the bearing, consequently there is an uninterrupted flow of oil to the crankpin bearing, which is of a similar form.

Because an engine has forced lubrication for the bearings, and metallic knocks caused by excessive working clearances are not so pronounced, it must not be thought that proper adjustment of the clearances is not so necessary. On the contrary, it is very necessary, since, although the knocks are partly deadened by the presence of abundant oil between the surfaces, yet the adverse effect upon the parts concerned, such as the oil films, connecting-bolts, etc. is much the same.

Particular attention should also be given to the tightening and locking of all bearing-nuts, but more especially the crankpin bearing-nuts. Slackening back a nut, no matter how small the amount, to facilitate the entry of the split pin, or the fitting of pieces of tin under a nut, should not be allowed. If through repeated re-adjustment of the bearing clearance, a nut goes beyond the split-pin hole, a new hole should be drilled. Special care should also be taken when refitting a bearing to see that the feather key in each bolt-head properly enters the recess provided for it, otherwise if the feather key should be partly sheared, the sheared portion will prevent the bolt-head from making proper contact with the bearing until after the engine has been in operation for some time, when the bolt will, of course, be slack. Slack crankpin bearing-bolts must be avoided at all costs, as the consequences are particularly serious.

When only one bolt of an enclosed engine crankpin bearing becomes slack it cannot readily be detected, so that the other bolt will be overstressed and eventually break. The inertia of the loose bottom half of the bearing will then at once bend the slack and only remaining bolt, and if the engine can be stopped in time, nothing more serious may result. But if the engine is not stopped in time, well, then, a badly broken bedplate and bent piston and connecting-rods are the least that can be expected. It would be better if both bolts became slack at the same time, as then neither of the bolts would be excessively stressed before the slack bolts made their presence known. It is generally one bolt which becomes slack, however, and the properly hardened-up bolt is immediately over-stressed and eventually breaks, creating the entirely wrong impression that this bolt, and not the bent bolt, was the originator of the trouble.

Serious damage caused by slack bearing-bolts is not altogether a rare occurrence, so that after each voyage it is wise to open the crankcase doors and examine the split pins and other locking devices. The main thing, however, is to see that the nuts are properly tightened, as split pins or pinching screws are of little use in retaining a slack nut, their purpose being to prevent a tight nut from becoming slack. This matter will be referred to again later.

The working clearances to be given to the principal bearings of a diesel engine vary as in other machinery, and it is only after actual running experience with any particular engine that the minimum clearances permissible can be determined. Since bearings are usually inaccessible when the engine is working, and overheated bearings cannot readily be detected, it is advisable to allow liberal clearance until experience has been gained. A safe rule is to allow at least one-thousandth of an inch per inch diameter of the bearing being adjusted.

Providing a bearing does not knock and subject the whitemetal and the bolts to undue shock, there is no real objection to bearings having clearances greater than those given below, although, as is well known, the clearance of a loosely adjusted bearing will increase much more rapidly than if finely adjusted. Moreover, the greater the clearance the more likely are the bearing-bolts to become slack, and a larger quantity of oil will require to be circulated owing to greater leakage from the ends of the bearings.

The usual diametrical working clearances given to the principal bearings of a marine engine of any type having a crankshaft of about 12 inches diameter are as follows:—

Crankshaft bearings	0·010 in. to 0·012 in.
Crankpin bearings	0·008 " " 0·010 "
Crosshead bearings	0·006 " " 0·008 "

When re-adjusting the working clearance of a bearing, it is customary to compress pieces of lead wire between the rubbing surfaces. Such a practice is convenient and gives an accurate indication of the amount of clearance between the surfaces, provided the clearances aimed at are not too small and the lead wire compressed to beyond its limit of usefulness. A piece of $\frac{1}{32}$-inch diameter lead wire, which is the size mostly used, may be relied upon to register accurately if compressed to not less than one-third of its diameter.

The following simple test carried out by the author will prove the foregoing statement. One crosshead bearing of a large marine engine was carefully re-adjusted until three pieces of $\frac{1}{32}$-inch diameter lead wire were compressed to 0·006 inch. After the pieces of lead wire had been removed and the surfaces well lubricated, the securing nuts were tightened to the position occupied when the pieces of lead wire were in place. The upper end of the connecting-rod was of the usual fork type, with double bearings, the outer ends of which were accessible for gauging. In neither of the bearings was it possible to enter a 0·002-inch thick gauge for any distance, nor was it possible to swing the connecting-rod with the crankpin bearing disconnected, because the crosshead bearings were gripping the crosshead pins so tightly.

The crosshead bearing-nuts were then slackened back until it was possible for one man to swing the connecting-rod, when it was found that a 0·003-inch gauge would enter between the underside of the crosshead pins and the bottom half of the bearings. At this adjustment, the nuts were marked, and the top half of the bearings lifted. Three new pieces of lead wire were then placed in position between the surfaces and the nuts put down to the marks last made. When these pieces of lead wire were removed, they were found to measure from 0·0075 inch as a maximum to 0·0068 as a minimum, so that it would appear that for clearances less than 0·008 inch $\frac{1}{32}$-inch diameter lead wire is not very reliable. Of course, the degree of reliability will depend to a certain extent upon the quality of the lead wire and, to a smaller extent, upon the hardness of the white-metal with which the bearing shells are filled, but in any case it is not wise to rely entirely upon lead wire when such fine clearances are required.

All crosshead and crankpin bearings have, and ought to have, a small amount of end clearance, so that after adjustment of either it is wise to carry out the common practice of trying to move the bearing end-wise along the journal by means of a crow-bar. In this way insufficient clearance will be indicated. In the case of crosshead bearings, it is generally possible to check the clearance by direct gauging, but it is always advisable to take leads off these bearings to make sure that the bearings are not binding on the sides of the crosshead pins.

Owing to the oscillating motion of crosshead bearings, the crosshead pins do not wear evenly, so that due allowance for this uneven wear must be made when re-adjusting the working clearances. The crosshead pins wear mostly on the bottom, and on the top also in the case of double-acting engines. The wear takes place very gradually, but when it is such that it interferes with the proper adjustment of the working clearances, it is necessary to scrape away some of the metal at the sides of the bearing. After about ten years' service it will be necessary to true up the crosshead pins and re-metal the bearings. In order to reduce the inconvenience caused by this uneven wear, crossheads should be made of specially tough steel. The usual practice is to make them of 38–42 ton steel having an elongation of 18 per cent.

The crankpins of four-stroke engines wear but little, and fairly evenly all round, and not, as might be expected, only on the part subjected to the compression and working pressures. As a matter of fact, it is sometimes found that the greatest wear has taken place on the underside of the crankpin, assuming the crank to be on top dead centre. The following theory may explain this.

As the crank rises on the compression stroke the pressure on the crankpin increases steadily, and on the working stroke the pressure decreases in a similar manner. The oil film on this part of the crankpin is, therefore, subjected to a gradually increasing pressure, under which condition it is most likely to serve the purpose for which it is intended, and minimum wear of the rubbing surfaces will result. Moreover, as the pressure on the crankpin at this part of the cycle is increased and then reduced at a uniform rate, no shock results.

At the end of the exhaust stroke and the beginning of the air-inlet stroke, however, the forces due to the inertia of the reciprocating masses, which may amount to as much as 50 per cent of the combustion load, are most active, and the sudden reversal of pressure at the end of the exhaust stroke will have the effect of thinning the oil film between the underside of the pin and the bottom half of the bearing, the effect being greater the larger the amount of slackness in the bearing. As this form of crankpin wear takes place only when the bearings have greater clearance than is necessary, it may be the hammering action on the oil film that is mainly responsible for the wear.

The wear in the crosshead and crankpin bearings of two-stroke engines occurs mostly on the underside of the former, and on the upper surface of the latter when the crank is on top dead centre. A great deal of trouble was at one time experienced with the crosshead bearings of two-stroke engines owing to the pressure being always in a downward direction, but with the improved quality of white-metal, and provided good tough steel is used for the crossheads, the wear is not excessive. In some Sulzer engines the oil is delivered to the crosshead bearings at a pressure of about 300 lb/sq.in. by means of a separate pump, it being assumed that this pressure is sufficient to force the oil between the underside of the crosshead pins and the bottom halves of the bearings when the crank is about the bottom dead centre position. One successful arrangement on an early diesel engine which came under the author's charge employed small plunger pumps attached to each crosshead, the plunger being attached to the connecting-rod in such a way that the angular movement of this part caused oil taken from the main supply passing up the connecting-rod to be forced between the rubbing surfaces as the crank passed over the bottom dead centre.

Although the wear takes place very gradually, each time a crosshead or crankpin bearing is opened up, the pins should be gauged for being true in an axial as well as a circumferential direction. If uneven wear has taken place, the correct position for the crank when taking leads is top dead centre, but, before finally closing-up, the crank should be rotated about 90° and the bearing tested by means of a crow-bar to make sure that it is free when in this position. At this position the larger diameter of an unevenly worn pin will, in most cases, be in line with the least worn part of the bearing.

When crankpins and crosshead pins have to be trued up, and the work cannot be done in a lathe, they will have to be filed and finally lapped. The implement for the latter part of the operation usually takes the form of a hard wooden block bored to the diameter of the pin to be trued up, and halved with clearance at the joint to allow its being kept up to the surface of the pin as the high places are ground away. The lap is firmly held between levers capable of being drawn together as the work proceeds, in order to exert a light pressure on the pin being ground, and is given a semi-rotary motion as it is worked around the pin. The surface of the lap should be given a fairly thick layer of fine carborundum powder worked into a paste with lubricating oil before being bolted around the pin. The securing bolts should first of all be made so tight that it is just possible to move the lap by means of a long lever, and the lap rotated backwards and forwards a very small amount until some of the grinding powder has become firmly embedded in the wood. In this way the wooden block becomes a very effective grinding tool.

In the case of crankshaft and crankpin bearings it is very rarely that the whitemetal is found cracked, but the same cannot be said of crosshead bearings of either two- or four-stroke engines. Some of the trouble in crosshead bearings is due to the crosshead pins being too small in diameter and flexing when subjected to the maximum load. The result of this slight bending upwards of the crosshead pins every revolution is that the inner half of the bearings becomes overloaded, and the whitemetal at this part becomes brittle. Cracking of the whitemetal then occurs, and although the metal will last a long time in a cracked condition it will eventually become detached from the shell, no matter how well and carefully the bearing has been lined, and will break up into small pieces. When this occurs the verdict generally is that the whitemetal was not adhering properly to the shell in the first place, but this is not always the case. The metal breaks away from the shell because the lubricating oil is forced into the cracks at great pressure and eventually finds its way between the metal and the shell. The foregoing will explain why it is that, in nearly every case, the inner surfaces only of crosshead bearings are affected.

Apart from re-adjusting the working clearances and checking the wear-down of the crankshaft occasionally, the crankshaft bearings require no attention. The amount that these bearings wear depends mainly upon the side clearance so necessary to allow the lubricating oil to be drawn into the most heavily loaded part of the bearing, provided, of course, that the oil is of good quality and free from impurities. As wear in these bearings affects the alignment of the crankshaft, everything possible must be done to prevent wear. If, therefore, a 0·003-inch gauge cannot be inserted for three inches or so down each side, the bottom half should be removed and the whitemetal scraped well back.

Crankshaft bearing-bolts very rarely break, but when they do the cause is always due to the top half of the bearing not being firmly held. The movement may be so small as to be unnoticeable, and the nuts may appear to be quite tight, but it may safely be assumed that movement is responsible for the failure. The movement may be caused by the crankshaft being slightly out of line, in which case the remedy is obvious.

Overhauling crankpin bearings

For the benefit of those not accustomed to overhauling such large and heavy bearings as are found on marine engines, a brief description of the procedure generally adopted may be included at this stage, taking for example the most difficult, namely, the crankpin bearing.

In many engines the crosshead shoe works in slipper guides with a total working clearance of about 0·010 inch. Owing to the absence of the astern shoe, special means are necessary for quick and easy lowering of the bearing into the crank-pit or on to the engine-room platform. The means to effect this are usually provided, but if the work is to be done in the shortest time, it is necessary for the lifting tackle employed to be perfectly in line with the crankpin bearing-bolts. As these bolts are, and should be, a good fit in the bearing, and if the lifting tackle is not properly aligned, time and labour will be wasted. A 2-in. square saddle-bar made to fit snugly over the fork end of the connecting-rod will be found to meet requirements.

After erecting the lowering gear, note the exact position of the bearing-bolt nuts and begin slackening them with a good-fitting spanner and a sufficiently heavy hammer. Light tools for this work are a waste of time and energy. When the nuts are slack, screw eye-bolts, which must be small enough to pass through the bolt holes, into the tapped holes provided in the end of each bolt. Then take the weight of the bottom half of the bearing with the lifting tackle, unscrew the nuts and lower the bottom half into the crank-pit, after carefully removing the shims, which should be tied together in their respective groups. It will then be necessary to lift the bottom half of the bearing out of the engine if it requires attention.

To remove the top half of the bearing, or merely to examine the bearing surface, it is necessary to suspend the piston, piston rod, connecting-rod, etc. by bolting a heavy bar across the ahead guide-bar, when the crank is on top centre, and turn the crankshaft very carefully until the crankpin is well clear of the top half of the bearing, which will be attached to the foot of the connecting-rod by two small bolts at opposite corners. The rubbing surface can then be cleaned and examined. If the bearing requires to be removed in order to scrape the surfaces, the crankshaft should be turned back to engage the bearing, the two tap-bolts previously referred to removed, and the crank turned in the direction of the crankcase door, when the bearing can be lifted on to the engine-room platform.

If the bearing surfaces are found to be extending toward the joint, the whitemetal will require to be scraped away as recommended earlier in this chapter. Then carefully gauge the crankpin for being true, and examine every part of it and the crank-webs for fractures. Crankpin fractures are rare, but when they do occur they are usually found at the junction of the crankpin and the webs, and extend in a circumferential direction. Any mark that looks like a crack should be filed to see if the mark has any depth. Also observe if the connecting-rod is in good alignment. In the case of the crank nearest the thrust block, the connecting-rod should be approximately central between the webs, but as crankshafts expand forward from the thrust block when heated up to the working temperature, the corresponding position of the other connecting-rods varies according to their position relative to the thrust block. In a shaft 40-feet long the expansion is about 6 mm.

Assuming now everything to be in order and the bearings thoroughly cleaned, oiled and refitted, tighten up the bearing bolt-nuts by spanner, leaving out the shims from between the two halves for the time being. Then carefully gauge the opening, add one and a half times the working clearance to be allowed, and select sufficient shims to give this measurement. This done, lower the bottom half of the bearing for a distance of about a foot and place the shims, which must, of course, be quite clean, in position. The thin shims, if any, should be placed underneath the thick ones, and the ends of the dowel pins should be at least 2 mm below the surface of the thick shim. The shims should fit close to, but not touch, the crankpin in order to prevent undue leakage of lubricating oil.

Four pieces of $\frac{1}{32}$-inch diameter lead wire, equal in length to rather less than half the circumference of the crankpin, should then be placed circumferentially in the bearing an equal distance apart. When employing such small-diameter lead wire it is advisable to anchor the wire by means of white lead. Now draw the bottom half of the bearing into position and drive the nuts hard up, care being taken to see that the contact surfaces of the two halves of the bearing and bolt-heads are quite clean, and that the feather keys in the bolts enter squarely in their recesses. After driving the nuts hard up, mark their position and slacken them away. Then, after lowering the bottom half of the bearing, remove and gauge the compressed pieces of lead wire, and, if compressed the desired amount, thoroughly clean the working surface and hammer up the nuts to the marks last made. The bearing should then be tested for being free endwise by means of a crow-bar.

The last, but by no means the least important, part of the operation is to lock the nuts carefully, making sure that the locking screws are right up to their work and not binding at the end of the threaded portion, a point which, when overlooked, has been the cause of more accidents than one. Locking screws should be case-hardened, and the end which bears against the nut cupped rather than pointed, the screw in turn being locked by a check-nut. Should the head of a locking screw be damaged by the use of improperly fitting spanners, so that it can be tightened only with difficulty, it should not be permitted to remain in service. A common fault among engine-builders is to make the locking screws dead hard. It is rather serious because such screws usually break off flush with the foot of the connecting-rod while the engine is operating, and it is a very difficult matter to remove the part left in. Being hardened, the screw cannot be drilled out in the ordinary way, and it is necessary to hammer back the nut until it has cleared the end of the screw, and then drill and tap a new hole. Where a welding plant is available, enough metal can sometimes be built up on the end of the screw to enable a wrench to be applied to unscrew the part of the screw left in.

Before finally closing up the crankcases, very careful search must be made to ensure that no cleaning rags or tools have been overlooked, and that the bar for hanging up the piston and rods has been removed. The use of cotton waste inside crankcases should be avoided and rags only used. The objection to cotton waste is that surfaces rubbed by it, particularly rough cast iron, are left covered by imperceptible fibrous matter which is washed off by the lubricating oil thrown from the revolving cranks, and accumulates, in which form it may cause trouble.

Crankpin bearing-bolts

Breaking of crankpin bearing-bolts, whilst most unusual, has in the past been one of the most frequently recurring accidents and, in view of the very extensive damage which always results, this important detail requires the particular attention of the operating engineer.

Sometimes these bolts break owing to faulty design, but more often the cause is due to their being overstressed, or having been permitted to remain in service too long and become fatigued. It is a wise plan to renew these bolts after 10 years' service in the case of four-stroke engines, since by that time the metal will be bound to have undergone a change. When faulty design is the cause of the failure, it is generally found that the bolts are renewals, and have not been made by the builders of the engine. This part in particular should always be supplied by the engine-builder whenever possible.

Owing to the great length of these bolts, and for another reason which will be given later, the diameter of the shank is reduced in places to rather less than that at the bottom of the thread, so that they can be more easily fitted, and made a good fit at the points where a good fit is necessary. Usually the bolt is a sliding fit at

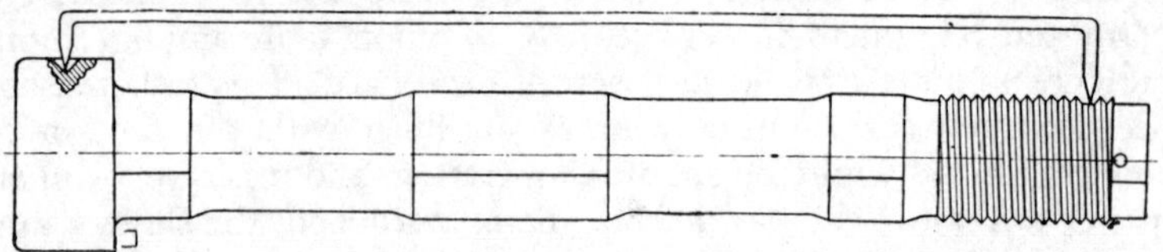

Fig. 193—Bearing bolt, with trammel for checking stretch

three places only, as shown in Fig. 193, namely, in way of the joining surfaces of the two halves of the bearing, and at each end. It is particularly necessary that these bolts should fit snugly in the holes at the points where two parts join, otherwise the bolt will move slightly while the engine is operating and wear of the bolt and enlargement of the hole will take place. When this occurs there is more likelihood of the bolt-nuts easing off.

Reducing the cross-sectional area of the shank in places also ensures that the stretching of the bolt when it occurs shall not take place wholly in the few disengaged threads below the nut, which would have the effect of further weakening the bolt at its weakest point. It is most important that the change in cross-section should be gradual, since bolts subjected to intermittent stresses, as these are, will first break at an abrupt change of section. This applies also to the point where the head joins the shank. The change at this point must, of necessity, be comparatively abrupt, but the fillet should always be of the greatest practicable radius.

Engine-builders are more or less agreed upon the foregoing, but quite a little variation is to be found at the point where the thread finishes, or where the thread joins the plain part, and here it is that bolts mostly break. In some cases the thread finishes on the larger diameter, while others run out on to a reduced part of the shank. Also, but much less frequently, bolts are found with a groove cut at the finish of the thread, and the important common practice of reducing the diameter gradually not attempted. To run the thread out on to a reduced part of the shank, as shown in Fig. 193, is recommended.

Another point occasionally overlooked is that the threaded portion of the bolts should extend sufficiently to allow for repeated letting together of the two halves of the bearing—even though under normal conditions the wear will be negligible, no one knows if normal conditions will prevail for 10 years—to avoid the possibility of the nut binding at the finish of the thread, and the necessity of fitting washers under the nuts, a highly undesirable practice. Another important point is in connection with the feather key always provided at the head end of the bolt to prevent the bolt from rotating when tightening and slackening the nut. The hole into which the key is fitted should never be drilled into the shank, as this has the effect of greatly weakening the bolt at a vital part. The same result without such an ill-effect is obtained by drilling into the head, as shown in Fig. 193, which is usual, but not always the case. A mistake sometimes made, however, is to drill the hole too near the shank. The hole should not penetrate the radius between the shank and the bolt-head. The best method of all is to fit a dowel pin in the face of the bearing against which the bolt-head lands and cut a corresponding groove in the side of the bolt-head.

Shock resulting in fatigue in four-stroke engine crankpin and crosshead bearing-bolts may be caused by the bearings being allowed to operate with too much clearance, the shock occurring at the end of the exhaust stroke. These bolts can also be seriously overloaded when tightening up the nuts, due to lack of judgment. The apparently simple operation of hardening up these nuts requires something more than mere brute force. It is impossible to state here what force should be applied to guard against the nuts becoming slack, but it requires only a brief study of the pitch of the thread, type of spanner, weight of hammer and strength of the man wielding the hammer, etc., to enable an experienced engineer to harden up without putting undue stress in the bolt while, at the same time, eliminating the possibility of the nuts slackening back whilst the engine is working.

When the average bolt is tightened up sufficiently to ensure that the parts are in good contact, and the nut will not slacken back, the tensile stress in the bolt is in the neighbourhood of 15,000 lb/sq.in., which is equivalent to a load of over 38 tons on a 2·5-inch diameter bolt, and the stretch may be as much as 0·010 inch, depending upon its length and the properties of the material. If undue flogging is applied after the nuts may rightly be called hard-up, it requires little effort to increase the tension by another 5,000 lb/sq.in., the only effect of which is to stretch the bolt still further, since if the various parts are already in solid contact, the only other explanation of an advance by the nut is that the bearing has been compressed or the threads of the bolt and nut strained.

It sometimes happens that a nut is found slack, and those responsible for the safe working of the machinery institute the practice of periodically opening the crankcases to test the nuts. Such a practice is to be recommended, but instead of, as is usual, testing by driving up the nuts, the spanner should be given a couple of good blows in the reverse direction. A certain type of human nature sometimes met with is prone to flog at a nut until no further advance is possible, irrespective of whether the hammer in use weighs 7 or 28 lb.

Unnecessary flogging not only causes undue tensile stress, but produces torsional stresses as well, which may increase the total initial stress in the bolt by as much as 20 per cent. Upon reflection, it will be apparent that the extent of this undesirable torsional stress depends upon the pitch of the threads; the coarser the thread the greater the torsional stress, and the finer the thread the greater the tensile stress for the same force applied when tightening up.

The threads, therefore, particularly coarse threads, should be well lubricated, in order to reduce the torsional stress set up as much as possible. From this it will be seen that both forms of threads have their disadvantages, but of the two, providing it is realised that there is nothing to be gained and much to be lost by injudiciously flogging at nuts, the finer form is to be preferred.

Much of the trouble arises from forcing the nuts, and consequently stressing the material unduly, to bring a slot in the castellated nut, when such are used, in line with the split-pin hole in the bolt,

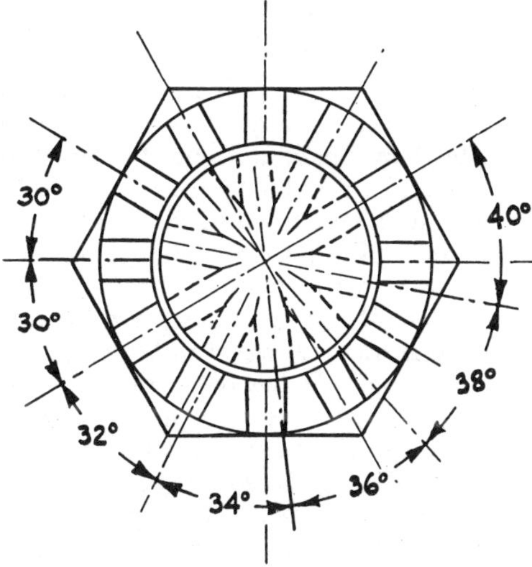

Fig. 194—Plan of bearing bolt nut showing how fitting of split pin may be facilitated

fitting the pin being the chief consideration, to avoid the trouble of filing a little off the face of the nut. To assist in this direction, as many split-pin holes as the bolt end will conveniently accommodate might be drilled in the same plane as the existing hole. If the angles between the holes are made as shown in Fig. 194, a slot will coincide with one or other of the holes thirty times in one revolution of the nut, as against six times when a single hole is provided. The centre line of each split-pin hole should be clearly marked on the end of the bolt, as a help to quickly finding the hole which coincides with a groove in the nut. The bolt in the sketch is $2\frac{1}{4}$ inches in diameter, slots in the nut are $\frac{3}{8}$-inch wide, and split-pin holes are $\frac{5}{16}$-inch in diameter, yet there is ample space for five holes, which should be sufficient to prevent injury to the bolt through injudicious flogging, which then becomes inexcusable.

Upon measuring bolts that have been broken, it is invariably found that they have been stretched beyond their elastic limit and have taken a permanent set before finally fracturing. This is always the case when the bolts have been excessively tightened. In view of this, and the fact that a period of time elapses between the fracture commencing and the bolt finally breaking, it is often in the power of a careful engineer to prevent serious damage arising from the bolts failing. Fractures always begin on the outer surface, so that, whenever a bearing is opened up for adjustment or any other reason, the bolts should be taken out of the bearing, cleaned and every part carefully examined, more especially the last thread engaged by the nut. Cracks always develop circumferentially, and if a crack, no matter how small, is found, the bolt should be made unfit for further use and a new bolt fitted. A good plan is to stamp on the bolt the date upon which it is first fitted.

In order that a bolt will not stretch without this being observed, periodical measurement in the following manner is recommended. Procure a piece of steel of not less than ¾-inch diameter or square, and make a good stout trammel equal in length to about 1½ inches less than the overall length of the bolt, so that it will reach from a point half-way up the bolt-head to the top thread but one, as shown in Fig. 193. After the ends of the trammel have been bent, well-pointed and slightly hardened, make a plate gauge of the exact distance between the points, for future reference and re-adjustment of the trammel in the event of its being damaged. On the side of the bolt-head that will be facing outward when in working position, penetrate the head to a depth of ¼ inch with a ½-inch diameter well-pointed drill, and centre dot the bottom of the countersunk hole thus made. Drilling the bolt-head in this way is advisable, as a centre punch-mark on the surface is likely to be obliterated in course of time, as this part of the bolt is sometimes hammered when fitting. Then, having filed down a portion of the second from top thread on the same side of the bolt as the mark on the head, measure off the distance with the trammel and mark with a centre punch.

With long bolts of comparatively small diameter and coarse-pitched threads there is a possibility of their being twisted when tightening the nuts. If this is likely, a line should be made on the bolt, as shown in Fig. 193, with a box-square. Upon subsequently applying the box-square any twist in the bolt will be apparent.

In cases when the free movement of an engine is suddenly checked, as by piston seizure, the propeller striking some heavy obstruction, or the engine racing due to the speed governor not being effective, all crankpin and crosshead bearing-bolts should be carefully examined at the first opportunity, since they may have been seriously overstressed. In certain circumstances the wisest thing to do is to renew the bolts. In any case all nuts should be tested before any attempt is made to start the engine again.

Whenever a bearing-bolt nut is found not exactly slack, but not as hard up as it ought to be, and is firmly held by whatever locking device is provided, most careful investigation should be made as to the cause. Maybe the bolt has been overstressed beyond its elastic limit, which would reduce the initial tension in the bolt and cause the nut to be found in the same position but slack; or perhaps the contact surfaces of the bolt and bearing were not properly cleaned when last the bearing was closed up. Sometimes careless screw-cutting is the cause of nuts being found slack.

Bearing bolts are made from 28–32 ton tensile (ordinary) mild steel, or from medium carbon steel or high-tensile (nickel-chrome) steel. The last is used because of its superior tensile strength, but experience suggests that a superior grade of mild steel, commonly called medium carbon steel, is the most suitable material for the purpose. This material, which has a tensile strength of 38–42 tons and a minimum elongation of 18 per cent, resists fatigue to a greater extent than the specially high-tensile steels. Mild and medium carbon-steel bolts may be annealed periodically if desired, but on no account may nickel-chrome steel bolts be annealed or heat-treated.

Anti-friction metal

The universal practice is to line the principal bearings with whitemetal because this metal has superior anti-frictional properties. If " fluid film " lubrication conditions could be constantly maintained and the bearing surfaces kept a reasonable distance apart, metals having specially high anti-frictional properties would not be so necessary, and brass would be used more extensively. " Boundary " lubrication conditions, however, occur at certain periods, and unless whitemetal is used the rubbing surfaces will wear at a greater rate. Moreover, the employment of whitemetal for the bearings of enclosed engines is essential, because in the event of a bearing becoming overheated very little harm is done, whereas if the surfaces were composed of brass and steel, the steel shaft as well as the brass bearing would be seriously damaged.

Not only is anti-friction metal necessary, but the nature of this metal is such that unless it is of good quality frequent renewal will be necessary. There is very little difference in the wearing qualities of the various leading brands, but in other respects some are better suited for the purpose than others. The only weakness of some of the present-day anti-friction metals is their inability to withstand cracking. Much of this is doubtless due to faulty running-in of the metal.

The metal should have the combined properties of toughness and ductility. There are two kinds of whitemetal in common use, one being the tin-base metal and the other the lead-base metal, both of which have high anti-frictional properties. It is, however, the former that are nearly always employed for lining the principal bearings of diesel engines, although the addition of not more than 1 per cent of lead is not detrimental. Tin by itself, being too soft, is hardened by the addition of copper and antimony, which when in the proper proportions form a tenacious and malleable alloy. The proportions of tin, copper and antimony in the various brands of anti-frictional metal vary, but a good mixture consists of 83 per cent tin, 7 per cent copper and 10 per cent antimony. A small percentage of variation in either of these component metals or the manner of mixing, however, exerts an influence upon the resulting alloy.

The melting or running out of bearings, although a common trouble in the early days of the open-fronted type of engine, is now a very rare occurrence; yet in view of the considerable number of ships which trade between foreign ports and have to undergo overhaul at places where whitemetalling of bearings is considered outside the realm of skilled occupations, the following hints on the subject may prove useful.

The first important part of the operation is to clean the bearing shell thoroughly, otherwise the whitemetal need not be expected to adhere properly, no matter how good the quality of metal or how carefully the remaining stages of the operation are carried out. To clean the bearing shells paraffin may be used, providing all trace of it is removed afterwards by a blow-lamp flame, and the surfaces finished off with a perfectly clean wire brush, or the bearings may be cleaned in a caustic soda bath composed of about 4 lb of caustic soda to each bucket of water. Burning off after washing with paraffin is, however, the best practice.

After the shell has been cleaned, it must be heated preparatory to tinning, which is the next stage in the operation. If a benzine blow-lamp or a gas blow-pipe is used, the flame may be directed on to the surface to be tinned, but if a paraffin blow-lamp is used, or the shell is heated in a fire, the flame must be applied to the back of the shell. The shell should be heated uniformly to a temperature that will make ground sal-ammoniac flow. Some anti-friction metals are self-tinning, that is to say, a strip of the metal itself can be used to tin the shell. Should the metal used not be self-tinning, the shell will require to be thinly coated with plastic metal, or a good-quality solder. Chloride of zinc (killed spirits of salts) or sal-ammoniac should be used as a flux. After tinning, all surplus flux must be removed.

The heating of the whitemetal is of particular importance, since, should it be overheated, the bearing will require to be remetalled in a very short time. About twice the amount of metal required for the bearing should be placed in a clean ladle and melted gradually on a slow fire, care being taken to see that no other whitemetal is mixed with it. The temperature of the metal when ready for pouring is about 550°F (288°C). At this temperature a piece of moderately stiff white (chart) paper will enter the metal freely and change its colour to light brown; or when the metal will brown a pine stick, it is ready for pouring. Whilst melting, the metal should be stirred continuously in order to prevent the metal at the bottom of the ladle from being overheated. When the surface of the metal in the ladle is skimmed, it should show perfectly bright; if a dark-coloured ash is present, it is a sign that the metal has been overheated, and if the paper test mentioned is carried out, the paper will probably catch fire. Overheated metal poured into a bearing will be very brittle when it solidifies and will quickly break up into small pieces when put into service.

While the metal is being melted, the bearing shell should be heated from the back until the tinning just begins to run. It is important that the shell be heated to the correct temperature, otherwise, if the temperature is too low, the metal will be chilled and will not adhere properly, or if too high the tinning will be oxidised and this part of the operation will require to be done over again. If a mandril is used, this too should be heated to about the same temperature as the shell, otherwise the metal will be chilled. When relining solid bush bearings, the mandril should be smoked or covered with paper to facilitate its removal.

Whenever practicable, the bearing should be standing on end when the metal is being poured into it. The ladle should have a rounded spout rather than one that is sharp or broad, as a broad thin flow of metal, or an intermittent flow, tends to produce blow-holes. Whilst pouring, continue to apply the heat to the shell, taking care not to overheat, and fill the bearing to the top. The metal in the bearing should be kept fluid for a few minutes, or until it has had time to settle down, when the bearing should be topped up. The heat should be directed in such a way that the metal sets from the bottom, and if in doing so it sinks, the flame should be applied to the upper part of the bearing until it is again sufficiently fluid to allow a piece of stiff paper to pass freely into it and the bearing should be topped up again. The metal should finally cool from the bottom upwards. Wet rags or a current of air may be used for this purpose.

The mandril should be firmly secured in the bearing shell before beginning to pour, and if the bearing is small it is advisable to secure this also. For sealing the ends of the bearing putty serves the purpose very well. Blow-holes can be prevented by venting with a piece of clean wire and allowing the air to escape to the surface immediately after pouring.

CRANKCASE EXPLOSIONS

The following notes have been taken from a paper presented by the author before the Institution of Mechanical Engineers in London and which was awarded the Akroyd Stuart Prize for 1952.

Explosions in enclosed crankcases seldom occur, but in view of the possible serious consequences operating engineers should know what causes them and be aware of the precautions to be taken in order to reduce the possibility of such explosions to a minimum.

Prevention of crankcase explosions resolves itself into two problems, the first being prevention of the formation of an explosive mixture; the second, elimination of the means of igniting such a mixture. Solution of either would effectively remove the possibility of an explosion.

As regards the former; if a crankcase were filled and kept charged with inert gas, such as carbon dioxide, an explosion could not occur. Chemists state that if the inert gas content could be maintained at 30 per cent or over, a crankcase would be in a safe condition, but there are objections to the presence of a gas that will not support life in a space where men may have to work at short notice.

Under normal working conditions a crankcase will first contain only air. As the lubricating oil becomes heated a portion of it is atomised by pressure and the churning action of the fast-moving parts. The small particles are thrown against the crankcase walls, where they combine and run down into the sump. Consequently the suspended oil-particles are constantly changing. These particles, called " oil droplets," give colour to the air, and the mixture is referred to as " crankcase mist," the density of which depends mainly upon the temperature of the oil.

If the oil-coolers are adequate, the highest average temperature reached by the bearing oil of a marine engine is about 140°F (60°C), which is not sufficient to vaporise the oil. The oil-particles suspended in air are, therefore, in liquid form and, whilst they alter the colour of the gaseous content of a crankcase, they do not alter its composition in the chemical sense. The composition may, however, be altered by local overheating.

Some minor explosions occur after an engine has been stopped and a crankcase door opened for inspection purposes. In such instances, even though some part of the engine was hot enough to ignite the oil-mist, it would seem that ignition was delayed until additional air entered through the open door.

When a bearing becomes hot in a crankcase containing oil-mist the engine should be stopped, and the maximum quantity of oil circulated through the bearings until the faulty bearing is at or near hand heat. Before a crankcase door is opened the circulation should be stopped and time given for the oil to drain from the bearings, as ignition may be brought about by oil dropping on to a hot bearing. The Ministry of Transport have very wisely issued a warning against the possible serious consequences of too hasty opening of crankcase doors when some internal part is known to be overheated. The taking of naked lights into the crankcase of a recently-stopped engine is another dangerous practice. No harm will be done to the engine in the event of the oil-mist being ignited because the open crankcase door prevents a serious build-up of pressure. Instances are, however, on record where men in the vicinity of the open door have been burnt by the resulting flame.

So far as the author is aware, there is no record of an explosion occurring after an engine has been stopped and before crankcase doors are opened. This would suggest that the possibility of inflammable mist making contact with an overheated part is greater when an engine is running than when at rest. The reason for this may be that when an engine is at rest and the gaseous contents are stagnant, oil vapour too rich to ignite surrounds the hot part and isolates it from the inflammable mist. This theory is supported by a recorded instance where, after an engine had been at rest for several minutes, a violent explosion occurred immediately it was restarted. During the time the engine was stopped, nothing was done to disturb the gaseous contents in the crankcase, and there would be practically no change in the temperature of the bearing.

When an explosion occurs in an engine at rest after a crankcase door is opened, the cause is probably not so much the entry of air, but the action of opening the door causing movement of the gaseous contents and varying the composition of the gases in the immediate vicinity of the hot bearing. It is not suggested that oil-mist can be too rich to burn; if the size of the suspended oil-particles is small enough they will ignite and burn like a gaseous mixture. The point the author wishes to bring out is that when heavier oil-particles are converted into vapour it is possible for the vapour to be so short of air that ignition will occur only when the rich vapour is disturbed and air allowed to mix with it, or to be replaced by oil-mist in an inflammable condition.

Frictional heat in bearings

A fundamental necessity of power-producers, or of any machine required to transmit motion, is the rubbing together of metals and the production of frictional heat. The quantity of heat produced can be kept within bounds by efficient lubrication, but it is quite another matter—and it is the responsibility of the engineer—to ensure this at all times and under all conditions. Experience has proved that overheated bearings are more likely to be avoided by the copious and continuous supply of oil to each bearing. This necessitates an enclosed crankcase.

The presence of free oil in a crankcase, no matter how finely the oil may be divided, is incapable of causing an explosion unless the temperature of some part is raised to the ignition temperature of the oil-mist. As, however, it is impossible to ensure that such a temperature will not at some time be reached, the only way to eliminate the possibility of an explosion would be to remove from the crankcase all oil in excess of the bare amount required to lubricate the bearings. This would mean reverting to drip lubrication, a practice that would be rightly looked upon as a retrograde step.

Ventilated versus sealed crankcases

Opinion is divided as to whether crankcases should be vented, ventilated by a current of air, or totally sealed.

The effect of venting, that is, the provision of openings to the atmosphere, can only be to avoid the building up of a greater pressure than atmospheric under normal working conditions, and so prevent leakage of oil from crankcase door joints, etc. In the event of an explosion these vents would be practically useless because of their relatively small diameter and location. It is highly improbable that the seat of an explosion would be in direct line with them. Moreover, such vents can have no material effect upon the inflammable properties of the oil-mist. They might indicate the presence of smoke in a crankcase, but when smoke issues from them the condition necessary to produce an explosion will already exist.

The practice of ventilating crankcases by a current of air has many adherents, but the fact that explosions have occurred in engines so treated is sufficient proof that it does not ensure immunity. Constant changing of a portion of the gaseous contents in this way will reduce the density of the mist and, in the event of an explosion, may reduce its violence, but it is highly improbable that ventilation within practical limits would put every part of the crankcase in a safe condition, because of the peculiar internal construction. To be effective the air would need to be admitted at so many points that this would be impracticable. Moreover, increased oil consumption is a further objection.

It is doubtful whether hermetically sealed crankcases would achieve the desired result, for the reason that a crankcase is full of air before the engine is started, and observations have shown that even after weeks of continuous operation, air forms a large proportion of the gaseous contents.

Another point to be considered in regard to large marine engines is the advantage of crankcases being provided, at crosshead guide-bar level, with small doors which can be readily opened while the engine is running. The first indication of an overheated inaccessible bearing is smoke, and periodical internal inspection of the crankcase is the best means of preventing serious damage to bearings and, incidentally, a crankcase explosion. Doors are preferable to small inspection windows because windows become fogged and, on occasions—in the tropics for instance—it is not easy to differentiate between oil-mist and smoke, even when crankcases are artificially illuminated.

Prevention of hot spots

If it is impracticable to prevent crankcase explosions by control of the gaseous contents, doubtless much can be done to prevent ignition of the inflammable contents. As such explosions can occur only if the oil-mist is ignited, and as ignition can result only from an overheated part, the obvious way to minimise the chances of an explosion is to—

(1) do everything possible to prevent a part getting hot;
(2) take steps to avoid dangerous pressure build-up in crankcases; and
(3) prevent flame issuing from the crankcase in the event of an explosion.

In regard to (1), it is most important to line all parts in which shafts revolve or slide with anti-friction metal of reasonable thickness. In addition to reducing the running temperature of a bearing, anti-friction metal is advantageous in so far as it melts at a temperature below the temperature necessary for igniton of lubricating oil, and produces slackness, which in a four-stroke type of engine can generally be heard, though in two-stroke engines a hot bearing is not always indicated in this way.

Other factors which make for the elimination of hot bearings are—

(1) Passages and pipes used to convey oil should have a bore not less than $\frac{3}{8}$-inch diameter.
(2) Duplex strainers should be provided on both suction and delivery sides of lubricating-oil pumps, and be located in easily accessible positions.
(3) Pipes inside crankcases should be (a) properly aligned to avoid strain when connected; (b) secured in a way that will prevent vibration; (c) free from sharp bends where dirt and other extraneous matter may collect; and (d) annealed periodically to reduce brittleness and eventual fracture when they are of small diameter and made of copper.
(4) All metal parts not intended to make contact, as for instance, a crankweb and flange of adjacent bearings, should have adequate clearance. The possibility of contact resulting from expansion when the part becomes heated to working temperature should not be overlooked.
(5) The point at which the oil leaves the crankcase should be covered by a grid of large area to prevent cotton waste, pieces of wood, etc. inadvertently left in the crankcase during overhaul, from choking the oil drain.
(6) Periodic removal of the oil to clean out sumps and oil drain-tanks is recommended, the oil being purified before it is returned to the system.
(7) Lubricating-oil pumps should discharge into a gravity tank large enough to ensure a supply of oil to the bearings for a reasonable time, in the event of pump failure. An alternative is the provision of an efficient alarm.

Generally when bearings overheat, the heating process is at first gradual, and if detected in time the engine can be stopped before a bearing becomes sufficiently hot to damage the anti-friction metal. When a temperature of about 500°F (260°C) is reached the anti-friction metal melts, and may run into the oil hole and stop the flow of oil. Should this occur the temperature of the bearing will from then onward increase very rapidly.

If, therefore, the oil hole could be prevented from choking, the rate of temperature increase would be reduced, which would give the attendants more time to become aware of the defect. A simple method to prevent oil holes becoming choked in this way would be to fit a channel-shaped ring in the annular oil groove, the ring being in halves and made of a material such as copper, which has a relatively high melting-point and which will not damage the surface of the revolving steel crankpin or shaft journal.

Overheated piston rods seldom occur in single-acting engines, but the author has known many double-acting engine piston rods become hot to the point of redness. In only one instance, however, did a crankcase explosion result. The practice of at least one well-known marine engine-builder, of surrounding the steel piston rod by a cast-iron sleeve and circulating water or oil through the annular space between these two parts, is commendable.

Piston rods which enter the crankcase rarely become hot owing to lack of lubricant. Generally the trouble arises from the rod making hard contact with some part of the stuffing-boxes provided at the lower end of the cylinder and top of the crankcase. In the design of such parts, therefore, it is wise to allow for liberal lateral movement of the piston rod, which occurs when the crosshead guide-bars become worn or parts are not refitted in strict alignment.

Crankcase relief valves

In the prevention of injury to personnel and damage to property as a result of crankcase explosions two problems are involved. The first is to obviate pressure build-up inside the crankcase by provision of an adequate escape for the rapidly expanding gases; and the second is to prevent personnel in the vicinity being burnt, or a fire from being started, either by diverting the hot gases to a point where they will do no harm or by reducing their temperature.

To prevent damage the requirements are (1) that the gases be released at a rate which will avoid the build-up of pressure likely to damage any part of the crankcase, and (2) immediately the excess pressure has been released the escape opening must be instantly closed to prevent entry of air and a second explosion. On occasions, an explosion has been immediately followed by another, sometimes of greater violence. This is attributed to the partial vacuum created by the momentum of the released gases causing air to rush into the crankcase and mix with the remaining oil-mist.

The advantage of the form of relief valve shown in Fig. 195 is that it is simple in construction, and when full open offers minimum resistance to the flow of excess gases. The disadvantages are that

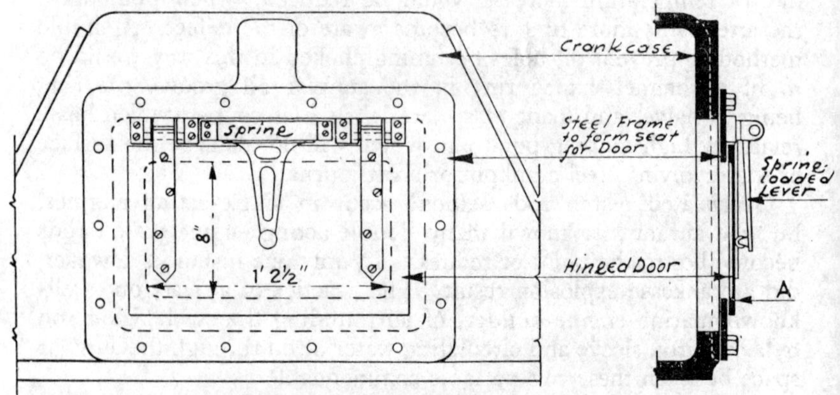

Fig. 195—Crankcase relief valve, spring type

if the spring load is sufficient to ensure the door closing with the speed necessary to prevent air from entering the crankcase, the load may be too great to ensure it opening with the speed necessary to prevent a serious build-up of pressure. The spring load holding the relief valve in closed position should be just sufficient to prevent movement and leakages of mist resulting from the pulsation caused by the moving parts in the crankcase. When tested by means of a sensitive spring-balance, a pressure of 4 lb applied at the point indicated by *A* in the diagram was found to be required to " crack " the valve, and $13\frac{3}{4}$ lb to hold it fully open.

The " Lightning " safety valve

A device which, it is claimed, will prevent an undesirable build-up of pressure in the event of an explosion, and close instantly, is shown in Fig. 196. This device, in slightly different form, has been used with good effect for many years in connection with the starting-air system of diesel engines and has the following special features:—

(1) it can be designed to open at any predetermined pressure above atmospheric;
(2) it opens instantly and to its fullest extent without shock when the predetermined pressure is reached; and
(3) it closes immediately the excess pressure is released.

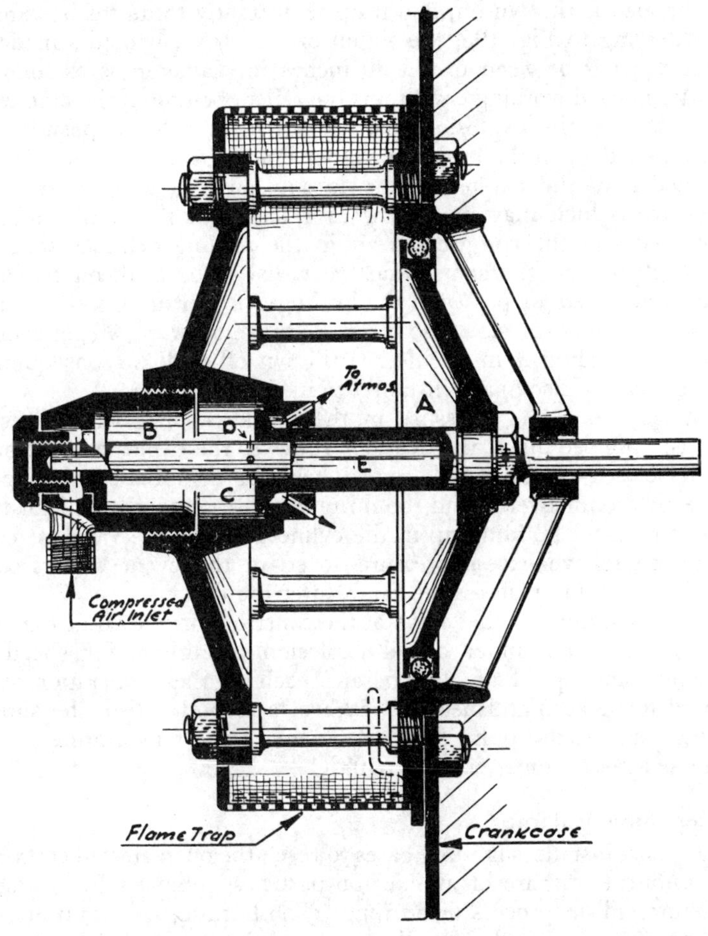

Fig. 196—Full-bore compressed-air-loaded relief valve for enclosed crankcase (" Lightning ")

Other good features, relating to the release of excess pressure from crankcases, are that it will operate equally well when disposed vertically, horizontally, or at an angle, while size does not affect its operation.

The main advantage of this valve over spring-loaded relief valves is that whereas in the latter the load is progressively increased as the valve opens, the load on the " Lightning " valve is decreased. Actually, at the moment the valve begins to open about 90 per cent of the load is thrown off, and it opens instantly to its fullest extent.

Referring to Fig. 196, the action of this valve, which is made in sizes varying between 6 and 30 inches in diameter, is as follows. Under normal working conditions the relief opening in the crankcase is closed by the explosion disc *A*, which is held in position by compressed air in the loading cylinder *B* acting on the mitre valve *C*. Immediately the explosion disc is subjected to a predetermined pressure (which may be as low as 1 lb/sq.in.) the mitre valve is unseated and the compressed air in the loading cylinder spills to atmosphere. At the same time the radial holes *D* through which the compressed air passes to the loading cylinder are closed. Thus, as soon as the explosion disc begins to move outward, 90 per cent of the load holding it in position is thrown off and, in consequence, the explosion disc opens instantly to its fullest extent.

When the excess pressure in the crankcase has been released, the compressed air in the cylinder *E* drives the explosion disc back to its closed position and immediately the compressed-air supply holes *D* are uncovered and the mitre valve re-seats, the full loading pressure again building up in the cylinder *B* and the valve is ready again to relieve excess pressure—even in the event of a second explosion taking place immediately after the first.

A " Lightning " relief valve of the construction shown in Fig. 196 has been tested under actual explosion conditions for speed of opening and speed of closing, and each of these operations was found to be accomplished in 1/50th of a second. Also, the simple flame-trap fitted around the outlet reduced the temperature of the released gases from 1,600°C to 108°C.

Quenching of flame

In most instances the first gases to reach the open air will comprise an unburnt mixture of air and oil-particles, followed by a similar mixture still in process of burning. The burning will continue, or, in other words, the flame will exist, until the whole of the inflammable mixture released has burnt or has been cooled below its ignition temperature by contact with the surrounding air.

The length of flame issuing from the crankcase exit will, therefore, depend upon two factors, one, the point in the crankcase at which explosion begins, and the other the position of the exit. Assuming that the pressure wave travels toward the exit, the nearer the seat of the explosion is to the exit, the smaller will be the quantity of unburnt mixture expelled and, consequently, the shorter will be the length of flame.

To ensure that every explosion that can occur in a multi-unit engine takes place near to an exit, so that the least possible quantity of unburnt mixture is expelled ahead of the burning gases, is impracticable. It would probably mean several exits on each crankcase door and at least two on each end of the crankcase. Even then there is no certainty that the excess pressure would be released through the nearest exit. Moreover, the greater the number of exits, the greater the risk to personnel of injury by burning.

The dangers attending the expulsion of burning gases could be overcome by trunking the gases from the exits to a point clear of the engine-room. The trunking would need to be of large size and free from bends if it were not to interfere with the free flow of the released gases. It would not, in fact, be practicable to provide such trunking in a ship's engine-room, and would not be favoured in installations where space is unlimited.

It would seem, therefore, that prevention of injury by burning can result only if the released gases are cooled as they leave the crankcase exits, and, as mentioned, this is achieved in the " Lightning " relief valve without in the least restricting the released gases. These good results are obtained with a flame trap made up of two layers of thick gauze and three layers of thin gauze, the thick layers being on the inside and first to meet the issuing flame. The reason for locating the gauze of thicker wire innermost is because it absorbs about 80 per cent more heat than the thinner wire, and because of its greater weight per unit area the temperature rise will be about 50 per cent only of that of thinner wire.

CHAPTER 23

Crankshafts, propeller shafts and thrust bearings

The crankshaft of any engine is the most costly and important part, and is generally the most difficult part to renew in the event of its becoming defective. If any part of a diesel engine is entitled to more care and attention in its construction and maintenance than any other, it is the crankshaft, and although the operating engineer has no control over the defects that are likely to arise from the employment of unsuitable materials or bad workmanship, yet much depends upon maintaining crankshafts in proper alignment. No matter how well constructed a crankshaft may be, neglect in this direction may cause a serious breakdown.

Crankshafts may be divided into three classes, namely, the solid-forged, the semi-built and the built crankshaft. In the former, one- to four-throw crankshafts are made from a single ingot, while in the semi-built type, each pair of webs and the crankpin joining them are in one piece, and the journals, which are separate, are shrunk in. The built-up crankshaft comprises separate webs, crankpins and journals. In engines having a comparatively short piston stroke, the built-up type of crankshaft is not suitable owing to there being insufficient material between the crankpins and journals to ensure a proper shrinkage grip.

The material used for crankpins and journals, when these parts are separate from the webs, is good-quality mild steel. The webs are made from Siemens-Marten open hearth steel, and are usually machined out of rolled or forged slabs. This practice involves a great deal of machining, and to obviate this many makers have adopted cast steel for crank webs. When high-quality steel is used, webs made from rolled slabs or forged ingot slabs are equally good, but if cheap basic steel is used, the slabs should be forged, as this method ensures the slabs being worked in the direction of both width and thickness, and the finished forging is less liable to contain latent defects.

Some engine-builders fit heavy weights to the cranks in order to balance the reciprocating masses, while others obtain the desired even turning movement by employing a heavy flywheel. Both methods prevent any uneven turning movement of multiple-cylinder engines, but the advantage of the unbalanced crank engine is that

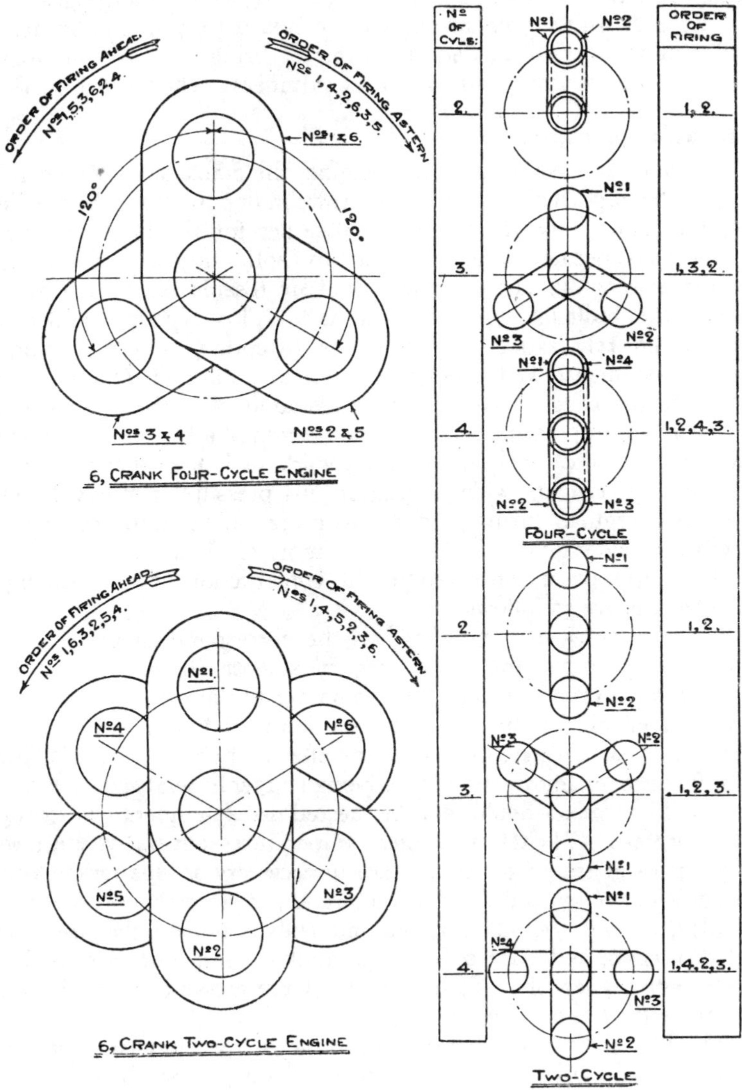

Fig. 197—Arrangement of cranks and firing order of cylinders

the various bearings on the crankcase are more accessible. When the crank webs are made of cast steel the webs and balance-weights are cast in one piece, and less space in the crankcase is occupied than when the webs and balance-weights are separate forgings.

The even turning of an engine depends mainly upon the firing order of the cylinders, and the order of firing of two- and four-cycle engines having from two to six cylinders is shown in Fig. 197.

Crankshaft construction

In the early days of the steam engine, the crankshafts were solid-forged, having usually one or two throws in one piece for the smaller engines, and single throws bolted together for the larger engines. As engines became larger, satisfactory solid forgings of the size required were difficult to obtain, and Sir Joseph Whitworth introduced the built-up type of crankshaft. This type of crankshaft proved entirely satisfactory from its inception, and one cannot but be astonished at the small number of failures in service when aware of the rough-and-ready methods adopted in the construction of such an important part by some engine-builders. The introduction of the diesel engine for marine work, with its greater maximum cylinder pressures, wider variation of pressure per revolution, and less regular turning effort than are obtained in the steam reciprocating engine, called for much more efficient methods.

The chief points observed in the construction of built-up type crankshafts are as follows:—

(1) The holes in the webs, and the corresponding parts of the pins and journals, must be perfectly smooth in order to ensure maximum surface contact. The smoother the finish of the surfaces the greater will be the shrinkage grip, and the better will the parts resist normal stresses, as well as the effects of shock resulting from the free movement of the engine being suddenly retarded.

(2) The webs should not be heated to a temperature greater than 1,380°F (749°C), as higher temperatures adversely affect the properties of the material, and are unnecessary as this temperature is sufficient to expand the holes the required amount.

(3) Each web should be heated uniformly to obviate the possibility of distortion, and once only, i.e. a crankpin and journal should be fitted simultaneously. To heat such a large mass of steel uniformly requires from 6 to 8 hours.

(4) The shrinkage allowance must be neither too large nor too small, as, if too large, the webs in the vicinity of the holes may be overstressed and the elastic limit of the material reached, in which

case not only is there a danger of fractures occurring, but the pins and journals are just as liable to become slack as when the shrinkage allowance is too small. A shrinkage allowance of 1·6/1,000 inch per inch diameter of crankpin or journal has been found to give the desired results.

Dowel pins

There are still some who advocate the employment of dowel pins even though past experience has definitely proved such to be quite unnecessary. There are a great many crankshafts at present in use, built years ago, which are giving entire satisfaction without the help of dowel pins. Moreover, the author has examined a few properly constructed crankshafts after they have been subjected to far greater shocks than could be set up by any sort of bad weather, and a single instance has yet to be found where the shrinkage grip has been overcome. Not only are dowel pins unnecessary, but the practice of boring holes at the ends of the journals between the webs and journals and relieving part of the shrinkage grip will have an effect contrary to that desired in a properly constructed crankshaft.

Dowel pins were doubtless necessary in the past when the method of assembling, and even the shrinking allowance in some cases, were left to the man doing the work. Judging by the shrinkage surfaces of many crankpins, journals and webs which have been inspected after failing in service, it is apparent that the dowel pins had been doing most of the work, and that, had they not been fitted, slack pins and journals would have resulted at an earlier date. But something more than dowel pins is necessary to meet the more exacting conditions in a diesel engine. This was proved in the early days, when crankshafts built in accordance with steam-engine practice quickly gave trouble, in spite of the time and trouble taken to make an extra good job of the fitting of dowel pins. At that time some of those responsible for the building of crankshafts even purposely left the shrinkage surfaces of the journals, crankpins and webs slightly rough-machined, instead of as smooth as possible, because it was thought that a better shrinkage grip would be assured by so doing. The fallacy of this practice is conclusively proved by the great number of engine crankshafts that have been in service for many years in which the shrinkage surfaces were made as smooth as possible and the shrinkage grip alone relied upon.

The only useful purpose a dowel pin can serve is to enable a ship to limp to port in the event of the shrinkage grip being overcome. The best practice, therefore, is to rely upon the shrinkage grip, if the method of constructing the crankshaft conforms with the best practice, and provide the ship with the material and the necessary gear to enable the ship's staff to fit dowel pins in the event of a journal or crankpin becoming slack owing to defective workmanship or material. Dowel pins to be of real service in such circumstances should be two in number, and be located about 90° apart, one on each side of the centre-line of the web. The holes and dowel pins should be as smooth as it is possible to make them, dead parallel, and of such diameter that the pins are a perfect driving fit. The dowel pins, which should be equal in length to at least half the thickness of the web, should be forced right home by a screw jack if a hydraulic jack is not available. A very small slot cut along the axis of the pins should be provided to release the imprisoned air.

Crankshaft alignment

The importance of keeping a line of bearings at the same height, and the crankshaft in good alignment, will be apparent to all. Whilst it is recognised that no matter how well constructed a crankshaft may be, it is bound to give trouble if the bedplate or engine seating is not sufficiently rigid to preserve the true alignment of the crankshaft whilst in operation, yet the operating engineer can do much to prevent crankshaft trouble by maintaining the crankshaft in proper alignment as far as it lies in his power to do so. There is no doubt that some crankshafts have broken owing to weak and flexible bedplates and engine seatings not maintaining alignment when the ship was encountering heavy weather.

When an engine leaves the builders, the bearings may be considered to be in perfect alignment, and will remain so if they should wear down evenly. That this is usual, but not always the case, has been proved by a number of crankshafts and coupling bolts breaking, and the cause being traced to misalignment of the bearings. The apparent causes of such uneven wear are (1) unequal power distribution in the various cylinders, (2) solid impurities in the lubricating oil, (3) overheating and melting of the whitemetal in some of the bearings, and (4) lining a set of bearings with different grades of anti-friction metal. How to prevent uneven wear resulting from any of the abovementioned causes will be obvious.

In the vast majority of ships, however, these causes are non-existent, and yet it is not uncommon to find that uneven wear has taken place. It would appear, therefore, that there must be some other cause. In a properly operated engine, all crankshaft bearings, with the exception of the bearing next to the flywheel, work under the same conditions as regards loading, amount of oil supplied, quality, etc., the only probable difference being in the facilities existing for enabling the oil to find its way to the loaded area of the bearings. It is suggested, therefore, that if uneven wear-down of a crankshaft is taking place, and the obvious causes mentioned cannot be held responsible, the cause is due to the bearings having a varying amount of side clearance. Should the bottom halves of the bearings that have worn the most be taken out, it will probably be found that they have little or no side clearance. The effect of their wearing excessively is to eliminate the original clearance, so that if the matter is not taken in hand when the uneven wear-down is first detected, the position will become rapidly worse, and the continual bending of the crankshaft will cause it to fatigue and eventually to fracture.

Contrary to what might be expected, the bearing next to the flywheel wears least of all. The reason for this is that the gyroscopic action of the rapidly revolving flywheel causes the shaft to take up a central position in the bearing, with the result that the oil film between the loaded surfaces of the bearing next to it is thicker and, consequently, less wear takes place.

Most operating engineers will agree that the alignment of a crankshaft is of vital importance, yet it is a fact that in a great many cases far more time and attention are given to cylinder-liner wear than to the wear-down of the crankshaft. This is quite wrong. Complete records of cylinder-liner wear must, of course, be kept, but if—assuming for the purpose of illustration an unlikely situation—it is required to have particulars of the cylinder-liner wear and the crankshaft alignment, and there is only time to deal with the most important, then it ought to be the crankshaft which receives attention. Cylinder liners will soon begin complaining and attract attention when they are reaching the end of their useful life, but crankshafts will endure, in absolute silence, continual bending, twisting and straining to the point of fracture. It is only when they can no longer endure the strain that they call the attention of those responsible for the burden that has been placed upon them, and, in less time than it takes to tell, the burden is transferred to the shoulders of the operating engineer.

Complete records of the exact position of the crankshaft at each bearing should, therefore, be on board every ship. When such records are not available it should be one of the first duties of an engineer taking over an engine that has been in service some time to ascertain the exact amount of wear which has taken place in the various bearings.

There are three ways to do this. First, if the engine-builder's bridge gauge is available—usually called Lloyds' gauge—and in good order, the top halves of the bearings can be removed and the height of each journal relative to the machined uppermost face of the bedplate, which is not likely to alter throughout the life of an engine, measured in the manner shown in Fig. 198. This method

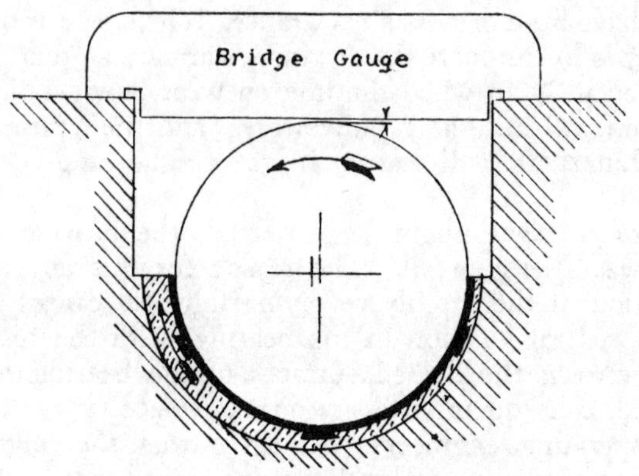

Fig. 198—Method of measuring wear-down of bearing

assumes that the crankshaft is sufficiently heavy and flexible to make contact with a bearing which has worn more than the bearings on either side of it. That there will be a limit to the amount of deflection will be apparent, so that this method will only accurately indicate a certain amount of uneven wear in a line of bearings. The exact amount that any crankshaft will sag can easily be found by selecting three consecutive bearings, the heights of which vary least, and, after measuring with the bridge gauge as described, remove the bottom half of the middle bearing and re-measure the height of the shaft at this particular bearing. The first measurement subtracted from the second will, of course, be the difference in the height of adjacent bearings that the bridge gauge is capable of registering accurately. The amount of sag depends upon many variable factors, such as distance between bearings, length of crank, etc., besides the diameter of the crankshaft, but it will generally be found that a shaft of 12 inches diameter deflects about 0·030 inch. As a rule, larger-diameter shafts deflect more and smaller-diameter shafts less, because the amount of deflection depends mainly upon the weight of the crank webs and crankpins.

The second method of detecting a low bearing is by placing the crank first on top and then on bottom dead centre, and measuring the distance between the crank webs at each position, as shown in Fig. 199. This method, as does the one previously described,

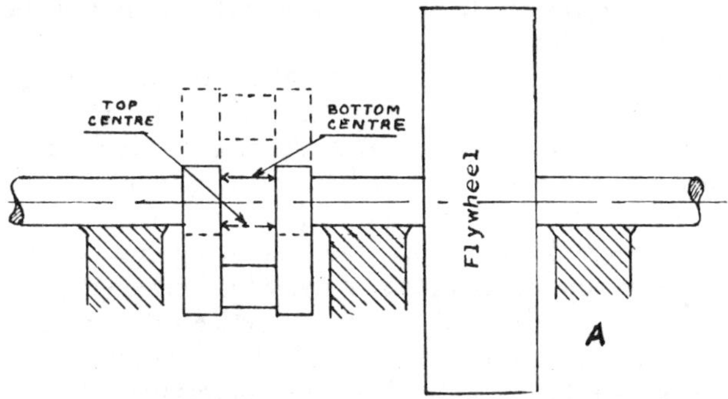

Fig. 199—Another method of testing for wear-down of bearing

assumes that a badly-worn bearing will reveal itself by causing the shaft to sag, and the distance between the webs to vary in consequence. When a bearing between two cranks is lower than those on either side of it, both sets of crank webs will tend to close in when the cranks are on the bottom centre, and open out when the cranks are moved to the top dead centre position. This method is suitable for indicating slight wear, or to test an end bearing with overhung flywheel. It is also the most suitable method for testing the height of the bearing at the opposite side of the flywheel, as shown at *A*, Fig. 199. To test this bearing for wear-down, place the crank first on bottom and then on top dead centre, and gauge in the manner shown in the sketch. If the flywheel bearing has worn down to a greater extent than the engine bearing, the first reading will be greater than the second. The nuts of the engine bearing should be slackened back while the gauging is being done, otherwise the deformation of the crank necessary to reveal a badly worn bearing may be prevented.

The third, and undoubtedly the most accurate, method is to remove the bottom half of each crankshaft bearing shell and measure its thickness on the vertical axis. Since, during construction, the cross-girders in the bedplate which carry the bearings are usually bored out in one operation, the surfaces on which the bearings rest may be taken to be in perfect alignment. If, therefore, the radial thicknesses of the bottom halves of the bearings are made the same in each case, the crankshaft is bound to be in good alignment, unless, of course, the bedplate or the engine seating is so weak that the bedplate has been distorted. In such an event nothing less than the lifting of the crankshaft and running a steel wire or straight-edge over the bearing landing surfaces to check their alignment will suffice to give the information necessary to put the crankshaft into proper alignment.

It occasionally happens that owing to a bottom-half bearing not being properly secured, the surface of the bedplate girder on which it rests becomes worn. In such an event it is necessary to know the extent of wear before the bearings can be properly adjusted, and in many cases this information can only be obtained by lifting the section of crankshaft concerned, removing the bottom halves of the bearings, and applying a straight-edge long enough to extend to the bearing on either side of the defective one. From this the importance of making quite sure that the bottom halves of all crankshaft bearings are firmly secured will be appreciated. In some cases it is possible to ascertain the amount of wear which has taken place without going to the trouble of lifting the crankshaft, in the following manner. First of all, select three consecutive bearings which are known to be in good alignment, and, after taking the bridge-gauge readings, remove the bottom half of the middle bearing. In this way the amount of crankshaft sags will be obtained. Passing now to the defective bearing, remove the bottom half and measure the distance between the underside of the journal and the landing surface. The radial thickness of the bearing necessary to put the shaft into proper alignment will be equal to this measurement plus the amount the shaft sags.

When the correct radial thicknesses of the bottom halves of the bearings to ensure the crankshaft being in good alignment have been obtained, the halves should be refitted, the position of the shaft at each bearing ascertained by means of the bridge gauge, and the measurements tabulated for future reference. While an engine is building, a good plan is to gauge the radial thicknesses of the bearings after the crankshaft has been finally bedded, and engrave the dimensions on a brass plate which should be bolted to the engine structure in a prominent position; or the original measurements should be stamped on the bridge gauge. In any case the matter is of sufficient importance to warrant a lasting record being made. In many cases the only record of the original gauge readings is on a piece of paper handed by the foreman fitter to the chief engineer a day or two before a ship sails. It is no wonder, therefore, that on subsequent occasions when it is necessary to have the original bridge-gauge readings so as to ascertain the exact position of a crankshaft as regards alignment, without going to considerable trouble, they cannot be produced.

As already mentioned, crankshaft bearings are sometimes made eccentric, as shown in Fig. 198, to facilitate removal of the bottom half. In such cases the bottom half is removed by rotating the crankshaft in the astern direction, or the opposite direction to normal rotation. Before attempting to remove such a bearing it should be ascertained if it is of the eccentric type, otherwise a powerful turning gear working in the wrong direction may bend the crankshaft or the adjacent bearing caps may be broken.

Renewing crankshafts

When a crankshaft breaks, a new section has generally to be connected to an old one, and unless the work is carefully done a further new section may be required at a not very distant date. The surest way of doing the work properly would be to remove the whole of the crankshaft, test the section to be refitted in the lathe for alignment, particularly the flange to which the broken shaft was connected, machine the crankpins and journals if necessary, join the sections together and fit the coupling bolts and, after re-metalling the crankshaft bearings, bed in the old as well as the new section, and adjust the heights of the bearings until the coupling flanges are fair at the periphery and the faces parallel.

This, however, is a long and expensive job, and is not really necessary if the remaining section of crankshaft is in good condition and in fair alignment. The alignment must be correct before an attempt is made to fit the new section as this must be aligned to the old section, and if this latter section is not in good alignment, further trouble may be expected. The alignment of the old section as a whole can be checked in various ways, but the simplest and most accurate is to check the coupling faces for being parallel with the centre of the nearest cylinder by means of long straight-edges. The piston and all running gear of this cylinder will have been removed in order to allow the lifting tackle to pass through to the section of crankshaft to be renewed, so that it will be possible to place one straight-edge against the cylinder wall extending down to about the centre of the crankshaft, and another against the flange face of the section of crankshaft, the alignment of which it is desired to check, as shown in Fig. 200.

If the cylinder liner has worn, packing equal in thickness to half the amount of the diametrical wear must, of course, be inserted behind the upper end of the straight-edge in the cylinder to make it lie parallel with the centre of the cylinder. Wooden straight-edges may be used, the one in the cylinder being held firmly in position

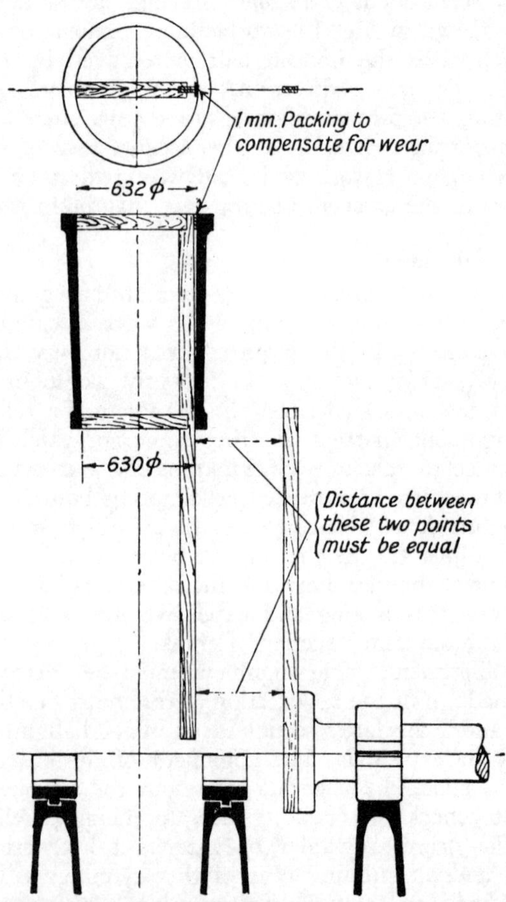

Fig. 200—Method of checking alignment of one section of crankshaft prior to fitting a new section

by shores, one end of each being slotted to take and hold the straight-edge as illustrated. The correct alignment of the old section of crankshaft will be indicated when the straight-edges are parallel.

To fit the new section of crankshaft, it should be lowered into position until the faces of the coupling are fair and parallel, care being taken to fit stays between the webs and sling the shaft in such a way that it is not distorted. The distance between each journal and the landing on which the bearing rests should then be measured, and the bottom halves of the bearings machined to these measurements, when the entire shaft will be in good alignment.

As an illustration of how necessary it is for the crankshaft to be in good alignment, and the serious and even precarious situation that may arise if this is not so, full details of the procedure adopted some years ago to correct the alignment of the air-compressor, main engine and thrust shafts of an oil tanker's six-cylinder air-injection engine may be of interest and value.

A new section of engine crankshaft had been fitted abroad, and according to the records the final gaugings between the flange faces of the various couplings were as follows:—

Coupling	Gaugings, mm			
	Top	Bottom	Port	Starboard
Compressor crankshaft	0·35	1·25	0·9	0·9
Main shaft middle ..	1·3	0·15	0·8	0·8
Thrust shaft	0·3	nil	0·3	0·1

With the shaft alignment as indicated by the foregoing measurements, the holes in the middle engine crankshaft coupling were reamered out and new bolts forced in by hydraulic pressure.

The engine operated satisfactorily so far as concerned the main shafting for six months, when two bolts in the middle coupling were found broken and all others slack. Two new bolts were fitted and the remainder of the bolts tightened up, but several of the bolts were again found slack a few days later. After this it was necessary to stop the engine every few days to examine the bolts and as the ship ran into heavy weather the mental strain put upon those on board can doubtless be well imagined. No trouble was experienced with the compressor or thrust-shaft coupling bolts, the nuts of which were perfectly tight when the vessel reached a home port.

Upon slackening away the bolts of the middle coupling, it was found that with one exception they were all slack and could be knocked out with a hand hammer, and all showed distinct evidence that the coupling flanges had been " working," the bolts being in many instances badly ridged. Also upon slackening away and withdrawing the last bolt, the flanges separated about 1·2 mm at the top only, and the after half of the coupling was found to be 0·3 mm higher than the forward half.

On discovering this considerable misalignment the author decided to strip down as necessary, so as to be able to lift the two halves of the crankshaft at Nos. 3 and 4 crankpins (the cranks at each side of the middle coupling) just sufficient to turn out the bottom halves of Nos. 3, 4, 5 and 6 main bearings, leaving two bearings at each end in place.

These bearings were then to be machined so as to bring the two flanges of the coupling into correct alignment—the amount to be machined off to be determined by removing these bearings and lowering the inner ends of each section of crankshaft until the coupling faces were parallel and measuring the amounts the shaft had been lowered by means of the wear-down gauge.

Before, however, commencing to strip down preparatory to lifting, it was decided to take accurate measurements of the middle coupling on the face and periphery—(1) with the ship on the blocks in dry dock, and (2) with the ship afloat. Readings taken with No. 1 engine crank on the four quarters in each case are shown in Fig. 201.

To obtain the second condition the dock was flooded just sufficiently to float the ship and subsequently pumped dry again. From the readings obtained it will be seen what effect the act of floating the ship had upon the middle coupling.

Stripping of the main engine then began, the various parts dismantled being as follows:—

(1) Nos. 3 and 4 cylinder liners, pistons and rods, cylinder extension pieces, crossheads, connecting-rods, with top and bottom ends disconnected and lifted clear.
(2) Nos. 2 and 5 pistons hung up from astern guide-shoes, bottom ends disconnected and removed and connecting-rod swung clear and secured.
(3) Nos. 1 and 6 units left intact.
(4) All (eight) crankshaft bearing-caps lifted and top halves removed on to platform.
(5) Crankshaft compressor coupling and thrust shaft forward coupling disconnected and coupling bolts removed.

The wear-down gauge was then applied at Nos. 3, 4, 5 and 6 bearings and the readings were noted.

Chain blocks were then rigged in line with Nos. 3 and 4 crankpins (the inner crank of each section) and the crankshaft was lifted just sufficient to enable the bottom halves of Nos. 3,

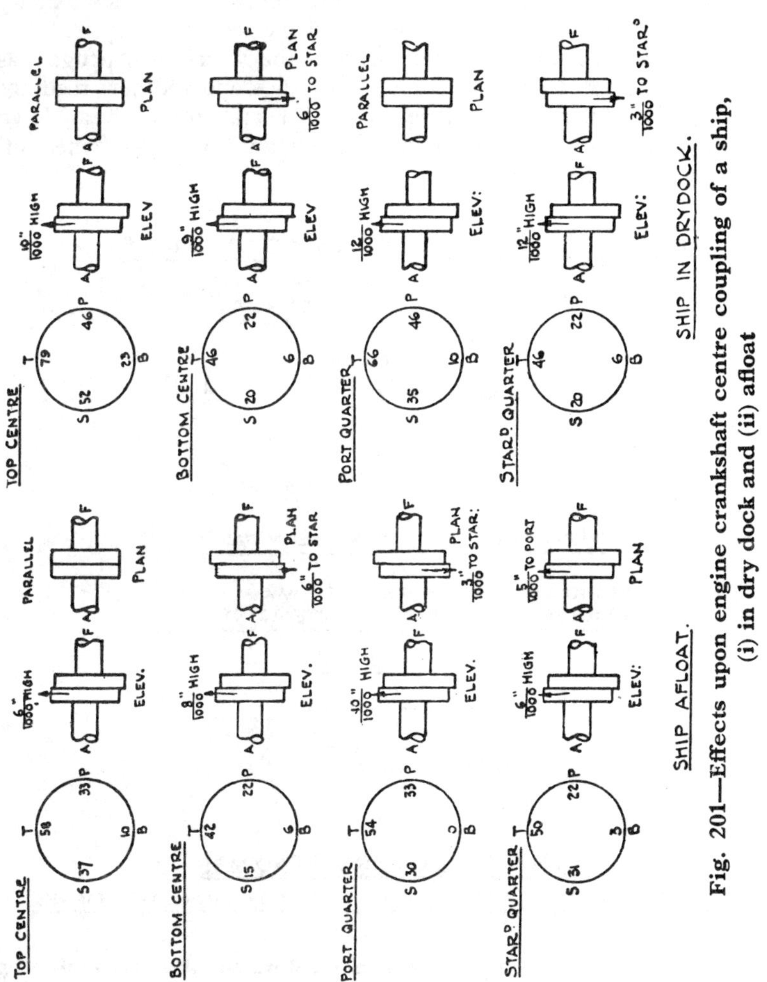

Fig. 201—Effects upon engine crankshaft centre coupling of a ship, (i) in dry dock and (ii) afloat

4, 5 and 6 crankshaft bearings to be turned out with wire strops and chain blocks.

With the bottom halves of these bearings out, the inner ends of the two halves of the crankshaft were lowered until the coupling faces were parallel and fair at the periphery.

Sliding wedges were arranged under the two halves of the coupling, to compensate for sag and prevent vibration set up by the auxiliary engines that were working at the time of the repairs.

After the coupling had been set fair, the wear-down gauge was again applied to Nos. 3, 4, 5 and 6 bearings and the new readings noted, the difference between the final and initial wear-down readings at each bearing giving the amount to be machined off that particular bearing.

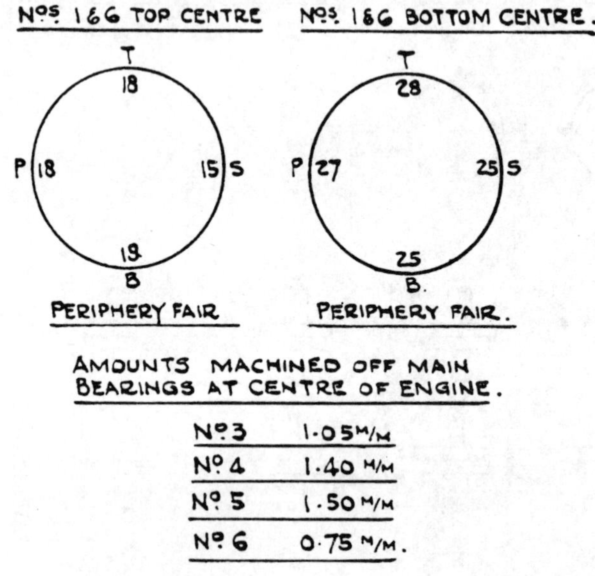

Fig. 202—Effect upon engine crankshaft centre coupling of machining bearings

The amounts obtained by the above method very closely corresponded with the calculated amounts (obtained by laying down the crankshaft—in its late position—on the drawing board) which were intended to be used as a check on the practical method.

The four bottom halves of the bearings mentioned were then sent to have the correct amount of whitemetal machined out of each, and the sides of the bearings "scraped" away as necessary to ensure a wedge-shaped clearance and the shaft bedding on the crown, assuming the alignment to be correct.

The amounts machined out were as follows:—

No. 3	1·05 mm	No. 4	1·4 mm
No. 5	1·5 mm	No. 6	0·75 mm

Upon refitting these four bearings, the flanges of the coupling were found fair on the periphery and parallel between the faces to the degree shown in Fig. 202, which is quite satisfactory.

The middle coupling was then hardened up with two of the old bolts and reamering of the bolt-holes commenced. The holes were finally lapped out to ensure their being perfectly parallel. New coupling bolts were fitted (by hydraulic ram) to suit each hole.

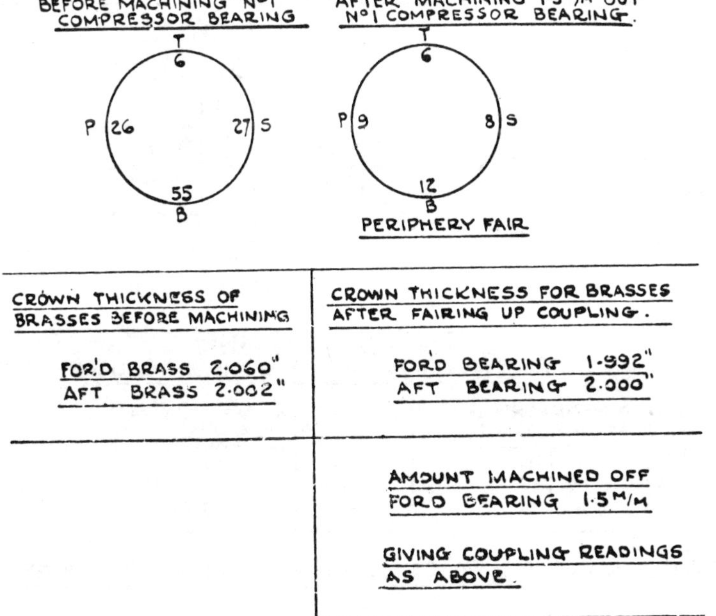

Fig. 203—Effect upon engine crankshaft coupling (at air-compressor crank) of machining forward bearing

The compressor coupling at the forward end of the crankshaft was found to be open at the bottom and slightly low to the engine crankshaft on the periphery. It was therefore decided to take 1·5 mm out of the forward compressor bearing. The amount to

BEFORE MACHINING Nº8 BEARING & BASE OF THRUST BLOCK.

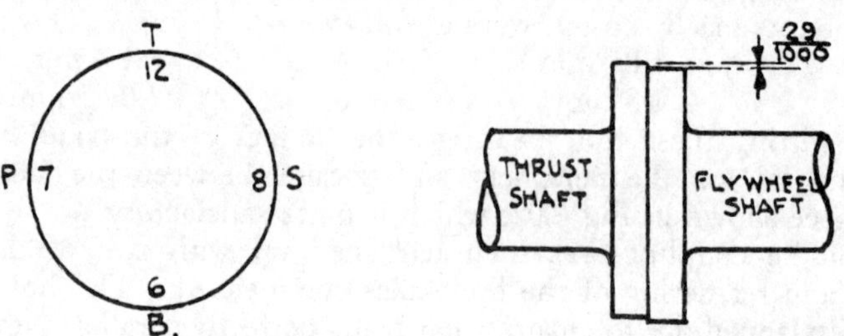

AFTER MACHINING Nº8 BEARING & BASE OF THRUST BLOCK.

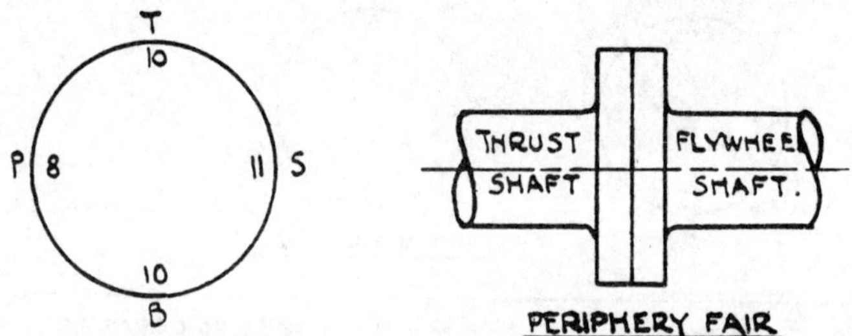

PERIPHERY FAIR

AFTER END COUPLING
(BETWEEN FLYWHEEL & THRUST BLOCK).

BEFORE MACHINING Nº 8 MAIN BEARING		AFTER MACHINING Nº8 MAIN BEARING	
Nº 6	0·175"	Nº 6	0·164"
Nº 7	0·136"	Nº 7	0·152"
Nº 8	0·054"	Nº 8	0·093"

BRIDGE GAUGE READINGS OF Nºs 6, 7, & 8 MAIN BEARINGS.

Fig. 204—Effect upon thrust-shaft coupling of machining aftermost engine bearing

be taken out was arrived at by taking the wear-down gauge readings with the shaft in its existing position, and then again with the bottom halves of the bearings removed and the shaft correctly lined up to the crankshaft coupling, necessitating stripping down compressor bottom ends and rigging chain blocks as necessary.

On refitting the forward bearing after machining, the face and periphery of the coupling gave the readings shown in Fig. 203. These being considered satisfactory, the coupling bolts were refitted and hardened up.

Turning now to the flywheel thrust coupling, the wear-down gauge reading showed No. 8 bearing to be high, and this was confirmed by gauging between the crank webs with crank first on top and then on bottom centre, the difference in these dimensions being 0·8 mm. It was therefore decided to machine 1 mm out of the bottom half of No. 8 bearing. This was done and the bearing refitted with the results shown in Fig. 204.

The flywheel-coupling flange was now lying considerably lower than the thrust-coupling flange and since it was not advisable to treat the thrust-shaft bearings in the same way as the crankshaft bearings by reducing the radial thickness of the bottom halves, it was decided that the underside of the thrust block must be machined and the block lowered bodily. From measurements taken on the thrust and flywheel couplings 2 mm was the amount to be taken off to bring the couplings fair. The readings taken on this occasion are shown in Fig. 204.

However, since the stern tube was to be re-wooded, it was deemed necessary to determine what effect the above alteration would have on the line of shafting aft of the thrust (the tail-shaft had already been withdrawn and the intermediate shaft was hung up in chain blocks). A wire was centred from the metal of the after end of the stern tube and stretched through the stern tube forward to the centre of the after coupling of the thrust shaft. It was found to be $\frac{1}{16}$-inch high at the forward end of the stern tube, and on squaring off the face of the thrust coupling it was found that the shaft line would benefit if the thrust block was lowered (this was also indicated at the forward end of the stern tube).

It was therefore decided to lower the thrust block 2 mm, and the bottom half of the block was sent away to be machined.

On returning the thrust block to ship, shipping same and re-bolting into place, the face of the forward coupling gave the reading shown in Fig. 204. These readings were considered satisfactory under the circumstances and the coupling bolts were refitted and hardened up.

During the lining up of the flywheel thrust-coupling, the normal sag of the shaft was taken out by means of a roller and sliding wedge arrangement fixed under the flywheel.

The stern tube having been re-wooded as necessary and re-bored to suit the spare tail-shaft, the tail-shaft was now shipped into the tube and the intermediate shaft replaced in position.

The readings at the forward and after couplings of the intermediate shaft were next carefully taken and are shown in Fig. 205.

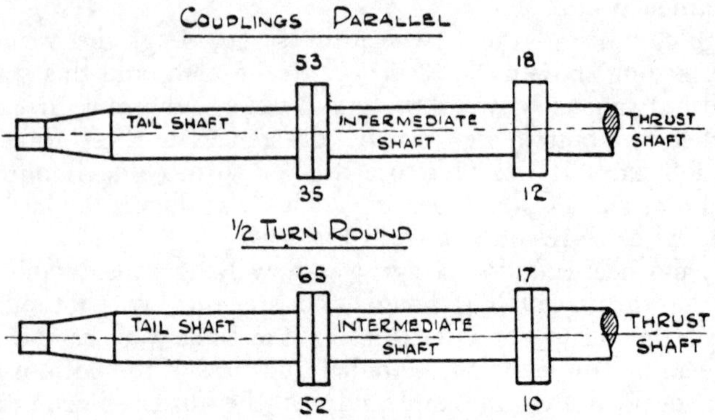

Fig. 205—Effect upon intermediate shaft couplings of lowering position of thrust block

No alteration was made to the height of the plummer-block packing, the block going back on the same chocks as before. The shaft line was approved and the coupling bolts at the forward end of the intermediate shaft fitted and hardened up, while the holes in the tail-shaft coupling were reamered through the after coupling of the intermediate shaft. The reamering being completed, the existing tail-shaft coupling bolts were refitted and the coupling hardened up.

After this repair was carried out no further trouble was experienced with coupling bolts.

Coupling bolts

A moment's thought only will suffice to convince any engineer of the importance of good-fitting coupling bolts. It is not sufficient that each bolt be a good driving fit, but when finally driven home every part of the hole in the coupling must be in good hard contact with the corresponding part of the bolt. If a bolt is not a good tight fit over its entire length it will be liable to become slack.

In view of the comparatively severe conditions to which the crankshaft coupling-bolts are subjected, the steam-engine practice of lining up the various sections and cutting out a large amount of metal by means of reamers is not good enough. It has been found that unless the holes in both flanges of a coupling are in fair alignment and practically of finished size, holes reamered with the shaft in a horizontal position are never perfectly parallel. The diameter of the holes is always larger at mid-length than at the ends by an amount varying from one to three thousandths of an inch, depending upon the care taken and the condition of the reamers and working gear. This is a very serious defect as it is at mid-length, or at the point where the flanges join, that the bolts require to be a particularly good fit.

Owing to the serious consequences which may result from these holes not being absolutely parallel, a boring bar or single-point tool should be used for opening out the holes to a few thousandths of an inch below the finished size, and a reamer put through for the final scrape. If desired, a series of drills may be used to open out the holes, but a reamer should only be used as a finishing tool. The holes will then be parallel, and there will be no tendency for slight working between the faces of the flanges to take place.

When coupling bolts break at the point in line with the joining faces of the flanges, the cause is nearly always due to the bolts being a bad fit at mid-length and allowing the flanges of the coupling to work slightly. When the bolts break at the end of the threaded portion, the cause is generally due to bad alignment of the two sections of crankshaft connected by the bolts.

Propeller shafting

The bearings of this shaft, sometimes referred to as the tunnel shaft, give no trouble apart from developing an abnormally high working temperature occasionally. Should a bearing give trouble in this way, it is always due either to the shaft being out of line or to the bottom half of the bearing having no side clearance. In such an event the bottom half should first be examined, and if showing hard contact at the sides should be well scraped in the manner already described for other bearings, in order to allow the lubricant to reach the loaded area. Should the rubbing surfaces be found in good order, it will be necessary to refit the bearing and test the shafting for alignment. Dirt is sometimes the cause of hand-lubricated bearings heating up. When dirt is the cause the bearing generally heats up suddenly, while the other faults mentioned will result in a high but steady working temperature.

To test the alignment of the shafting one of three methods may be adopted: first, by removing the coupling bolts and observing the position of the two flanges relative to each other; secondly, by removing the bearing caps and stretching a long fine wire above the shafting, and measuring the distance between the wire and the shaft at each bearing; and, lastly, by sighting. The last only of these three methods requires explanation.

To test the alignment by sighting, first of all procure three square pieces of thin sheet-iron, the size of which should be an inch or so larger than the diameter of the shafting. Clamp them firmly together, and V-cut one side so that it will sit astride the shaft and preferably be self-supporting by making contact with the pedestal of each bearing; or they may be made to stand upright by the use of putty (a mixture of red and white lead) built up on each side of the plates from the shaft. Then drill an $\frac{1}{8}$-inch diameter hole in line with the centre-line of the part cut out of the plates, and at such a height that when the plates are placed in position the hole will be an inch or more above the coupling. Next separate the three plates and mark the upper side of each, remembering that, when in use, the mark on each plate should be facing in the same direction.

Now place one plate on the shaft at a bearing well removed from the troublesome one, and place another plate similarly but at the other side of the troublesome bearing. A screened light should then be placed behind one or other of these plates. This done, the remaining plate is placed on the shaft at each bearing in turn located between the two outer plates. If the shafting is in good alignment, and the sighting plates have been carefully made and placed in such a way that the holes in them are in line with the vertical axis of the shaft, the light will be seen through the holes in all three plates. If the shafting is out of line, the bearing causing the misalignment, and the direction in which it ought to go, will be readily revealed by the middle plate.

Tail-end shafts

A section of a tail-end shaft, to which is attached the propeller, and the stern tube through which the shaft passes and which is firmly secured to the ship's structure, are shown in Fig. 206. The most suitable material for tail-end shafts is wrought iron or mild steel, the latter being mostly used; since they are exposed to the corrosive action of sea-water, means must be provided to protect them. Means must also be provided to prevent sea-water leaking past the moving tail-end shaft and the stationary stern tube into the ship, as well as to furnish a reasonably low-friction bearing for the tail-end shaft.

The most common method of protecting the tail-end shaft is to fit a brass liner over that part of the shaft which lies within the stern tube. This liner serves the double purpose of protecting the shaft from the sea-water and forming a suitable bearing surface in conjunction with the strips of lignum vitae wood with which the stern tube is lined. The lubrication of the tail-end shaft is effected by sea-water, which is allowed access to the inside of the stern tube, in combination with the oily surfaces of the wood.

The above method is not entirely satisfactory owing to the comparatively rapid wear rate of the wood bearing, and when a ship

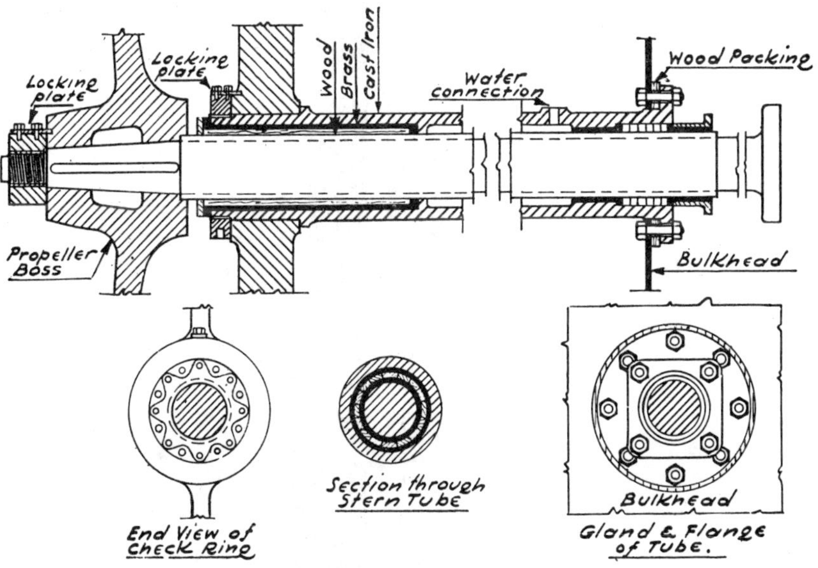

Fig. 206—Stern tube and propeller shaft

is constantly engaged in water containing a large proportion of sand and mud, other methods have to be employed. In such cases the usual practice is to run an uncovered steel tail-end shaft in a whitemetal-lined stern bush, the rubbing surfaces being lubricated with oil under slight pressure. An essential feature of this arrangement, which is illustrated in Fig. 207, is the provision of efficient

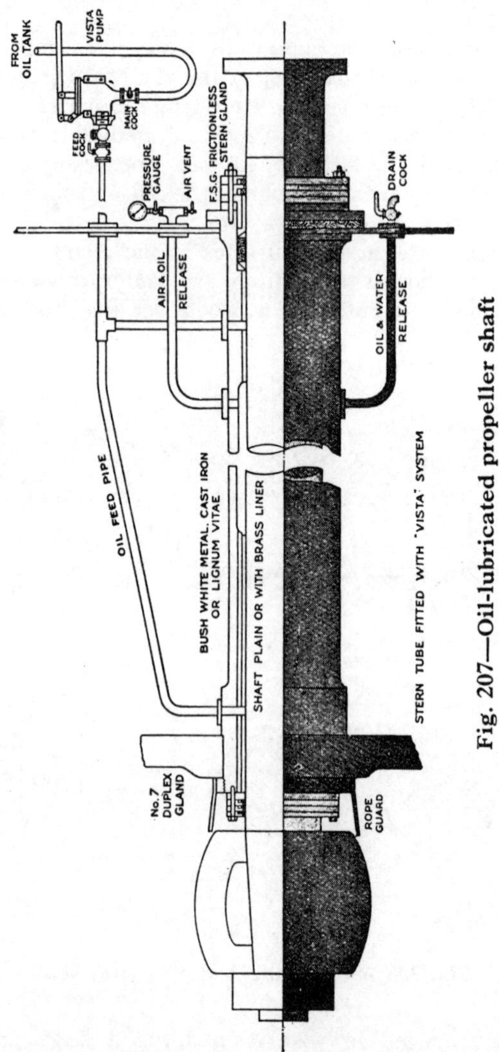

Fig. 207—Oil-lubricated propeller shaft

glands at each end of the stern tube to prevent leakage of lubricating oil. While such an arrangement is more mechanically sound and is more satisfactory, provided the parts are properly fitted, than the brass-covered shaft and lignum vitae bearing, the latter combination is still mostly favoured for deep-sea ships, and this type will be chiefly dealt with here.

The brass liners of tail-end shafts are usually from 15 to 20 feet long, but liners 30 feet long have been employed. The composition of the most suitable material for this purpose is gunmetal: 88 per cent copper, 10 per cent tin, and 2 per cent zinc. The liner is firmly secured to the shaft by boring it out to a diameter slightly less than that of the shaft, and, after expanding it by heat, placing it in position on the shaft, which it grips as it cools. The shrinking on of brass liners is not an easy operation, as not only must the liner be bored out to a size and heated to a temperature that will ensure its slipping easily over the shaft, but if bored out to too great a diameter it will not grip the shaft sufficiently, and if heated to too high a temperature the properties of the material may be adversely affected. The liner should cool out evenly. Should the ends cool down more rapidly than the middle portion, the metal may be overstressed and crack circumferentially as it contracts in length. Some cool the middle portion by compressed air to prevent this, but if the liner is allowed to cool down evenly there is no risk of the metal being overstressed. The usual shrinkage allowance is $\frac{1}{1000}$-inch per inch diameter. It is not good practice to pin the liners to the shaft as, apart from the possibility of water leaking past the pins and reaching the shaft, holes drilled into the shaft are liable to start fractures.

Obviously, the longer the liner the more difficult is the shrinking operation, so that when the shaft is very long a common practice is to fit two short liners, one at each end of the stern tube, the portion of the steel shaft between the liners being uncovered. As an alternative to this practice the bore of the liner and the tail-end shaft are stepped to provide two or more shrinking diameters. In the case of small-diameter shafts the brass liner is forced on by hydraulic pressure. The liners and shaft are always stepped with this method of fitting, and air-release holes must be provided in the liner at the point where the diameter changes. When the liner is in position red lead putty is forced into one of the air-release holes, and when it begins to issue from the other hole the holes are fitted with screwed pins cut flush with the liner.

Stern tubes

The circular stern tube is generally made of cast iron, and in deep-sea ships is from 1·5 to 2·5 inches thick. The tube is flanged at the forward end for attaching to the bulkhead, as shown in Fig. 206, and must therefore be inserted from the inside of the ship. The diameter of the after end is made slightly less than that at the forward end to facilitate fitting. A stuffing-box filled with greasy hemp packing is arranged at the forward end to prevent sea-water from leaking into the ship. The after end of the stern tube passes through the stern frame, and the length of the tube is such that when the circular nut screwed on the end of the tube is hardened up, the stern frame is sandwiched between the nut and a shoulder formed on the stern tube. In this way the stern tube is rigidly secured to the hull of the ship.

A flanged brass bush is inserted in the after end of the stern tube, and secured to it by countersunk screws passing through the flange into the stern tube. Strips of lignum vitae about 2 inches wide and ¾-inch thick are dovetailed into the bush, waterways being left at four or more points to allow sea-water to have free access to the rubbing surfaces. The lignum vitae is prevented from rotating with the shaft by four projecting longitudinal strips cast on the inside of the bush, while forward movement is prevented by a lip on the inner end of the bush shown in Fig. 206. To prevent the lignum vitae from working outboard, a check ring secured by means of tap-bolts to the flange of the brass bush is provided.

After the lignum vitae strips have been fitted and secured in the after end of the stern tube, they are bored to the required diameter. The amount of diametrical working clearance to be allowed depends upon the diameter of the shaft: the larger the diameter the greater the clearance and vice versa. If insufficient clearance is allowed the shaft may jam, while if too great the sooner will the tube have to be re-wooded. The best results are obtained with a diametrical clearance of 0·5 mm for shafts below 10 inches diameter and 1·0 mm for those above. If the strips of lignum vitae are cut across the grain the wear rate will be much less than if cut with the grain. The usual practice is to fit end-grain wood in the lower half and straight-grain wood in the upper half of stern tubes, since in the latter position the wood is not subjected to such severe conditions. The usual practice is to re-wood the stern-tube bush when the wear-down reaches ¼ inch.

Propeller attachment

The after end of the tail-shaft, to which the propeller is joined, is tapered, the usual amount being ¾-inch per foot length of taper.

A key half in the shaft and half in the propeller is attached to the shaft by countersunk screws. The forward end of the tapered hole in the propeller is recessed to fit over the end of the brass liner on the tail-shaft; thus no part of the steel shaft is in contact with sea-water. In order to make the point where the propeller joins the brass liner watertight, a rubber ring is sandwiched between the propeller and the end of the brass liner. The propeller nut, as well as the nut on the after end of the stern tube, are provided with locking plates, and the former is screwed left-hand when a right-hand propeller is used, and vice versa, so that the tendency will be for the nut to tighten when the parts are revolving.

Although a properly fitted rubber ring sandwiched between the propeller and the end of the brass liner is effective in preventing water from reaching the steel shaft, yet it is surprising how many shafts are damaged by corrosion owing to the rubber rings leaking. The only reason can be that insufficient care is taken when fitting the rubber rings. The rubber should, of course, be of good quality, but more important still is the size of the rings. If the cross-section of a ring is too great, the propeller will be prevented from being driven hard up, and the propeller will quickly become slack, since, as stated in an earlier chapter, confined rubber is practically incompressible. It is doubtless on account of the fear of such a serious thing happening that the cross-section of many rubber rings fitted is rather small, and, consequently, they do not properly seal the space. The remarks made in Chapter 7 regarding rubber rings are applicable to rings for this purpose.

The propeller nut and the end of the tail-shaft should be protected in some way against the corrosive action of the sea-water. The practice is to fit a hollow cone-shaped casting over the nut and bolt it to the propeller boss. Thus no part of the steel tail-end shaft will be in contact with sea-water if the various parts have been properly fitted. If no cone is fitted over the propeller nut it should be cemented over. Only the best Portland cement should be used, as the least amount of sand present will cause the cement to crack and let the sea-water reach the steel parts. To prepare the cement first dissolve 4 lb of common washing soda in two gallons of almost boiling water, and then mix 7 lb of cement at a time with this amount of soda solution and apply it to the nut whilst hot in the shortest possible time. Whilst one 7 lb of cement mixed with the soda solution is being applied, the next 7 lb should be prepared so that the operation of covering the nut and the end of the tail shaft is continued without interruption.

Corrosion of tail-end shafts

Even though the Classification Societies require single-liner tail shafts to be exposed for examination every three years, and double-liner shafts every two years, yet broken tail-end shafts are by no means unknown. Cracks are generally preceded by corrosion, and when fracture occurs the cause is stated to be what is called corrosion fatigue. It is necessary, therefore, that the design of the various parts should be such that no part of the steel shaft is exposed to sea-water, and that the various parts to be fitted together with extreme care in order that leakages of sea-water past any of the joining surfaces be prevented.

The tendency of steel tail-end shafts to corrode is greatly accentuated by the immersion of steel and brass in sea-water, which, owing to the employment of dissimilar metals, sets up galvanic action. Galvanic action is usually concentrated at or near the ends of the brass liners. Sometimes the wastage takes place just inside the brass liner and is not readily apparent. When, therefore, the point at which the liner joins the shaft is pitted or is slightly open, further investigation should be undertaken.

Whenever the tail shaft is withdrawn, the brass liner should always be sounded by tapping with a hammer to ascertain that all parts of the liner are in close contact with the shaft. Liners occasionally become slack at the propeller end, and in such cases it is generally wise to renew the liner. Should a liner be found cracked circumferentially, as sometimes happens, it is wise to renew it no matter how fine the crack may be, as cases are known where sea-water has penetrated to the shaft and caused very serious corrosion. In the case of one liner inspected by the author, which had cracked for a distance equal to about half the circumference, the shaft was found badly corroded in the vicinity of the crack and the shaft had commenced to fracture.

Sometimes when two short liners are fitted on a tail-end shaft, the exposed parts of the shaft between the liners are tightly wrapped with spun yarn or other material soaked in white lead and tallow to prevent sea-water from getting at the shaft. Such coverings are not very durable, and may easily keep a ship in dry dock for a few tides longer than would otherwise be necessary owing to the loose wrapping making the tail-end shaft difficult to withdraw. It is because of the possibility of corrosion taking place between the liners that the Classification Societies require this type of shaft to be withdrawn for examination once every two years, as against once every three years when one long liner is fitted.

Thrust bearings

As the whole of the power developed by a marine engine must be transmitted through the thrust bearing or block, the importance of maintaining this part of the installation in proper order requires no emphasis.

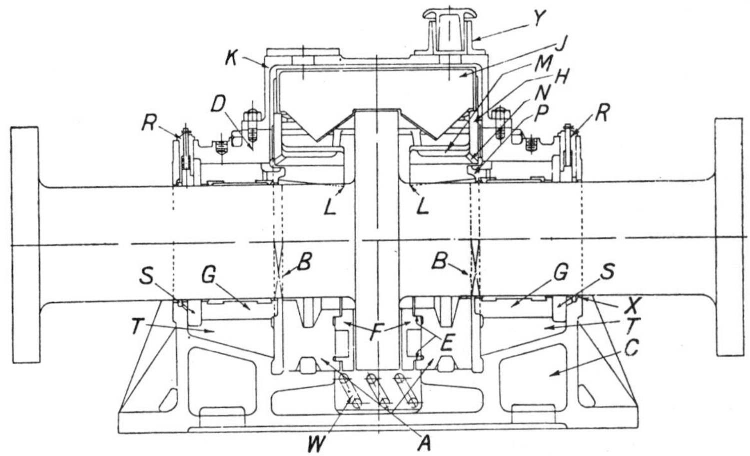

Fig. 208—Michell thrust bearing, " B " type

Fig. 208 illustrates the Michell thrust block. In this type of thrust block there is only one collar on the shaft. At each side of the collar is a thrust shoe *A*, of inverted horseshoe form. These shoes are exact duplicates, one for ahead and the other for astern operation. On the back of each shoe are two facings, on which are secured two steel adjusting liners *B*. The centre of effort of the total thrust on each shoe lies within these facings, which abut on the lower half-casing of the block *C*, thus ensuring that the whole of the thrust load is transmitted through the lower half of the block. The upper half of the casing *D* and the bolts connecting it to the lower half are thus relieved of all load. The design, therefore, permits of the complete upper half being removed for inspection of the rubbing surfaces without interfering with any of the principal working parts. The liners *B* are adjusted for thickness when the parts are first fitted, and no further adjustment is necessary, unless for some unusual reason excessive wear has taken place.

The front of each thrust shoe next to the collar face is provided with a machined recess *E*, concentric with the shaft. The thrust pads *F*, of which there are usually six on the ahead side and six on the astern side, are slid into position between the rubbing face of the collar on the shaft and the recess *E*. These pads are made of cast iron or bronze, and are faced on one side with whitemetal, which is finished to a true flat surface with a slight radius on the leading-in edge. The back of each pad is machined in a way to provide a radial shoulder in a certain definite position, and on the edge of the shoulder thus formed each pad is free to rock, and thereby automatically adjust its position relative to the face of the collar, so that a wedge-shaped space is formed between the parts and the lubricating oil is thus drawn in between the loaded surfaces.

The points upon which the pads rock are not at the centre of each pad, but are "offset" according to the rotational direction of the shaft. The handing of the pads, however, on the ahead and astern sides of the collar is the same, so that all pads in a bearing are similar and interchangeable, but for a right-hand propeller all pads are right-handed, and vice versa. Therefore, for a twin-screw installation with propellers turning outboard the Port thrust block has left-handed pads, and the Starboard right-handed pads.

At each end of the thrust block a journal bearing *G* lined with whitemetal is provided, so that each complete thrust block is a self-contained and truly aligned unit. The upper half of the casing *D* is provided with two cast-iron stops *H*, for the ahead and astern sides respectively. These stops serve three purposes, namely, (1) to prevent rotation of the thrust shoes and pads, (2) to act as oil-catchers and distributors, and (3) to form supports for the oil scraper *J*.

In the majority of cases lubrication of these thrust blocks is on the self-contained bath principle, the oil-bath being formed in the lower part of the block. The level of the oil should be such that the revolving collar on the shaft dips into it, but not so high that it will leak from the ends of the journal bearings when the shaft is at rest. Oil is lifted up from the bath on the outer surface of the rotating collar, and the bulk of the oil lifted is removed from the collar after the shaft has made half a revolution or so by the oil scraper *J*, which deflects it into the oil-catchers *H*. Each of these oil-catchers, one on the ahead side and the other on the astern, further diverts the oil, the major portion of which flows over the two lower corners *L* on to the revolving shaft at the root of the collar, where it is whirled round and outwards, providing a copious supply to the wedge-shaped clearances between each pad and the collar face. A smaller quantity of oil is caught in the reservoir *M*, cast on the stops *H*. This portion of the oil flows through the hole

N into a lip *P*, formed on the upper half of the bearing, whence it is carried by channels to the journal bearings.

Since a steady stream of oil flows around each journal bearing it is necessary to prevent it from escaping from the ends. Such leakage is prevented by the oil deflectors *R*, which scrape it off the shaft and deflect it to the groove *S*, whence it gravitates through the channels *T* back to the bath at the lower part of the block. These deflectors are extremely efficient, so that packing or the like, which is liable to wear, is quite unnecessary round the shaft.

Operation of thrust bearings

As the multi-collar type of thrust bearing is now obsolete, and the single or double collar type has been universally adopted, the following remarks apply to the latter, which has proved so efficient and reliable.

The lubricating arrangements of the Michell thrust bearing just described are such that the loaded parts work under ideal " fluid-film " conditions of lubrication; consequently, with ordinary attention, such bearings operate for years without any appreciable wear taking place. As there is no metallic contact between the bearing surfaces, the only heat generated is that caused by the passage of the oil films between the pads and the collar face. The working temperature of the bearing is not materially affected by the thrust load, provided that a suitable grade of oil is used, but is mainly influenced by the speed of rotation: the higher the speed the greater the working temperature, all other conditions being equal. In some cases the outer surface of the block is alone sufficient to dissipate by radiation to the atmosphere the heat generated, but in the majority of ships' installations it is advisable to provide other means of carrying off some of the heat and so keep the working temperature within moderate range. The usual working temperature is from 100° to 120°F (38° to 49°C). Slightly higher temperatures are not detrimental to the efficiency of the thrust block, nor are any of the parts likely to be affected by a temperature 30° or 40°F (16–20°C) higher than that stated, but as it is more difficult to detect by touching with the hand (the common method of judging the temperature at sea) any change in temperature arising from some fault when the temperature is of such an order, it is wise to keep the temperature below 120°F (49°C) if possible.

The heat produced can be carried off either by providing a cooling coil immersed in the oil, or by circulating oil from the main engine bearing system through the thrust block. A cooling coil in the oil-bath meets the case very well under all operating conditions, providing there is no possibility of water mixing with the oil. This must be guarded against at all costs for obvious reasons. The usual practice is to make such cooling coils of non-corrodible cupro-nickel, and they should be fitted in such a way that they are easily accessible for inspection and cleaning. " Staybrite " steel is an even more suitable material for these coils. The consequences of thrust-block cooling coils leaking may be so serious that it is wise to clean and test them hydraulically to twice the working pressure every two years.

For some reason not quite apparent, the pipes conveying the cooling water to thrust blocks corrode very rapidly, and frequently require to be renewed, unless they are made of non-corrodible material such as " Staybrite " steel. The explanation may be that in most cases the pipe arrangement is such that the cooling water must be forced down from a higher to a lower level, since the author has found that both copper and steel pipes corrode much more rapidly when the water flows in this direction than when flowing upwards.

When water flows upwards through a pipe the air in suspension remains more or less evenly distributed, and travels at the same rate or even faster than the water nearest to the walls of the pipe, and, consequently, is not given the opportunity to attack the surrounding metal wall. Moreover, owing to the friction of the metal surfaces, that portion of the water next to the pipe will move at a slower rate than the centre of the column, in the same way as a river flows more rapidly at the middle than near the banks. The buoyant nature of the particles of air makes them seek the fastest moving portion of the water in a pipe and they are, consequently, kept away from the metallic walls.

When, on the other hand, water is forced through a pipe in a downward direction, the particles of air, being much lighter than the water, naturally resist being forced in this direction and seek the slowest flowing portion of the water column. As in the previous example, the slowest moving portion of the water will, owing to frictional resistances, be that nearest to the walls of the pipe, so that when water is being forced downwards, the particles of air will get close to the surrounding metal surface and tend to resist being pushed forward by even the slowest moving portion of the column of water. The result will be that the speed of the air particles will be slow compared with the speed of the slowest moving portion of the water and they will, in consequence, be given the time and opportunity to attack the metal surfaces.

It will have been observed by all those operating diesel engines that the cooling-water outlet pipes of cylinder jackets, exhaust valves and even fresh-water piston-cooling pipes corrode more rapidly when the arrangement is such that the water is forced to a lower level. The corrosive elements are particularly active when the water is hot, because the air particles are more buoyant than when cold and resist being carried in a downward direction by the water to a greater extent. In such cases the corrosion usually takes place at the upper end of the pipe, or at the point where the direction of flow is changed from an upward to a downward one, whereas when the water is cold, the corrosion is more general in the pipe leading the water in a downward direction.

An alternative to cooling thrust blocks by water is to carry off the heat generated by connecting the thrust block to the bearing lubricating-oil system of the engine and passing a continuous stream of cool oil through the block. The only objection to this method is that the oil is not so free from impurities as when the block is self-contained, but provided the oil is given the attention recommended in Chapter 21, the wear rate will be no greater. It only means that the oil-bath should be cleaned out fairly frequently. Even when the block is self-contained the oil-bath should be cleaned out and re-charged with new oil every two years, as dirt enters the block in some mysterious way no matter what precautions are taken to keep it out. When, however, the oil is taken from the engine bearing system, the connection should be made at the highest point of the system, and, of course, only oil which has passed through the strainers should be led to the thrust block.

With this method of lubricating thrust blocks, it is essential for the oil outlet to be arranged in such a way that immediately the oil leaves the block it falls to a lower level, and that thereafter the drain pipe to the lubricating oil double-bottom tank be free from bends and the like that might obstruct the free flow of the oil. If the part of the drain pipe nearest to the thrust block is located horizontally, the height of the outlet is raised in proportion to the length of the horizontal portion when the ship is rolling or pitching. If the horizontal portion of the drain is located in an athwartship direction, the flow of oil from the block will be stopped momentarily when the ship is rolling, and if it is located in a fore-and-aft direction, the same thing will happen when the ship is pitching. As the flow of oil to the block continues without interruption in such circumstances, a momentary stoppage of the outflow means that the amount of oil contained in the block becomes excessive, and under certain conditions of weather not only will the oil level become so high that oil leaks from the ends of the journal bearings, but the oil will be violently churned and the block will attain an abnormally high working temperature.

Thrust bearing maintenance

After a time the diametrical clearance of the journal bearings, as well as the oil clearance between the thrust pads and shaft collar, increase, and require to be re-adjusted. The side clearance of the journal bearings will also need increasing, otherwise if a wedge-shaped clearance is not provided to allow the oil to enter and be carried round with the shaft the whole block will work at an unduly high temperature.

The correct diametrical clearance of the journal bearings depends upon the diameter of the shaft and should be as follows:—

6 inches and under	0·020 inch
6 ,, to 10 inches	0·025 ,,
10 ,, ,, 18 ,, ...	0·030 ,,
18 ,, ,, 21 ,, ...	0·035 ,,
21 ,, and upwards	0·045 ,,

When re-adjusting the diametrical clearances of the journal bearings, the clearance between the ends of the block casing and the underside of the shaft, shown at *X*, Fig. 208, should be observed. If this clearance is insufficient, contact between the shaft and the casing will take place and the shaft will be grooved. A lip at this point is necessary to prevent oil from overflowing.

To check, and re-adjust if necessary, the oil clearance between the thrust pads and collar, assemble the thrust shoes *A* and the pads *F*. Then with these in working position, force the thrust shaft endwise, by means of screw jacks placed between the back of the thrust shaft coupling and thrust block casing, until the collar is hard up against the thrust pads, taking care that the shaft is truly central in the journal bearings, and that both liners *B* are bearing equally hard on the casing. The position of the shaft should now be noted. This is best done by measuring the distance between the collar and a fixed internal surface of the casing with a micrometer gauge. Then repeat the foregoing operation in the opposite direction and measure the distance the shaft is moved. This measurement, which is the total fore-and-aft oil clearance, varies with the diameter of the shaft and should not be less than the following:—

6 inches and under	.. ..	0·025 inch
6 „ to 10 inches	.. ..	0·030 „
10 „ „ 18 „	.. ..	0·035 „
18 „ „ 21 „	.. ..	0·040 „
21 „ and upwards	.. ..	0·050 „

Should the clearance be less than that recommended, the liners *B* must be adjusted to give the correct amount, care being taken that both liners are bearing equally on the casing. If the clearance is slightly greater than that recommended, it will in no way affect the working of the thrust block, but the clearance must not be excessive, otherwise trouble with the crankshaft bearings may result.

The oil recommended in Chapter 20 for the principal bearings is suitable for the lubrication of these thrust blocks.

Finally, do not neglect thrust bearings because they do their job efficiently and silently month in and month out. All they ask is to be kept supplied with sufficient good clean lubricating oil. If this simple task is not attended to the consequences can be very serious. For instance, a few months before this paragraph was written a thrust bearing was allowed to run short of oil, and the position of the crankshaft was altered so much in consequence that one of the cranks made such hard contact with the adjacent bedplate girder that not only was the crank bent, but the heat produced ignited the gaseous contents of the crankcase and an explosion occurred.

CHAPTER 24

Cylinder pressure indicators and indicator diagrams

It is usual to state the power of an engine in terms of indicated horse-power or brake horse-power, the former being the power produced in the cylinders and the latter the power produced at the thrust bearing. The indicated horse-power is always the greater of the two because, in calculation, no account is taken of the power required to overcome the frictional resistance in the engine or to drive accessories which may be driven by it.

In order to arrive at the indicated horse-power of a multiple-cylinder engine it is necessary to ascertain the power produced in each of the cylinders, which, for successful operation, must be the same, assuming that the whole of the power produced in a cylinder is transmitted to its respective crank. Should one cylinder have to drive a scavenge air-pump or some such accessory then that cylinder should produce the same power as each of the other cylinders plus the power required to drive the pump, if the engine is to be balanced as regards power distribution.

To find how much power is being produced in a cylinder certain particulars regarding the engine must be known. One is to know the pressures prevailing in the cylinder. The terminal compression pressure and the maximum combustion pressure can be found in a number of ways, and whilst it is important to be able to ascertain readily the value of these pressures, for the purpose of calculating the power produced, it is necessary to know the pressure prevailing at every point of the cycle. The instrument used for this purpose aboard ship is the "pressure indicator," and when fitted to an engine cylinder, with the engine running on fuel, it makes a continuous record on paper of the pressures prevailing in that cylinder throughout all strokes of the cycle.

It affords a ready means, also, of computing the average pressure exerted on the piston, for if from the average pressure acting on the piston during the working stroke we deduct the pressure acting in opposition during the compression and idle strokes, we obtain what is called the " mean indicated pressure." The mean indicated pressure, in combination with other known factors, enables the indicated horse-power (i.h.p.) of the engine to be calculated.

Fig. 209—Cylinder pressure indicator (Dobbie McInnes)

It is a valuable instrument also, in detecting irregularities in the combustion process, as will be shown later.

In general appearance a pressure indicator suitable for diesel engines resembles those used in connection with steam engines, but in constructional detail a few modifications have been found to be necessary owing to the higher pressures and temperatures encountered in the diesel engine. In the first place, since very much higher pressures have to be recorded the area of the piston is only about half that of a steam-engine indicator piston; also, to obtain an accurate reading, the spring is placed outside and above the indicator cylinder, so that it will not be affected by the intense heat of combustion.

The Dobbie McInnes indicator is shown in Fig. 209. This instrument consists of a cylinder in which works a case-hardened steel piston, loaded by a helical spring. The spring controls the upward motion of the piston and returns it towards its original position as the gas pressure on the piston decreases. Since these springs are accurately calibrated, the pressure in the cylinder causes the indicator piston to rise through a distance proportional to the pressure exerted, and therefore a certain distance travelled by the indicator piston represents a certain pressure exerted. Usually the scale of the spring used is such that 1 mm travel equals 1 atmosphere, or 1 inch travel equals 350 lb/sq.in. Stronger or weaker springs may, of course, be used, depending upon the desired height of the diagram. The spring must be strong enough, however, to overcome inertia forces and cause the indicator piston to respond instantly to the slightest change of gas pressure exerted.

The motion of the indicator piston is transmitted to a pencil by a small piston rod and a combination of levers, the pencil being attached to the end of the top, cranked lever.

The paper on which the pressures are to be recorded is held closely around the drum by clips. This drum is made to oscillate on its axis by a pull on the cord which is wound around the lower part of it. When the pull on the cord is released, a spring located inside the drum, which has a large number of coils to give it an even movement, returns the drum to its original position. This drum spring must be of the correct strength; if it is too weak the inertia forces will not be overcome, particularly in high-speed engines, and if too strong the cord will be stretched. As the indicator must register the pressure in the cylinders in relation to the position of the engine piston, the motion of the drum must coincide with that of the engine piston, but, of course, the travel of the drum is much less. The full movement of the drum in one direction is completed in the same time as one stroke of the engine piston.

The desired semi-rotary motion of the drum is obtained by connecting the cord to a moving part of the engine, which gives a sufficiently correct reproduction on a reduced scale of the motion of the engine piston. The drive is usually taken from either the engine camshaft or the crosshead.

One arrangement of camshaft drive is shown in Fig. 210, while Fig. 211 shows a typical crosshead drive. The former is mostly used at the present time, but as it is not unlikely that engines of the future will not require camshafts extending the full length of the engine at cylinder-head level, the crosshead drive will become more widely used. The reason for this possible trend is indicated in Chapter 17, pages 329 and 339.

A cam with a single peak mounted on the camshaft can be used for two-stroke engines, but for four-stroke engines the cam requires a double peak, since in this type the camshaft works at half the speed of the crankshaft, and the indicator drum must be pulled and released twice during one revolution of the camshaft, to register

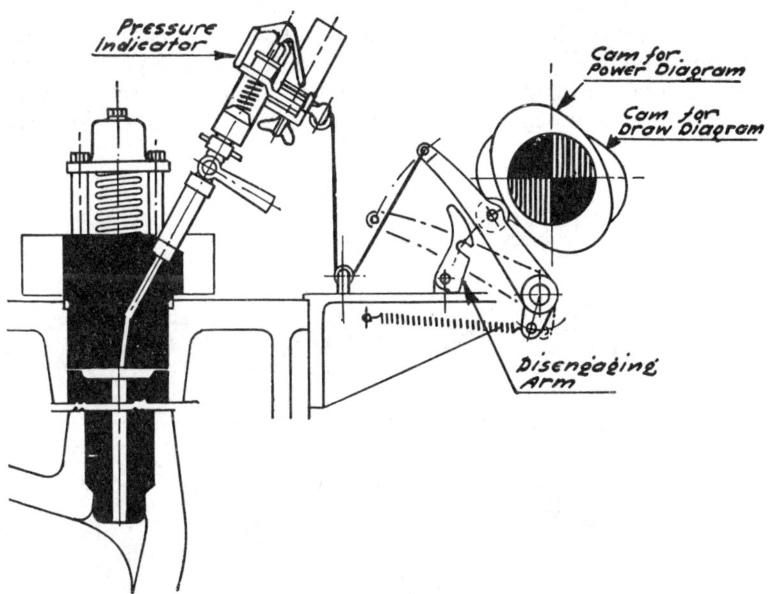

Fig. 210—Camshaft drive for operating drum of pressure indicator, 4-stroke engine

the four strokes of the piston. Whichever type of drive is employed, slackness in the gear must be avoided as it will give a distorted diagram.

A parallel motion the whole way from the piston to the indicator drum is ideally necessary to give an accurate reproduction of the piston position on the diagram drawn, but this, as will be appreciated, is practically impossible to obtain. Diagrams taken with the gears usually found, however, are sufficiently correct for all practical purposes, provided they work as intended.

The cord used for transmitting the motion to the drum should be of a specially braided kind to prevent distortion under tension. Before using a new cord it should suspend a moderately heavy weight for an hour or so, more especially if long cords are required, as the amount of stretch even in good cord may produce an error. The best cord is one containing a core of fine wire. For very long leads, such as will be required on double-acting engines, steel tape is superior. The best results, no matter what kind of cord is used, are only obtained by leading the cord from the operating gear to the indicator in the shortest and most direct way possible. When the direction of the cord is changed, it should ride on a perfectly free pulley. The cord may be bent any number of times to clear the usual obstructions about an engine, but the fewer the better, since the

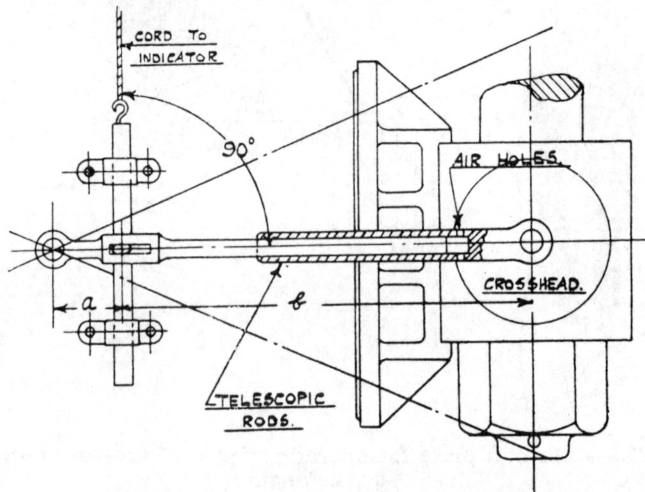

Fig. 211—Crosshead drive for operating drum of pressure indicator

less the friction the more true the diagram. It is important, however, that the part of the cord between the point from which motion is

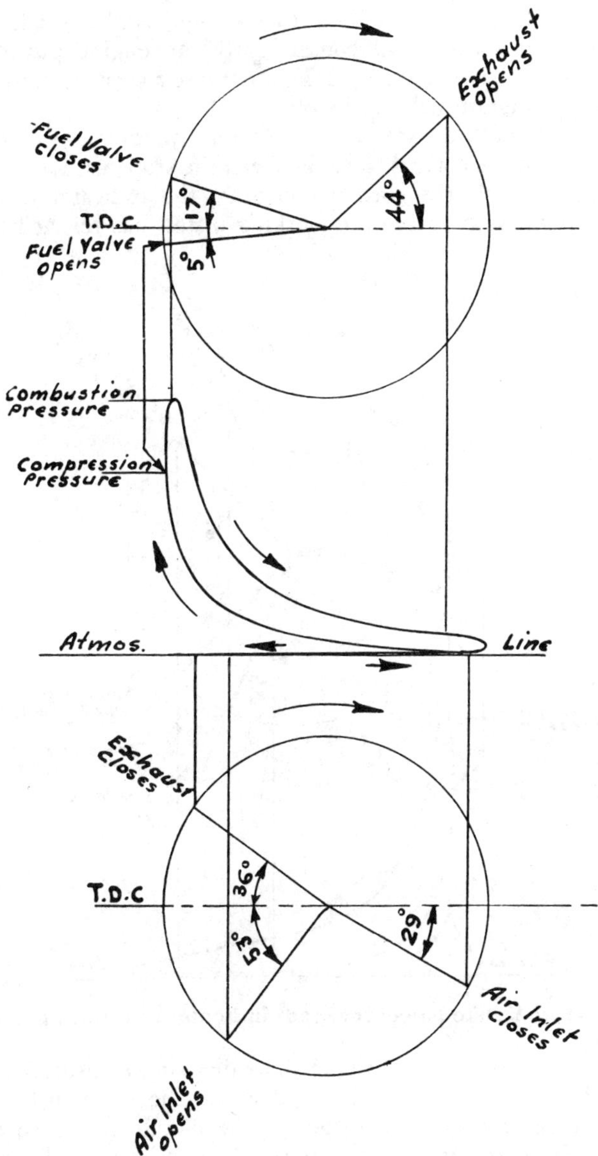

Fig. 212—Four-stroke (supercharged) valve timing diagrams and corresponding indicator diagram

derived and the first pulley should be at right angles to the driving lever when the latter, and consequently the engine piston, is at mid-position (as shown in Fig. 211), otherwise a correct reproduction of the piston motion will not be obtained.

The length of the cord must be carefully adjusted to give the indicator drum the correct travel between the stops without touching either of them. If the cord is too long, the indicator drum will come against a stop before the working piston has reached the end

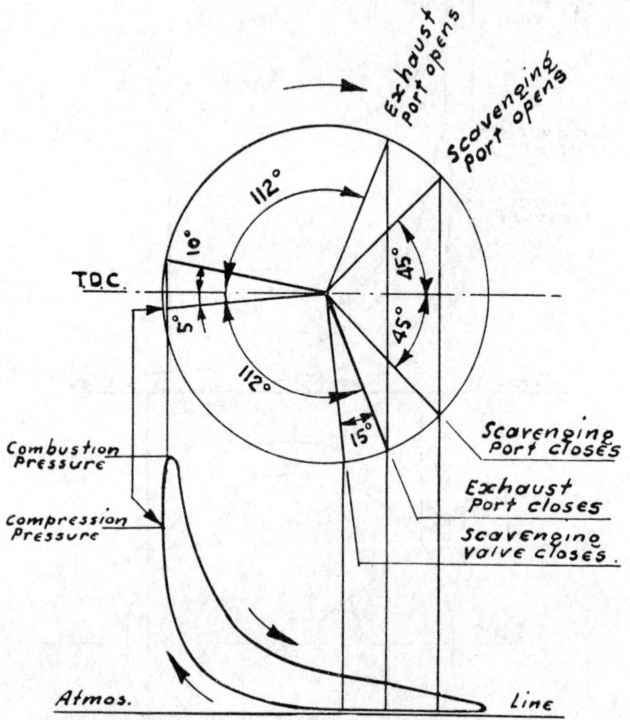

Fig. 213—Two-stroke (supercharged) indicator and timing diagrams

of its stroke, with the result that a short diagram, measured horizontally, will be obtained. If the cord is too short it will be broken or the indicator may be damaged. The length of the cord must be adjusted before it is connected to the indicator. To do this, allow the drum to rest against its stop, and with the hook shown in Fig. 209 in one hand, take hold of the end of the cord with the other hand and exert a light pull upon it. The length of the cord should then be adjusted until the ends come to within $\frac{3}{8}$-inch of each other.

A four-stroke indicator diagram, for a supercharged engine, with the corresponding timing diagrams, is shown in Fig. 212. Two timing diagrams are given, to represent the two revolutions, or four strokes, of this cycle. As the camshaft revolves at only half the speed of the crankshaft, the angular movement of the camshaft is but half the amount shown in the sketch. It is usual to speak of timing angles as referred to the crankshaft, and not the camshaft.

A two-stroke diagram is shown in Fig. 213, for a supercharged engine, with the corresponding timing diagram. In this type of engine the camshaft revolves at the same speed as the crankshaft, therefore the angular measurements are the same, the cycle of operations being completed during one revolution of the crankshaft.

The springs most commonly used in indicators give a diagram about $1\frac{1}{4}$ to $1\frac{1}{2}$ inches in height, the length of the diagram being $2\frac{1}{4}$ to 3 inches. This size of diagram will be obtained with springs of the strength previously mentioned, on page 532. A stronger spring may be used, but since such would reduce the height of the diagram, slight errors in measuring up would be more serious. The best results are obtained by using the lightest spring possible. From slow-running engines a good diagram is obtained with a 250 (250 lb to the inch) spring, but for high speeds a stronger spring is necessary to prevent errors due to inertia of the moving parts of the indicator.

Taking indicator diagrams

The cause of many troubles in diesel-engine operation is unequal power-distribution in a line of cylinders. The increased pressures resulting therefrom in some cylinders have little effect, but the accompanying higher mean-temperatures may have serious consequences.

Before commencing to take diagrams, the indicator should be dismantled and all working parts thoroughly cleaned and lubricated with a thin oil. The piston must be quite free in the cylinder, and able to drop through by its own weight. A slight leakage of gas past the piston is preferable to the possibility of the piston sticking, even though ever so slightly. The pencil point should be sharp enough to give a fine clear line—if too sharp it will tear the paper—and the stop-screw adjusted so that when the pencil touches the paper the screw point is $\frac{1}{32}$-inch or so from the stop.

Before attaching the indicator, the indicator cock on the cylinder must be opened to blow out any dirt lodging in the passage. It is essential that the passage be quite clear, not only of loose dirt, which may cause the indicator piston to stick, but of any matter that will reduce the area; a large straight passage is necessary if the pressure exerted in the indicator is to be identical with the pressure in the engine cylinder. Small indirect passages restrict the flow of gas.

When satisfied that the hole is perfectly clear the indicator may be attached, care being taken to see that a sufficient number of the connecting-nut threads are engaged to hold the instrument firmly against the pressure which it must withstand. The length of the cord must next be adjusted in the manner already described, the paper or card placed in position on the drum, and the cord attached.

Before taking the diagram, open the indicator cock and allow the piston to make about half-a-dozen strokes to warm up the instrument; then, when the pencil is at its lowest position, press it to the paper just long enough to make one outline. After this shut the indicator cock, making sure that the indicator cylinder is open to the atmosphere, and disconnect the cord from the drum, then press the pencil against the paper again and pull the drum cord once only, by hand, to get the atmospheric line. This line should be extended beyond each end of the power diagram so that, if the engine is of the four-stroke type, it will be distinct from the air-inlet and exhaust lines.

On each diagram taken should be marked the number of the cylinder, injection pressure, revolutions, etc., and whether it was the first, second or third diagram taken. The indicator should then be dismantled, cleaned and oiled before it is attached to the next cylinder—unless one is quite satisfied that the piston is working freely.

Mean indicated pressure

In order to calculate the indicated horse-power of an engine it is necessary to find the mean indicated pressure from the indicator diagram. The mean indicated pressure may be found in two ways, (1) by finding the area of the diagram in square inches by means of a planimeter, and dividing the area by the length of the diagram in inches, when the mean height will be obtained; or (2) when a planimeter is not obtainable, the mean height of the diagram can be obtained in the following manner. Divide the length of the diagram into any number of equal parts, ten being the most convenient; set off half a part from each end—or one-twentieth—

and nine equal parts of one-tenth between; erect ordinates perpendicular to the atmospheric line at the points of division to the upper line of the diagram; add together the lengths of these ordinates intercepted between the upper and lower lines of the diagram, divide by the number of measurements made, and multiply the quotient by the scale of the spring; the result will be the mean indicated pressure.

Planimeter

There are various types of planimeters in use which differ in construction but operate in much the same way. The one most commonly used is the Amsler polar planimeter, illustrated in Fig. 214, which gives a reading in square inches, tenths of a square

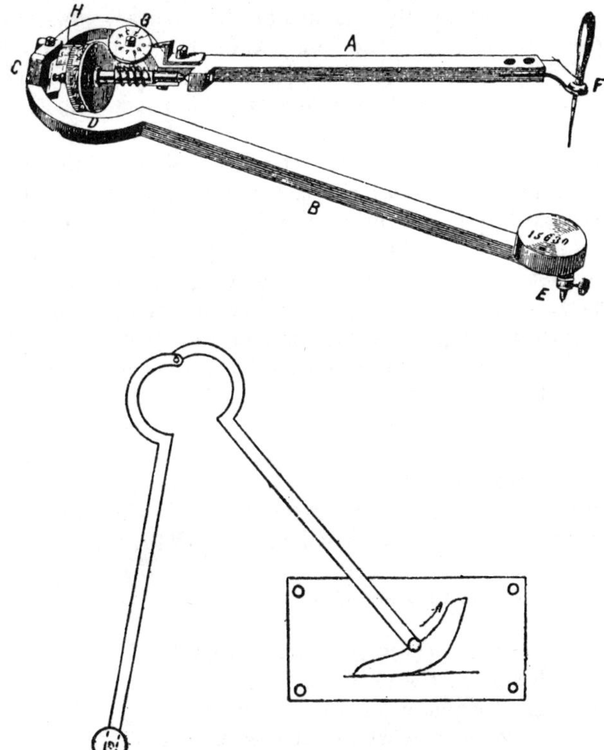

Fig. 214—The Amsler polar planimeter and its working position

inch, and hundredths of a square inch. It consists of two bars *A* and *B* hinged at *C*. At the end of the bar *B* is a needle-point *E*, which is pressed into the table and loaded by a weight to hold this part in position during operation. The tracing point *F* on the bar *A* is moved over the outline of the diagram. The graduated roller *D*, which is in contact with the table, revolves as the outline of the diagram is traced. The dial *G* is divided into ten parts, each part representing one complete revolution of the roller *D*, and is only used when large areas are to be measured.

The planimeter should be used on a level, unglazed but smooth surface, the indicator card being pinned to the board. The planimeter is then set with the bar *B*, Fig. 214, about parallel to the left-hand side of the card, as shown in lower figure, and the needle-point pressed down just sufficiently to hold it in place. Set the tracer point at any given point on the outline of the diagram, mark it as the starting point, and adjust the roller wheel to zero. Now follow the outline of the diagram carefully with the tracing point moving in a clockwise direction, care being taken to stop exactly on the starting point.

The area of the diagram is read off from the recording wheel and vernier as follows. Suppose the largest figure on the roller wheel *D* that has passed zero on the vernier *H*, Fig. 214, to be one (units), and the number of spaces that have also passed zero on the vernier to be one (tenths), and the number of the graduation on the vernier that exactly coincides with the graduation on the roller wheel to be two (hundredths), then the area of the diagram is 1·12 square inches. Divide this by the length of the diagram, which we will say is 3 inches, and we have 0·37 inch as the mean height of the diagram. This multiplied by the scale of the spring, which we will assume is 250, gives 92·5 lb/sq.in. as the mean indicated pressure acting on the piston during one cycle.

Having found the mean indicated pressure, the indicated horse-power can now be obtained by substituting in the following formula:

$$\text{Indicated horse-power} = \text{i.h.p.} = \frac{P.L.A.N.}{33{,}000}$$

where P = mean indicated pressure in lb/sq.in.,
L = length of the stroke in feet,
A = area of piston in square inches,
N = number of working strokes per minute.

In four-stroke engines N is equal to half the number of revolutions multiplied by the number of cylinders, if the total output is to be based on the power developed in one cylinder, and in an engine of the two-stroke type the number of revolutions multiplied by the number of cylinders.

When calculating the power developed in the lower cylinders of double-acting engines it must be remembered that the effective piston area is the area of the piston less the cross-sectional area of the piston rod.

Stating that an engine develops a certain horse-power is apt to convey a wrong impression regarding its actual capabilities, unless the type of engine and the manner of driving the scavenging and cooling-water pumps, etc. is also given. For instance, in some designs these components are driven by the main engine, while in others they are independently driven. Also, in the case of air-injection engines of the same indicated horse-power, one operating on the two-stroke and the other on the four-stroke principle, and each having the air-compressor directly coupled, the four-stroke engine will be capable of doing more useful work than the two-stroke engine, since, in the latter, part of the indicated power will be expended in driving the scavenging pumps, unless, of course, they are independently driven.

For these reasons the power of engines is generally stated in terms of actual power developed on the brake test, that is, the b.h.p.

The brake horse-power of an engine depends upon its mechanical efficiency, as shown by the formula—

b.h.p. = i.h.p. multiplied by the mechanical efficiency.

If we assume two-stroke and four-stroke diesel engines to be 75 and 85 per cent mechanically efficient, respectively, the following formulae are obtained:—

$$\text{Two-stroke:}\quad \begin{cases} \text{i.h.p.} \times 0{\cdot}75 = \text{b.h.p.} \\ \text{b.h.p.} \times 1{\cdot}333 = \text{i.h.p.} \end{cases}$$

$$\text{Four-stroke:}\quad \begin{cases} \text{i.h.p.} \times 0{\cdot}85 = \text{b.h.p.} \\ \text{b.h.p.} \times 1{\cdot}176 = \text{i.h.p.} \end{cases}$$

Besides making possible the equalising of the power in a line of cylinders, and ascertaining the indicated horse-power of an engine, the indicator diagram also discloses faults in the timing of the various parts which affect the cycle of operations.

Two- and four-stroke theoretical indicator diagrams were explained in Chapter 2, so we will now proceed with an explanation of the various lines which form the indicator diagram.

Atmospheric line

The atmospheric line indicates whether the pressure at any part of the cycle is greater or less than the pressure of the atmosphere. Before drawing the atmospheric line the indicator should be warmed, and care taken to see that the piston is subjected only to the pressure of the atmosphere. It is not necessary—though it is advisable—to draw this line after the diagram has been taken; the indicator will then be thoroughly warmed up.

Air inlet

As the engine piston moves out of the cylinder, air, in the case of unsupercharged four-stroke engines, is drawn through a finely-slotted pipe, in order to silence the inrush of air and prevent as far as possible any impurities being drawn into the cylinder. If these slots are partly choked or the air-inlet valve lift insufficient, the air-inlet line of the diagram will fall below the atmospheric line, and the final compression pressure will be below normal. Even when the slots are quite clear the air-inlet line tends to fall below the atmospheric line until near the end of the stroke, when the speed of the piston is reduced and the air-inlet line rises and coincides with the atmospheric line.

In a normal diagram taken with a spring of a scale commonly employed, the air-inlet line so far as can be seen with the naked eye, follows along the atmospheric line unless the defect is very great.

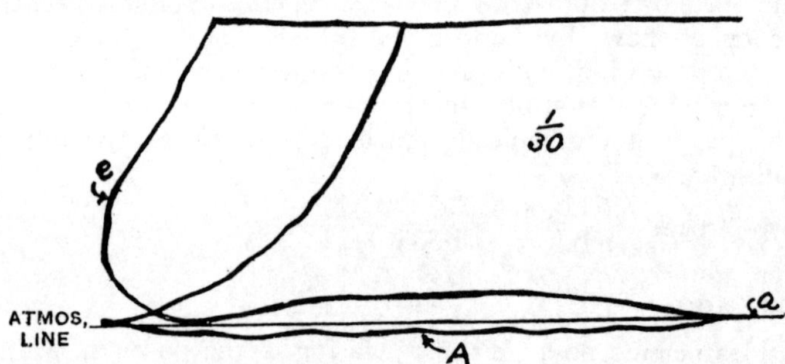

Fig. 215—Light-spring indicator diagram, 4-stroke engine

If it is desired to know exactly what is taking place in the cylinder during this stroke, it is necessary to take what is called a light-spring diagram. As the term implies, a low-scale spring is used, which will register about 30 lb to the inch; such a diagram is shown in Fig. 215. Owing to the employment of a weak spring the lines are naturally inclined to be wavy, and due allowance must be made for the inertia of the indicator piston, etc.

The air-inlet stroke *A*, which begins at *a*, will be seen to start on the atmospheric line, then fall below it, and finally rise to it again. The reason for this is that when the piston is at the top of the cylinder and beginning the air-inlet stroke, the compression clearance space is filled with a mixture of burnt gases and air at about atmospheric pressure. As the crank leaves the top dead centre the speed of the piston is relatively slow and the air is able to follow it up, consequently the pressure in the cylinder remains at about atmospheric pressure for the first part of the stroke. But as the crank gets away from the top centre the piston speed increases and it is more difficult for the air to follow up the piston, consequently the pressure in the cylinder falls slightly below atmospheric. It is, however, a neck-and-neck race between the piston and the air until the crank approaches the bottom dead centre, when the piston speed decreases. The air rushes on, catching up to the piston, and crushes into it, as it were, with the result that not only does the pressure rise to atmospheric but slightly exceeds it, due to the momentum of the inrushing air. In a low-speed unsupercharged engine the average pressure in the cylinder during this stroke is about 1 lb/sq.in. below atmospheric.

Compression

The compression line should curve quite regularly until it meets the fuel-injection line. The terminal compression pressure is sometimes taken as represented by the maximum height of the diagram measured from the atmospheric line. This, however, is not the correct value, since there is always an increase in pressure upon injection of fuel. To obtain the correct compression pressure, therefore, the fuel (and injection air in the case of air-injection engines) to the cylinder concerned must be shut off and what is called a compression diagram taken.

The distance from the atmospheric line to the highest point on the single-line compression diagram multiplied by the scale of the spring will give the terminal compression pressure. Thus, if the height of the compression curve is 1·25 inches, and the scale of the spring used 1/400, the terminal compression pressure is 500 lb/sq.in.

Wear in the bearings produces a drop in the compression pressure, so that as wear in the crankshaft, crankpin, and crosshead bearings takes place the piston has to be raised by fitting liners of suitable thickness underneath the crosshead bearings to reduce the piston end clearance. A partially choked indicator-cock passage will also cause a lower terminal compression pressure to be recorded. A power diagram taken under such conditions will be low and broad, as shown dotted in Fig. 216—the full line representing the normal diagram.

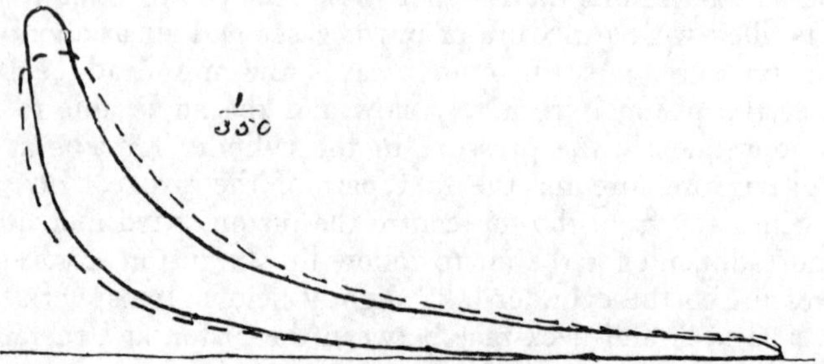

Fig. 216—Indicator diagram showing effect of partly choked passage to indicator

It is essential, both as regards fuel economy and proper working, that the correct compression pressure be maintained; not only is a high pressure necessary to ensure a temperature sufficient to ignite the fuel, but if the pressure is not up to what it should be it may mean that the amount of air necessary to burn a normal charge of fuel is not in the cylinder, imperfect combustion will result, and the mean temperature will consequently be increased. Sluggish starting is sometimes due to this fault.

An engine should be thoroughly warmed up before diagrams are taken. If an engine is cold the compression pressure recorded may be from 20 to 30 lb lower than when heated up and working normally.

In all marine diesel engines, whether they be four-stroke, two-stroke, supercharged, or unsupercharged (certain Doxford engines excepted), the designed terminal compression pressure is in the region of 500 lb/sq.in., or roughly 35 kg/cm. Such a pressure has been found high enough to give a good thermal efficiency without the need to make the cylinder castings unduly heavy, and to ensure that sufficient heat of compression will be produced to give prompt ignition of all fuels commonly used when an engine is started from cold or the piston speed is as low as 20 per cent of normal full speed.

When supercharged engines are running unsupercharged the compression pressure will be about 100 lb/sq.in. below the normal pressure, The compression pressure varies in direct proportion to the supercharge air pressure. For instance, in the 500 i.h.p. (rated) cylinder from which the diagrams shown in Fig. 217 were taken, the compression pressure when unsupercharged was 400 lb/sq.in., and when supercharged to 3·5 lb/sq.in. the compression pressure became 500 lb/sq.in. It will be realised that 3·5 lb is 1·25 atmospheres per square inch, and that the supercharged compression pressure is 1·25 times the pressure produced under unsupercharged conditions.

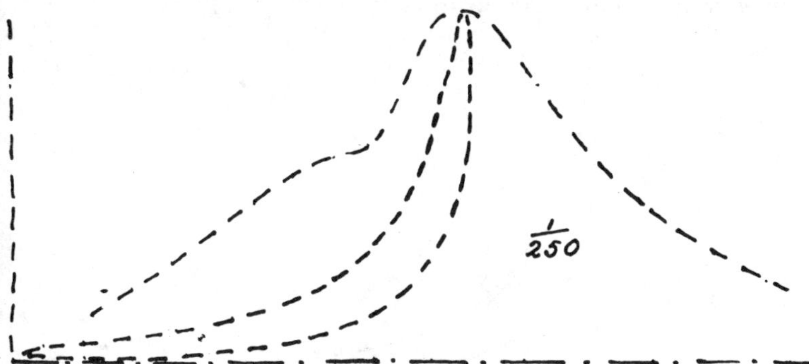

Fig. 217—Indicator diagram (draw card) from a 500-h.p. cylinder, 4-stroke engine

The compression pressure depends, therefore, upon the supercharge air pressure, which varies in different makes of engines but is generally of a value which under full-speed conditions will produce a compression pressure of about 500 lb/sq.in. When in doubt about the correct supercharge air pressure the compression pressure is therefore a useful guide. A further effect of altering the supercharge air pressure is to cause a variation in the exhaust gas temperature: the higher the pressure the lower the temperature, and vice versa. In most two- and four-stroke supercharged engines the correct supercharge air pressure produces an exhaust temperature in the region of 800°F (427°C), assuming, of course, that all parts of the engine which may have an effect upon the exhaust temperature are in good order.

Fuel injection

Injection of fuel commences just before the end of the compression stroke (Figs. 212 and 213).

When an engine operating on the true diesel heat cycle is running under full load conditions the pressure in the cylinder is nearly constant during the period of fuel injection, which is about one-tenth of the working stroke. Experience has shown, however, that the highest efficiency is not obtained in this way, so the practice is to time the injection of fuel so that there is an appreciable rise in cylinder pressure when injection begins. This results in the upper end of the indicator diagram taking a pointed form, as shown by the full line in Fig. 218; in some cases it becomes almost a peak. The pressure rise upon injection of fuel varies in different makes of engines from 100 lb to 200 lb/sq.in.

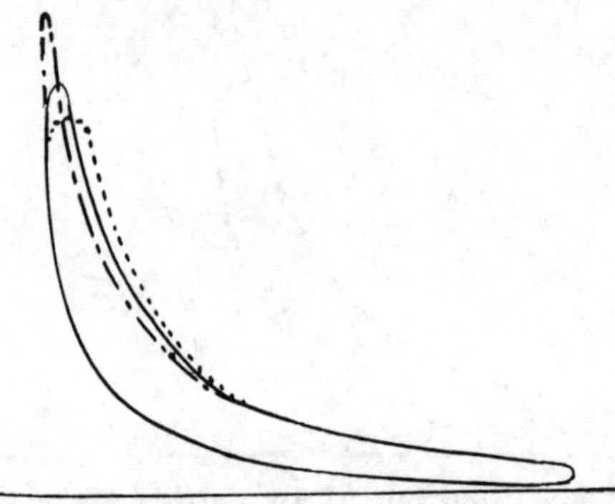

Fig. 218—Indicator diagram showing effect of varying the injection timing: normal (full line), too late (dotted line), and too early (dot and dash line).

If injection takes place too late the height of the diagram is reduced and the body of the diagram becomes fuller, while if injection takes place too early the reverse is the case. In the same diagram, the dotted line shows the effect when injection takes place too late, and the dot-and-dash line when injection takes place too early.

The above statements refer to airless-injection engines. In air-injection engines the pressure rise upon injection is only about 50 lb/sq.in. and the upper end of the diagram is relatively flat (Fig. 216), but the effect of too early and too late injection is similar.

Expansion

The expansion line should curve regularly towards the toe of the diagram. If an expansion line is obtained where the line drops by a series of steps, sticking of the indicator piston will probably be the cause. A similar line, but more in the form of waves, is produced by the inertia of the moving parts of the indicator, and is a sign that the piston is working freely. If the wave is very pronounced, vibration of the indicator cord may be the cause, or too light a spring is being used.

Exhaust

The exhaust opens near the end of the expansion line, or just before the end of the working stroke, and if the timing is correct the toe of the four-stroke diagram will be finely rounded, as shown

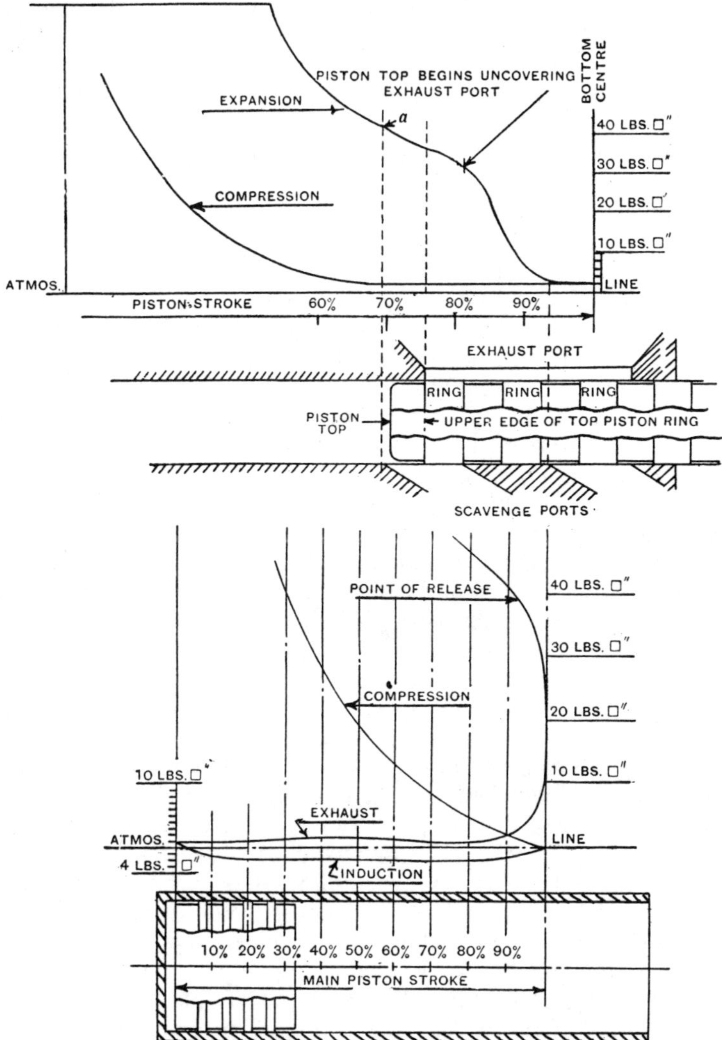

Fig. 219—Ideal light-spring indicator diagrams (2-stroke at top, 4-stroke below)

in Fig. 218. If the exhausting process commences too late, the expansion line will be prolonged towards the end of the stroke, while if it is too early the fall towards the atmospheric line will take place sooner.

As the exhaust gases are released at a pressure well above that of the atmosphere—i.e. 30 to 40 lb—the exhaust line of the diagram is slightly above the atmospheric line. Slight alteration in the timing of the exhaust valve can be carried out whilst the engine is running by altering the roller clearance. If the exhaust commences too late, the clearance between the cam and rocking-lever roller should be reduced, or if too early, increased.

As will be seen from Figs. 212 and 213, the indicator diagram of the two-stroke engine is very similar to that of the four-stroke, the only difference being at the toe where the exhausting and recharging processes occur.

The light-spring diagram is very useful in finding faults in the exhaust and air-inlet processes. Referring to the four-stroke diagram in Fig. 219, a rapid fall in the pressure when the exhaust valve opens will be observed; also, that during the first part it nearly joins the atmospheric line, then rises above it until near the end, when it runs into it again.

The reason for this is that when the burnt gases are released the piston is travelling slowly and the exhaust valve is rapidly opening, consequently a sudden fall of pressure in the cylinder results. The slow speed of the piston at this point allows the pressure to fall to almost atmospheric pressure; then, as the crank gets away from bottom dead centre, the piston gathers speed and the gas in the cylinder is slightly compressed. As the crank approaches the top centre the piston speed is again reduced, but the gases continue to flow out until the pressure in the cylinder is reduced to that of the atmosphere. It is said that the momentum of the burnt gases is sufficient to create a slight partial vacuum in the cylinder, which facilitates the entry of the fresh charge of air.

From the two-stroke diagram, in Fig. 219, it will be observed that toward the end of the expansion line at *a* the pressure drop is increased slightly. This results when the piston uncovers the upper scavenging ports *e* and allows gas to enter and fill the passage. The increased rate in drop of pressure is only momentary, however, since the valve controlling the other end of this passage is closed at this period of the cycle. The release of the exhaust gases begins when the top piston ring passes the upper edge of the exhaust port, as indicated in the diagram, but the pressure in the cylinder does not fall very rapidly until the top of the piston begins to uncover the exhaust port.

In two-stroke port-scavenged engines the piston top begins to uncover the exhaust ports when the crank is about 50° from the bottom centre. When the scavenge air is controlled other than by the piston, the air is admitted at about 30° from the bottom centre, and is cut off when the crank is about 65° over bottom dead centre.

The foregoing remarks on indicator diagrams will have served to convey an idea of what diagrams taken from a diesel engine should be like, but since in the actual diagram faults are not so apparent, we will pass on to a study of some actual diagrams which show the effect of various faults.

Power balancing

Indicator diagrams play a very important part in the operation of an engine. The fuel valve and other adjustments are so fine, and a slight alteration has such a serious effect, that the taking of indicator diagrams cannot be neglected. They provide the only means of ascertaining whether the total load on the engine is equally distributed throughout the cylinders, which is a matter of the first importance. They also assist in ascertaining what alterations are necessary to obtain proper combustion of fuel.

Upon leaving port, diagrams should be taken as soon as possible after the engines have warmed up to their running temperature, since no matter how much care is taken to adjust the fuel pump when the engine is at rest, further adjustments are often necessary when the engine is running, due to unequal wear and expansion in the actuating mechanism. From this it must not be inferred that the clearances between the cams and rollers are of only secondary importance; on the contrary, these should be checked and adjusted with the greatest care before an attempt is made to start an engine, otherwise certain parts of the engine may be overstressed and the foundation laid for a serious accident.

When the engine is properly warmed up and working at full load, diagrams should be taken at each cylinder in turn with the fuel shut off at the fuel pump, so as to ascertain the actual compression pressure in each cylinder. Provided everything is in order, the compression pressures will be 450 to 550 lb/sq.in. This applies to either four-stroke or two-stroke engines, but the actual pressure varies in different makes of engines. An exception is the early Doxford engine, wherein the terminal compression pressure is only 350 lb/sq.in.

In a correct compression diagram the compression and expansion curves appear almost as a single line: if they are separate the indicator should be dismantled, and the piston examined for freedom in the cylinder. A double line can also be produced by a faulty indicator drive. A compression line obtained with the indicator drum disconnected and stationary will not disclose such faults, and if an accurate assessment of the power developed in a cylinder is to be made, the area, if any, enclosed between the compression and expansion lines with the fuel shut off must be known.

Having made the adjustments to the indicator or the drive found necessary to ensure a single-line compression diagram, the cylinder should be set to work under full load, after which a power diagram should be taken. Before doing this, however, the cylinder should be allowed to work under full-load conditions for about ten minutes so that all parts are again at the working temperature. The indicator drum should then be connected to the operating gear, when a diagram as illustrated in Fig. 220 will be produced. In this particular case the terminal compression pressure is 510 lb/sq.in. and the maximum combustion pressure 700 lb/sq.in., the pressure rise upon injection of fuel being 190 lb/sq.in. Other conditions prevailing at the time this diagram was taken are given at the right of the diagram.

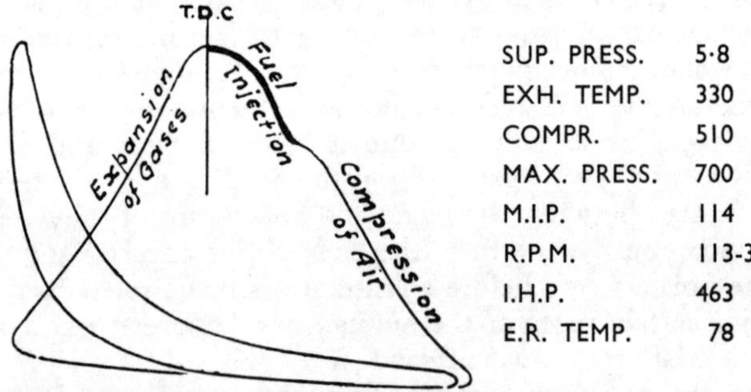

Fig. 220—Power and out-of-phase indicator diagrams of a 4-stroke supercharged engine

Taking draw diagrams

The power diagram does not show very clearly what is taking place in the cylinder during the fuel-injection process, because the engine piston, and consequently the indicator drum, are almost stationary at this period of the cycle of operations. In modern engines which operate on the dual-combustion principle, i.e. partly at constant volume and partly at constant pressure, rather than wholly at constant pressure, fuel injection begins well before the piston has completed its compression stroke, so that the end of compression and beginning of fuel injection are indistinguishable on a power diagram. It is, therefore, customary to take an out-of-phase or " draw " diagram which records the fuel-injection process when the drum of the indicator is at about mid-travel. Such a diagram, with the corresponding power diagram, is shown in Fig. 220.

To obtain such a diagram the indicator drum is operated by hand, thus: open the indicator cock and take the drum cord in one hand, holding the pencil in the other; when the pencil arm of the indicator is seen to begin its upward movement, pull on the drum and press lightly on the pencil simultaneously, endeavouring to time the stroke of the drum so that it comes into contact with the opposite stop just as the pencil arm again reaches its lowest position. After a little practice it will be found possible to get quite good draw diagrams even from high-speed engines.

Draw diagrams can also be obtained by driving the indicator drum from a cam which is out-of-phase. Most engines are now provided with two cams for each cylinder, one for power diagrams and the other for " draw " diagrams. Two such cams for a four-stroke engine are shown in Fig. 210. When studying the relative positions of these cams it must be remembered that when taking a power diagram, the roller of the driving gear is riding on the highest point of the cam-peak as injection of fuel is taking place, whereas when taking a draw diagram the roller is only half-way to that point. In other words, when taking a power diagram the indicator drum has almost completed its movement in one direction when injection of fuel begins, while it is in the middle of its travel at this point of the cycle of operations when operated by the cam provided for the taking of draw diagrams. As the gear shown in Fig. 210 is for a four-stroke engine in which the camshaft works at half the speed of the crankshaft, the angle between the peaks of the cams is only 45° as this corresponds to 90° angular movement of the crankshaft. In two-stroke engines each cam would require one peak only and the angle between the peaks would be 90°.

Fuel-valve faults

Commencement of fuel injection must begin when the crank of the respective cylinder reaches a point which will ensure the fuel-injection line of the draw diagram being *almost* a continuation of the compression line, as shown in Fig. 220. Should the two lines appear as one, the maximum combustion pressure will be greater than it ought to be, and if there is a slight dip in the compression line before fuel injection begins (late injection), as shown in Fig. 221, the power output will be below normal, the combustion

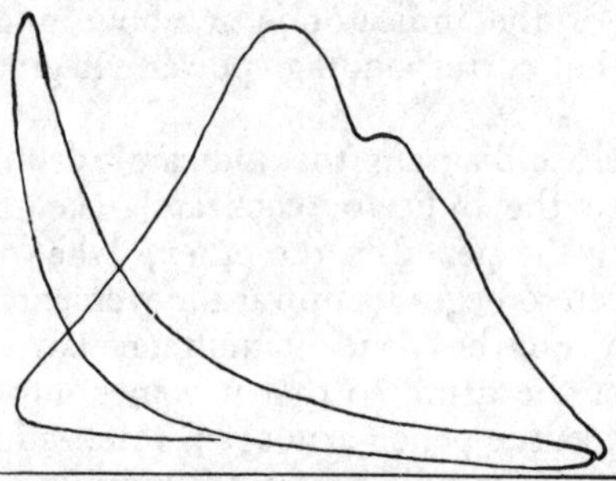

Fig. 221—Indicator diagram taken from a 4-stroke supercharged engine, showing late injection of fuel

pressure will be less than it ought to be, and the exhaust temperature will be above the normal figure. The remedy for such a fault is, of course, to cause the fuel to be injected earlier, and as a guide to the amount of adjustment required it may be taken that, in the average engine, one degree advance will cause the combustion pressure to be increased about 25 lb/sq.in.

As will be appreciated, the manner in which the compression line joins the fuel-injection line on a draw indicator diagram depends upon the speed with which the drum is operated. The correct speed is, as already mentioned, for the drum to travel from one stop to the other in the same time that the engine piston makes one stroke. Should the drum be operated by hand and too quickly, the peak of the diagram will be relatively narrow and the point where the compression line joins the fuel-injection line will not be clearly defined. The drum can in fact be operated so quickly that a fault of the magnitude shown in Fig. 221 would pass unnoticed.

The construction of the normal type of fuel-injection pump is such that the whole of the fuel discharged for a particular setting must enter the engine cylinder each cycle. Should there by any undue obstruction to the flow in the form of partly choked spray holes in the fuel-valve nozzle, or insufficient needle-valve lift, the only effect will be to increase the injection pressure. Any obstruction offered by a partly choked strainer, where fitted, will produce an abnormally high pressure between the pump and the strainer but the injection pressure will be about normal, although the beginning of injection will be late.

An abnormally high injection pressure resulting from either of the above faults will increase the degree of atomisation and decrease the degree of penetration. Should the fault be pronounced, the cylinder pressure rise will begin at the correct time but the maximum combustion pressure will be below normal. This is due not so much to the first part of the fuel charge entering the cylinder at a slightly reduced rate, but rather to low penetration resulting in the very finely-atomised particles of fuel not mixing intimately with the requisite proportion of pure air and, consequently, taking a longer time to burn completely. Taking the normal injection pressure as 6,000 lb/sq.in., a 25-per-cent increase will not materially affect the efficiency of the engine nor the mean working temperature of the parts surrounding the burning gases, but higher injection pressures may result in after-burning and its attendant adverse effects upon lubrication of the piston. Under such conditions indicator diagrams of the shape shown by the full lines in Fig. 222 will be obtained. The dotted lines represent the normal diagrams.

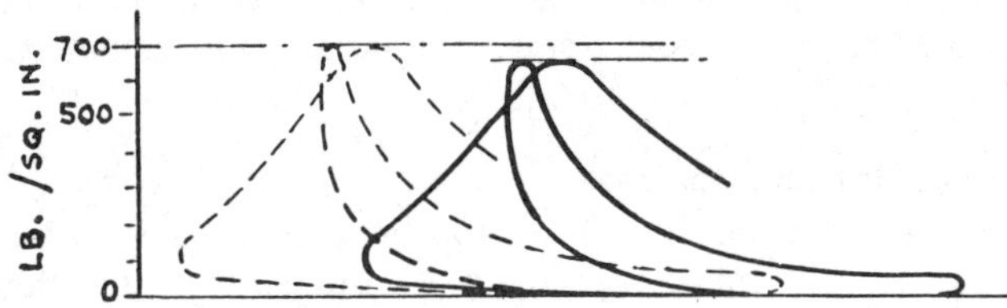

Fig. 222—Indicator diagram showing effect of reduced needle-valve lift or partially choked spray holes

Choked strainers

If the fuel strainer usually situated between the fuel pump and the fuel valve becomes partially choked, injection of the whole fuel charge will be adversely affected. First of all, as the fuel-pump plunger begins its discharge stroke the pressure on the pump side of the strainer will be built up much more rapidly than the pressure on the fuel-valve side of the strainer. This will mean that commencement of injection will be late and the speed at which the needle valve opens will be relatively slow. Also, the initial portion of the fuel charge will be injected at a pressure, and consequently velocity, well below the normal injection pressure, the extent depending, of course, upon the proportion of the passage still open for the flow of fuel. A further effect would be that when the spill valve opens, the pressure between the strainer and the fuel-valve nozzle would fall relatively slowly and the needle valve would not close sufficiently smartly to ensure a clean cut-off of the fuel to the cylinder. An indicator diagram taken under such conditions would look something like the one shown in Fig. 223.

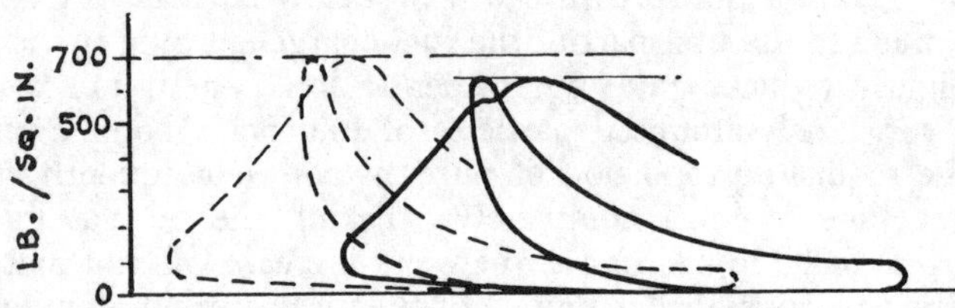

Fig. 223—Indicator diagram showing effect of partially choked high-pressure fuel strainer

The effect of a partially-choked strainer in the high-pressure fuel line could be so serious that mechanical difficulties due to after-burning would soon occur, and the wisdom of examining the strainers at regular and frequent intervals thus cannot be overstressed.

Broken needle-valve springs

If the load on a needle valve is too light, due either to a broken spring, or insufficient compression of the spring, injection will begin before the full injection pressure has been built up, and therefore too early. In all other respects the diagram will be normal.

In considering such a fault it must be remembered that the main function of the needle valve is to control the flow of fuel through the spray holes. The holes must be blanked until the fuel on the discharge side of the pump has been compressed and the full injection pressure built up, so that the initial portion of the fuel charge will enter the cylinder at the same rate as the remainder. The needle valve also ensures a clean cut-off at the end of the injection period and so prevents the formation of oil drops on the nozzle tip. This is the reason why it is so important for the needle valve to be a good fit in its guide and to re-seat squarely, and for the needle-valve lift to be no greater than the designed amount.

The actual pressure during injection is mainly governed by the viscosity of the fuel and the total area of the spray holes.

Let us take an extreme case and assume that the spring collapses completely and the needle valve becomes jammed in the full open position. The first effect would be for injection to begin long before the normal injection pressure has been built up, and, consequently, too early. Secondly, the pressure produced will not be sufficient to give the correct degree of atomisation, and a much slower burning rate, and its undesirable consequences, will result. When the spill valve opens, the spray holes will remain uncovered, and some of the fuel left in the fuel valve will percolate through the holes and probably form a drop on the nozzle tip. As mentioned in a previous chapter, this drop of fuel would carbonise and combustion troubles would eventually occur due to interference with the direction of the fuel sprays.

In considering faults of this kind it should be remembered that fuel is compressible, and that the fuel-pump plunger will complete a small proportion of its discharge stroke before the pressure has been built up to the normal amount, which for *low-viscosity* distilled fuel is around 4,000 lb/sq.in. Actually, therefore, the process of building up the pressure takes time, and the more lightly loaded the needle valve may be the longer will be the time. In the extreme case just quoted it is not unlikely that the bulk of the fuel charge will be injected at or near the normal injection pressure, since it is the area of the spray holes which determines the injection pressure; but if the pressure at the beginning and end of the injection process is below normal, the desired good results cannot be expected. As a general rule the spring load on the needle valve is approximately half the normal injection pressure.

Leaks in fuel pump

In the event of a fuel-pump suction valve leaking, the pump plunger will have advanced further on its discharge stroke before the pressure necessary to open the needle valve and inject the fuel has been built up. This fault will therefore have the effect of delaying the beginning of injection. Moreover, as a proportion of the fuel will pass back to the pump suction through the defective valve during the whole discharge period of the plunger's stroke, less fuel will be discharged and the power output of the cylinder concerned will be reduced.

Any fault which prevents the rapid build-up of pressure immediately the pump plunger begins its discharge stroke, such as fuel leaking past a loose-fitting plunger or a defective spill valve, will result in late injection and a reduction in the quantity of fuel injected into the cylinder. A leaking fuel-pump discharge valve does not have this effect. The purpose of this component is merely to retain the fuel standing in the discharge pipe after the pump has finished discharging and during the suction stroke of the plunger. As the pressure on the discharge valve during this period is almost nil, the defect would require to be bad before fuel in the discharge pipe would pass back to the pump during the suction stroke of the plunger.

The effect on an indicator diagram of a leaking pump suction valve, spill valve, or plunger will be the same, i.e. the point at which injection begins will be clearly seen, the maximum pressure will be below the normal, and the power diagram will be thin or of reduced area. Other methods would therefore have to be adopted to determine which of these three faults is responsible. In the event of the cause being a slack-fitting pump plunger it will be apparent, while if the spilled fuel passes back to the pump suction through a pipe external to the pump, the pipe will become overheated if the spill valve is leaking, though this applies, of course, to unheated fuel only.

In order accurately to assess the effect of the various faults discussed in this chapter and illustrated on the indicator diagrams, readers are recommended to trace the normal diagrams on a piece of thin paper and lay them over the diagrams which record the faults.

Performance on residual fuel

The main engines in most ships now operate on residual or high-viscosity fuels, and it may be interesting and useful to give the performance of a single-acting supercharged two-stroke engine

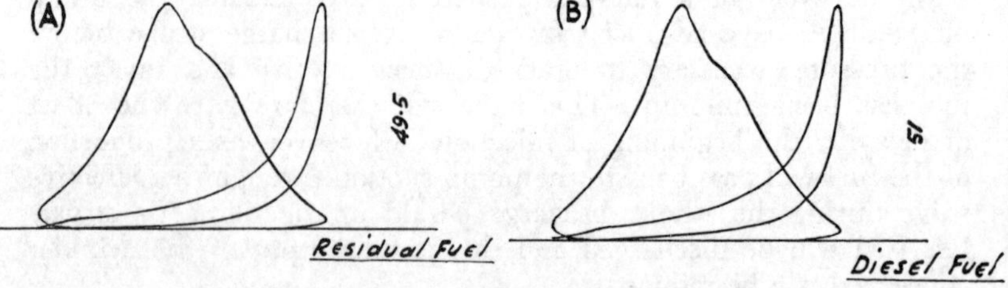

Fig. 224—Indicator diagrams taken from a 2-stroke engine when operating on (A) residual fuel, and (B) diesel fuel

when operating first on diesel fuel of 95 seconds and then residual fuel of 3,390 seconds Red. No. 1 at 100°F (37·8°C). All conditions likely to affect the powers developed by the five-cylinder engine and the speed of the ship were similar.

	Average of 5 cylinders	
	Diesel fuel	Residual fuel
Compression pressure, lb/sq.in. ..	550·3	554·6
,, ,, kg/sq.cm ..	38·7	39·0
Combustion pressure, lb/sq.in. ..	726·6	703·9
,, ,, kg/sq.cm ..	51·1	49·5
Mean indicated pressure, lb/sq.in. ..	88·9	87·5
,, ,, ,, kg/sq.cm	6·25	6·15
Indicated horse-power	1,012	976
Exhaust temperature	572°F (300°C)	608°F (320°C)
Revolutions per minute	106	104
Fuel temperature at pump	Atmos.	200°F (93°C)
Total daily fuel consumption, tons ..	16·15	16·65
Fuel consumption per i.h.p./hr/lb ..	0·298	0·318

Two indicator diagrams taken from the same cylinder when operating on residual fuel and then diesel fuel are shown in Fig. 224. The remarkable similarity of the diagrams, which proves the fuel flexibility of this Burmeister & Wain engine, will be observed.

Exhausting and re-charging

What has been written earlier regarding fuel-valve faults refers, of course, to either four- or two-stroke engines. The only difference between the two engine types is the manner of expelling the burnt gases and filling the cylinder with air. As these processes take place in two-stroke engines near the end of the working stroke when the piston is travelling relatively slowly and pressures in the cylinder are low, light-spring diagrams only will disclose any fault that may exist. A 30 spring (30 lb per inch), which is the one usually employed, will magnify the various stages of the processes occurring during the low-pressure period of the cycle of operations sufficiently to disclose incorrect timing of valves or partial choking of ports in the cylinder liners. To begin with we will consider light-spring diagrams taken from an unsupercharged four-stroke engine.

Fig. 225 is a light-spring diagram taken from a four-stroke unsupercharged engine. From this diagram it will be observed that when the exhaust valve opens at the point A the pressure in the cylinder falls to nearly atmospheric pressure, as it should do; then as the expulsion of the burnt gases proceeds, the pressure rises. When the end of the exhaust stroke is approached the exhaust line

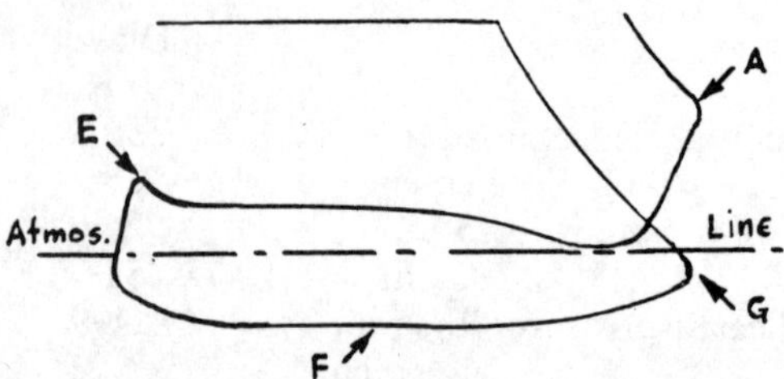

Fig. 225—Light-spring indicator diagram of a 4-stroke engine showing late opening and early closing of exhaust valve

should turn towards the atmospheric line (as shown in Fig. 215) instead of which the pressure rises to a point E and then suddenly falls.

The cause of this abnormal rise of pressure in the cylinder at the end of the exhaust stroke is due to the exhaust valve closing too early and compression of the burnt gases left in the cylinder. At the point E the air-inlet valve opens, and during the last portion of the stroke the pressure falls suddenly because the compressed gas flows into the air-inlet pipe. Thus a mixture of inert gas and air will be drawn into the cylinder on the next stroke. In such cases the release of the compressed gases through the air-inlet valve will be distinctly heard at the air-inlet pipe.

It will also be noted from the diagram shown in Fig. 225 that the air-inlet line F falls too far below the atmospheric line, and that

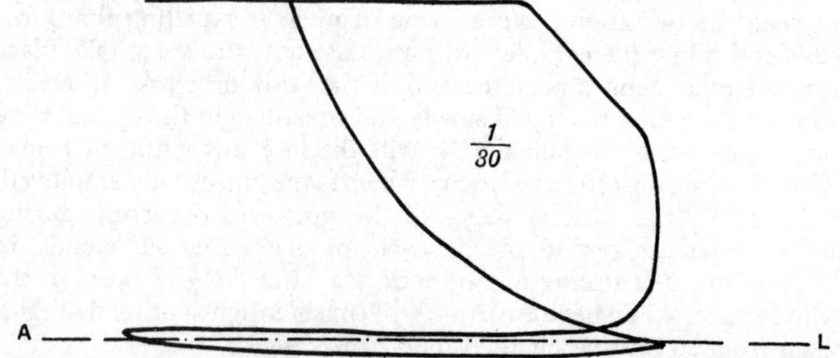

Fig. 226—Good example of a light-spring indicator diagram of a 4-stroke unsupercharged engine

at the point G, when compression begins, the pressure in the cylinder is well below atmospheric; this may be due to either insufficient air-inlet valve opening, resulting from incorrect roller clearance, or to a partly-choked air intake. If the fault is pronounced, the compression curve of a power diagram taken under such conditions will fall below the normal curve and the terminal pressure will be low. If the flow of exhaust gases is similarly restricted, the exhaust line will take up a higher position relative to the atmospheric line, but in other respects the diagram will be normal. A good example of a light-spring indicator diagram is shown in Fig. 226.

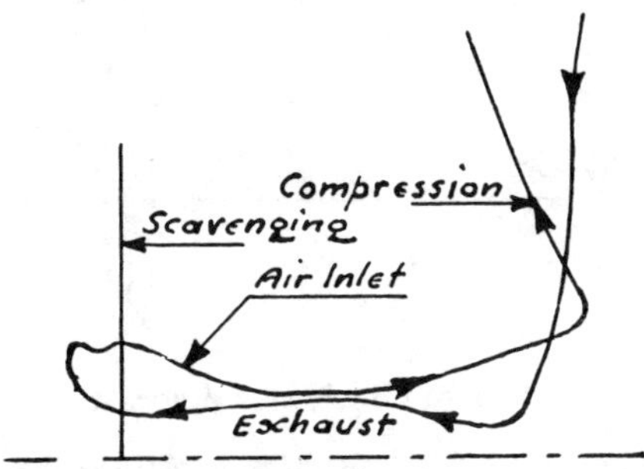

Fig. 227—Light-spring indicator diagram of a 4-stroke supercharged engine

In Fig. 227 is shown a light-spring diagram of a four-stroke supercharged engine, the supercharge air pressure being 4·5 lb/sq.in. At the end of the working stroke the pressure reaches a minimum, and as the piston gathers speed during the exhaust stroke the pressure rises slightly, only to fall again as the piston nears the end of the exhaust stroke and its speed is again reduced. Before the piston reaches the end of the exhaust stroke, however, the air-inlet valve opens and admits air at the full supercharge pressure. This is indicated by the upward turn of the exhaust line, the pressures being a maximum at the moment the piston begins the air-inlet stroke. As the piston gathers speed the pressure falls, but rises again to the full supercharge air pressure before the compression stroke begins.

To some it may seem a little strange that the exhaust line and the air-inlet line do not run parallel with the atmospheric line. If they did so it would undoubtedly reduce the pumping losses, but larger openings for the egress of burnt gases and entry of supercharge air would be necessary. To provide larger openings would offer design difficulties and would not improve these processes because the slowing-down of the piston at the end of the exhaust and air-inlet strokes ensures that the whole of the burnt gases are expelled and the cylinder re-charged with air at the full supercharged pressure before the piston begins its compression stroke.

A normal light-spring diagram taken from a two-stroke engine is shown in Fig. 228. When the indicator pencil begins producing the line *A* the piston has uncovered the exhaust ports in the cylinder

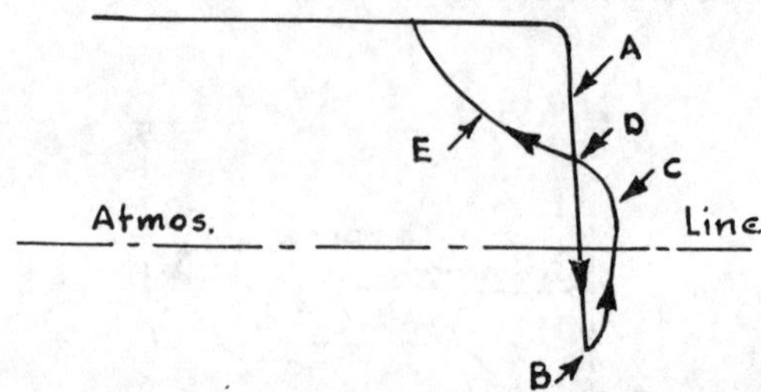

Fig. 228—Normal light-spring indicator diagram of a 2-stroke engine

liner and the pressure in the cylinder is falling rapidly, continuing to fall to a point *B* which is well below the atmospheric pressure. This rapid and extensive fall in pressure is due to the exit being of such large area and to the momentum produced in the released gases being so great that a partial vacuum is created in the cylinder before the scavenging air enters. When studying this part of the cycle of operations it must be remembered that when the sudden release of the burnt gases begins, the pressure in the cylinder is in the region of 40 lb/sq.in. In cases where the burnt gases leave the cylinder through a poppet valve in the cylinder head which does not offer such a large exit so quickly, the fall in pressure is not so rapid or extensive. At the point *B* the scavenging ports are uncovered and air begins to enter the cylinder as the piston proceeds towards the end of the working stroke.

The inrushing scavenging air quickly builds up the pressure in the cylinder until the piston reaches the end of its stroke, indicated by *C*, when the pressure is slightly above atmospheric. As the piston begins its compression stroke the pressure in the cylinder continues to rise until at *D* the cylinder is charged to the full scavenging or supercharge air pressure. At this point the scavenging air ports are closed by the piston and compression of air begins.

Since the timing of the exhausting and re-charging processes are governed by the engine piston there is nothing one can do to alter the timing. However, should carbon resulting from bad combustion of fuel, or excessive lubrication, deposit in the cylinder exhaust ports, the beginning of the exhausting process will be late and the fall in pressure when they are uncovered will not be so rapid. Moreover, the pressure in the cylinder will not reach such a low value before the scavenging air begins to enter. Each of these effects is

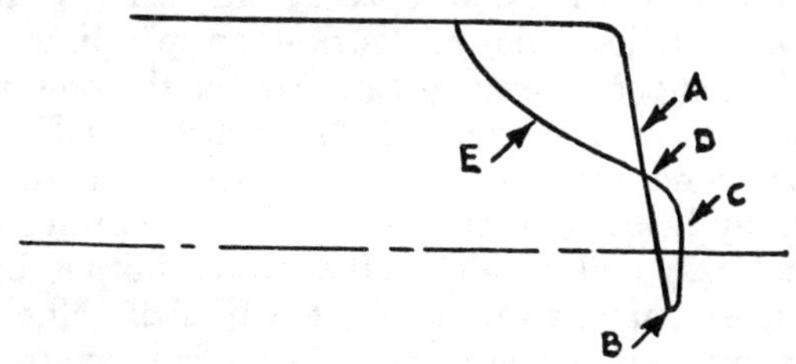

Fig. 229—Light-spring indicator diagram of a 2-stroke engine, showing restriction in the exhaust ports

shown in Fig. 229, except the late beginning of the exhaust process which is in progress when the exhaust line *A* of the diagram begins.

Should the flow of scavenging air into a cylinder be restricted or the pressure be below the normal figure the exhausting process will be unaffected, as shown in Fig. 230, but when the piston reaches the end of the stroke the pressure in the cylinder indicated by *C*

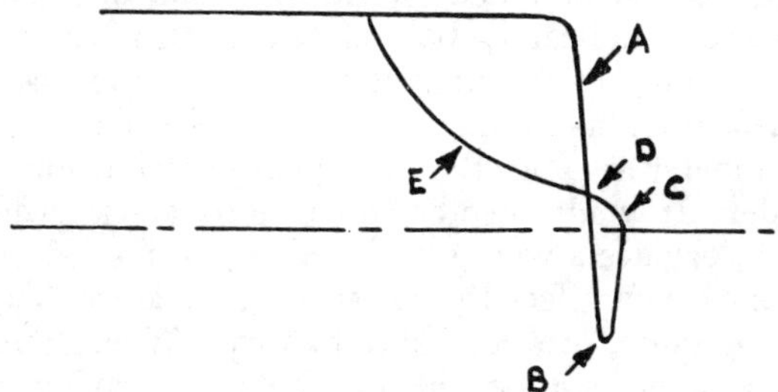

Fig. 230—Light-spring indicator diagram of a 2-stroke engine, showing too low a scavenging air pressure

will be below the normal, as will be the terminal compression pressure. The greater sweep of the compression line indicating slow compression will be noted.

Partially-choked exhaust ports will result in a higher proportion of burnt gases being left in the cylinder, and a low scavenging air pressure will result in an insufficient quantity of air being in the cylinder when fuel is injected. Either of these faults may cause the mean temperature of the cycle to be increased, the serious consequences of which have already been stated.

Exhaust-gas temperature as a means of power balancing

The temperature of the exhaust gases from the individual cylinders can be a useful guide to power distribution in a line of cylinders; the higher the temperature the greater will be the power developed, provided the parts of the engine which affect the combustion process are in proper condition and correctly timed. For instance, if the fuel-valve spray holes have enlarged, the fuel will not be correctly atomised and this will result in the power output being below, and the exhaust temperature above, the normal value. The same will occur if injection of fuel takes place too late, while the pressure of supercharge air also influences the exhaust temperature without having a material effect (within limits) upon the power output. In the case of four-stroke engines, if an exhaust valve opens too early, power output will be reduced but the exhaust temperature will be increased.

In view of the foregoing—and other instances could be quoted—it will be seen that too much reliance must not be placed upon exhaust temperatures for power balancing purposes. As to the manner in which the fuel is being atomised and injected, this information can be obtained by out-of-phase diagrams produced by the pressure indicator, but as either insufficient atomisation or incorrect timing of injection is reflected in the maximum combustion pressure it is sufficient for the daily check to know the exhaust temperature and the maximum combustion pressure of each cylinder. It would then be sufficient to take indicator diagrams once a week, or once a voyage if the engine is in good order and the other factors which affect the exhaust temperature, such as supercharge air pressure, are not likely to vary. Where the installation comprises a large number of cylinders the taking of indicator diagrams is a lengthy operation, but fortunately there are other much simpler and quicker methods of ascertaining the maximum combustion pressures, and the compression pressures also, one of which will be described later in the chapter.

For certain reasons thermometers of the ordinary type are unsuitable for measuring the exhaust temperature, the chief being that they are frequently broken when starting up an engine from cold. In view of this, pyrometers of the thermo-electric type have been extensively adopted, although these are also delicate instruments and require very careful handling.

The action of these pyrometers is as follows. When the junction of two dissimilar metals forming part of a circuit is heated, a low electrical difference of potential is set up and a current is thus produced. If pieces of bismuth and antimony, platinum and platinum alloy, or copper and copper-nickel alloy (known as constantan), or other metals be soldered together and form part of a circuit, then if the junction of the two dissimilar metals be heated to a temperature greater than the rest of the circuit, a current will flow in the direction from the positives—bismuth, platinum, or copper, as the case may be. If the junction be cooled below the temperature of the rest of the circuit, a current will flow in the opposite direction; the current will continue to flow so long as the temperature difference in the circuit is maintained, while the wider the range of temperature, the greater the strength of current produced, and vice versa. Currents thus produced are called thermo-electric currents.

Pyrometers working on this principle consist of two rods of dissimilar material, which are insulated but brazed together at one end, to form what is termed the hot junction, which is exposed to the heat of the gas whose temperature is to be measured. The opposite end of each rod is connected to separate terminals from which cables are run to the terminals of a sensitive, magnifying galvanometer, thus forming a complete circuit.

The electric current set up at the hot junction of the dissimilar metals passes to the moving coil of the galvanometer, to which is connected a pointer, and the electrical current set up is read off against a scale calibrated in degrees of temperature. Any increase in temperature at the hot junction will result in corresponding increases in the strength of the current, and consequently the deflection of the pointer will be greater, and vice versa. If the pointer of the apparatus is adjusted to zero when not in operation, the temperature of the atmosphere, which is the temperature of the cold metal-junction, must be added to the indicator reading to arrive at the correct temperature of the exhaust gases.

During recent years the mercurial thermometer has been improved and made more suitable for registering the temperature of exhaust gases. The bulb ends are well protected and the stems are better supported. In some the space above the mercury is filled with nitrogen, which prevents the common trouble of the mercury column breaking up. A space is provided at the top of the stem, into which the gas is compressed as the mercury expands, preventing the tube from bursting.

Hitherto the thermo-electric pyrometer, as just described, has been used extensively, but to meet the demand for a more robust

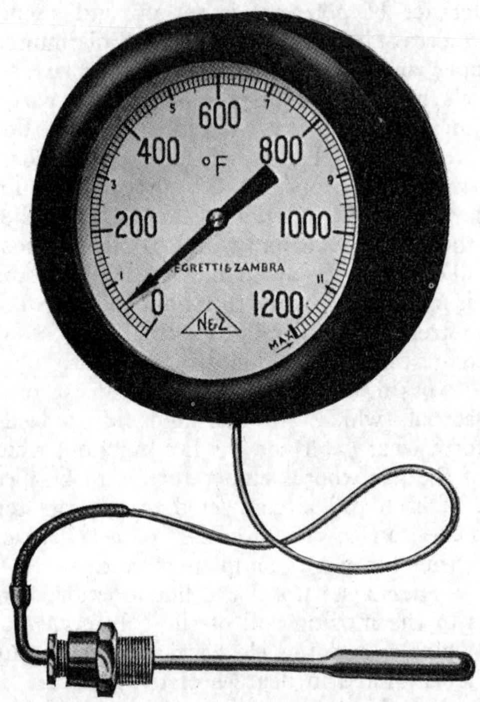

Fig. 231—Dial thermometer (Negretti and Zambra)

type of instrument the mercury-in-steel dial thermometer has come into increased favour for marine use. Such an instrument has proved to be very accurate, and sensitive to the slightest variation in temperature of the exhaust gases, and with reasonable care does not require much attention. The instruments are of two types, one being the distant-reading type, the dial of which is placed in the most convenient position for easy reading, and the other that in which the complete instrument is attached directly to the engine exhaust-pipe. In each case one complete instrument is used for each engine cylinder.

Negretti and Zambra's mercury-in-steel thermometers are constructed with a steel bulb built up from solid-drawn tube. The capillary tubing which connects the bulb in the exhaust pipe to the dial is also of steel, with a bore of 0·006 inch. In the distant-reading type (Fig. 231) the steel tubing is encased in copper to prevent corrosion. The bulb and capillary tubing are filled with mercury under pressure. The dial pointer is operated by a Bourdon tube to which it is directly connected, so that with an increase in temperature the mercury in the bulb expands and produces a greater pressure in the Bourdon tube, thus causing the tube to uncoil or straighten out and operate the pointer.

The " Lightning " relief valve and cylinder pressure indicator

The cylinder relief valve used in connection with this equipment is loaded by compressed air instead of a spiral spring. A sectional

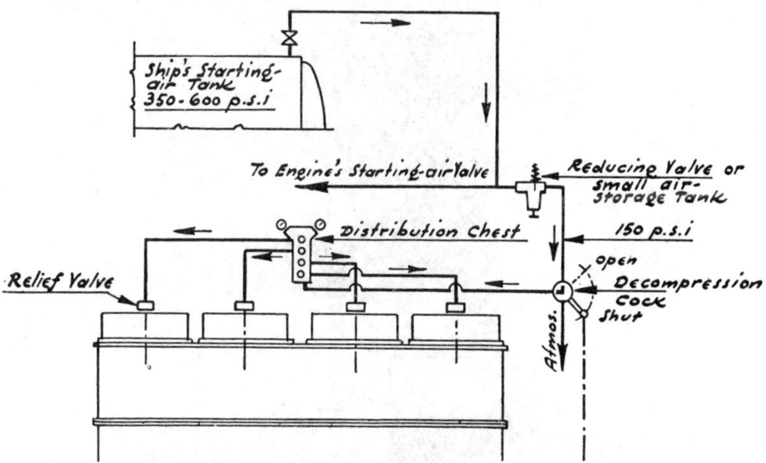

Fig. 232—Pipe arrangement of compressed-air-loaded cylinder pressure indicator (" Lightning ")

view of this valve is shown at (b) in Fig. 83, while an outline of the whole equipment is shown in Fig. 232.

In view of the ease of reducing the load on this type of relief valve it can be used to ascertain the terminal compression pressure or the maximum combustion pressure prevailing in the cylinder, because as the loading (compressed-air) pressure is reduced, a point is reached when the loading pressure and terminal pressure in the cylinder are in equilibrium.

Fig. 233—Distribution chest of compressed-air-loaded cylinder pressure indicator (" Lightning ")

This is effected by directing the compressed air as it passes from the source of supply, usually the starting-air tank, to the relief valve through a distribution chest, which may be situated at any convenient position in the engine-room. The distribution chest, shown in both Figs. 232 and 233, contains one change-cock for each cylinder of the engine and has mounted upon it two pressure-gauges. The only difference between these gauges and ordinary Bourdon gauges is that the dial of one is specially calibrated.

To ascertain the pressure in any cylinder all that is necessary is to turn the handle of the change-cock corresponding to the cylinder in which it is desired to know the pressure, through an angle of 180°. The pointer of the left-hand gauge (Fig. 233) will at once rise from the zero position to the normal loading position, indicated constantly on the right-hand gauge, and then move very slowly in the direction of the zero position.

As the pointer of the left-hand gauge moves slowly and steadily back towards the zero position a point is reached when the loading pressure on the relief valve is directly proportional to the pressure in the engine cylinder, and the relief valve will lift lightly but audibly. When this occurs the terminal pressure in the cylinder is registered on the left-hand gauge in lb/sq.in. The handle of the change-cock is then returned to its original position and each change-cock is operated in turn until the pressure in all cylinders has been ascertained. Terminal compression pressures are ascertained in the same way after the fuel has been cut off to the cylinder being gauged for pressure.

This equipment serves other useful purposes. First, it can be used to decompress automatically all cylinders whenever the engine is stopped while manœuvring a ship in and out of port. This is effected by a decompression cock (see Fig. 232), situated in the compressed-air line between the reducing valve and the distribution chest. The function of this decompression cock is to cut off the supply of compressed air and put the cylinder relief valves in communication with the atmosphere. The relief valves are instantly unloaded and any pressure in the cylinders is allowed to escape freely, merely by moving the handle of the decompression cock through an angle of 90°.

As the decompression cock can be situated in any convenient position, the obvious choice is near the engine controls. It may therefore be operated by hand or connected to the engine-control lever in such a way that when the lever is brought to the " Stop " position the cylinders are automatically decompressed.

Operation of this decompression cock will, moreover, result in an engine being brought to rest almost immediately the fuel is cut off, since unloading the relief valves releases the air compressed in the engine cylinders during the compression strokes of the pistons, and as the relief valves automatically close when the pistons begin the outward normal working strokes, the partial vacuum created in the cylinders has a powerful braking effect upon the engine.

Contrary to what might be expected, experience in a large number of ships has proved that even when this equipment is used daily to check cylinder pressures the relief valves require no more attention in port than do ordinary spring-loaded relief valves. If the three-ply stainless-steel bellows are not subjected to more than double the normal pressure they will last indefinitely, but if a reducing valve is used the makers do recommend the renewal of the rubber diaphragms every twelvemonth.

CHAPTER 25

Materials of construction; and Corrosion

The object of this chapter is to explain to the junior members of the profession the composition of the more important materials they are handling daily. Since it is written by one with a limited knowledge of metallurgy the information given is of an elementary character, but it may serve as a prelude to a more thorough study of this interesting subject which, with the introduction of diesel engines of greater power, is becoming increasingly important.

The metals mostly used in engineering can be grouped into two categories, namely ferrous and non-ferrous. The former include cast iron, wrought iron, and steel, while in the latter group are copper, lead, tin, zinc, manganese, aluminium, nickel, and other lesser-known metals. Certain other elements which are not true metals, such as carbon, silicon and phosphorus, are used to modify as required the properties of the finished metals.

An alloy may be ferrous or non-ferrous. It is made by melting and mixing together two or more metals with the object of producing a metal having properties differing from those of the constituent metals. Among the most extensively used non-ferrous alloys are bronzes (tin and copper) and whitemetal (tin, antimony, lead). Alloy steels and cast irons are obtained by adding definite proportions of other elements, such as nickel, chromium, and tungsten.

The basis of cast iron, steel, malleable or wrought iron and malleable cast iron is the metal iron. Pure iron is bright and very ductile, but on heating and then cooling it becomes tough. As usually mined and smelted, however, iron contains impurities, and has not the appearance or qualities of the pure metal. The purest iron obtainable is Swedish wrought iron, the best of which contains only 0·2 per cent of impurities. All other commercial irons contain a larger proportion of impurities.

Pig iron is the product of the blast furnace, roughly cast into masses called " pigs " for convenience of handling. Pig iron is of known composition, and when remelted and cast is called "cast iron." Steel is the same material with some of the impurities removed, hence the reason why it is more like pure iron. Cast iron contains the greatest amount of impurities, the total varying from 5 to 10 per cent, and the carbon content alone amounting to 3 to 4 per cent. Steel contains varying quantities of the same impurities, but the carbon content is very much lower, that of mild steel being less than 0·1 per cent.

The effects which the various so-called impurities have on the metal are briefly as follows:—

Carbon

This impurity is present in iron in two forms, namely *free carbon* and *combined carbon*. The former is that part of the carbon content which has failed to combine or been prevented from combining with the other elements, and exists in the form of *graphite*. The extreme softness and weakness of graphite is well known, so that the effect of free carbon is to weaken the iron as a whole. Combined carbon, as the name implies, is that part of the carbon content which has combined with the other elements present. The effect of combined carbon is to strengthen and harden castings. In addition to depending upon the amount of carbon put into the mixture, the combined and free carbon contents of a finished article depend upon the time taken to cool out after casting, and consequently upon the size of the casting; also upon the influence by other elements present in the mixture.

Silicon

This element plays a very important part in the manufacture of cast-iron castings because of its effect upon the carbon content. It tends to inhibit combination of the carbon, so that, all other things being equal, the higher the percentage of silicon in the mixture, the lower will be the percentage of combined carbon and more carbon in a free or graphitic state will be present in the finished casting. If too much of the carbon in a mixture combines, the casting will be very brittle; a certain amount of silicon is necessary to prevent this. In the case of small castings, which naturally cool down more quickly than large castings, a greater amount of silicon is required to prevent more than the desired amount of carbon from remaining as combined carbon. The difficulties of the foundry-man in producing a casting of varying section and uniform strength throughout will therefore be appreciated.

Manganese

As in the case of silicon, the presence of manganese in the mixture influences the final state of the carbon, but while silicon tends to increase the amount of free carbon, manganese has a tendency to keep more of the carbon in a combined form. These two elements are sometimes referred to as the hardening and softening elements respectively, silicon having a softening effect and manganese a hardening effect upon the finished casting.

Phosphorus

With the percentages generally used for engine castings, phosphorus has little or no effect upon the final condition of the carbon in a casting. It increases the fluidity of cast iron, as does carbon, and gives it a fine skin. Thus the greatest value of this element is in connection with ornamental castings. Phosphorus decreases the tensile strength of castings so that for engine work the percentage is kept as low as possible. In the case of large castings it tends to make the thicker sections spongy. Hence for large castings, or small castings of uneven section which will be subjected to pressure, its presence except in very small quantities is harmful.

Sulphur

This is present in the form either of sulphide of iron or sulphide of manganese, the quantity of the latter depending upon the amount of manganese the mixture contains. If present in the form of sulphide of iron it tends to make the castings harder; sulphide of manganese will separate from the iron and float to the surface when the metal is in a molten state, and it is a softener. Thus if sulphur and manganese, which are both hardeners, are brought together in the correct proportion they may combine, and the resulting casting will be exceedingly soft. Sulphur also tends to make a casting brittle, and for this reason the amount is kept as small as possible.

Before going on to give a list of the materials generally used and the mechanical properties required for various parts of diesel engines, a brief description will be given of how the quality of the material as cast is measured.

Tensile strength

The tensile strength of the material is found by machining down a piece of the metal to a certain length and diameter and finding the force required to pull the two ends asunder. This force is generally expressed in tons per square inch.

Elongation

Before the tensile test bar referred to above is pulled, two marks—usually 2 or 3 inches apart—are made equidistant from the mid-length position. After the bar has been broken and the tensile strength determined, the two parts are joined together by hand pressure and the distance between the marks measured. It will be found that the test bar has stretched before breaking. The amount of stretch is expressed as a percentage of the distance between the marks before testing. Thus an elongation of 28 per cent on 2 inches means that the test bar stretched 0·56 inch before breaking. Cast iron is a brittle metal, so that its elongation is practically nil and is seldom measured.

Transverse strength

This test is usually carried out by placing a bar of the metal, 1 inch square in cross-section, on two sharp edges, 12 inches apart, a third sharp edge being brought down exactly midway between the other two and a gradually increasing force applied to it until the bar breaks. The transverse strength of the bar is expressed in pounds or tons per square inch; the *deflection* is the amount the bar bends before breaking. This test is applied to cast iron parts only, for reasons that will be obvious.

Hardness

The " Brinell hardness figure " is a measure of the hardness of a metal. It is obtained by indenting the metal with a hardened steel ball subjected to a predetermined load for not less than a certain time. The diameter of the ball generally used is 10 mm, the time the force is applied being not less than 30 seconds, while the load depends upon the material. For hard material such as cast iron, the load is 3,000 kilograms, and 500 kilograms for soft materials. The diameter of the indentation is measured by means of a special microscope fitted with a scale.

ENGINE PARTS

Bedplates—These parts when made of cast iron have the following composition and mechanical properties:—

Tensile strength	11 to 14 tons/sq.in.
Transverse strength	2,000 to 3,000 lb/sq.in.
Composition:	
Carbon	3·3 to 3·6 per cent
Silicon	1·5 „ 1·8 „
Phosphorus	0·6 „ 0·8 „
Sulphur	0·1 „ 0·13 „
Manganese	0·5 „ 0·8 „

The bedplate is subjected to many severe stresses, chiefly of a bending nature, since it is bolted to a foundation much less rigid than a cast-iron structure. Apart from being sound and homogeneous throughout, however, the material used has no special properties.

Columns—These parts when made of cast iron are of the same composition and mechanical properties as that used for bedplates.

The stresses are compression, due to tightening of the through tie-bolts and the combustion load in the bottom cylinders in the case of double-acting engines. Cast iron of ordinary quality is strong in compression, so that the material used has no special properties.

Cylinder beams—These parts are generally made of cast iron of the same composition and mechanical properties as that used for bedplates and columns.

Crosshead guide bars—Generally, these parts are made of ordinary good-quality cast iron, but sometimes a better quality is employed, since the bars must resist wear. The composition of such a material is:—

Combined carbon	0·6 to 0·75 per cent
Free carbon	2·2 „ 2·8 „
Silicon	1·0 „ 1·3 „
Sulphur	0·1 „ 0·2 „
Phosphorus	0·3 „ 0·5 „
Manganese	0·4 „ 0·7 „

Cylinder liners—These form one of the foundryman's most difficult propositions, since they must not only withstand severe stresses due to differences in temperature and pressure, but must resist the abrasive action of the piston rings. The composition of the material of cylinder liners which have given good service is given on page 274, but it must be remembered that the foundry methods employed, the pouring temperature, and the time taken to cool out after casting are also important.

Composition:

Combined carbon	0·8 to 0·9 per cent
Free carbon	2·2 ,, 2·4 ,,
Silicon	0·8 ,, 1·0 ,,
Manganese	1·0 ,, 1·7 ,,
Phosphorus	0·2 ,, 0·3 ,,
Sulphur	0·08 ,, 0·1 ,,

Mechanical properties:

Tensile strength not less than 14 tons/sq.in.

Transverse strength not less than 2,500 lb/sq.in.

Brinell hardness figure, over 200.

Pistons—These are generally made of close-grained cast iron. The material must be capable of withstanding the great heat stresses to which it will be subjected, and must be sufficiently hard to resist enlargement of the piston-ring grooves. The composition and mechanical properties of the cast iron used for pistons of normal design, which have given good service, are as follows:—

Composition:

Combined carbon	0·9 per cent
Free carbon	2·4 ,,
Silicon	0·8 ,,
Manganese	1·7 ,,
Phosphorus	0·3 ,,
Sulphur	0·1 ,,

Mechanical properties:

Tensile strength not less than 14 tons/sq.in.

Brinell hardness figure, over 180.

It is generally agreed that one of the properties which give resistance against fracture in cast-iron pistons is growth of the material after repeated heating and cooling. The growth of cast iron under these conditions depends greatly upon the amount of silicon which the iron contains; the lower the silicon content the less the growth, and vice versa. Other factors have an effect, but the predominating influence is that of the silicon content. The silicon content cannot, of course, be reduced too much, for reasons given at the beginning of the chapter.

Piston rings—The duty of these rings calls for a very high quality of cast iron. In addition to being sufficiently hard to resist wear, the rings must not be brittle, otherwise they will break when sprung over the piston; they must also be capable of being pulled out of their true shape sufficiently to enable them to be sprung over the piston and yet not to take a permanent set. So far as hardness is concerned, it is usual to make the rings slightly softer than the cylinder liners. The rings must not be too soft, however, otherwise the fine metallic dust produced as they wear will grind away the hardest cylinder liners.

The composition and mechanical properties of the material for piston rings, giving reasonably good service, are as follows:—

Composition:

Combined carbon	0·6 per cent
Free carbon	2·8 ,,
Silicon	1·8 ,,
Manganese	1·0 ,,
Phosphorus	1·1 ,,
Sulphur	0·1 ,,

Mechanical properties:

Tensile strength not less than 12 tons/sq.in.

Brinell hardness figure, 175 to 185.

Exhaust valves—The housings of these valves are always made of good-quality cast iron, since the flanges must resist the bending force produced by the combustion load. The spindles are made of mild steel of 28–32 tons tensile strength, since they must resist a tensile force when the valve re-seats. The seat and valve head (or lid) are made of either special cast iron or steel, since they must resist the erosive action of high-temperature, high-velocity gases.

Cast iron has been found not entirely satisfactory for exhaust-valve lids and seats. A notable feature regarding all grades of cast-iron valves is that during the early part of their life they resist the injurious action of the exhaust gases quite well. After the skin of the metal has been removed, however, the material offers less and less resistance to the action of the gases as the softer metal at the middle of the valve lid is reached. The skin is probably due to more rapid cooling of the metal next to the mould during casting, the metal nearer the surface having a higher combined carbon content—which makes for hardness—than the metal near the middle of the casting, which takes longer to cool and therefore contains more free carbon. In the manufacture of cast-iron exhaust-valve lids and seats, one of the aims should be to cast as near as possible to the finished dimensions.

Now that higher powers without a corresponding increase in size are being demanded, the question of suitable material for exhaust valves is receiving more than usual attention. The only difference in the conditions to which the exhaust valves of an ordinary form of engine and a supercharged engine are subjected is that in the latter the burnt gases are released at a higher pressure and, consequently, velocity, the scoring action taking place at the very beginning of the opening period.

There are many special steels now made for exhaust valves and seats, the best of which appears to contain the correct combination of carbon, silicon and chromium necessary to resist the cutting action of the high-temperature, high-velocity gases.

Crankshafts—*Built-up type*—Siemens-Marten open-hearth mild annealed steel is used, the ultimate tensile strength being 28 to 32 tons/sq.in. and the elongation 25 to 29 per cent. In some instances the webs are made of cast steel.

Connecting-rods—Siemens-Marten open-hearth or ingot mild annealed steel is used; ultimate tensile strength 28 to 32 tons/sq.in.; elongation 25 to 29 per cent.

Piston rods—The same steel as for crankshafts and connecting-rods is used.

For double-acting engines this material is sometimes used, but generally a nickel–chrome steel having a higher tensile strength is employed, to keep down the diameter of the rods. Particulars of this higher-grade steel are:—

nickel, 1·5 per cent; chromium, 0·5 per cent; ultimate tensile strength, over 40 tons/sq.in.; elastic limit, not less than 25 tons/sq.in.; elongation, 18 per cent.

Crossheads—The following steels are used:—

Siemens-Marten open-hearth ingot or mild steel of ultimate tensile strength 28 to 32 tons/sq.in., elongation 25 to 29 per cent; or Siemens-Marten open-hearth ingot or mild steel of ultimate tensile strength 36 to 38 tons/sq.in., elongation 20 per cent; or nickel–chrome steel, nickel 1·5 per cent, chromium 0·5 per cent, ultimate tensile strength 42 tons/sq.in., elastic limit not less than 27 tons/sq.in., elongation 25 per cent.

Bearing-bolts—Nickel–chrome steel is used, nickel 3 per cent, chromium 0·7 per cent, ultimate tensile strength not less than 45 tons/sq.in., elongation 22 per cent; or mild steel of the properties already given.

Through tie-bolts—Siemens-Marten open-hearth mild steel is used, ultimate tensile strength 28 to 32 tons/sq.in., elongation 26 to 28 per cent.

Camshafts—Made of the same material as through tie-bolts. The cams are made of hard cast iron and the keys of cast steel or high-carbon steel, but in small high-speed engines the cams are made of high-carbon case-hardening steel.

Crosshead guide shoes—Of cast iron or cast steel. When of cast steel the ultimate tensile strength should be 25 to 30 tons/sq.in. and the elongation 18 to 20 per cent.

H.P. fuel pumps—The *bodies* are made of Siemens-Marten open-hearth ingot or mild steel, ultimate tensile strength 28 to 32 tons/sq.in., elongation 25 to 29 per cent. The *plungers* are of 3 per cent nickel case-hardening steel of the following composition and mechanical properties:—

Carbon not exceeding		0·15	per cent
Silicon	,,	0·30	,,
Sulphur	,,	0·05	,,
Phosphorus	,,	0·05	,,
Manganese	,,	0·60	,,
Chromium	,,	0·30	,,
Nickel	,,	3·50	,,

Ultimate tensile strength, over 42 tons/sq.in.; elongation, not less than 18 per cent. The *valves and seats* are of stainless steel or high-grade cast iron. The *fuel-pump cams* are usually made of the same material as the plungers. The *rollers and tappets* are generally made of case-hardening carbon steel of the following composition and mechanical properties:—

Carbon, not more than		0·20	per cent
Silicon	,,	0·30	,,
Sulphur	,,	0·07	,,
Phosphorus	,,	0·07	,,
Manganese	,,	1·00	,,

Tensile strength 32 tons/sq.in.; elongation, over 20 per cent.

Fuel valves—The *spindles* are of 3 per cent nickel case-hardening steel, as for fuel-pump plungers. The *housings* are made of good-quality cast iron or mild steel, whilst the *spray nozzles and nuts* securing them are generally of special heat-resisting steel.

Compressed-air valves and seats—As these parts are exposed to moist air and other corrosive elements they are generally made of special steel: a copper–nickel alloy, such as Monel metal, having the following approximate composition is used:—

Copper	27·00	per cent
Nickel	67·10	,,
Iron	3·85	,,
Silicon	0·14	,,
Manganese	1·87	,,
Lead	trace	

CORROSION

Numerous theories have been advanced to explain the cause of corrosion, but, as operating engineers, they do not concern us particularly. We know that water is the universal solvent and that there are few forms of matter which are not to some extent dissolved, disintegrated or otherwise changed by it in course of time. Moreover, we know from experience that hot sea-water is more destructive than cold fresh-water, that if air held in suspension can be separated from the water its corrosive properties are reduced, and that the direction and manner of the flowing of the water have an important bearing upon the preservation of the metal walls enclosing it.

At one time it was common practice to deliver the cooling water to tanks situated well above the cylinder heads, from which it flowed, partly by gravity and partly by pressure from the pump, to the cylinder jackets and pistons of the engine. (The primary object was to obviate the sudden stoppage of cooling water in the event of the pumps failing, the capacity of the tanks being large enough to ensure several minutes' supply of cooling water after the pumps had stopped functioning.)

More corrosion of iron castings and copper pipes in contact with cooling water takes place now that the practice is for the pumps to deliver the water direct to the cylinder jackets and pistons, which would suggest that the old practice of delivering to gravity tanks had a beneficial effect in this respect. That a considerable amount of air was separated from the water whilst in the gravity tanks was very apparent, because unless the air-release cocks situated at the top of the tanks were left open, the tanks soon became filled with air.

Designers have to a certain extent counteracted the ill-effect of air in the cooling water, when the water is delivered direct to the engine, by arranging its passage through the cooling spaces in such a way that stagnant or dead water is avoided, and pockets in which air becomes trapped are eliminated. The present practice of employing rotary cooling-water pumps also makes the provision of gravity tanks less advantageous, because with reciprocating pumps a certain amount of air must be drawn in with the water to prevent hammering in the pump and delivery pipes. Nevertheless, a careful study by the operating engineer of the shape of all cooling-water spaces is essential, and if pockets in which dead water is likely to occur or air to accumulate exist, a leak-off should be provided, or, if this is not possible, these particular parts should periodically be well cleaned and the surfaces protected by anti-corrosion paint or compound.

A better example of the destructive action of aerated water could not be found than in bilge pumps, which in most cases draw water part of the time and a mixture of air and water most of the time. There will be few operating engineers who have not seen the inside of these pumps so disintegrated that formerly cast-iron parts had developed into a plumbago-like substance which could be cut with a penknife. Generally in such cases the brass seats become loose, and the cast iron in way of them so badly corroded that a repair, if not impossible, is a difficult and costly matter.

This wastage is mainly due to allowing the bilge pump to continue working after the bilge becomes dry. In many ships, the after-well bilge suction is never wholly covered with water from the beginning to the end of every voyage, and the pump is allowed to draw a little water and much air by day and by night, and those responsible remain completely oblivious to the harm that is being done to what is probably an expensive casting. The damage done in this way is so great and occurs so often that it would doubtless pay to provide a regulating cock operated by a float in this particular bilge suction, and so make it impossible for the end of the suction pipe to become uncovered.

Mud also contributes to the corrosion of certain parts of engines. For instance, the lower ends of cylinder water-jackets in way of the rubber sealing rings are often found corroded, and unless steps are taken to stop the action it will eventually be impossible to prevent water from leaking past the rubber rings without effecting extensive repairs. When an engine is working and the cylinder jackets are being properly circulated with water, it is unlikely that air will find its way to the lowest part of the jacket as it is generally admitted with the water at a higher point. The corrosion therefore must, if it is due to air in the cooling water, take place when cooling water is not circulating. What actually happens is that mud accumulates at the bottom of the water jackets, and when port is reached and water is drained from the jacket to attend to some part, or if it escapes owing to leakages past valves or glands, the air percolates through the wet mud, with which it more or less combines, and begins its destructive work.

From this it is evident that if corrosion of engine parts in contact with the circulating cooling water is to be prevented, as far as it lies in the operating engineer's power to do so, mud must be excluded, or air must not be allowed to reach the mud. In other words, the mud must not be allowed to become dry. As it is not always possible completely to exclude mud from such parts as the bottoms of cylinder water-jackets, the only alternative is to keep the jackets full of water when a ship is in port and the engines are not in use. It is, of course, necessary on occasion to empty the jackets to effect repairs or adjustments, but when the work is done the jackets should be filled with water and not allowed to remain empty—as is frequently the practice—until the ship is ready to proceed to sea a week or even longer after the work on the jackets has been completed.

If the cooling system of an engine is properly designed and the operating engineers do all in their power to reduce to a minimum the amount of air entering with the water, renewal of parts owing to corrosion will not be necessary for a considerable time if the cast iron is of good quality and the castings are homogeneous. On occasion, however, a casting in contact with the cooling water is seriously affected after a comparatively short time in service. In such cases it is generally found that other, but similar parts of the engine which are subjected to exactly the same conditions are not affected in the least degree. Furthermore, it invariably happens that the corrosion is confined to a very small proportion of the casting even though there is no apparent reason why a much greater proportion of the surface should not be similarly affected.

This would suggest that if the casting had been homogeneous throughout, the whole instead of part of it would have resisted the action of the circulating water. The inference is, therefore, that local wastage of this kind is due to porous patches in the casting, which the ordinary method of water-pressure testing the casting during manufacture of the engines failed to reveal.

Any steel or cast-iron part found corroding should be very thoroughly cleaned, the final part of the operation being carried out by a steel-wire brush, and given a coat of Bitumastic solution which has been heated to a temperature of 200°F (93·3°C). After the first coat is quite dry a second coat at normal atmospheric temperature should be applied. This in most cases will arrest the corrosion, but if there is a cause the better plan is to look for it and remove it.

CHAPTER 26

Preparing an engine for sea

As is the case with all other classes of machinery, the working parts of a diesel engine require to be opened up periodically for examination, cleaning, and re-adjustment of parts subject to accumulation of deposit and to wear. It is not possible to generalise as to how long the various parts will operate before opening up becomes necessary, or shall we say advisable, as the period depends to a great extent upon the manner in which the engine is operated and how the fuel and lubricating oil are used. Moreover, some shipowners unwisely demand more power from an engine than it is really capable of developing at maximum efficiency for long periods, while others realise that the tendency is to rate diesel engines rather highly and are content with about 95 per cent of the full rated power. This 5 per cent reduction in the power output lessens considerably the amount of opening up required.

A good deal depends, of course, upon the design of certain parts, and the quality of the materials of which those parts are made, but with any of the well-known makes it is safe to say that the amount of opening up required by an engine that is not overworked depends mainly upon the skill of the operating engineer. The author has in mind one engine the pistons of which were taken out and the piston rings renewed regularly every six months, not because it was thought to be advisable, but because it was absolutely necessary. The cylinder lubricating-oil consumption was excessive, the bearing wear much more than it ought to have been, and the engine-room was in a dirty condition. Another chief engineer was appointed, and the result of this change was that the pistons operated for eighteen months before it was even desirable to open up the cylinders, while the general condition of the engine-room was all that could be desired. The trade this ship was on necessitated the utmost power practicable being got out of the engines, and it was, consequently, a rather difficult job to operate. The first chief engineer was widely experienced and conscientious, but it was evident that his successor had made a closer study of this type of machinery and knew exactly how to attend to the details referred to throughout this book, and so prevent endless work and worry to himself and expense to the owners.

Arriving in port

After the signal " Finished with engines " has been received certain formalities require to be carried out. The nature and extent of these depend upon the position of the ship and the state of the weather. For instance, if the ship is anchored in a position exposed to bad weather, or near other ships at anchor or on the move, the engines must be " kept handy " as they may be required at a moment's notice. In such cases all that is necessary is to stop circulation of the lubricating oil and cooling water after the heat from combustion has been carried off. In cold climates, however, it will be advisable to keep the cylinders and pistons warm by heating the cooling water to about 100°F (37·8°C) and circulating it through these parts. It is not necessary to circulate the lubricating oil when the engine is standing idle, but there should be no doubt about the capacity of the pumps to pick up the oil instantly and circulate it. The starting-air and fuel systems should be left open, but it is wise to lash the starting lever lightly with rope as a precaution against the engine being inadvertently set in motion.

When informed that the engine will not be required for some time the starting-air, fuel, lubricating-oil, and cooling-water systems will require to be shut off; and after making quite certain that starting air cannot reach the cylinders the engine turning gear should be engaged. The engine should then be given about a dozen revolutions by auxiliary power in order to carry oil up to the dry parts of the cylinder liners and avoid rusting during the stay in port. To make sure there is sufficient oil between the piston rings to ensure this, it is good practice to operate the cylinder lubricators by hand as each piston is in line with the injection holes in the cylinder liner. If no work has to be done on the cylinders or their connections it is advisable to keep the cooling-water jackets full to avoid corrosion taking place. When the pistons are cooled by lubricating oil such a precaution is unnecessary, as a protecting film will always be left on the internal surfaces of the pistons and the parts conveying the cooling oil to and from the pistons, many of which are made of steel.

Temperature of engine-room

In ports where the temperature is likely to fall to freezing-point and below, and means are not provided to keep the temperature above that point, care must of course be taken to see that the cooling water is drained from the cylinder jackets, pistons, and the entire pipe system, so as to prevent fracture of castings and bursting of pipes. Drain-cocks and valves are generally provided for this purpose, but all parts containing water should receive consideration, and if there is any doubt about water not being completely drained out a careful examination should be made.

The temperature of ships having steam-driven auxiliaries is never likely to fall to freezing-point, but it may on occasion be advisable to keep all openings into the engine-room closed and set in motion steam-driven machines that are not really required for the work in hand. The best safeguard against damage by frost is to provide arrangements to enable the cylinder-jacket cooling system to be circulated by warm water. This will keep the whole engine-room warm and prevent water in pipes situated in every part of the engine-room from freezing. Even if warm water is allowed to circulate through half the total number of cylinders the engine-room will be maintained at such a temperature that freezing is most unlikely. Such an arrangement allows the work of overhauling parts of cylinders to proceed.

Fuel settling-tanks

Not only must these tanks be full upon leaving port, but the strainers or filters situated between the tanks and the main engine fuel-pumps must be quite clean in order that there will be no undue resistance to the flow of fuel when the engine is set in motion. Involuntary stops have occurred and serious situations arisen when leaving port, owing to the engine fuel-pump suctions running dry after ten minutes or so. The cause of this is generally due to the settling tank running dry or to choked strainers, but on occasions the cause has been due to the low temperature of the fuel. Everything in this direction may appear to be in order when a ship arrives in port, but then the fuel is warmer and will more readily flow through a partly choked strainer. When leaving port, however, the fuel is colder and more viscous, and a partly choked strainer may not allow sufficient fuel to flow, with the result that when the engine has consumed the fuel in the pipe connecting the strainer with the fuel pumps, the engine stops for want of fuel. The fact that there appears to be a sufficient supply of fuel when the fuel pumps are being primed is not a sure indication that the supply will be sufficient when the engine is set in motion.

Fuel settling-tanks, being generally placed out of sight, high up in the engine-room, are apt to escape attention until a ship has put to sea and begins to roll. The engines may then begin to work irregularly, due to fine grit, which, not being allowed to settle on the tank bottom owing to the movement of the ship, finds its way to the engine fuel-pumps. Efficient strainers may be provided, but somehow fine grit finds its way to the engine in spite of them, and while these particles may not be large enough to interfere with the working of the engines, they will have a bad effect upon the valve faces. When in port it is, therefore, advisable to open up, steam out, or well air and then thoroughly clean those tanks occasionally.

The steam-heating coils, when fitted, should be examined for corrosion, and while the tank is open the coils should be tested by admitting steam at the full working pressure. Steam-heating coils are invariably located so low that the sediment which accumulates on the tank bottom can only be removed with difficulty, and in some cases the tank can be properly cleaned only by removing the heating coils. This, of course, would be unnecessary if the coils were located not less than 6 inches from the bottom of the tank, and there is no reason why they should be located lower than this.

Cylinder-head valves

If the cylinder-head valves or any parts of the operating gear have been changed, overhauled or simply removed for access to some other part, it will be necessary to check, and re-adjust if required, the clearances between the rocking-lever rollers and the plain parts of their respective cams. Before carrying out this operation it is advisable to insert a crowbar under the roller end of the rocking lever and prise open the valve two or three times, allowing it to re-seat smartly to make sure that it is working freely and re-seating properly. A slight upward pressure should then be exerted on the roller end of the lever by means of the crowbar whilst adjusting the roller clearance in order to take up all slackness in the operating gear. The clearance must always be checked again after the locking nut on the adjusting screw has been tightened, as this operation sometimes has the effect of altering the clearance.

Even though the air-inlet and exhaust valves have not been disturbed since the previous run, it is advisable to prise them open a few times with a crowbar to make sure that they are free to open to their fullest extent and re-seat properly, and so make certain, so far as these parts of the engine are concerned, of the engine starting properly. The starting valves also should be tested in the same way and for the same reason, while the indicator cocks should be shut to prevent escape of starting air and loss of compression when the engine is started. Open indicator cocks are frequently the cause of a false start.

After making sure that all valves are free and in working order, a careful inspection of the cylinder heads should be made for tools or the like that may become jammed under the rocking levers, or fall, when the engine is started. All parts of the valve gear should then be lubricated.

In some makes of engines, the rocking levers work on eccentrics mounted upon a fulcrum shaft, which is rotated through a certain angle, usually 180°, during the reversing operation. In such cases, the eccentrics naturally wear mostly on one half of the circumference only—i.e. the half which takes the load during ahead operation—so that to maintain uniform timing of the valves for both directions of rotation with the same roller clearance the eccentrics require to be trued up occasionally. The extent of wear, if any, is readily ascertained by measuring the roller clearance with the reversing gear in the ahead and then the astern position. Generally, as wear takes place and the desired roller clearance for ahead operation is maintained, the clearance with the gear in the astern position becomes less and less, and if not attended to, the roller will eventually ride on the plain part of the cam when the engine is operating in the astern direction. If the parts are properly lubricated, the wear rate will not be great, but it should nevertheless be checked from time to time, particularly in the case of engines with mechanically-operated fuel-injection valves, as a reduction in the roller clearance means earlier admission, later cut-off, and consequently higher cylinder pressures when working in the astern direction.

Piston-cooling system

After opening and closing the various valves as necessary to cause the cooling oil or water, as the case may be, to flow in the desired direction, the stand-by piston-cooling pump will require to be put into operation, and the flow from each piston observed. The fluid should issue from each outlet in a steady stream. If the presence of air is indicated by bubbles or an unsteady flow, the whole of the pump output should be passed through one piston at a time until all air has been expelled and the desired condition of flow obtained, after which a final examination should be made to make quite sure that the valves are in their correct working positions, and that each piston will receive its proper supply when the engine is started. It is wise to keep the stand-by pump working until the " full away " order is received.

After the cooling medium has been circulating properly at the normal working pressure, the drain tank should be sounded, and replenished if the pump suction is not well covered. When adding to the contents of the piston-cooling tank with the pumps in operation, it must be remembered that space must be left for the fluid in the system, otherwise when the pump is stopped the tank will overflow and much lubricating oil or fresh water, as the case may be, will be wasted.

The practice of some engineers is to by-pass the piston cooler until the engine has been working some time, and the cooling medium has approached normal working temperature, the object being to facilitate starting and reduce the stresses set up in the pistons due to temperature difference. There is no doubt that this practice has both these effects to a small extent, and would be commendable if it were unaccompanied by objections. The main objection is that, as a rule, the change-over to the cooler must be made when all hands are fully occupied manoeuvring the engine and attending to the thousand-and-one things that must be attended to when a ship is leaving port, with the result that the rising temperature of the piston-cooling medium may not be noticed. When lubricating oil is the medium employed this would be a serious matter. In view of this, and the fact that modern engines start readily enough with unheated pistons, the wisest plan is to start with the piston cooler in operation, unless the sea temperature is extremely low. Moreover, the design of modern pistons is such that the additional stresses arising from circulating the pistons with cool water or lubricating oil are so very small that they are not worth consideration.

The mechanism conveying the cooling medium to the piston should then be examined for leakages. When of the telescopic type, the glands and the joints between the pipes and the pistons should be carefully examined. As telescopic pipes sometimes break at the point where they join the flange, or pull out of the flanges, it is wise to tap each pipe lightly with a hammer or similar tool. The sound produced will indicate whether the pipe is firmly attached to its flange. If telescopic-pipe glands are found leaking, it is not advisable to tighten them too much, as the leakage generally takes up when the fluid and the parts concerned become heated. Should the glands be tightened when an engine is at rest and the parts are cold, there is a danger that when the engine is working normally the telescopic pipes will be gripped with undue pressure, and they may be damaged at the point where they are joined to their flanges. Many telescopic pipes have been broken or pulled out of their flanges in this way.

Telescopic pipes which work through packing should always be well lubricated before an engine is set in motion. The best time to do this is when the engine is being turned just prior to disengaging the turning gear. These pipes tend to become dry in port and, if the engine is started with the pipes in this condition, a strain so great will be set up at the point where they are attached to the flanges that the pipes may be damaged. The very quick acceleration natural to diesel engines is responsible for many leakages which occur at the upper ends of telescopic pipes, so prevent this as far as possible by not nipping up the glands too tightly and by lubricating the pipes before an engine is set in motion.

Cylinder cooling system

The stand-by jacket-cooling pump will then require to be set to work after all necessary valves in the system have been opened and closed as required. The flow through each cylinder jacket should be observed, and care taken to see that the exhaust pipes, if water-cooled, are being properly circulated. It is an advantage when the flow from each cylinder can be viewed, as then there is no fear of the engine being set in motion until all air has been expelled from each cylinder jacket. In cases where the flow from each cylinder jacket cannot be seen it is advisable, especially when the jackets have been emptied, to circulate one jacket at a time. If a good steady flow through a particular cylinder jacket cannot be obtained, presence of air will probably be the cause. In such cases, partly closing the outlet valve to create a greater pressure in the jacket, and then opening quickly, may dislodge the air.

The inlet cooling-water valves provided at the lower end of each cylinder jacket should always be full open while an engine is in operation, and the amount of water circulating varied by regulation of the outlet valves. After the water has been made to circulate properly through each of the cylinder jackets, the outlet valves should be shut down until they are from one-half to three-quarters of a turn open, and then regulated as necessary to give the required outlet temperature after the engine is set in motion. Whilst on the subject, it would be as well to point out the importance of making quite sure that the valves are properly fitted, i.e. that the water approaches the valve from the underside of the lid, where same are of the globe type. Where sluice or gate valves are used, the valve should be located in such a way that in the event of a gate becoming detached from its spindle it will not fall and stop the flow of cooling water. These regulating valves are generally, but not always, fitted in the right way when an engine leaves the builders, but during subsequent repairs they are sometimes refitted wrongly. It is quite an easy matter to arrange the bolt holes in the flanges of the valves so that they can only be fitted in the right way, but some engine-builders do not yet fully appreciate the importance of guarding against these valves being refitted in the wrong way and causing a sudden stoppage of cooling water to a cylinder jacket.

In cold weather it is advisable to preheat the cylinders. The common method for doing this and the care to be exercised have already been described. There is nothing to be gained by preheating to a high temperature. All circulating valves should be left open during the operation, as it is just possible that one may be overlooked until after the engine has been set in motion. The cooling water should be circulating when the engine is started. The practice of preventing the pumps from delivering until the engine has been operating for a few minutes is unwise. Air or steam might accumulate in these few minutes and interfere with the flow of water when the pumps begin delivering. The quantity of water to be circulated depends, of course, upon the speed of the engine. The quantity should be small until the temperature begins to rise, but so long as the water is moving, trouble arising from local overheating is not likely to occur.

Lubricating-oil system

The stand-by lubricating-oil pump should really be the first auxiliary machine to be set in motion when preparing an engine for sea, in order that time is allowed for the solid impurities in the oil to be separated and collected in the strainers before the engine is required to operate. Whenever the crankcases have been opened for the overhaul of internal parts, much dirt will have been carried in, and in addition to cleaning out the crankcases it is advisable to arrange to begin circulating the lubricating oil continuously for six hours before the engine is started, cleaning the strainers as required meanwhile, so that when the engine is started the pressure of the oil at the bearings will not be reduced owing to dirty strainers. Heating the oil to about 100°F (37·8°C) whilst it is circulating will facilitate the separation of the impurities, and prevent greasy matter from depositing on the cooler tubes. Raising the temperature of the oil in cold climates greatly assists the pumps also.

Lubricating-oil strainers should always be provided with pressure gauges connected in such a way that the condition of the cartridges can be seen at a glance. The best practice is to provide a pressure gauge at each side of the discharge strainers and a vacuum gauge at the pump side of the suction strainer. When the cartridges of the discharge strainer are clean, both pressure gauges will register the same pressure, but when dirt collects the gauge connected to the pump side of the strainer will register a higher pressure than the one on the outlet side. In the case of the suction strainers, dirty cartridges will be indicated by a higher vacuum reading.

The dirt accumulates on the outside of the cartridges, so that they require to be carefully removed from the strainer in order not to allow any of the dirt to fall back into the strainer-box. The best way to clean these cartridges is to immerse them in fuel contained in a drum larger in diameter and length than the cartridge; after the dirt has been brushed off, compressed air should be blown through the gauze from the inside of the cartridge. For the supply of compressed air it is generally possible to connect a hose pipe to some part of the starting-air system.

In nine cases out of ten when a stand-by lubricating-oil pump fails to lift the oil from the double-bottom tank or maintain a steady pressure, the cause is either due to the oil being too cold and viscous, or to leakage of air into the suction pipe. Slight leakages in these pipes sometimes pass unnoticed until the oil is cold, and a higher vacuum must be created in the pipe to cause the oil to flow to the pump. Because of this it is wise to test these pipes by hydraulic pressure occasionally. In the case of new engines, all bolted joints should be tightened soon after the lubricating oil has attained its working temperature.

The tanks in which the new lubricating oil is stored are usually located high up in the engine-room, and the oil in them can be used to test the lubricating-oil pump suction pipe. As a rule, these tanks are connected to the pump suction pipe, in which case all that is necessary to test the suction pipe is to shut the valve at its extreme end, in order to stop the new oil from passing into the double-bottom tank, and admit the new oil to the suction pipe. When making such a test, however, see that all air is allowed to escape from the suction pipe. This can usually be arranged for by opening the air-release cock generally provided on all such pumps.

The lubricating oil in the system should be examined and, if considered necessary, purified. Most engineers will have an idea of the condition of the oil before port is reached. If not, draw off a sample of oil while it is circulating, and test it by adding to it twice the amount of paraffin and pouring the mixture through a piece of blotting paper. The amount of sediment left on the blotting paper will convey an idea of how much solid matter is contained in the oil.

When the principal bearings are lubricated on the pressure system, it is usual to have a large quantity of oil in the system or, to be more correct, a small quantity in circulation compared with the quantity in the drain tank or sump. This is conducive to proper lubrication, since, as the oil can remain longer in the sump before being circulated through the bearings, there is a better chance for the impurities to separate from the oil and fall to the bottom of the sump out of reach of the pump suction. The not uncommon practice, therefore, of keeping only sufficient oil in the sump to cover the pump suction pipe is not good.

Some engineers seem to think that they save oil by keeping the absolute minimum in the system. Such reasoning is difficult to understand. Actually the consumption will, if anything, be higher, since the smaller the quantity of oil in circulation, the higher will be the working temperature, and consequently the greater will be the amount of vapour produced in the crankcase. Therefore, while there is no advantage whatever in "starving" the system, there are three disadvantages, namely, the impurities are given less time to settle out, more oil is vaporised and lost, and as oil in the vaporised form is more easily oxidised the oil will deteriorate more rapidly.

The best arrangement for the oil sump is shown in Fig. 187, but where one compartment only is provided the end of the pump suction pipe and the end of the return pipe from the engine should be as far away from each other as possible, and the end of the latter pipe should be beneath the working level of the oil in the sump. The object of this is to ensure that as little as possible of the impurities coming from the engine will be delivered back to the bearings. It must be remembered that there are many injurious impurities in the oil which will not be collected by the common form of gauze strainer, but which will settle out in the sump if time is allowed for them to do so.

With this form of sump, the returned oil should enter at a point near the bottom of the sump, and be drawn from a point as high as practicable. The pump should be provided with a high and a low suction, the former being used generally, and the latter only in cases of emergency or when it is necessary to empty the tank for cleaning or other purposes. The desired results will be obtained if the high suction ends about one foot from the bottom of the tank, and the low suction from half to one inch.

Crankcase inspection

After the piston-cooling water and lubricating oil are circulating at the normal working pressure, the crankcase doors should be opened, and all pipes and fittings conveying these media carefully examined for leakages.

Lubricating oil should issue from the ends of every bearing fed from the pressure system. As a rule, if oil issues from the ends of the crosshead bearings it may safely be assumed that the crankshaft and crankpin bearings will get sufficient oil, since the oil must pass through these bearings before it reaches the crosshead bearings. It is, however, more satisfactory to see the oil flow from both ends of all bearings, and this can generally be brought about—provided, of course, that all the passages are clear of obstructions—by turning the engine with auxiliary power while circulating the oil.

All pipes in engine crankcases should be firmly secured in order to prevent them from vibrating while the engine is operating. Copper pipes should be annealed periodically as they tend to become brittle and may fracture. Pipes used to convey oil to the camshaft driving-chains should receive attention also. While these pipes must sometimes be led to within a few inches of the chain in order to deliver the oil where it is wanted, they must not be so near that they will foul the chain in the event of its becoming slack through stretching.

Priming the fuel-injection system

One of the most important operations of preparing an engine for sea is the priming of the fuel pumps and fuel valves, as it is a fact that more false starts are due to insufficient attention being given to this than to any other cause. Much has been written upon the subject in a previous chapter, so that it is not necessary to say more at this stage than to impress upon readers the vital importance of continuing the priming operation until all air has been expelled, and the fuel flows from the various vents provided on the pumps and valves in a steady stream and its natural colour. When the fuel issuing from the vents is of a light-brown colour, it generally indicates the presence of air. Pressure resulting from a priming valve being only partly open will cause the issuing fuel to be a light colour also, but it is, of course, presumed that these valves are fully open before the priming operation is begun.

Cylinder lubrication

Not only must the cylinder lubricators begin delivering oil into the cylinders immediately an engine is set in motion, but a certain amount of oil should be contained between the piston rings. When a ship is entering port, a great deal of manoeuvring is generally necessary, and the moist starting air admitted on these occasions tends to wash the oil film off the cylinder walls and leave them more or less dry. For this reason it is advisable to adjust the lubricators to discharge about three times the normal quantity whilst manoeuvring into port. Moreover, during the time a ship is in port the oil film oxidises, and there is no doubt that more cylinder-liner and piston-ring wear takes place during the time a ship is leaving port than in many hundreds of hours of normal running at sea.

The cylinder lubricators and the pipes connecting them with the cylinders must, therefore, be fully primed prior to starting, and some oil injected into the spaces between the piston rings if the engine has been idle for more than a couple of days. The best time to do this is when the engine is being turned to make sure that all is clear before the turning gear is disengaged, the lubricators being worked by hand during the period when the oil-injection holes are covered by the piston.

When working the lubricators by hand, observe that the ball valves are functioning properly. If in doubt, the pipes should be disconnected from the cylinder, and the lubricator plunger worked while a finger is pressed against the end of the pipe. If the valves and all other parts are in good order, it will be impossible to stop oil issuing from the disconnected end of the pipe. If oil is showing in the sighting glass—that is oil which has displaced water or glycerine, whichever is used—it indicates that one or both of the joints at the ends of the sighting glass are leaking. If the joints have become hard they should be renewed, as undue pressure on the securing nut will probably break the glass if it is of tubular form. These joints are made of leather, and must be fairly thick in order that only moderate pressure on the nut holding the parts together will ensure fluid-tightness, When one of these joints becomes defective, it is wise to renew the joints at both ends of the glass.

The lubricators should be set to deliver from three to four times the normal quantity before an engine is started, and allowed to continue doing so for the first three hours or so that the engine is operating at full power. When the cylinder liners are new, the amount of oil delivered should be reduced to the normal amount very gradually over a period of three to four days, but in the case of old cylinder liners the amount delivered can be adjusted in one operation.

Starting systems

The starting-air compressor will require to be set to work at an early part of the proceedings, in order to ensure that the tanks are fully charged some time before the main engines are required. The usual pressures are 350 to 600 lb/sq.in.

The compressor cylinder-lubricators require the same attention as those feeding the main engine cylinders. It is not, however, necessary to increase the rate of feed or, in fact, do more than make sure that the whole of the pipes connecting the lubricators and the cylinders are fully charged with oil, so that delivery into the cylinders will take place immediately the compressor is set in motion.

Because of the very small piston-end clearances in air-compressors, one of the greatest dangers to be guarded against is water in the cylinders. Very serious damage has resulted on occasions due to this. When preparing an engine for sea, therefore, an important duty is to open fully the cooler drains and observe if water drips from them as the compressor is turned at least two complete revolutions by hand power. If no water is observed it may be taken for granted that the coolers and cylinders are free of water, but as there are usually pipes connecting the various stages in which water can collect, and from which it can be dislodged only when the compressor is set in motion, the cooler drains should be left open for a few minutes, i.e. until there is no doubt about the compressors being entirely free of water.

While the starting-air tanks are being pumped up, the drains should be opened momentarily to make sure that the tanks are free of water. The drains on the starting-air manifold pipe should also be opened for the same reason. As corrosive liquids are liable to collect in these pipes, it is wise always to keep these valves slightly open and prevent accumulation of these undesirable liquids. The valves may require more frequent overhaul if left slightly open, but it will prevent corrosion of the starting-air manifold, which is a much more serious matter. The amount of air that will leak through the partly-open valves is of no account, whilst if they are not opened too much the noise produced when starting will not be objectionable.

The safety devices on the starting-air system must be in good order, as when starting an engine there is always the possibility of a starting valve jamming and causing an abnormally high pressure in the starting-air manifold. If bursting-diaphragms are employed one must be sure that they are not weakened by corrosion, as should these diaphragms rupture, the engine will be out of commission, so far as manoeuvring is concerned, until a new diaphragm has been fitted. And since it takes time to fit a new diaphragm a serious position may easily arise. One must therefore be quite sure that the bursting-diaphragms will not rupture unless it is to relieve an abnormally high pressure and so prevent damage to the starting-air pipes and fittings. See page 328 for details of alternative relief devices.

As the starting-air automatic valve, or relay valve as it is sometimes called, is liable to become denuded of lubricant owing to moisture in the starting air and may jam, one must be satisfied that this valve is in good order before an engine is set in motion. The construction of these valves varies, but in most cases it is possible to test the valve for being free without disconnecting or dismantling any part. All such valves are generally provided with means of injecting grease to the rubbing surfaces, and a little should be injected each time an engine is made ready for sea. When no such provision is made, the moving parts of the valve should be removed occasionally and lightly greased.

When decompression valves are fitted, they must be in proper working order. If they do not open owing to the operating gear being incorrectly adjusted, the air-inlet or exhaust-valve rocking levers may be broken; or should one or more of the valves jam in the open position, it will be necessary to stop the engine to free them.

These valves are generally operated mechanically from the reversing shaft or some other part which is set in motion during the reversing operation, and the rods and levers employed to transmit the motion are generally arranged in such a way that when the reversing gear is in either extreme position the decompression valves are closed, the open period occurring for a few degrees on each side of the mid-position of the reversing gear.

The conditions under which these valves work are such that they tend to become dry and may jam in the open position. They should, therefore, be opened up occasionally and overhauled, as the consequence of a valve that will not function properly may be a false start. In some engines the cylinder relief-valve or the exhaust-valve is made to serve as a decompression valve.

In the case of most two-stroke engines, there are no rocking levers to break in the event of the decompression gear failing to function, but unless the pressure in the cylinders is released during the reversing operation there is a possibility of the engine not starting promptly when the starting gear is operated. Suppose, for instance, that two cranks of a multiple-cylinder engine are diametrically opposite, and that upon stopping the engine comes to rest these two cranks are in the horizontal position. In the cylinder whose piston is moving upwards will be air under pressure, and the other cylinder will contain burnt gases, also under pressure. If the engine remains at rest long enough, the gas in both cylinders will escape and the pressure be reduced, but if the engine is to be instantly reversed it means that the piston which was moving downwards during the preceding run will now have to move upwards. As this cylinder will contain burnt gases under pressure, and any upward movement of the piston will compress them still further, it will be seen that resistance will be offered to the turning effort of the starting air in the cylinders. If the starting air is at its maximum working pressure the resistance will be overcome, and the only effect will be sluggish starting and an increased consumption of starting air, but if the starting-air pressure is low, the engine may not start.

The starting-air valves in the cylinder heads should also be tested for being free, care being taken to see that starting air cannot enter the cylinders whilst this is being done. All such valves can generally be prised open by means of a crowbar. Any valve that does not re-seat smartly should be removed and freed, as it is almost sure to jam when an attempt is made to start the engine. It is not advisable to rotate such valves when testing them for being free, or at any other time, as this causes them to leak. The leakage is not noticed until the engine has been operating on fuel for a few days, when the valve faces will be found burnt.

Starting and reversing gears

All rubbing surfaces of these gears should be well lubricated, and run over several times before the engine is required to operate. The action of the reversing gear should be carefully observed, and any stiffness or jerkiness of movement investigated and the cause removed. The brake or buffer cylinder of the reversing gear may require replenishing with oil, or some of the reversing-shaft bearings may have become dry.

The starting gear of a diesel engine cannot, unfortunately, be tested like that of a steam engine, so that it is necessary to know that every single part of the gear is in proper working order. The compressed air for operating the starting gear is generally taken from the starting-air tank side of the automatic valve, and this valve can be closed by hand. With such an arrangement the starting gear can be operated and its action carefully observed without admitting starting air to the working cylinders.

Thrust bearings

This part should be filled with clean oil up to about one inch from the shaft, and the sump tested for the presence of water. If the bearing is lubricated by a continuous stream of oil under pressure from the bearing-oil system, see that the oil is flowing properly when the stand-by lubricating-oil pump is started up.

Thrust blocks are generally provided with oil-level indicators. These should be tested occasionally by letting the oil run out of the glass and allowing it to fill up again immediately to make sure that they are registering correctly. When these indicators are located under the floor level, as they very often are, and the oil in them is not clearly visible, it is wise to convert them into level indicators of the dip-stick type. On occasions the tubular glasses of these level indicators have broken for no apparent reason, allowing the oil to escape and the thrust block to run dry, causing serious damage before being noticed.

Speed governors

This part should also be given attention before the engine is set in motion. The governor itself and the working joints of the various links and levers should be lubricated and tested for being free to function correctly in the event of their being required to act during the voyage.

Turning gears

The final part of the operation of preparing an engine for sea is to start the turning gear and turn the engine two complete revolutions, after which the turning gear should be disengaged. On occasions the disengaging of the turning gear has been forgotten and, as can be imagined, serious damage done. To many such a lapse of memory may seem unforgivable, but those who are fully aware of the arduous duties of engineers in charge of such vast and complicated machinery, and the mental strain that is sometimes imposed upon them, realise that there can be extenuating circumstances.

On the other hand the damage done may be due to want of proper thought or to gross carelessness. For instance, on one occasion it was necessary to stop an air-injection engine at sea to investigate a slight knock in the crankcase, and while some of the staff were attending to this others were instructed to take the opportunity to change a fuel valve. The turning gear had been engaged, as it always ought to be when men have to enter the crankcase, no matter how long the examination or repair is likely to take, or whether or not it is necessary to turn the engine by auxiliary power, and the reversing gear was run over to its mid-position with the object of opening the decompression valves. (This is a very necessary precaution to take on such occasions as it obviates the possibility of pressure accumulating in any of the cylinders owing to starting-air valves leaking.)

The work of changing the fuel valve was finished first, and those engaged upon it decided to test the valve faces by injection air. To carry out such a test it was necessary to shut the starting-air relay valve, or rather prevent it from working automatically, in order to prevent starting air from reaching the cylinders, and to run the starting gear over to the normal working position to allow injection air to pass to the fuel-injection valves, the reversing gear remaining in the mid-position. This is, of course, the correct procedure with air-injection engines, and nothing untoward would have happened had those responsible put the starting gear back to its stop position after the testing of the fuel valve had been carried out. This, however, was not done, with the result that when one of the engineers, who was unaware of the starting gear having been moved from its stop position, prepared to re-start the engine, he failed to notice that the starting gear was in its normal working position and operated the lever which put the reversing gear into the " Ahead " position. This had the effect of opening one of the fuel-injection valves and allowing injection air to enter the corresponding cylinder. The engine was immediately set in motion, the turning gear was completely wrecked and many of the teeth in the flywheel were broken. Fortunately the last man had just climbed out of the crankcase.

In modern engines the starting and reversing gears are interlocked, so that it should not be possible to operate the reversing gear until the starting gear is in its stop position, but it must be remembered that owing to neglect or structural weakness such safety devices may fail to function, and a serious accident such as the one just described may happen unless proper thought is given to the possible consequences of such foolproof devices not serving the purpose intended.

Piston rod packing

Whilst a ship is in port, rusting of piston rods must be prevented by keeping them well greased. This is of particular importance in the case of double-acting engines if the gas packing is not to prove troublesome when the engine is next set to work.

The usual form of packing is very simple, and consists of about nine rings contained in a water-cooled stuffing-box. Each packing ring comprises a solid cast-iron ring bored to the diameter of the piston rod and cut into four or six equal parts, the parts or segments being assembled around the piston rod and held against it by means of either garter springs or inward-springing steel rings. Each packing ring is carried in a cage ring or carrier, in which it has, when all rings are firmly secured in place, about 0·006 inch clearance in a vertical direction in order to allow it to follow, laterally, the slight movements of the piston rod. The packing rings are held firmly together in the stuffing-box by a gland, and lubricating oil is fed to the packing by mechanically-operated lubricators.

The simplest form of packing ring is exactly similar to a piston ring but is hammered in such a way that it springs inward instead of outward. The disadvantage of this type of packing ring is that, in the event of a ring breaking, the piston rod must be disconnected at the crosshead to place a new ring in position. Cast iron is the most suitable material for these packing rings, so that this difficulty of comparatively fragile cast-iron rings breaking cannot be overcome by using steel, as such material causes excessive wear of the piston rods.

If each of the packing rings is given 1 mm total end clearance, and is properly lubricated whilst in operation, not only will leakage of gas be prevented, but the wear rate of the packing and piston rods will be very small. Efficient lubrication is most essential, and provision should be made to allow the oil to get between the rubbing surfaces by chamfering both inner edges of the packing rings. The best results are obtained when the oil is injected between the second and third rings from the top. If the oil is injected lower down, the pressure in the bottom cylinder—which occurs on every up-stroke of the piston of two-stroke engines—tends to force the oil downwards, with the result that the upper packing rings run more or less dry and cause the upper end of the piston rod to wear excessively.

CHAPTER 27

General operation and watch-keeping

Having arrived at this stage, most readers will, no doubt, have concluded that there are many parts in a diesel engine likely to give trouble if not properly attended to; that much skill and care are required if such engines are to operate efficiently; that a faulty adjustment after the overhaul of a small part may be the cause of such an engine failing to start, or something more serious; and finally, that the diesel engine, from an operating point of view, is a most interesting form of ship's propelling machinery, and that this type of machinery offers good chances for an engineer to prove his worth, because there are so many directions in which he can exhibit his knowledge and resourcefulness.

Air-injection engines are now obsolescent but there are still a number in service, and whilst the following notes refer mainly to modern airless injection engines it is thought wise to point out possible difficulties with air-injection engines, particularly in connection with fuel valve operation where a wrong move may have very serious consequences.

The causes of most troubles likely to be encountered in diesel engines are, if caught in time, readily capable of remedy once they are located, and many can be avoided if the various parts are attended to as recommended throughout this book when a ship is in port. The not-uncommon belief that a man must be born and brought up, as it were, with this class of machinery in order to understand it fully is altogether wrong. Familiarity with this particular class of machinery is, of course, necessary, but it is in the power of any man of average intelligence who has had a sound training in marine engineering to diagnose promptly the cause of the vast majority of operating troubles, provided he realises that a diesel engine cannot be successfully operated by merely observing, and adjusting when required, the temperatures and pressures as registered by attractively mounted gauges.

The contents of this book will probably have dispelled such a notion if it existed. It is not necessary for an engineer to have actual experience of all the difficulties that may occur to be able to determine the cause of any particular one. With modern engines it is doubtful if such an experience could be gained in a lifetime, but as any one of those mentioned hereafter may occur at any time, it behoves all those desirous of acquiring the necessary knowledge to make an exhaustive study of this and similar books written by men who have experienced more troubles at sea in a month than are now likely to be experienced in twenty years.

When anything goes wrong with a diesel engine it is necessary to think and act quickly, otherwise a serious situation may arise. Should anything unusual occur at sea and the cause cannot be diagnosed at once, the wisest course is to stop the engine and then investigate, remembering that there are certain important things (mentioned later) to do when an engine is suddenly stopped.

To ascertain the cause of irregularities quickly and correctly, the first essential is to know the exact condition of every part of the engine, because many causes have the same symptoms, and if the condition of every part is known many possible causes can be dismissed at once and so a great deal of time saved in diagnosing the real cause. Next to this is the ability to tell by sound, and the instinctive quality called intuition, whether, for instance, the cause of the trouble lies in the starting-air or fuel system, or whether the defect is of a mechanical nature.

To take a simple example, suppose nothing happens when the starting gear is operated. A capable engineer will be able to say at once by the sound produced whether the starting air has reached the starting valves in the cylinder heads, and tell by intuition—a desirable quality which many operating engineers acquire—not only if the starting air has entered the active cylinder, but whether or not it is exerting the necessary force therein. Such an engineer, if his intuition tells him that starting air has reached the unit in starting position and is exerting the required force, would go straight to the starting valve of the unit next in turn for starting air and find the starting valve jammed in the open position, or the rocking-lever roller riding on the plain part of the cam. A less capable engineer would have to start at the automatic starting-air valve and follow the starting-air line until he reached the seat of the trouble, all of which would take up much valuable time.

On one occasion a single-screw ship got into difficulties whilst leaving port owing to the main engine failing to start. After everything else had been inspected the automatic valve was found to be closed. Had those responsible accustomed themselves to the different sounds produced when an engine is being set in motion, the valve would have been opened in a matter of seconds and nothing more would have been heard of the incident.

Practically the whole of this work is devoted to the operating side of diesel engines, and the bulk of it deals either with difficulties likely to be encountered or the means to be adopted to prevent such difficulties from occurring. Although every care has been taken not to overlook any part of this vast subject, completeness so far is too much to expect, since the work has been done in spare time with many enforced interruptions, so this chapter is included in the hope that points so far overlooked will be remembered and dealt with. If, therefore, a certain amount of duplication is found, the author would ask readers to make allowances for any such repetition.

Failure to start on air

If an engine is not set in motion when the reversing gear is in its correct position and the starting gear is run over to the starting position, one of the following will most probably be the cause:—

(1) If the starting valves are of the pneumatically-operated type, the valve of the cylinder whose crank is in the starting position may have jammed in the closed position owing to dryness of the rubbing surfaces, or the control valve which admits operating air to the starting valve may be jammed or be incorrectly timed.

When the starting valves in the cylinder heads are of the mechanically-operated type, failure to start will not be due to the valve in the active cylinder being jammed in the closed position, as any resistance to opening would be overcome, even to the extent of breaking the rocking lever.

If the recommendations made in the previous chapter with regard to these valves are carried out, failure to start will not be due to a starting valve jamming when same are of the pneumatically-operated type, but if this important part of the operation of preparing an engine for sea has been neglected and it is necessary to free the valve, lubricating oil should be sparingly applied. Paraffin should not, of course, be used for this purpose.

As a rule, the force of air applied to open pneumatically-operated starting valves is great enough to overcome friction between dry or corroded rubbing surfaces and open the valve, the effect of this fault being usually to prevent the valve from closing properly, as these valves are generally of the spring-return type, and as, since the spring must be overcome before the valve can be opened, there is a limit to the spring load that can be put upon them.

When, however, the starting valves are of the simple spring-loaded non-return type and are opened by the starting air itself, the cause of a valve failing to open may be due to the lid or head being a neat fit in the lower part of the valve pocket, and if the valve is not perfectly central it may jam. On one ship fitted with this type of starting valve, the engines manoeuvred satisfactorily when leaving port, but on arrival at the next port the engine was stopped and failed to restart owing to the starting valve being jammed in the closed position. The reason was that the lid of the valve was flush with the underside of the cylinder head, and when the parts were cold the lid was just clear of the side of the pocket and the valve operated satisfactorily. But when the parts became hot the lid expanded and jammed.

(2) The clearance between the starting cam and the rocking-lever roller of the unit whose crank is in a starting position may be incorrect. If the clearance is excessive, the starting valve will open late and close early, maybe to such an extent that there is no overlapping of the starting valves. Should the roller clearance be insufficient, the cylinder may receive its charge of starting air before its respective crank reaches the top dead centre, but this should not prevent an engine from starting unless the fault is at the unit whose crank is next in starting position. Even then the rocking-lever roller of the first unit would have to be riding on the plain part of the cam before an engine would fail to start, owing to an equal but opposite force being applied in the cylinder next in turn for starting air.

(3) The most common cause of an engine not starting is escape of starting air from the active cylinder, and the most probable source of leakage is the exhaust valve. If the air escapes through the air-inlet valve it will be at once apparent, unless the engine is of the supercharged type in which the air intake is enclosed. In any case the starting air will be heard to pass through the exhaust- or air-inlet valve in the event of either of these valves leaking to such an extent that the engine is prevented from starting.

Leakage of starting air past other cylinder-head valves, or leakage externally owing to the valve housings not being properly fitted in the cylinder head, may cause sluggish starting but is not likely to prevent an engine from starting.

Should an engine fail to start on air and the cause not be apparent, the following should be the procedure. Leave the starting gear in the starting position, then ascertain from the position of the camshaft which unit is in starting position, and open the indicator cock of this unit. If, upon opening the cock, air rushes from the cylinder at great force, it indicates that the force necessary to set the engine in motion is present, but that there is an equal force acting in the opposite direction. This equal but opposite force in the form of compressed air will probably be found upon opening the indicator cock of the cylinder whose crank is next in starting position. The presence of compressed air in this cylinder will most likely be due to the starting valve leaking badly. Had the starting gear been run back to the stop position before the indicator cock of the active cylinder was opened, release of starting air from this cylinder would have caused the engine to turn a few degrees in the reverse direction to that for which the reversing gear was set, proving the existence of a force acting in the opposite direction.

On very rare occasions failure to start on air is due to the decompression valve not functioning properly, but this can be so only if it is required to start an engine within a few seconds of the previous run. When starting for the first time after a period of idleness, no pressure exists in any of the cylinders. When an engine fails to start on air after a recent run, however, the non-functioning of the decompression valve, though unlikely, must be considered as a cause. These valves are sometimes the cause of sluggish starting, but to stop an engine from starting, not only would the pressure in each cylinder (the active cylinder and cylinder next in turn) have to be equal, but the cranks would have to be an equal distance on each side of the top dead centre. This can never happen when a ship is at rest, because if the starting gear is brought to the stop position at the moment one piston has only half completed its compression or working stroke, and a fairly high pressure exists in the cylinder, the pressure would send the piston towards the bottom of the cylinder, and if the piston does not travel far enough to release the gases, their pressure will be considerably reduced by expansion. When an engine revolves a half revolution or so in the opposite direction to that of the preceding run upon being stopped, the reason is that the engine has been stopped when one piston has almost completed its compression stroke.

When, however, a ship is moving at a fair speed in, say, the ahead direction, and the engine is stopped after operating in the astern direction, it is quite possible and even probable that an appreciable pressure will be left in one or two cylinders. Suppose, for instance, that when the engine comes to rest one piston has completed only a portion of its working stroke; the further expansion of the gases will be resisted by the pressure of water on the propeller which will tend to rotate the propeller and with it the engine in the reverse direction, or the direction in which the ship is moving through the water.

Assuming that the engine in question is of the two-stroke type and has six cranks spaced 60° apart, and that at the moment of stopping one crank is 60° over the top centre on the working stroke, the next crank is on top centre, and the third crank 60° from the top centre on the compression stroke. As release of burnt gases takes place at about 120° after the top centre, and as the pressure in the cylinder on the compression stroke will not have risen appreciably when the crank is 120° from the top centre, the pressure in all other cylinders will be of no account. The pressure in the cylinders whose cranks are nearest the top centre will be in the neighbourhood of the starting-air pressure, so that if starting air is admitted to the cylinder which contains partially-burnt gases, and the decompression gear fails to release the compressed air in the other cylinder, the engine may fail to start when the gear is operated.

These then are the causes of an engine failing to start when starting air rushes out of certain cylinders upon the indicator cocks being opened. In the event of only moderate pressure being found in the active cylinder, and all other cylinders being free of pressure, the cause will probably be that the starting air is escaping from the active cylinder through a partly-open cylinder-head valve. The exhaust valve is usually the worst offender.

When an engine turns a few degrees and then stops as the starting gear is run over, the cause of its stopping is generally one of two things—namely, a jammed exhaust valve or a badly-timed starting-air valve. If the former, it will be found in the cylinder in the starting position, while if the cause is a badly-timed starting valve, the faulty valve will be found in the cylinder whose piston has almost completed the starting period, the cause of the engine stopping being that the rocking-lever roller clearance is so great that the

- Engine fails to start on air
  - Starting air escaping from active cylinder
    - Exhaust valve partly open
    - Air-inlet valve partly open
    - All piston rings jammed
  - Automatic starting-air relay valve not functioning
    - Hand gear engaged
    - Piston not operating valve
    - Rubbing surfaces dry
    - Operating air valve on starting gear jammed
  - Starting valve of next active cylinder leaking
    - Roller clearance insufficient
    - Control valve leaking
    - Valve faces burnt
    - Valve jammed in open position
  - Starting-air control valve not functioning
    - Valve jammed
    - Operating air joint leaking
    - Incorrectly adjusted
  - Starting valve of active cylinder not opening
    - Rocking-lever roller clearance too great
    - Starting gear not right over
    - Valve jammed if pneumatically operated

Fig. 234—Reasons for engine failing to start

valve closes before the starting valve of the cylinder next in turn to receive a charge of starting air is sufficiently open.

Other possible causes of an engine failing to start on air are indicated in the " family tree " diagram shown in Fig. 234.

Sluggish working on air

An engine should begin revolving without hesitation immediately the starting gear reaches the " on air " position, and the speed " on air " should be uniform. If all parts concerned are in good order it is necessary for the engine to make a half-revolution or so only before running the gear over to the " on fuel " position. Should it be necessary to run for a longer period, and the rotational speed of the engine be uneven, it is a sure indication that the valves in some of the cylinders are not functioning properly. The fact that a piston is on the compression stroke should not affect the even turning of the engine when " on air " as some seem to think, at any rate not in the case of marine engines which have many cylinders.

When the condition of the valves in some of the cylinders is such that the engine is set in motion but revolves slowly and almost stops at certain points, the cylinder containing the faulty valve can be located by watching the starting valves as the engine revolves " on air." When the speed is lowest the fault will most probably be in the cylinder whose starting valve is then in operation. The only exception to this is a leaking starting-air valve in the cylinder next in turn to receive starting air at the moment when the rotational speed of the engine is lowest. Should this valve be at fault, compressed air will be admitted to the cylinder during the greater part of the compression stroke, and result in an abnormally high compression pressure, which will, of course, cause the engine speed to be reduced when the piston of this particular cylinder is performing the compression stroke.

The other causes of an engine working sluggishly on starting air are indicated in Fig. 235, and further explanation will be found unnecessary.

Failure to start on fuel

When an engine fails to begin working on fuel it can be due to only one of two things, namely, that the fuel is not being injected into the cylinders, or that the compression pressure in all the cylinders is so low that the temperature necessary to ignite the fuel is not being attained.

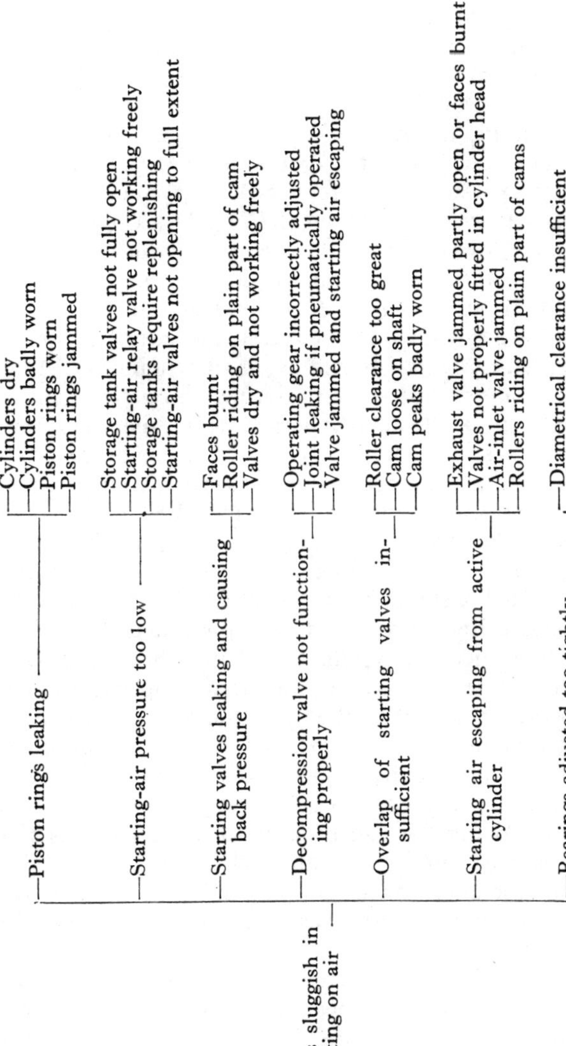

Fig. 235—Reasons for slow rotational speed on starting air

It is inconceivable that an engine could be so neglected that the compression spaces in the cylinders become so great that a pressure of 400 lb/sq.in. at least cannot be produced when the engine is working on starting air. The only other cause of a low compression pressure is cylinder-head valves or piston rings leaking, but as such faults would be very apparent and cause difficulties when starting on air, the most likely cause of an engine failing to begin working on fuel is that the fuel is not being injected into the cylinders owing to a fault in the fuel-injection system.

As, however, the cause of an engine not " picking-up " on fuel may be due to a low compression pressure, it may be as well to mention that the causes of the compression pressure being reduced are: (1) piston rings leaking; (2) cylinder-head valves leaking; (3) wearing of bearings which increases the clearance volume at the end of the compression stroke; (4) if the engine is of the four-stroke unsupercharged type the air inlet may be partly choked.

If the engine is of the supercharged type, the cause may be that the necessary supercharge air pressure is not being produced. The difference in the compression pressure when such an engine is working at atmospheric pressure is about 100 lb/sq.in., so that if such an engine is started without the necessary supercharge air pressure, the compression pressure may be so low that the fuel will not be ignited, especially if the atmospheric temperature is very low and the cylinders have not been preheated.

When the fuel-injection system is at fault, the trouble is nearly always due to the system not having been properly primed, and if after a false start this part of the operation of preparing an engine for sea is carried out as recommended earlier in this book, the engine will in all probability " pick-up " on fuel right away. It is not wise to keep on trying to get an engine to " fire " without locating and removing the cause, as it so often happens that the whole of the starting air is used up in doing so, and, in the end, not only must the fuel system be properly primed, but an hour or so must elapse before there is again sufficient compressed air to start the engine.

Furthermore, fuel being injected into the cylinders in this way may have very serious consequences. In the case of four-stroke engines the fuel will strike against the cold surrounding walls and resume its liquid state and accumulate in the cylinder, while in two-stroke engines the liquefied fuel will be blown into the exhaust pipe by the scavenging air, and when the engine does begin working on fuel and heat is generated, the accumulated fuel may be ignited and burn at an explosive rate. This has happened on at least one occasion. Repeated attempts were made to start a two-stroke engine working on fuel, the valve gear of which was not properly adjusted. When the fault was discovered and removed and the engine began working, the hot burnt gases ignited the accumulated fuel in the exhaust pipe and sent pieces of it flying in all directions.

The cause of fuel not being injected into the cylinders may be due to: (1) air in the fuel pumps, (2) fuel-pump valves leaking, (3) fuel pumps not properly adjusted as regards quantity delivered, (4) the fuel priming valves may have been left open, (5) water in the fuel, (6) choked fuel filters or the fuel may be too viscous. It is only necesary for the valves of one fuel-pump unit of an air-injection engine to leak in order to put the whole battery of fuel pumps out of action, and so prevent an engine from beginning to work on fuel. In the case of airless injection engines the corresponding cylinder only will be affected.

When an engine fails to begin working on fuel, open the priming valves on the fuel-injection valves; if no fuel issues, or if it takes several strokes of the fuel priming pump to cause the fuel to issue from the overflow, it is a sure indication either that the fuel-injection system has not been properly primed, or that the fuel-pump valves are leaking. If the fuel valves of an airless injection engine lift, fuel must be going into the cylinder, since it is the pressure on the fuel which lifts the valve; but as the valves of air-injection engines are mechanically operated, movement of the valve will take place whether or not fuel is being injected into the cylinder.

Immediately after an engine begins working on fuel, it should be ascertained whether all cylinders are firing. It sometimes happens that, owing to a cylinder-head valve not re-seating properly, the compression pressure of one or more cylinders is not sufficiently high to ignite the fuel injected. If the cylinders are warm, much of the fuel will remain in a vaporised state and be discharged into the exhaust pipe during the exhausting process without ill-effect. The hot burnt gases from the other cylinders will carry the vaporised fuel into the atmosphere, and the only effect will be a regular puff of black smoke. If, however, the parts are cold, a serious state of affairs may arise, as already mentioned.

The author was once sent to witness the trial of a large airless injection engine, the fuel valves of which were mechanically operated. The engine began working on fuel without hesitation, but after a minute or so it was noticed that one cylinder was not working. Thinking that the valve was not lifting sufficiently, an engineer

- Engine fails to begin working on fuel
  - Fuel-pump valves leaking
    - Valve cages leaking
    - Dirt in fuel
    - Governor gear jammed and holding valves off seats
    - Faces require grinding
  - Fuel system not properly primed
    - Water in fuel
    - Air left in system
    - Injection air forcing fuel back through leaky valves
    - Priming connections left open
  - Fuel supply restricted
    - Suction strainers dirty
    - Gravity tank empty
    - Vacuum in gravity tank
    - Valve in suction line not fully open
  - Fuel-injection pressure too low
    - Injection air pressure too low
    - Spill valve jammed, airless injection
    - Priming valves left open
  - Rotational speed on air too low
    - Starting-air pressure too low
    - Starting air restricted
    - Cylinder-head valve leaking
    - Tight bearings
  - Compression pressure too low
    - Piston rings leaking
    - Indicator cocks open
    - Cylinder-head valves leaking
  - Timing of fuel pumps incorrect
    - Suction valves, if air injection
    - Fuel-pump plungers not functioning correctly, if of spring-return type
    - Spill valve, if airless injection
  - Speed governor jammed
    - Inertia weight jammed
    - Trip pawl not engaging
    - Connecting mechanism not properly adjusted

Fig. 236—Reasons for engine failing to begin working on fuel

- Engine sluggish in starting on fuel
  - Compression of certain cylinders too low
    - Cylinders dry
    - Clearance volume too great
    - Cylinder-head valves leaking
    - Piston rings leaking
  - Fuel-pump valves leaking slightly
    - Faces require grinding
    - Dirt in fuel
    - Valves not working freely owing to viscous fuel
  - Fuel valves leaking
    - Faces require grinding
    - Priming valves leaking
    - Valves not re-seating properly
  - Injection pressure too low
    - Spill valve leaking, if airless injection
    - Insufficient pressure at fuel-pump suction, if airless injection
    - Air injection, air valves not fully open
    - Blast pressure too low, if air injection
  - Fuel system not properly primed
    - Water in fuel
    - Air in fuel
  - Fuel injection occurring too early
    - Faces require grinding
    - Operating cam too far advanced
    - Valve spindle not working freely
    - Spindle bent
  - Fuel-pump plungers, if spring-return type, not working freely
    - Plungers tight in liners
    - Springs broken or too weak
    - Fuel cold and viscous

Fig. 237—Reasons for engine failing to begin working promptly on fuel

increased the lift a small amount. As this did not have the desired effect, orders to shut off the fuel to this particular cylinder were given. After the engine had been stopped, fuel was observed passing the piston, and when the fuel valve was removed fully a gallon of fuel was found on the top of this piston. The cause of the cylinder not firing was due to the starting valve of this cylinder jamming in the open position; fortunately it remained jammed as long as the engine was working. Before re-starting the engine, it was decided to remove the starting-air valve and supply pipe. This proved a wise decision, as quite a lot of fuel had found its way into these parts. Had the fuel in the cylinder ignited, some of the hot burning gases would have passed the partly-open starting valve and entered the supply pipes, and an explosion would have occurred. As the starting-air system was protected against explosions by nothing better than a spring-loaded relief valve, the starting-air pipes and fittings would have been blown to pieces, and lives probably lost, because there were many workmen and visitors in the engine-room at the time.

Further causes of an engine failing to start working on fuel are shown in Fig. 236, while the causes of an engine being sluggish in picking-up on fuel are given in Fig. 237.

Piston-rod gas packing

Surprisingly little trouble has been experienced with the piston-rod packing of double-acting engines. There have been, of course, designs which proved totally unsuitable, but present-day designs are effective in preventing the escape of gases, while the wear and tear of the packing and piston rods are small when carefully fitted and properly cared for whilst in use.

It is important that piston rods of any type of engine should be in good alignment, but in double-acting engines it is essential. This means that, as well as being properly aligned with the crosshead guide bar, the athwartships working clearance of the crosshead must not be more than necessary for efficient lubrication.

When operating, therefore, the rods should be checked for side movement by placing a finger on the crankcase oil-scraper packing gland and just touching the piston rod. Movement of the rod fore and aft generally indicates misalignment, and movement athwartships excessive clearance in the crosshead guides.

As regards the crankcase oil-scraper packing, leakage of oil is to be looked for. If the rings have been properly fitted, the cause will probably be choking of the drain holes at the bottom of the stuffing-box, or the rings have jammed upon attaining working temperature.

If leakage is due to choking of the drain holes nothing can be done while the engine is operating, but if due to jammed packing rings they may be freed by slackening the gland a little. This, however, must be carefully done by easing the nuts evenly and not more than a quarter of a turn. After an hour or so the nuts should be re-tightened. If the results are negative, the leakage must be due to choked drain holes, or the packing rings requiring readjustment.

Hot piston rods occur in single-acting engines only when they rub against a fixed part of the stuffing-box. The cause is rarely due to lack of lubricant, since ample oil is picked up when the rod is in the crank-case. The rods of double-acting engines, however, may become over-heated due to inefficient lubrication or for the reason just given. Either cause will quickly produce a red streak on the rod, in which case the engine speed should be reduced to the minimum possible and the rod swabbed alternately with fresh water and oil. Oil should be applied sparingly, otherwise it will ignite and the flame may cause a crank-case explosion. After the redness has disappeared oil only should be applied, and if only a small part of the rod's circumference has been affected it may be possible to carry on to the next port of call before the packing rings must be reconditioned.

For satisfactory operation it is most important that the piston rods be well greased before an engine is set in motion after a period of idleness, and that delivery of lubricating oil to the rubbing surfaces should take place immediately. As the packing cage rings must be an easy fit in the stuffing-box to facilitate their removal for overhaul, the space between these two parts must be full of oil before the oil will flow through the holes in the lantern ring to the rubbing surfaces. The method of introducing the oil varies in different makes of engines, but whatever the method may be, make quite sure that the piston rods are well swabbed before starting, and that an adequate quantity of oil will reach the piston rods immediately upon starting.

Double-acting engine piston leakage

As is to be expected, the cylinder liners of double-acting engines wear mostly at the ends, the least wear taking place about mid-length. The rate of wear at each end is about the same in properly lubricated cylinders and is no greater than in the case of single-acting engines.

In the case of two-stroke double-acting engines, the first indication of piston-ring leakage will be revealed by the cylinder pressures, since the greater part of the gases which pass the piston rings flows into the exhaust ports and not into the opposite end of the cylinder as in four-stroke engines. The compression and combustion pressures at both ends of the cylinder will be reduced if both sets of piston rings are defective. If one set of rings only is defective, the pressures in the corresponding end of the cylinder only will be affected.

The troubles that might be expected to result from uneven enlargement of double-acting cylinder liners, in addition to the effect of gas leaking past the piston rings, are: (1) weakening and ultimate breaking of piston rings due to the constant opening and closing action; (2) excessive enlargement of the piston-ring grooves due to lateral movement of the piston rings consequent upon the opening and closing action; (3) greater wear-and-tear of the piston-rod packing owing to lateral movement of the piston rod when the piston is in the most worn part of the cylinder, with the possibility of overheated piston rods due to the rods making contact with the packing cage rings and glands when the crank passes over the bottom dead centre; and (4) greater wear rate of the cylinder liners and piston rings as the liners become enlarged at the ends, due to greater gas pressure acting behind the rings as a result of the gaps being larger when at the ends of the cylinders.

A double-acting engine, the cylinder liners of which had enlarged 6 mm at the ends, was kept under close observation to ascertain the effect of the enlargement, and the following was noted. As regards leakage of gas past the piston rings, of which there were a total of nine on each piston, there was no noticeable effect upon the working of the engine. The top cylinder compression pressures were an average of 18 lb/sq.in. lower than when the liners were new and parallel eight years before the observations were made, but the bottom cylinder compression pressures were about the same.

Strictly speaking, enlargement of the end of the cylinder liner should produce a higher compression pressure because the volume of air drawn in is larger by the amount of metal worn away, but the amount is so small in proportion to the total volume swept by the the piston that it would not be registered by the pressure indicator. The reduction of the top cylinder compression pressure in this case would be due partly to the wear-down in the running gear at the various bearings, which amounted to 1·5 mm, and partly to leakage past the piston rings. Had the reduction in the top cylinder compression pressure been wholly due to wear-down at the various bearings, the bottom cylinder compression pressures should have shown a corresponding increase. As, however, the bottom cylinder compression pressures were practically the same as when the liners were new and parallel, it is evident that a small amount of leakage past the piston rings was taking placc.

The amount must have been very small, however, since when new cylinder liners were fitted to this four-stroke engine the compression pressures were practically the same, and no difference in the power output or the fuel consumption per unit power developed could be observed. It would seem, therefore, that cylinder liners worn to the extent mentioned have no noticeable effect upon the combustion efficiency of an engine.

Doxford engines

The following notes refer mainly to engines built prior to 1957. A full description of the modern Doxford opposed-piston engine is given in the following chapter.

The makers of these opposed-piston engines issue comprehensive working instructions which should be carefully studied if trouble-free operation is desired. The following notes are mostly additional to those instructions.

Except in recently-built engines the pistons are cooled by fresh water, the recommended outlet temperature being 160°F (71°C). The water is conveyed to the bottom pistons by means of link gear having rotating glands at the joints. The glands are spring-loaded, so that as the packing loses its resilience the pressure on the packing is automatically maintained, within limits. Cooling water is conveyed to and from the top pistons by flexible rubber hoses bent over circular grooved quadrants—two for the inlet and two for the outlet hose. The location of the quadrants and the arrangement of the link gear carrying the hoses is such that the length of the hoses remains practically constant at all positions of the piston. In other words, although the water is conveyed from a stationary point to a moving point the hoses do not become slack nor are they stretched.

The hot cooling water passing through the flexible hoses tends to cause swelling of the rubber, which will in time restrict the flow. The swelling occurs mostly at the ends, and more frequently in the case of the outlet hose. As there are no outward indications of defective hoses restricting the flow of water, apart from an increase in outlet temperature of the water, the ends of these hoses should be disconnected and examined every two or three months, particularly as a slightly swollen hose may run quite a long time and then suddenly disintegrate internally, causing a complete stoppage of the flow of water. All cooling-water temperatures should be checked at intervals of not more than one hour so that any increase in temperature will be observed and the fault looked for before serious overheating occurs. An ample supply of spare flexible hoses should be on board.

To obtain the best results the cooling water should flow steadily through the pistons. In the Doxford engine this is usually the case, but on one ship apprehension was caused by the flow from one cylinder being irregular, the flow sight-glass gradually filling up and suddenly emptying at regular intervals. Altering the opening of the inlet regulating valve and adjusting the air-snifting valves on the cooling-water pump did not have the desired effect. The reason was that the branch pipe of the piston affected was the one nearest the point of the manifold where the water discharged by the pump entered, and a greater quantity of air and water vapour entered that particular branch pipe. The trouble was overcome by altering the inlet end of the branch pipe in such a way that the water entered it from the bottom instead of from the top of the manifold.

During routine inspection of the inside of the crankcase in port, the gear conveying the cooling water to the bottom pistons should not be overlooked. In engines which have the pipes connected by the cone-and-nut type of fastening, it is not sufficient to hammer-test the nuts, as a wrong impression may be gained by this means. It is much better to test the nuts for tightness by means of a spanner.

Doxford's have until recently used the accumulator system of fuel injection, wherein a multiple ram pump forces fuel into a pipe or accumulator, from which it is measured out to the cylinders by mechanically-operated valves, the lift of which, and consequently the quantity of fuel which passes them, can be varied collectively at the control platform or individually at the valves. The normal working injection pressure of about 6,000 lb/sq.in. is maintained constant by a number of pumps grouped together, usually one pump per working cylinder. With this fuel-injection system, however, any number of pumps can be employed so long as the total output is adequate and the pressure in the accumulator is not caused to fluctuate owing to the number being insufficient. In other words, the number of fuel pumps bears no relation to the number of cylinders.

The operation of these pumps should be carefully observed when the engine is running. A leaking delivery valve can be detected by feeling the air vessel situated at the top of each pump. Should the vessel become unusually warm it means that the corresponding valve is leaking and should be given early attention, otherwise the faces of the valve will become so badly scored that it will be difficult to recondition them in the normal way.

On one occasion when manoeuvring a Doxford engine a bell-crank lever was found bent due to the corresponding delivery valve leaking so badly that the full injection pressure of 6,000 lb/sq.in. acted on top of the suction valve, with the result that when the engine was started the load on the bell-crank lever was so great that it failed to stand up to the strain. It is important that bell-crank levers and the rods operating the suction valves should be well lubricated.

Fuel-pump suction and delivery valves should be examined at intervals of not more than six months and ground-in if the faces appear to be bearing lightly in places. Only the finest of grinding powders should be used. The timing of the suction valves is rather difficult to check by means of feelers in the manner recommended by the engine-builders, but an alternative and easier method is to wrap lead wire around the suction valve and strike a sharp blow on the end of a piece of good-fitting wood inserted in the hole in the valve. The lead wire will be squeezed to the clearance, which can then be gauged.

The fuel valves are mechanically operated. The arrangement of the fuel valve and actuating gear is shown in Fig. 61, from which it will be seen that each cylinder is provided with two fuel valves located diametrically opposite on the transverse centre-line. Both fuel valves are used for ahead running, but only one is used for the astern direction of rotation.

The horizontally disposed and somewhat complicated (when compared with other airless injection fuel valves) valves of Doxford engines operate satisfactorily provided they are removed for cleaning and testing for oil-tightness at intervals of two to three months. The effect of leakage at the conical end of the spindle is the same as in other airless injection fuel valves, but whereas in the latter slight leakage around the parallel part of the spindle or needle does not have any serious effect, such leakage in the Doxford engine will cause difficulties when manoeuvring. This is due to the fuel passages of these valves being constantly under a pressure of 6,000 lb/sq.in., and only a very slight leakage will appreciably reduce this pressure. When, therefore, frequent use must be made of the fuel priming pump to maintain the pressure when the engine is stopped for a short period, possible leakage from the point indicated should be looked for and stopped.

The pilot ram for re-seating the fuel valve is spring-loaded. These rams sometimes jam, in which event they should be removed and rubbed down with metal polish applied on a soft rag while being rotated at high speed in the lathe. Before the engine requires to be manoeuvred it is good practice to go round all the fuel valves with the forked spanners provided by the engine-builders and make sure that all parts are free and the valves re-seating smartly. This operation requires to be done when there is no pressure in the fuel system, otherwise, as the valves are lifted during the test, fuel may enter the cylinder, with undesirable consequences. Upon the engine being first stopped after a long voyage it is advisable to release the pressure on the fuel system and test the valves for re-seating properly in the manner suggested.

Some engineers are inclined to over-prime the fuel system when manoeuvring. When all parts are in good order an initial priming only is required. Should some of the parts be worn slightly, and more frequent priming be necessary to ensure prompt starting, the priming pump should not be operated until after the telegraph order has been received from the bridge. The operation can be performed so quickly that such a procedure will not cause delay in executing the order. If failure to maintain the pressure is due to leakage at the conical end of one or more valves, frequent priming during a lengthy stop will cause fuel to enter the corresponding cylinders and result in the cylinder relief valves lifting violently each time the engine is started.

The fuel valves are cooled by fresh water, and the construction is such that it is not impossible for the fuel, which is at a very much higher pressure than the water, to find its way into the cooling-water passage as a result of leaking joints. The cooling-water outlets from the various valves should therefore be inspected for fuel leakage every hour when the engine is operating. If fuel is present the faulty valve should be replaced by a spare valve at the earliest opportunity. Also, the fuel-valve locking nuts should be inspected for slackness every two hours or so as the slight jarring action of the operating gear tends to make them loose, and as such would either increase or decrease the quantity of fuel entering the cylinder, a fault of this kind should be attended to without delay.

Before fitting a spare fuel valve it should be tested to the full working pressure and all parts checked to make sure that they are freely workable. When a valve has been fitted in position in the cylinder and all clearances checked, the water-jacket gland should be hand-tight only. A little water may leak at first, but when the parts attain normal working temperatures the leak will in all probability take up. Most ships are provided with a complete set of spare fuel valves. In such cases it is good practice to change both valves in a cylinder at the same time and keep two spare valves for that particular cylinder. This makes recording of the number of working hours of the various valves easier, and avoids certain little difficulties which arise when fitting a valve which first does service in one cylinder and later is transferred to another.

Before dismantling fuel valves for overhaul the conical end of the spindle should be tested for fluid-tightness. If the leakage is substantial the valve should be put on one side for attention by those with the proper facilities. If the leakage is slight matters may be put right by rotating the spindle with metal-polishing paste between the surfaces. No coarse abrasive should be used. The holes in the spray plate should be afterwards checked for size as they have a tendency to enlarge. All copper washers or joint rings should be annealed each time a valve is overhauled.

The hardened steel striking-pins at the valve end of the fuel-valve rocking levers tend to wear. When badly worn a pin can be driven out and turned through an angle of 90° before refitting. When this new contact point becomes worn the pin can be given another quarter of a turn on two further occasions.

It is important to check the maximum cylinder pressures regularly in any make of diesel engine, but it is of greater importance in the Doxford engine where the fuel valves are mechanically operated by a system comprising so many links and levers. If all parts of the gear are not properly lubricated while the engine is working, excessive wear will take place and alter the timing of the fuel valves, or some part may jam and prevent a valve from re-seating properly, with the result that excessive quantities of fuel will enter a cylinder and cause unduly high maximum pressures.

The spring-loaded relief valves of Doxford engines tend to burn at the mitre faces if allowed to operate violently or too often, and as this inevitably means an involuntary stop, everything possible must be done to avoid excessive cylinder pressures. When cylinder relief valves lift violently it means that there is something wrong. It may be that owing to a fault in the measuring gear a fuel pump is delivering too much fuel or that a fuel valve is leaking and allowing fuel to enter the cylinder before its time. Should the relief valves lift for one or two revolutions only when starting, over-priming is usually the cause, but with mechanically-operated fuel valves slight leakage past a valve while the engine is stopped will have the same result.

When the relief valves act while the engine is working normally a jammed fuel-valve spindle is nearly always the cause. The purpose of relief valves is to act in such circumstances and generally no harm is done, but, on the other hand, securing bolts may be strained and the pressure between joining surfaces reduced as a result. Especially is this likely to happen in the case of spring-loaded valves, because to ensure gas-tightness such valves must be heavily loaded initially, and when acting the load is progressively increased. With air-loaded relief valves such as are described in Chapter 11, the initial loading is lower and the loading on the valve remains constant even when lifted to its maximum extent.

Correct timing of the fuel valves can be maintained only if the camshaft has a fixed angular relationship to the crankshaft, so that when the drive is by chain it must not be allowed to become too slack. In one ship a serious accident resulted owing to the engine starting in the opposite direction to that for which the reversing gear was set. The cause of this wrong movement was found to be excessive slackness in the chain driving its two camshafts.

In some Doxford engines the camshaft bearings are lubricated by grease. As grease which has been in the bearings too long tends to harden, they should be opened up periodically to remove all such grease, otherwise the bearings may be scored. It will be found that if the grease cups are given one-eighth of a turn each watch the bearings will be properly lubricated. As the front camshaft must slide axially during reversal, this is a further reason why the bearings should be clean and well lubricated. Particularly is this necessary in the case of the sliding coupling at the after end of the engine.

Correct adjustment of the side rods is essential if the top pistons are to operate in good alignment. The connection to the transverse beam must be adjusted as finely as practicable so that, when working, shock due to slackness is not transmitted to the beams, which have been known to break. Moreover, excessive clearances at these points tend to slacken the side rod nuts, which may result in the side rods being stretched.

In addition to the general inspection at each port recommended by the engine-builders, the following parts should be given particular attention. The bottom piston cooling-water telescopic-pipe elbows should be examined to see that the spring-loaded glands are free to follow up the packing. The packing for these stuffing-boxes must not be over-size, that is to say, it should be possible to insert each turn of packing with the fingers. If the packing is of such a size that greater force than this is necessary, the spring-loaded gland cannot be expected to serve the purpose intended, and leakage of cooling water is bound to occur. Moreover, tight packing tends to score the pipes.

WATCH-KEEPING

In the following pages the aim is to suggest a routine which, if followed—and it will, of course have to be added to or varied to suit individual jobs—will save the watch-keeping engineer many shocks, the chief engineer much worry, and the shipowner considerable expense. It is also hoped that by following an imaginary methodical engineer on watch, no detail necessary for the successful operation of the machinery will be overlooked. To keep a good, watch, an engineer must, first of all, realise that he has a very important duty to perform, and he must be very much on the alert every minute of his period of responsibility.

A few minutes before eight bells, the relieving engineer should be on deck to observe the exhaust gases from the main and auxiliary engines, the various cooling-water discharges overboard, the direction of the wind and the position of the engine-room ventilators, and the state of the sea; so that at eight bells he will be at the engine-room entrance, where he should be met by the senior engineer of the retiring watch, the latter having begun a final examination of all the running machinery, starting from the bottom platform and working upwards, about one bell, to make sure that everything is in order for handing over. It is assumed, of course, that there are two engineers at least on a watch together. If this is not the case, the only engineer will have to complete the entries in the scrap logbook, and hand over the watch to the relieving engineer on the starting platform.

The exhaust gases from the main and auxiliary engines should be quite colourless and free from sparks. If the exhaust is clear and at the correct temperature, there will not be much wrong inside the cylinders. There are, however, some engines which always have a slightly discoloured exhaust and yet give results which compare favourably with an engine having a colourless exhaust. The author had charge of such an engine for a year, and was unable to prove conclusively the cause of it. The fuel consumption per i.h.p. per hour was good but not the best possible, while the parts likely to be affected by a low combustion efficiency, even to the exhaust passages, were always found in reasonably clean condition. The cause may have been due to the shape of the combustion space not being strictly in accordance with thermodynamic considerations, but whatever it was it had no ill-effect upon the working of the engine. More will be said regarding the causes of discoloured exhausts later.

Sparks from the exhausts should be stopped, as not only do they spoil the paintwork on deck, but they may burn the lifeboat covers and even start a fire. Consisting as they do of incandescent soot, they indicate that partially burnt fuel or lubricating oil is reaching the exhaust passage; thus they are generally caused by imperfect combustion of fuel or excessive lubrication of the cylinders. Sparks will also be caused by an exhaust valve leaking and allowing burning gases to pass into the exhaust. When an engine exhausts through a boiler, the sparks may be caused by high-velocity gases from the engine dislodging soot from the fire spaces of the boiler.

The relieving and retiring engineers should then begin a systematic tour of the engine-room, the relieving engineer making a thorough inspection of all parts of the machinery, and the retiring engineer receiving complaints, if any, and putting right whatever is wrong to the satisfaction of the relieving engineer. A relieving engineer should never be put off with the remark that "it was like this, or like that, at the beginning of my watch." What concerns him is what it is like at the beginning of *his* watch. A remark such as this being accepted by a relieving engineer has more than once had very serious consequences, and no one except the engineer on watch at the time when anything goes wrong can justly be held responsible. If disagreement arises, the chief engineer should be consulted, and if he considers that the abnormal condition of any part may safely continue, he should insert a note in the scrap logbook to that effect. A chief engineer should encourage junior engineers to bring their differences to him, no matter what the size or nature of them may be, since only by so doing can he know exactly how things are going below.

Steering gear

In most ships, the first machine in turn for inspection will be the steering gear. If this is of the electric-hydraulic type, the points which should be noted are: (1) the amount of oil in the replenishing tank, (2) the temperature of the electric motor and pump, (3) all glands for leakage, (4) ammeter for load and (for D.C.) commutator for sparking, and (5) pressure in hydraulic cylinders, bearing in mind the state of the sea. The telemotor replenishing tank and glands should be inspected also, the former for the amount of non-freezing liquid contained, and the latter for leakage.

Observing how the steering gear answers the telemotor will generally reveal all that is required regarding the control mechanism. All working parts should, of course, be efficiently lubricated. Greasers should be properly instructed in this matter, and not merely sent with an oil can to put oil into all the holes they can find about the machine. They cannot be expected to know just where and how much oil is required by the various parts, with the result that some important and out-of-the-way part is neglected, and will wear excessively, or may eventually seize and put the gear out of action suddenly, whereas a little of the oil wasted on other easy-to-get-at parts would have prevented what might prove a serious accident.

On one occasion when a ship was entering port, the steering gear refused duty owing to a pin on the underside of the tiller, to which the hunting gear rod was attached, breaking off. The cause of the pin breaking was due to the connection not being lubricated and eventually seizing, with the result that when occasion arose to put the helm hard-over, the pin was twisted and broken off. On the underside of the tiller was not the proper place for this connection to be made, but nevertheless the operating engineer could not be excused because of this, as he must have known that such a connection existed, and it was his duty to lubricate and examine it periodically.

Fuel settling-tanks

Before descending to the engine-room the relieving engineer should examine the fuel settling-tanks, or daily service tanks, as they are sometimes called. The level of fuel in each tank should be noted, and the drain cocks opened momentarily to test for the presence of water. If the ship is rolling, the movement of the level indicators will reveal if these are in order. When the ship is steady, float indicators should be pulled down and then released to make sure that they are working properly and registering the correct level. It might be mentioned here that when changing over from an empty tank, the valve or cock on the full tank should always be opened before the valve on the almost empty tank is shut. This will allow any gas, which sometimes accumulates in the pipe leading to the tank not in use to escape to the empty tank, and thus prevent the risk of the engine stopping due to an air-lock in the fuel system.

Both fuel settling-tanks should be full at the beginning of each watch, the best practice being for the tanks to be changed over a quarter of an hour before the end of the watch, and the partly emptied tank replenished ready for the next watch. Before a fuel tank is brought into use it should, of course, be tested for the presence of water.

Upon reaching the main engine cylinder heads, the method of inspection to be adopted will depend upon the make and type of engine, but the main points to be observed in all engines will be set out below.

Cylinder cooling system

The temperature of each cylinder head must be noted. It will be sufficient to touch these by hand, and note the discharge-water temperatures recorded in the scrap logbook by the previous watch. The usual practice is to judge the temperature of the cylinders by touching the cooling-water outlet pipes from each cylinder. When taking over a watch it is wise also to check how much each cooling-water regulating valve is open, as on one occasion the temperatures were in order when an engine was taken over, and within a quarter of an hour the oil on top of one of the cylinders was observed to be vaporising owing to excessively high temperature. It transpired that just a few minutes before eight bells one of the junior engineers found the temperature of this cylinder below normal, and quite rightly shut down the cooling-water regulating valve, after satisfying himself that the cause was too much cooling water. He, however, forgot to report the alteration, or to observe the effect of the alteration in the amount of cooling water circulating, with the result mentioned.

When sea-water cooling is employed, the outlet temperatures should not exceed, from cylinder jackets 120°F (49°C), and from pistons 110°F (43·5°C). With fresh water as the cooling medium, these temperatures should be, cylinder jackets 140°–160°F (60°–71°C), and pistons 130°F (54·5°C). When pistons are cooled by lubricating oil, the outlet temperature should not exceed 140°F (60·0°C).

A fault which may lead to trouble, is operating the cylinder jackets at far too low a temperature. The object is apparently to reduce the risk of overheating, and consequently fracture of the castings; whereas in doing so, not only is the efficiency of the engine reduced, but the engineers are courting trouble, because the cooler the cylinder jackets the wider the range of temperature in the metal, and consequently the stresses set up are greater. On the other hand, the temperature of the outlet cooling water should not be too high, otherwise the rubber sealing rings employed at various parts of the engine cylinders may be damaged, and—when sea-water is used—because of the possibility of scale being deposited on the cooled surfaces.

Some engineers are under the impression that so long as the cooling-water outlet temperature is maintained well below the boiling-point of water no scale will form, but it must be borne in mind that the outlet cooling-water temperature as recorded by the thermometer is the mean temperature of the whole of the water passing through the cylinder jacket, and that the small proportion of this water which makes actual contact with the surfaces of the parts surrounding the combustion space is raised to a much higher temperature.

When at sea, so long as ordinary attention is given to the cooling systems, no trouble beyond perhaps a slight leak at some of the glands is likely to occur, but when entering and leaving port, particularly in cold weather, special attention must be given to this important part of a diesel engine.

When an engine is stopped suddenly after running for some time, the cylinders and pistons would become very hot and the lubricating oil on the cylinder walls and pistons would be carbonised, and the rubber sealing rings damaged, if circulation of cooling water were stopped with the engine. This is due to the heat in the metal nearest the burning gases continuing to flow from the gas to the water side and raising the temperature of the stagnant water. The fact that the cylinder jacket is cool or cold when the engine is stopped does not preclude the possibility of overheating. It is therefore necessary, in cases where the cooling-water pumps are not independently driven, to set the stand-by pumps in motion immediately the engine is stopped.

In the event of a cylinder becoming too hot or too cold without known reason, the cause should be located before the amount of cooling water circulating is re-adjusted. If the cylinder is very hot, then more water must, of course, be given at once. Abnormal temperatures in the case of one or two cylinders do not always signify that there is too much or too little water circulating. An abnormally high temperature may be the result of a cylinder being overloaded, or the fuel not being burnt efficiently, while an abnormally low temperature may be caused by a piece of grit lodging on one of the fuel-pump valve seats, or other faults already mentioned which have the same effect. If the change in temperature is due to such causes the temperature of the piston-cooling water will show a corresponding change, as will that of the exhaust gases. Should these temperatures be normal, then the cooling-water supply to the cylinder concerned may safely be re-adjusted.

When a change in temperature of the jacket cooling-water occurs, the possibility of a piece of scale breaking away and restricting the flow by becoming jammed in the regulating valve should be considered. When, therefore, a cylinder heats up for no apparent reason, close the regulating valve momentarily to see how much it is open, then open the valve to its fullest extent. This will probably allow the piece of scale to pass through the valve, but in case it does not, close the valve again and then open it to its normal working position. Closing the valve will doubtless break up the scale into pieces sufficiently small to pass through the valve.

Having felt the cylinder heads on the way down, an engineer will know if the correct quantity of water is being circulated through the cylinder jackets before he notes the pressure recorded on the gauge situated on the bottom platform level. The pressure in the cooling system is generally taken to indicate the amount of water flowing, but it must be remembered that, under the usual method of controlling the supply, certain conditions can exist whereby the correct pressure is being recorded but insufficient or too much water is being circulated.

Speaking broadly, the temperature of the metal surfaces in contact with the burning gases depends upon the outlet temperature of the cooling water. To control the temperature of the cooling water as it leaves the cylinder jackets, the usual practice is to adjust the cooling-water pump output until the amount delivered is approximately correct, then adjust the temperature of the cylinders by opening or closing as required the regulating valves always provided for each cylinder. If, when the required outlet temperature is recorded, the pressure on the system is too high, say, 40 lb/sq.in., then the pump output will require to be reduced and the cylinder cooling-water regulating valve opened a little more.

As a rule, especially in cold weather, these regulating valves require to be screwed down until they are only a quarter of a turn or so open. Owing to the flow of water being restricted in this way, sediment may accumulate in the valves, and make it difficult to keep the temperature steady. It is, therefore, advisable during a long voyage to open fully each valve for a few minutes once each day in order to wash through any sediment that may have deposited.

Should a cylinder become excessively hot owing to shortage of cooling water, the fuel to the cylinder concerned must be shut off at once, but if the engine is of the air-injection type, the injection air should be allowed to continue entering the cylinder, as with a cylinder in such a condition a fuel valve may jam or something else happen, and fuel may be ignited in the fuel-valve casing. Should the overheating be due to an insufficient quantity of water circulating,

Fig. 238—General arrangement of safety devices fitted to a diesel engine

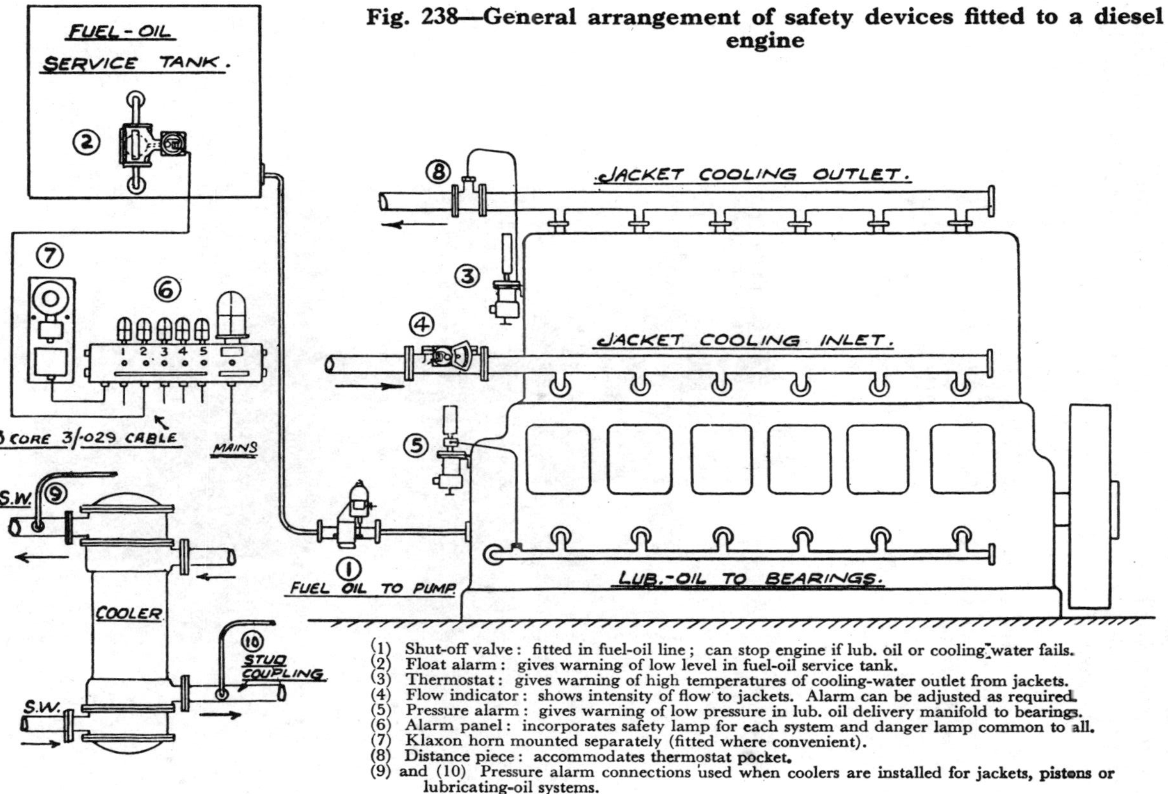

(1) Shut-off valve: fitted in fuel-oil line; can stop engine if lub. oil or cooling-water fails.
(2) Float alarm: gives warning of low level in fuel-oil service tank.
(3) Thermostat: gives warning of high temperatures of cooling-water outlet from jackets.
(4) Flow indicator: shows intensity of flow to jackets. Alarm can be adjusted as required.
(5) Pressure alarm: gives warning of low pressure in lub. oil delivery manifold to bearings.
(6) Alarm panel: incorporates safety lamp for each system and danger lamp common to all.
(7) Klaxon horn mounted separately (fitted where convenient).
(8) Distance piece: accommodates thermostat pocket.
(9) and (10) Pressure alarm connections used when coolers are installed for jackets, pistons or lubricating-oil systems.

the matter may be righted by slowly increasing the supply of cooling water, but should the trouble be caused by the water jacket being empty, or only partly filled, the engine should be stopped immediately and allowed to cool down by radiation to the atmosphere. There

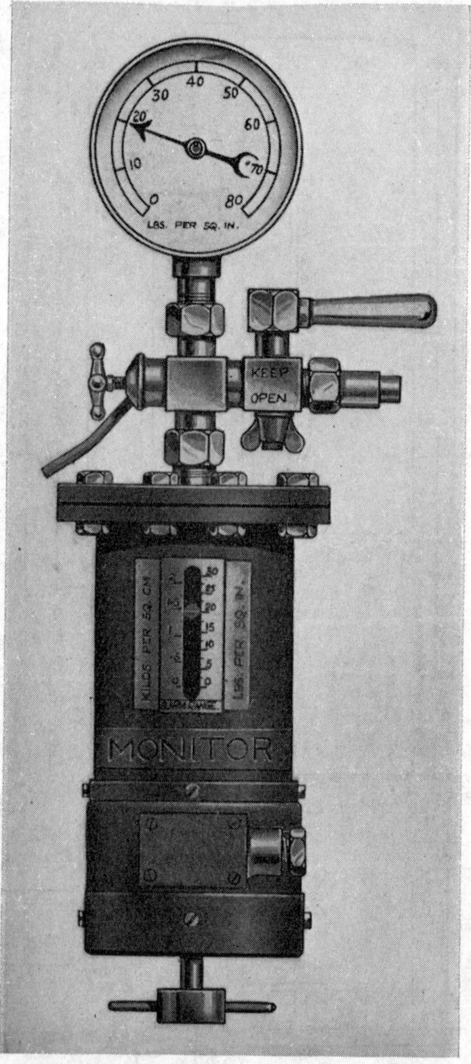

Fig. 239—Pressure alarm, electric type (Monitor)

is no surer way of cracking a casting than by heating it and then quenching it with cold water.

Devices are sometimes incorporated in the cooling water, lubricating oil and fuel systems, their purpose being to give audible or visual warning of something wrong with those essential services. Fig. 238 shows where these safety devices, when fitted, are usually situated. Some of these are made to stop the engine should the pressure in the system fall below a predetermined figure. This, in the author's view, is an unwise precaution, as under certain circumstances the taking of the engine out of the control of those in charge may have far more serious consequences than would result from allowing an engine to run for the short time it takes to remedy the fault after audible warning has been given.

Fig. 239 illustrates the " Monitor " pressure alarm of the electric type, applicable to the jacket cooling, piston cooling, and lubricating oil systems, etc., where fall in pressure denotes insufficiency of cooling water or oil. The alarm may be adjusted to come into operation at any predetermined pressure drop, the alarm point—which should be midway between the pressure in the system when the pump is delivering its normal capacity and when the pump

Fig. 240—Flow indicator, electric type (Monitor)

has just stopped—being shown on the visible indicator at the front of the fitting. The pressure in the system is indicated on the gauge at the top of the fitting, provision being made for testing the alarm without actually reducing the pressure by closing the fluid shut-off cock and opening the small test tap at the left-hand side of the fitting, observing at what falling pressure the alarm sounds.

An alternative for the fresh-water circulating systems is the "Monitor" flow indicator, illustrated by Fig. 240, this fitting being incorporated in the actual pipe-line, to give the alarm

Fig. 241—Alarm panel, for five circuits (Monitor)

should the flow be reduced to danger point. The standard dial is graduated from 0 to 10, the engineers soon learning to visualise the comparative flow passing, by the corresponding position taken up by the indicator pointer. The alarm point can be easily set to any position on the indicator scale by means of a small adjustable tappet inside the electric contact case, the point of alarm then being shown on the tappet.

Three-terminal electric contact gear is provided for both the "Monitor" pressure alarm and flow indicator, which provides for a safety lamp in addition to a danger lamp and Klaxon horn. A typical "Monitor" alarm panel is illustrated by Fig. 241, which shows five circuits. The safety lamps are normally "on"; failure of any circulating system extinguishes the respective safety lamp and at the same instant audible and visible warning of the failure is given.

A simple and very popular form of alarm, alternative to the electric type, is by whistles operated from the compressed-air system. Whistle alarm gear can be provided for either the " Monitor " pressure alarm or " Monitor " flow indicator.

" Monitor " float alarms are also in general use for attaching to the outside of oil service tanks, overflow tanks, etc. These give warning when the level reaches danger point, in the one case electrically and in the other by compressed-air whistles (see Fig. 242).

Fig. 242—Float alarm, electric type (Monitor)

Cylinder-head valves

Whilst at the top of the cylinders, the opening and closing action of the cylinder-head valves should be observed. If the engine is of the ordinary two-stroke airless injection type there will be no valves to observe, unless the makers have provided means for indicating the distance the fuel-valve needles lift. This is not usual, so that improper working of these small parts must be ascertained, as indicated in Chapter 10. The fuel-valve body, however, should be observed for movement relative to the cylinder head, and placing a hand on the fuel pipe will give some idea of the action of the fuel pump.

When an engine is operating it should be possible to stop the valve rocking-lever rollers revolving by holding them between the fingers when the valves are operating, in order to check that, after expansion of the various parts, the rollers are not riding on the plain parts of the cams and preventing the valve from re-seating properly. In this way excessive roller clearance due to a partly jammed valve may also be detected, since the cam peak will strike the roller with a more pronounced tap. The rocking-lever rollers should revolve quite freely, otherwise they and the cam peaks will wear excessively.

Any cam and roller producing more than the usual amount of noise, which indicates excessive roller clearance, should be investigated before the roller clearance is re-adjusted. The cause may be due to the valve spindle jamming in a partly open position, or to some obstruction which has the same effect. With some designs of exhaust- and air-inlet valves the roller clearance has been known to increase due to a lid becoming slack on the spindle and unscrewing. These valves should re-seat smartly but without shock. When such valves, usually exhaust valves, almost re-seat and then pause momentarily before finally closing, it is a sign that the spindle is gumming up, and the valve may be expected to jam at any moment.

In modern engines, exhaust valves rarely if ever jam when operating, provided the spindle has sufficient working clearance in its guide, but for the benefit of those in charge of engines not so modern in which the exhaust gases are not entirely free from carbonised oil, and the cooling of the exhaust valve is not so efficient, the following note is included. If a valve bounces or vibrates on its seat at the instant of closing, it generally indicates insufficient spring load. A spring broken in one place may be the cause. When a spring is broken in several places, the valve generally vibrates during the whole of the active period, and makes such a noise that the cause will be apparent. A hammering noise, and a valve re-seating with great shock but without much vibration, indicate that the valve spindle is jamming almost to the point of seizure. The hammering noise is caused by the piston striking the valve lid and driving it on to its seat with great force. Such a state of affairs should not be allowed to continue a moment longer than necessary, as there is a grave danger of the valve spindle being bent owing to the concave or convex (as the case may be) piston crown striking the valve lid on one side. In such an event, the fuel should be shut off the cylinder concerned, and the rocking-lever roller clearance of the defective valve increased until the amount the valve opens is reduced sufficiently to prevent the piston from striking it. This will probably prevent the piston from striking the valve, since in such cases the valve usually jams at the point of maximum opening, and by increasing the roller clearance the travel of the valve is reduced. The valve spindle should be freed by injecting a little paraffin, and then lubricated with a mixture of fuel and lubricating oil.

During the inspection of the cylinder heads the camshaft bearings, roller pins and nuts about the valve actuating gear and the camshaft driving gear should not be overlooked, when taking over a watch. In some engines the fuel pumps are driven directly off the camshaft, and will require to be inspected at this stage. The points to observe about this part are that all joints are perfectly fluid-tight, that no leakage is taking place at the various plugs or priming valves, and that the driving mechanism is in proper order. Lubrication of the cams operating airless injection fuel pumps is of particular importance.

Air-injection fuel valves

The fuel valves must be examined for leakage. If the spindle gland requires to be tightened, the operation must be carried out with care to minimise the chances of the spindle jamming in the open position. It is not advisable to shut off the injection air or fuel while doing so. As a rule a valve spindle that tends to jam will, before doing so, become sluggish in closing and will not re-seat smartly. The outward indication of this sluggish action is slight, but perceptible to one who, while slowly tightening up the gland, places the tip of a finger and thumb on an exposed part of the spindle.

When a fuel valve jams in the open position and fuel enters the cylinder during the compression stroke, dangerously high pressures in the cylinder will be reached, owing to the fuel being injected into a rapidly decreasing volume. The fuel must, therefore, be shut off immediately. The injection air will require to be shut off also, because high-pressure injection air entering the cylinder during the whole of the compression stroke will cause the final compression pressure to be increased very considerably. The fuel should always be shut off first, however, not only because it causes the greatest pressure in the cylinder to be reached, but to ensure that the fuel valve is cleared of fuel before the means of injecting it are removed. Should injection air be shut off first, fuel will remain in the injection valve and there is a danger of hot compressed air from the cylinder igniting the fuel in the fuel valve. The seriousness of such a thing happening has already been mentioned in a previous chapter.

The first indication of a fuel valve jamming is the cylinder relief valve acting violently. As an engineer must go to the top of the engine to ascertain which of the valves is at fault, the quickest way to shut off the fuel is to open the priming valve on the fuel-injection valve, but the corresponding fuel pump should be put out of action before the injection air is shut off, as even with the priming valve open a little fuel may be discharged into the valve casing. Although very high cylinder pressures are reached by this form of pre-ignition, yet there is no fear of the cylinder head or any part of it blowing off. The reason why quick action on the part of an engineer is necessary is because such high cylinder pressure may start certain joints leaking.

The first indication of a fuel valve leaking is discoloured exhaust gases, and if sighting cocks opposite the outlet from each cylinder are not provided, the fuel should be shut off each cylinder, one at a time, until the faulty valve is located. In the case of both air- and airless injection engines, the indicator diagrams will reveal a greater pressure rise upon injection of fuel because fuel will enter the cylinder before the pressure necessary to open the valve has been built up by the pump. The fuel is, of course, already in the injection valve well before the end of the compression stroke, and the means to force it into the cylinder is ever present. The exhaust temperature is not affected until carbon begins to deposit on the fuel-valve nozzle, because the pressure behind the fuel is released after the injection period in the case of airless injection engines—unless, of course, the fuel valves are mechanically operated—while the valve is cleared of fuel during the injection period in air-injection engines. When carbon deposits on the fuel-valve nozzles and interferes with the fuel sprays, the combustion efficiency is reduced and the exhaust temperature increased.

Fuel-injection pumps

The temperature of the fuel pump bodies should be ascertained by feeling with a hand. Owing to the very high working pressure of airless injection engine fuel pumps, the valve chambers will become warm if any of the valves or their cages are not quite fluid-tight. The heat is generated by the fuel being forced back to the low-pressure side of the defective valve at great velocity. Such fuel-pump valves sometimes work in removable cages to facilitate grinding of the faces and renewal, so that, if the joint between a valve cage and the pump body is not perfectly fluid-tight, the effect will be the same as if the valve was leaking, and the valve chamber will heat up. If a small piece of grit should lodge on a valve seat and prevent the valve from re-seating properly, the fuel-injection pressure will not be affected unless the leakage is very great, but the amount of fuel injected into the corresponding cylinder will be reduced, and the valve chamber will heat up.

In view of the effect which the smallest pieces of grit have upon these pumps, it is essential that the low-pressure part of the fuel system should be kept in clean condition. It is also important that the valves be a good fit in their cages to ensure accurate re-seating. Therefore, if the output of a pump should be reduced suddenly and the valve chamber heat up, do not jump to the conclusion that it is due to the valve jamming in its cage and try to remedy the trouble by filing the surfaces guiding the valve, since this may have the effect of converting a temporary leak into a permanent one, or until the parts have been renewed.

Bottoms of cylinders

The next part of the engine to be inspected will be the bottom ends of the cylinders. In the case of single-acting engines, the cylinder liners and pistons should be examined as far as possible to see that they are being properly lubricated. In the case of double-acting engines the piston rods should feel only slightly greasy, and in both types it should be observed whether any oil lifted from the crankcase is passing the scraper packing.

The cylinder lubricators should have been fully charged with oil, and be delivering regularly and consistently. The lubricating-oil pipes and connections conveying the oil to the cylinders should be observed, to make sure that the whole of the oil delivered by the lubricator is entering the cylinder.

The piston-cooling telescopic pipes can generally be observed from this position. These should be covered with a thin greasy film. Leakage of cooling water from the glands is very undesirable, and should not be allowed to continue. Even with small leaks the water is likely to be splashed on the piston-rod flange of single-acting engines, and it will eventually find its way between the piston and piston rod and corrode the surfaces. In one particular make of engine it was necessary to interpose 0·5 mm thick packing between the pistons and piston rods to stop the water, more in the form of vapour, from getting between these parts and playing havoc with the surfaces.

Knocking in cylinders

While at the bottom of the cylinders any unusual noise in the cylinders should be listened for. Piston slap occurs in four-stroke engines where the piston rods are comparatively long, and the cylinder-liner wear approaches 6 mm, but since in many engines no noise is produced by such wear, one must be quite satisfied that the noise is not due to the piston being slack in the upper end of the cylinder. As a rule, shutting off the fuel makes a slight but noticeable difference to the noise when this is the cause. Should the knock occur when the piston is at the upper end of the cylinder—this can be ascertained by touching the piston rod or piston-cooling telescopic pipes with the fingers and listening—the cause will be one of three things, namely, pre-ignition, piston slap, or the piston connecting bolts becoming loose. If pre-ignition is the cause the knocking will, of course, stop when the fuel is shut off, while if loosening of the piston connecting bolts is the cause, the noise produced will be greatest at the end of the exhaust stroke, when there is practically no pressure in the cylinder to keep the joining surfaces of the piston and piston rod together.

Should the knock occur when the piston is at the bottom of the cylinder, the cause will be due to the piston rings having insufficient end clearance, piston connecting bolts fouling some part of the crankcase top, or, if the cylinder liner is divided into two parts, gas escaping from between the piston rings into the space between the ends of the liners. Should the knocking be due to the first or second cause, the knock will take place each time the piston is at the bottom of the cylinder.

It is rarely that piston slap occurs in two-stroke crosshead type engines because the piston skirt is always in a practically unworn part of the cylinder, while loose piston-connecting bolts are not easy to detect because at the end of each up-stroke there is pressure on the top of the piston tending to keep the joining surfaces in contact. A light clicking noise is due to the piston rings riding over the scavenging air and exhaust ports, or if the cylinder liner consists of more than one part, to the parts not being absolutely in line. Such a fault is not really harmful, and the projection causing it will probably be worn off in a day or two. When, however, a decided knock occurs each time the piston reaches the bottom of the cylinder due to newly-fitted piston rings not having sufficient end clearance, it is not wise to allow the engine to continue working since there is a grave danger of the piston seizing or the cylinder liner being broken.

A grunting noise in a cylinder suggesting that the piston is running dry is generally due to gas passing the rings which are not a perfectly good fit in the grooves and causing them to vibrate. When this is the case the noise occurs during each fuel-injection period.

Crosshead guides

The crosshead guides should be given attention whilst passing along the middle platform. It is sufficient to lay a hand on the ahead guide bar to tell if everything is in order or not. The guides of forced lubricated engines rarely become overheated, but they and the whitemetal rubbing surfaces of the crosshead shoe wear slightly, and the bolts connecting the parts together might become loose. Knocking on the guide bars should therefore be investigated. Should the knocking be caused by wear it will occur each time the crank passes over the top dead centre. A loose crosshead shoe will have the same effect, but as this fault will develop rapidly it ought not to be difficult to diagnose the cause of the knocking.

The crosshead shoes should be a reasonably good fit in the guides, otherwise not only will the alignment of the piston be adversely affected, but the piston-cooling telescopic pipes will be strained and the piston-rod oil-scraper packing in the top of the crankcase will require more frequent attention. This is, of course, particularly necessary in the case of double-acting engines on account of the piston-rod gas packing. Most engines will work satisfactorily with a clearance, when the parts are cold, of 0·1 mm between the face of the shoe and the guide, making a total clearance of 0·2 mm. It is not necessary as in steam practice to give the crosshead less clearance at the top to allow for the radial expansion of the cylinder. As a matter of fact, the upper ends of guides should, if anything, be made a closer fit, as it is this part that wears most.

Bottom platform inspection

The chief points requiring attention when the bottom platform is reached by the relieving engineer, and the operating irregularities likely to be experienced on this level, will now be dealt with.

The following pressures and temperatures are, of course, simply a rough approximation for diesel engines in general, the correct values for any particular make of engine being obtained by experience. For instance, there is nothing to be gained by operating the piston-cooling system at 30 lb/sq.in. if 20 lb will keep the outlet temperature of water or oil, as the case may be, within moderate range when the engine is operating. The reduction in power absorbed by the pump at the lower pressure may not be of much account, but a low pressure has decided advantages in that conditions under which the telescopic pipe glands work are less severe, with the result that the packing will require less attention.

The following are the approximate pressures and temperatures recorded by the various instruments usually located at the starting platform, when the engine-room atmosphere is at about 90°F (32·2°C) and the sea temperature 60°F (15·6°C):—

	lb/sq.in.	°F	°C
Starting air	600	—	—
Cylinder cooling outlet (fresh water) ..	25	140	60
,, ,, ,, (sea-water)	25	110	43·3
Piston cooling outlet (fresh water)	30	130	54·4
,, ,, ,, (sea-water)	30	100	37·8
,, ,, ,, (lubricating oil) ..	30	120	49
Bearing lubricating oil (supply)	20	80	26·7
,, ,, ,, (return)	—	100	37·8
Supercharge air	2–4	120	49
Scavenging air	1–2	100	37·8
Exhaust gases	—	850	454
Injection air compressor H.P. discharge ..	900	290	143
,, ,, ,, H.P. suction ..	240	95	35
,, ,, ,, I.P. discharge ..	240	250	121
,, ,, ,, I.P. suction ..	40	80	26·7
,, ,, ,, L.P. discharge ..	40	260	127
,, ,, ,, C.W. discharge ..	25	90	32·2

Piston cooling

When taking over a watch, the engineer must observe the cooling water or oil leaving each piston; not only should the temperature be correct, but the fluid should flow in a steady stream. An unsteady stream indicates either that air has got into the system, or that there is some obstruction in the passages. When telescopic pipes are used to convey the cooling medium to and from the pistons, the air-vessels usually provided to prevent hammering sometimes become filled with air and then partly empty themselves suddenly. The air from the air-vessels is then carried along with the liquid and causes the flow from the outlets to become unsteady for a few minutes. Solid obstructions in the piston-cooling passages develop only when lubricating oil is the cooling medium, due to the oil being allowed to carbonise in the pistons, but irrespective of the medium used, the possibility of cotton waste and even bolts being accidentally left in the passages by engine repairers must not be overlooked.

As the temperature of the oil or water leaving the pistons is always between 100° and 140°F (37°–60°C), vapour rises from the outlets when the fluid is discharged into open troughs. A certain amount of vapour in such cases cannot be avoided, but since it represents loss of either oil or fresh water the temperature should not be allowed to become so high that the loss is appreciable. The first indication of a cracked piston is generally smoke in the piston-cooling water followed by a drop in the exhaust temperature; when inspecting the cooling outlets, therefore, it is a good plan to smell the vapour also.

The usual practice is to regulate the output of constant-speed piston-cooling pumps at the suction, if of the reciprocating type, and at the discharge if of the centrifugal type. The temperature of the water or oil leaving the pistons is regulated by valves at the inlet to each piston, while the outflow is through open-ended pipes. As the pressure gauge is connected to the system at a point between the pump and the inlet regulating valves, it does not indicate that sufficient oil or water is being circulated through the pistons, but merely gives an indication of the amount available. The construction of most types of piston-cooling conveying mechanism is such that definite pressure produced in the passages by regulating the amount of medium circulated at the outlets would cause very severe water-hammer action, and not only would it be difficult to keep the telescopic pipe glands fluid-tight but the parts would doubtless quickly break.

In the event of a piston overheating, the fuel should be shut off the cylinder concerned and the piston allowed to cool before the water supply is increased. Should the temperature of water flowing from a piston be found low, and alteration of the regulating valve not bring about the desired change, short-circuiting of the water must be suspected. This can occur only when the cooling water passes to and from the piston through the centre of the piston rod as shown in Fig. 119, and if the water passes straight through the crosshead owing to the lower end of the internal pipe in the piston rod corroding or wearing and not sealing the inlet and outlet passages properly. It will thus be seen that in certain types of engines a piston may become dangerously hot without any outward indication, and this proves once again how very necessary it is for an engineer to investigate and ascertain the cause of the least irregularity. Every fault is indicated in some way. In a great many instances the indications are small and would pass unnoticed by any but a properly observant operating engineer.

Although short-circuiting of the cooling water has been known to occur only in the type of conveying mechanism just referred to, yet when telescopic pipes attached direct to the piston and working side-by-side in a common casting, called the stand-pipe, are employed, the possibility of this casting corroding or fracturing and allowing the inlet and outlet water to mix must be considered when an increase in the amount of water circulated does not reduce the temperature of the water flowing from the open-ended return pipes. When oil is used to cool the pistons, the possibility of corrosion is eliminated, but it is still possible for certain parts of the conveying mechanism to wear or break and either short-circuit the oil or stop the flow.

The quantity of cooling water or oil in the drain tanks must be ascertained at the end of each watch, and the cause of any increase or decrease located and remedied without delay. As a rule, the pressure of the piston-cooling medium is always slightly higher than that of the sea-water circulating the cooler, but when the sea-water passes through the tubes and the cooling medium is on the outside of the tubes and leakage occurs between the two sides of the cooler, it is the sea-water which finds its way through the opening. When, therefore, the level of the liquid in the piston-cooling tank rises, the cause is invariably due to leakage in the cooler, while loss of cooling medium, if the cause is not apparent, may be due to leakage into the crankcase. When this occurs the level of the bearing lubricating oil in the drain tank will, of course, rise.

In the event of sea-water mixing with the piston-cooling oil prompt action is necessary, otherwise solid matter will be formed in the pistons and the passages are likely to become choked. If convenient, the speed of the engines should be reduced to lower the working temperature of the pistons, and the water removed from the bottom of the piston-cooling oil tank by the hand pump usually provided.

In the event of a ship running short of fresh water for piston-cooling purposes, sea-water may safely be used in the closed system. If sea-water is cooled and used over and over again, the working outlet temperature need not be reduced as the amount of solid matter contained in such a small quantity of sea-water is negligible, even if it did all deposit in the pistons, which is very unlikely. The sea-water should, however, be replaced by fresh water at the first opportunity, as sea-water corrodes the internal parts of the system more quickly than fresh water.

On one occasion the author had to convert, hurriedly, a fresh-water piston-cooling system over to sea-water owing to the piston cooler casing fracturing so badly that it could not be immediately repaired. The pipes were altered to cause the piston-cooling water pump to draw from one of the auxiliary sea suctions, and the bilge pump to draw from the piston-cooling tank. The piston-cooling pump then drew water from the sea and forced it through the pistons, the water flowing from the pistons into the piston-cooling tank. The bilge pump lifted the water from the piston-cooling tank and discharged it overboard. The engine operated at full power in this way for seven months until a new cooler casing had been made and sent to the ship. No deposit was found in two of the pistons opened up while the permanent repair was being carried out, but parts of the piston rods through which the cooling water was led to and from the pistons were beginning to corrode.

If, for some unlikely reason, lubricating oil has to be substituted for fresh water, then it would not be possible to operate the engine at full power, because it would not be possible to pass sufficient oil through the passages which had been designed for water unless the pressure on the oil was substantially greater than the normal pressure for water, and, if such high pressures were employed, mechanical difficulties in the direction already indicated would result.

Bearing lubricating oil

As the pressure on the bearing lubricating-oil system is regulated at the pump only, the pressure recorded on the gauge indicates whether or not an adequate supply of oil is reaching the bearings. It is true that the gauge pressure denotes the force of the oil in the main supply pipe, or before it enters the bearings—the lowest point of the system—but it requires only a simple mental calculation to assure one that the pressure is sufficient to cause the oil to reach the highest point supplied in the system.

The pressure shown on the gauge depends mainly upon the viscosity of the oil. The slackness in the bearings will also affect the pressure unless the pump has a good reserve capacity, which is not always the case. The viscosity of the oil depends upon its temperature, and the amount of impurities it contains. When starting a lubricating-oil pump with oil that is abnormally viscous, the pressure in the system is liable greatly to exceed the normal working pressure with certain types of lubricating-oil pumps, unless the pump speed is carefully controlled and allowed to reach the normal speed gradually.

Such sudden rises in pressure are very often responsible for pipe joints being strained, and leakage occurring after the oil has become warm and less viscous. If the pipe joints strained in this way are located outside the crankcase, much valuable oil may be wasted before the leakage is noticed. It is therefore wise always to examine the pipe joints located under the floor plates when this occurs, and not wait until the loss is registered on the drain-tank level indicator. For this and other reasons mentioned in an earlier chapter, it is advisable to heat the lubricating oil to about 100°F (37·7°C) prior to starting the pump in a cold climate, or when the oil is abnormally viscous.

Relief valves, when provided on the delivery side of lubricating-oil pumps, should be so arranged that the escaping oil is visible and is returned to the crankcase or drain tank. It is not good practice to lead the escaping oil into the pump suction pipe, as it is quite possible for the pressure in this pipe to be raised thereby, and the joints strained sufficiently to cause them to leak and adversely affect the proper working of the pump. This occurred in one ship which came under the writer's notice. Frequent trouble was caused by the lubricating-oil pump failing to draw the oil from the double-bottom tank in sufficient quantities, and this was eventually found to be due to very small air leaks occurring in the suction pipe. The escaping oil from the relief valve was led into the pump suction pipe, and the conditions were such that each time the pump was started, the relief valve acted and allowed such quantities of oil to enter the suction pipe that the non-return valve on the tank end was forced on to its seat, and a fairly high pressure momentarily built up in the suction pipe, even though the pump was working.

Cases there are where no drain pipe is provided to lead the oil away from the relief valves. In such cases an engineer is naturally afraid of losing oil as well as making a mess of the engine-room and sometimes loads the valves so much that they will not function at any pressure, with the result that some of the pipes are broken or joints are strained and oil leaks into the bilges. If a ship is rolling, three or four hundred gallons of oil may be lost before leakage is suspected.

Lubricating oil is always strained and cooled before it is returned to the bearings. Sometimes the pump draws the oil through a strainer, and sometimes the strainer is situated on the discharge side of the pump. The cooler is always located on the discharge side. More effective separation of the solid impurities in the oil is obtained when the strainer is on the suction side of the pump, because, when it is located on the discharge side, much of the fine grit that would be trapped at the suction side is forced through the gauze on the discharge side. Moreover, the gauze is more likely to be damaged on the discharge side when a difference in pressure results owing to the strainers requiring cleaning.

The bearing oil pressure should remain perfectly steady no matter which type of pump is employed, so long as it is in good order. Even single-acting reciprocating pumps maintain a steady pressure if they are provided with an efficient air-vessel. Should the pressure fluctuate, the most likely cause is an insufficient quantity of oil in the drain tank. If the oil is contaminated with impurities and very viscous, the pressure will fluctuate. All other faults which have the same result will be found in the pump.

Should the pressure drop suddenly, the cause, apart from pump defects, may be due to a broken pipe inside the crankcase. When copper pipes are used to convey the oil to the crankshaft bearings, they are liable to become brittle, especially if they are allowed to vibrate, and they have been known to break while an engine was operating. Such pipes should be annealed every four years. A sudden increase in pressure is generally caused by the gauze in the strainers rupturing due to their not being cleaned often enough, or to the wire gauze having deteriorated and being in need of renewal.

The oil generally passes through grids on its way from the crankcase to the drain tank. Sometimes these grids become choked with waste, carelessly left in the crankcase, and this obstructs the flow of oil. In such an event, not only is there a danger of the drain tank becoming dry, but the level of oil in the crankcase may rise so much that the cranks will dip into the oil. This must be avoided, because if the oil is cold and viscous the stresses set up may damage the plate forming the bottom of the oil sump. These plates are sometimes quite thin and not intended to withstand such treatment.

When taking over a watch, an engineer should observe the amount of lubricating oil in the drain tank and compare it with the amount logged at the end of the previous watch, as, in fact, he should do with the whole of the temperature and pressure readings. Should the pressure on the gauge and the quantity of oil in the drain tank remain more or less constant, there cannot be much wrong with the system. Regular sounding of the drain tank should be carried out, as variation in the level of oil is the first indication of water leaking into the system at the cooler or through a broken piston cooling-water telescopic stand-pipe, of oil leaking from the system, or of the oil not flowing freely from the crankcases. The pressure gauge should be tested occasionally to make quite sure that it is registering correctly, as the small-bore pipes sometimes become choked with dirt. When this occurs it will generally be found that the pressure gauge pipe is connected to the underside of a horizontally located oil-pipe.

No matter what precautions are taken it is impossible to keep the lubricating oil entirely free of solid impurities, with the result that when a ship reaches port and circulation of oil is stopped, the fine particles of solid matter settle out and lie on the bottom of horizontally located pipes. When next the oil is put into circulation, the cold viscous oil sweeps the dirt along the bottom of the pipe and into any openings that may be there. For this reason it is not good practice to connect branch pipes to the underside of a main supply pipe.

Discoloured exhaust

This fault may be caused by: (1) fuel-injection pressure too low; (2) fuel valve lift too small, if the engine is of the air-injection type; (3) fuel valves leaking; (4) combustion air intakes partly choked, if engine is of the unsupercharged type; (5) too liberal lubrication of the exhaust valve, or exhaust valve leaking; (6) fuel atomisers choked or requiring adjustment; (7) carbon deposit on fuel spray nozzles interfering with the fuel sprays. Black smoke is generally due to imperfect combustion of fuel, blue smoke to over-lubrication of the cylinders, and white smoke to the presence of water in the gas spaces. The water may be in the fuel or leaking into the cylinders, but water leaking into the exhaust pipe would have the same effect.

The cylinder in which imperfect combustion is taking place will probably be located by opening the gas sighting-cocks usually provided at the outlet of each cylinder. If the fault is only slight, and doubt exists as to which is the cylinder causing the discoloration, it can usually be determined by letting the gases impinge on a piece of white paper.

The most frequent cause of a discoloured exhaust is one of the fuel valves leaking. The leakage may be so slight that the working of the engine is not affected, but such faults should not be allowed to continue as they become rapidly worse and may seriously affect the working of the engine. In such cases the smoke in the exhaust is caused by a drop of fuel forming on the spray nozzle after the valve has closed. The smoke results from the partial combustion of this drop of fuel during the expansion and exhaust periods, and will eventually cause carbon to deposit on the nozzle. This will not prevent the entry of the fuel, but it may cause improper spraying and consequently imperfect combustion of the main charge.

Breakdowns

A contingency to be reckoned with is the possibility of laying off one unit in the event of some of the working parts being seriously damaged. This can be more easily accomplished in a diesel engine, because each unit is practically independent instead of all units being interdependent as in the steam reciprocating engine.

Suppose, for instance, that owing to the failure of a crosshead bearing bolt the damage resulting necessitates the removal of the piston, piston rod and connecting rod in order that the engine could be set to work on the remaining units. Beginning at the bottom of the engine it would first of all be necessary to stop the lubricating-oil supply to this unit. This will be done by driving a well-fitting wooden plug into the hole in the crankpin. To make the plug more secure it should project ¼-inch or so above the surface of the pin and have a V-shaped groove cut in the end. If then a few turns of fine wire are wound around the pin and the plug secured by it there will be no danger of the plug being forced out by the pressure of the lubricating oil. The cylinder lubricators will also require to be put out of action.

If the engine is of the two-stroke type, the scavenging air and exhaust ports will next require attention. Had the piston been undamaged, these would have been easily dealt with, since the ports could have been effectively blanked by placing the piston in such a position that all the ports were masked. If, however, the piston must be removed, it is an easy matter to blank the ports by a number of piston rings sprung into the cylinder, which when in contact with each other completely cover the ports. The gaps between the ends of the rings should, of course, be located opposite the bars between the ports. Piston rings fitted in the manner described will be sufficient to prevent escape of burnt gases and scavenging air into the engine-room, and obviate the troublesome job of fitting blank flanges at the points where air and burnt gases enter and leave the cylinder.

If the cylinder head can remain in place, the only other work necessary is to disconnect the gear operating the cylinder-head valves, and stop the corresponding fuel pump from discharging. The cooling water to the cylinders and pistons offers no difficulty, since this can usually be shut off by stop-valves.

When for some reason it becomes necessary to disconnect and hang up a piston in the cylinder and operate with it thus, the starting air as well as the fuel and injection air of the defective unit must be blanked off to prevent compressed air from entering the cylinder and blowing the piston out when the engine is set in motion. Strange as it may seem, this important matter has been overlooked on more than one occasion and very serious damage done to costly parts of the engine.

In the case of four-stroke engines, the air-inlet and exhaust-valve rocking levers must be disconnected. Further precautions are necessary to prevent exhaust gas pressure from the other cylinders from finding its way into the cylinder in which the piston is hung up, by firmly securing the exhaust valve in the closed position. It is also advisable to secure the air-inlet valve in the open position, in order to allow any compressed air or gas under pressure that may mysteriously find its way into the cylinder easy access to the atmosphere, and thus prevent accumulation of pressure.

When setting an engine in motion, the first few charges of fuel injected into the cylinders are greatly in excess of the amount injected under normal working conditions. Consequently the exhaust pressures are higher than at normal full load, and the pressure in the exhaust manifold may be high enough to overcome the exhaust-valve spring of the defective unit—when gases under pressure will enter the cylinder and act on the piston unless the precautions recommended are taken. Moreover, it may happen that an unburnt charge of fuel is exhausted from one of the other cylinders and ignited in the exhaust manifold by the hot gases therein, thus causing an explosion and a rapid local increase of pressure which may reach the exhaust valve of the defective unit.

It is not so long ago that one piston and connecting rod of a trunk piston engine were hung up in their cylinder owing to a broken lubricating-oil pipe causing one of the gudgeon bearings to " run out." The starting air, fuel and injection air were correctly blanked off, and the air-inlet and exhaust-valve rocking levers disconnected. Upon starting the engine, the piston, and with it the connecting rod, although well secured by wire ropes, were blown into the crankcase, doing, as can doubtless be imagined, very serious damage. The blank flanges in the starting and injection air lines were found intact, so that the conclusion reached was that the exhaust gases under pressure must have overcome the exhaust-valve spring, and, the air-inlet valve being closed, the pressure of gas in the cylinder accumulated and, acting on top of the piston, caused the wire ropes to break, with the result mentioned.

When selecting a blank flange for the starting-air line, remember that the pressure it must withstand is high, and that the impact with air is sudden. Such flanges should, therefore, be $\frac{1}{4}$-inch thick at least. On one occasion when a $\frac{1}{16}$-inch thick flange was fitted, repeated starting caused the centre of the flange to be blown out and the inevitable happened.

Fires in engine-room

Wherever liquid fuel is employed there is a possibility of a fire occurring unless the simple precaution is taken of stopping all leakages into the bilges and other open spaces where naked lights may be used. When a fire occurs in the engine-room of a motorship at sea the cause can only be due to two acts of carelessness, i.e. allowing fuel to be present in places where it ought not to be and/or the careless use of naked lights in places where fuel is normally stored. On occasions the cause has been due to fuel pipes leaking and allowing fuel to impinge on hot exhaust pipes.

Should fuel take fire in the bilges or on the tank top, water poured on the fire is very little use as an extinguisher, since the fuel, being in most instances lighter than water, will simply float on the surface of the water and continue burning. Water applied in this way may even increase the danger, by causing the fire to spread if the water is allowed to accumulate. If water must be used, the obvious way to prevent the fire from spreading is to start the bilge pump immediately the fire hose is brought into action. When water is used, it will prove more effective if applied in the form of a fine spray. A greater area of the fire will then be covered and there are better chances of cooling the fuel to below its ignition temperature.

When the fire is in the open the best way to extinguish the flames, in the absence of proper fire-extinguishing apparatus, is to smother the flames with sand, asbestos matting, or other inert material. Gases which do not support combustion, and are heavier than air, on being liberated will descend to the surface of the burning oil and smother the flames. The contents of certain liquid fire-extinguishers have this property and are very effective.

Whenever liquid fuel is used, not only should chemical fire-extinguishers be provided, but an engineer should be appointed and held responsible for their efficient working, as there is no doubt that many serious fires would have been prevented had the extinguishers been maintained in proper order. Moreover, as a precaution against fire it should be the practice to wash down the engine-room double-bottom tank top every week by means of a powerful water jet. If suitable hose connections to enable this to be done do not exist, they should be provided. The practice of some shipowners, of having the spaces under the engine-room floor permanently lighted, has much to commend it, as not only can the condition of the tank top be kept under constant observation, but it obviates the use of naked lights.

CHAPTER 28

Description of modern diesel engines

At the time of concluding the writing of this book the general trend among shipowners was to propel their new ships by two-stroke supercharged engines operating on either the single- or double-acting principle. In the majority of these engines the supercharge air is supplied by gas turbine-driven centrifugal compressors—or turbo-blowers as they are generally called—the motive power being obtained from the products of combustion exhausted by the engine.

The supercharging of marine diesel engines began in the 1920's when the Swiss engineer Buchi introduced the principle of exhaust gas turbo-charging in four-stroke engines; this, it was found, could raise the mean indicated pressure from 90 lb to 135 lb/sq.in. without ill-effect. This 50 per cent increase in the power developed for a given size and number of cylinders was not surpassed for over twenty years.

The M.I.P. of two-stroke engines has, by supercharging, been raised, in recent years, from an average of 70 lb to 105 lb/sq.in., so that the rated power output of a given engine has been increased 35 per cent. It is probable that the powers of both four-stroke and two-stroke engines will be further increased in the not far distant future by supercharging to a higher degree than is now practised, but because of its inherently simpler construction it is more than likely that the four-stroke type will maintain its lead.

Sulzer

A sectional view of a Sulzer two-stroke, single-acting supercharged engine is shown in Fig. 243. This engine, which has cylinders of 760 mm bore and 1,550 mm stroke, is built with from 4 to 12 cylinders, the rated output per cylinder being 1,300 b.h.p. Operating particulars of one of these 9-cylinder engines are as follows:—

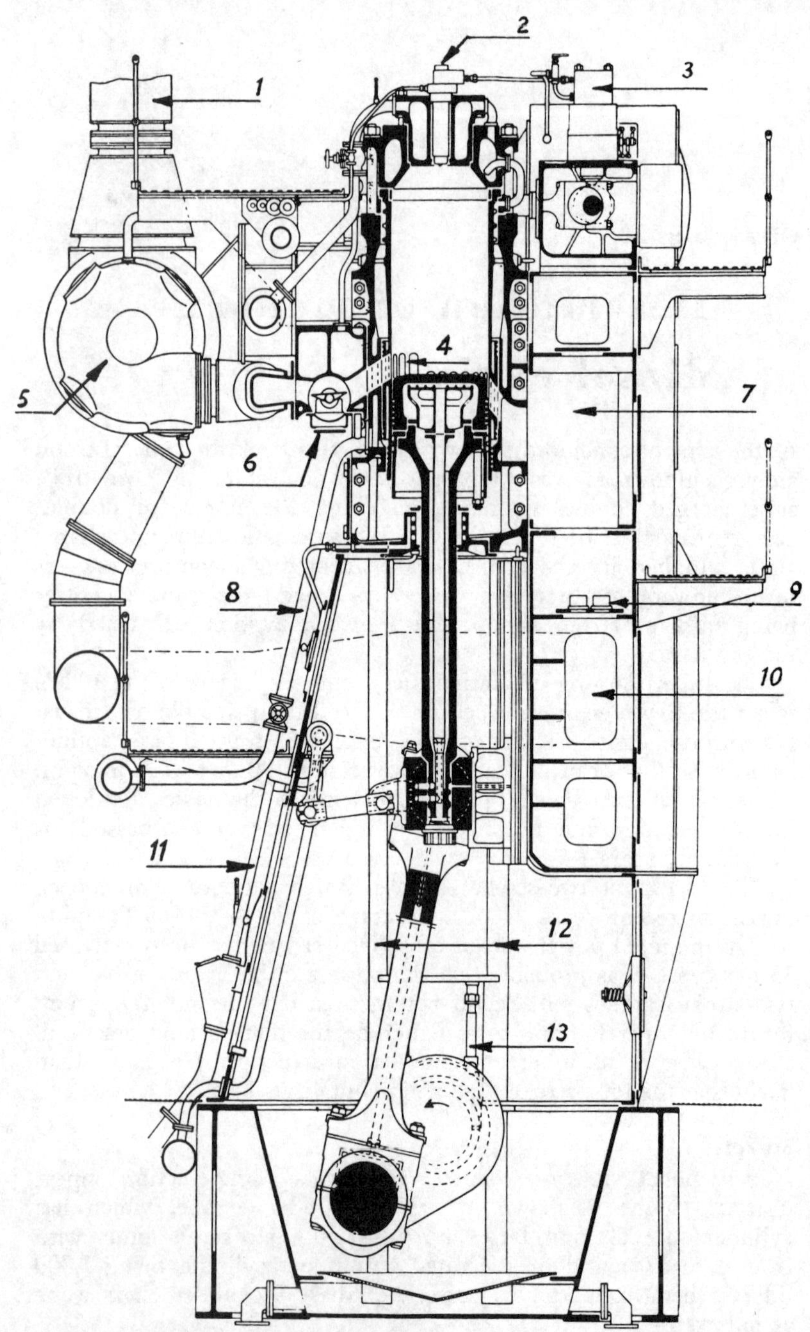

Fig. 243—Single-acting, 2-stroke supercharged engine (Sulzer)
(For key to reference letters see foot of opposite page.)

Rated power output at 119 r.p.m.	11,700 b.h.p.
Service power output at 115 r.p.m.	10,250 ,,
Supercharge air-pressure, lb/sq.in.	7
Exhaust-gas temperature before turbine ..	800°F (427°C)
,, ,, after ,, ..	575°F (302°C)
Cylinder compression pressure, lb/sq.in. ..	525
,, combustion ,, ,, ..	810
Mean effective (brake) pressure, lb/sq.in. ..	85
Mechanical efficiency, per cent	88
Fuel consumption, lb/b.h.p./hour	0·332
Weight of engine, lb per b.h.p. developed ..	88

The bedplate and framing are made either of cast iron or fabricated steel; Fig. 244 shows the first type of construction, while fabricated steel construction is shown in Fig. 245. In the latter form the bedplate, framing and cylinder beam are held rigidly together by long tie-bolts. With a view to keeping the crosswise distance between the tie-bolts to a minimum the crankshaft bearing caps are held down by jack-bolts, one of which can be seen in Fig. 243. This arrangement simplifies the inspection of the crankshaft journals and reduces the bending stresses in this part of the bedplate when the tie-bolts are being tightened.

The cylinder scavenging and supercharging system is shown diagrammatically in Fig. 246. *A* is the turbo-blower, *B* the exhaust-gas turbine, *C* the oscillating exhaust-gas control valve, *D* the piston, *F* the air receiver, and *G* the air cooler. The cylinders are scavenged on the loop principle and turbo-charged on the pulse principle. The advantage of this form of scavenging over the uniflow form is that where the upper ends of the cylinders are closed by a fixed head, as in all Sulzer engines, the head can be of very simple construction. If uniflow scavenging is desired with fixed heads they would have to be provided with a large pocket in order to contain the exhaust valve.

In unsupercharged engines of this make the scavenging air is supplied by double-acting reciprocating pumps, the piston rods of

---

1. Exhaust to atmosphere
2. Fuel valve
3. Fuel-injection pump
4. Exhaust ports
5. Turbo-blower
6. Exhaust control valve
7. Scavenge air-receiver
8. Jacket cooling water
9. Non-return flap valves
10. Supercharge air-receiver
11. Piston cooling oil return
12. Tie-bolts
13. Bearing-cap jack-bolts

which are connected to an arm rigidly bolted to the engine crosshead. Each cylinder has its own pump but all deliver into a common receiver to ensure a uniform pressure. Scavenging air from this receiver flows into the cylinders through a single row of ports, the opening and closing of which is controlled by the engine pistons.

Fig. 244—Cast-iron bedplate, frames, and cylinder beam of an 8-cylinder engine (Sulzer)

The exhaust gases leave the cylinders through a row of ports located at a slightly higher level than the scavenging air-ports. In supercharged engines the exhaust ports are controlled by an oscillating valve (*C*, Fig. 246), the drive incorporating a spring which prevents the driving mechanism from being damaged in the event of a piece of piston ring or other hard object jamming the valve. The movement of this valve is timed in such a way that communication between the cylinder and exhaust pipe is closed early on the up-stroke of the piston, thereby ensuring that the cylinder is filled with air at the full supercharge air-pressure.

In the supercharged engines of Sulzer make the separate engine-driven scavenge pumps are omitted, scavenging air being supplied

Fig. 245—View of part of an engine having fabricated steel structure (Sulzer). (Note piston, piston rod, crosshead, and connecting-rod in foreground)

by enclosing the lower end of the cylinder and using the down-stroke of the engine piston to produce the necessary pressure, as shown in Fig. 246 and described in Chapter 18. Supercharge air from the turbo-blowers passes through coolers before entering the receiver from which it passes to the cylinders. Non-return flap valves are placed between the scavenging air-receiver and the

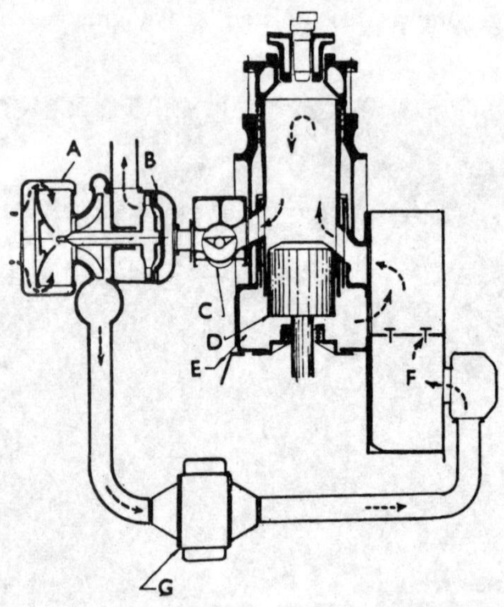

Fig. 246—Cylinder scavenging and supercharging system of Sulzer 2-stroke engine

supercharge air-receiver. During the down-stroke of the piston the air underneath is compressed and flows into the cylinder when the scavenging air-ports are uncovered by the piston. In this way scavenging and partial supercharging of the cylinder is effected when starting the engine and the turbo-blowers are not operating at a speed which ensures the requisite quantity of low-pressure air being supplied. A further advantage of this arrangement is that in the event of the turbo-blower becoming unusable the engine can still be operated at about 70 per cent of the normal service power.

The exhaust ports begin to open 112° after and are fully closed 112° before the top dead centre, the scavenging air-ports begin to open 135° after and are fully closed 135° before the top dead centre, while the oscillating exhaust valve begins to open at 90° after and is closed 120° before top dead centre. Supercharging, being on the pulse system, requires an earlier exhaust opening than other types of engines. The exhaust ports must, therefore, be situated relatively high, and alternate means must be provided to cut off communication between the cylinder and the exhaust passage before the piston completely closes the exhaust ports. It is for this reason that the oscillating exhaust valve is provided, which cuts off communication with the exhaust pipe 8° before the exhaust ports are fully closed.

In studying the various operations of this system it must be remembered that when the exhausting and re-charging processes are completed the scavenge air-receiver, as well as the supercharge air-receiver (7 and 10, Fig. 243), contain air at the supercharging pressure, i.e. about 7 lb/sq.in. On the up-stroke of the piston the air pressure in the scavenge air-receiver is reduced by expansion, and air will flow into it from the supercharge receiver; consequently when the piston begins the down-stroke the non-return flap valves close, and when the scavenging ports open the pressure in the scavenge air-receiver will be slightly greater than the supercharge air-pressure. As the pressure in the scavenge air-receiver is reduced and scavenging begins, it is replenished by air flowing from the supercharge air-receiver. Thus the peak pressure of scavenging air assists the sudden release of the burnt gases to drive the turbo-blower.

The scavenge air and exhaust ports can be readily inspected by opening conveniently situated hinged doors, while the piston rings can be viewed and tested for freedom through the ports. Each piston is lubricated at eight equi-spaced points located about one-quarter of the stroke from the top of the cylinder, the mechanical lubricators being situated above the camshaft and driven from it. A special feature of these lubricators is that their output can be varied simultaneously, from a minimum to a maximum, by a single hand-lever. In addition, the units of each lubricator can be adjusted separately.

The pistons are cooled by oil which is conveyed by pipes mounted on swinging links from a common supply pipe. The independently driven pump supplying oil to the pistons at a pressure of 55 lb/sq.in. supplies oil to the crosshead and crankpin bearings and to the turbo-blower bearings also. The crankshaft bearings are lubricated from a separate supply working at 20 lb/sq.in.

The one-piece cylinder liner is made of close-grained grey cast iron, while the cylinder head comprises two parts, as shown in

Fig. 247. The main outer part is a circular water-cooled casting which, when bolted down, firmly secures the cylinder liner in position. The separate centre portion of the head, which is also water-cooled, contains the fuel-, starting, and relief valves—the

Fig. 247—Cylinder head of Sulzer engine

starting valve being pneumatically operated. The fuel-valves are water-cooled from an independent source, and a special valve is provided to enable the high-viscosity fuel, when used, to be circulated and its temperature raised prior to starting the engine.

The fuel-injection pumps are of the design shown in Fig. 47, each pump being provided with a suction, delivery, and spill valve.

Sulzer's contention is that this type of pump is more easily maintained in good order than the rotating plunger type. The pumps are located at cylinder-head level and are operated from the crankshaft by chain drive. The same cam is used for ahead and astern

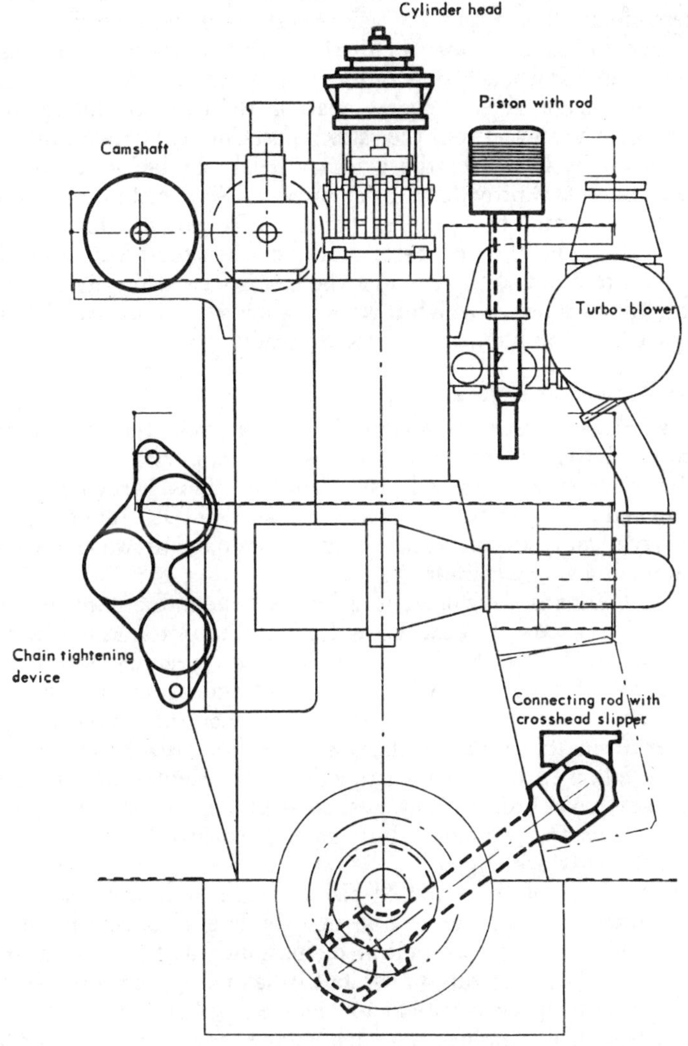

Fig. 248—Method of exposing running gear for overhaul (Sulzer)

running by arranging for its position relative to the engine crankshaft to be altered by an oil-operated rotary servo-motor built into the camshaft driving-wheel. The speed governor is of the centrifugal type.

Manoeuvring of the engine is carried out on the bottom platform, the controls being at the forward end of the engine. There are two levers mounted on a quadrant, one for starting and direction control, and one for speed control. All the usual interlocking devices are incorporated in the starting and reversing gears.

Sulzers have given a good deal of thought to the important question of accessibility of the various parts for maintenance purposes. As shown in Fig. 248, the cylinder head can be lifted clear and landed on a stool provided for the purpose. A special torque spanner, which is operated by an hydraulic pump, is provided for slackening (and tightening) the piston-rod nut and when the piston and piston rod are lifted out of the cylinder the rod is passed through a permanently fixed pipe, in which it rests in such a position that the piston rings and piston connecting nuts are readily accessible.

Opposed-piston engines

An engine which works on the diesel cycle but which, when compared with all other forms, has very important constructional differences, is the opposed-piston engine. This particular form of construction originated in Germany, and to Dr. Junkers of that country must go the credit for the idea of employing two reciprocating pistons in a single cylinder.

The Germans developed to a limited extent the Junkers engine for road transport, but its successful application to marine transport was due to the late K. O. Keller, for many years chief designer at Doxford's, Sunderland, whose persistent endeavours began to bear fruit about the year 1920. In the method of transmitting the power from the reciprocating pistons to the revolving crankshaft Keller followed the German practice. In recent years Burmeister & Wain have brought out a successful engine operating on the opposed-piston principle, but having constructional differences from the Doxford engine.

Advantages of the opposed-piston engine not possessed by the more orthodox form of engine may not be at once apparent. It is undoubtedly more complicated, inasmuch as there are a greater number of large moving parts, and it has no appreciable advantage in weight or space occupied for a given power output over some other two-stroke engines, yet such engines have become exceedingly popular. The reason may be that at the beginning of the motorship era when diesel engines were not entirely satisfactory for ship propulsion, the opposed-piston form of construction had several attractive features. For instance, having open-ended cylinders a source of weakness and consequently expense in renewing cracked heads was eliminated; pistons, which required more frequent overhaul than they do now, could be given attention in much shorter time and with considerably less effort; the ideal uniflow system of scavenging could be employed; finally, such engines could be more easily dynamically balanced. The opposed-piston form of construction had other less important attractions, and the reasons why Keller persisted in his endeavours to overcome the many difficulties in adapting such an engine to ship requirements are perhaps not far to seek. That success attended his efforts is evidenced by the very large number of ships propelled by opposed-piston engines at the present time.

Opposed-piston engines of Doxford construction operate on the two-stroke principle and are single-acting. They could be made double-acting but the practical difficulties would be great, and the height of the engine such that it is unlikely that double-acting will be built for a long time, if at all.

Messrs. Harland & Wolff produce under licence from Burmeister & Wain a double-acting opposed-piston engine. The height of this engine is not unduly great for the power developed because the stroke of the top piston is considerably less than that of the corresponding piston in a Doxford engine. In the Burmeister & Wain engine the stroke of the top piston, usually referred to as the exhaust piston, is only about one-third that of the main piston, whereas in the Doxford engine the strokes of the top and bottom pistons are in ratio of 3 to 4, respectively, in order to ensure primary balance of the reciprocating parts.

Where the top piston is connected to cranks or eccentrics on each side of the main crank each unit is independent, so that any number of cylinders can be employed. When the top piston is connected to the bottom piston of the adjacent cylinder, as in the now obsolete Fullagar engine, the number of cylinders must be even. The smallest number of cylinders to ensure an engine starting from any position of the crank in either direction is three in Doxford and Burmeister & Wain engines. In the Fullagar engine not less than four cylinders would be required to achieve the same results.

Doxford

As will be observed from the diagram of one cylinder of a Doxford engine, shown in Fig. 249, two identical pistons reciprocate in opposition in a single cylinder, the lower piston being connected to a crank in the usual way while the upper piston is connected to two additional cranks, one on either side of the main crank. The

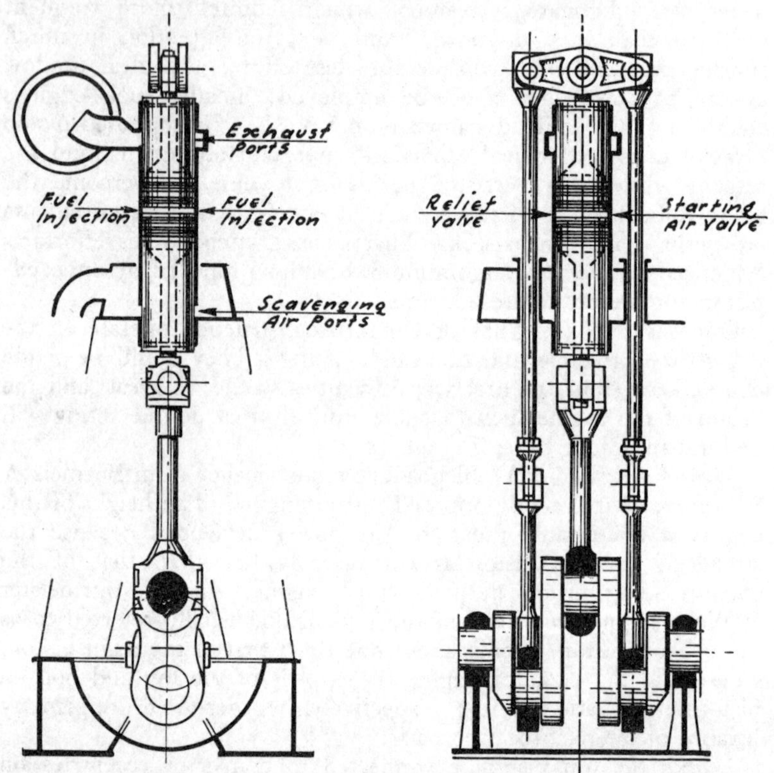

Fig. 249—Diagram of one cylinder of a Doxford opposed-piston engine

fuel is burnt in the space enclosed by the inner end of each piston and the cylinder liner. Two fuel-valves (see Fig. 61) are located horizontally at a point about mid-length. Air for combustion is admitted near the bottom of the cylinder and the burnt gases are released near the top of the cylinder. The air is admitted and the burnt gases expelled through two separate rows of ports cut in the wall of the cylinder liner, which are covered and uncovered as required by the pistons, the lower piston controlling the admission and cut-off of air and the upper piston acting similarly in regard to the burnt gases.

In the most recently-built Doxford engines certain alterations have been made, chiefly with a view to bringing the fuel-injection process into line with more common practice, and enclosing the top of the crankcase, again in accordance with usual practice, in order to prevent solid matter from the cylinders contaminating the crankcase lubricating oil, when operating on residual fuels. Other developments have been supercharging and oil cooling of the lower piston.

Fig. 250 will give a general idea of the construction of the Doxford opposed-piston engine. The only important difference between the small engine illustrated and larger engines of this make is that the reciprocating scavenging air-pump is sometimes located in line with the working cylinders, the piston being operated by a crank on the crankshaft instead of beam levers connected to the engine crosshead.

The bedplates, columns, and entablatures of Doxford opposed-piston engines built since about 1935 are of fabricated steel construction, the material used being ordinary mild steel of 28–32 tons tensile strength. The bedplate is given the required degree of rigidity by adopting deep girder formation and making the top, side, and bottom plates continuous where practicable. Several other engine-builders have since adopted the fabricated steel type of bedplate—although there does not appear to be any marked advantage in weight or cost when compared with cast-iron bedplates. The possibility of rejection because of casting faults is, however, eliminated.

The cylinders of Doxford engines have always been cooled by fresh water circulated in a closed system.

In any make or type of diesel engine it is wise to pre-heat the cylinders and pistons before starting, but such a practice is necessary in the pre-1958 Doxford engine if prompt and reliable starting is to be assured, because of the relatively low cylinder compression pressure (350 lb/sq.in.). Fuel injection, however, begins unusually early (28° before and continues until 22° after top dead centre) so that the combustion pressure of 650 lb/sq.in. is more in accordance with usual practice.

In order to maintain the internal surfaces of the cylinder liners at a relatively low temperature and so assist lubrication, the liners are only about one-inch thick. To enable them to withstand safely the combustion pressure the liners are reinforced at mid-length, i.e. in way of the combustion space, by shrinking on a cast-steel jacket and cast-steel rings above and below the jacket. The bores

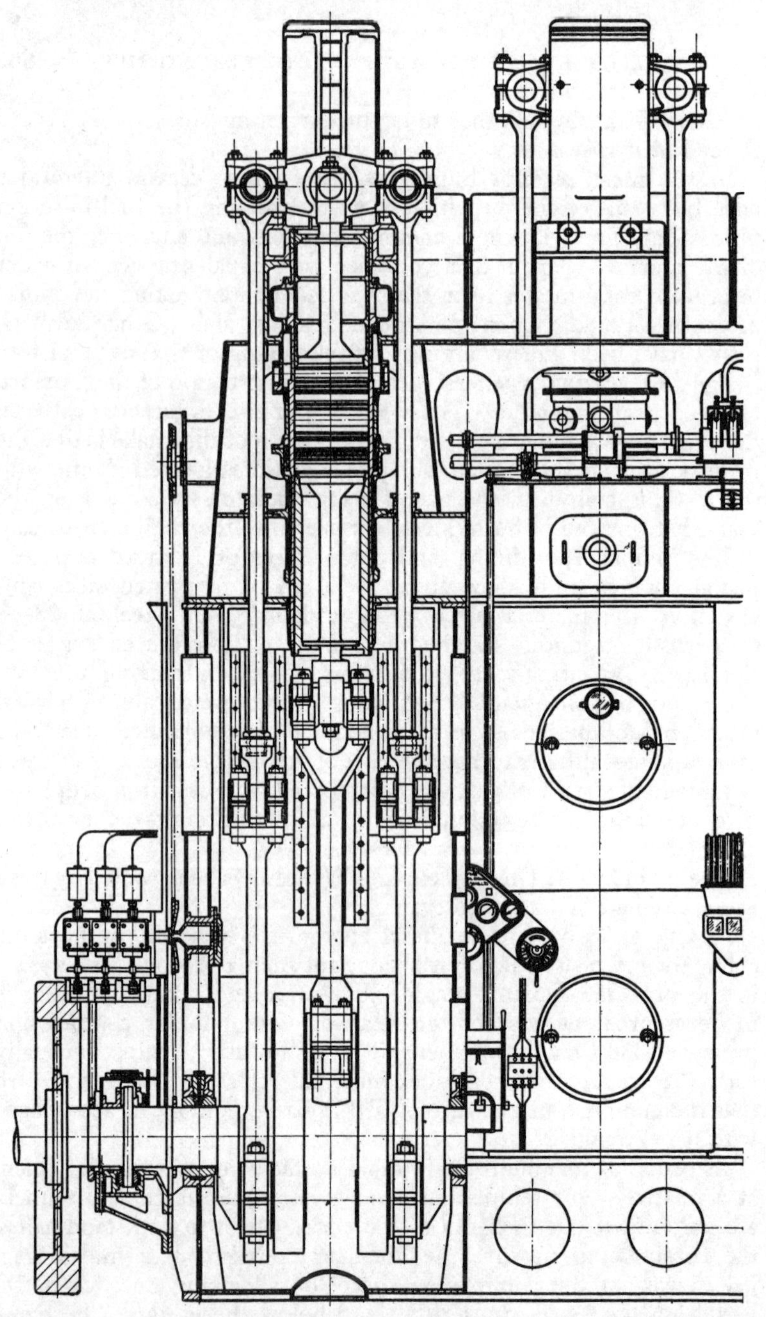

Fig. 250—The Doxford opposed-piston engine: section and elevation

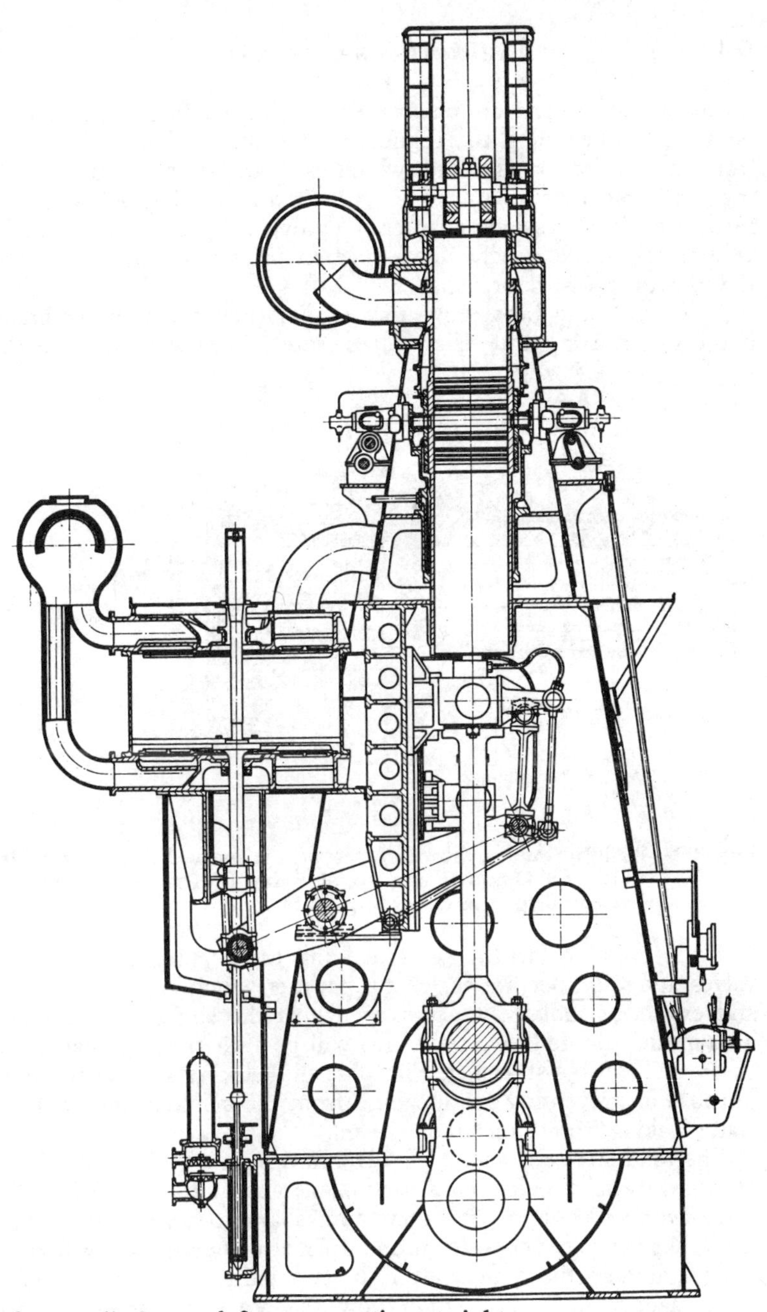

of two cylinders at left, cross-section at right

of the cast-steel parts are channelled to allow cooling water to pass between the liner and the reinforcing members. Apart, therefore, from the portions of the liner which carry the rubber sealing rings the wall thickness is uniform. The more usual practice is, as mentioned in a previous chapter, to provide a greater thickness in way of the space in which combustion takes place and in which the greatest pressure prevails.

As there would be a grave risk of distorting the cylinder liners if the fuel starting and relief valves were caused to land upon the

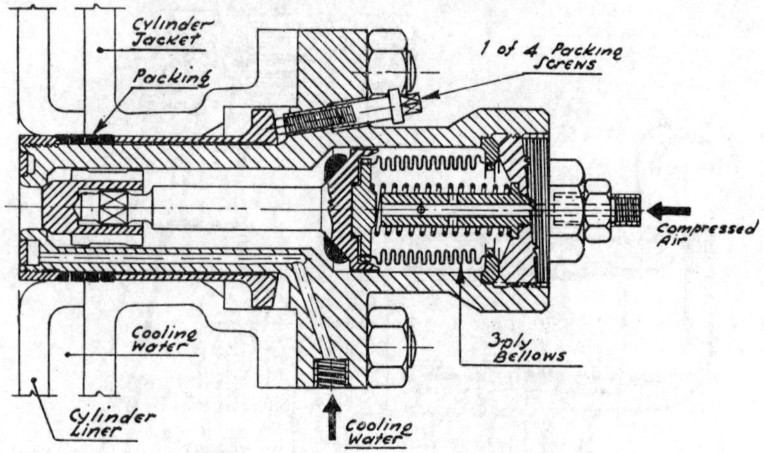

Fig. 251—"Lightning" type compressed-air loaded cylinder relief valve on Doxford engine, showing method of preventing escape of gas and cooling water

liners in order to form a gas-tight joint, the openings between the valves and the liner are sealed by packing which can be squeezed and expanded radially if necessary whilst the engine is operating. The means adopted to achieve this will be clear from an inspection of the relief valve shown in Fig. 251, the packing serving the dual purpose of preventing gas escaping from the cylinder and cooling-water leaking from the cylinder jacket.

The mild steel crankshaft of a Doxford opposed-piston engine is of necessity of peculiar construction, as shown in Fig. 252. The three-cylinder engines have their crankshaft, complete with thrust shaft, shrunk together to form one unit. In engines having four or more cylinders the crankshaft is in two parts connected together in a manner depending upon how the scavenge air-pumps are driven. In engines with one crank-driven pump, or four- and six-cylinder engines the pumps of which are driven by rocking levers from the engine crosshead, the connection of the two portions of the crankshaft is by means of a flexible coupling piece. Fig. 252 shows alternative means of connecting adopted by Doxford. The method of conveying lubricating oil from the crankshaft journals to the crankpins will be observed. A point worthy of note is that drilling of an oil hole through a shrunk joint is avoided by conveying the oil through pipes external to the crankwebs.

The crankshaft and crankpin bearing shells are spherical in shape, and the housings in the bedplate cross-girder and the foot of the connecting-rods are bored to correspond. The reason for this unusual arrangement is that to accommodate a three-throw crank between two supporting bearings necessitates a great distance between the bearings, consequently the crankshaft is bound to distort a small amount when subjected to bending and torsional stresses. With the more usual form of bearing such distortion, even though slight, would cause the crankshaft journals to tilt in the bearings and throw the connecting-rod out of alignment. As will be readily imagined, particular care is necessary when adjusting these special bearings. Not only must the whitemetal-lined bearings be carefully bedded on the pins and journals, but they must be bedded with equal care in their housings. The working clearances require to be slightly greater than for ordinary bearings (see Chapter 22), and the pintles provided to prevent the bearing shells from rotating must be a free fit in the crankshaft bearing-cap and foot of connecting-rod, so that the bearings will be free to accommodate themselves to the constantly changing alignment of the respective journals and crankpins.

As can be imagined, the flexible nature of the Doxford crankshaft tends to set up high-frequency torsional vibrations. To damp out these vibrations, which are more pronounced in the larger engines, a device called a " detuner " is provided, consisting of a flywheel mounted on the hub of a similar flywheel rigidly connected to either the forward or after end of the crankshaft. The latter is referred to as the fixed flywheel, and the former the floating flywheel. The fixed flywheel drives the floating flywheel through a heavy grid-shaped spring fitted in grooves in the rims of both wheels. The parts are lubricated from the bearing lubricating-oil system and a casing is fitted to contain the oil.

The pistons are machined from mild steel forgings. The grooves for the piston rings are either flame-hardened or have thin cast

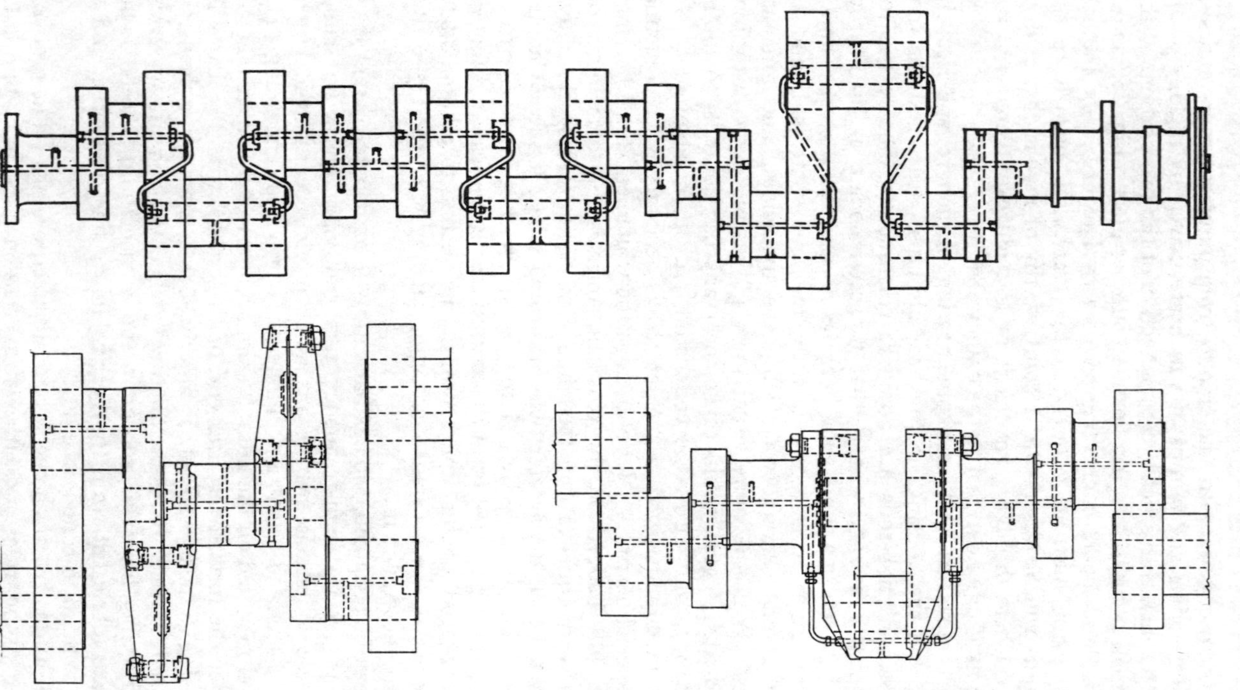

Fig. 252—Three-unit crankshaft of a Doxford engine and (below) details of flexible coupling for larger engine, and coupling with integral scavenge pump crank

steel rings electrically welded to the lower face of the grooves to increase resistance to wear. A cast-iron skirt is provided on each piston to blank the scavenge air and exhaust ports when the pistons are at their innermost positions. The skirt on the lower piston is of heavier construction for the purpose of primary vertical balancing. In three-cylinder engines the first two piston rings are situated nearer the crown of the pistons, as with such a small number of cylinders available for starting it is necessary to retain the starting air for a longer proportion of the stroke so that the engine will start from any position of the crankshaft. The pistons are provided with a broad renewable copper wearing ring situated under the nest of piston rings, the purpose of which is to centralise the piston in the cylinder and act as a rubbing strip.

The largest Doxford opposed-piston engine so far constructed has a cylinder bore of 750 mm and a combined piston stroke of 2,500 mm. Such a cylinder is capable of developing 1,500 h.p. at 110 r.p.m. and an M.I.P. of 90 lb/sq.in., but when supercharged a maximum output of 2,150 h.p. is obtained. It is also stated that if a six-cylinder 750 mm bore non-supercharged engine were replaced by a six-cylinder 650 mm bore supercharged engine the same power, namely 9,000 h.p. would be developed with a reduction in overall length of 10 ft, i.e. from 64 to 54 ft. Moreover, the weight of the engine would be reduced from 525 to 420 tons. Since in all supercharged engines a smaller proportion of the power developed is absorbed in friction, the mechanical efficiency of such engines is higher. In the Doxford engine this results in a reduction of 4 per cent in the fuel consumption per unit power developed at the thrust bearing.

Operating particulars obtained on the sea trials of a Doxford three-cylinder supercharged engine are as follows:—

Power developed	3,580
Revolutions per minute	120
Average M.I.P.	116
Exhaust temperature at cylinders	780°F (416°C)
,, ,, ,, turbine	740°F (393°C)
Turbo-blower r.p.m.	6,700
Cylinder combustion pressure lb/sq.in. ..	750
Supercharge pressure lb/sq.in.	4·6

The turbo-blowers operate in series with the normal reciprocating scavenge pumps. As in systems already described, the exhaust from different cylinders is separated and the turbine provided with two inlets to avoid interference due to pressure waves. In six-cylinder engines two turbo-blowers are employed, the exhaust from three of the cylinders entering the single inlet of one turbine, and the other three cylinders exhausting into the second turbo-blower.

Doxford's later fuel-injection system is shown diagrammatically in Fig. 253, from which it will be seen that a crank-operated fuel pump discharges into the head of a steel, bottle-shaped vessel, the pressure in which is maintained at 6,000 to 7,000 lb/sq.in. When injection of fuel into the cylinder is required the small cam-operated

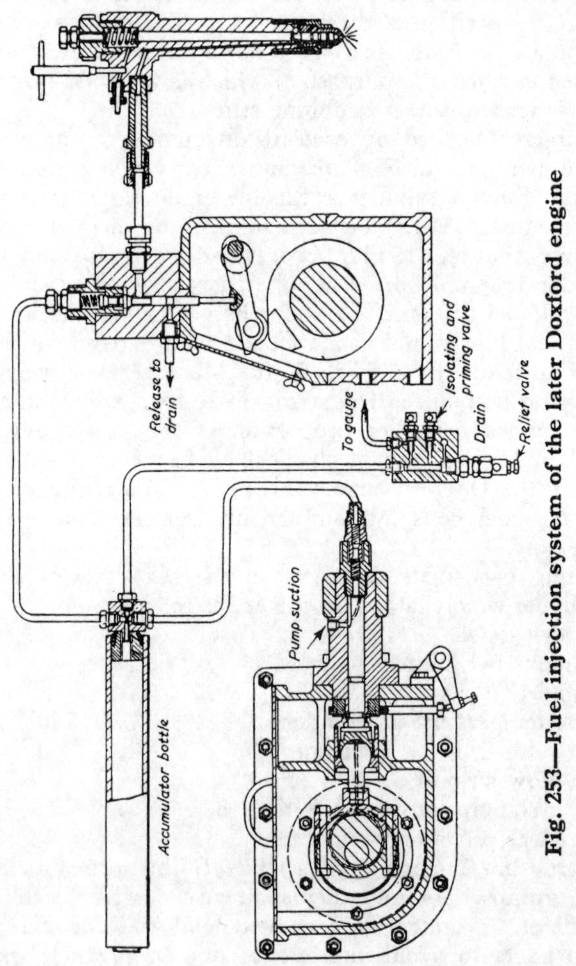

Fig. 253—Fuel injection system of the later Doxford engine

valve is lifted and fuel is allowed to flow to the fuel-valves. The fuel entering the fuel-valve at injection pressure opens the differential needle valve and fuel is sprayed into the cylinder. The beginning and end of injection is governed by the lever through which the small cam-operated valve, suitable for either direction of rotation, is lifted. This lever, it will be noted, is pivoted on an eccentric which, when rotated, raises or lowers the lever and varies the duration of injection.

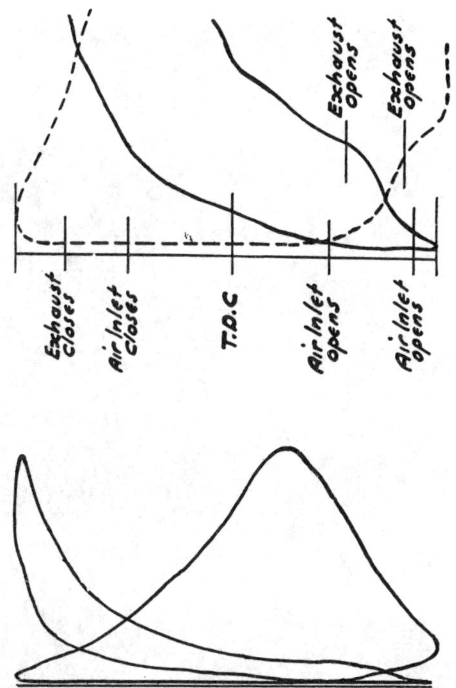

Fig. 254—Indicator diagrams taken from a Doxford supercharged engine

One pump, bottle, and timing valve are required for each cylinder. As there are two fuel-valves per cylinder in this engine both are supplied with fuel by the same pump. The quantity of fuel delivered to each cylinder is determined by the fuel pump, and there is a separate adjusting screw for regulating the quantity going to each valve. The bottle acts merely as an accumulator, the internal pressure being maintained by the pump. Variation in the speed of the engine is effected by adjusting the quantity of fuel delivered by the pump and at the same time the period of opening of the timing valve.

Indicator diagrams taken from a Doxford supercharged engine are shown in Fig. 254. At the bottom are the normal power and out-of-phase diagrams, while at the top are light-spring diagrams, the dotted line being the out-of-phase diagram.

Fig. 255 shows the top cylinders and the exhaust turbo-blowers of a six-cylinder Doxford supercharged engine.

Fig. 255—View of top cylinders and exhaust turbo-blowers of a Doxford 6-cylinder supercharged engine

Burmeister & Wain (Harland & Wolff)

This is another notable engine which operates on the opposed-piston principle. It is of the two-stroke type and may be either single-acting or double-acting, a cross-section through the latter type being shown in Fig. 8 (p. 36) and an enlarged sectional view of one cylinder in Fig. 256. As will be seen, this engine embodies many unique features.

It will be observed that unlike the Doxford engine, there is only one orthodox piston per cylinder, this being named the main piston in the illustration. There are, however, other pistons of unusual construction in the same cylinder, one in single-acting and two in double-acting engines. They are referred to as " exhaust pistons," since their main function is to cover and uncover the exhaust ports in the cylinder liner relative to the position of the main piston. The top and bottom exhaust pistons are connected together and are held a fixed distance apart. They reciprocate together, the cast-steel yokes secured to the pistons being connected together by four rods. As, however, the exhaust pistons are connected by two connecting rods to eccentrics secured to the crankshaft, they contribute to the rotation of the crankshaft, as in the Doxford engine. The stroke of the exhaust pistons is about one-third that of the main piston.

The main and exhaust pistons are of the same diameter, and as the running gear of both lead back to the crankshaft all vertical forces are balanced within the moving parts of the engine. In the latest design of engine, therefore, the long, heavy tie-bolts (described in Chapter 5) which in earlier designs relieved the main structure of tensile stresses, are no longer necessary. The bedplate and framing are welded steel structures of a strength sufficient only to withstand the forces produced when a ship is labouring in a heavy sea. The employment of eccentrics instead of cranks for the operation of the exhaust pistons enables the centres of adjacent crankshaft bearings to be kept reasonably close, so that the orthodox form of bearing is used. Actually, each cast-steel crank-web incorporates an eccentric, so that for a given speed and power this engine is very little longer than an engine with one crank per cylinder.

The uniflow system of scavenging is adopted, that is to say, the scavenging air enters one end of the cylinder and the exhaust gases are expelled from the opposite end. Scavenging air at about 2 lb/sq.in. is supplied by positive displacement rotary type blowers (Fig. 176) mounted on the back of the engine and driven by roller chains, the driving sprocket wheel being secured to the engine

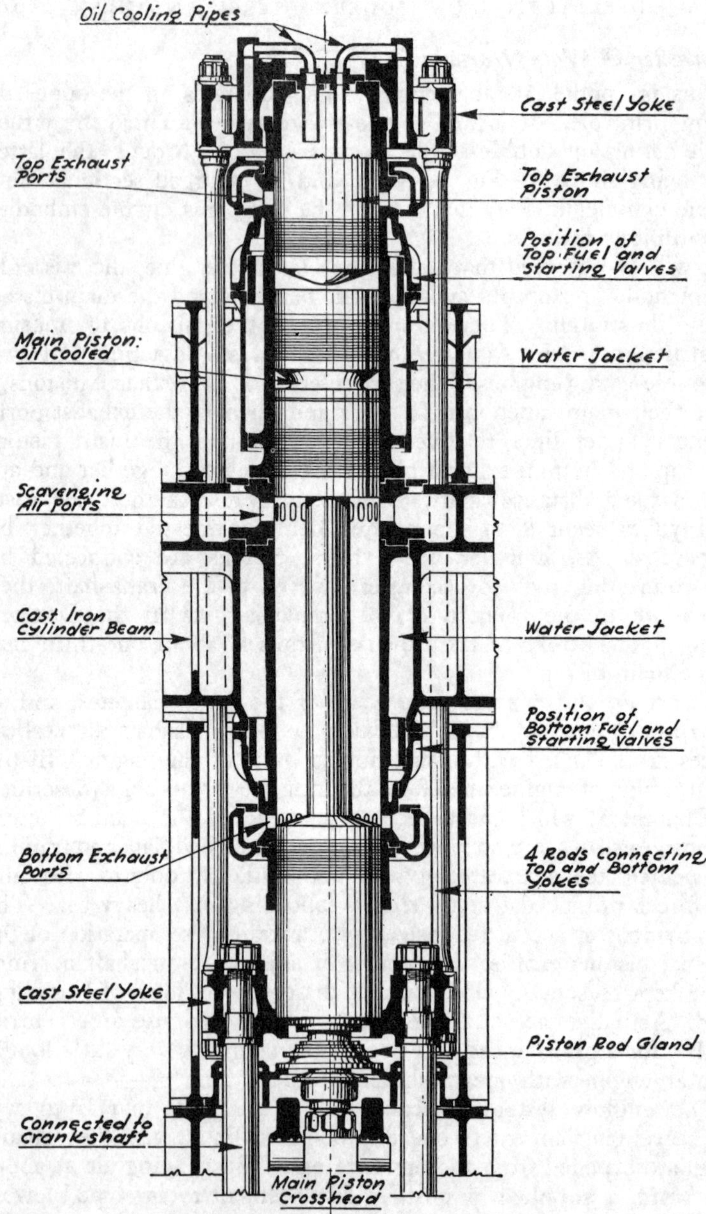

Fig. 256—Sectional view of one cylinder of a 2-stroke double-acting engine (Burmeister & Wain)

crankshaft. In the single-acting engine the bottom of the cylinder is enclosed by the scavenging air-receiver, so that the piston-rod packing situated at the top of the crankcase must prevent scavenging air entering the crankcase, in addition to preventing lubricating oil leaving the crankcase.

The main and exhaust pistons are internally cooled by lubricating oil from the bearing system, and the cylinder jackets by fresh water circulating in a closed system. The piston rods of the double-acting engines are enclosed in cast-iron sleeves, which protect the steel rods from the burning gases in the bottom cylinder. The cooling oil passes through an annulus between the piston rod and the sleeve on its way to the main piston, so that the oil serves the dual purpose of cooling the sleeve as well as the piston. After circulating the piston the oil returns through a central hole in the piston rod.

As will be noted upon referring to Fig. 256, the piston rod passes through the lower exhaust piston, so that the packing necessary to prevent leakage of gas from the cylinder into the engine-room is incorporated in the outer end of this exhaust piston. Since the conditions under which the packing must operate are very similar to those prevailing when the packing is situated in a fixed bottom cylinder cover, the design of packing is similar. The fact that the exhaust piston is moving in an upward direction at the same time as the piston rod is moving downwards has no deleterious effect upon the packing.

The cylinders are secured at mid-length to a robustly constructed entablature in which is incorporated the scavenge air-receiver. The cylinders are free to expand above and below the entablature. The cylinder liners are made of vanadium cast-iron and are provided with cast-iron jackets through which fresh water is circulated. Each main piston is lubricated at two diametrically opposite points located near the end of the top half of the piston and at two similar points for the bottom half of the piston, but at right-angles to those for the lower half of the piston. Each exhaust piston is lubricated at three equi-spaced points located about the middle of the nest of piston rings when the pistons are at the end of their outward stroke.

Scavenge air enters the cylinder through ports situated at mid-length and passes longitudinally through the cylinder, the burnt gases leaving through ports near the top and bottom of the cylinder. The scavenge air-blowers are of the rotary type and are driven by a chain from the main crankshaft. The chain-drive arrangement is shown in Fig. 257.

As in the Doxford engine, each cylinder is provided with two fuel-valves situated diametrically opposite each other. The valves of the Burmeister & Wain engine, however, are of the automatic type operated by pressure built up by the fuel pump. Both these components are fully described in Chapters 8 and 10.

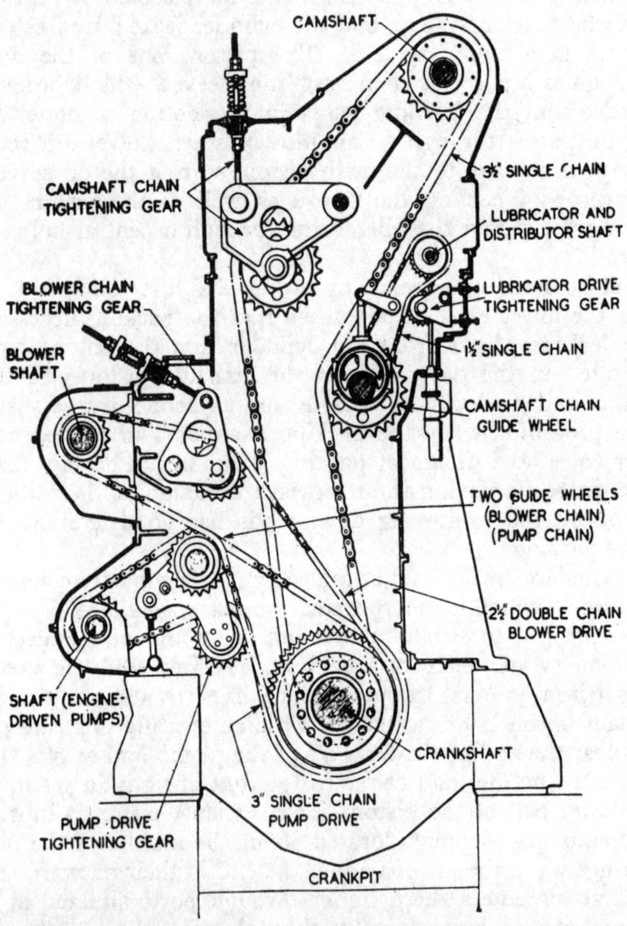

Fig. 257—Chain-drive arrangement in Harland & Wolff engines

The two-stroke single-acting Burmeister & Wain engine is made in two forms. In the first the upper end of the cylinder is the same as the double-acting opposed-piston engine just described and illustrated, the return of burnt gases being effected by an exhaust piston reciprocating in the cylinder. In the other form the cylinder head is fixed, the burnt gases being expelled through a cam-operated poppet or mushroom valve in the cylinder head. A diagrammatic, sectional view of one of these engines is shown in Fig. 258. As in the case of the double-acting opposed-piston engines, both forms of single-acting engines can be supercharged to a degree which will result in about 35 per cent increase in power output over the same engine when not supercharged.

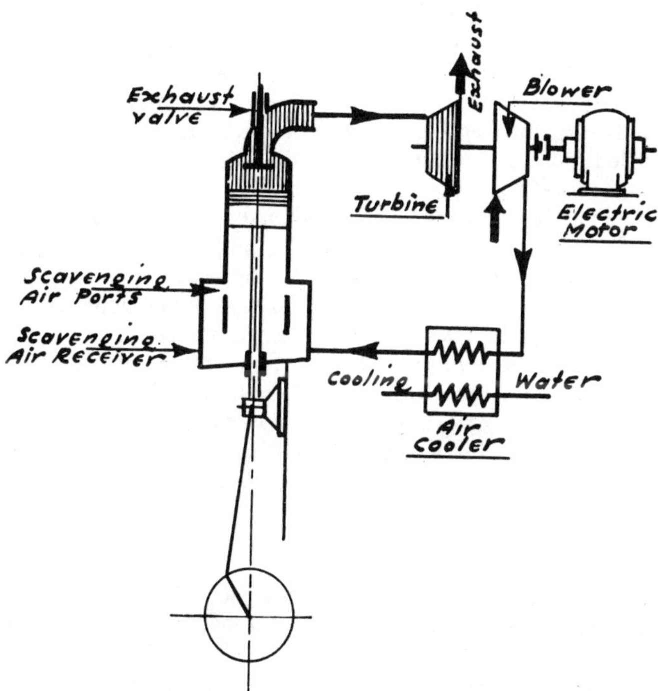

Fig. 258—Diagram of Burmeister & Wain supercharged system

As will be seen from Fig. 258, the lower end of the cylinder is enclosed by the scavenge air-receiver. A rotary blower mounted on the back of the engine delivers air at about 2 lb/sq.in. pressure into this receiver from which is passes into the cylinder through the row of ports shown in the illustration when the piston nears the end of its working stroke and uncovers them. The scavenge air ports are evenly spaced around the cylinder and are shaped in a way which gives the air a swirling motion as it enters the cylinder. The scavenge air-receiver, which forms a rigid longitudinal girder, accommodates and supports the cylinders. The exhaust manifold is made of welded steel plating, heavily lagged to prevent radiation of heat and provided with flexible fittings to allow free expansion and contraction.

The cylinder heads and piston crowns are made of chrome–molybdenum cast steel and the piston skirt of alloy cast-iron. The exhaust valve is made from a single forging of special heat-resisting steel and the valve seat of pearlitic cast-iron, while the valve body is made of close-grained grey cast-iron and secured in position in the usual manner. The pistons are oil-cooled, the oil being supplied from the bearing system; the cylinders and exhaust valve are cooled by fresh water and the fuel-valve is oil-cooled from a system separate from the bearing system.

The cams and rollers of the exhaust-valve operating gear are made of steel and are case-hardened. The camshaft is situated on a level with the bottom of the cylinders and is chain-driven from the crankshaft in the usual way, the exhaust valve being actuated through long push-rods, the advantage being a shorter chain drive. During the reversal of the engine a lost-motion clutch enables the same cam to be used for both directions of rotation.

The Burmeister & Wain impulse system of supercharging their engines is also shown diagrammatically in Fig. 258, while a sectional view of a single-acting poppet valve engine is shown in Fig. 259. To illustrate the diversity of the methods adopted to achieve the same end a diagram of the supercharging arrangement on Bremer–Vulkan/M.A.N. engines is shown in Fig. 260.

In the first Burmeister & Wain supercharged engines the exhaust turbo-blowers and the engine-driven Rootes blower (Fig. 176) were connected in series, the air being drawn from the atmosphere by the turbo-blower and delivered via an air cooler to the Rootes blower, which in turn delivered it to the scavenge air space in a manner somewhat similar to the arrangement shown in Fig. 260.

In more recent Burmeister & Wain engines the Rootes blower is not fitted, the scavenging air, when starting or running at speeds too low to drive the exhaust-gas turbine, being supplied by driving the normally exhaust-gas-driven blower by an electric motor, as shown in Fig. 258. This electric motor is fitted with automatic disengaging mechanism, so that after the engine has attained a speed

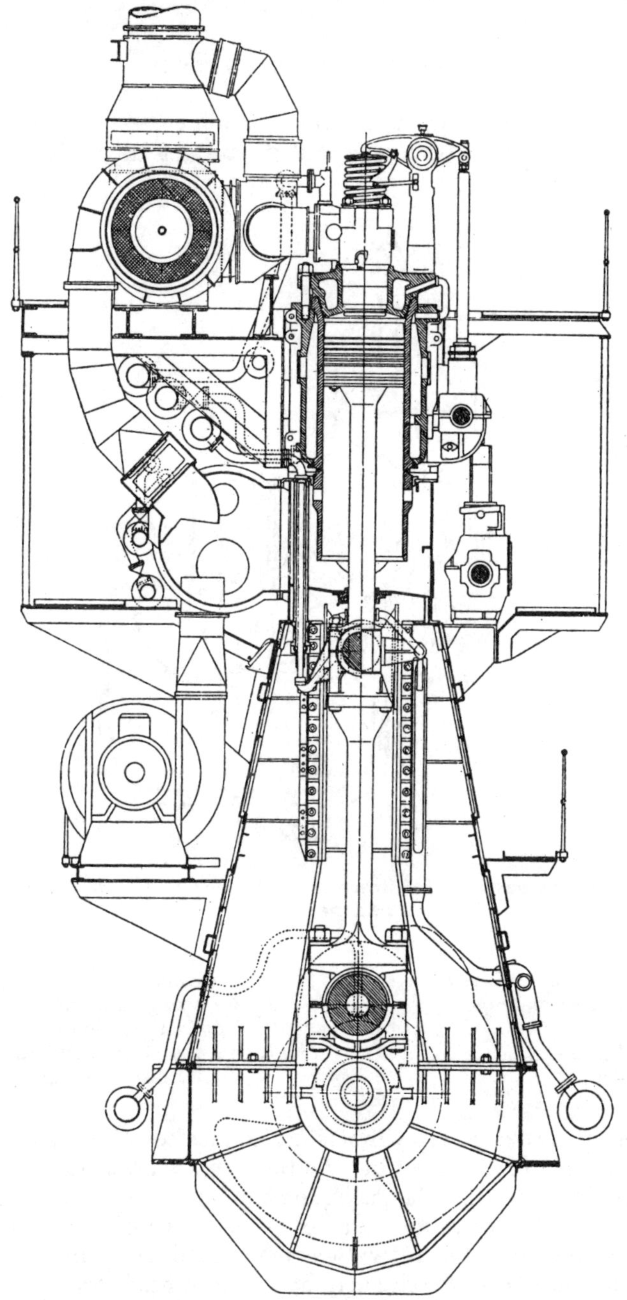

Fig. 259—Two-stroke single-acting turbo-charged poppet valve engine (Burmeister & Wain)

sufficient to drive the exhaust turbine, at a predetermined speed, the electric motor drive disengages and the turbine takes over the duty of driving the blower.

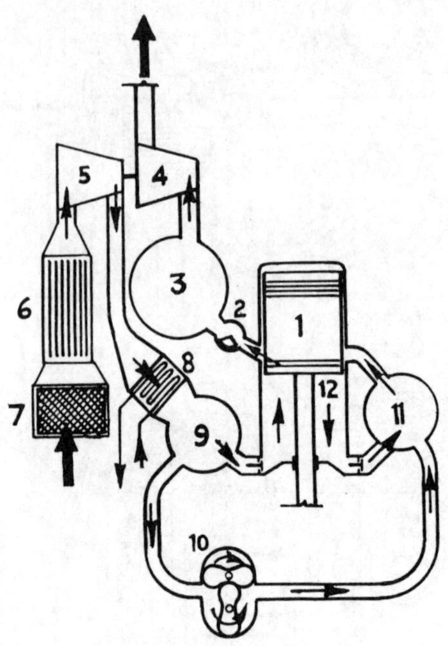

Fig. 260—Diagram of the Bremer-Vulkan-M.A.N. scavenging supercharged engine

1. Piston
2. Rotary slide valve
3. Exhaust manifold
4. Turbine
5. Blower
6. Silencer
7. Air filter
8. Air cooler
9. First stage manifold
10. Rootes type blower
11. Second stage manifold
12. Under piston pump

Not more than three cylinders are connected to the same turbine inlet and the pipes conveying the burnt gases are made as short as possible to ensure that the maximum amount of energy is transmitted to the rotor blades of the turbine. This is one of the reasons why large engines are provided with as many as three turbo-blowers, all of which are usually situated at cylinder-head level, as shown in Fig. 255.

The free-piston engine

This type of power producer is a combination of a diesel engine and an open-cycle gas turbine. Its principal advantage over the gas turbine proper is that combustion of fuel takes place under conditions similar to those prevailing in the diesel engine, with the result that the turbine portion of the plant is subjected only to gas at moderately high temperatures. The disadvantage is that it is much more complicated than the gas turbine and introduces reciprocating parts subject to wear and tear.

The simplest form of this plant consists of a generator in which gas produced from the combustion of a mixture of liquid fuel and air is delivered into a turbine which transmits power through a speed-reduction gear to the ship's propeller. The gas generator comprises two stepped opposed pistons, mechanically linked to ensure synchronisation, and reciprocating in a single two-diameter cylinder. As the pistons approach each other the large-diameter portions compress air for charging the smaller power cylinders and afterwards scavenging them.

Fig. 261 shows, diagrammatically, the various stages in the operation of a free-piston engine, working on the two-stroke principle. The gas generators are started by admitting compressed air to the extreme ends of the cylinder from an external source—as in the case of the diesel engine. Beginning at (A), it will be seen that the two differential pistons are in their extreme outward positions. At this point, urged by compressed air above the larger-diameter pistons, they begin to move inward, closing the inlet ports (1) and then the exhaust ports (2), and compressing the air trapped between the two power pistons. At a certain point on the in-stroke the air in the compressor cylinders is discharged into a chamber surrounding the power cylinder.

When the pistons reach the innermost position, as shown in (B), the air between the ends of the power pistons has been compressed to a pressure and temperature sufficient to ignite and burn the atomised fuel injected. The consequent increase in pressure forces the pistons apart and towards the outer ends of the cylinder. After the pistons have completed about three-quarters of the outward stroke the exhaust ports and then the inlet ports are uncovered, as shown in (C). The opening of these two sets of ports releases the products of combustion—still at a pressure of about 45 lb/sq.in.—and the scavenging air sweeps out the remaining burnt gases. The power cylinder is therefore left full of pure air ready for the next combustion process.

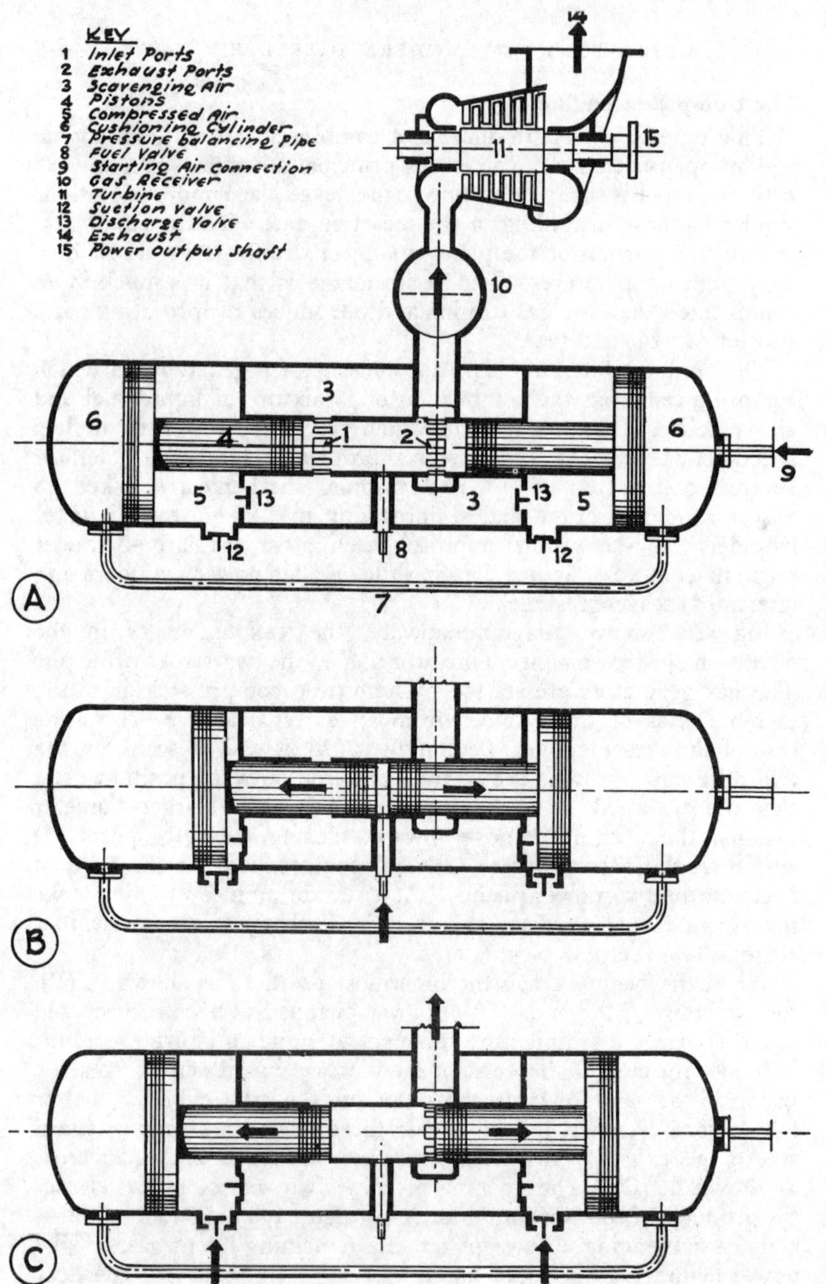

Fig. 261—Diagrammatic views of free piston engine

At the moment the pistons begin their outward stroke the air-delivery valves close and the suction valves open. When, therefore, the pistons reach the extreme outward position the compressor cylinders are full of air at atmospheric pressure ready to be compressed and delivered into the chamber surrounding the power cylinders, wherein a low pressure is maintained.

The pistons are brought to rest at the end of the outward stroke and driven in the reverse direction by enclosing the outer ends of the cylinder and utilising them as cushion, or "bounce," cylinders. These bounce cylinders are connected by an equalising pipe, and the various parts concerned with the operation are so proportioned that the energy transmitted to the air is sufficient not only to limit the travel of the pistons but to return them to the inner position ready for the next combustion stroke.

The generator unit is therefore a source of gas at a pressure of about 45 lb/sq.in. and a temperature of 850°F (454°C); mechanical power is obtained by passing the gas through a turbine, into which is incorporated an astern turbine for reversing the direction of motion of the propeller. The loss due to the windage of the astern blading when running ahead is about 2 per cent. Alternatively, the turbine can be coupled to the propeller shaft through a reversing reduction gear-box.

For an installation giving 10,000 s.h.p. it is claimed that the fuel consumption for all purposes would be 0·40 lb per s.h.p. per hour. Twelve gas generator units would, however, be required to feed the two turbines, and it is doubtful whether the maintenance work on the reciprocating components would be much less than on conventional diesel machinery.

CHAPTER 29

Useful workshop hints

The workshop of the modern motorship is generally equipped with efficient machine tools, so that practically all running repairs between periodical dry docking can be done on board, if the engineers are able to use the tools properly. Since many engineers are not fortunate enough to obtain machine-shop experience during their apprenticeship, the following practical notes on the principal machining operations may prove useful.

The principal machine tools used in an engineering workshop are the lathe, drilling, milling, grinding, planing, shaping and slotting machines. The four former are continuous-running machines, while the remaining three machines have a reciprocating motion—i.e. a cutting and a non-cutting or return stroke.

The lathe

This is undoubtedly the most useful of the machine tools installed on board ship. It is called upon to remove stock from various classes of metal, such as steel, cast iron, bronze, gun-metal, etc. of a varying degree of hardness.

To operate on these metals successfully, tools of a variety of shapes are required, also a large range of speeds are necessary. The sketch (Fig. 262) and the following table give the average angles for round-nosed tools used for rough-cutting steel and cast iron:—

Material	Clearance angle	Back slope	Side slope
Mild steel	6°	8°	22°
Hard steel	6°	8°	14°
Cast iron, medium hard ..	6°	8°	14°
,, ,, very hard	6°	6°	Horizontal

For rough-cutting very soft steel and iron of approximately 22 tons tensile strength, the most efficient tool is one having a lipped cutting edge with a back slope of about 30°.

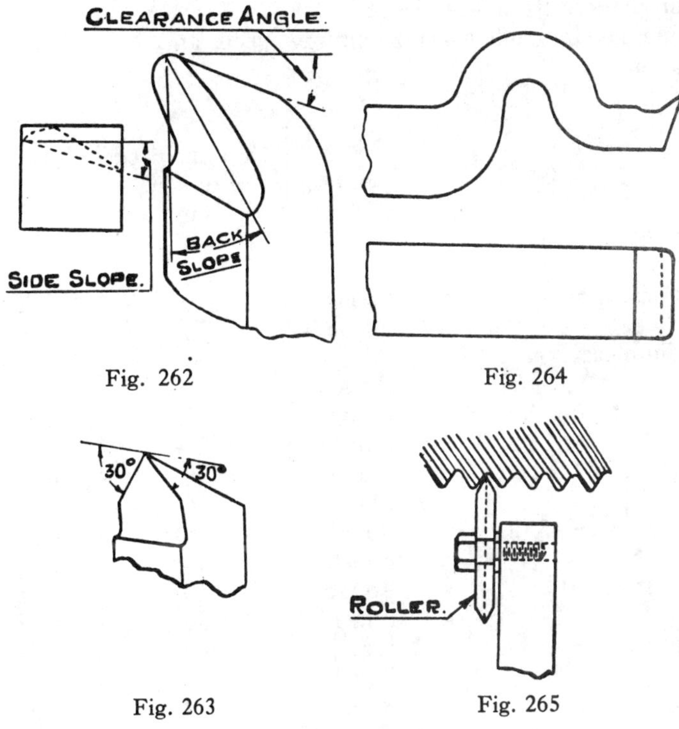

Fig. 262

Fig. 264

Fig. 263

Fig. 265

Figs. 262—265
Lathe cutting tools

For rough-cutting alloy, a diamond-shape tool is usually preferred, as illustrated in sketch (Fig. 263), having a clearance angle of 30°, a back slope of 30°, and no side slope. Sometimes no back slope is given to such a tool, which is then easier to make.

For finish-turning either cast iron or steel, a broad flat-nosed tool is generally used with a coarse feed; if a bright finish is desired on steel, a spring tool should be used of similar shape to that shown in Fig. 264, with a cutting compound which can be made of soft soap dissolved in water, with a little common soda added to prevent rusting.

As far as possible, all tools should have as broad a cutting edge as possible, in order that the heat generated may quickly be dissipated.

The most efficient tool steel for rough-cutting is high-speed steel, but for finishing with a spring tool (Fig. 264), a good-quality carbon tool steel should be used.

The following table gives the cutting speeds and feeds for various materials:—

Material	Operation	Cutting speed in feet per min.	Feed per rev., in.
Soft cast iron	Rough	40	0·25
	Finish	70	0·05
Medium cast iron ..	Rough	25	0·25
	Finish	40	0·03
Hard cast iron	Rough	15	0·25
	Finish	25	0·02
Soft steel, 22 tons ..	Rough	40	0·375
	Finish	80	0·06
Medium steel, 35 tons	Rough	20	0·25
	Finish	45	0·05
Hard steel, 70 tons ..	Rough	10	0·25
	Finish	30	0·03
Brass	Rough	60	0·25
	Finish	100	0·02
Copper	Rough	200	0·25
	Finish	300	0·015

In the above table, the feed per revolution for finishing depends on the width of the tool. The figures given can be considerably increased with a broad-nosed tool.

Frequently very hard material has to be operated upon. A useful cutting compound, which will be found very helpful in such cases, is a mixture composed of half a gill of castor oil, one tablespoonful of sulphur, and one tablespoonful of cylinder oil. A drip composed of two parts paraffin and one part turpentine also ensures easy cutting. A suitable lubricant is essential to maintain good sharp edges on the tools, which would otherwise break, owing to the excessive power required to cut with blunt tools. The shape of the tool may also be modified, giving a smaller clearance angle, back slope, and side slope, to facilitate the operation on very hard metals.

For screwing with a single-point tool, the surface speed for brass should be 20 to 32 feet per minute, and for steel and cast iron from 8 to 16 feet per minute. Lard oil will be found very good as a cutting medium, and will give a good finish.

If a thread is found too small on the diameter, a useful tool for swelling the thread is shown in Fig. 265. The angle of the roller requires to be less than the angle of thread, as illustrated, and same should be worked from side to side of thread until the correct diameter is obtained.

The depth of cut for any material depends, of course, upon the size and power of the lathe, and can be ascertained from the actual machine. Naturally, if the edge of the tool is kept in good condition, less power will be required than if the edge of the tool is dull. When setting a tool in the tool rest, the point of the cutting edge should be in line with the lathe centres; if high or low in relation to the centres, the tool will not cut freely, and the work will have a tendency to ride out of the centres.

When it is desired to turn long cylindrical work, such as valve spindles, a steady should always be used, otherwise true turning is impossible. A steady is usually supplied with the machine, as is also a face-plate, driving plate, and independent four-jaw chuck. A useful tool, although not generally included in the standard lathe equipment, is a drill chuck to fit into the spindle of the loose headstock. Where holes are required to be bored in pieces of an unsymmetrical nature, which are gripped in the chuck or mounted on the face-plate of the lathe, balance-weights should be attached, in order that the holes may be truly cylindrical.

Drilling

The drilling machines usually found in ships' workshops are of the vertical type, capable of drilling holes up to 1½ inches in diameter. The lower end of the spindle is bored a Morse taper, generally No. 4, suitable sleeves being available for the smaller-sized drills.

Drilling a hole is quite a simple matter, but if accuracy is desired it is important that the drills should be ground correctly on the cutting edges. If a drill is ground with the point central, but the cutting edges at different angles, a condition as illustrated in Fig. 266 is obtained. It will be obvious that with a drill ground in this way, the cutting edge *b* will do no work, and the edge *a* double the work. Consequently, it will take a much longer time to drill a given hole, and the overworked edge may fail to stand up to the strain. Further, the drill will have a tendency to press on that side of the hole opposite the effective cutting edge and make the finished hole larger in diameter than desired.

If both cutting edges are ground to the same angle, but the point of the drill is not central, as illustrated in Fig. 267, the drill

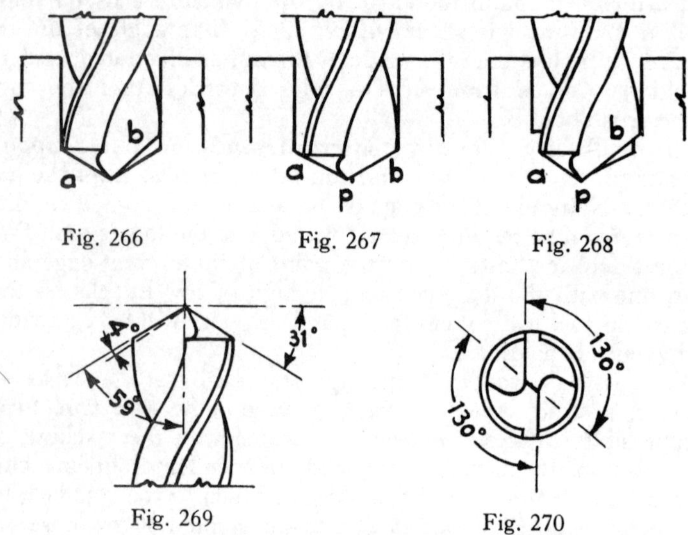

Fig. 266 Fig. 267 Fig. 268

Fig. 269 Fig. 270

Figs. 266—270
Cutting edges of drills

will revolve about its own axis, and since this axis is not directly in line with the point of the drill a bending action is set up in the drill, which may break. Also, the shoulder *b* being further away from the point *p* than the shoulder *a*, the diameter of the finished hole will be proportionately larger than the diameter of the drill. This is sometimes useful when it is desired to drill a hole slightly larger than the available drill. The feed in such cases, however, should be carefully applied.

Fig. 268 illustrates the result obtained by a combination of the two previous errors in grinding a drill. In this case the point of the drill *p* is out of centre, the two cutting edges are of unequal lengths, and are also at different angles to the axis of the drilling-machine spindle. With such a drill it will be apparent that the short cutting edge *a* will drill a hole of a size determined by its distance from the point *p*, while the other cutting edge *b* will merely open the hole out to a larger diameter. In such cases the finished hole will be larger than the drill, one cutting edge will do nearly all the work, and a bending strain will be set up in the drill.

The correct cutting angles are shown in Fig. 269. The backing, as shown by the dotted line, is important, and should amount to about 4°.

On a properly ground drill there are three cutting edges, the relative angles of which are shown in Fig. 270. It will be noted that what is commonly called the point of a drill should really be a cutting edge.

The table on p. 688 gives drilling speeds and feeds for the materials indicated:—

An efficient lubricating medium for drilling holes in steel is a solution of soft soap and water with soda added to prevent rusting. For hard steel, an efficient lubricant is a mixture in the following proportions:—2 gills of castor oil, one tablespoonful of powdered sulphur, and one tablespoonful of heavy steam-cylinder oil. In tempered steel, a hole can be bored by leaving the drill dead hard, and using turpentine as a lubricant. In such cases, the feed should be very light, otherwise the drill will be broken. Cast iron should be drilled without any lubricant. To drill hard cast iron or steel, the drilling speed should be reduced.

It is sometimes found useful to have a boring attachment for the drilling machine. It consists of a cutter bar, having one end turned to suit the spindle of the machine, the other end to have a rectangular hole to take the cutting tools. The cutter bar may be guided in a pilot hole in the work, or if a cored hole is to be cleaned out, the cutter bar may be guided by a hole in the drilling-machine table.

To drill small holes in very hard steel which it is not desired to heat-treat, cover the surface of the steel to be bored with melted beeswax; when coated and cold, make a hole the required size in the wax with a pointed instrument, and fill it with strong nitric acid. After allowing it to soak for an hour, rinse off and apply again. It will gradually eat through.

A quicker method is to use a piece of copper rod, the size of the hole required, one end being gripped in the lathe or drilling machine chuck and the other fed with emery powder of moderate fineness. In such cases, a guide is usually necessary to prevent

Speeds and feeds for high-speed drills

Drill Size	Cast iron of average quality			Medium steel			Hard or very tough steel		
	r.p.m.	Feed		r.p.m.	Feed		r.p.m.	Feed	
		In. per rev.	In. per min.		In. per rev.	In. per min.		In. per rev.	In. per min.
¼	1,500	·010 to ·015	15 to 23	1,200	·008 to ·012	9 to 14	600 to 900	·006 to ·008	3½ to 6
⅜	1,000	·012 to ·020	12 to 20	800	·008 to ·012	6 to 9	400 to 600	·006 to ·008	2½ to 5
½	750	·015 to ·025	11 to 19	600	·010 to ·015	6 to 9	300 to 460	·008 to ·010	2 to 4½
⅝	600	·015 to ·025	9 to 15	500	·010 to ·015	5 to 8	220 to 360	·008 to ·010	2 to 3½
¾	500	·018 to ·030	9 to 15	400	·010 to ·020	4 to 7	200 to 300	·010 to ·012	1¾ to 3½
⅞	440	·018 to ·030	8 to 13	350	·010 to ·020	3½ to 7	180 to 260	·010 to ·012	1¾ to 3¼
1	380	·018 to ·030	7 to 11	300	·010 to ·020	3 to 6	150 to 225	·010 to ·015	1½ to 3
1⅛	340	·020 to ·030	7 to 11	270	·015 to ·020	4 to 5½	140 to 200	·012 to ·020	1½ to 4
1¼	300	·020 to ·030	6 to 9	240	·015 to ·020	3½ to 5	120 to 180	·012 to ·020	1½ to 3½
1⅜	275	·020 to ·030	5½ to 8	220	·015 to ·020	3 to 4½	110 to 165	·012 to ·020	1¼ to 3¼
1½	250	·020 to ·035	5 to 8	200	·015 to ·020	3 to 4	100 to 150	·012 to ·020	1¼ to 3
1⅝	235	·020 to ·035	5 to 8	185	·015 to ·020	2¾ to 3¾	95 to 140	·012 to ·020	1 to 2¾
1¾	220	·020 to ·035	4½ to 7½	170	·015 to ·020	2½ to 3½	90 to 130	·012 to ·020	1 to 2½
1⅞	205	·020 to ·035	4 to 7	160	·015 to ·020	2½ to 3	80 to 120	·012 to ·020	1 to 2¼
2	190	·020 to ·035	4 to 7	150	·015 to ·020	2¼ to 3	75 to 114	·012 to ·020	1 to 2¼
2⅛	180	·020 to ·040	3½ to 7	140	·020 to ·030	2¾ to 4	70 to 108	·012 to ·020	¾ to 2
2¼	170	·020 to ·040	3½ to 7	130	·020 to ·030	2½ to 4	65 to 102	·012 to ·020	¾ to 2
2⅜	165	·020 to ·040	3¼ to 6½	120	·020 to ·030	2½ to 3½	60 to 95	·012 to ·020	¾ to 2
2½	155	·020 to ·040	3 to 6	115	·020 to ·030	2¼ to 3½	60 to 90	·012 to ·020	¾ to 1¾
2⅝	145	·020 to ·040	3 to 6	110	·020 to ·030	2¼ to 3¼	55 to 85	·012 to ·020	¾ to 1¾
2¾	140	·020 to ·040	2¾ to 5½	108	·020 to ·030	2 to 3¼	55 to 80	·012 to ·020	¾ to 1¾
2⅞	130	·020 to ·040	2½ to 5	104	·020 to ·030	2 to 3	52 to 77	·012 to ·020	¾ to 1½
3	125	·020 to ·040	2½ to 5	100	·020 to ·030	2 to 3	50 to 75	·012 to ·020	¾ to 1½

the copper rod bending. This can be made from a piece of hardwood, with a hole in it the size of the copper rod, and fixed so as to keep the rod in position. Oil should be used to keep the emery in place. After a little while, the grains of emery will bed themselves into the end of the copper rod, thus forming a very effective grinding tool.

Drilling holes in glass is a very delicate operation, but for holes up to ½-inch diameter an old three-cornered file is suitable. It should be ground near the end, gripped in the chuck, and rotated at high speed, using a mixture of camphor and turpentine as a lubricant.

The glass should rest on a piece of felt or rubber not much larger than the hole to be drilled. When half-way through, the glass should be turned over and drilled to meet the first cut, otherwise there is every likelihood of the glass being broken.

For larger holes, use a brass or copper tube having an outside diameter equal to the size of the required hole. Revolve the tube at high speed, and feed with carborundum and light machine-oil between the end of the tube and the glass.

To file glass, use a smooth file wet with turpentine.

Shaping

The shaping machine is a very useful tool on board ship, the most convenient size having a 12-inch stroke. With such a machine tool, numerous jobs can be done, such as facing flanges, taking stock from the joints of bearings when it is desired to compensate for wear in the bore, cutting keyways, etc.

The cutting speed for various materials is as follows:—

Brass or bronze	150 ft/min.
Cast iron	90 ,,
,, steel	80 ,,
Mild steel	70 ,,
Nickel–chrome steel	60 ,,

Grinding

For dressing-up lathe tools no special skill is required if an ordinary or double-headed grinding machine is available, but where it is desired to do precision grinding, either external or internal, it is necessary that certain conditions be strictly observed if satisfactory results are to be obtained.

In a few of the larger motorship workshops there are correctly-designed grinding machines, having the necessary rigidity to grind truly cylindrical, and to any practical limits of accuracy. Successful grinding, however, does not finish with the machine.

The emery or abrasive wheel must be in perfect balance, as otherwise the work will show vibration or chatter marks, also the work will not be cylindrical. In either external or internal grinding, the wheel should never travel off the work. If it is allowed to do so, the result in external grinding will be that the face of the wheel will be sheared away by the sharp edges of the work, and, in internal grinding, the hole will be bell-mouthed. The traverse of the wheel should be just sufficient to allow not more than one-third of the width of the wheel to project beyond the work.

The wheel surface speed for external grinding lies between 5,500 and 6,500 ft/min.; below 5,500 ft/min. excessive wheel wear is liable. These speeds apply to steels of all grades. The most efficient speed for low tensile materials, such as cast iron, is 5,000 ft/min., while the travel of wheel should be about two-thirds the width of wheel per revolution of the work. This ensures the wheel preserving a flat face, since if the traverse of the wheel is less than one-half of the width of the wheel, the latter will wear convex.

For external grinding, the surface speed of the part being ground should average 60 ft/min.

The cross-feed for external grinding should be from 0·0005 to 0·0015 inch per each reversal of table, depending upon the material being ground and the quality of the wheel used. For ship work the lowest dimension is recommended.

The water supply for external grinding should be of ample volume, say, not less than 5 gallons per minute for a 14-inch wheel. Soda should be mixed with the water to prevent rusting of the polished surface.

The amount left on for grinding varies according to the quality and state of material. For material in a soft state and rough turned, the amount left on can vary from 0·02 to 0·04 inch, according to the diameter of material. For case-hardened work the turned finish must be finer and a much smaller grinding allowance made, say 0·005 to 0·02 inch, as the question of the depth of case has to be considered. For holes less than 6 inches diameter, the diameter of the wheel will be from 0·6 to 0·9 of the hole diameter. On holes above 6 inches diameter the diameter of the wheel will be governed by the strength of the spindle.

The most efficient wheel surface speed for internal grinding is from 1,000 to 4,000 ft/min.

For internal grinding, the surface speed of the part being ground should be from 100 to 120 ft/min., and the cross-feed should be hand-operated, as the spring of the spindle due to the wheel being generally overhung has to be considered. It is a good plan to fit a stop on the hand adjustment and set it to the diameter required. The surfaces of the grinding wheel should be kept clean, and should not be allowed to glaze; the best tool for truing-up the wheel surface is a diamond, mounted in a shank or handle.

Two wheels of about 6 inches diameter should cover the amount of grinding required to be done on board ship, one for cast iron and the other for steel.

Increasing the speed of a wheel makes it appear harder and decreasing its speed gives it the effect of being softer.

Grinding wheels are tested to a surface speed of 9,000 ft/min.; the stress in the wheel is then about 250 lb/sq.in. The stress in a wheel running at 6,000 ft/min. is about 108 lb/sq.in.

If a portable grinder is available, which can be mounted in a lathe tool rest, a considerable amount of work may be accomplished with a fair amount of success, but owing to the lack of rigidity in the lathe and fittings, it is very difficult to do precision grinding. When using a portable grinding machine, care must be exercised to exert a light constant pressure when the wheel is in contact with the work. Especially is this necessary when dressing up cylinder walls, since if a varying pressure is applied spasmodically, the result will be a series of undulating grooves, which may ruin the cylinder surface.

Heat treatment of steels

With the rapid development of the various branches of the engineering industry, such as the manufacture of petrol and diesel engines, high-pressure steam turbines, etc. comes the demand for steels of varying physical properties to withstand the new exacting conditions.

These steels may be divided into three classes, as follows: steels for cutting metals, alloy steels for various duties, and stainless steels.

The cutting steels which we are concerned with here can be subdivided into two classes, namely high-speed steels and carbon steels. The alloy steels can also be subdivided into steels having a tensile strength up to 100 tons/sq.in., and steels used for case-hardening purposes to minimise wear of rubbing surfaces. Even in stainless steel there are several qualities.

High-speed steels contain various proportions of tungsten, vanadium and chromium, and are usually known as air-hardening steels. These steels are very efficient for cutting purposes, as they have the peculiar property of retaining the cutting edge at moderately high temperatures.

To anneal this material, it is necessary to place it in a box in the fire, and gradually bring up the heat to a temperature of approximately 1,570°F (942°C), and maintain at this temperature for about four hours. Then allow the fire to cool out slowly and when cold remove the steel. To harden, heat the steel up in the ordinary fire to about 2,290°F (1,253°C), and cool it out in an air-blast. During the heating operation, care should be taken to remove the steel when this temperature has been attained, since if it is allowed to remain for more than a few seconds, the point will be destroyed.

This high-speed steel requires to be forged at a temperature of 1,840°F (1,004°C). On no account should it be hammered after the temperature has dropped to 1,750°F (954°C).

It is important that carbon steel should not be forged below 1,480°F (804°C), because, at such low temperatures, forging strains are produced which would render the tool liable to burst and become flawed in the centre; and if not normalised, it would probably crack when attempting to harden it.

The " heat colours " corresponding to these temperatures are given in the Table on page 712.

Carbon steels which vary in carbon content from 0·75 to 1·5 per cent are widely used for cutting tools. Steels containing 1·5 per cent of carbon are used chiefly for making razor blades and the like. Steels containing the following percentages of carbon are used for the purposes indicated:—

Steels containing:

1·25 per cent carbon	Turning, slotting, planing tools, etc.
1·12 " "	Drills, reamers, milling cutters, etc.
1·00 " "	Taps, screwing dies, ball races, pneumatic tools, etc.
0·87 " "	Caulking tools, shear blades, punches, hand chisels, etc.
0·75 " "	Hammers, mason's tools, miner's drills, etc.

Steels containing more than 1 per cent of carbon will not weld; those containing from 0·875 to 1 per cent will weld with great care, while steels containing 0·75 per cent of carbon and less will weld easily.

The process of annealing carbon tool steels should preferably be carried out in a muffle furnace, the part to be annealed being contained in a steel box properly sealed to exclude air. The temperature of the furnace should be gradually raised to 1,420°F

(771°C) and the box containing the steel allowed to remain at this temperature for about three hours. The furnace should then be allowed to cool down, and the box with the steel removed only when cold.

A quick and more or less effective method of annealing small pieces of steel, such as a machine tool, it to put it into a blacksmith's fire and heat for an hour in a bright red flame, then take it out of the fire and cover over with lime, sand or ashes, and allow it to remain covered until cold. Another method, which is almost as simple, and more effective, is to procure a piece of pipe 2 or 3 inches in diameter and insert the steel that is to be annealed, first heating one end of the pipe and closing it, leaving the other end open for sighting purposes. The whole should then be heated in a charcoal fire until the steel in the pipe is a cherry-red. Maintain it at this temperature for half an hour, then cover the fire with ashes or sand and allow the steel to remain until cold.

The hardening temperatures for various carbon steels are as follows:—

Steels containing:

1·5 to 1·25 per cent of carbon	1,350°F (732°C)
1·12 ,, 1·0 ,, ,, ...	1,380°F (749°C)
0·87 ,, 0·75 ,, ,, ...	1,430°F (777°C)

For hardening, a good clean fire is essential. A charcoal fire gives a clean heat. The tool to be treated should be placed in a slow fire, and the temperature afterwards gradually raised until the desired temperature is attained, when the tool should be at once removed. Then quickly plunge the tool vertically into pure water, in such a way that the smallest cross-section of the tool enters the water first. The whole of the tool should be immersed. Distilled water, which is generally available on board ship, is an excellent cooling medium. As large a quantity of water as practicable should be used in order to dissipate the heat quickly.

The tempering temperature of carbon steels varies according to the duty for which the tool is required, the range of variation being from 428°F (220°C) (light straw) to 572°F (300°C) (pale blue). The following are the tempering points for different cutting tools:—

Turning, slotting and planing tools	428°F (220·5°C)	(light straw)
Drills, reamers and milling cutters	464°F (240°C)	(dark straw)
Taps, screwing dies and pneumatic tools	482°F (250°C)	(brown–yellow)

Caulking tools, shear blades and punches	491°F (254°C)	(brown–yellow)
Hammers, cold chisels and mason's tools	536°F (280°C)	(purple–blue)

After the tool or piece of steel to be treated has been hardened in the manner previously described, one side should be well polished with emery paper, so that the different colours which correspond to the changing temperature will be more easily seen.

An effective and safe way to temper is to heat a fairly large piece of ordinary iron in a fire to well over the tempering temperature, then withdraw it from the fire, and lay the tool which is to be tempered upon it with the polished side up. Allow the tool to heat up, and when the correct colour appears, plunge it into water.

Case-hardening

The object of case-hardening is to alter the composition of the surface of comparatively soft iron so that by subsequent heat-treatment, it will become hard, and be better able to resist wear and tear. The alteration consists in raising the carbon content of the exterior of the article from about 0·15 to 1 per cent.

This is accomplished by first packing the article to be treated in a cast-iron box with a carbonising compound and placing the box in a furnace, the whole being maintained at a predetermined temperature, which is about 1,730°F (943°C), for a period of time depending upon the depth of case required. The result is an article possessing a hard case and a comparatively soft core.

Many firms manufacture carbonising, or what are termed case-hardening, compounds under various trade names. The principal ingredients in each of these compounds are charred leather, string, horn, bone and charcoal, mixed with some fusible compound such as salt. Very satisfactory results can be obtained with a simple mixture of sodium carbonate (washing soda) and charcoal.

There are many case-hardening steels on the market, but the best are those which have a carbon content of between 0·10 and 0·20 per cent. If the content is greater than 0·20 per cent, a decided hardening effect is produced throughout, which will tend to make the core brittle and easily broken. If the carbon content of the steel is less than 0·10 per cent, the core after treatment is usually crystalline.

To obtain a good depth of case, say of about 0·10 inch, which will generally meet all ship's requirements, the airtight box containing the article to be case-hardened should remain for at least five hours in the furnace at the temperature already stated. The time, however, depends to a great extent upon the size of the article being treated. Steel air-starting cams, for instance, would probably require twelve hours, while a roller pin would acquire the desired case in less than half that time. This measure of time is taken from the moment the box containing the article has attained the correct temperature, and until the furnace is allowed to die down. The box should not be removed from the furnace until it is quite cold.

In order to refine the core of the case-hardened article, it should be heated and allowed to cool out gradually. After this it should be heated again and quenched in water, which will have the effect of hardening the case. Great care must be exercised when packing the article in the carbonising box, and hardening in water, if distortion is to be avoided.

It is sometimes desired to case-harden a portion only of the article, such as, for instance, a valve spindle, and for this it is necessary to prevent the transfer of carbon to the parts which are to be left in a normal condition. There are a number of ways of doing this, the most common practice being to cover the parts which are to remain in normal condition with fireclay before packing the article in the carbonising box. Another effective method is to fit pipes over the parts it is desired to protect.

It is sometimes necessary to make a cutting tool, and if no suitable material is at hand, a fairly successful substitute may be made of wrought iron by converting the exterior into steel by case-hardening.

To do this, take equal parts of prussiate of potash, sal-ammoniac and salt. Powder and mix them. Heat the piece of iron to a dull red heat, dip it in the powder, and put it back into the fire so as to melt the mixture. Remove, and repeat the process several times, then harden and temper in the manner already described.

Alloy steels

There are numerous alloy steels, each of which is used for certain duties. In these notes we will confine ourselves to those parts about a diesel engine which are most likely to wear and have to be dealt with on board.

Generally, what is called 3 per cent nickel case-hardening steel is used for fuel-injection valve spindles, cam toe-pieces, and valve rocking-lever tappets. Case-hardening carbon steels are also used for rollers, roller pins, and general purposes, while stainless or rustless steel is used for bolts and other parts exposed to the action of water, and for air-compressor valves.

The method of heat-treating 3 per cent nickel case-hardening steel is as follows. For cementing or absorbing carbon, pack the articles to be treated with case-hardening compound in a box. There should be at least 2 inches of compound around each article—that is to say, any part of the article should be at least 2 inches from the sides of the box, and if there is more than one article being treated at the same time, there should be more than 2 inches of case-hardening compound between them. Whan the articles are packed and the box lid put on, the joint between the lid and the box should be sealed with fireclay to exclude air. The temperature of the box should then be raised to 1,730°F (943°C), and maintained at this figure for about six hours or more. The furnace should then be allowed to cool out, and the box removed only when cold.

To refine the cores of the articles just case-hardened, heat up each piece separately to 1,560°F (849°C) for about 20 minutes and quench in oil. To harden the converted surface, heat up the article again to 1,380°F (749°C) and quench in water.

Stainless steel

To normalise this material, it should be heated in a box to 1,560°F (849°C) for about three hours and allowed to remain in the furnace until cold. To harden, the article should be heated to 1,800°F (982°C) and then quenched in oil. The tempering temperatures of stainless steels vary for different duties, but for air-compressor valves and such-like the pieces to be treated should be heated to 930°F (499°C) and then quenched in oil.

Winding small springs

Small springs may be wound successfully by means of a simple tool, which can be made in a few minutes, as follows.

Take a piece of $\frac{1}{8}$-inch sheet steel about 12 inches long and 1 inch wide. Near one end, mark off a distance from one edge equal to the pitch of the required coils. Then drill a hole on this line large enough for the wire to pass through freely.

Drill a hole near the other end of the plate about twice the diameter of the wire. The tool now requires threading. To do this, place the plate flat, and put the wire up through the larger hole and down through the smaller hole. The tension during winding is governed by the thumb of the operator.

Next procure a piece of round metal, the diameter of which is equal to the inside diameter of the spring coils. Grip this in the lathe chuck, together with one end of the spring wire (the end through the smaller hole). Now place the winding tool flat on the spindle, the edge of the plate from which the distance of the small hole was measured being the following edge. Rotate the spindle slowly, exerting no pressure on the winding tool other than by the thumb on the wire. The tool will be guided by its edge touching the last complete coil, which will give the correct and uniform spaces between the coils.

Tempering springs

A very handy method, which can be carried out on board ship, is to heat the spring to redness, and to quench in cold water to harden. The spring should then be dipped in raw linseed oil, and held in a fire until it blazes up, when all the oil will be burnt off; it should then be quenched in cold oil.

Another method, suitable for small springs, is to heat the spring slowly and very carefully to a dull red, and quench in lukewarm water. The spring should then be placed in an iron ladle and covered with tallow containing a little resin. Heat until the mixture of tallow and resin flares up, then set aside to cool.

Brazing

Solders for joining metallic surfaces are composed of an alloy of two or more metals. The solder used must have a lower melting-point than the metals to be joined by it, but the fusion point should be as near as possible to that of the metals to be joined, so that a more tenacious joint is effected.

Solders are divided into two general classes, hard and soft. The former fuse at a red heat, and the latter at a comparatively low temperature. The hard soldering of copper, brass, iron, etc. is generally known as brazing, and the solder used is called spelter. The spelter used for general brass work is composed of equal parts of copper and zinc; for light sheet iron, one-and-a-half of copper to one of zinc; and for general ironwork, two of copper and one of zinc.

Brazing brass or copper

A petroleum brazing lamp, or blacksmith's forge, may be used, but a smokeless flame is essential. The parts to be joined must be thoroughly cleaned, otherwise a good joint is impossible. Paraffin oil should not be used to clean the parts, as it spreads into so thin a film as to pass unnoticed, and the parts are thought to be clean when they are not, which prevents a good joint being made. All trace of oil should be removed by burning off.

Assuming the parts to be quite clean, they should then be bound or clamped together, and laid on broken coke, which should be heaped around the work in the immediate vicinity of the prepared joint.

The spelter is first of all mixed with crushed borax and water into a paste, after which it is placed carefully in position.

The heat should be applied gradually until the water is evaporated, and then directed on to the spelter until it fuses.

Brazing cast iron

First remove all grease and dirt from the pores of the metal by heating to a dull red. The surfaces should be cleaned with a wire brush. The parts should then be fastened together by the use of wire, screws, bolts or clamps. If possible, they should be secured in such a way that they can be turned over during the process of brazing, to facilitate the application of the flux and spelter.

A good formula for cast iron brazing is as follows:—boric acid, 16 oz.; chloride of potash (pulverised), 4 oz.; carbonate of iron, 3 oz.

This mixture should be kept dry and airtight. Grain spelter should be added before using. The metals should be heated to a bright red colour, and the flux and spelter applied with an iron rod flattened at the end. After brazing cast iron it should be allowed to cool slowly.

Soldering steel to cast iron

After having cleaned and polished the surfaces to be joined, the cast iron surface should be copperised with sulphuric acid. Allow the surface to dry, and then solder the steel to the copperised cast iron as in ordinary brazing.

Cementing iron

For joining two pieces of iron by cementing, the following is a very useful recipe.

Mix equal parts of sulphur and white lead with one-sixth of borax. When about to apply, wet it with strong sulphuric acid, place a thin layer of it on the faces to be joined, and press them together by the use of clamps or other suitable means. After about five days it will be perfectly dry, and the joint will have the appearance of having been welded.

Welding

Charcoal is the best fuel for iron working, but small coke may be used with success, or a good-quality coal, provided it is free from sulphur.

On board ship, coal is usually the only suitable fuel available. When coal is used, it should be burnt until it no longer gives a light before the iron to be welded is placed in the fire. A blue flame is a sign of sulphur, and the fire should be kept quite clean and at a bright red.

For welding, the iron should be white hot, at which heat it will be in the pasty condition necessary for a good joint. Do not leave it in the fire after it has reached the right heat, or it will be burnt.

When the iron is at a red heat, it should be dipped in clean sand, and returned to the fire. This will prevent the formation of scale. It also protects the outer surface from the action of the fire while the heat penetrates to the middle of the mass of iron.

The correct welding heat of a metal is reached just before the fusing point. As a flux for welding, borax or sand and salt may be used.

Do not quench a welded joint in water, but allow it to cool slowly. The surfaces to be joined should be crowned to ensure that the centre of the iron is welded together.

Pipe bending

To prevent a pipe from being flattened while bending, it is necessary to support it from the inside. For most cases generally met with on board ship, sand may be used for hot bending and water for cold bending. If the pipe is to be bent hot, two blank flanges should be made and one bolted in place. The sand—which should be fine and quite dry—is then put into the pipe a little at a time, and rammed tight until the pipe is full.

A cylindrical piece of wood, with diameter slightly less than the pipe bore, should then be forced into the pipe by screwing up the flange and exerting a pressure on the sand.

If the pipe is not flanged, softwood plugs, well tapered, may be used.

To form a sharp bend in a pipe, it should be heated to a bright red (care being taken not to overheat) and gripped in the vice; then slightly cool the outer curve with water, so that the inside, being hot and plastic, is compressed. By this method of bending the cubical capacity of the pipe is slightly reduced, and the pipe walls are, in consequence, better supported by the filling material. If the outside of the curve is left hot, and allowed to stretch, the cubical capacity would be increased, with the result that there would be a lack of support on the inside of the pipe.

It is essential that the sand be quite dry, otherwise, when heat is applied, steam will be generated.

To bend a pipe with water as a filling, one end must be closed, and the other fitted with a cock and connected to a pump to obtain a slight pressure in the pipe.

Before attempting to bend brass or copper tubing, it should be first annealed by heating it to red at the part to be bent, and quenching in cold water. Brass tubing should not be bent hot. It should be filled with resin or lead to prevent flattening. Seams in tubes to be bent should be kept on the inner curve.

Cracks in iron

As is well known, the best way to prevent a crack from extending further is to drill and plug at the ends, but with some fractures there is sometimes great difficulty in locating the ends of the rent. The exact points can usually be found by applying paraffin to the crack, wiping it, and immediately dusting it over with powdered chalk.

Stopping leaks in oil-tanks, etc.

There are many oil-proof cements, but the most simple composition is a stiff paste of molasses and flour. The most useful lute for small leaks, etc. consists of the following ingredients: two parts of glue, one part of glycerine, and seven parts of water. This preparation should be applied warm.

Cardboard is widely used for making oil-pipe joints, but liquored leather is more suitable, provided that moderate temperatures are not exceeded.

To prevent bolts and screws from rusting in

Bolts, screws, etc. that are exposed to heat or damp soon become rusted, even when oil has been used liberally, and entail a good deal of time and trouble when taking adrift. To prevent this, a thin paste of graphite and oil should be mixed, and the bolts and screws dipped before use, when they can be readily taken out.

To remove a tight nut

Before going to the trouble of splitting a tight nut, heat the end of the spanner, and place it on the nut for a little while before turning. This will have the effect of expanding the nut only.

Testing lubricating oil

To determine the amount of solid impurities in oil, half fill a tumbler with the oil, and add kerosene until the whole becomes quite thin. The mixture should then be poured through a sheet of white blotting-paper, followed by a little pure paraffin to clean the paper. The residue, if any, will give an idea for what purpose the oil is suitable. By testing filtered oil in this way, the efficiency of the filtering medium is ascertained.

A simple method of testing oil for acids is to place a drop of the oil on a sheet of copper or brass, and leave it there for a few days. If the oil contains acids, there will be a green spot on the metal.

Water in oil is more easily separated when the oil has been heated than when it is cold, because on the application of heat there is a greater expansion of oil than water, and, therefore, the water has a relatively greater specific gravity.

Temporary dies

To make dies, proceed as follows. Take a piece of good steel the required size to fit the stocks. Cut the grooves on the sides of the block to fit the ridges in the stocks. Then mark the centre of the block, and describe a circle the size of the tapping hole required. On the circumference of the circle, and in line with the handles of the stocks, drill and tap two small holes.

These should then be plugged with iron, flush with one side of the block, and protruding from the other to facilitate removal. The centre hole should then be drilled and tapped the required size, and the iron plugs removed.

The threads will then need to be dressed-up with a small ward file, and the centre hole tapered at the bottom, to enable a start to be made when screwing. Then cut the block in two with the hacksaw, and after again dressing the threads, the die is ready for hardening and tempering.

To harden the die thus made, first fill the threads with hard soap, to prevent the formation of scale; then heat a block of iron to nearly white, laying the dies on it until the latter are a cherry-red, when they should be dipped flat into water.

To temper the dies, the iron block should be re-heated, and the dies, after cleaning the surface with emery cloth, placed upon it until they show a light chestnut-brown, when they should be quenched in water.

To true grindstones

When a cup-type dresser is not provided, turn the stone at a moderate speed and hold a piece of iron tubing at right-angles to the grindstone spindle, turning the tube as the edge grinds away. The stone should be quite dry.

APPENDIX

CONVERSION TABLES AND USEFUL CONSTANTS

Comparison of temperatures on the Centigrade and Fahrenheit scales

°C	°F	°C	°F	°C	°F
0	32	55	131	110	230
5	41	60	140	115	239
10	50	65	149	120	248
15	59	70	158	125	257
20	68	75	167	130	266
25	77	80	176	135	275
30	86	85	185	140	284
35	95	90	194	145	293
40	104	95	203	150	302
45	113	100	212	155	311
50	122	105	221	160	320

To convert Centigrade to Fahrenheit, multiply by 9, divide by 5, and add 32.

To convert Fahrenheit to Centigrade, subtract 32, multiply by 5, and divide by 9.

Quantity of heat

British Thermal Unit—In the United Kingdom and America, quantities of heat are measured in British thermal units (B.t.u.). One B.t.u. represents the amount of heat required to raise the temperature of 1 lb of water 1°F.

Heat being another form of energy can also be measured thus:—

1 B.t.u. = 778 ft/lb of work = 1·055 kJ
1 h.p. hour = 2,545 B.t.u. = 2·685 MJ
1 kilowatt hour = 3,412 B.t.u. = 3·600 MJ
= 1·34 h.p. hour, roughly

Calorie—This unit of heat (the "large calorie") is used on the Continent with the metric system, and represents the amount of heat required to raise the temperature of 1 kilogram of water 1°C (i.e. from 15° to 16°C).

(B.t.u.) × 0·252 = Calories
Calories × 3·968 = B.t.u.

Oil fuel measurements

(sp. gr. 0·9)

1 ton of oil is equal to	39·8 cu.ft
1 " " "	249 gallons
1 " " "	6 barrels (nearly)
1 " " "	1,140 litres (approx.)
1 " " "	1·31 tons of coal (in heat units)
1 gallon " "	4·545 litres
1 " " "	0·16 cu.ft
1 " " "	9 lb
1 cu.ft " "	0·025 ton
1 " " "	56·3 lb
1 " " "	28·316 litres
1 " " "	6·229 gallons

British and Metric conversion tables

British to Metric		Metric to British	
1 inch	= 25·4 mm	1 mm	= 0·0394 inch
1 sq.in.	= 6·45 sq.cm	1 sq.cm	= 0·155 sq.in.
1 lb	= 0·454 kilogram	1 kilogram	= 2·205 lb
1 gallon	= 4·545 litres	1 litre	= 0·22 gallon
1 lb/sq.in.	= 0·0703 kg/sq.cm	1 kg/sq.cm	= 14·22 lb/sq.in.
	= 0·0678 atm.		= 0·965 atm./sq.in.
(1 atmosphere	= 14·7 lb/sq.in.)	(1 atmosphere	= 1·033 kg/sq.cm)

FRACTIONS OF AN INCH TO DECIMALS AND MILLIMETRES

In.	Decimal	Mm	In.	Decimal	Mm
$\frac{1}{64}$	= 0·0156	= 0·397	$\frac{3}{8}$	= 0·3750	= 9·525
$\frac{1}{32}$	= 0·0313	= 0·794	$\frac{1}{2}$	= 0·5000	= 12·700
$\frac{1}{16}$	= 0·0625	= 1·588	$\frac{5}{8}$	= 0·6250	= 15·875
$\frac{1}{8}$	= 0·1250	= 3·175	$\frac{3}{4}$	= 0·7500	= 19·050
$\frac{1}{4}$	= 0·2500	= 6·350	$\frac{7}{8}$	= 0·8750	= 22·225

THOUSANDTHS OF AN INCH TO MILLIMETRES

Thousandths of an inch	Millimetres	Thousandths of an inch	Millimetres
1	0·0254	20	0·5080
2	0·0508	30	0·7620
3	0·0762	40	1·0160
4	0·1016	50	1·2700
5	0·1270	60	1·5240
6	0·1524	70	1·7780
7	0·1778	80	2·0320
8	0·2032	90	2·2860
9	0·2286	100	2·5400
10	0·2540		

Millimetres to Inches

Millimetres	Inches Decimal	Inches Fractions
0·1	0·0039	$\frac{3}{1,000}+\frac{9}{10,000}$
0·2	0·0079	$\frac{7}{1,000}+\frac{9}{10,000}$
0·3	0·0118	$\frac{11}{1,000}+\frac{8}{10,000}$
0·4	0·0157	$\frac{15}{1,000}+\frac{7}{10,000}$
0·5	0·0197	$\frac{19}{1,000}+\frac{7}{10,000}$
0·6	0·0236	$\frac{23}{1,000}+\frac{6}{10,000}$
0·7	0·0276	$\frac{27}{1,000}+\frac{6}{10,000}$
0·8	0·0315	$\frac{31}{1,000}+\frac{5}{10,000}$
0·9	0·0354	$\frac{35}{1,000}+\frac{4}{10,000}$
1·0	0·0394	$\frac{39}{1,000}+\frac{4}{10,000}$

Millimetres and Inches

Millimetres to inches		Inches to millimetres	
Mm	Inches	Inches	Mm
1	0·03937	0·1	2·54
2	0·07874	0·2	5·08
3	0·11811	0·3	7·62
4	0·15748	0·4	10·16
5	0·19685	0·5	12·70
6	0·23622	0·6	15·24
7	0·27559	0·7	17·78
8	0·31496	0·8	20·32
9	0·35433	0·9	22·86
10	0·3937	1·0	25·40
20	0·7874	2·0	50·8
30	1·1811	3·0	76·2
40	1·5748	4·0	101·6
50	1·9685	5·0	127·0
60	2·3622	6·0	152·4
70	2·7559	7·0	177·8
80	3·1496	8·0	203·2
90	3·5433	9·0	228·6
100	3·937	10·0	254·0
200	7·874	20·0	508·0
300	11·811	30·0	762·0
400	15·748	40·0	1,016·0
500	19·685	50·0	1,270·0
600	23·622	60·0	1,524·0
700	27·559	70·0	1,778·0
800	31·496	80·0	2,032·0
900	35·433	90·0	2,286·0
1,000	39·37	100·0	2,540·0
2,000	78·74	200·0	5,080·0

Gallons and Litres

Gallons to litres		Litres to gallons	
Gallons	Litres	Litres	Gallons
1	4·546	1	0·22
2	9·092	2	0·44
3	13·638	3	0·66
4	18·184	4	0·88
5	22·730	5	1·10
6	27·276	6	1·32
7	31·822	7	1·54
8	36·368	8	1·76
9	40·914	9	1·98
10	45·460	10	2·20
20	90·92	20	4·4
30	136·38	30	6·6
40	181·84	40	8·8
50	227·30	50	11·0
60	272·76	60	13·2
70	318·22	70	15·4
80	363·68	80	17·6
90	409·14	90	19·8
100	454·60	100	22·0
200	909·2	200	44·0
300	1,363·8	300	66·0
400	1,818·4	400	88·0
500	2,273·0	500	110·0
600	2,727·6	600	132·0
700	3,182·2	700	154·0
800	3,636·8	800	176·0
900	4,091·4	900	198·0
1,000	4,546·0	1,000	220·0

Kilograms per Square Centimetre and Pounds per Square Inch

(1kg/sq. cm = 14·223 lb/sq. in. = 0·98 bar)

Kg/sq.cm	Lb/sq.in.	Kg/sq.cm	Lb/sq.in.	Kg/sq.cm	Lb/sq.in.
0·1	1·422	4·8	68·271	9·5	135·120
0·2	2·845	4·9	69·693	9·6	136·542
0·3	4·267	5·0	71·116	9·7	137·965
0·4	5·689	5·1	72·538	9·8	139·387
0·5	7·111	5·2	73·960	9·9	140·809
0·6	8·534	5·3	75·382	10·0	142·232
0·7	9·956	5·4	76·805	10·5	149·343
0·8	11·378	5·5	78·227	11·0	156·455
0·9	12·801	5·6	79·649	11·5	163·566
1·0	14·223	5·7	81·072	12·0	170·678
1·1	15·645	5·8	82·494	12·5	177·790
1·2	17·068	5·9	83·916	13·0	184·901
1·3	18·490	6·0	85·339	13·5	192·013
1·4	19·912	6·1	86·761	14·0	199·124
1·5	21·335	6·2	88·183	14·5	206·236
1·6	22·757	6·3	89·606	15·0	213·348
1·7	24·179	6·4	91·028	15·5	220·459
1·8	25·602	6·5	92·450	16·0	227·571
1·9	27·024	6·6	93·873	16·5	234·682
2·0	28·446	6·7	95·295	17·0	241·794
2·1	29·869	6·8	96·717	17·5	248·906
2·2	31·291	6·9	98·140	18·0	256·018
2·3	32·713	7·0	99·562	18·5	263·129
2·4	34·136	7·1	100·984	19·0	270·240
2·5	35·558	7·2	102·407	19·5	277·352
2·6	36·980	7·3	103·829	20·0	284·464
2·7	38·403	7·4	105·251	20·5	291·575
2·8	39·825	7·5	106·674	21·0	298·687
2·9	41·247	7·6	108·096	21·5	305·798
3·0	42·670	7·7	109·518	22·0	312·910
3·1	44·091	7·8	110·940	22·5	320·021
3·2	45·514	7·9	112·363	23·0	327·132
3·3	46·936	8·0	113·785	23·5	334·243
3·4	48·359	8·1	115·207	24·0	341·357
3·5	49·781	8·2	116·630	24·5	348·468
3·6	51·203	8·3	118·052	25·0	355·580
3·7	52·626	8·4	119·474	25·5	362·691
3·8	54·048	8·5	120·897	26·0	369·802
3·9	55·470	8·6	122·319	26·5	376·913
4·0	56·893	8·7	123·741	27·0	384·026
4·1	58·315	8·8	125·164	27·5	391·137
4·2	59·737	8·9	126·586	28·0	398·250
4·3	61·159	9·0	128·008	28·5	405·361
4·4	62·582	9·1	129·431	29·0	412·472
4·5	64·004	9·2	130·853	29·5	419·583
4·6	65·426	9·3	132·275	30·0	426·696
4·7	66·849	9·4	133·698	31·0	440·919

KILOGRAMS PER SQUARE CENTIMETRE AND POUNDS PER SQUARE INCH—*continued*

Kg/sq.cm	Lb/sq.in.	Kg/sq.cm	Lb/sq.in.	Kg/sq.cm	Lb/sq.in.
32	455·142	55	782·27	78	1,109·40
33	469·364	56	796·49	79	1,123·63
34	483·589	57	810·72	80	1,137·85
35	497·812	58	824·94	81	1,152·07
36	512·034	59	839·16	82	1,166·30
37	526·258	60	853·39	83	1,180·52
38	540·480	61	867·61	84	1,194·74
39	554·705	62	881·83	85	1,208·97
40	568·928	63	896·06	86	1,223·19
41	583·15	64	910·28	87	1,237·41
42	597·37	65	924·50	88	1,251·64
43	611·59	66	938·73	89	1,265·86
44	625·82	67	952·95	90	1,280·08
45	640·04	68	967·17	91	1,294·31
46	654·26	69	981·40	92	1,308·53
47	668·49	70	995·62	93	1,322·75
48	682·71	71	1,009·84	94	1,336·98
49	696·93	72	1,024·07	95	1,351·20
50	711·16	73	1,038·29	96	1,365·42
51	725·38	74	1,052·51	97	1,379·65
52	739·60	75	1,066·74	98	1,393·87
53	753·82	76	1,080·96	99	1,408·09
54	768·05	77	1,095·18	100	1,422·32

Useful constants

CHEMICAL FORMULAE AND MOLECULAR WEIGHTS OF GASES

	Formula	Molecular Weight
Water vapour ..	H_2O	18·0
Oxygen	O_2	32·0
Nitrogen	N_2	28·0
Hydrogen	H_2	2·0
Carbon dioxide ..	CO_2	44·0
Carbon monoxide ..	CO	28·0
Ethylene	C_2H_4	28·0
Methane	CH_4	16·0
Chlorine	Cl_2	70·0

H_2O, the chemical formula for water vapour, means that it consists of two volumes of hydrogen gas combined with one volume of oxygen gas at the same temperature and pressure. By weight, however, the proportion is 2 of hydrogen to 16 of oxygen, since their atomic weights are hydrogen 1 and oxygen 16, or, in other words, oxygen is 16 times heavier than hydrogen. Thus the composition of water vapour being H_2O, the molecular weight is $1 \times 2 + 16 \times 1 = 18$.

Specific Gravities of Gases

Atmosphere as 1·0; barometer 30 inches; temperature 60°F

Hydrogen	0·0694
Oxygen	1·1111
Nitrogen	0·9691
Sulphur dioxide ..	2·2639
Carbon monoxide ..	0·9720
Carbon dioxide ..	1·5196
Steam	0·6220
Town gas	0·4000

Explosive Ranges of Fuels

	Percentage	Range
Ether	2·9 to 7·5	4·6
Petrol	1·1 to 5·3	4·2
Benzene	2·7 to 6·3	3·6
Alcohol	4·0 to 14·0	10·0
Acetylene	3·2 to 52·2	49·0

The percentages given above are the minimum and maximum proportions of gas which, when mixed with air and ignited, will cause an explosion. As an example, ether will require not more than 97·1 per cent and not less than 92·5 per cent of air to secure an explosive mixture.

For constant volume (explosion) engines, a wide explosive range is desired, since it minimises the danger of the engine stopping due to misfiring, consequent upon an over-rich or too weak a mixture of gas, as well as making an engine easier to start.

Air Required for Combustion of Fuels

A certain amount of air is essential for the proper combustion of any fuel, the amount varying with the composition of the fuel employed.

The quantity of air required affects the thermal efficiency of the engine, since with a fuel which requires little air, less heat is lost in the exhaust gases.

Theoretically, the approximate weight of air required for the combustion of any fuel can be calculated by the following formula if the chemical composition of the fuel is known:—

$$W = 0{\cdot}116\,[C + 3\,(H - \tfrac{1}{8}O)],$$

where W = weight of air in lb per lb of fuel;
C = percentage of carbon in fuel;
H = ,, hydrogen in fuel;
O = ,, oxygen in fuel.

1 lb of petrol requires about 15·3 lb of air.
1 lb of benzene ,, 13·4 ,,
1 lb of alcohol ,, 9·5 ,,
1 lb of air at atmospheric pressure and at a temperature of 60°F occupies about 13 cubic feet.

The average composition of air is 23 per cent of oxygen by weight or 21 per cent by volume, the remainder being almost entirely nitrogen.

Average Composition of Various Fuels

Petrol	Carbon, 84 per cent; hydrogen, 16 per cent.
Benzene	Carbon, 92 per cent; hydrogen, 8 per cent.
Alcohol	Carbon, 52 per cent; hydrogen, 13 per cent; oxygen, 35 per cent.
Paraffin	Carbon, 85 per cent; hydrogen, 15 per cent.
Solar or gas oil ..	Carbon, 87 per cent; hydrogen, 12 per cent; oxygen, 1·0 per cent.
Diesel oil	Carbon, 87 per cent; hydrogen, 11 per cent; oxygen, 1 per cent; impurities, 1 per cent.
Heavy fuel ..	Carbon, 86 per cent; hydrogen, 10·5 per cent; oxygen, 1·5 per cent; impurities, 2 per cent.

Specific Gravity of Oils: Correction for Difference in Temperature

Since all classes of oils expand upon being heated, a known specific gravity is correct only for a certain temperature. The necessary correction for a difference in temperature is made by allowing for the expansion of the oil. For " gas oil " or " diesel oil," the coefficient of expansion is generally taken as 0·0004 per degree F rise in temperature, or 0·00072 per degree C. The specific gravity of the oil decreases with a rise in temperature and vice versa.

Fuel Coefficients

Fuel coefficients are used to measure and compare the overall performances of ships under service conditions. The coefficient now generally used is found by the following formula:—

$$C \doteq \frac{D^{2/3} \times S^3}{F}$$

where C = fuel coefficient;
D = displacement of ship in tons;
S = speed of ship in knots;
F = fuel consumption per day in tons.

Colours Corresponding to Temperatures

	°F	°C
Faint red	960	516
Dull red	1,290	699
Brilliant red	1,470	799
Cherry red	1,650	899
Bright red	1,830	999
Orange	2,010	1,099
Bright orange	2,190	1,199
White heat	2,370	1,299
Bright white heat ..	2,550	1,399
Welding heat	2,800	1,538

INDEX

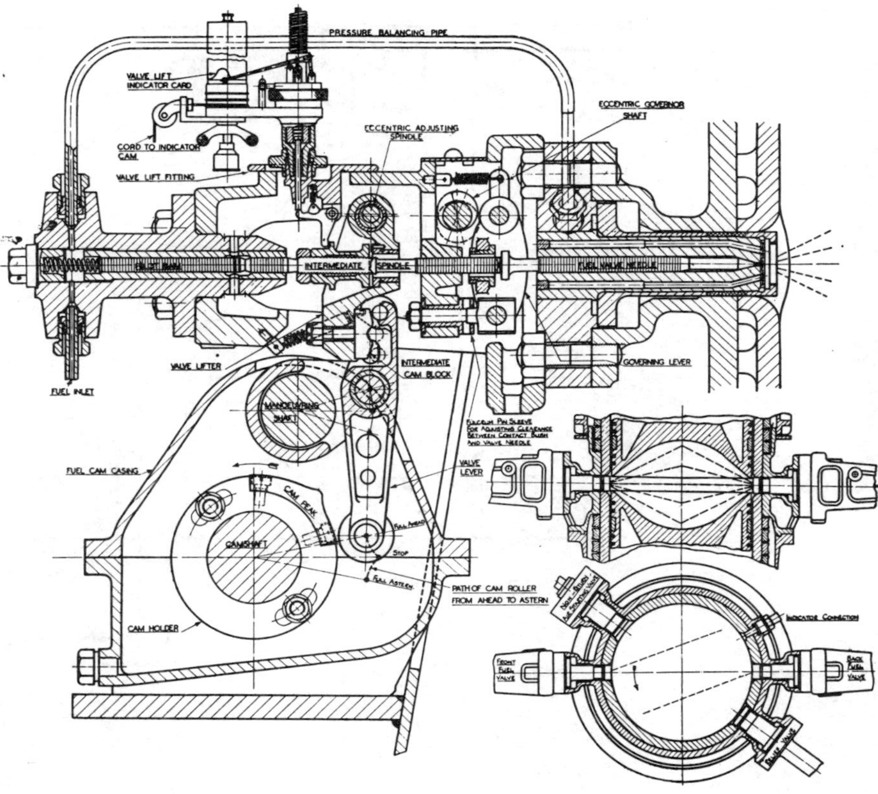

Fig. 61—Mechanically operated fuel valve (Doxford opposed-piston engine)

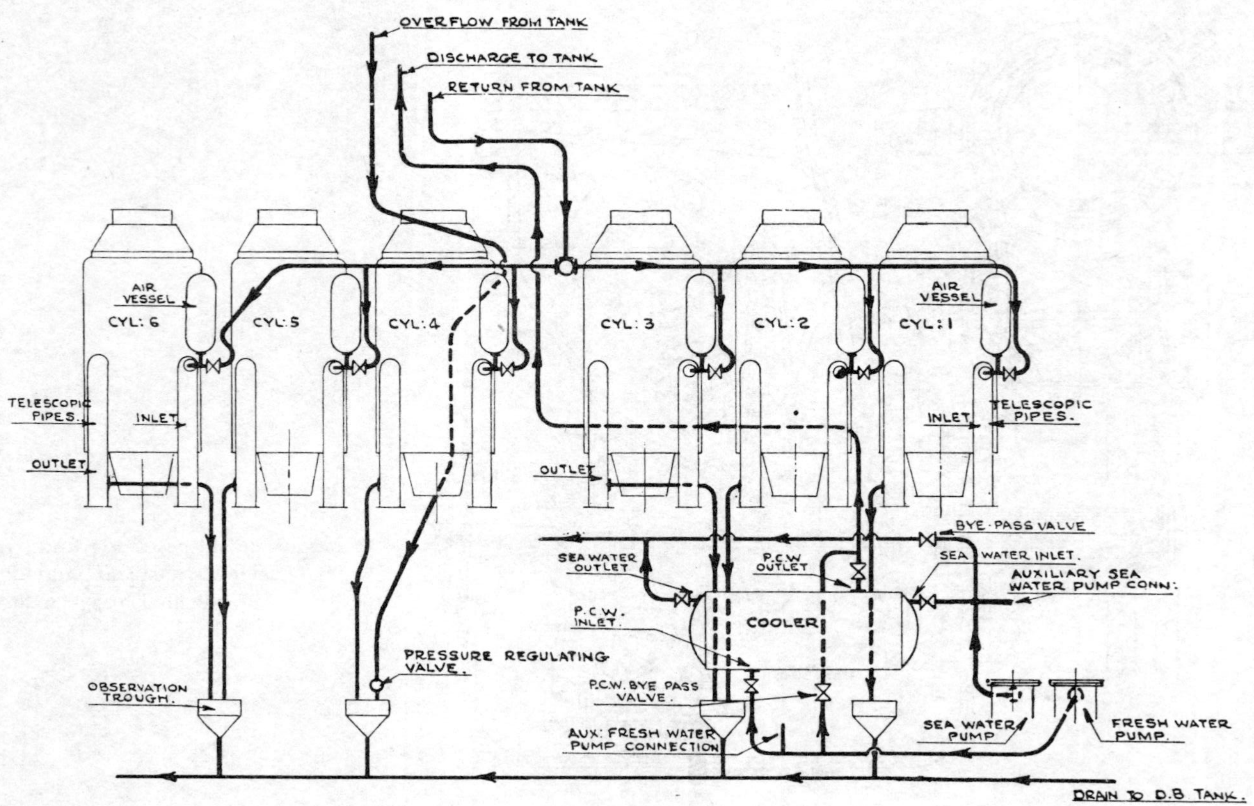
OVERFLOW FROM TANK
DISCHARGE TO TANK
RETURN FROM TANK
AIR VESSEL
CYL: 6
CYL: 5
CYL: 4
CYL: 3
CYL: 2
AIR VESSEL
CYL: 1
TELESCOPIC PIPES.
INLET
OUTLET
OUTLET
INLET
TELESCOPIC PIPES.
BYE-PASS VALVE
SEA WATER OUTLET
P.C.W OUTLET
SEA WATER INLET.
AUXILIARY SEA WATER PUMP CONN:
P.C.W. INLET.
COOLER
PRESSURE REGULATING VALVE.
OBSERVATION TROUGH.
P.C.W. BYE PASS VALVE.
AUX: FRESH WATER PUMP CONNECTION
SEA WATER PUMP
FRESH WATER PUMP.
DRAIN TO D.B TANK.

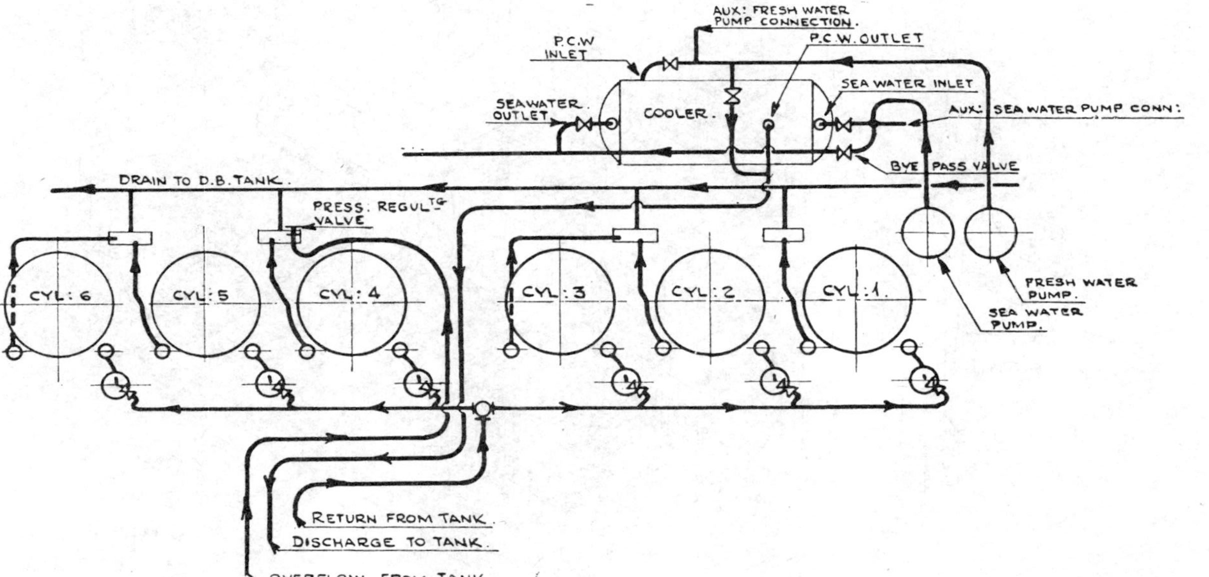

Fig. 129—Arrangement of a piston-cooling system

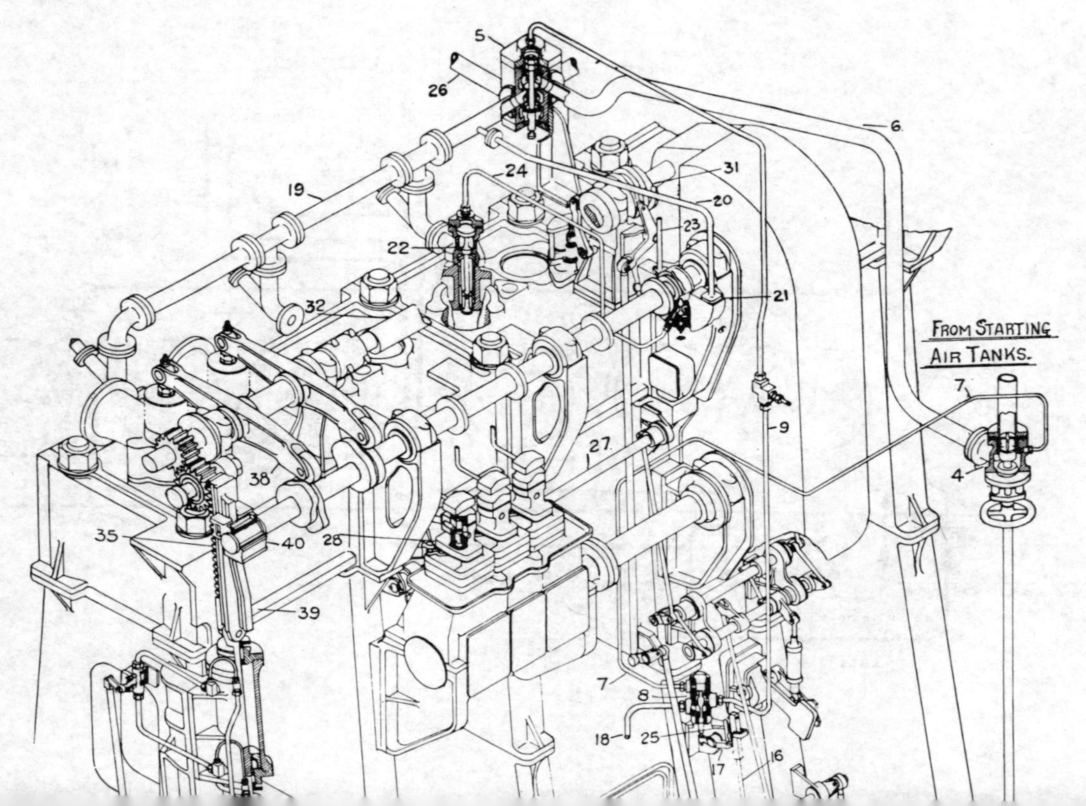
FROM STARTING AIR TANKS.
5
26
6
19
24
31
20
23
22
21
32
7
4
9
27
38
35
40
28
39
7
8
18
25
17
16

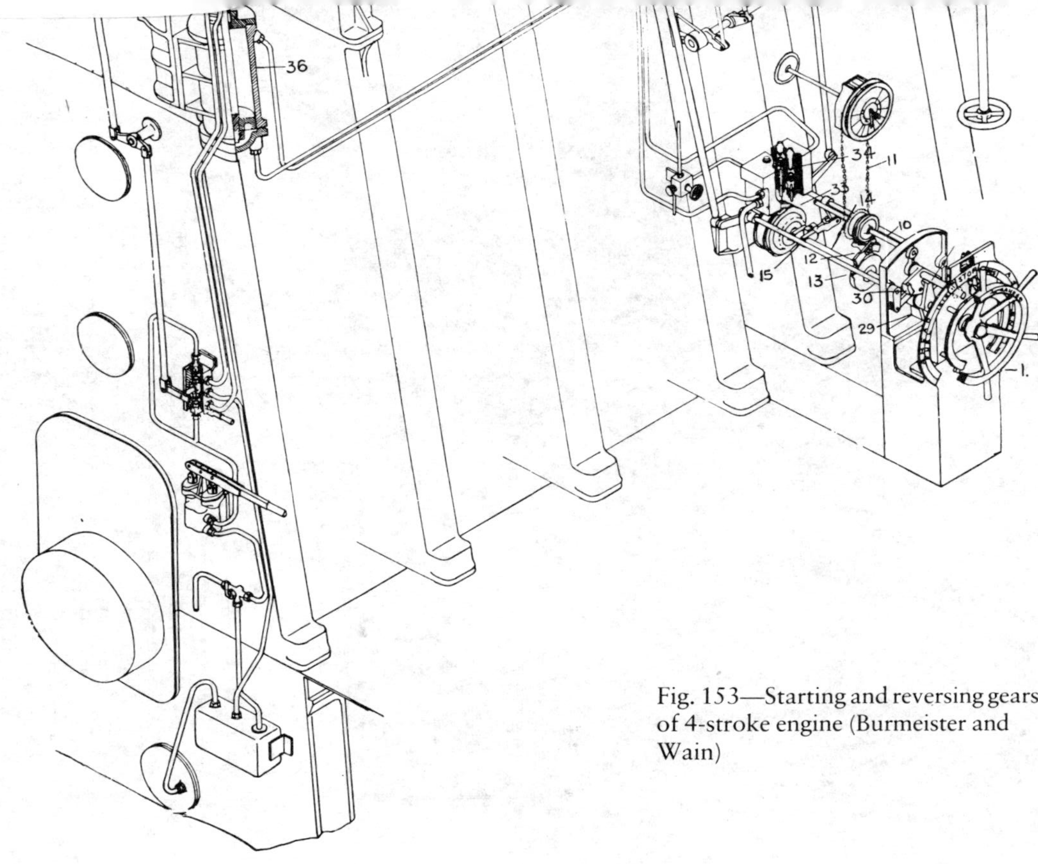

Fig. 153—Starting and reversing gears of 4-stroke engine (Burmeister and Wain)

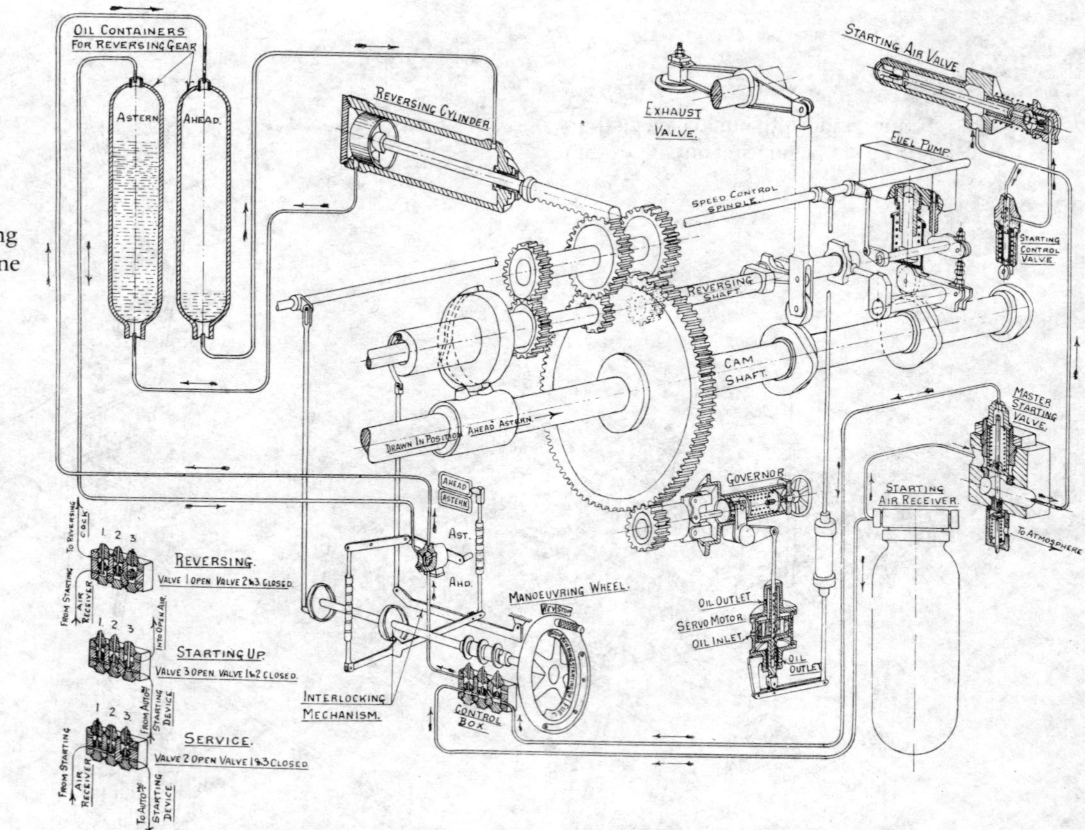

Fig. 156—Manoeuvring gear of a 4-stroke engine (M.A.N.)